Innovative Design and Creation of Visual Interfaces:

Advancements and Trends

Ben Falchuk
Applied Communication Sciences, USA

Aderito Marcos
Universidade Aberta, Portugal

Information Science
REFERENCE

Managing Director:	Lindsay Johnston
Senior Editorial Director:	Heather A. Probst
Book Production Manager:	Sean Woznicki
Development Manager:	Joel Gamon
Development Editor:	Heather Probst
Acquisitions Editor:	Erika Gallagher
Typesetter:	Adrienne Freeland
Cover Design:	Nick Newcomer, Lisandro Gonzalez

Published in the United States of America by
Information Science Reference (an imprint of IGI Global)
701 E. Chocolate Avenue
Hershey PA 17033
Tel: 717-533-8845
Fax: 717-533-8661
E-mail: cust@igi-global.com
Web site: http://www.igi-global.com

Library of Congress Cataloging-in-Publication Data

Innovative design and creation of visual interfaces: advancements and trends / Ben Falchuk and Aderito Marcos, editors.
   p. cm.
 Includes bibliographical references and index.
 Summary: "This book offers the cutting edge in research, development, technologies, case studies, frameworks, and methodologies within the field of visual interfaces, offering a holistic picture of the state of the art in the field"--Provided by publisher.
 ISBN 978-1-4666-0285-4 (hardcover) -- ISBN 978-1-4666-0286-1 (ebook) -- ISBN 978-1-4666-0287-8 (print & perpetual access) 1. Computer graphics. 2. User interfaces (Computer systems) 3. Human-computer interaction. I. Falchuk, Benjamin. II. Marcos, Aderito, 1968-
 T385.I4743 2012
 005.4'37--dc23
                                    2011051463

British Cataloguing in Publication Data
A Cataloguing in Publication record for this book is available from the British Library.

Table of Contents

Section 2
Volume 2

Detailed Table of Contents

Section 1
Volume 1

Chapter 1

Mathias Dahlström, lastminute.com labs, UK

Richard Lewis Jones, lastminute.com labs, UK

Marko Balabanović, lastminute.com labs, UK

NRU ("near you") is a new mobile phone application for finding nearby activities. The application displays restaurants, bars, cafes, and so forth close to the user, on a display that updates as the user rotates it and moves it around his or her body, encouraging real-world interaction. This device is a simplified form of augmented reality that works on an existing consumer phone handset, combining location and orientation sensors with a touchscreen interface. In this paper, the authors explain the design of the system and the technologies involved, and share some experiences from the application's first 6 months in operation.

Chapter 2

Anna Ursyn, University of Northern Colorado, USA

This article explores the landscape of creative endeavors in the new media art and reflects on aesthetics of information visualization. When using computer based information visualization to show data interactively in many dimensions, the user can navigate across big data sets, find patterns, relationships, and structures that would be invisible if presented numerically. The authors also explore ways of combining information visualization techniques with the principles of creative design, enhancing artistic influences on the technical implementations, and raising the level of training in design. Finally, the authors offer suggestions for creating knowledge visualizations with the use of art and graphics to strengthen the readiness of computer scientists to fulfill aesthetic expectations and gain recognition from art world specialists for factual solutions done in visualization projects and new forms of art.

Chapter 3

Robert J. Hendley, University of Birmingham, UK

Barry Wilkins, University of Birmingham, UK

Russell Beale, University of Birmingham, UK

This paper presents a mechanism for generating visually appealing but also effective representations for document visualisation. The mechanism is based on an organic growth model which is driven by features of the object to be visualised. In the examples used, the authors focus on the visualisation of text documents, but the methods are readily transferable to other domains. They are also scaleable to documents of any size.The objective of this research is to build visual representations that enable the human visual system to efficiently and effectively recognise documents without the need for higher level cognitive processing. In particular, the authors want the user to be able to recognise similarities within sets of documents and to be able to easily discriminate between dissimilar objects.

Chapter 4

    Leonardo Bonanni, MIT Media Laboratory, USA

    Maurizio Seracini, University of California at San Deigo, USA

    Xiao Xiao, MIT Media Laboratory, USA

    Matthew Hockenberry, MIT Media Laboratory, USA

    Bianca Cheng Costanzo, MIT Media Laboratory, USA

    Andrew Shum, MIT Media Laboratory, USA

    Romain Teil, MIT Media Laboratory, USA

    Antony Speranza, MIT Media Laboratory, USA

    Hiroshi Ishii, MIT Media Laboratory, USA

Few people experience art the way a restorer does: as a tactile, multi-dimensional and ever-changing object. The authors investigate a set of tools for the distributed analysis of artworks in physical and digital realms. Their work is based on observation of professional art restoration practice and rich data available through multi-spectral imaging. The article presents a multidisciplinary approach to develop interfaces usable by restorers, students and amateurs. Several interaction techniques were built using physical metaphors to navigate the layers of information revealed by multi-spectral imaging, prototyped using single- and multi-touch displays. The authors built modular systems to accommodate the technical needs and resources of various institutions and individuals, with the aim to make high-quality art diagnostics possible on different hardware platforms, as well as rich diagnostic and historic information about art available for education and research through a cohesive set of web-based tools instantiated in physical interfaces and public installations.

Chapter 5

    Sha Xin Wei, Concordia University, Canada

Since 1984, Graphical User Interfaces have typically relied on visual icons that mimic physical objects like the folder, button, and trash can, or canonical geometric elements like menus, and spreadsheet cells. GUI's leverage our intuition about the physical environment. But the world can be thought of as being made of *stuff* as well as *things*. Making interfaces from this point of view requires a way to simulate the physics of stuff in realtime response to continuous gesture, driven by behavior logic that can be understood by the user and the designer. The author argues for leveraging the corporeal intuition that people learn from birth about heat flow, water, smoke, to develop interfaces at the density of matter that leverage in turn the state of the art in computational physics.

Chapter 6

Ramón Trueba, MOVING Group, Universitat Politècnica de Catalunya, Spain

Carlos Andujar, MOVING Group, Universitat Politècnica de Catalunya, Spain

Ferran Argelaguet, MOVING Group, Universitat Politècnica de Catalunya, Spain

Object occlusion is a major handicap for efficient interaction with 3D virtual environments. The well-known World in Miniature (WIM) metaphor partially solves this problem by providing an additional dynamic viewpoint through a hand-held miniature copy of the scene. However, letting the miniature show a replica of the whole scene makes the WIM metaphor suitable for only relatively simple scenes due to occlusion and level of scale issues. In this paper, the authors propose several algorithms to extend the idea behind the WIM to arbitrarily complex scenes. The main idea is to automatically decompose indoor scenes into a collection of cells that define potential extents of the miniature replica. This cell decomposition works well for general indoor scenes and allows for simple and efficient algorithms for preserving the visibility of potential targets inside the cell. The authors also discuss how to support interaction at multiple levels of scale by allowing the user to select the WIM size according to the accuracy required for accomplishing the task.

Chapter 7

Ya-Xi Chen, Media Informatics, University of Munich, Germany

Rodrigo Santamaría, University of Salamanca, Spain

Andreas Butz, Media Informatics, University of Munich, Germany

Roberto Therón, University of Salamanca, Spain

Many online communities use TagClouds, an aesthetic and easy to understand visualization, to represent popular tags collaboratively generated by their users. However, due to the free nature of tagging, such collaborative tags have linguistic problems and limitations, such as high semantic density. Moreover, the alphabetical order of TagClouds poorly supports a hierarchical exploration among tags. This paper presents an exploration to support semantic understanding of collaborative tags beyond TagClouds. Based on the results of the authors' survey of practical usages of collaborative tags, they developed a visualization named TagClusters, in which tags are clustered into different groups, with font size representing tag popularity and the spatial distance indicating the semantic similarity between tags. The subgroups in each group and the overlap between groups are highlighted, illustrating the underlying hierarchical structure and semantic relations between groups. The authors conducted a comparative evaluation with TagClouds and TagClusters based on the same tag set. The results confirmed the advantage of TagClusters in facilitating browsing, comparing and comprehending semantic relations between tags.

Chapter 8

Paulo Castro, CITI-DI, FCT, Universidade Nova de Lisboa, Portugal

Adriano Lopes, CITI-DI, FCT, Universidade Nova de Lisboa, Portugal

Magnet Mail (MM) is a visualization system for emails based on a zoomable interface and on manipulation of objects. Users are able to search, analyze and understand relations among email messages as long as they provide searching keywords to do so, as well as interact with graphical objects in the display in a pro-active manner. The underlying concept is a magnet metaphor that relates user interaction, searching keywords and relations among emails. In this paper, the authors present a prototype that interacts with a mass-market email system and most of its graphical implementation relies on the Piccolo toolkit.

Chapter 9

Sosuke Okamura, University of Tokyo, Japan
Takeo Igarashi, University of Tokyo, Japan

This article describes an assistant interface to design and produce pop-up cards. A pop-up card is a piece of folded paper from which a three-dimensional structure pops up when opened. The authors propose an interface to assist the user in the design and production of a pop-up card. During the design process, the system examines whether the parts protrude from the card or whether the parts collide with one another when the card is closed. The user can concentrate on the design activity because the error occurrence and the error resolution are continuously fed to the user in real time. The authors demonstrate the features of their system by creating two pop-up card examples and perform an informal preliminary user study, showing that automatic protrusion and collision detection are effective in the design process.

Chapter 10

Christian Jacquemin, LIMSI-CNRS, University of Paris Sud 11, France
Rami Ajaj, LIMSI-CNRS, France
Sylvain Le Beux, LIMSI-CNRS, France
Christophe d'Alessandro, LIMSI-CNRS, France
Markus Noisternig, IRCAM, France
Brian F.G. Katz, LIMSI-CNRS, France
Bertrand Planes, Artist, France

This paper discusses the Organ Augmented Reality (ORA) project, which considers an audio and visual augmentation of an historical church organ to enhance the understanding and perception of the instrument through intuitive and familiar mappings and outputs. ORA has been presented to public audiences at two immersive concerts. The visual part of the installation was based on a spectral analysis of the music. The visuals were projections of LED-bar VU-meters on the organ pipes. The audio part was an immersive periphonic sound field, created from the live capture of the organ sounds, so that the listeners had the impression of being inside the augmented instrument. The graphical architecture of the installation is based on acoustic analysis, mapping from sound levels to synchronous graphics through visual calibration, real-time multi-layer graphical composition and animation. The ORA project is a new approach to musical instrument augmentation that combines enhanced instrument legibility and enhanced artistic content.

Section 2
Volume 2

Chapter 11

Hans Dehlinger, University of Kassel, Germany

A straight line, pen-drawn and executed on a pen-plotter, is by default sharp and crisp. This is the nature of a straight line between two points. Likewise, drawings generated from such lines are by definition sharp. This paper considers generative line drawings, executed on a pen-plotter which *appears* to be wholly or in part *unsharp* when viewed. Described here are some strategies based on systematic experiments with geometric transformations to produce such drawings. The topic is approached from an artist's point of view with a focus on the generative and algorithmic issues involved, and the results are demonstrated by examples.

Data mapping is the essence of being human. This report follows the process of data mapping; the transmission of a structured utterance from one domain to another. It starts with signals in the world and moves through experience and engagement with the world through those signals. The paper develops descriptions of the materials and mechanisms of data mapping. The descriptions are aids and conveniences in the effort to understand the systemic workings of the process of communication. From a systems perspective one might find points of leverage in their own involvement with the processes of communication and data mapping. Recognizing these leverage points can help in activities of art making, information design and in simply living.

Chapter 13

The valence of any visual paradigm and its accompanying technologies is subject to the contingencies of political regimes and cultural shifts. The instigation, implementation and even reconfiguring of any associated technological system effects a translation and adjustment to the structure and use of these supporting mechanisms that both re-defines the relationship between object and viewer and ultimately influences its translation into material form. The permeation of digital systems throughout contemporary urban space is typified by Internet Protocol webcam systems, instigated by civic authorities for surveillance and the imagistic promotion of iconic city form. This paper examines how this system's reception and subsequent translation of transmitted data signals into digital information not only presents new material to mediate people's engagement with public space, but moreover, how it presents new opportunities for the designer to materialize its three-dimensional form within the spatial ambiguity of virtual and real-time environments.

Chapter 14

Recent developments in process interaction solutions are helping companies and educational institutions to reduce training costs, enhance visualization, and increase communication. Service personnel can make more informed decisions by allowing a broad range of employees to access data instantly. New 3D interactive technologies incorporated into training applications and learning environments together with the introduction of the one projector 3D solution is rapidly changing the landscape for education. Over the last 10 years, virtual reality applications have been applied in various industries; medical, aircraft computer modeling, training simulations for offshore drilling platforms, product configuration, and 3D visualization solutions for education and R&D. This paper examines emergent visualization technologies, their influence on market growth and on new perceptions of learning and teaching. It describes the interrelationship between technology development, technology providers, product launches, R&D, and the motivation to learn and teach new skills. The paper incorporates social, technological, and global markets growth drives, describing the pull and drag synergy between these forces.

Interaction in modern human-computer interfaces is most intuitively initiated in an image-based way. Often images are the key components of an interface. However, too frequently, interfaces are still designed by computer scientists with no explicit education in the aesthetic design of interfaces and images. This article develops a well-defined system of criteria for the aesthetic design of images, motivated by principles of visual information processing by the human brain and by considerations of the visual arts. This theoretic disquisition establishes a framework for the evaluation of images in terms of aesthetics and it serves as a guideline for interface designers by giving them a collection of criteria at hand; how to deal with images in terms of aesthetics for the purpose of developing better user interfaces. The proposed criteria are exemplified by an analysis of the images of the web interfaces of four well known museums.

A hundred years ago officers entering the Royal Navy took an exam where they had to draw a mouse-trap. At the time there was much discussion, and some despair, about competence, and about teaching. For amateurs, drawing manuals provided instructions on how to render a still life in 3D, or draw a running figure, tasks that would now be effortless given current software. Today much debate about drawing, its purpose, and about 'digital drawing', and de-skilling. Graphics programs are designed for 'realism'. But contemporary drawing looks in the opposite direction: into the processes of drawing; the expressive mark; and the structure and character of the line. Those who deal with the evolving gadgetry of digital drawing have had to contend both with unhelpful software, and with an art world that has yet to realise the scope of this new visual universe.

This paper proposes an empirical approach to the visualization phase of architectural images, employing established concepts, methodologies, and measurement techniques found in media psychology and user-centered studies. The paper proposes a human-centered approach for conceptualizing visualization technologies and evaluating the quality concept of images to simulate a satisfactory architectural experience. The authors use psychophysiological measures to capture the affective component of image quality experience facilitated by different displays, including immersive and nonimmersive displays. These types of visualizations are important for empirically evaluating the experiential aspects of an architectural space and other types of images.

Anna Puig-Centelles, Universitat Jaume I, Spain
Nicolau Sunyer, Universitat de Girona, Spain
Oscar Ripolles, Universidad Politécnica de Valencia, Spain
Miguel Chover, Universitat Jaume I, Spain
Mateu Sbert, Universitat de Girona, Spain

Rain is a complex phenomenon and its simulation is usually very costly. In this article, the authors propose a fully-GPU rain simulation based on the utilization of particle systems. The flexibility of CUDA allows the authors to include, aside from the rainfall simulation, a system for the detection and handling of the collisions of particles against the scenario. This detection system allows for the simulation of splashes at the same time. This system obtains a very high performance because of the hardware programming capabilities of CUDA.

Gonçalo N. P. Amador, Universidade da Beira Interior, Portugal
Abel J. P. Gomes, Instituto de Telecomunicações, Portugal

Navier-Stokes-based methods have been used in computer graphics to simulate liquids, especially water. These physically based methods are computationally intensive, and require rendering the water surface at each step of the simulation process. The rendering of water surfaces requires knowing which 3D grid cells are crossed by the water's surface, that is, tracking the surface across the cells is necessary. Solutions to water surface tracking and rendering problems exist in literature, but they are either too computationally intensive to be appropriate for real-time scenarios, as is the case of deformable implicit surfaces and ray-tracing, or too application-specific, as is the case of height-fields to simulate and render water mantles (e.g., lakes and oceans). This paper proposes a novel solution to water surface tracking that does not compromise the overall simulation performance. This approach differs from previous solutions in that it directly classifies and annotates the density of each 3D grid cell as either water, air, or water-air (i.e., water surface), opening the opportunity for easily reconstructing the water surface at an interactive frame rate.

Filipe Gaspar, ADETTI-IUL / ISCTE-Lisbon University Institute, Portugal
Rafael Bastos, Vision-Box & ADETTI-IUL / ISCTE-Lisbon University Institute, Portugal
Miguel Sales, DiasMicrosoft Language Development Center & ISCTE-Lisbon University Institute, Portugal

In large-scale immersive virtual reality (VR) environments, such as a CAVE, one of the most common problems is tracking the position of the user's head while he or she is immersed in this environment to reflect perspective changes in the synthetic stereoscopic images. In this paper, the authors describe the theoretical foundations and engineering approach adopted in the development of an infrared-optical tracking system designed for large scale immersive Virtual Environments (VE) or Augmented Reality (AR) settings. The system is capable of tracking independent retro-reflective markers arranged in a 3D structure in real time, recovering all possible 6DOF. These artefacts can be adjusted to the user's stereo glasses to track his or her head while immersed or used as a 3D input device for rich human-computer interaction (HCI). The hardware configuration consists of 4 shutter-synchronized cameras attached with band-pass infrared filters and illuminated by infrared array-emitters. Pilot lab results have shown a latency of 40 ms when simultaneously tracking the pose of two artefacts with 4 infrared markers, achieving a frame-rate of 24.80 fps and showing a mean accuracy of 0.93mm/0.51° and a mean precision of 0.19mm/0.04°, respectively, in overall translation/rotation, fulfilling the requirements initially defined.

Preface

Computer graphics and human-computer interfaces can be paradigm-shifting fields. Computer Graphics, through the design, manipulation and processing of extremely varied types of pictographic data using computers, has provided a rich vision of innovative applications. It has fostered such diverse areas as multimedia, virtual environments, simulations and data visualisation, to mention a few.

Over the past decade we have seen incredible changes in the Web, the mobile device landscape, and software services. Of course, innovations in hardware design and performance bring us ever shrinking form-factors, storage, and ever-increasing clock-speeds, but it is the computer graphics and interfaces that confront the end user and present information. The principles of computer graphics are largely based upon mathematics while the art of human-computer interface is based, at least partly, on the sometimes quantitative effects of multimedia presentation upon the completion user tasks.

On the software side, innovation in computer graphics can take the form of new algorithms or new building blocks, or new applications of graphics to practical problems. On the human computer interface side, innovations take the form of new ways to visualization important information, new ways to navigate through information spaces (such as audio or video libraries), and new fundamentals such as new widgets and other means to help users achieve information tasks. There is a distinct artistic trend in computer graphics and interfaces as both are the basis for various digital artistic endeavors ranging from digital photography to performance art enhanced by graphics. Thus, while we see it is easy to think of computer graphics to be solely the territory of Web pages and iPhone applications, there is much more.

In assembling this Journal of Creative Interfaces and Computer Graphics (IJCICG), we strove to find a talented team of researchers who could steer us into the depths of these fields. Indeed we found folks with deep expertise and experience and a passion for graphics and interfaces. In defining the scope of this journal we allowed for a fairly wide swath of submissions in this space because we consider almost any revolutionary improvement to be viable and interesting regardless of its context. Mathematical graphics folks have an appreciation for practical innovations in visualization, for example. For our first two volumes we have succeeded in arranging many interesting submissions on areas such as computer art, aesthetics, interactions techniques, and applications of graphics including visual simulation. The following sections describe these articles.

VOLUME 1

In the Volume 1 article about *NRU*, authors Dahlstrom et al (UK) describe an innovative new approach to using a mobile device to mitigate the objects around you at any given time. Their system provided an advanced interface on a mobile device that was reminiscent of a radar screen. Effectively, the radar was to detect interesting places near you at any given time by searching data feeds correlated to the users' location and the interaction technique proved novel and valuable to end-users in trials.

In the Volume 1 article about aesthetic expectations, Ursyn (USA) provides a deep analysis about the role and value of aesthetics in computer graphics research and interface design. Describing metaphors and looking back at past and current trends in visualization, Ursyn provides some experiences on conveying meaning with images and the important role of aesthetics today.

In the Volume 1 article about the system called *Organix*, Hendley et al (UK) describe a visually appealing way to represent textual document content using scalable organically modeled entities. These entities morph with the changing structure of the document, allow insight into its contents, and allow comparison between sets of documents by visual inspection of the graphical artifacts. The results are familiar – almost creature-like –and aesthetically pleasing.

In the Volume 1 article about computer interfaces for art restoration, Bonanni et al (USA) describe a fascinating use of table-top computing devices to allow users to explore artistic restorative processes. The computer system allows end users to engage in painting scraping to explore it, much like a restorer might scrape off layers of paints from an old canvas. In the digital version various scans comprise the layers and the human finger can be used to touch the interface to remove these layers (e.g., false color, x-ray, UV fluorescence). The system – *WetPaint* – takes art restoration, analysis, and exploration to a new level.

In the Volume 1 article about video, Wei (Canada) describes his vision for the incorporation of primitive physical things like flow, water, and smoke into digital interfaces to help us create and use them in new ways. Real-time visual displays were used with subjects whose motion was captured and fused with computer graphics to create dramatic installations.

In the Volume 1 article about World in Miniature (WIM) and Virtual Reality (VR), Trueba et al (Spain) devise an improved method to allow users immersed in VR settings to see the context of their position through a 2nd miniature virtual model of the setting called a WIM. The authors have come up with an algorithm to automatically decompose VR settings (e.g., rooms) into cells such that navigation and tasks within the VR setting are simplified for the user.

In the Volume 1 article about Tag Cluster-based visualizations the authors Chen et al (Germany, Spain) propose a clustered view of tag clouds in which font-size, color, and other semantics better inform the user of the cluster's meaning and where visual distance between tags represents semantic similarity between tags. The authors perform a user-study to determine the effectiveness of this visualization using a realworld tag set from last.fm Website.

In the Volume 1 article about Magnet Mail the authors Castro et al (Portugal) describe an email visualization technique in which novel magnet-metaphor is activated within email inboxes to better help users sort and keep track of email messages. Different magnets attract or repel messages in custom ways and the overall effect, according to the authors, is an improved email management experience.

In the Volume 1 article about popup cards the authors Okamura et al (Japan) describe a fascinating application of graphics in which the visual interactions are used to convey to users the technique to make pop-up cards (the cards that reveal themselves when opened). The authors base their work conceptually upon some of Andrew Glassner's pioneering work and create a functional interface that they run users studies on; the studies show that their automatic protrusion and collision detection are effective.

In the Volume 1 article about classical instrument augmentation Jacquemin et al (France) describe a project that comprised an audio and visual augmentation of a historical church organ. Part of an immersive interactive presentation in France the exhibit featured visual projections upon the organ's pipes and periphonic sound created from live organ sounds. The expo was performed in France and the project comprises an interesting intersection of performance art and multimedia.

VOLUME 2

In the Volume 2 Dehlinger (Germany) presents an article about generative line drawings that hold the characteristic to appear fully or partially unsharp when displayed. The author explores some computing strategies based on systematic experiments with geometric transformations to achieve them. The work has been implemented taking into account the artist's point of view which focuses on the generative and algorithmic concerns adopted and less on the computing efficiency. Some exemplary results are presented.

In the Volume 2 article about the process of communication and data mapping, Evans (USA) examines the materials and mechanisms of receiving messages while following the process of data mapping that starts with signals of the world and moves towards our experience and engagement with that world via those signals. The author argues that the process of data mapping a portrayal of the complexity is a point of leverage and can be adopted as the basis of visualization and sonification in information design and in digital art.

In the Volume 2 article about the digital images generated by CCTV webcam systems, Perin and Matthews (Australia) discuss how these open-source digital software can be explored to process and interpret raw virtual qualitative data to generate again a formal response to civic space. The conversion of the webcam's generated images of the real world into the virtual provides the viewer with a facility to convert the surveillant role these webcam systems into a qualitative and experiential intervention within both virtual and urban space.

In the Volume 2 article about creative interfaces through the integration of new visual solutions, Arminano (Sweden) discusses the adoption of 3D interactive technologies in training applications and learning environments. These new approaches are rapidly changing the landscape for education. The author presents some approaches aimed to provide effective visual communication and knowledge transfer in cooperation, models prototyping, among others, in several major areas such are: learning and training, medical and pharmaceutical industries, design studios, urban planning, etc.

In the Volume 2 Peters (Germany) presents a survey for scientist about criteria for the creation of aesthetic images for human-computer interfaces. This survey provides a system of criteria for the aesthetic design of images, motivated by principles of visual information processing by the human brain as well as inspired by considerations of the visual arts. This article is a theoretic disquisition aimed at establishing a framework for the evaluation of images in terms of aesthetics, serving also as a guideline for the interface designers.

In the Volume 2 Faure Walker (UK) presents some thoughts about digital drawing in a form of an essay. The essay is illustrated by the author's own works and personal comments on his own venture in digital drawing. He delves into the queries often discussed: why it was that fine art drawing has been so little affected where new tech replaces old technology? Or, are we a de-skilled society when it comes to handicrafts compared with a hundred years ago? The author recounts the story of the connections and disconnections between traditional and digital drawing.

In Volume 2 Fonseca et al (Spain) analyze user experiences and differences detected in viewing architectural images in various interfaces. The authors propose an empirical approach to the visualization of architectural images based on established concepts, methodologies and measurements techniques found in media psychology and user-centered studies. It explores psycho-physiological measures to capture the affective component of the image quality experience facilitated by different displays, including immersive and non-immersive displays. *The approach allows also for empirically evaluating the experiential* aspects of an architectural space.

In Volume 2 Puig-Centelles et al (Spain) propose a fully-GPU rain simulation based on particle systems. The solution presented explores CUDA flexibility in order to include, aside from the rainfall simulation, also a system for detection and handling the collision of the particles against the scenario. The collision detection permits to further simulate the splashes at the same time. Through this solution the potential of CUDA in terms of its capabilities for hardware programming is tested into its limits allowing obtaining results of very high performance in rain simulation.

In Volume 2 Amador and Gomes (Portugal) present a novel solution to water surface tracking and simulation. The traditional navier-stokes-based methods for liquid simulation are computationally intensive and require rendering the water surface at each step of the simulation process, which is usually inappropriate for real-time scenarios. The authors' novel approach does not compromise the overall simulation performance since it differs from previous solutions in that it directly classifies and annotates the density of each 3D grid cell as either water, air, or water-air (i.e., water surface), allowing for an easier reconstruction of the water surface at an interactive frame rate.

In Volume 2 Gaspar et al (Portugal) describe the theoretical foundations and engineering approach adopted in the development of an infrared-optical tracking system designed for large scale immersive Virtual Environments (VE) or Augmented Reality (AR) settings. The system is capable of tracking independent retro-reflective markers arranged in a 3D structure in real time, recovering all possible 6DOF. The article presents in great detail all the hardware and software settings, calibration of the solution, 3D reconstruction as well as tests and final results.

SUMMARY

In the coming months and years please look to IJCICG for continued coverage of these and other related fields in computer graphics and interfaces.

Ben Falchuk
Applied Communication Sciences, USA

Aderito Marcos
Universidade Aberta, Portugal

Section 1
Volume 1

Chapter 1
NRU ("near you"):
Real–World Interaction
with a Mobile Phone

Mathias Dahlström
lastminute.com labs, UK

Richard Lewis Jones
lastminute.com labs, UK

Marko Balabanović
lastminute.com labs, UK

ABSTRACT

NRU ("near you") is a new mobile phone application for finding nearby activities. The application displays restaurants, bars, cafes, and so forth close to the user, on a display that updates as the user rotates it and moves it around his or her body, encouraging real-world interaction. This device is a simplified form of augmented reality that works on an existing consumer phone handset, combining location and orientation sensors with a touchscreen interface. In this paper, the authors explain the design of the system and the technologies involved, and share some experiences from the application's first 6 months in operation.

INTRODUCTION

A common challenge for people in cities is to find places to go and activities to do. Where to eat? Is there a nice cafe nearby? How about a bar or pub? These questions are especially valid in an unfamiliar city, for instance when travelling, but we also have them in our home cities. Part of

the joy of visiting and living in the world's big cities is the ever-changing flow of new places to be discovered and unfamiliar neighbourhoods to explore. One solution is a guidebook or magazine, with recommendations of places to visit, maps, photos and additional information. Clearly, however, the printed page is a static information source, increasingly out of date as establishments open and close, and is of limited size. With the advent of mobile technologies the move began

DOI: 10.4018/978-1-4666-0285-4.ch001

to migrate this guidebook content onto small devices users could carry with them. Initially these were straightforward interfaces to the same static content. It has become common to carry a mobile phone with both a very large memory capacity and a connection to the internet. This enables the content to be delivered on-demand, so the user has access to a large and ever-changing source of data about a city, drawing on web sites ranging from content supplied by writers and editors to reviews and ratings supplied by users. Visitors to a city don't just need an idea about where to go or what to do, they will also need to know where they are and how to reach their destination. Once again mobile technologies are becoming an increasingly common solution, supplanting or replacing printed maps that are carried or available in the environment. A variety of positioning technologies are in common use:

- Detecting nearby mobile phone cell towers and using a map of known locations of cell towers
- Using a Global Positioning System (GPS) receiver
- Detecting nearby WiFi access points and using a map of known locations of access points

In the last few years detailed street mapping imagery has also become widely available, driven by the adoption of internet services such as Google Maps[1]. Today's visitor to a city has in their pocket a device capable of retrieving a vast array of information relevant to their location.

At lastminute.com we help customers find and book places to visit and things to do, chiefly through our web site. We feature both travel products (such as flights, hotel rooms, car rentals, package holidays, cruises, train tickets) and entertainment products (such as theatre tickets, restaurant bookings, spa treatments, music or comedy tickets, etc). Although today our customers transact their business from a desktop or laptop computer, we see that over time the mobile phone is a much more natural channel. After all, everything we do is for people travelling or out and about in cities. The goal of our lastminute.com labs innovation team is to explore what kinds of interaction we can create to help people visiting cities make the most of their time.

This paper will explain the design of our new nru ("near you") mobile application and our initial findings since its launch. The goal of nru is to help a visitor to a city find nearby things to do. For us this is also an exploration of the newest mobile phone technologies available to today's consumers, to see whether the kind of immersive, physical interaction often prototyped in research labs is a feasible and usable paradigm in the real world today.

The remainder of the paper is structured as follows. First we introduce the challenges of designing and building mobile user interfaces for location-based systems. We then introduce some technologies that enabled and motivated our design. Next we explain the design concept that motivated the nru application, followed by a detailed walk-through of the nru interface. Finally, we summarise the lessons we've learned from its first six months of operation

THE CHALLENGES OF MOBILE USER INTERFACES FOR LOCATION-BASED SYSTEMS

In a typical simple interaction, a location-based system will fetch a number of nearby results (for instance in nru these might be restaurants), and display them to a user. The very simplest interface is just a list of nearby things, still often used in mobile applications. A more common approach taken in recent years is to show a street map with graphical "pins" for each result, with an accompanying list to show more detail for each item. For example see Figure 1 showing the results from the lastminute.com "fonefood" mobile web service[2]. This approach has become a common interaction pattern, well understood by users, with the massive popularity of the Google Maps interface. Although Google Maps was originally designed for desktop or laptop computers, it has been successfully implemented on many of the larger-screen mobile phones such as the iPhone or Blackberries.

Although users are familiar with this approach, it does have some clear problems. First, it is hard to orient oneself relative to the map, to understand which way one is facing. The maps are generally shown from above with north to the top of the screen, in a fixed orientation, irrespective of the direction the user is facing. Second, it confuses what are really three separate problems:

- Where am I?
- What is nearby?
- How do I get there?

An alternative to the birds-eye view provided by the interface above is to assume that the screen of the device is a viewport onto a world of data superimposed over the real world. This is a very simple example of an "augmented reality" system (Azuma, 1997), so called since by blending the real world with location-based data it is stepping outside a purely virtual "virtual reality" system. Perhaps because of their origins in the immersive virtual reality research, many augmented reality systems have used custom hardware to create various forms of head-tracking, head-mounted displays, projected interfaces, often showing location-based data in headsets or on modified glasses (Starner et al., 1997). "Handheld" augmented reality using off-the-shelf hardware has only been practical more recently (Schmalstieg & Wagner, 2007), often using markers placed in specific environments for easy recognition with a camera. Trials have therefore typically been limited to smaller user groups, niche applications or specific geographic areas. However there has been a strongly creative thread of work in that

Figure 1. Screenshot of the "fonefood" search results screen

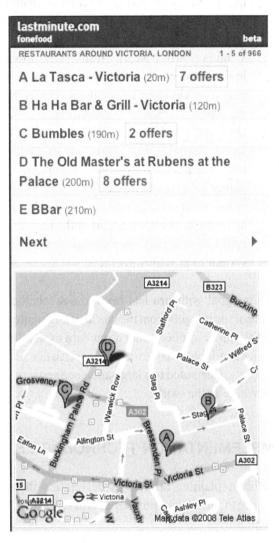

field imagining many applications, both useful and more futuristic, of augmented reality systems, and indeed these interactions are a staple ingredient of much science fiction literature and cinema.

An augmented reality interaction will address our three problems as follows:

- Where am I? The user's position and orientation are not shown relative to a street map, so in a way this question is not answered. However the augmented reality approach also makes this a less important question to answer. If the user knows where the nearby things are relative to his or her position and orientation, why would he or she need to know where he or she is?

- What is nearby? Nearby results are shown in their real-world positions, using the display as a viewport to see them relative to the user's position and orientation.
- How do I get there? Depending on the speed, accuracy and obtrusiveness of the interface, a constantly-updating augmented reality interface could guide the user to his or her destination by updating its display as he or she walks. Or this part of the problem could be delegated to a conventional map system to provide directions.

Our goal with nru has been to see whether some of the insights from the world of augmented reality can be applied using a standard consumer device available today, to create a service that can be freely distributed to a large audience and work anywhere in the world.

IMPLEMENTATION TECHNOLOGIES

Before explaining nru and its design, it will be helpful to introduce a number of crucial enabling technologies.

Android

Android is an open source operating system for mobile devices developed and maintained by Google and the other members of the Open Handset Alliance (Oliver, 2009). Android was launched in November 2007 with the first hardware available to the public in October 2008. The Android development environment is freely available for Windows, Mac OS X and Linux. It is based on Java (Gosling, Joy, Steele, & Bracha, 2005), the widely-used programming language originally developed by Sun Microsystems. Android devices however do not run the Java virtual machine, rather a similar but incompatible VM called Dalvik. The Android Market is the principal means of distributing Android applications.

T-Mobile G1

For most of the time since Android's launch the T-Mobile G1 (otherwise known as the HTC Dream) has been the main target for Android development. This phone is equipped with the following notable features:

- 480x320 LCD touchscreen
- GPS receiver
- Accelerometer
- Magnetometer

These are all used by nru, and when combined allow for a rich physical interface.

Location Based Services

As noted earlier, there are three core methods for determining position on a commercial scale today: GPS, WiFi networks in proximity, and triangulating cell phone towers around the user. Until recently, the design of new services needed to access separate Application Programming Interfaces (APIs) for each of these services, creating a very dissatisfying user experience on the typical mobile phone operating system. With the introduction of CoreLocation and GeoLocation APIs for platforms such as Android and the iPhone, this barrier has been removed. These APIs cover all three main approaches and simply return a latitude/longitude location and estimated precision. With these APIs in place, it is possible to create a good experience that is fairly precise in most occasions, and to indicate to the user the degree of error.

Accelerometer

Multi-axis accelerometers are increasingly used in consumer devices. They measure acceleration and can be used to sense the orientation of a device in the vertical plane (pitch and roll). Accelerometers can be found in digital cameras, where they detect whether the device is being held in portrait or landscape orientation. This information is used at the point of image capture and image display. Several smartphones are now equipped with accelerometers (e.g., Nokia N95, Apple iPhone as well as the T-Mobile G1), where, again, they can be used to display the user interface in the appropriate orientation. Notably the controllers for the Wii games console (Wiimotes) contain accelerometers (Turner, 2007).

Magnetometer

Magnetometers measure the influence of Earth's magnetic field. They can therefore be used to sense orientation of a device in the horizontal plane (yaw). At the time of writing this mobile phone feature is not widespread. It is available on the Android mobile phones released so far (the T-Mobile G1 and the similar HTC Magic), and on the new iPhone 3GS. Given the appeal of interfaces using the magnetometer we expect this to become an increasingly common feature.

THE NRU CONCEPT

Design Rationale

The aim of nru is to show users nearby things to do, in order to help them decide on an activity. In order to concentrate on this display and decision-making interaction, and given the small size of mobile phone screens, we have attempted to remove as much visual clutter as possible. Our design rationale has been to find the very simplest

form of this interface that is usable and functional. We have employed this principle in two areas:

1. The visual design of the interface, where we've kept the view as simple and minimal as possible
2. The interaction with the user, where we've minimised clicks or button presses, and tried as far as possible to use the phone's orientation to provide a natural mapping to access the information in space.

Unlike early mobile applications that tended to look like miniature web sites, there is a clear trend with newer mobile application interfaces to maximise the screen area devoted to content (e.g., photos, maps, videos, depending on the application) and to replace on-screen buttons and controls with touchscreen gestures, or physical gestures through moving the device itself. In part this stems from the recent popularisation of the Nintendo Wii interface, where the game controllers are often used in a way that mirrors a real-world interaction (e.g., a swinging gesture for a tennis stroke). Note also that unlike most augmented reality systems, we have chosen *not* to show a live camera feed or a map under the nru display, in the interests of a clean and simple interface, and we are not rendering 3D models of any kind. Of course a device as small as a phone doesn't occupy much of the users' field of view, so the real world itself can still be seen all around.

Touchscreen

Touchscreen interfaces are a new paradigm amongst manufacturers of mobile devices. They have completely changed the landscape and desires of consumers. In essence they allow for a more direct manipulation of on-screen representations of data; enabling users to focus on performing action directly on objects, rather than selecting actions through menus and thus splitting the user experience into selecting actions and seeing the actions being applied.

Mobile devices are currently using a variety of styles of touchscreen. Google Android devices rely on a desktop metaphor (Figure 2), Nokia Series 60 devices use grid based interactions evolved from older Nokia systems (Figure 3). Primarily they are designed to be used with on-screen keyboards. Nokia and Android based phones are often delivered with hardware keyboards as well.

At lastminute.com labs we decided to adopt a more explorative and gesture driven approach to our UI. The decision was driven by the fact that we had access to a magnetometer, accelerometers and a touchscreen. By combining these we are able to create gesture driven designs and as a result there is no need to rely on a traditional grid design. Many designers in this field are designing mobile solutions for existing products with well-established UI frameworks where this kind of innovative approach would be harder to achieve.

Gesture as Navigation Structure for Mobile UIs

Gesture-driven interaction design, in our view, strongly stems from the research conducted on tangible computing, where physical objects are manipulated to generate a stimulus to a virtual on-screen object. A good introduction is presented in the paper on Tangible Bits (Ishii & Ullmer, 1997). At its very core is the feeling that moving a physical object (or making a gesture with an object) conveys meaning that we as humans can interpret with ease. The abstract on-screen representations that have come with the introduction of computer systems with graphical user interfaces have removed this direct mapping to physical experience, making interpretation less natural for us as humans.

In order to fully leverage the new generation of mobile devices, encompassing both magnetometers and accelerometers, it is important to understand the importance of and take advantage of these physical interactions. As will be seen in the next section, all the primary navigation functions of nru are controlled by physical movements of the phone. The authors have removed any indicators of how the user can turn the device; instead the responsiveness of the interface to movement invites the user to move the device around in space. Since the feedback is immediate when the device is lifted or rotated, there is no need for further on-screen instructions.

THE NRU USER INTERFACE

In this section we will walk through the main elements of the nru interface.

Initially the user is presented with a list of categories to choose from. When the user selects a category, a search takes place using the user's current position as reported by the positioning system. The nearest 10 points of interest in the category are displayed on the screen (the search will automatically repeat at a later stage if the user's position changes significantly). Depending on the orientation of the device, one of two different views is shown to the user–in the following subsections we will study them in depth. Since we decided to design a UI based on motion and rotation of the device for navigation, the touchscreen interaction can be very simple; a single touch to select an entry, or a rotation gesture to swing the view around, to defy the laws of physics and browse the surrounding areas without actively turning around.

"Compass" View

The compass view is presented to the user when the phone is flat i.e. within 20 degrees of horizontal, as reported by the accelerometer (Figure 4). The magnetometer reading is used to display a representation of a compass at the correct ori-

Figure 2. The Android phone "desktop"

Figure 3. A typical Nokia Series 60 grid display

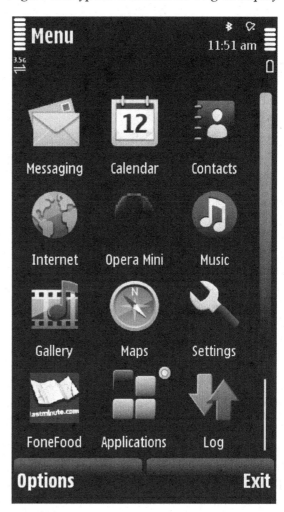

entation with respect to magnetic North. Around the compass are plotted the points of interest as 'blobs' at their respective bearings and distances from the user's position (as reported by the positioning system), the distances from the user represented by the distance from the centre ring of the compass on a linear scale. The names of the points of interest are plotted next to the blobs, radiating outward.

Various early forms of this view used the size, shape and colour of the blobs to represent additional dimensions such as category, distance or the price and quality ratings. However the final design as shown cut these options back to the simplest view.

"Scanner" View

The scanner view is presented when the phone is held upright i.e., within 20 degrees of the vertical (Figure 5). Rather than a compass, the 'blobs' appear on a horizontal line, their positions on the line representing the direction of the point of interest from the user's position. Distances are represented by the sizes of the blobs (larger being

Figure 4. nru compass view

shown on this view. To aid orientation of the user, a smaller version of the compass view is shown at the top right of the scanner view.

Interacting with NRU

As the user changes his direction (or rather, changes the direction of the phone) the compass or scanner view will change accordingly, the blobs changing position to reflect their new bearings. This is enabled by leveraging the compass functionality of the Android phones. The user can also "spin" the view by dragging his finger around or along the display; the blobs will move accordingly, disconnecting from the current direction (Figure 6). After a short delay, the blobs will return to their 'true' positions. If a blob is tapped, a web page for that point of interest will appear. If the user taps in an area which contains a group of blobs that are close together, the user will see a list of blobs and their distances. The user can then select from this list and see a web page with more information. This method of dealing with overlapping data points, although functional, can result in a messy display in dense areas.

closer). The names of the points of interest are plotted above the blobs, the distances below. On the US version of nru, ratings and prices are also

Figure 5. nru scanner view

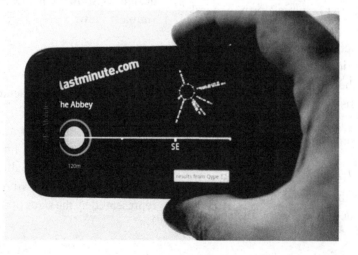

Figure 6. Using a touchscreen gesture to rotate the compass view

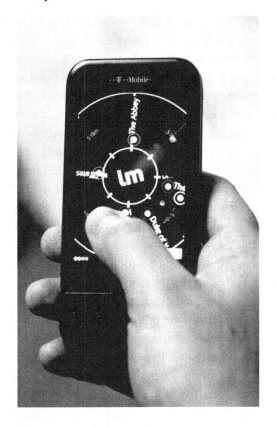

CONTENT SOURCES

The nru application draws on content from a variety of sources depending on the users' country of origin. For a customer originating in the UK (i.e., someone who as a handset purchased in the UK), the location-based content comprises:

- Restaurants, from the lastminute.com "fonefood" mobile restaurant booking service (covering approximately 6000 restaurants in 12 European countries)
- Bars, Bowling Alleys, Cafes, Cinemas, Clubs, Comedy Clubs, Music Venues, Pubs, Snooker & Pool Clubs all from Qype[3] (covering over 100 countries worldwide)

For a customer originating in the USA the location-based content comprises:

- Restaurants, nightlife and shopping, all from Zagat[4] (covering 95 countries worldwide)

Since the application retrieves content from various APIs that all have differing capabilities and schemas, we have created an intermediate service called "geoff" (the **geo**graphic **f**eed **f**inder). The geoff service takes a standardised request from a location-based client such as nru, and then delivers the nearby content aggregated from multiple providers. Some providers are queried in real time (such as Qype) while others provide a periodic transfer of data (such as Zagat). One of the functions within the geoff service is to standardise the data from different provides so that it is delivered in a consistent format to the nru client.

LESSONS LEARNED

The T-Mobile G1 handset was the first Android handset launched in the UK, in October 2008. nru was launched into the UK Android Market in January 2009, and into the US Android market in June 2009. Rather than conduct formal user testing as we normally do, we opted to make the system publicly available to the early adopter community who were among the first purchasers of the Android handsets, and to iterate and improve the system based on their feedback. We took advantage of the functionality of the Android market for applications that allows users to be informed of and easily upgrade their nru applications as we release updated versions. At the time of writing we have had approximately 11000 downloads in the UK and 5000 in the USA. Uptake has been quick partly because of Google's decision to give this application prominent billing as one of the few "featured" in the Market, and partly because the novelty of the interface. At the time the G1 was the only compass-enabled phone available and so this kind of functionality had never been seen before by most customers.

So what lessons have we learned since launch? Broadly we can categorise them into those to do with the content available or those to do with the interaction and user interface.

Content

In creating nru, and our earlier "fonefood" location-based mobile web service for booking restaurants, we had assumed that most users were very familiar with local listings and booking services as desktop web sites. For instance the regular lastminute.com site already has a restaurant search and booking service, and similar services have been commonplace for many years. This assumption was proved correct—users were indeed familiar with the terminology and the nature of the data available. However we hadn't anticipated the consequences of putting data from these listings services into a mobile location-based system. As soon as the user is seeing just the nearby things, particularly in an application such as nru where there is a real feeling of proximity, then there is a much greater expectation that there will indeed be many results nearby, wherever the application is used. As most of the content services we use have heavy concentrations in larger cities, and are much sparser in smaller towns or villages, this leads to disappointment and violated expectations for users where there aren't many nearby results. In order to trust, believe in and use the service, users want all of their local establishments to be listed. If, when looking around them using the nru interface, they can see restaurants or bars that nru isn't showing, they feel it isn't working correctly. This is a problem of setting expectations inappropriately, through our messaging and the workings of our interface. It also means we must pick content sources where we understand the areas of concentration very well so we can make them clear to users.

Interaction

Since the launch of the iPhone, touch interfaces have become a major new trend in mobile design. For designers, it gives them a clear benchmark for how users perceive touch interactions and how things should behave. The flip side of having such a dominant device in the market is that the designer has to create unique experiences if he or she wants a user to accept a change in the design rationale. For example, if the designer is working with a map and presenting data overlaid on it, he or she will be judged against the currently dominant interaction style. Through touch interfaces especially, interactions are coupled with the design, shape and position of elements within a UI. For example, the Google Maps interactions dominate the map expectations of iPhone users.

Using movement of the entire phone for navigation means the application is not overloaded with touch gestures to be learned. The simplicity of moving the device or the user around is elegant compared to artificially moving one's finger across the device. The authors designed the compass and scanner views to overcome the issues of competing with the existing Google Maps interaction paradigm for presenting location-based data, and this is one of the reasons why the authors have resisted displaying a map layer under the compass view.

Our feedback has been very positive for both the compass and scanner views, and the rotation of the phone around the body has proven to be intuitive in the sense that users have understood the interaction immediately. What has been less obvious is the switch between the compass and scanner view as the phone is lifted, with some users taking a little while to realise this was possible, and even then not always understanding what it was that caused the switch. Users have also been very forgiving when the compass accuracy has been poor, as it often is indoors, seeing the interface as quite playful and novel rather than judging it on accuracy alone.

An obvious problem, particularly with the compass view, is that the text can be hard to read as it rotates, especially for longer names of establishments or where there is significant overlap. This is an area for further research into visualisation and layout, to find a more legible arrangement.

Through our constraints a nice design feature emerged. As we limited the scope of the application to retrieve the 10 closest things within a category, without the possibility for the user to use a pinch gesture to zoom in the interface, we discovered that occasionally the results would be further away and within a specific direction. This means we are effectively not only the showing the location of places but also indicating which parts of a city are interesting for a specific category. For instance in Figure 7 all the nearest comedy clubs are in a single direction, so there is clearly a concentration in that part of the city and thus it makes a good destination.

Although nru is only applied to city activities, any geographic data source could be plugged in to create any number of new services. For instance, retail chains are looking for applications to locate the nearest shop and by projects hoping to guide visitors toward various cultural attractions within cities. A clear constraint is that users do expect nru to work on a very local level, so whatever data is used needs to have sufficient density so that within the region of interest the nearest point is not more than a few minutes' walk.

CONCLUSION

The authors have introduced various methods to present location-based data in a mobile application and explained the capabilities available on an Android phone handset. Bringing those together, the authors created nru ("near you"), a mobile application running on a consumer phone handset that starts to introduce some of the interaction style and insights from the world of augmented reality. NRU has been available to the public for

Figure 7. nru compass view showing lots of comedy clubs all in the same direction

approximately six months, and the authors have summarised some of the lessons learned, both about the content and about the interface itself.

The strong positive reaction expressed by users does suggest that the application may benefit from picking up ideas from the philosophical traditions of Merlau-Ponty (1945) and Hathaway (1985), where the central notion is how we understand meaning through objects, their configuration in space and our own body's relationship to them. With the introduction of powerful mobile platforms such as Android, designers have a chance to re-explore the notions of ready-at-hand, present-at-hand once again. A modern mobile UI is more than meets eye. It is the combination of the motion, the gestures, the form of the physical device and the visual screen interface that creates the immersive experience; that makes us feel a mobile UI is elegant and simple. A good introduction for designers and computer scientists to this philosophy and its intrinsic relationship with computer science and interaction design over the last decade is Embodied Interactions (Dourish, 2001), where Dourish outlines what potential the body has in interactive systems.

This style of real-world interaction will come to dominate location-based services for phones in the near future, both using the positioning, accelerometers, magnetometers and touchscreen as described, and using the camera as an additional input device for shorter-range recognition. When engaging with this new style of interaction, users expectations about the density of content available are increasing rapidly, and in many cases more rapidly than can be met with existing sources of content. This challenge, together with that of refining the interfaces and interactions themselves, provide many good directions for further research.

REFERENCES

Azuma, R. (1997). A Survey of Augmented Reality. *Presence (Cambridge, Mass.)*, 6(4), 355–385.

Dourish, P. (2001). Where the Action Is. Cambridge, MA: MIT Press.

Gosling, J., Joy, B., Steele, G., & Bracha, G. (2005). *Java(TM) Language Specification* (3rd ed.). Reading, MA: Addison-Wesley.

Hathaway, D. (1985). A Manifesto for Cyborgs: Science, Technology and Socialist-Feminism in the 1980s. *Socialist Review*, *80*, 65–108.

Ishii, H., & Ullmer, B. (1997). *Tangible bits: Towards seamless interfaces between people, bits and atoms*. Paper presented at the Conference on Human Factors in Computing Systems.

Merleau-Ponty, M. (1945). *Phenomenology of perception*. London: Routledge.

Oliver, E. (2009). A survey of platforms for mobile networks research. *ACM SIGMOBILE Mobile Computing and Communications Review*, *12*(4), 7. doi:10.1145/1508285.1508292

Schmalstieg, D., & Wagner, D. (2007). Experiences with Handheld Augmented Reality. In *Proceedings of the Symposium on Mixed and Augmented Reality* (pp. 12).

Starner, T., Mann, S., Rhodes, B., Levine, J., Healey, J., & Kirsch, D. (1997). Augmented Reality Through Wearable Computing. *Presence (Cambridge, Mass.)*, *6*(4), 386–398.

Turner, D. (2007). Hack: The Nintendo Wii. *MIT Technology Review, July*.

ENDNOTES

[1] http://maps.google.com
[2] http://m.lastminute.com
[3] http://www.qype.co.uk
[4] http://www.zagat.com

This work was previously published in International Journal of Creative Interfaces and Computer Graphics, Volume 1, Issue 1, edited by Ben Falchuk, pp. 5-18, copyright 2010 by IGI Publishing (an imprint of IGI Global).

Chapter 2
Aesthetic Expectations for Information Visualization

Anna Ursyn
University of Northern Colorado, USA

ABSTRACT

This article explores the landscape of creative endeavors in the new media art and reflects on aesthetics of information visualization. When using computer based information visualization to show data inter-actively in many dimensions, the user can navigate across big data sets, find patterns, relationships, and structures that would be invisible if presented numerically. The authors also explore ways of combining information visualization techniques with the principles of creative design, enhancing artistic influences on the technical implementations, and raising the level of training in design. Finally, the authors offer suggestions for creating knowledge visualizations with the use of art and graphics to strengthen the readiness of computer scientists to fulfill aesthetic expectations and gain recognition from art world specialists for factual solutions done in visualization projects and new forms of art.

INTRODUCTION

Generally speaking, an opinion is now well established that art, graphic design, visual storytelling, and the use of signs and metaphors support visual communication by combining creative imagery with the analytic rationality of conceptual diagrams. Computer graphics are often used to translate into pictures data about events and processes, so the data is easier to understand. A fisheye view, a tree-map, or a pile metaphor may serve as examples of classic representations used for pictorial data presentation. By the way of illustration, a BumpTop prototype for desktop organization is a pile metaphor that integrates interaction and visualization techniques optimized for pen input (Aragawala, 2006).

DOI: 10.4018/978-1-4666-0285-4.ch002

Despite advances in information visualization it remains difficult to locate information and explore its structure. For example, the linkage structure of the World Wide Web would be valuable to understand but is extremely difficult to visualize. Consider also that despite billions of bytes of video data sharing Internet sites such as YouTube and Hulu, that understanding and exploring within the content is still near impossible. Visual presentation of large data sets is in demand because Web became the main carrier of information. When we use the search engine, too much data must be scrolled on the screen, so new browsers are necessary to present information visually. It can be done with the use of information visualization, data mining, and semantic Web. It seems reasonable to assume that merging verbal and visual ways of communication makes the central part in scientific visualization and simulation, virtual reality environments, Web based environments, Web graphics, game design, visualizations of big sets of data, semantic Web, data mining, and many other tasks and areas of interest. (Visualization can be described as the creation and algorithmic manipulation of graphic images directly from the 1D, linear, 3D world, and multidimensional data. Information visualization is usually defined as the presentation of pictures showing easy-to-recognize objects, which are connected through some well-defined relations, to amplify cognition. It is usually done with the use of computer supported, interactive, sensory (mostly visual) representations of abstract data (Card et al., 1999; Bederson & Shneiderman, 2003). In knowledge visualization, it is generally accepted that visual representations are used to improve the creation and transfer of knowledge between people. In contrast to information visualization that supports the retrieval and organization of large data sets about facts and numbers, knowledge visualization helps to augment communication about knowledge-related relations and principles).

The following text comprises some issues concerning art and aesthetics in the context of information visualization domain and the new media art. First, it discusses the changing landscape of creative endeavors in new media art and information visualization: the decisive role of visual literacy and visual science, application of metaphorical thinking about concepts and data, and the position of aesthetics in new media art and information visualization. Secondly, it analyzes some ways of enhancing artistic influence on the technical implementations by combining knowledge visualization techniques with the principles of creative design and insights of cognitive neuroscience, as well as some tools that may support such endeavors. In the third place, this article offers suggestions about creating knowledge visualizations with the use of art and graphics. Proposals for visual problem solving in displaying information and data comprise several kinds of activities aimed to improve one's power of conveying meaning with images, along with conclusions coming from the research and direct observation done in the educational setting.

THE CHANGING LANDSCAPE OF CREATIVE ENDEAVORS

A wide variety of available technologies may allow people from various disciplines strive to unite the artistic content of a work with presentation and organization of the data. How both are solved graphically and aesthetically, poses an important question. The evolving presence of computer graphics created many opportunities for people not necessarily trained in visual arts. Visualization projects are mostly done by specialists in computer science having small amount of background in art or design, while artists and designers often work on visualization without much knowledge in computer science (Kosara, 2007). According to Kosara, a minimal set of requirements for any visualization comprises an image based on data that is readable and recognizable.

Information visualization specialists, software programmers, scientists, musicians, system architecture developers, and many other technology-oriented people find their production intertwined with the visual flow of their thoughts. They acquire means to communicate knowledge by changing tacit knowledge into explicit one—as mental representations and images, and then by finding meaningful patterns and structural relations in graphical displays of data. However, computer scientists may not receive the level of training in design that artists and architects do.

Some hold that art background is not important because there may be cooperation with artists. As artists often demonstrate quite different frame of reference, acquiring one's own sufficient level of visual literacy and skills might appear more satisfying. For scientists, collaboration with visual artists opens new opportunities, while others strive to develop their own ways of artistic expression. Some Website and software designers often apply ready clipart images, stock photos or backgrounds, and relay on artistic skills of people who designed these resources. Some authors create generative art by adding visual sequences and soundscapes to their visualizations. Many times visualization experts, after finding patterns in visual metaphors, ascribe to their products a rank of aesthetic quality, even when color composition is executed in a printer-derived cyan-magenta-yellow-black) set of colors. Developing one's own creations and building confidence in one's own choices and solutions depend often on practice. Projects one may want to create become often an open stage for experimentation with finding new paradigms in visual problem solving.

Programmers and software developers have been going a U-turn shape way: from having a good self-confidence about the superiority of their field of expertise over the art- and design-related skills (thus saying, for example, "I can only draw stick figures, and I feel good about it") to a rude awakening by becoming fully aware that effectiveness and aesthetics may not be as independent as they initially seem (Vande Moere, 2008). According to Peters (2007), the aesthetic appeal of interfaces becomes more important because users are more willing to adopt a product if it evokes pleasurable feelings. Visualizations that are captivating are easier, and thus find bigger audience. For example, Seifert et al. (2008) present a family of algorithms for a tag cloud layout. Evaluation in terms aesthetic quality of tag clouds, obtained from an extensive user study, confirms that aesthetic values correlate with product usability. Analysis of the visual patterns in networks may result in finding analogies along with an aesthetic experience. According to Ricard Solé (2008, p. 243), "the natural description of complex systems involves a network view where each system is represented by means of a Web. Such graphs have been shown to share surprisingly universal patterns of organization ... When studying human genome architecture, and looking for the logic of genes or proteins interactions, the scientists find a familiar pattern: the way molecules interact within cells is not very different from the way the Internet is organized".

A research study revealed that the perceived data visualization aesthetics produced an effect on specific measures of usability of 11 different visualization techniques: the most aesthetic data visualization technique performed relatively high in metrics of effectiveness, rate of task abandonment, and latency of erroneous response (Cawthon & Vande Moere, 2007).

VISUAL LITERACY AND VISUAL SCIENCE

Visual literacy has become clearly seen as an essential step for producing efficient knowledge visualizations, with a growing body of knowledge confirming this approach; for example, last year the International Visual Literacy Association has convened for the fortieth time. Lengler (2006) argues that a more profound understanding of the vision competencies constituting visual literacy will enable practitioners and researchers to produce more effective knowledge visualizations. He considers visual literacy a prerequisite and an essential step for producing efficient knowledge visualizations, because visual literacy allows expressing concepts with visual means and constructing meaning by integrating visual messages.

One may discuss the aesthetics of visualization as related to the visual competence in the art, design, and technological solutions in visualization. Visual competence may depend on the balance between the digital art literacy and the technological literacy. Gaining competencies in digital imaging and visualization may create a need of a handbook, in a similar way as Edward Tufte did for all of us many years ago. It is possible to discern several areas for overlapping between thinking in terms of art and computer graphics. Thanks to the master work of Edward Tufte (1983, 1990, 1997), the mode of applying the visual along with the verbal way of communication has been accepted, developed and taught in the precise and thoughtful way, with all advantages coming from the chances for experiencing the insight and using mental shortcuts provided by this way of thinking. Visual quality of the data-, information-, and knowledge-visualization projects depend on the skillfully applied imagery. This may lead to one unambiguous conclusion that images, symbols, and metaphors should be created, or taken from the arts, both from the iconography of masterpieces and contemporary work of artists using technology.

Visualization experts postulated that a body of knowledge called Visual Science, with at least three major categories: geometry, spatial perception, and imaging, should be studied, practiced, and scientifically verified as a discipline, with its own knowledge base, research, history, and public perception (Hartman & Bertoline, 2005). Visual framework of the visualization science, which provides a way of dealing with massive amounts of data, draws from art, science, (mostly interac-

tive) technology, and employs visual thinking to study the processes that produce real images or images in the mind (Burkhard, 2006).

METAPHORICAL THINKING ABOUT CONCEPTS AND DATA

Assigning Visuals to Abstracts

Many hold that some themes related both to art and science can be negotiated easier as abstract concepts. Developing abstract thinking abilities is essential both in countless areas of life and in education, as abstract thinking can be seen indispensable when one strives to be virtuous in mathematics, philosophy, poetry, or science. Non-physical, numerical data (such as network system data or stock market values) often refers to naturally occurring objects and related events. In such cases metaphors are often applied to process complex information. Interdisciplinary concepts, such as design cognition, user engagement, aesthetics, and art can enhance information visualization (Vande Moere, 2008). Many times information visualizations have been obtained by assigning visuals to abstracts. Abstract data are often described as lacking a notion of position in space. Some hold that visualization helps to link immaterial concepts to images because "the ability to perceive objects and events that have no immediate material existence made possible the visualisation and creation of tools" (Ittelson, 2007). According to Vande Moere (2008), visual metaphors serve for representing the structure of and the relationships within abstract datasets; the interaction paradigms enable navigation inside representations that map abstract data as physical artifacts, with different degrees of 'data physicality:' ambient display, pixel sculptures, object augmentation, data sculptures and alternative modality.

Conceptual Metaphors

Metaphor is generally considered a basic structure for communicating messages. George P. Lakoff, a cognitive linguistics professor, says that metaphors address cognitive abilities to abstract the essence of the idea. Conceptual metaphors allow for understanding an abstract or unfamiliar domain in terms of another, more familiar concrete domain (Lakoff, 1990). Visual metaphors, which make such concepts visible, are inherent in our thought, and thus enable visualization of abstract concepts. The use of suitable metaphor is crucial in program visualization, while a successful retrieval of data for visualization depends on the availability of right metaphor. Numerous kinds of metaphorical forms, which are also present in literature, visual arts, and music, make possible visualization of concepts derived from mathematics, cognitive science, and philosophy. Symbols may support developing the systems of ideas, recognizing particulars, discerning relations and concepts. By introducing symbols and metaphors, an artist may help to incorporate some concepts and complex data into a larger entity and hold the user's attention on cognitive processes.

Metaphors are often shaped upon natural forms, such as an ammonite, a Nautilus shell, or a double helix of the DNA molecule (Figure 1a, b). For example, helix, a curve drawn on a conical or cylindrical plane, can be found on Nautilus shells or the extinct ammonoid fossils from the Devonian or Cretaceous periods, However, the spiral chains of polymers characteristic of the nucleic acids, such as the deoxyribonucleic acid (DNA), or other protein molecules have also a helical form.

On the other hand, the same forms may present geometrical curves or mathematical equations. Mathematical knots, that have been inspired by our everyday experience related to fastening hitches, shoelaces, or strings, are the knots closed without any open end to be untied, and have to be embedded in higher-dimensional space to be properly examined. They provide inspiration to sculptors, architects, graphic artists, and designers (Figure 2). At the same time, those working on graph visualization or analyses of many kinds of topological objects may take advantage of applying the knot theory, a branch of mathematics that studies knots.

Figure 1. a) A mollusk shell (© Anna Ursyn); b) A double helix of the DNA molecule (© Olson group)

a.

b.

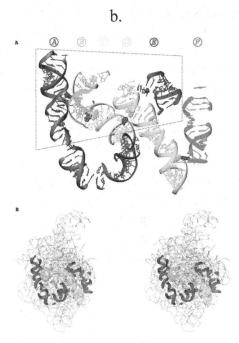

Figure 2. Helaman Ferguson, Twisted Knot (© Helaman Ferguson) This paper restaurant napkin sculpture is based on the 27,000 year-old algorithm. The impressions of cordage in ceramic materials were discovered and dated at Dolni Vestinice. The algorithm is iterative and has three steps: twist, twist, and counter twist. It is a very important algorithm, fundamental in all the clothes we were making of rope, cable, etc.

Natural Metaphors

An opinion is well established that natural metaphors may provide the best basis of scientific and technological visualization (Paton et al., 1991). Authors active in the field of cognitive science hold that natural metaphors, as well as words, reside in thought as instinctively understandable concepts (Mateo & Sauter, 2007). They are based on our basic experience; for example, the domain of quantity is represented as verticality: 'more is up' and 'less is down' (Lakoff & Núñez, 2001; Science Forum, 2009). The concept of natural architecture (e.g., Rocca, 2007) addresses two aspects of the natural and the manmade: the conceptual split and the relationship of architecture to its surroundings. Mateo and Sauter present diverse design approaches; nature has rendered poetic potential to stimulate, as a metaphor, the design process. From formal, conceptual, geometrical to literal engagements, the scope of potential correlations between nature and design is as far reaching as the human imagination.

Visual Metaphors

We may find an extensive use of metaphors in literature, visual arts, and music. In a visual mode of articulation, images that have iconic properties or serve as generally accepted symbols could be considered crucial to visualization of the hard to explicate objects and notions. Such simple subjects are often being pictured in art works, serving as metaphorical statements about the theme and the artist's thoughts on the theme. Common, primary, simple elements of our environment, such as raindrops, snowflakes, and simplified animal shapes might serve as a carrier of a notion. Extensive use of natural metaphors might yield art works that are massively structured in cognitive terms.

Metaphors that are widely used in visualization projects include a city, a house, parking lot, metro, library, street, and also facial expressions. Clouds and trees can be seen as metaphorical forms conveying both qualities and quantities presented in visual way. The use of signs and metaphors in art, graphic design, and visual storytelling may support visual communication, organize and structure information graphically and convey human insight about the represented information through the key characteristics of the visualization metaphor. When we deal with several kinds of data, we may describe with metaphors the structure and the relations among data.

Ralph Lengler and Martin Eppler (2006) applied as a metaphor a grid-like, tabular form of displaying chemical elements, first devised in 1869 by the Russian chemist Dmitri Mendeleev, and known as the Mendeleev's periodic table. They designed an impressive interactive presentation of one hundred visualization methods, "A Periodic Table of Visualization Methods". They have also designed other metaphorical visualizations, such as an interactive visualization on visual literacy: "Mapping the Stairs to Visual Excellence," an interactive map, "Knowledge Domain Visualization Studies," and "Knowledge Domain Map.

Auditory Metaphors

Natural metaphors seem even more essential for music theory and appreciation. Zbikowski (1998, 2005) stressed how much cognitive science research on metaphor has to offer music theory, "There seems little doubt that musical analyses are not scientific explanations, but metaphorical ones. It remains to explore the nature and depth of these metaphors, and, in doing so, to come to a better appreciation of the processes through which we organize our understanding of music" (Zbikowski, 1998). According to Desain and Honing (1992, 1996), metaphors in music theory inform and shape the ways we theorize about music. In music theory, tempo is often compared to walking or moving, while the harmonic, melodic, rhythmic, and time related progression of music is characterized by flow or motion. Natural, physical metaphors are also abundant in music psychology. Brian Evans (Figure 3) creates visualization of sound as an image and sonification of an image into sound, thus creating the visual rendition of a music form as

music for the eyes. He wrote, "Sound to image—a visualization. Image to sound—a sonification. In mapping numbers into sensory experience, aesthetic decisions are made. The sound should be seen, the image audible" (Evans, 2007a).

A SHIFT IN THE POSITION OF AESTHETICS IN NEW MEDIA ART AND INFORMATION VISUALIZATION

Much in the same way as general definition of art may be shifted due to the transformed aesthetic perception of new media arts, the position and definition of aesthetics in new media art may become problematic. Tools and paradigms that the new media art have absorbed from new technologies have changed the notions and understanding of aesthetics and art in general. The developments in the new media art involve digital, participatory, multisensory, creative activities. Participatory art engage viewers into the role of producers, not only passive observers (Bishop, 2006). For this reason,

Figure 3. Brian Evans, Green pods (Evans, 2007b)

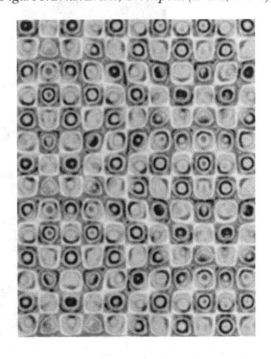

in a foreword to the Moggridge'a book (2007), Gillian Crampton Smith states that designers of digital technology products no longer regard their job as designing a physical object—beautiful or utilitarian—but as designing our interactions with it. With this approach, Corwin Bell (Figure 4) produced interactive computer video games with biofeedback sensors that measure heart rate and skin conductance; players learn to control their breathing, build mental serenity, and reduce stress.

A need became evident, of forging aesthetic principles related to new media art and tools for criticism that are in dialogue with new technologies and the visual vocabulary they invent. These studies would allow gaining the capacity to shape existing criteria in the art world aesthetics and criticism. Some hold that aesthetics of new creative media cannot be analyzed in terms analogous to traditional artistic practices, especially when such analysis is based on misinterpretation of aesthet-

ics as equivalent to art. Few would challenge the Andres Gaviria's (2008, p. 481) assumption that "aesthetics is concerned with the theory of sensual perception, while art is a social practice involved in certain forms of research and investigation processes and in the construction of particular types of artifacts." Lau and Vande Moere (2007) refer the concept of aesthetics to the degree of artistic influence on the visualization technique, the amount of interpretative engagement it facilitates, and the context in which the data should be interpreted, which is in contrast with 'aesthetics' as the visual appeal and quality of visual artifacts, which largely depend on human subjective judgment. However, perception of digital, participatory, multisensory art has become even more transformed with the growing spectrum of domains included into the general notion of art. Blais and Ippolito (2006) confront generally accepted definition of art by adding several fields of creative

Figure 4. Corwin Bell, Journey to the Wild Divine, interactive game (the University of Northern Colorado Master of Arts project) along with his next games.

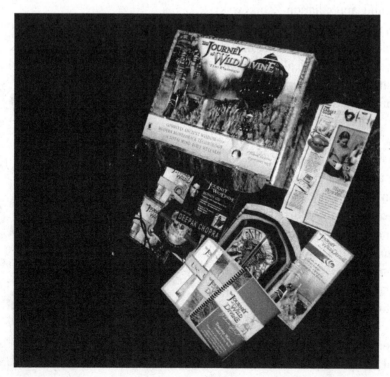

activity, such as computer code-based art, games, online autobiography, haktivism, computer virus making and preservation, and community building.

Some hold that the aesthetic and cultural principles of the new media should not dissociate themselves from earlier media, but mediate and refashion the approaches to earlier media (Bolter & Grusin, 2000). Indeed, the combined commitment of artists and visualization specialists to aesthetics and technology makes happen that the distinctions between the artists who practice the traditional aesthetic art and the informative functional art tend to be vanishing (Vande Moere, 2005). Cultural theorists, philosophers of new media (e.g., Hansen, 2006), and media artists are developing new critical tools for discussing media art and critically examining their aesthetics-related features (Rieser & Zapp, 2008; Popper, 2005). After tryouts and experiments, project solutions should be good enough to hang them on the living room wall and live with them comfortably for at least a month. In a similar way, in a good time-based project, one can see every frame óf an animation as a masterpiece.

Few thought to challenge the assumption that aesthetics is essential in visualization. The theory and practice of art criticism can support visualization criticism; they can be appropriated and modeled to provide building blocks for a visualization theory acceptable for a scientific discipline (Erbacher, 2007). Masters of information visualization are working on developing some principal rules about information aesthetics. For several years, books (for example, Maeda 2004; Manovich, 2008; Fishwick; 2008; Vesna, 2007), courses, and conference presentations convey this knowledge to the computing community. A need for developing appealing visualizations applied for information visualization have prompted the attempts to formulate the aesthetics of visualization in terms of its functional value in inquiry, research, and experimentation (Gaviria, 2008). Lau and Vande Moere (2007) map the relationship of information aesthetics with different visualization techniques according to three factors: data, aesthetics, and interaction. Research results about perception and visual cognition suggest that the foundation of aesthetics is in cognitive neuroscience, because aesthetic preferences correlate with specific brain structures and processing systems. According to Peters, a physicist and photographer (2007) (Figure 5) both cognitive neuroscience and artistic principles give us clues to define dimensions of visual aesthetics. Each dimension, called by the author the aesthetics primitive, such as color,

Figure 5. Gabriele Peters, New York: Dark Days (© Gabriele Peters). The negative has been scanned with high resolution (4000 ppi), and before the enlargement of the image, artificial grain was added to exaggerate the pointillist effect of the film grain.

form, spatial organization, motion, depth, and the human body, can evoke an aesthetic experience.

Definition of aesthetics in computing refers not only to the formal quality of computing, but also to ideas of creative expression and pleasure in the context of computer science (Fishwick, 2006). Some visualization projects earn prestigious artistic awards. "Processing"—an open source programming language and integrated development environment (Reas & Fry, 2007; Fry, 2008), created by Reas and Fry for the electronic arts and visual design communities, won a 2005 Golden Nica award at Prix Ars Electronica—International Competition for CyberArts

ENHANCING ARTISTIC INFLUENCE ON TECHNICAL IMPLEMENTATIONS

Advantages Coming from Engineering New Tools

The question has been around whether advancements in information visualization may necessitate artistic input. Examination of the possible solutions brings about suggestions about combining information visualization techniques and tools with the principles of creative design. This may be seen as a dual task: taking full advantage of available tools and encouraging programmers, software developers, and other professionals to present information and data through art and graphics. For this reason, cognition science and visual aesthetics experts support visualization specialists, Webpage designers, and interface constructors in identifying the needs of the user and selecting the tools to represent, map, and interpret the data. Concerns about aesthetics of visualization correspond somehow with an interest in the aesthetics of the new media art derived from its technical characteristics: being digital, networked, multisensory, immersive, or interactive. According to Ippolito (2002), the Internet artists who employ online protocols including

the World Wide Web, e-mail, peer-to-peer instant messaging, videoconference software, MP3 audio files, and text-only environments like MUDs and MOOs, enriched the scope of electronic media.

The information visualization professionals are now focusing on visual content analysis, thus shifting from a visual and presentational exploration to visual analytics techniques that aim at broadening our awareness of knowledge. This shift creates potential for new application domains and evolving scientific disciplines. A new framework for information visualization includes cooperation of researchers involved in information-rich disciplines, such as humanities, psychology, sociology, architecture, natural sciences, business and management, rather than just technology-rich disciplines (Banissi, 2008). Indeed, visualization machinery is now available to anyone with a dataset and Internet connectivity. For example, the Many Eyes Website, a free site where anyone can may upload their own data, create interactive visualizations, and carry on conversations about data, has been created with a goal to "democratize" visualization, and experiment with new collaborative techniques (Wattenberg, 2007).

The spectrum has been widened with the evolvement of the critical theory of bio art using biotechnology as its medium (Kac, 2006), and of the evolutionary computing that harnesses the power of natural selection to turn computers into automatic optimization, design tools, and evolutionary art (for instance, works of EvoArt at the European Network of Excellence in Evolutionary Computing (2008). Artists manipulate in many ways life processes and invent or transform living forms, but also develop ecosystem engineering and simulations of biotic and abiotic habitats (Dorin & Korb, 2007). By adding visual sequences and soundscapes to generative art creation, they contribute to advances in the art- and aesthetics-related concepts.

Generative architecture is designed as a genetic code of artificial events. The codes of transformation resemble the natural structure of DNA. Celestino Soddu (2009) used generative software to start generative approach for designing artificial DNA of Italian medieval towns (Figure 6 a, b). His works include intelligent industrial productions and cities identity design.

Some artists map the data into sensory experience. For example, Brian Evans provides visual presentation of sounds and music; he creates visualization of sound as an image and sonification of an image into sound. Thus the visual rendition of a music form might be considered music for the eyes. He states, "Sound to image—a visualization; Image to sound—a sonification. In mapping numbers into sensory experience, aesthetic decisions are made. The sound should be seen, the image audible" (Evans, 2007 a, b).

In educational setting, virtual reality technologies that make available interactive three-dimensional virtual reality software and visual content management (for example, Eon Reality, Inc.), provide a much-appreciated learning environment for enhancing artistic input to knowledge visualization projects. Interactive learning became widely encountered with online training tutorials, such as Lynda.com. Simulation tools, video games, and virtual reality environments can reshape children's mathematical crafts (Eisenberg et al., 2005). The use of design software, such as JavaGami or HyperGami (Figure 7 a, b), allows children to go beyond recipes in the creation of original mathematical-and-artistic creations. According to Eisenberg, by placing computers inside craft objects we can make them programmable, interactive yet with autonomous behavior.

Exploring the Context and Culture of Knowledge Visualization

Extensive research studies result in finding ways supporting individuals in their effort to solve problems visually while dealing with data to be mapped onto visual space. Research work is aimed to understand the language of visualization,

Figure 6. a) Celestino Soddu, Basilica (© Celestino Soddu) b) Building by Celestino Soddu (© Celestino Soddu)

a.

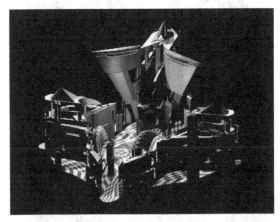

b.

along with interactive context and culture of media supporting the new approaches. Information visualization conference proceedings provide the visual content analysis applied to data and knowledge visualization.

Discussion of the aesthetics of information visualization draws from existing approaches to information art and, even earlier, digital art. Moreover, tracing the evolution of digital art cannot be

Figure 7. a) Michael Eisenberg, A Hypergami project; b) Michael Eisenberg, A JavaGami project

a.

b.

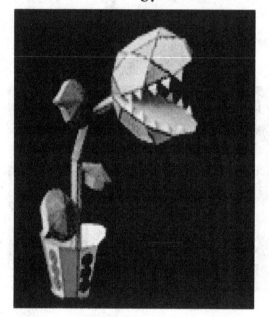

done without placing it within the context of art history, and in relation to other disciplines, such as cognitive science, computer science, philosophy, media studies, art history and criticism, and sciences dealing with images (Grau, 2004, 2007; Wardrip-Fruin, 2003; Lovejoy, 2004).

Artists' cooperation could amplify possible imagery from which visualization metaphors

may be selected to evoke an aesthetic experience. With inspiration coming from nature and/or mathematics, realities created with the use of programming refer to our imagination and experience based on physiological reality of the mind. With this perspective, one may anticipate an impact of information visualization practices on aesthetic experience and the existing views about representation through art. As stated by Erbacher (2007), artistic component is required in effective visualization techniques, to fulfill both the aesthetic and technical requirements. Quite few would challenge the belief that ability to create visualizations in compliance with the creative principles of design comes with learning through creating art, contrary to the hands-on, step-by-step, or rote learning by memorization and repetition. The hands-on learning may involve concrete operational thinking mode, while integrating visuals and computer graphics may cultivate higher-order thinking skills.

VISUAL PROBLEM SOLVING IN DISPLAYING INFORMATION AND DATA

Visualizing knowledge in graphical form may contribute to combining both the precise and expressive way of thinking and emboldening visualization professionals to link creative imagery with the analytic rationality, invent the visual vocabulary in dialogue with new technologies, and enhance artistic influences on the technical implementations. Texts are linear and static, while pictorial and time-based constructions of net media are dynamic and often interactive. Everyday environments (such as computers, communication media, TV, multimedia, online protocols, and games) serve as a container for a story. From traditional texts, we go toward the effective storytelling with verbal-with-visual working style that utilizes electronic media. Research results and first hand observations in educational setting provide material for suggestions about the ways to learn imaging data through art and graphics. Drawing inspiration from science for exercises in creating art is one of possible ways, because everything we encounter is interdisciplinary.

It seems activities aimed at improving one's power to conveying meaning by merging information visualization with the principles of creative design may comprise several kinds of tasks:

1. Visual Presentation of Scientific Concepts

Visual, verbal, and time-based approaches can be best combined when art and science related themes are integrated, to engage one in combining the precise and expressive way of thinking. Presenting difficult concepts through visual metaphors make easier learning and understanding of abstract ideas and processes. With cognitive approach to mental imagery, one can visualize science concept and create image representation of it. This can be done through hand drawing or, even better, by creating computer art graphics. Visual representation of scientific data related material in both pictorial and verbal way involves thinking about selected events or processes in order to present them visually. Content analysis includes deriving meaning from the data, a study of techniques and concepts (such as examining its independent and dependent variables), and possible comparisons in time and space. Activities of this type are aimed to evoke a holistic, synaesthetic mode of learning and engage visual, verbal, and manual modes of action. Metaphorical imaging and abstract thinking prevail over hands-on instruction and mere memorization when it comes to learning higher-level thinking concepts and accomplishing tasks such as writing programs, creating computer graphics, or designing a visualization project (Figure 8 a, b).

In educational setting, a research study conducted in cooperation with a physicist (Ursyn & Sung, 2007) involved integrative instruction in science and examined the effect of non-restrained, spontaneous creation of sketches, versus writings, on the effectiveness of student learning. In a University of Northern Colorado master's level research, Jennifer Neal Brill (2009) linked the study of visual arts with the improved reading comprehension in elementary school students. Yet another research study related to integrated instruction in teaching art and various subfields in physics. Mental visualization of the main fields in physics may facilitate problem solving, and enhance the content and nature of mental imagery in cognition and learning. The rationale for this program has been confirmed by the results of previous experimental studies that applied art in technical instruction in programming (Ursyn & Scott, 2007; Ursyn et al., 1997). Student achievement in science was tested after students received integrative instruction in computer graphics, Web construction, and Web site design, and then created their knowledge-based art, drawing upon concepts from programming, Web design, computer graphics, art, and design.

2. Creating Art by Finding Inspiration in a Science-Based Topic

This approach involves one's visual response to a scientific concept after exploration of its meaning, and creating science-based art with the use of computer graphics software or programming. Data, processes, products, and events serve as a theme for art. It may be a challenging and rewarding activity to create an artistic presentation of concepts taken from various disciplines and thus show one's visual power and understanding of underlying processes, products, and forces. It may mean turning data into pictures by mapping from abstract description to images. One may use a metaphor as a form of thought and present knowledge with the use of electronic media for retrieving and visualizing data (Figure 9 a, b, c).

Figure 8. a) Trevor Pfaff, A Journey to the Center of the Earth – University of Wyoming student work. This is concept visualization. The face area is a representation of the density of the material as the trip progresses toward the center of the earth. Density is also represented by the shading. The thickness of the block indicates the thickness of each layer. The trip begins at the upper left at the multi- composition surface, and ends at the solid core in the center of the picture. The student included this description into the drawing, at the same time as a part of its background composition and the process explanation, so it shows his learning process; b) Ben Hobgood, A Cow program. Work of the University of Northern Colorado Student. This is a graphical representation to assist the learning of the C⁺⁺ computing language by somebody with little or no programming experience. It shows how the basic structure of C⁺⁺ works by connecting its user-defined elements with visual symbols by visualizing abstract data perceived in a simple C⁺⁺ program that asks for the pounds of food that one wishes to feed the cow, and which then reveals how many steaks can be provided in return.

a.

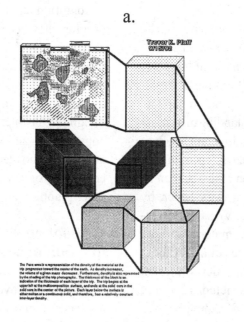

b.

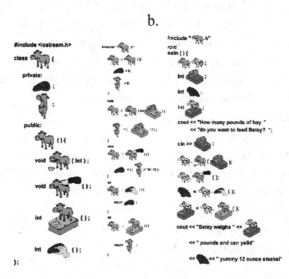

Figure 9 a) Brian Phelps, Unification (Work of the University of Northern Colorado Student); b) Andrea Carvalho, Concert. Work of the University of Northern Colorado Student. This computer art graphics was inspired with an invited lecture about nuclear fusion delivered by a physicist; c) Sam Dailey, Big Bang (Work of the University of Northern Colorado Student). This abstract work was inspired with an invited lecture about the Big Bang theory delivered by a physicist.

a.

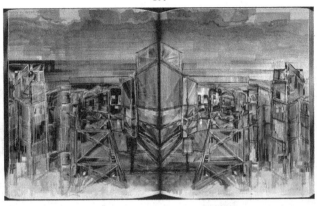

b.

c.

Figure 10 a) Craig Howie, Group Theory (Work of the University of Northern Colorado Student). This project related to the Abstract Algebra class. The basic idea of a Group is laid in the middle and all the abstraction of a Group is built from there. Color is used to show properties of symmetry in a group Caley table. The author created symbols for the concepts, for example, an algebraic operation as a sort of input-output machine. The learner may play with item configurations; b) Nathan Lowel, My Virtual Town (Work of the University of Northern Colorado PhD candidate). Visual presentation of communication media and related concepts and processes.

a.

b.

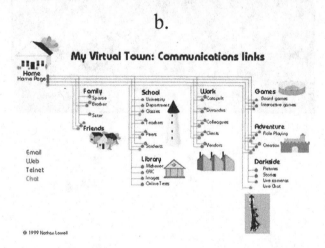

Effects of instruction with the art–science–computer graphics connection were examined in the quantitative and qualitative research studies (Ursyn, 1997). A research study in the experimental computer art graphics classes examined if students' achievement in geology could be improved by creating art and how quality of students' artwork may be influenced by their scientific experiences. Students explored geological concepts and processes through creating computer art graphics. The results of their active investigations of physical and natural phenomena served as an inspiration for creating computer art graphics assignments. Analyses of variance and covariance showed significant difference between the mean score on physical geology course taken concurrently by the students completing the science-related art assignments and those from the control group. Jurors' evaluations of the students' art quality in the form of a forced q-sort correlated with the order of art creation. In a qualitative study (Ursyn, 1994), the questionnaire answers revealed that the creation of geology-related art provided the students with confidence about their artistic abilities and increased students' understanding of scientific concepts. The results of this study indicated that building representations of scientific concepts through computer art graphics improved students' achievement in science and enhanced the students' artistic production.

3. Visual Learning by Arranging Data Visually into a Structured Whole

By applying computer art graphics techniques, one can visualize how things are working, simulate the process, and convey the meaning of a selected scientific concept. By drawing and writing everyone can transform what one just explored both into iconic (visual) and semantic (verbal) codes. The intellectual task of choosing images and words relevant to the theme just examined results in creating something useful or beautiful. According to Edward Tufte (1983, 1990, 1997), graphical display of information enhances density, complexity, dimensionality, and beauty of communication. Visual style of presentation may also reduce the intrinsic cognitive load of the users in structuring information, by somewhat shifting the explanatory task from abstract to meaningful parts, which may be easier to understand and remember. In terms of active involvement, one may draw

sketches in order to capture the essence of the selected process, and control composition of the project as well. It may be helpful in mastering the arts-related skills and putting them in service of an active, inventive, and personal way of creating information visualizations, rather than sticking to a purely technical approach.

In the educational setting, a model of visual approach to learning was created and the effectiveness of this approach to teaching and learning was tested in a "Visual Learning" class. Students designed projects about the material learned in various classes they were taking simultaneously and considered difficult. The model was aimed to support students' success in other subject areas. Production of the final projects, which visualized ideas and data in a graphical form, was preceded by instruction in visual thinking. This model of visual learning was designed as a means for analyzing the phenomenological world of the individual without sacrificing the power of analytical thinking (Figure 10a, b).

CONCLUSION

The landscape of creative endeavors has changed in terms of the role played by the aesthetic requirements of information visualizations. It became well established among programmers and software developers that effectiveness and aesthetics may not be independent, and aesthetic values correlate with product usability. It caused a need to combine information visualization techniques with the artistic principles and enhance artistic influences on the technical implementations. This task requires forging aesthetic principles related to creative media. The paper provides suggestions about ways of improving one's power of conveying meaning with images and the readiness to fulfill the aesthetic requirements of new media art and information visualization projects.

REFERENCES

Agarawala, A. (2006). *Enriching the Desktop Metaphor with Physics, Piles and the Pen* (Master's Thesis, University of Toronto). Retrieved May 10, 2009, from http://www.dgp.toronto.edu/~anand/big/Thesis-BumpTop.pdf

Banissi, E. (2008). *Preface, 12th International Conference Information Visualisation.* Retrieved April 22, 2009, from http://www2.computer.org/portal/web/csdl/abs/proceedings/iv/2008/3268/00/3268toc.htm

Bederson, B., & Shneiderman, B. (2003). *The Craft of Information Visualization: Readings and Reflections*. San Francisco: Morgan Kaufmann Publishers.

Bishop, C. (2006). *Participation (Documents of Contemporary Art)*. Cambridge, MA: MIT Press.

Blais, J., & Ippolito, J. (2006). *At the Edge of Art*. London: Thames & Hudson.

Bolter, J. D., & Grusin, R. (2000). *Remediation: Understanding New Media*. Cambridge, MA: MIT Press.

Burkhard, R. (2006). Is it Now Time to Establish Visualization Science as a Scientific Discipline? In *Proceedings of the 10th International Conference on Information Visualisation* (pp. 189-194). Washington, DC: IEEE Computer Society

Card, S. K., Mackinlay, J. D., & Shneiderman, B. (1999). *Readings in Information Visualization. Using Vision to Think*. San Francisco: Morgan Kaufmann.

Cawthon, N., & Vande Moere, A. (2007). The Effect of Aesthetic on the Usability of Data Visualization. In *Proceedings of the 11th International Conference on Information Visualisation* (pp. 637-643). Washington, DC: IEEE Computer Society.

Desain, P., & Honing, H. (1992). Music, Mind, and Machine: Studies in Computer Music, Music Cognition, and Artificial Intelligence (Kennistechnologie). *Thesis Pub*. ISBN-10: 9051701497.

Desain, P., & Honing, H. (1996). Physical motion as a metaphor for timing in music: The final ritard. In *Proceedings of the 1996 International Computer Music Conference,* San Francisco (pp. 458-460). ICMA.

Dorin, A., & Korb, K. (2007). Building Artificial Ecosystems from Artificial Chemistry. In *Proceedings of the 9th European Conference on Artificial Life* (pp. 103-112). Berlin, Germany: Springer-Verlag.

Eisenberg, M., Eisenberg, A., Blauvelt, G., Hendrix, S., Buechley, L., & Elumeze, N. (2005). Mathematical Crafts for Children: Beyond Scissors and Glue. In *Proceedings of the Art + Math = X, Special Year in Art & Mathematics International Conference* (pp. 61-64).

Erbacher, R. F. (2007). Exemplifying the Inter-Disciplinary Nature of Visualization Research. In *Proceedings of the 12th International Conference on Information Visualisation* (pp. 623-630). Washington, DC: IEEE Computer Society.

European Network of Excellence in Evolutionary Computing. (2008). *EvoWeb*. Retrieved January 04, 2009, from http://evonet.lri.fr

Evans, B. (2007a). Artist Statement. *Electronic Art and Animation Catalog, A Computer Graphics Annual Conference Series*, 264-265.

Evans, B. (2007b). *Visual Music*. Retrieved May 11, 2009, from http://www.lightspace.com

Fishwick, P. (Ed.). (2006). *Aesthetic Computing*. Cambridge, MA: MIT Press.

Fry, B. (2008). *Visualizing Data: Exploring and Explaining Data with the Processing Environment*. Sebastopol, CA: O'Reilly.

Gaviria, A. R. (2008). When Is Information Visualization Art? Determining the Critical Criteria. *Leonardo*, *41*(5), 479–482. doi:10.1162/leon.2008.41.5.479

Geiss, R. (n.d.). *Milkdrop*. Retrieved November 5, 2009, from http://www.nullsoft.com/free/milkdrop

Grau, O. (2004). *Virtual Art: From Illusion to Immersion*. Cambridge, MA: MIT Press.

Grau, O. (Ed.). (2007). *Media Art Histories*. Cambridge, MA: MIT Press.

Hansen, M. B. N. (2006). *New Philosophy for New Media*. Cambridge, MA: MIT Press.

Hartman, N. W., & Bertoline, G. R. (2005). Spatial Abilities and Virtual Technologies: Examining the Computer Graphics Learning Environment. In *Proceedings of the 9th International Conference on Information Visualisation* (pp. 992-999). Washington, DC: IEEE Computer Society.

Ippolito, J. (2002). Ten Myths of Internet Art, Tenth New York Digital Salon. *Leonardo*, *35*(5), 485–498. doi:10.1162/002409402320774312

Ittelson, W. H. (2007). The Perception of Nonmaterial Objects and Events. *Leonardo*, *40*(3), 279–283. doi:10.1162/leon.2007.40.3.279

Kac, E. (2006). *Signs of Life: Bio Art and Beyond*. Cambridge, MA: MIT Press.

Kosara, R. (2007). Visualization Criticism – the Missing Link between Information Visualization and Art. In *Proceedings of the 11th International Conference on Information Visualisation* (pp. 631-636). Washington, DC: IEEE Computer Society.

Kosara, R., Bendix, F., & Hauser, H. (2006). Parallel Sets: Interactive exploration and visual analysis of categorical data. *Transactions on Visualization and Computer Graphics*, *12*(4), 558–568. doi:10.1109/TVCG.2006.76

Lakoff, G. (1990). The Invariance Hypothesis: Is Abstract Reason Based on Image-Schemas? *Cognitive Linguistics*, *1*(1), 39–74. doi:10.1515/cogl.1990.1.1.39

Lakoff, G., & Núñez, R. E. (2001). *Where Mathematics Comes from: How the Embodied Mind Brings Mathematics Into Being*. New York: Basic Books.

Lau, A., & Vande Moere, A. (2007). Towards a Model of Information Aesthetics in Information Visualization. In *Proceedings of the 11th International Conference on Information Visualisation* (pp. 87-92). Washington, DC: IEEE Computer Society.

Lengler, R. (2006). Identifying the Competencies of 'Visual Literacy' - a Prerequisite for Knowledge Visualization. In *Proceedings of the 10th International Conference on Information Visualisation* (pp. 232-236). Washington, DC: IEEE Computer Society.

Lengler, R., & Eppler, M. (2006). *Towards A Periodic Table of Visualization Methods for Management*. Retrieved April 22, 2009, from http://www.visual-literacy.org/periodic_table/periodic_table.pdf

Lovejoy, M. (2004). *Digital Currents: Art in the Electronic Age* (3rd ed.). London: Routledge.

Maeda, J. (2004). *Creative Code: Aesthetics + Computation*. London: Thames & Hudson.

Manovich, L. (2008). *Software Takes Command*. Retrieved April 26, 2009, from http://lab.softwarestudies.com/2008/11/softbook.html

Mateo, J., & Sauter, F. (Eds.). (2007). *Natural Metaphor: Architectural Papers III*. Zurich, Switzerland: ACTAR & ETH Zurich.

Moggridge, B. (2007). *Designing Interactions*. Cambridge, MA: MIT Press.

Neal Brill, J. L. (2009). *Linking the Study of Visual Arts and Improved Reading Comprehension*. Unpublished master's thesis, University of Northern Colorado.

Paton, R. C., Nwana, H. S., Shave, M. J. R., Bench-Capon, T. J. M., & Hughes, S. (1991). Transfer of Natural Metaphors to Parallel Problem Solving Applications. In *Parallel Problem Solving from Nature* (LNCS 496, pp. 363-372).

Peters, G. (2007). Aesthetic Primitives of Images for Visualization. In *Proceedings of the 11th International Conference on Information Visualisation* (pp. 316-325). Washington, DC: IEEE Computer Society.

Popper, F. (2005). *From Technological to Virtual Art* (2nd ed.). London: Thames & Hudson.

Reas, C., & Fry, B. (2007). *Processing: A Programming Handbook for Visual Designers and Artists*. Cambridge, MA: MIT Press.

Rieser, M., & Zapp, A. (Eds.). (2008). *The New Screen Media: Cinema/art/narrative*. London: British Film Institute.

Rocca, A. (2007). *Natural Architecture*. Princeton, NJ: Princeton Architectural Press.

Seifert, C., Kump, B., Kinreich, W., Granitzer, G., & Granitzer, M. (2008). On the Beauty and Usability of Tag Clouds. In *Proceedings of the 12th International Conference on Information Visualisation* (pp. 17-25). Washington, DC: IEEE Computer Society.

Skog, T., Ljungblad, S., & Holmquist, L. E. (2003). Between aesthetics and utility: Designing ambient information visualizations. In *Proceedings of the IEEE Symposium on Information Visualization (InfoVis)* (pp. 30-37).

Soddu, C. (2009) *Argenia, Generative Art and Science*. Retrieved April 23, 2009, from http://www.celestinosoddu.com/

Solé, R. (2008). On Networks and Monsters: The possible and the actual in complex systems. *Leonardo, 41*(5), 456–460.

Tufte, E. R. (1983). *The visual display of quantitative information*. Cheshire, CT: Graphics Press.

Tufte, E. R. (1990). *Envisioning information*. Cheshire, CT: Graphics Press.

Tufte, E. R. (1997). *Visual explanations. Images and quantities, evidence and narrative*. Cheshire, CT: Graphics Press.

Ursyn, A. (1994). *Student Perception of Computer Art Graphics Integration of Art & Science*. Washington, DC: American Educational Research Association. (ERIC Document Reproduction Service No. ED 374 773)

Ursyn, A. (1997). Computer Art Graphics Integration of Art and Science. *Learning and Instruction, 7*(1), 65–87. doi:10.1016/S0959-4752(96)00011-4

Ursyn, A., Mills, L., Hobgood, B., & Scott, T. (1997). Combining Art Skills with Programming in Teaching Computer Art Graphics. *Computer Graphics, 25*, 3.

Ursyn, A., & Scott, T. (2006). *Overlap between thinking in terms of art and computer science*. Paper presented at the Consortium for Computing Sciences in Colleges (CCSC), Durango, CO.

Ursyn, A., & Scott, T. (2007) Web with Art and Computer Science. In *Proceedings of the ACM SIGGRAPH Education Committee*. ISBN 978–1–59593–648–6.

Ursyn, A., & Sung, R. (2007). Learning Science with Art. In *Proceedings of ACM SIGGRAPH Education Committee Proceedings*. ISBN 978–1–59593–648–6.

Vande Moere, A. (2005). Form follows Data: The Symbiosis between Design and Information Visualization. In *Proceedings of the International Conference on Computer-Aided Architectural Design (CAADfutures '05)*, Vienna, Austria (pp. 31-40). Retrieved January 3, 2009, from http://Web.arch.usyd.edu.au/~andrew/publications/caadfutures05.pdf

Vande Moere, A. (2008). Beyond the Tyranny of the Pixel: Exploring the Physicality of Information Visualization. In *Proceedings of the 12th International Conference on Information Visualisation* (pp. 469-474). Washington, DC: IEEE Computer Society.

Vesna, V. (2007). *Database Aesthetics: Art in the Age of Information Overflow (Electronic Mediations)*. Twin Cities, MN: University of Minnesota Press.

Wardrip-Fruin, N. (2003). *The New Media Reader*. Cambridge, MA: MIT Press.

Wattenberg, M. (2007). *Many Eyes*. Retrieved May 11, 2009, from http://www.bewitched.com/manyeyes.html

Zbikowski, L. M. (1998). Metaphor and Music Theory: Reflections from Cognitive Science. Music Theory Online. *Online Journal of the Society for Music Theory, 4*(1).

Zbikowski, L. M. (2005). *Conceptualizing Music: Cognitive Structure, Theory, and Analysis*. Oxford, UK: Oxford University Press.

This work was previously published in International Journal of Creative Interfaces and Computer Graphics, Volume 1, Issue 1, edited by Ben Falchuk, pp. 19-39, copyright 2010 by IGI Publishing (an imprint of IGI Global).

Chapter 3
Organix:
Creating Organic Objects from Document Feature Vectors

Robert J. Hendley
University of Birmingham, UK

Barry Wilkins
University of Birmingham, UK

Russell Beale
University of Birmingham, UK

ABSTRACT

This paper presents a mechanism for generating visually appealing but also effective representations for document visualisation. The mechanism is based on an organic growth model which is driven by features of the object to be visualised. In the examples used, the authors focus on the visualisation of text documents, but the methods are readily transferable to other domains. They are also scaleable to documents of any size. The objective of this research is to build visual representations that enable the human visual system to efficiently and effectively recognise documents without the need for higher level cognitive processing. In particular, the authors want the user to be able to recognise similarities within sets of documents and to be able to easily discriminate between dissimilar objects.

1.0 INTRODUCTION

Information visualisation has been defined as "The use of computer-supported, interactive, visual representations of abstract data to amplify cognition" (Card et al., 1999). This can involve many processes, such as filtering, abstracting or re-organising the data. Critically, though, it requires the generation of a visual representation which makes best use of the human visual system to allow efficient interpretation of the information.

It is important to note the difference between physical and abstract data. Physical data has some physical form on which the visualisation can be

DOI: 10.4018/978-1-4666-0285-4.ch003

based, for example archaeological data, human body (medical) data, earth data, etc., and this type of data is represented by scientific visualisations. In contrast abstract data has no such basis, examples include World Wide Web data, software modification logs, etc., and is represented by information visualisations. Effective information visualisation methods produce cognitive amplification, in which visualisation methods help to shift the work load from the cognitive to the perceptual system, expand the working memory and allow a high level of interaction. The user is thus aided in their goals of the confirmation and discovery of knowledge.

As the use of the internet increases the amount of information becoming accessible to users grows rapidly. A large percentage of this data is in text form. Often it is unstructured which makes it difficult for users to find specific information in a single document let alone in collections containing hundreds of documents. A common task faced by users is to identify documents similar in content to a particular document they already know is relevant. The most common tool for undertaking this task on the Web is the search engine. Unfortunately, having submitted a query the user is often faced with a high recall to precision ratio. Results tend to be formatted as lists of text 'snippets' which the user then has to scan through in the hope of finding something useful. We propose a novel system that attempts to visualise documents within a collection as organic shapes. It is hoped that by producing visual representations of documents users can identify similar documents more easily. Within the context of search engine results this system could be used on the 'snippets' themselves, or on the entire document. Alternatively the system could be regarded on a more artistic level as simply producing visually interesting shapes.

The following sections describe related work, the model used in the system, results obtained, future work and conclusion.

2.0 RELATED WORK

A wide variety of document collection visualisations have been developed. Bead (Chalmers & Chiston, 1992) uses physically based modelling techniques to produce document clusters. This approach can be computationally complex, an alternative and more efficient algorithm has been developed (Chalmers, 1996). WEBSOM as described by Lagus et al. (1996) uses a self organising map (SOM) algorithm to produce a map of documents with similar documents located in closely related regions of the map. Themescapes (Wise et al., 1995) visualises the thematic content of a document collection as a 3D landscape, stronger themes are give a higher elevation. A network is used by Singhal and Salton (1995), Salton (1995), the resulting structure of the network and the number of incident lines (or degree) at a particular node can give insights into the core documents or paragraphs within a particular article. The research and approaches used for text visualisation are extensive. Card et al. (1999, p409-461) contains a selection of papers discussing 1D, 2D and 3D text visualisation. A comprehensive review of document visualisation has been written by Morse (1998).

A novel system is described by Roher et al. (1998). This approach generates a document feature vector, maps the weights for each feature to distances along each axis and the eight bisecting quadrants, place spheres at the end points and finally produce a 3D amorphous shape. This allows up to 14 dimensions of the document to be viewed as a single shape. Documents can then be compared, with similar documents having similar shapes. It was this idea that inspired the current work.

Chernov faces are very simple 2D line drawings of faces where the features of the face are determined by the data. Since humans are good at recognising faces and facial expressions, it was reasoned that this may be an appropriate strategy for representing data in a form other than a face.

The system presented here is based on the same principles. Morris et al. (1999) discuss the merits of such a strategy, and indicate that in theory objects other than faces could be used to represent data in this way.

3.0 MODEL

3.1 Document Feature Vector Extraction

It should be noted that the current system considers individual words within the document to be the base unit. However, it has been written so that two or three consecutive words, sentences or even paragraphs could be consider the base unit of a document and for this reason a *term* may be a more appropriate definition rather than a *word*.

Initially a table of words and their frequencies is built for each document. As each word is read from the document it is compared to a list of predefined stop words e.g. *the*, *in*, *at*, etc., and discarded if a match is found. The word is then stemmed, this means that words such as *replace*, *replaced*, *replaceable*, etc., are equated to *replac* and treated as one word. The stemming algorithm used is based on Porters (1980). The stemmed word is then searched for in the table. Existing entries have the frequency incremented, new entries are added to the table.

A complete cumulative word/frequency table is then constructed by combining each individual document word/frequency table in the collection. This is then sorted so that the most commonly occurring words are at the top. (Table 1)

3.2 Feature Vector Weight Assignment

It is insufficient to use the frequency of the term within any particular document as an indicator of its importance. This is due to differences in document sizes. For example consider a word occurring 50 times in a document with 100 words and the same word occurring 10 times in a document of 20 words, within which document is the word more important?

Cosine normalisation is a method that generates comparable term weights. A document frequency (df) is calculated by summing the presence of a term within a document for each document in the collection. For example, if the word 'class' occurs in 20 documents out of 100 in the collection, the document frequency is 20. The inverse document frequency (idf) is 1/df, an alternative to this is to use log(df).

The weights for each term in the collection are then calculated using the following formula:

$$weight = \frac{tf * idf}{\sqrt{\left(tf_1 * idf_1\right)^2 + \left(tf_2 * idf_2\right)^2 + ... + \left(tf_n * idf_n\right)^2}}$$

Table 1. An example of a cumulative word/frequency table

Term, Cumulative Frequency	Document 1 Frequency	Document 2 Frequency	.....	Document *n* Frequency
Class, 75	25	5	.....	10
Jive, 70	1	7	.....	1
.	.	.	.....	.
.	.	.	.....	.
.	.	.	.....	.
Data, 17	0	2	.....	8

Figure 1. The order cells are added using the depth-first algorithms. Decrementing the weightIndex (left), incrementing the weightIndex only (right)

left   *right*

where *tf* is the term frequency within the document.

Once the feature vector weights for each document have been generated the organix can be grown.

3.3 Cellular Model

In the cellular growth model, the organic is grown a 'cell' at a time, each cell is associated with a weight in the vector. Cells are represented as spheres or sphere variants, as this produces a more organic effect (see cell types section 3.3.4). Cell attributes such as number of child cells or branching factor, cell distribution, cell type and cell colour are initially determined by the weights. Other attributes are determined algorithmically. These attributes may then be altered by a set of rules that are applied to the cell taking the local environment of the cell into consideration. A cell may then survive unaltered, be adapted to fit the environment or die (see rules section 3.3.5). Once the environment can no longer support cell growth the process stops and an organic shape is the result.

Several variations on the core growth algorithm have been implemented. In the following algorithms the weightIndex is the index of the weight to use from the document feature vector.

Depth-first:

```
GrowCell(parentCell, weightIndex)
generate number of child cells
for each potential child cell
        apply pre-survival rules
```

```
generate cell location
        generate cell colour
apply post-survival rules
for each surviving child cell
        increment weightIndex
        bound weightIndex to valid
range
        growCell(child,,weightIndex)
        decrement weightIndex
        bound weightIndex to valid
range
```

A second version of the depth-first algorithm has been implemented which neglects to decrement the weightIndex (line shown in bold). (Figure 1)

In the current algorithms *all* the immediate child cells of a parent are tested for survival before being added to the system. This means that the descendants of each cell have a greater chance of survival. It may be interesting to see the effect of adding cells immediately it is known they have survived rather than waiting for all siblings to be checked before proceeding. (Figure 2 and 3)

Breadth-first (see Box 1):

The results of the different growth algorithms can be seen in section 4.0.

3.3.1 Child Cells (Branching Factor)

The weights are used to determine the number of child cells a particular cell will have. However, small weights at the beginning of the vector can

Figure 2. Limb growth prevented by allowing first limb to complete

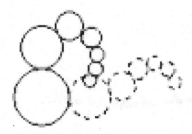

Figure 3. The order cells are added using the breadth-first algorithm

cause cell growth to stop. This can result in two organics looking similar because growth was stopped early on. If growth had been allowed to continue a divergence of forms may have resulted as more influential weights further down the vector are allowed to take effect. The simple solution employed by the system was to force each cell

to have at least one child and stop cell growth by other means. (Figure 4)

The current system forces the number of children to range from 1 to 10. Larger weights allow a cell to have more children and so a higher branching factor. Document vectors that have large weights in similar locations within the vector will result in high branch factors at similar (x,y,z) locations within the organic.

3.3.2 Distribution

Having determined the number of child cells the problem arises of how to distribute them around the parent cell. Several alternatives can be considered. Child cells could be distributed evenly around the parent. However evenly distributing points around a sphere can be computationally intensive. A prototype system was tried using this method with a maximum of six child cells, this allowed child cells locations to be easily computed as they are placed along each local axis of the parent. (Figure 5)

Another alternative is to distribute child cells evenly around a particular axis (e.g. around the y-axis, in the x-z plane), resulting in a circle of child cells around the parent. Unfortunately this produces very flat organics with many overlapping

Box 1.

```
Put root cell on queue
While (queue not empty)
generate number of child cells
for each potential child cell
      apply pre-survival rules
   generate cell location
      generate cell colour
   apply post-survival rules
   increment weightIndex
   bound weightIndex to valid range
   place child cell on queue
remove current cell from queue
```

```
// only surviving cells
// placed on queue
```

Figure 4. Stopping growth prematurely hides organic features. Growth stopped (left) and growth allowed to continue (right).

left   *right*

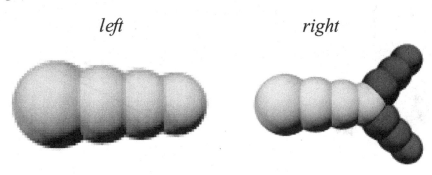

and obscured cells. However, this method is used in the current system for the children of the first 'core' cell since it helps to promote the initial growth in several directions.

The method finally adopted was to distribute the first set of child cells uniformly in the x-z plane around a single 'core' cell and then position each child cell at an angle to its parent proportional to the weight that the child cell represents. Since the system is three dimensional it is necessary for the child cell to be rotated around two axes. In this case rotations about the z and y axes were chosen, although any two axes (or even all three) could be used. (Figure 6)

A particular feature of this method arises if the weights at the beginning of the document vector are small. Small weights produce a small number of child cells and small angles, so initially the organic will grow in a straight line. Technically this is correct and if two documents each have small weights at the beginning of their vectors then they will look similar. However, this can lead to a visually uninteresting organic. One solution may be to split the vector into six parts and begin each part along a different axis.

A final alternative may be to allow several different types of distribution and use the weight to actually pick the distribution type.

3.3.3 Colour Assignment

Cell colour is assigned by weight. Several techniques have been considered. Once again low weights can cause problems, in this case depending on how the weights are used, very dark or very light (near white) organics can be grown. Using one minus the weight value can overcome this problem.

The most basic method is to use the weight for each RGB (red, green, blue) value which produces a greyscale organic. A similar method is to use three consecutive weights (w_i, w_{i+1}, w_{i+2}) although this can also produce greyscale results if the consecutive weights are similar.

The method chosen was to set each child cell to the colour of its parent if the parent only had one child. A parent with more than one child is an indication that the weight for that parent is large. The value of this weight is then used to assign the colour in the following way.

w_i = the current weight index for the cell
remainder = $(w_i \% 3)$
if remainder = 0
R: proportional to w_i
G: proportional to $(1-w_{i+2})$
B: proportional to $(1-w_{i+3})$
if remainder = 1
R: proportional to $(1-w_{i+1})$

Figure 5. Cell distribution along each axis

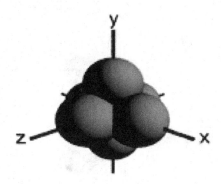

Figure 6. Child cell location

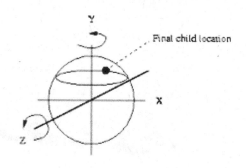

G: proportional to w_i

B: proportional to $(1-w_{i+3})$

if remainder = 2

R: proportional to $(1-w_{i+1})$

G: proportional to $(1-w_{i+2})$

B: proportional to w_i

This technique produces on average colours that are neither too dark, too light, or greyscale.

3.3.4 Cell Types

Cell type is assigned by weight. Various cell types have been implemented in the system. Each cell type is currently based around a sphere that helps to produce a more organic looking shape. In addition, using spheres is useful for generating organics made from blobs rather than discrete spheres. Blobs can be defined as "iso-surfaces of scalar fields, i.e. their surface is defined by the strength of the field in each point. If this strength is equal to a threshold value you're on the surface otherwise you're not" (POV-Ray Documentation). (Figure 7)

A selection of cell types is shown in Figure 8, the default cell type is a sphere.

The use of different cell types can help to give visual focus to particular areas of the organics.

3.3.5 Rules

Rules can be introduced to the system to produce varying effects. Rules fall into two different categories, *pre-survival* and *post-survival*. Pre-survival rules are executed before a cell is created and may prevent a cell from growing. Post-survival rules can affect a cell in one of three ways, a cell can survive unaltered, be changed to fit its local environment, or die.

The basic form of a rule is as follows:

if *condition operator threshold* then *effect*

Example of a pre-survival rule:

if *cell radius < threshold* then *cell dies*

Examples of post-survival rules:

if *number of cells in neighbourhood (radius r) > threshold* then *cell dies*

if *dominant cell colour in neighbourhood (radius r) != cell colour* then *cell dies* OR *cell* changes colour to match neighbourhood

The first post-survival rule listed is useful for 'thinning out' a highly branched organic. When applied to organics with low branching factors it has no effect.

Figure 7. Overlapping spheres represented as a blob

left   *right*

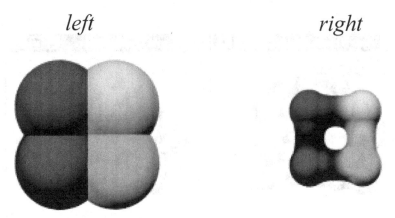

3.3.6 Stopping Organic Growth

Various methods have been considered in stopping organic growth. The most obvious one is to allow growth to continue until all the weights have been used. This method has been used but can generate organics with extremely long limbs, the ends of which are too small to have a useful visual impact.

The system could begin with a fixed amount of energy which is gradually reduced as cells are grown. A variant of this is to define a critical mass beyond which an organic cannot grow. This could be particular useful when large weights appear at the beginning of the document vector. Large weights would produce greater numbers of large cells thus increasing the mass of the organic early on and hence stopping the system sooner.

A fixed number of iterations could also be used, for example a percentage of all the weights. However, this can lead to problems as described in section 3.3.1. Rules such as the pre-survival rule described in section 3.3.5 can be used to stop organic growth and it was this method that was used in the system implemented. (Figure 9)

3.4 Architecture Model

An alternative to the cellular growth model described in section 3.3 is the architecture model. This involves having a fixed architecture of body parts e.g. head, body, arms, legs, tentacles, etc., and using the weights to pick which parts make up the final organic. The attributes of these body parts e.g. size, shape, colour etc., may also be determined by the weights. (Figure 10)

Figure 8. Various cell types

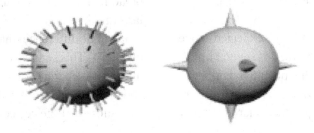

Figure 9. Organix using cellular automata method. Comparing object oriented design articles to article about agents.

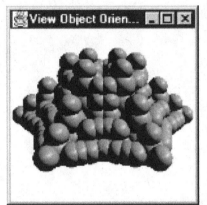 

4.0 RESULTS

Figure 11 *a-i* shows a comparison of organics generated using the three algorithms described in section 3.3. The first two columns relate to documents describing science and technology in the public sector, the third column relates to a document dealing with Brazilian agriculture. Document lengths ranged from 12,765 to 37,602 words.

It can be seen from Figure 11 that the two depth first algorithms (DFV1, DFV2) generate very different organics. This is expected since DFV1 will visits the same weights several times, if these weights are large the potential number of cells will also be large. DFV2 visits each weight once, so if a weight will produce a large number of cells, it will only have the opportunity to do so once. It is for this reason that DFV2 and the breadth-first algorithm generate organics of similar density.

All three algorithms generate a very different organic for the Brazilian Agriculture document. This is due to the low occurrence of high frequency words found in this document in comparison to those in the rest of the collection.

It is interesting to note that DFV2 and the breadth-first algorithms although producing similar organics for similar documents do allow for more subtle differences than the organics generated by DFV1. This suggests that DFV1 could be used initially to separate documents in a coarse fashion and then one of the other algorithms could be used on a sub-set of the collection to give finer detail.

Figure 10. Examples using the architectural model

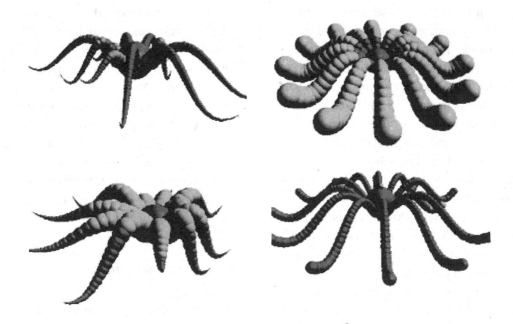

Figure 11. Comparison of depth vs. breadth first algorithm results

	Science and Technology in the Public Eye	Promoting Public Understanding of Science and Technology	Brazilian Agriculture: Recent Policy Changes and Trade Prospects
<u>Depth-First Version 1</u> The index for the weight to use increases *and* decreases during the growth of each limb. This allows large weights to be visited more often.	 a	 b	 c
<u>Depth-First Version 2</u> The index for the weight to use increases *only* during the growth of each limb.	 d	 e	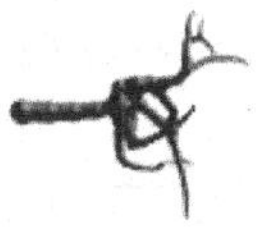 f
<u>Breadth-First</u> The weight index is used per cell in turn and increases *only*.	 g	 h	 i

Figure 12 *a-j*, *k-t* shows another set of organics grown using the cellular growth method described. These documents were selected based on the keyword 'jive'. However, documents *a-j* relate to the dance meaning of the word whereas *k-t* deal with astronomical terms and use jive as an acronym. The documents *a-j* contained between 5-87 words, documents *k-t* ranged from 12-143. This document length is typical of that found in search engine 'snippet' result lists.

It can be seen that there are similar organics within each subset of documents *a-j*, *k-t*, this is expected as each set refers to a particular subject. However, it is interesting to note that documents *a* and *b* exhibit peculiarities not present in the other members of the *a-j* group.

There are also similarities between the two sets of documents for example *o*, *p* and *t*, are similar to many members of the *a-j* group. Similarities between the two sets is caused by common words, primarily the words *jive* and *class*. The need to avoid stopping organic growth prematurely is highlighted by *i* and *n*, if *n* had been stopped sooner it would have been far less distinguishable from *i*.

On the whole, the two sets appear quite different, with the *k-t* set having more branches. This too is expected, the *k-t* set contains very precise terminology, for example the terms 'evn' and 'vlbi' are close to the top of the cumulative frequency table and yet neither of these terms appears in the *a-j* set.

The documents represented by *r* and *s* are significantly different to all the rest in both *a-j* and *k-t*. Upon investigation it was discovered that these documents were composed of a series of bullet points almost all of which contained the words 'jive', 'evn' or 'vlbi'. Each of these words has a high frequency within the entire collection and produce strong weights in both *r* and *s*, thus the initial branching factor of these documents is high.

The organix in Figure 12 were created using DFV1 and it is apparent that this algorithm produces 'organisms' which have symmetrical halves although they are laterally inverted.

5.0 FUTURE WORK

This work could be taken in a number of directions. Detailed improvements to the algorithms used include:

- Using the weights for other attributes of the cells e.g. cell size.
- The current system creates child cells at 90% of their parent size and positions them so an overlap occurs between child and parent. This could be altered in numerous ways so that parent and child cells are more distinct.
- Using alternative child cell distribution methods.

Figure 12. Document collection based on 'jive' keyword

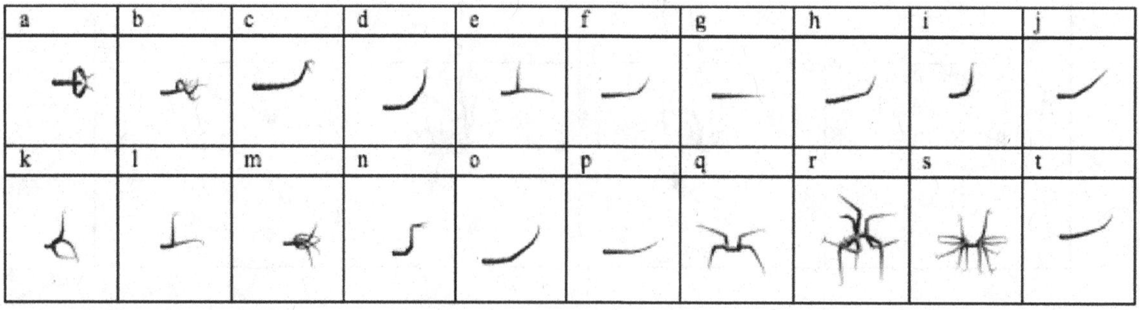

- Generating more pre and post-survival rules and determining the effects on the organic formed.
- Introducing a gravity field which would alter the direction of cell growth based on the gravity strength at a certain point. This gravity field could be determined by a function related to the document feature weights.
- Introducing static points of attraction/repulsion whose location is based on some function of the weights and whose effect is to influence growth direction.
- At present the colour assignment algorithm is not entirely satisfactory. An algorithm that is able to produce a more distinct set of colours is required.
- Using a combination of spheres and cylinders to form a more branch like structure, spheres could be used as nodes of high weight and cylinders as low weights.
- Only selecting terms that occur in more than 20% of the collection and less than 80%, the current system uses all terms.
- Document similarity can be measured in a way similar to the described by Singhal and Salton (1995), however, it should be possible to measure similarity based on the number of coincident cells, colour, size, etc., that make up the organic. Each particular attribute could be weighted, the results could then be summed to produce a similarity value, e.g. s = sum(dist between cells + 0.5*colour diff + 0.25*size diff).

Beyond this, there are several directions in which the work could be developed. At present, there is no user interaction with the organix. They are objects used for recognition and through which a user accesses a document. Providing an element of interaction with the organix would allow the user to further refine their understanding of the document represented and explore the alternatives through drilling down into more detail.

Although the current domain is text documents there is no reason, of course, why other domains could not be used as long as an appropriate set of features could be extracted. Some preliminary work has been undertaken in some other domains.

Experimental results have confirmed that this is an effective way of supporting users in discrimination and identification tasks when compared to more conventional (and familiar) representations of the same data. It would be interesting to experiment with alternative organic forms in order to identify just which features are important in cueing efficient discrimination and also whether the use of a different form (e.g. a representation which is closer to faces) would be more effective.

6.0 CONCLUSION

Within this paper we have described work on the generation of organic visual forms (termed *Organix*) from document feature vectors. The aim is to build a representation which is aesthetically appealing and engaging to the user—but more importantly, a representation which allows users to very quickly survey a collection of objects and identify similarities and differences without imposing a significant cognitive load. It appears that by using a representation which has elements of the familiar, even though the *organix* are far from authentic creatures, we are able to produce effect visualisation of abstract objects (documents).

There are many low level aspects of the mechanism that it would be interesting to explore further in order to improve the authenticity and effectiveness of the visualisations. More important, perhaps, is the question of just what features are important in cueing this discrimination and just what features of low-level human visual processing are involved. By supporting this mapping between the visual representations and the visual processing system we should be able to generate organic forms which are more effective.

REFERENCES

Card, S., Mackinlay, J., & Sheniderman, B. (1999). *Readings in Information Visualization: Using vision to think*. San Francisco: Morgan Kaufmann.

Chalmers, M. (1996, October 27-November 1). A Linear Iteration Time Layout Algorithm for Visualising High-Dimensional Data. In *Proceedings of IEEE Visualization,* San Francisco (pp. 127-132).

Chalmers, M., & Chitson, P. (1992, June 23). Bead: Explorations in Information Visualisation. In *Proceedings of SIGIR '92,* Copenhagen, Denmark (pp. 330-337). ACM Publishing.

Lagus, K., Honkela, T., Kaski, S., & Kohonen, T. (1996, August 2-4). Self-Organizing Maps of Document Collections: A New Approach to Interactive Exploration. In *Proceedings of KDD '96: Second International Conference on Knowledge Discovery and Data Mining,* Portland, OR (pp. 238-243).

Morris, C., Ebert, D., & Rhengans, P. (1999, October 13-15). *An Experimental Analysis of the Pre-Attentiveness of Features in Chernoff Faces*. Paper presented at Applied Imagery Pattern Recognition '99, Washington, DC.

Morse, E. (1998). *Document Visualization*. Retrieved June 13, 2000, from http://www.lis.pitt.edu/~elm2/DocumentVisualization.htm

Porter, M. F. (1980). An algorithm for suffix stripping. *Program, 14*(3), 130–137.

POV-Ray Documentation. (2000). *Version 3.1g "Blob" POV-Ray Scene Language Help*.

Rohrer, M. R., Ebert, D. S., & Sibert, J. L. (1998, October 19-20). The Shape of Shakespeare: Visualizing Text using Implicit Surfaces. In *Proceedings Information Visualization 1998,* Durham, NC (pp. 121-129).

Salton, G. (1995). Automatic Analysis, Theme Generation, and Summarization of Machine-Readable Text. *Science, 264*(3), 1421–1426.

Singhal, A., & Salton, G. (1995, May 22-25). Automatic Text Browsing Using Vector Space Model. In *Proceedings of the Dual-Use Technologies and Applications Conference,* Utica, NY (pp. 318-324).

Wise, J. A., et al. (1995, October 20-21). Visualizing the Non-Visual: Spatial Analysis and Interaction with Information from Text Documents. In *Proceedings of IEEE Information Visualization '95,* Atlanta, GA (pp. 51-58).

This work was previously published in International Journal of Creative Interfaces and Computer Graphics, Volume 1, Issue 1, edited by Ben Falchuk, pp. 40-53, copyright 2010 by IGI Publishing (an imprint of IGI Global).

Chapter 4
Tangible Interfaces for Art Restoration

Leonardo Bonanni
MIT Media Laboratory, USA

Bianca Cheng Costanzo
MIT Media Laboratory, USA

Maurizio Seracini
University of California at San Deigo, USA

Andrew Shum
MIT Media Laboratory, USA

Xiao Xiao
MIT Media Laboratory, USA

Romain Teil
MIT Media Laboratory, USA

Matthew Hockenberry
MIT Media Laboratory, USA

Antony Speranza
MIT Media Laboratory, USA

Hiroshi Ishii
MIT Media Laboratory, USA

ABSTRACT

Few people experience art the way a restorer does: as a tactile, multi-dimensional and ever-changing object. The authors investigate a set of tools for the distributed analysis of artworks in physical and digital realms. Their work is based on observation of professional art restoration practice and rich data available through multi-spectral imaging. The article presents a multidisciplinary approach to develop interfaces usable by restorers, students and amateurs. Several interaction techniques were built using physical metaphors to navigate the layers of information revealed by multi-spectral imaging, prototyped using single- and multi-touch displays. The authors built modular systems to accommodate the technical needs and resources of various institutions and individuals, with the aim to make high-quality art diagnostics possible on different hardware platforms, as well as rich diagnostic and historic information about art available for education and research through a cohesive set of web-based tools instantiated in physical interfaces and public installations.

DOI: 10.4018/978-1-4666-0285-4.ch004

Figure 1. A traditional approach to art diagnosis and restoration. In this example, a sample region was scraped to determine what lay beneath the wall paint (see the patch on the right side of the image). At one depth, the diagnosticians found a fresco, and the restorers chose to uncover the entire wall to that layer.

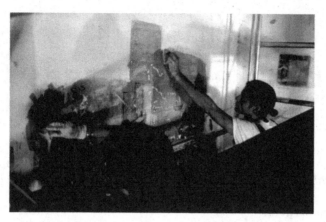

INTRODUCTION

When you gaze upon a painting in a museum, your eyes could be misleading you. The appearance of a work of art only reveals the current state; its true significance could lie beneath the surface. Traditionally the only means of diagnosing the history of a painting was destructive, but over the past three decades medical imaging techniques have been applied to ancient artwork to peer beneath the surface non-invasively. Many of these studies have revealed a pastiche of sketches, re-workings, alterations and misguided restoration attempts that complicate the authorship and authenticity of the work. These studies are rare; their findings are closed to interpretation; and they are rarely re-evaluated. We believe that the history of our cultural heritage should be open and accessible to a wide audience to motivate conservation efforts and to increase the likelihood of further discovery. Our team is building tangible interfaces for art restoration to make modern diagnostic information widely available and to broaden the interpretation and appreciation of art history.

ART DIAGNOSTICS

The field of art diagnostics is concerned with revealing the history of a work of art to assess its condition and to help direct conservation efforts. Traditional techniques require technicians to abrade the surface of an image using scalpels and solvents to locate details and layers of interest (see Figure 1). While these techniques are seldom used with important works of art, direct physical interaction is time-tested, intuitive, and almost always collaborative.

Alternatively, medical imaging equipment can be used to produce high-resolution images of the artwork at different wavelengths (e.g. infrared, ultraviolet, x-ray). These represent various materials deposited over the course of the painting's history, from original sketches to layers of pigment and varnish. While safe, multi-spectral scans require specialized training to analyze, and the work is almost entirely carried out on single-user graphics workstations. When analyzing a multi-spectral scan, the diagnostician begins by precisely aligning the co-located high-resolution images with a multi-layered photo editing software on a powerful computer. Then, she looks for anomalies between the layers by zooming into a detail and superimposing two scans in transparency. By gradually adjusting the opacity of one image relative to another, the diagnostician can more easily perceive differences between the scans. These are usually analogous to alterations made over the history of the artwork. The diagnostician then saves the image detail, together with information about the layers and the level of opacity used (see Figure 2).

Once complete, art diagnosis can inform restoration and conservation efforts. In many cases, diagnosis will reveal the condition of a painting to indicate vulnerabilities and to direct conservation. Sometimes the diagnosis will reveal a 'pentimento,' or an early change of mind by the artist. In other cases, art diagnosis reveals interventions made by other artists and restorers which hide or destroy part of the original work. Depending on the philosophy of restoration, the artwork is conserved in its present state, returned to its original condition, or left as a pastiche of old and new.

Art diagnostic practice relies on practitioners from multiple disciplines—historians, curators, technicians—working individually or in teams to assess and make decisions about artwork. There are virtually no software tools in existence to facilitate these diagnoses or collaborations, save custom programs made by individual restoration laboratories (Möller & Seracini, 1996). We are building a suite of tools that reinforce art diagnostic practice to make it available for diverse multidisciplinary groups, including students and amateurs.

GRAPHIC TECHNIQUES

The multi-layered analysis that characterizes art diagnostics is akin to visualization techniques common in a number of fields: designers, engineers, and doctors all rely on a sectional stack of image layers to visualize dense three-dimensional volumes (Bonanni, Alonso, Chao, Vargas, & Ishii, 2008). In medical imaging, physical masses are often visualized as a sequence of slices through the body. In archaeology, layers are used to depict temporal progression, and in architecture they help to design for spatial coincidence. In every case, the relationship between layers can be as telling

Figure 2. A detail from multi-spectral analysis of a painting. This detail of a Raphael's painting Young Woman with Unicorn is a composite of the visible image and an x-ray scan. It reveals that the columns framing the subject were added what was once a simple window.

as the individual images themselves, and it can be useful to compare one layer with another to determine persistence of features over time and space.

Physical metaphors help users intuitively understand the position of image layers in three-dimensional space. The ubiquitous 'desktop' operating system metaphor represents file structures through a series of stacked 'windows.' Depth cues—such as shadows and occlusions—are commonly used to help organize the layers; these can facilitate reading and comparison of more than one layer at a time (Sekuler & Blake, 2002; Zhai, Buxton, & Milgram, 1996). Drop shadows create the illusion of superposition, and semi-transparent windows allow two layers of information to be viewed simultaneously (Harrison, Ishii, Vicente, & Buxton, 1995; Ishak & Feiner, 2004).

Physical behaviors can also help to navigate multi-layered images. In one interface, application windows behave as pieces of paper that can be folded back to reveal underlying content (Dragicevic, 2004). This would allow a diagnostician select between co-located scans. In another, objects can be shuffled and stacked like playing cards to establish order (Agarawala & Balakrishnan, 2006). This might afford the ability to confront scan layers in subjective order.

Whereas traditional graphical interfaces have been designed for single-user workstations, tangible and interaction could allow interdisciplinary groups to work together as they would in traditional art diagnostics. Using physical tools and gestures on a real artifact provides a group with a shared frame of reference, co-located feedback and the ability for experts from various disciplines to make decisions on a work of art at the same time. Tangible User Interfaces (TUIs) use real-world objects to control digital interfaces, so that the affordances of the familiar items make the interaction more intuitive. When dealing with a sequential series of slices through a volume, TUIs make it possible to navigate through physical space with real-world tools to make the interaction more natural (Ishii & Ullmer, 1997). For example, a model of a skull can be used as a reference to navigate scans of the brain (Hinckley, Pausch, Goble, & Kassell, 1994). An outstretched palm can help to define the cut plane when peering inside an object (Bonanni et al., 2008) (see Figure 3). Physical interfaces make room for novel types of interaction, as in one interface that allows users to take a non-planar slice through numerous sections by deforming a flexible projection screen (Cassinelli & Ishikawa, 2005).

The layers of pencil, paint and varnish that constitute most paintings add up to no more than a millimeter of thickness, making it difficult to perceive their true volume. A new generation of gesture-based tangible interfaces can facilitate navigating their relative thinness. Multi-touch interfaces enable people to deal with high-resolution content on large screens (Brown, 2008).

Figure 3. A Tangible User Interface for Medical Visualization. The patient can refer to an MRI scan of his shoulder by touching the location on his body during a consult with a doctor.

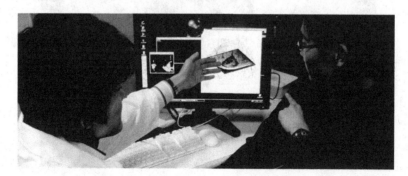

There, they can use both hands as they would on a real object, and multiple people can participate in the diagnostic process. Fingers are no longer restricted to behaving as a mouse pointer, making it possible to take advantage of the tactile expertise in a restorer's hands.

Making interaction with three-dimensional volumes intuitive and collaborative relies on the careful use of physical metaphors. In turn, these can make it possible for groups to perform complex manipulations to multi-layered images intuitively enough to broaden the reach of professional interfaces.

MUSEUM INTERFACES

Museums are increasingly using interactive techniques to enrich the audience experience. In general, museum interfaces need to be discrete so as not to distract from the art on the walls. Audio guides, video guides and small screen-based kiosks are among the most common systems in place. The content, which is generated by curators, usually consists of pre-recorded audio and video clips. Building these interfaces is time-consuming and expensive, often requiring external consultants.

Interactive systems have also been designed for museums; these combine expository information with game-like interaction techniques. One archaeological interface has been designed so that image layers can be peeled away from each other (Benko, Ishak, & Feiner, 2004). A museum installation allows users to uncover a mosaic by brushing away virtual dust on a touch screen (Dunn, 2002). These interfaces give users the impression that they are participating in an act of discovery.

Social networks can make it possible for users to actually participate in the art diagnostic process. In general, only the curators and diagnosticians working for a particular institution can study and publish findings about its collection. Leveraging collective intelligence could vastly expand the pool of analysts to include professionals at other institutions, academics, students and the general public. Popular resources such as Wikipedia reveal the extent to which a global pool of experts can form authoritative reference documents (Wikipedia, n.d.). A number of examples of 'citizen science' point to the ability for even novices to contribute to a research project by taking advantage of their unique point of reference (Cohn, 2008; Schnoor, 2007).

Considering the paucity of collective efforts aimed at art in general, even a very simple amateur collaboration stands to make a significant impact. When the U.S. Library of Congress began publishing its collection of photographs on the popular photo-sharing site Flickr, fans contributed annotations and tags by the thousands—enough to make the entire collection searchable and editable by anyone. Making art diagnostic information publicly available could prompt a wealth of findings by neglected individuals around the world.

WETPAINT

So far, very few paintings have been subjected to comprehensive analysis through multi-spectral imaging. These are the most famous painting in the world, paintings so popular that they exhibited behind physical barriers that make them difficult to see—even in person (see Figure 4). One approach is to place a large display that affords up-close views near the work of art in the museum. This is the case with Michelangelo's *David*, which is flanked by a large screen where viewers can rotate a three-dimensional model of the statue to see it from new perspectives (Levoy et al., 2000).

With this approach in mind, we selected a large, high-brightness plasma display with glass surface and infrared touch detection to build an interface that complements Leonardo Da Vinci and Andrea del Verrocchio's *Annunciation* (see Figure 5), on display at the Uffizi Museum in Florence, Italy.

Figure 4. Viewing a famous painting. The viewing gallery for Da Vinci's Mona Lisa, showing the protective barrier and tinted glass separating the audience of hundreds from the 21"x30" (53cm x 77cm) painting

Figure 5. Leonardo Da Vinci and Andrea del Verrocchio's Annunciation, 1472-5. This work is typical of Renaissance painting in that it was modified by several artists, including Verrocchio, Leonardo's master, da Vinci himself, and subsequent painters and restorers.

We have five high-resolution scans available from this masterpiece at various wavelengths (see Figure 6). Although the painting is only several hundred microns thick, varying wavelengths of light are able to discern materials deposited at various stages through the painting's history. Among other details, these scans reveal two similar compositions painted over each other. Further exploration reveals original sketches as well as many signs of age.

In our first interface—called *Wetpaint*—we sought to create an experience akin to traditional restoration methods using a detail from the painting. (Bonanni et al., 2009). Five scans are stacked in order from shallowest (visible light) to deepest (x-ray). Using a finger, the viewer can scrape off part of one layer to reveal the next. Replacing the finger allows one to excavate the subsequent layer (see Figure 7). The subtracted area has a ragged edge with a drop shadow meant to evoke the abrasive technique used by restorers, usually with a scalpel or a brush. Once an area has been removed, it slowly fades back or 'heals.' This animation, while not as precise as the controlled fading used by professionals, nevertheless highlights some inconsistencies between two layers. Users can select another layer to depart from by tapping page edges on the side of the screen. The

Figure 6. Multi-spectral scans. In the case of the Annunciation, five wavelengths of imaging are available to us, representing five relative depths into the surface of the painting.

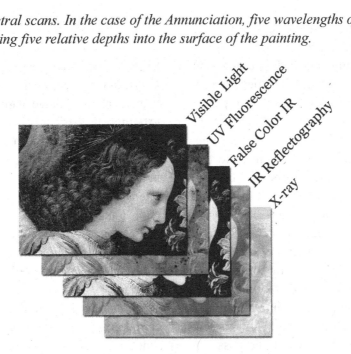

Figure 7. Wetpaint. Our first touch-screen interface for comparing multi-spectral scans of a painting uses the metaphor of scraping through layers to reveal the progression of the artist. The photograph shows two layers being scraped off by the user, as well as the page edges on the right of the screen used to navigate between scans.

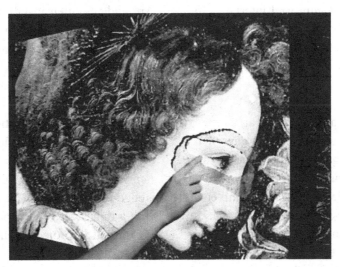

large image fades globally to a new layer from which a new investigation can begin.

We performed a user study of the Wetpaint interface and exhibited it in two public contexts. In our study of this interface, we concluded that defining arbitrary regions for comparison was beneficial in cases when images had particular significance or the different layers were not intended to be superimposed. Public exhibitions revealed that the scraping metaphor is intuitive, and the fixed scale and orientation of the artwork makes it legible to many people at once. On the other hand, the lack of controlled fade or zoom and the fixed layer order makes it difficult to use in a professional research context. The limitation of single-touch detection was significant as multiple people tried to use the screen at the same time. The scraping diameter was limited to the size of a fingertip, which is too small for uncovering large areas. On the other hand, the tactile nature of the touch interaction, the sense of discovery and the compulsion to scratch off layers made it an enjoyable if short-term experience.

By virtue of exhibiting in several contexts, we found a need for modularity and flexibility in the specifics of implementation. Most interactive museum interfaces are stand-alone, built from scratch by dedicated consultants; it should be possible to develop interfaces that can be customized by amateurs. Touch-screens and large displays are rare and varied, so any interface relying on them needs to provide a number of points of entry. Based on these findings and the user studies, we are building a series of improved interfaces for distributed hands-on interaction with art history.

PICTOUCH

Based on the desire to attract a wider audience to the art diagnostics, we are building a comprehensive system for investigating multi-spectral scans in galleries and museums and on the web. Our current prototype, called *Pictouch*, is a universal tool that allows professional-quality interaction with multi-spectral scans of any painting. Pictouch can be viewed using a web browser with traditional mouse and keyboard, as well as on single- and multi-touch screens of various sizes. Curators can configure the interface through an on-line database; style sheets configure the content based on the specific device being used.

TOUCH SCREEN

Based on the lessons learned from deploying the Wetpaint interface, we have made improvements that can take advantage of multi-touch techniques to be more user-friendly in a public context. There are several advantages to a multi-touch approach: several people can work on different parts of the image at once; multiple fingers can be used to interact with a larger area; and the texture of a multi-touch display is compliant, providing a physical accompaniment to the visual feedback. Early evaluation in the lab suggests that this is a vast improvement over the original Wetpaint interface.

On the other hand, a large touch-screen monitor can be an eyesore in a gallery of ancient paintings. Since multi-spectral scans benefit from being shown at a large size and high resolution, we are experimenting with ways to more seamlessly integrate the object in a gallery context. Pictouch was designed to engage the museumgoers in a tactile interaction with the painting on the wall. Art students often install an easel in front of a painting to copy it and learn from the techniques used by the original painter(s). We built a wooden easel to support a digital canvas (see Figure 8). A short-throw projector paints an image on the canvas, which consists of an acrylic sheet covered with a flexible rear-projection screen membrane. The acrylic sheet is modified to work as a multi-touch display based on *Frustrated Total Internal Refraction* (FTIR) (Han, 2005). The acrylic sheet is edge-illuminated with infrared LEDs and coated with a thin layer of transparent silicone rubber. Pressing on the projection surfaces compresses the rubber, diffusing the infrared light. A video camera with an infrared band pass filter behind the canvas detects the points where the screen is touched and communicates them to a Flash program using the Community Core Vision multi-touch library (Sekuler & Blake, 2002). The tactile projection screen and its slope invite direct interaction.

Figure 8. Our multi-touch screen prototype. This easel design was intended to offer a natural multi-user, ambidextrous touch interface that would complement a museum exhibit.

Next, we designed a professional-quality interface to explore multi-spectral scans in great detail. We were inspired by the workflow of art diagnosticians, but carefully designed the interaction to be universal and to preserve the beauty of the work of art. Traditionally, an art diagnosis consists of zooming into various details of a painting at high resolution. Various scans are compared by adjusting their relative opacity. Areas of particular interest are saved for later study. Over time, the annotations of several diagnosticians create a composite image highlighting relevant areas for interpretation by historians and conservationists.

USE SCENARIO

Raphael's *Young Woman with Unicorn* (1506) is a curious painting: a traditional Renaissance portrait, this depiction of a woman before an idealized landscape is made incongruous by the baby unicorn she holds in her arms. Gazing at the diminutive painting in Rome's Borghese Gallery affords little in the way of an explanation. Alongside it, however, a high-resolution display shows same painting full-size with a number of outlined areas. When you touch one of these, it zooms to fill the screen. The unicorn begins to fade, and

it is revealed to be nothing more than a puppy. Dragging the slider beneath the detail allows you to blend the visible image of the unicorn and the x-ray of the puppy. Folding over the edge of the detail shows the other layers available: infrared, ultraviolet, the rough sketch that preceded the painting. Comparing the visible image with this sketch reveals that Raphael never painted anything in the young woman's arms; she held them folded on her lap. Later, the dog was added; it was subsequently replaced by religious artifacts, and finally by the unicorn. Touching outside the detail returns you to the full-size original (see Figure 9).

This interface was designed to be symmetrical: an expert has the same ability to create composite views as a museumgoer. Dragging across the full-size painting allows a user to define any rectangular area to zoom into. The slider and page corners then allow him to select which layers to explore, and at exactly what opacity. Whether or not amateurs contribute significant composites, their usage patterns are a meaningful gauge of the overall perception and understanding of the work of art.

Pictouch should be easy to customize by any curator. The Flash application that renders the visual effects communicates through the Flickr API with an image collection stored on-line. Us-

Figure 9. Our professional art diagnostic interface design. From left to right: faint outlines highlight areas of interest; selecting an area causes it to pop out of the background; the area expands to fill the screen and begins to fade between the uppermost layers; users can select which layers to fade between by turning over an image edge and selecting from the page corners (the page corner interaction is derived from the Fold n' Drop technique, see Dragicevic, 2004).

ing Flickr allows curators to easily upload photos and to annotate specific areas for visitors to examine. The on-line photo collection automatically samples the originals at multiple resolutions, useful for producing image tiles for zooming seamlessly into various details. By the same token, areas of interest on the touch screen are uploaded to the on-line repository, informing curators which parts are of most interest to visitors.

FUTURE WORK

Pictouch was designed as a complement to exhibits, laboratories and classrooms. Our interface is being developed alongside user studies and long-term evaluation with professional diagnosticians, art history students and museum visitors. Beyond refining the interface, it is important to understand whether it is possible to motivate a sustained appreciation of conservation efforts.

While the software behind Pictouch is modular and intended to work in a variety of different contexts, the physical installation will vary according to the specific setting. In a classroom context, for example, the interface could be useful on students' individual computers, with the instructor able to aggregate the samples being explored. In

professional practice, conventional touch-screen interaction would be sufficient for small groups, while an even larger display with remote control would serve for presentations. Since multi-touch displays are still not widely available, museum galleries seeking them could use custom installations designed to fit into the exhibit design. In the future, we will seek to develop fabric-based multi-touch sensing, as well as display technologies that forgo the need for rear illumination.

CONCLUSION

The open and collective traditions of the interaction community can have a vast impact on the way art history is analyzed and discussed. Open source communities are fostered by the symmetry of computation: the tools used to create software and the same tools that use it, so anyone can be a programmer. Collective tools exist for the exchange of text, software code, even photos and videos. We are building tools specifically targeted to encourage sustained and distributed sharing of art history information. Cultural heritage is a shared resource; by making available its 'source code' we can broaden the community actively engaged in its preservation and dissemination.

ACKNOWLEDGMENT

We are grateful for the generous support of Joe Branc, Seth Hunter, and the sponsors of the Things That Think consortium at the MIT Media Lab.

REFERENCES

Agarawala, A., & Balakrishnan, R. (2006, April 22-27). Keepin' it real: Pushing the desktop metaphor with physics, piles and the pen. In R. Grinter, T. Rodden, P. Aoki, E. Cutrell, R. Jeffries, & G. Olson (Eds.), *Proceedings of the SIGCHI Conference on Human Factors in Computing Systems (CHI '06)*, Montréal, Québec, Canada (pp. 1283-1292). New York: ACM Publishing. Retrieved from http://doi.acm.org/10.1145/1124772.1124965

Benko, H., Ishak, E. W., & Feiner, S. (2004, November 2-4). Collaborative Mixed Reality Visualization of an Archaeological Excavation. In *Proceedings of the 3rd IEEE/ACM International Symposium on Mixed and Augmented Reality* (pp. 132-140). Washington, DC: IEEE Computer Society. Retrieved from http://dx.doi.org/10.1109/ISMAR.2004.23

Bonanni, L., Alonso, J., Chao, N., Vargas, G., & Ishii, H. (2008, April 5-10). Handsaw: Tangible exploration of volumetric data by direct cut-plane projection. In *Proceedings of the Twenty-Sixth Annual SIGCHI Conference on Human Factors in Computing Systems (CHI '08)*, Florence, Italy (pp. 251-254). New York: ACM Publishing. Retrieved from http://doi.acm.org/10.1145/1357054.1357098

Bonanni, L., Xiao, X., Hockenberry, M., Subramani, P., Ishii, H., Seracini, M., et al. (2009, April 4-9). Wetpaint: Scraping through multi-layered images. In *Proceedings of the 27th international Conference on Human Factors in Computing Systems (CHI '09)*, Boston (pp. 571-574). Retrieved from http://doi.acm.org/10.1145/1518701.1518789

Brown, S. F. (2008). Hands-On Computing: How Multi-Touch Screens Could Change the Way We Interact with Computers and Each Other. *Scientific American, July*.

Cassinelli, A., & Ishikawa, M. (2005, July 31-August 4). Khronos projector. In D. Cox (Ed.), *ACM SIGGRAPH 2005 Emerging Technologies*, Los Angeles (pp. 10). New York: ACM Publishing. Retrieved from http://doi.acm.org/10.1145/1187297.1187308

Cohn, J. P. (2008). Citizen Science: Can Volunteers Do Real Research? *Bioscience, 58*(3). doi:10.1641/B580303

Dragicevic, P. (2004, October 24-27). Combining crossing-based and paper-based interaction paradigms for dragging and dropping between overlapping windows. In *Proceedings of the 17th Annual ACM Symposium on User interface Software and Technology*, Santa Fe, NM (pp. 193-196). Retrieved from http://doi.acm.org/10.1145/1029632.1029667

Dunn, R. (2002, July 21-26). The virtual dig. In *Proceedings of the ACM SIGGRAPH 2002 Conference Abstracts and Applications*, San Antonio, TX (pp. 122-123). Retrieved from http://doi.acm.org/10.1145/1242073.1242139

Han, J. Y. (2005, October 23-26). Low-cost multi-touch sensing through frustrated total internal reflection. In *Proceedings of the 18th Annual ACM Symposium on User interface Software and Technology*, Seattle, WA (pp. 115-118). New York: ACM Publishing. Retrieved from http://doi.acm.org/10.1145/1095034.1095054

Harrison, B. L., Ishii, H., Vicente, K. J., & Buxton, W. A. (1995, May 7-11). Transparent layered user interfaces: An evaluation of a display design to enhance focused and divided attention. In I. R. Katz, R. Mack, L. Marks, M. B. Rosson, & J. Nielsen (Eds.), *Proceedings of the SIGCHI Conference on Human Factors in Computing Systems*, Denver, CO (pp. 317-324). New York: ACM Publishing. Retrieved from http://doi.acm.org/10.1145/223904.223945

Hinckley, K., Pausch, R., Goble, J. C., & Kassell, N. F. (1994, April 24-28). Passive real-world interface props for neurosurgical visualization. In C. Plaisant (Ed.), *Conference Companion on Human Factors in Computing Systems,* Boston, (pp. 232).New York: ACM Publishing. Retrieved from http://doi.acm.org/10.1145/259963.260443

Ishak, E. W., & Feiner, S. K. (2004, October 24-27). Interacting with hidden content using content-aware free-space transparency. In *Proceedings of the 17th Annual ACM Symposium on User interface Software and Technology,* Santa Fe, NM (pp. 189-192). New York: ACM Publishing. Retrieved from http://doi.acm.org/10.1145/1029632.1029666

Ishii, H., & Ullmer, B. (1997, March 22-27). Tangible bits: Towards seamless interfaces between people, bits and atoms. In S. Pemberton (Ed.), *Proceedings of the SIGCHI Conference on Human Factors in Computing Systems,* Atlanta, GA (pp. 234-241). New York: ACM Publishing. Retrieved from http://doi.acm.org/10.1145/258549.258715

Levoy, M., Pulli, K., Curless, B., Rusinkiewicz, S., Koller, D., Pereira, L., et al. (2000). The digital Michelangelo project: 3D scanning of large statues. In *Proceedings of the 27th Annual Conference on Computer Graphics and interactive Techniques* (pp. 131-144). Retrieved from http://doi.acm.org/10.1145/344779.344849

Möller, C., & Seracini, M. (1996, August 4-9). The third dimension of "Ritratto di gentiluomo". In B. Blau, C. Dodsworth, L. Branagan, J. Ippolito, K. Musgrave, & W. Waggenspack (Eds.), *ACM SIGGRAPH 96 Visual Proceedings: the Art and interdisciplinary Programs of SIGGRAPH '96,* New Orleans, LA (pp. 11). Retrieved from http://doi.acm.org/10.1145/253607.253614

Schnoor, J. L. (2007). Citizen Science. *Environmental Science & Technology, 41*(17), 5923–5923. doi:10.1021/es072599+

Sekuler, R., & Blake, R. (2002). *Perception* (4th ed.). Boston: McGraw Hill.

Wikipedia. (n.d.). Retrieved June 20, 2009, from http://wikipedia.com/

Zhai, S., Buxton, W., & Milgram, P. (1996). The partial-occlusion effect: Utilizing semitransparency in 3D human-computer interaction. *ACM Transactions on Computer-Human Interaction, 3*(3), 254-284. Retrieved from http://doi.acm.org/10.1145/234526.234532

This work was previously published in International Journal of Creative Interfaces and Computer Graphics, Volume 1, Issue 1, edited by Ben Falchuk, pp. 54-66, copyright 2010 by IGI Publishing (an imprint of IGI Global).

Chapter 5
Calligraphic Video:
Using the Body's Intuition of Matter

Sha Xin Wei
Concordia University, Canada

ABSTRACT

Since 1984, Graphical User Interfaces have typically relied on visual icons that mimic physical objects like the folder, button, and trash can, or canonical geometric elements like menus, and spreadsheet cells. GUI's leverage our intuition about the physical environment. But the world can be thought of as being made of stuff as well as things. Making interfaces from this point of view requires a way to simulate the physics of stuff in realtime response to continuous gesture, driven by behavior logic that can be understood by the user and the designer. The author argues for leveraging the corporeal intuition that people learn from birth about heat flow, water, smoke, to develop interfaces at the density of matter that leverage in turn the state of the art in computational physics.

INTRODUCTION: COMPLEX DISPLAYS IN THE LIMIT

Decision-making activity with complex displays impose a cognitive load that generally increases with complexity. On the other hand, the experientially richest visual displays generally come from sampled video textures. The challenge of manipulating such textures in their full density can overwhelm the human capacity for interpreting, remembering, and manipulating icons or object-based graphical structures. Our basic conceptual contribution is to realize that richness comes from corporeal experience, and is independent of combinatorial structure, which is a formal property not amenable to intuitive grasp. We apply this to the problem of fully exploiting ubiquitous two-

DOI: 10.4018/978-1-4666-0285-4.ch005

dimensional computer graphic interfaces leveraging intuitions derived from corporeal experience.

On the computational side, large processor resources are needed to generate 3D or higher dimensional models (in the case of particle dynamics or animated object physics) but ultimately the results must be projected back to a two-dimensional array for display. Object-oriented graphics algorithms must contend with combinatorial complexity as a function of the number of objects and of dimension. Our array-based computational physics techniques use (variably sized) lattices with various underlying data representations, but are robustly invariant in the number of objects and points of user manipulation because each pixel effectively can be a manipulable particle.

AN APPROACH BASED ON KINESTHETIC INTUITION

In 2001, I built with colleagues[1] a responsive environment in which wireless sensors beamed accelerometer data to OpenGL textures that were mapped onto a polygonal mesh. This textured mesh was projected onto the floor from a height of 20 feet, which produced moving "wings" registered to body of the participant (see Figure 1).

The mesh width varied according not to some programmed clock but to a function of the actual instantaneous movement of the participant's body.

Despite the crude graphics, jumping on the hard floor onto which this responsive mesh was projected, one felt as if one were jumping on an elastic rubber sheet. Sha concluded that what gave such a strong sense of elasticity to the projected mesh was the nearly zero latency synchrony of the mesh's grid size with the vertical displacement of the participant's body. This motivated the strategy of using semantically shallow models that do not infer the cognitive, intentional or emotional state of the participant, but instead simulate the physics driving the graphics animation, with perceptibly negligible latency. A major limitation of that early work was the coarse resolution of the 3D geometry that we could render and drive in realtime from sensor data. In subsequent work, strategically forgoing 3D graphics freed up computational overhead to compute and present much richer 2D textures.

Normal mapping, for example, uses precomputed perturbed normals from a bump map stored within a texture. The advantage of this method is that it adds extra detail that reacts to light without altering geometry, very useful for adding small details such as reliefs on a textured surface. For example, Cohen (1998) shows how a complex mesh can have the number of polygons reduced while maintaining detail.

If we were to take this simple technique divorcing it from its 3D context and apply it to a 2D surface covering the screen then the geometry

Figure 1. Participants in the TGarden:TG2001 responsive environment, under projected OpenGL meshes that morph according to their movement. Ars Electronica 2001.

would no longer be an issue. The detail would be restricted to the size of the source texture that can provide the richest amounts of detail possible as it reaches the limit case of the number of on-screen pixels.

We are interested in physics-based processing of video textures for both engineering and scientific reasons. In practice, our screen-based visual interfaces can become so dense that hierarchical and visual-iconic representations saturate our human faculties. We hypothesize that we can tap the user's large pool of corporeal intuitions about the behavior of continuous physical material to build interactions with dense visual textures in novel, and complementary applications. Every person acquires corporeal intuitions from infancy, over a lifetime, so it seems reasonable to leverage that sort of lifelong, pre-verbal capacity. We emphasize that these applications complement and do not replace conventional visual interfaces based on object models or, formally, graphs of objects. Texture-based interfaces may also have value in manipulating very large numbers of time-based streams as well.

The other principal motivation for *calligraphic video* is to experiment with the construction of corporeal kinesthetic intuition via continuous gesture in continuous media. This is aligned with a phenomenological approach to embodied cognition that draws on the work of Edmund Husserl (1982), Eugene Gendlin (1997), and Humberto Maturana and Francisco Varela (1980). Gendlin's work re-introduced into psychology the phenomenological study of "how concepts (logical forms, ..., rules, algorithms,...., categories, patterns .....) relate to experiencing (situations, events, therapy, metaphoric language, practice, human intricacy ....)" (Gendlin, 1997, p. i) Biologists Maturana and Varela have introduced the study of organisms as *autopoietic systems,* providing insights into living and social organisms as continuously self-reproducing systems.

KINESTHETIC INTUITION COMPLEMENTS COGNITIVE WORK

In the limit case where the number of manipulable objects approaches the number of pixels in the display, we introduce a kinesthetic approach to video-based interfaces that also leverages the physical intuitions of continuously manipulating continuous matter. Using a phenomenological approach may sidestep the cognitive load imposed by complex visual displays.

Entertainment applications such as gesture-based games with video feedback rely on sensuous-aesthetic as well as cognitive decision-making activity. Our approach is one attempt to simultaneously aesthetic and sensuous intuition arising from prior reading of designed graphics, and from the body's tacit, expert, lifelong negotiation of the physical environment. The sort of intuition we leverage is that of *continuous* matter and *continuous* dynamics.

PHENOMENOLOGY AND GESTURE

We are building these *calligraphic video* interfaces as platforms for research in gesture along phenomenological lines. (Sha, 2002) Gendlin complements the logical structure of cognition with what he calls *felt meaning,* which has a precise structure: "Experiencing is 'non-numerical' and 'multischematic' but never just anything you please. On the contrary, it is a more precise order not limited to one set of patterns and units." (Gendlin, 1997, p. v). Moreover, categories may be logically but not experientially prior to instances.[2] This is a strong motivation for seeking a non-object-oriented approach to manipulable, active graphics. Human experience is material and corporeal, and is intrinsically structured as temporal processes. (This motivates our turn to dynamical fluids.) Based on fundamental work with immune and nervous systems, Maturana and Varela moved from the discussion of cellular organisms to autopoietic systems, loosely and briefly defined as continuously self-reproducing sets of processes in an ambient environment, whose relationships remain dynamically intact across changes of constitutive matter.

Given that, at the everyday scale, experience is *continuously* composed of temporally evolving matter, we wish to have an experimental platform for creating objects of experience that do not have to be selected from a pre-existing category. For example, graphic objects in our manipulable system must not appear to the user as built out of a pre-existing set of geometric primitives. It is essential, of course, that these be manipulable in some improvised way, and essential that these manipulations be continuous in time, to permit us to study the evolution of material form—*morphogenesis*, to use a term of René Thom (Thom, 1983, 1989; Petitot, 2004). We build *calligraphic video*—video texture that responds to manipulation by human gesture as interpreted from camera-based input—as apparatuses[3] in which we can conduct studies of how humans imagine, create, and perceive dynamical "objects" from *fields* that are *effectively continuous* in time and space. Working with continuous fields of video permits us to construct experiments in which objects can be formed by improvised manipulation and allowed to return to general substrates. The manipulations must be as free as possible of class-based tools or menu structures (else they would imply pre-existing logical, functional, or geometric categories). The video texture substrate may not appear uniform at all, but it is continuous in space and time. Now, rather than use arbitrary dynamical systems to animate the responsive video, we choose to study the structure of corporeal-kinesthetic-visual intuition[4] via improvised manipulations of media that leverage corporeal-kinesthetic-visual experience of continuous matter commonly encountered from childhood.

COMPUTATIONAL PHYSICS

I describe three computational models of physical material that we have implemented for realtime video processing. These lattice models are based on the Laplace heat equation, the Navier-Stokes equation for turbulent fluids, and Ginzburg-Landau equation for magnetic domains. Most of these were implemented on conventional machine architectures. These three models cover a range of physicality that provided some sense of the phenomenal richness required and the limits of perception.

Over the past four years, we have successfully built a suite of realtime, array operators on video streams for each of these PDE's. Each PDE operator treats a frame of video as initial data and generates a new stream of arrays as short time evolution solutions of the corresponding PDE intercalated into the incoming video. The numerical simulation is intercalated in between frames of incoming video, balancing computational complexity, computation grid size, video resolution, and video i/o bandwidth. Put another way, each incoming frame of video is used to set instantaneous 'initial' conditions that re-trigger the evolution of the PDE.

In the following three sections, we present the models proceeding from the simplest to the most sophisticated material model. In each section we present the model in compact physics language. For details on implementation of these models in efficient manner, I survey some of the literature on computational physics and simulations in Sections 4 and 6.

INTRODUCTION TO LATTICE METHODS: HEAT

Simulating the diffusion of heat through a homogeneous medium provides the canonical and simplest physical model for a lattice computation.

This initial data is integrated by our realtime implementations of these simulations in between frames of video, so these effects are seen in real-time, in concert with the activity of the performer or participant. If $\phi(\mathbf{x}, t) : \mathbb{R}^n \times [0, \infty) \to \mathbb{R}$ is a scalar field on spacetime

$$\frac{\partial \phi}{\partial t} = \Delta \phi \qquad (1)$$

This partial differential equation, known as the Laplace equation, can be approximated on a discrete rectangular lattice using finite differencing, and numerically integrated using a relaxation method. Where $C_{i,j}$ is the value of the (i,j)-th cell, the method in essence is given by (Figure 2):

$$C_{i,j} \to \frac{1}{4}(C_{i-1,j} + C_{i+1,j} + C_{i,j-1} + C_{i,j+1})$$

$$(1)$$

MATTER INTUITION: NAVIER-STOKES MODEL OF FLUIDS

More recent results are based on the Navier-Stokes equation (Chorin and Marsden, 1998). A fluid whose pressure and temperature are nearly con-

stant can be characterized by a velocity field $\mathbf{v} : \mathrm{R}^n \to \mathbb{R}^n$ and scalar pressure field $\mathrm{p} : \mathrm{R}^n \to \mathbb{R}$, where n = 2 or 3. We can characterize the assumption that the fluid conserves mass by the condition that there are no sources or sinks in the velocity field. By Stokes theorem, this is equivalent to the condition that the velocity field is divergence-free:

$$\nabla \cdot \mathbf{v} = 0$$

Our second physical assumption is that the momentum is conserved. Let ρ be the density, p the scalar pressure, v the viscosity coefficient, F the external force. Newton's Second Law states that force is the rate of change over time of momentum:

$$F = \frac{d(m\mathbf{v})}{dt}$$

Applying the chain rule for the total change of a function $u(v(x,t))$ of velocity field v which is in turn a function of position and time, one can show that the total derivative of u is given by:

$$\mathbf{D}[\mathbf{u}] = \frac{\partial \mathbf{u}}{\partial t} + (\mathbf{v} \cdot \nabla)\mathbf{u}$$

Figure 2. The center cell's value is replaced by the average of its neighboring cells' values

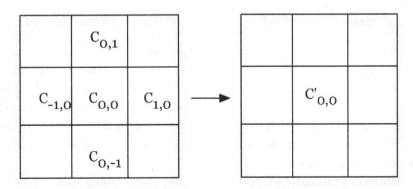

$$C_{0,0} \to C'_{0,0} = 1/4 * (C_{-1,0} + C_{1,0} + C_{0,-1} + C_{0,1})$$

Figure 3. A test case used to test the implementation of the Navier-Stokes model. Top-left is the initial state of the test case, gray walls with a white block that continually has a downward force applied to it. The force follows the block as it gets advected.

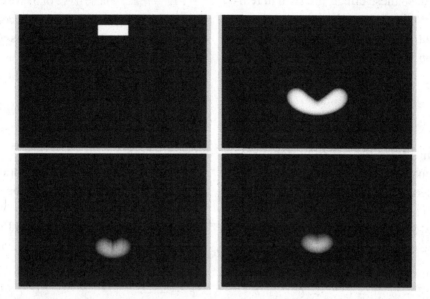

Equation \ref{specialMaterialDerivative} defines the material derivative of u, which yields the physical change of some material field u that is carried along by the velocity field v with respect to time. We can write the total force acting on an infinitesimal fluid element as:

$$\frac{\partial(\rho \mathbf{v})}{\partial t} + (\mathbf{v} \cdot \nabla)(\rho \mathbf{v}) = \nabla p + \nu \triangle(\rho \mathbf{v}) + \rho \mathbf{f}$$

Solving for the time derivative of the velocity field, we obtain the Navier-Stokes equation (Chorin & Marsden, 1998):

$$\frac{\partial \mathbf{v}}{\partial t} = -(\mathbf{v} \cdot \nabla)\mathbf{v} - \frac{1}{\rho} \nabla p + \nu \triangle \mathbf{v} + \mathbf{f}$$

For the densities, we just deal with the first term, known as the advection equation. This moves the densities according to the velocity field. There are many versions of this equation in the literature. Stam (1999) includes a diffusion term for the fluid itself.

$$0 = \frac{\partial \mathbf{u}}{\partial t} + (\mathbf{v} \cdot \nabla)\mathbf{u}$$

LIMITS OF PHYSICAL INTUITION: MAGNETIC SPIN MODELS

We have extended this work to magnetic domains and consider Ising spin models in order to traverse and study the limits of embodied intuition. The Ising model (Figure 4a) for magnetic domains—and its generalization from discrete range {0,1} to continuous range of the circle $\mathbf{S}^1$ in the Ginzburg-Landau model—provide quite different physical models for the continuous, realtime manipulation of a continuous texture:

$$lu_t^\epsilon + \triangle u^\epsilon = \frac{1}{\epsilon^2}(|u^\epsilon|^2 - 1)u^\epsilon$$

Figure 4. a) Silhouettes of two people under Ising model texture b) Visitor jumping rope transforms herself into 'fire' based on movement.

a.

b.

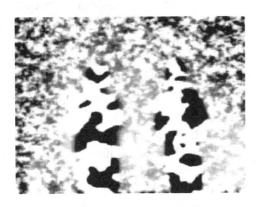

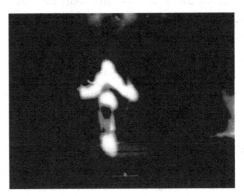

in which vortices form as $\in \to 0$.

The simplest way to model this is to use the relaxation method as for the Laplace heat equation, but where the values are taken in S^1 rather than R^1. Further experiment is needed to determine whether these simulations of magnetic spin domains driving re-synthesis of the input video, can constitute substrates for intuitive manipulation of time-varying textures.

In any case, we now have at hand a variety of pseudo-physical textures with which to construct experimental "matter" for phenomenological experiments.

IMPLEMENTATION

A good software engineering strategy to follow is to program in the environment that is the most expressive and has the most support from its professional community for the type of logic that is most readily implemented in a given area, and use lower level languages exactly where extra access to machine resources is needed. We optimize the use of our programmer time between coding behavior in a more expressive but less efficient (in terms of machine resource) language, versus coding in a more efficient, but much less expres-

sive language, remembering that machine cycles can be faster and cheaper than human "cycles" by six orders of magnitude or more, depending on how we measure the comparison. Following this strategy, we have implemented our video instruments, as well as the Ozone (Sha, 2009) media choreography framework in Max/MSP/Jitter (Max) a graphical programming environment for realtime media processing.[5] This is the *lingua franca* and the professional environment of choice for all realtime media and sensor development, and has a global community with active archives of toolkits maintained by both researchers and professionals. Thus, our realtime media systems are coded using multiple frameworks: high-level but expressive Max abstractions (sub-programs) that can be modified at will by media programmers and students, mid-level Java and C externals written by the core research team, and OpenGL shaders written by specialists.

SENSING HUMAN ACTIVITY

Having used a variety of wireless sensing modalities over the past decade, including optical, acoustic, accelerometers, sound level, magnetic field, pressure, ultrasound, and others, we are guided by two considerations: (1) since it is difficult even for humans to interpret physiological features of other humans, and the correspondence between physiological data and internal consciousness and experience is not understood, we stick to physical data; (2) we wish to encumber the participant in our environments with the least extra instrumentation.

Therefore our tracking method of choice, following our general strategy of using field (lattice-based) methods wherever possible, has been the Lucas-Kanade optical flow method available from a standard computer vision library inside Jitter.[6] Instead of tracking discrete points, or barycenters of blobs, we track motion across the entire visual field, which gives continuous spatial information that is much more robust and general than blob tracking and provides dense data that we can stream into the rest of the video processing network.

LINKING INSTRUMENTS TOGETHER

One of our main goals has been to make it easy for composers to link video and sound instruments together and to orchestrate sets of instruments. Figure 5 shows a typical front-end for a set of video instruments as an interface to the set of fluid externals described previously in this paper.[7] The MeteorShower instruments, for example generate not only graphics, but also particle data, which we pack as a Jitter matrix streamed over the local network to sound instruments on a different instance of Max. A particle matrix can contain for example 12 planes of data: id, positions, velocities, accelerations, charge, and mass. The heart of the challenge then becomes designing an effective, and interesting mapping. In the past we have successfully mapped particles positions and velocities to a number of "voices" using a Max/MSP granular synthesis instrument created by Tim Sutton, the principal responsive sound instrument designer at the Topological Media Lab.

Figure 5. Chainable realtime video re-synthesis instruments and OpenGL processing in Max framework: Timespace pixel-level time-shifting, MeteorShower general particle system, Furgrass vector field, as well as Navier Stokes fluid simulation engines.

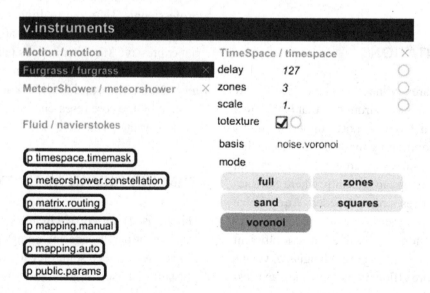

Figure 6. Ouija Experiments: Dancers under projection of live brushwork by Filip Radonjik, composited with processed video of their own movement.

BALANCING CPU AND GPU

Using Jitter's matrix array data structure the composer can quickly and efficiently manipulate an array of floating point or integer (char) data, and visualize or process its planes as video images. Furthermore Max/Jitter provides facilities for acquiring and broadcasting such arrays as streams on networks between CPU's. We broke the computational physics PDE solver into independent Jitter plugging, allowing us to easily swap out individual components of the fluid solver and use them in varying contexts. Since we can work with the native data format of Jitter, it means that an application programmer can easily manipulate the underlying fields as they evolve through the simulation using Jitter's built-in functions.

Another way to operate on 2D rectangular data like images and videos is to use OpenGL textures, slabs and shaders, which are all available in Jitter. Once transferred to OpenGL textures, we can do computation on the GPU. Our instruments and other modules for realtime video provide a large range of abstractions that leverage the capabilities of the GPU without the need to code customized shaders, though we have written custom shaders as necessary. Numerous shaders are already part of the Max release, and others have been written for specific purposes.

Combining live video, synthesis and GL shading modules, we readily synthesize video as structured light-fields to augment the movement of paper (after Figures 6, 7, and 8, see Figure 9) or elastic membrane (Figure 10) in live performance.

Currently, all calculations executed prior to rendering are done by the CPU, while the GPU is being used for rendering, shading and compositing. Most CPU calculations that are happening

Figure 7. A MeteorShower installation, and a visitor creating and playing with the meteors in realtime.

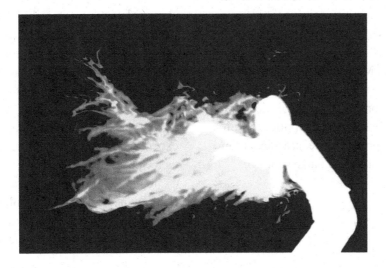

Figure 8. Cosmicomics installation in two different epochs, Elektra Festival, Montreal 2007.

inside the visual instruments are done using Jitter matrices. While this is still not as fast as doing GPU hardware processing, doing operations on Jitter matrices is significantly faster than using expressions or *for* / *while* loops which incidentally do not exist in Max as native constructs. By leveraging Max's unique model, we are able to maintain realtime processing capabilities while providing simple interfaces for application programmers who are primarily media designers and performers who wish to use our system.

APPLICATIONS

Our applications primarily lie in the domain of live performance and associated phenomenological experiments. These applications include: (1) the MeteorShower instrument based on particle systems for sound as well as video, (2) the Cosmicomics installation fusing an implicit cosmological narrative, (3) the Ouija phenomenological experiments cast as movement exercises, (4) Touch dance performance.

Testing and developing applications for live performances and phenomenological experiments involving diverse, varying groups of participants notably pushed the development of scalable real-

Figure 9. Blending realtime video into paper to create composite temporal material for a chrysalis containing the dancer, in Touch2 performance, Remedios Terrarium, Montreal 2008.

time visual instruments as part of our Ozone media choreography system (Sha, 2009). We view our realtime media programs not as a set of software libraries that need to be compiled into applications, nor as toolkits, but as instruments that can be played by an instrumentalist accompanying an installation, or a performance—an event with an audience, a place, and a definite beginning and end. An instrument is not a singular piece of code tied to a specific performance or installation, but a "verticalized" bundle of expected ranges of gesture, sensing or controller hardware, sensing modality, feature extraction, mapping, and media (sound, video, lighting, actuation) synthesis.

Meteors and Particle Systems

One example of a visual instrument using continuous input to generate a graphical output is MeteorShower (Figure 7). This instrument uses a 2D lattice of attractors to influence a set of freely moving particles. Being driven by a custom gravitational model, the particles circulate over the entire field of attractors. The attractor masses

Figure 10. Movement artist working under elastic membrane illuminated by realtime video synthesized from his movement. We blend physical, topographic shadow with projected dynamical texture.

are scaled according to the motion gradient from the realtime camera feed. Scaling the masses of the attractors modifies the accelerations of the particles. Each particle evaluates the force exerted on it for every attractor of the lattice for each frame. Unlike a flocking algorithm, the moving particles do not interact, and therefore computation of the forces occurs only between particles and attractors.

A key aspect of this application is that a subset of the particles is associated with distinct sound synthesis processes parameterized by functions of position and velocity in a rich way. When the particles are scattered, their voices sum to what seems like noise. But as their motion becomes more spatially or temporally correlated, the voices develop more harmonic relationships with each other.

Cosmicomics

Building on the *MeteorShower*, and integrating a significantly richer spectrum of realtime video instruments, we created an installation partly inspired by Italo Calvino's Cosmicomics, that combined a pre-composed sequence of three epochs with contingent responses to visitors' activity as tracked by an overhead camera (Figure 8). Each epoch presented customized set of video for plasma display and spatialized sound instruments that blended a prepared animation with localized responsive behavior.

Ouija

In June-July 2007 we conducted 4 weeks of a series of dance experiments called *Ouija* in a theatrical blackbox at Concordia University (see Figure 4b and Figure 6). This series of phenomenological experiments was designed with a choreographer Michael Montanaro[8] to see (1) how we could distinguish between intentional and non-intentional gesture, and (2) how such movement is modulated

by the presence of responsive or pre-edited video and sound. The next subsections introduce some of the tools and methods we used during those experiments and look at other similar developments in realtime video involving performance.

Touch

Touch was a dance performance shot for a video in which the Navier-Stokes smoke/fluid simulation played an integral role in the concept of the work: to act as a material as well as symbolic medium in which the performers could enact evolving ethical and aesthetic relationship. The performers acted under a membrane onto which the video was projected from above. Their bodies and movements could be tracked through the translucent membrane, using infrared cameras and sources. In a second version of the performance, one dancer started the performance encased in a chrysalis made of tissue paper that was painted by mix of our realtime video instruments. The video blended with the optical qualities of the paper to create a hybrid physical-computational material that had a composite iridescence and response to movement that could not be achieved by either paper or lighting alone. See Figure 9.

RELATED WORK

There is a large literature on the use of physical models for graphic animations, distinguishing between "phenomenological" and "causal" (e.g. "spatio-temporal shape or force field") effects, where phenomenological is equated with 'mere' appearance to use for example Neyret \& Praizelin (Neyret & Praizelin, 2001). However it is important to observe that most of these computer graphic applications are primarily concerned with ocular inspection of some representation, rather than kinesthetic, embodied experience. We use phenomenology in its original sense (Husserl,

1982; Gendlin, 1997) to emphasize embodied, felt experience, distinct from visual representation. Loke et al. argued on similar phenomenological grounds that "movement is constituent of perception" (2007, p. 693). Their study of the Sony Eye Toy is restricted to reduced game schemas of *a priori* objects and movements. Rather than restrict our interaction to abstracted conversational turn-taking models, we treat events that are dense with *concurrent, continuous* movement by humans and media.

Will.0.W1sp (Woolford & Guedes, 2007) is "an interactive installation using realtime particle systems to generate characters which move with human motion, but have no set form." However, Will.0.W1sp uses a mass-spring system model whose physics is much reduced. In this case, the motion capture data is manually processed via rotoscoping into virtual skeleton joints. Attractors are associated with the joints. We do not need prior geometry, prior manual processing of data. Our dynamics (Figure 7) place relatively few *a priori* spatial-temporal constraints on the movement, so the textures can be moved autonomously by the participant, and with more painterly gesture.

Jacquemin (2008) used a technique by Georgii and Westermann to implement particle dynamics as texture computations on the GPU, in order to animate graphs. Our strategy is to skip the translation into and out of the relatively sparse graph representations required by particle models, and work directly at the full density of a bitmap.

Although it is natural to use increased computational resources to simulate 3D graphics and 3D physics (see Irving et al., 2006), we focus on 2D techniques to maximize machine resources and algorithmic power, but also for the key reason that we are delivering our results through two-dimensional projection devices: displays and video projectors. In our experience working with participants in live responsive environments, the experiential, i.e. phenomenological, impact of causal models of three-dimensional physics is dwarfed by the impact of kinesthetically plausible,

perceptually negligible-latency dynamics on two-dimensional surfaces.

Our implementation is based on the GPU version of Stam's unconditionally stable solver (1999) as extended by Harris (2004) using a Mac-Cormack method for the advection as implemented in Crane *et al.* (2007) for more accurate results (see Kim, 2008; Harris, 2004, for more detailed techniques). See Figure 10.

CONCLUSION

Physical Models Leverage Body Intuition

Replacing cognitive models mastered by the user with simulations that have shallow semantics, but rich physics, produce textures that can be driven at video rates in response to user movement and gesture. Such responsive video textures can be projected as fields of structured light that can be shaped as palpable matter by the inhabitants of the environment.

The heat and Navier-Stokes models offer rich affordances, *continuous in space and time*, by which the user can manipulate video as structured light. These leverage his/her own tacit, lifelong, corporeal experience of whole classes of physical material like water or smoke. However, the Ising model for magnetic domain does not seem as accessible, because it references magnetic material, which is familiar to most people in the form of compact magnets, rather than continuous volumes of distributed magnetic matter. It is a subtle question whether and how a model such as Ginzburg-Landau equation, whose primitive—a spin vector—corresponds to nothing perceivable by human senses, could scaffold intuitive manipulation at the macro-scopic scale of the phenomena it simulates, in this case a piece of generalized magnetic material. In any case, what we gain by using computational simulation rather than the actual physical material itself as the interface medium, is the potential for modifying the behavior of the computational matter to non-ordinary, *quasi*-physical behavior for the purposes at hand, while still accessing the participant's physical intuition. We can then design new forms of matter that respond in interesting and dynamically varying ways to activity.

Future Work

We can explore classes of movement and gesture to condition parameter spaces and mappings that yield powerful, interesting, and evocative computational material. We can also explore higher order phenomena. For example, adding temperature and quenching temperature as parameters can offer a sense of *phase change*, a class of material phenomena that we are exploiting more systematically in our media choreography framework.

As these techniques mature, we can expect more elaborate, professional applications working together with artists from the performing arts on one hand and with architects on the other. For example, one such application is the full scale augmented performance work, *Frankenstein's Ghosts*, partly inspired by Mary Shelley's novel, with the Blue Rider contemporary music ensemble (Adams et al., 2008). Architecture theorists have been rhetorically arguing for dynamic, mobile, interactive, and responsive environments, or in more sophisticated terms (Lynn, 1999; Leatherbarrow, 1993; Bullivant, 2006). We can redeploy some of the insights gathered from our realtime media work under the unforgiving conditions of live performance, and extend them in a different direction: long-term, durable installation in relatively uncontrolled, public environments (see Figure 11).

There are several promising directions in which to expand on our computational approach. We are interested in improving the simulation by working

Figure 11. Exterior LED lighting modulated by activity and script, with induced interior lightfield. "20 years: 20 hours" at the Canadian Centre for Architecture, Montréal, Saturday, 2 May, 2009. Photo: Benoît Desjardins.

a.

b.

with velocities located on the sides of the grid cells Fedkiw (2001), using level set equation to simulate the interaction between fluids and air (Crane et al., 2007), taking advantage of data level parallelism as found in modern processors, and distributing the simulation across a network of machines to provide richer detail.

ACKNOWLEDGMENT

Michael Fortin was responsible for the implementations of the Navier-Stokes model, Yannick Assogba for the Ising model, and Jean-Sébastien Rousseau for the design and implementation of the video-processing framework in Jitter. We thank the other members of the media choreography team: Tim Sutton, Harry Smoak, Morgan Sutherland, and Emmanuel Thivierge, and the TML (2006). We thank Prof. Peter Grogono, the Computer Science Department, the Faculty of Fine Arts, and Hexagram for their support. And we thank Soo-yeon Cho for working on movement and choreography related to this research.

REFERENCES

Adams, L., Montanaro, M., & Sha, X. W. (2009). *Frankenstein's Ghosts*. Montreal, Quebec, Canada: Blue Riders and Topological Media Lab.

Barad, K. M. (2007). *Meeting the universe halfway: Quantum physics and the entanglement of matter and meaning*. Durham, NC: Duke University Press.

Bullivant, L. (2006). *Responsive Environments: Architecture, Art and Design*. London: Victoria and Albert Museum.

Chorin, A. J., & Marsden, J. E. (1998). *A Mathematical Introduction to Fluid Mechanics* (3rd ed.). Berlin: Springer.

Cohen, J., Olano, M., & Manocha, D. (1998). Appearance-preserving simplification. In *SIGGRAPH '98: Proceedings of the 25th Annual Conference on Computer Graphics and Interactive Techniques* (pp. 115-122). New York: ACM Publishing.

Crane, K., Llamas, I., & Tariq, S. (2007). Realtime Simulation and Rendering of 3D Fluids. In *GPU Gems 3* (1st ed., pp. 633-675). Reading, MA: Addison-Wesley.

Cycling '. 74. (2009). *jit.repos*. Retrieved June 14, 2009, from http://www.cycling74.com/docs/max5/refpages/jit-ref/jit.repos.html

Fedkiw, R., Stam, J., & Jensen, H. W. (2001, August). Visual simulation of smoke. In *Proceedings of SIGGRAPH Computer Graphics Annual Conference* (pp. 15-22). New York: ACM Publishing.

Gendlin, E. T. (1997). *Experiencing and the Creation of Meaning: A Philosophical and Psychological Approach to the Subjective*. Evanston, IL: Northwestern University Press.

Harris, M. J. (2004). Fast Fluid Dynamics Simulation on the GPU. In *GPU Gems - Programming Techniques, Tips, and Tricks for Realtime Graphics*. Reading, MA: Addison-Wesley.

Husserl, E. (1982). *Ideas pertaining to a pure phenomenology and to a phenomenological philosophy. Vols. 1-2. Collected works of Edmund Husserl*. The Hague, The Netherlands: M. Nijhoff.

Irving, G., Guendelman, E., Losasso, F., & Fedkiw, R. (2006). Efficient simulation of large bodies of water by coupling two and three dimensional techniques. *ACM Transactions on Graphics*, *25*(3), 805–811. doi:10.1145/1141911.1141959

Jacquemin, C. (2008). Allegra: A new instrument for bringing interactive graphics to life. In *Proceedings of the 16th ACM International Conference on Multimedia* (pp. 961-964). New York: ACM Publishing.

Kim, T. (2008). Hardware-aware analysis and optimization of stable fluids. In *I3D '08: Proceedings of the 2008 Symposium on Interactive 3D Graphics and Games* (pp. 99-106). New York: ACM Publishing.

Loke, L., Larssen, A. T., Robertson, T., & Edwards, J. (2007). Understanding movement for interaction design: frameworks and approaches. *Personal and Ubiquitous Computing, 11*(8), 691–701. doi:10.1007/s00779-006-0132-1

Lynn, G. (1999). *Animate Form*. New York: Princeton Architectural Press.

Maturana, H. R., & Varela, F. J. (1980). Autopoiesis and Cognition: The Realization of the Living. In *Boston Studies in the Philosophy of Science* (Vol. 42). Dordrecht, The Netherlands: D. Reidel Publishing Company.

Mostafavi, M., & Leatherbarrow, D. (1993). *On Weathering: The Life of Buildings in Time*. Cambridge, MA: MIT Press.

Neyret, F., & Praizelin, N. (2001). Phenomenological simulation of brooks. In *Proceedings of the Eurographic Workshop on Computer Animation and Simulation* (pp. 53-64). New York: Springer-Verlag.

Petitot, J. (2004). *Morphogenesis of meaning*. Bern, Switzerland: P. Lang.

Sha, X. W. (2001). *Topological Media Lab* (Tech. Rep.). Atlanta, GA: Georgia Institute of Technology.

Sha, X. W. (2002). Resistance is fertile: Gesture and agency in the field of responsive media. *Configurations, 10*(3), 439–472. doi:10.1353/con.2004.0006

Sha, X. W., Sutton, T., Rousseau, J. S., Smoak, H. C., Fortin, M., & Sutherland, M. (2009). *Ozone: A continuous state-based approach to media choreography* (Tech. Rep.). Montreal, Quebec, Canada: Concordia University, Topological Media Lab.

Stam, J. (1999). Stable fluids. In *SIGGRAPH '99: Proceedings of the 26th Annual Conference on Computer Graphics and Interactive Techniques* (pp. 121-128). New York: ACM Publishing.

Thom, R. (1983). *Mathematical models of morphogenesis*. Chichester, UK: Ellis Horwood.

Thom, R. (1989). *Structural stability and morphogenesis: An outline of a general theory of models*. Reading, MA: Addison-Wesley.

Woolford, K. A., & Guedes, C. (2007). Particulate matters: Generating particle flows from human movement. In *Multimedia '07: Proceedings of the 15th International Conference on Multimedia* (pp. 691-696). New York: ACM Publishing.

ENDNOTES

[1] Sponge and FoAM art research groups, based in San Francisco and Brussels, respectively. http://www.topologicalmedialab.net/xinwei/sponge.org, http://f0.am

[2] Gendlin stands in for a vast literature of related work in psychology and phenomenology, including Leibniz, Husserl, Merleau-Ponty, Peirce, and James. But for compactness we refer to a few bridging scientists.

[3] We interpret apparatus in Karen Barad's richer sense of a hybrid of matter, expectation and theory. See chapter 4 of Barad (2007).

[4] Such experiments are an empirical approach to Husserlian studies of intuition and experience. See Husserl (1982).

[5] Max/MSP/Jitter version 5, 2008, http://www.cycling74.com (Cycling74, 2009).

[6] cv.jit by Jean-Marc Pelletier, IAMAS.

[7] See Touch 2 video of dancer http://www.topologicalmedialab.net/video/movement/touch_2_fx.mov.

[8] Michael Montanaro, Chair of Contemporary Dance at Concordia University, designed the structured improvisation structure of the experiment. Assistant choreographer Soo-yeon Cho supervised the actual movement exercises. See video documents on the *Ouija Experiment On Collective Gesture In Responsive Media Spaces*, http://www.topologicalmedialab.net/joomla/main/content/view/159/74/lang,en/

This work was previously published in International Journal of Creative Interfaces and Computer Graphics, Volume 1, Issue 1, edited by Ben Falchuk, pp. 67-83, copyright 2010 by IGI Publishing (an imprint of IGI Global).

Chapter 6
World-in-Miniature Interaction for Complex Virtual Environments

Ramón Trueba
MOVING Group, Universitat Politècnica de Catalunya, Spain

Carlos Andujar
MOVING Group, Universitat Politècnica de Catalunya, Spain

Ferran Argelaguet
MOVING Group, Universitat Politècnica de Catalunya, Spain

ABSTRACT

Object occlusion is a major handicap for efficient interaction with 3D virtual environments. The well-known World in Miniature (WIM) metaphor partially solves this problem by providing an additional dynamic viewpoint through a hand-held miniature copy of the scene. However, letting the miniature show a replica of the whole scene makes the WIM metaphor suitable for only relatively simple scenes due to occlusion and level of scale issues. In this paper, the authors propose several algorithms to extend the idea behind the WIM to arbitrarily complex scenes. The main idea is to automatically decompose indoor scenes into a collection of cells that define potential extents of the miniature replica. This cell decomposition works well for general indoor scenes and allows for simple and efficient algorithms for preserving the visibility of potential targets inside the cell. The authors also discuss how to support interaction at multiple levels of scale by allowing the user to select the WIM size according to the accuracy required for accomplishing the task.

INTRODUCTION

During the last few decades much research has been devoted to develop new strategies for facilitating user interaction with complex, densely-occluded virtual environments. Among the different approaches that have been proposed for measuring scene complexity, the most relevant one, from the point of view of 3D user interfaces, is *depth complexity*, which depends on the number of occluding objects. Occlusion is a big handicap for the efficient accomplishment of 3D interaction tasks, including selection and manipulation, as most interaction techniques for these tasks require

DOI: 10.4018/978-1-4666-0285-4.ch006

the object, along with relevant context information, to be visible. Navigating to a location where potential targets are visible is a common solution to this problem, but requiring the user to navigate every time an occluded object must be selected hinders performance in manipulation-intensive applications.

In this paper we address the problem of facilitating the interaction with highly-occluded, indoor scenes, focusing on applications running on spatially-immersive displays such as CAVEs. This work is based on the World in Miniature (WIM) (Stoakley, Conway, & Pausch, 1995), which is particularly appropriate for performing tasks requiring relevant context information to be visible. The WIM complements the first-person perspective offered by typical Virtual Reality applications with a second dynamic view of a miniature copy of the virtual world (Figure 1). This second exocentric view of the world helps users to understand the spatial relationships of the objects and themselves inside the virtual world. Objects in the miniature replica of the scene are referred to as *proxies*. Typically the miniature is hand-held, the non-dominant hand being used for rotating the WIM, thus establishing the frame of reference for further interaction tasks, and the dominant hand is used for selection, manipulation, and navigation tasks. Its hand-held feature also allows it to be quickly explored from different viewpoints without modifying the immersive point of view.

The WIM metaphor supports most 3D user interaction tasks, including selection, manipulation and navigation. Objects can be selected either by pointing directly at them or by pointing at their WIM proxy. For simple scenes, a rotation of the non-dominant hand is enough to view and pick objects that are occluded from the immersive viewpoint. Likewise, objects can be manipulated either at the one-to-one scale offered by the immersive viewpoint, or at the WIM scale. By representing the virtual camera with a 3D avatar,

the WIM provides a convenient way to quickly change its location inside the virtual environment.

Unfortunately, the WIM metaphor has two important limitations regarding its scalability which have prevented its widespread use. The first one is concerned with the level-of-scale at which different interaction tasks have to be accomplished. Different interaction tasks require, broadly speaking, different levels of accuracy. Since the WIM covers the whole scene, it is appropriate only for rough, coarse-level interaction tasks. For example, a WIM showing a full house might be suitable for quickly moving the camera from a room to another, but it lacks accuracy for finer tasks, such as laying out furniture pieces. Most extensions to the WIM are concerned with this problem. A second major limitation of the WIM is occlusion management, i.e. how to keep relevant objects simultaneously visible while preserving important context information.

A key observation is that many user interaction tasks are *local*, i.e. they can be accomplished with a minimum amount of context information. For instance, adjusting the position of a piece of equipment in a room might be accomplished disregarding the contents of other rooms. This suggests that the part of the scene covered by the miniature replica should be adapted according to the user task. Therefore two key problems have to be addressed. On the one hand, decide which part of the virtual environment must be included in the replica. As stated above, using a replica of the whole environment is only feasible for simple scenes like a single room. Some authors have extended the WIM metaphor to cope with complex models (Chittaro, Gatla, & Venkataraman, 2005; LaViola et al., 2001; Wingrave, Haciahmetoglu, & Bowman, 2006). These approaches define a region of interest (ROI) and put in the miniature copy only those objects inside this ROI. The user is allowed to scale and move the ROI, either automatically or manually. Although these techniques allow the accomplishment of user tasks at different levels of scale, the solutions

Figure 1. User interacting with the WIM

adopted are valid for a limited class of models, or assume the input scene already provides some information about its logical structure. On the other hand, the adoption of the WIM for complex scenes requires some strategy to handle 3D occlusion. Bounding geometry such as walls must be conveniently removed to make interior objects visible. Notice that backface culling techniques (Stoakley, Conway, & Pausch, 1995) are suitable only for simple models. General 3D models require more sophisticated techniques for handling 3D occlusion (Diepstraten, Weiskopf, & Ertl, 2003).

In this paper we extend the WIM metaphor so that it can be used in arbitrarily-complex, densely-occluded scenes. Our approach, dubbed Dynamic Worlds in Miniature (DWIM) is based on a selection of the region to be included in the miniature copy through a subdivision of the scene into logical structures such as rooms, floors and buildings. These elements are computed automatically from the input scene during a preprocessing step. The rationale here is that matching the WIM content with logical entities of the environment will help the user to accomplish interaction tasks. A logical decomposition provides additional cues to better understand the spatial relationships among the parts of the scene, and facilitates bounding those regions which provide the context information required to accomplish a local task. Furthermore, this subdivision offers a more intuitive and clear view of the nearby environment, suitable for precise object selection and manipulation. Indeed, our subdivision greatly simplifies the generation of cut-away views of the miniature copy, so that enclosing geometry does not occlude interior objects (Figure 2). The main contributions of the paper to the WIM metaphor are (a) an algorithm to automatically compute which region of the scene must be included in the miniature copy, which takes into account a logical decomposition of the scene, and (b) an algorithm for providing a cut-away view of the selected region so that interior geometry is revealed. These improvements expand the application of WIM to arbitrarily-complex, densely-occluded scenes, and allows for the accomplishment of interaction tasks at different levels of scales.

PREVIOUS WORK

In this section we briefly review previous work related to the problem being addressed (enhancements to the WIM metaphor) and to our adopted solution (cell decomposition and occlusion management).

Worlds in Miniature

The WIM was proposed originally by Stoakley, Conway, and Pausch (1995) who discussed their application to selection, manipulation and traveling tasks. They found that users easily understood the mapping between virtual world objects and their proxy counterparts in the WIM. Unfortunately, using a replica of the whole environment in the miniature limits its application to simple models like a single room, due to the occlusion and level-of-scale problems discussed in the preceding section. Several WIM extensions have

been proposed to overcome these limitations. The STEP WIM proposed by La Viola et al. (2001) puts the miniature replica on the floor screen so that it can be interacted with the feet. The main advantage is the freeing of the hands for other tasks. The method provides several methods for panning and scaling the part of the scene covered by the miniature. The Scaled and Scrolling WIM (SSWIM) (Wingrave, Haciahmetoglu, & Bowman, 2006) supports interaction at multiple levels of scale through scaling and scrolling functions. SSWIM adds functionally and hence complexity because the user has to scale the model manually. The scrolling is automatic though when the user moves to a position outside of a dead zone. Chittaro, Gatla, and Venkataraman (2005) propose an extension to support user navigation through virtual buildings, allowing users to explore any floor of a building without having necessary to navigate. Unfortunately, it requires an explicit identification of all the polygons on the different floors, which can be a time-consuming task for complex models. Unlike previous WIM extensions, we select the region covered by the miniature using an automatically computed decomposition of the model into cells.

Figure 2. Examples of our improved WIM rendering. The miniature replica provides a cut-away view of a part of the model according to the user's position.

 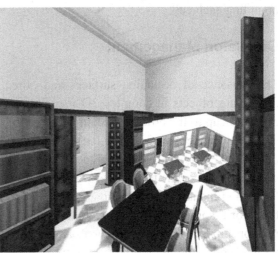

Cell and Portal Decompositions

Portal culling techniques (Airey, 1990) accelerate the rendering of indoor models by dividing the scene into cells (that usually correspond to rooms and hallways) connected by portals which represent the openings (for example doors and windows) that connect the cells. The resulting structure is called a cell-and-portal graph (CPG) and encodes the visibility of the scene. Only a few papers refer to the automatic determination of CPGs. Furthermore, most of them work under important restrictions (Cohen-Or et al., 2003), such as axis-aligned walls (Teller & Séquin, 1991). Hong, Muraki and Kaufman (1997) take advantage of the tubular nature of the colon to automatically build a cell graph by using a simple subdivision method based on the center-line (or skeleton) of the colon. To determine the center-line, they use the distance field from the colonic surface. Very few works provide a solution for general, arbitrarily-oriented models with complex, non-planar walls. Notable exceptions are those approaches based on a watershed transform of the scene (Haumont, Debeir, & Sillion, 2003; Andújar, Vázquez, & Fairén, 2004). Our approach for cell detection is based on the scene subdivision proposed in (Andújar, Vázquez & Fairén, 2004). Note however that we do not need to recover the exact geometry of the portals, but only to approximate the geometry bounding each cell.

Occlusion Management

The presence of occluding surfaces and other distracting objects in complex 3D models is a big handicap to the efficient accomplishment of discovery, selection, manipulation and navigation tasks. Current 3D selection techniques, for example, require the target object to be visible. Occlusion management techniques are valuable tools for helping viewers understand the spatial relationships between the constituent parts of complex scenes. Elmqvist and Tsigas (2008) identify five main design patterns for occlusion management: Multiple Viewports (using multiple views of the scene), Virtual X-Ray (turning occluded objects visible), Tour Planners (camera animations reveal the otherwise occluded geometry), Interactive Exploders (adopted for the WIM in (Chittaro, Gatla, & Venkataraman, 2005) through a floor sliding mechanism) and Projection Distorter (using nonlinear projections to combine multiple views into a single view). Among these, Virtual X-Ray techniques are particularly relevant for WIM-based manipulation as they make the discovery task straightforward and facilitate access to the potential targets by selectively removing occluders. Occluders can be removed by turning them semi-transparent or invisible (Elmqvist & Assarsson, 2007). Transparency is particularly simple to implement as it eliminates the need for identifying distracting objects, but rendering semi-transparent objects increases the visual complexity of the scene and the cognitive load to the user. Occluder removal techniques can be view-independent (Coffin & Hollerer, 2006) or view-dependent (Chittaro, Gatla & Venkataraman, 2005; Burns & Finkekstein, 2008). Since the WIM replica is hand-held and can be rotated by the user interactively, we only discuss view-dependent techniques.

Early cut-away papers used depth buffer and image processing techniques to replace occluding surfaces by semi-transparent representations (Feiner & Seligmann, 1992). Diepstraten, Weiskopf, and Ertl (2003) propose a number of efficient algorithms for generating cut-away views, provided that the scene objects have been labeled as interior or exterior. Some approaches use CSG rendering techniques so as resulting holes are rendered as if they were actually cut into the obstructing geometry, making the interior of solid objects visible by the cutaway action (Coffin & Hollerer, 2006). Recent works on interactive cutaways (Burns & Finkelstein, 2008) introduce an image space algorithm based on jump flooding to generate a depth-image representation of the cutaway surface at interactive rates. Note that the above techniques require the user to manually define the shape of the cutout volume, or to explicitly identify the objects to be exposed. We will show that our cell subdivision of the scene greatly simplifies the task of removing occluding objects.

OUR APPROACH

Overview

We aim at improving the WIM metaphor by addressing three main problems:

(a) **Delimitation:** instead of putting the whole scene in the miniature, we compute the part of the scene to be included according to the user's location. The region of the space covered by the WIM is represented by a polyhedral cell.

(b) **Clipping:** Our clipping solution can be seen as a particular case of Constructive Solid Geometry (CSG) rendering, as we must render the intersection of the scene with a polyhedral approximation of the current cell.

(c) **Revealing:** we keep the walls of the cell from occluding interior objects without sacrificing the outer context entirely.

A key ingredient of our approach is the automatic decomposition of the scene into a collection of *cells*. Roughly speaking, a cell is a region with approximately-constant visibility, with no significant occluding surfaces on its *interior* (i.e. all occluding surfaces must be on the *boundary* of the cell). Using cells as basic units for defining the extents of the miniature replica provides several advantages. First, cells often match with the intuitive notion of rooms of a model. Second, since no large occluding surfaces occur inside cells, occlusion management in a cell can be solved by

selectively removing parts of the enclosing boundary, so that interior objects are visible.

Our WIM delimitation strategy has two main steps (described in detail in next subsections): *cell detection*, where the scene is discretized into a voxelization and then voxels are grouped into cells with approximately constant visibility, and *polyhedral approximation*, where a low-polygon approximation of the cell boundary is computed. Our subdivision scheme produces cells which roughly correspond to rooms and hallways.

The user will be provided with a miniature containing only the objects inside the current cell. Since regions are detected during preprocessing, we could clip the scene geometry to each cell and store the resulting geometry during preprocessing. However, this approach would add complexity to the integration with already existing applications using their own scene graph. Therefore, we have adopted a runtime approach. Our solution (described in next subsections) can be seen as a particular case of CSG rendering which can be implemented easily on the GPU (Kirsch & Döllner, 2005). Finally, we apply a view-dependent cut-away technique for removing the frontmost geometry of the cell so that internal objects are visible (revealing). An important benefit of using cells with approximately constant visibility is that they greatly simplify the occluder removal task, as removing the enclosing geometry will be enough to reveal interior objects.

Preprocessing

As a preprocess, we compute a cell decomposition of the scene and create a rough polygonal approximation for each cell. We first convert the input model into a voxelization where voxels intersected by the scene geometry are detected. This conversion can be performed in the GPU (Dong et al., 2004). Our current implementation is based on the voxelization algorithm by Eisemann and Décoret (2006). The algorithm builds the voxelization by simply rasterizing the geometry with a fragment shader that computes the depth of each fragment. Although the algorithm is not exact and misses some intersected voxels (about 0.2% in the test models) due to inherent features of graphics hardware rasterization, we have chosen it because it is extremely fast: voxelizations up to 2048^3 of a 2M faces model can be computed in less than one second. Missing voxels are unlikely to have a large impact on the distance field and cell detection steps, making more conservative algorithms for GPU voxelization not appropriate for this task.

We then compute a discrete distance field (Figure 3(b)). Distance fields have been used for generating cell-and-portal graph decompositions (Haumont, Debeir, & Sillion, 2003; Andújar, Vázquez, & Fairén, 2004) as the valleys of the distance field approximately correspond to the portals of the scene. We approximate the distance field using a 5x5x5 Chamfer distance matrix (Jones & Satherley, 2001) which requires only two traversals.

Voxels are grouped into cells through a region-growing process. We start from the voxel having the maximum distance value. During this process, all conquered voxels are assigned the same cell ID. The propagation of the cell ID continues until the whole cell is bounded by voxels having either negative distance (meaning already-visited voxels), zero distance (non-empty voxels) or positive distance greater than the voxels at the cell boundary. When the growth of one cell stops

we simply choose a new unvisited maximum and repeat the previous steps until all voxels have been classified (see Figure 3(c)). Since geometric noise produced by furniture pieces severely distort the distance field, we filter out small cells (Figure 4) as proposed in (Andújar, Vázquez, & Fairén, 2004).

We approximate each cell (consisting of a collection of voxels) with a polyhedron using the surface extraction algorithm proposed by Andújar, Ayala, and Brunet (2002). This step is made for the solely purpose of accelerating the GPU-assisted clipping of the geometry outside the cell during runtime. Before extracting the surface, a dilation operation is performed to each cell to include adjacent non-empty voxels. After dilation, cells are no longer disjoint. For example, a wall separating two cells will belong to both cells. The dilation step is required for the cell to include the geometry enclosing it, such as walls (see Figures 6(c) and 6(f)). This surrounding geometry will be selectively drawn or removed depending on the viewpoint, so as to keep as much context information as possible, as discussed in next sections.

Delimitation and Clipping

At runtime, we identify the cell containing the user's viewpoint, using random-access to the voxelization described in the preceding section. We use the associated polyhedral representation of the cell to define the extents of the WIM: the

Figure 3. Cell detection example:(a) input model; (b) distance field; (c) detected cells

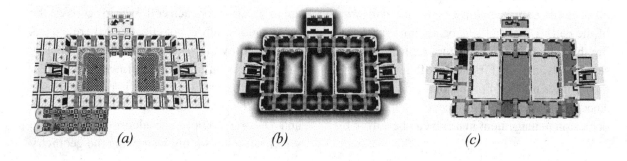

(a)   *(b)*   *(c)*

Figure 4. A partial view of a building and its color-coded cell decomposition, prior to the dilation operation

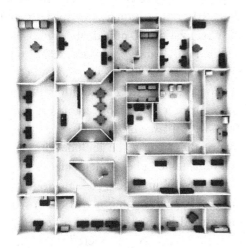 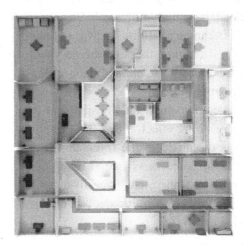

user will be presented with a miniature replica comprising only the objects inside the current cell.

Since regions are detected during preprocessing, the clipping can be performed either during preprocessing or at runtime. Our current implementation adopts a runtime approach for clipping the scene geometry to the polyhedral approximation of the current cell. The main advantage of this approach is that it supports recomputing the cell decomposition whenever some large occluding surface such as a wall is modified as a result of a user manipulation task.

Our clipping solution can be seen as a particular case of CSG rendering, as we must render the intersection of the scene with a polyhedral approximation of the current cell. We use a coarse-level, CPU-based culling to the region's bounding box to quickly discard geometry not to be included in the miniature. However, this coarse-level clipping must be combined with a fine-level clipping to the polyhedral cell. Fortunately, there are efficient algorithms for rendering CSG models using the GPU (Hable, Rossignac, & Blister, 2005; Kirsch & Döllner, 2005), whose implementation can be greatly simplified when the CSG tree consists of a single boolean operation, as in our case. The algorithm we propose is based on building a Layered Depth Image (Shade et al., 1998) of

the polyhedral approximation from the current WIM viewpoint. Layered Depth Images (LDIs) can be efficiently constructed using depth-peeling (Everitt, 2001). We use OpenGL framebuffer objects (FBOs) to render each layer directly into a depth texture. Since the cell detection algorithm tends to produce regions with very low depth complexity, these regions can be encoded with just a few LDI layers and one rendering pass for each layer (note that the LDI is build from a low-polygon description of the cell's boundary, which is geometrically much simpler than the part of the scene inside the cell). Once the LDI has been computed, the coarsely-culled scene is rendered using a fragment shader that checks the fragment's depth against the LDI and discards fragments outside the LDI (and hence outside the cell). Our current implementation uses the OpenGL's texture array extension to encode the LDI, so that the fragment program is allowed to access an arbitrary number of LDI layers, although the LDI representation of a typical cell does no require more than 4-6 layers (Figure 5).

Revealing

Note that cells include the bounding walls of the rooms they represent. Fortunately, our clipping strategy can be trivially extended to keep front-most enclosing geometry from occluding interior objects. This can be accomplished by adding an offset to the frontmost faces of the polyhedral region in the opposite direction of their normals. Indeed, we apply the offset as an epsilon used during the depth comparison with the first LDI layer. The resulting effect is that the frontmost geometry is discarded in the fragment shader, leaving interior objects visible (Figure 6(f)). Furthermore, this strategy can be easily extended when adding support to multiple levels of scale, as discussed below.

RESULTS AND DISCUSSION

We conducted a user-study to evaluate potential advantages of our *WIM delimitation* and *WIM revealing* strategies in comparison with competing approaches. We focused on selection and manipulation tasks performed in spatially-immersive displays such as CAVEs. The test model was a three-story building with about 60 rooms and 150k polygons. Figure 3(c) shows the results of the cell decomposition step on the test model, using a 128^3 voxelization. The running time for the cell decomposition was 3.8 seconds, including the voxelization (80 ms), distance transform (120 ms) and polyhedral approximation (3.6 s) steps, measured on a 2.66GHz QuadCore PC.

Concerning WIM delimitation, we compared our approach (based on automatic cell detection) with a *user-adjustable cube* defining the part of the scene to be included in the replica. Our adjustable-cube implementation is inspired in SSWIM (Wingrave, Haciahmetoglu, & Bowman, 2006) with some modifications to match our Virtual Reality system. At the beginning of the task, the cube was centered at the user's position and covered a fraction of the model (in the experiments the cube covered about a 10% of the model). Users were able to manually scale up and down the cube at constant speed (2.5 m/s for the experiments), using two Wanda buttons. Similar to (Wingrave, Haciahmetoglu, & Bowman, 2006), the cube center was updated when the user navigated to a location farther away from the initial position (we set the distance threshold to a 60% of the cube size). The adjustment of the cube size and position only affected the WIM coverage; the apparent size of the WIM remained constant

Figure 5. The LDI is built from a polyhedral approximation of the current cell (left). For each viewing ray, the LDI defines alternating intervals of outside (blue) and inside (red) geometry, which allows clipping the scene to the cell's boundary (right)

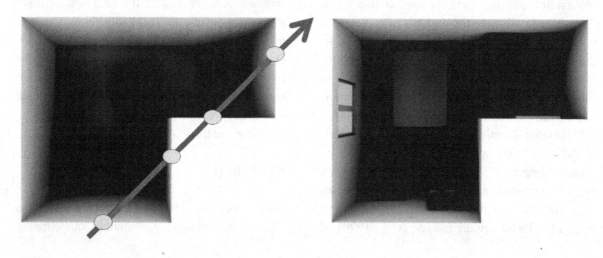

Figure 6. Different strategies for WIM rendering

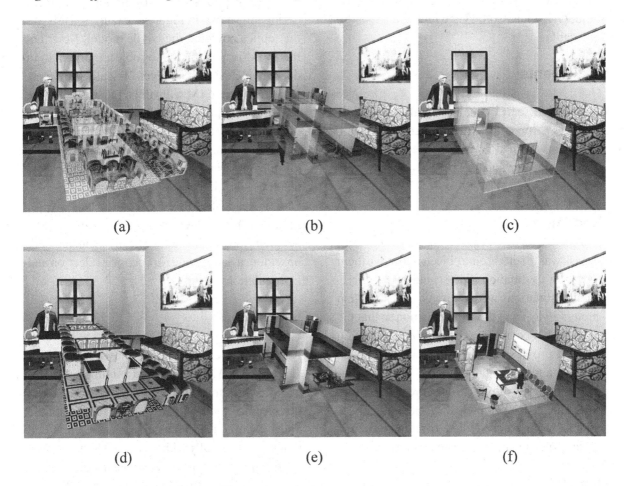

<table>
<tr><td>(a)</td><td>(b)</td><td>(c)</td></tr>
<tr><td>(d)</td><td>(e)</td><td>(f)</td></tr>
</table>

during the experiment (about 30cm³). Regarding WIM revealing, we considered two options for distractor removal: turning them invisible (using our *z-offset* approach) or semi-transparent (using unsorted alpha blending with depth buffer write operations disabled).

Given that our WIM delimitation strategy automatically matches the WIM extents to the current cell, in the best case scenario one could expect DWIM delimitation to have a positive impact on selection performance. In practice, however, this may not be the case. On the one hand, DWIM's lack of manual adjustment can keep the user from finding a suitable level of scale for performing the spatial task. On the other hand, DWIM's cells include enclosing geometry

which might distract the user unless efficiently removed. We also expected the WIM revealing strategy to have a varying impact depending on the WIM delimitation strategy and the amount of intervening distractors. In any case, rendering semi-transparent objects increases the visual complexity so we expected the transparency option to have a negative impact on selection performance.

Apparatus

All the experiments were conducted on a four-sided CAVE with active-stereo projectors at 1280x1280 resolution. The input device was a 6-DOF Ascension Wanda and a tracking system with 2 receivers providing 60 updates/s with 4 ms latency. The experiment was driven by a cluster of 2.66GHz QuadCore PCs with Nvidia Quadro 5500 cards.

Participants

Eleven volunteers (1 female, 10 male), aged from 24 to 35, participated in the experiment. Some participants (4) had no experience with VE applications; 5 had some experience and 2 were experienced users.

Procedure

The task was to select some objects and move them to a target destination represented by a sphere. Target destinations were chosen to be more than 4 meters away from the initial position so that the task could be accomplished more efficiently using the WIM proxies rather than the actual objects. Selection and manipulation in the WIM was accomplished using the virtual hand metaphor. Users were requested to complete the task as quickly as possible. Users were allowed to navigate at 2m/s constant speed using the wanda's joystick.

Design

A repeated-measures within-subjects design was used. The independent variables were WIM delimitation (adjustable cube, current cell) and WIM revealing (transparency, z-offset), resulting in four combinations. Each participant performed the experiment in one session lasting approximately 15 min. The session was divided into four blocks, one for each technique.

Before each block users were provided with a short training session which required them to complete practice trials. We measured the time to complete the task, distinguishing between selection, manipulation and navigation times (some users decided to navigate to find a better view to accomplish the task).

Various options for WIM delimitation and rendering are shown in Figure 6. Figure 6(d) shows the replica covering the whole model. Note that this WIM is not suitable for object manipulation due to occlusion and level-of-scale problems. Rendering the WIM with alpha blending (Figure 6(a)) does not provide a sufficiently clear view of the model and still provides a scale unsuitable for object manipulation. Figures 6(b) and 6(e) show sample renderings with the adjustable cube. The result of our clipping algorithm (with transparency instead of z-offset revealing) is shown in Figure 6(c). Now the miniature includes only the geometry inside the automatically-detected cell, providing a better scale for accurate selection and manipulation

Results

Results of the experiment are shown in Figure 7. The two-way ANOVA showed a significant effect ($p < 0.01$) for the WIM delimitation factor, users performing much better (30% less time) with the WIM delimited automatically to the current cell rather than manually with the cube. This result was expected as our approach eliminates the need to manually adapt the WIM extent to the task. We also found a significant effect ($p = 0.04$) for the WIM revealing factor, and a clear interaction effect ($p < 0.01$) between delimitation and revealing. When the WIM was delimited automatically to the current cell, the choice of the revealing strategy had a significant effect, users performing much better when removing occluding walls with the z-offset approach. This seems to confirm our hypothesis on the limitations of the transparency option for performing spatial tasks (see Figures 6(c) and 6(f)). However, when delimiting the WIM with the adjustable cube, the revealing strategy had little impact on overall user performance. Our explanation for this is that rendering the WIM with transparency resulted in higher visual complexity of the resulting images, but this was compensated by the fact that users were not forced to perform a fine adjustment of the cube to avoid occluding walls (see Figures 6(b) and 6(e)).

We conducted a second experiment with identical setup except for the object to be manipulated, which was moved to an adjacent room. This change implied that, when using our approach, users were required to navigate to the target room, whereas for the adjustable cube users were able to choose whether to navigate or to scale-up the cube. We also chose a target room with less occluding objects to favor transparency against our z-offset approach. The results of the second experiment are shown in Figure 7 (right). Despite being a worst-case scenario for our approach, we still found a significant effect for WIM delimitation ($p = 0.01$), users performing better with DWIM. Our best explanation is that, in densely-occluded environments, scaling-up the cube rapidly increases the number of distractors, adding occluders from neighboring cells and keeping it from providing a clear view for carrying out spatial tasks. Concerning WIM revealing, we did not found a significant effect on completion times ($p=0.1$). This seems to confirm our hypothesis that the alpha blending option is only usable with a low number of occluders.

Runtime Overhead

Our technique introduces some performance overheads with respect to competing WIM implementations. Our rendering algorithm requires building the LDI of a low-polygon approximation of the cell and drawing the objects with a simple fragment shader. Notice that the LDI is built using a FBO with the size of the WIM viewport, which is much smaller than the immersive viewport. The overhead was found to be less than one millisecond, which had no noticeable impact on the application frame rate. When compared with WIM implementations putting a replica of the whole scene, our approach clearly wins as only a fraction of the geometry is rendered every frame.

Supporting Several Levels of Scale

Our technique can be extended to provide a miniature replica at multiple levels of scale, allowing the user to select the extents of the WIM according to the accuracy of the intended interaction task. The WIM delimitation strategy can be modified so as to allow the user to interactively expand the extent of the miniature copy by adding cells adjacent to the current cell. This can be easily accomplished

Figure 7. Box plots for task 1 (left) and task 2 (right)

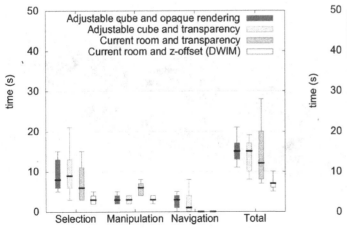
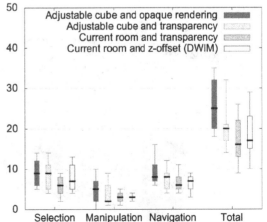

as cell adjacency information can be computed as a subproduct of the cell detection algorithm (Andújar, Vázquez & Fairén, 2004). The main advantage with respect to continuously scaling a cube is that the WIM is expanded in a discrete manner, showing always a complete subset of cells, i.e. cells are not splited during zooming operations. Of course, putting more than one cell on the replica implies modifying the WIM revealing strategy, so as to keep potential targets visible in the presence of large occluding surfaces *inside* the WIM. A simple solution consists in extending the WIM revealing algorithm as follows. Suppose the WIM contains a set of neighboring cells $\{C_1, ..., C_n\}$. Let C_k be the cell containing the user's hand position. We build the LDI by rendering cells in $\{C_1, ..., C_n\}$, but giving visibility priority to C_k, so that the frontmost geometry of C_k belongs to the first LDI layer. Using such LDI would provide a clear view of the objects inside C_k. Assuming that potential targets are limited to the cell containing the user's hand, this strategy would provide a clear view of potential targets while preserving most context information (see Figure 8).

Limitations

Our approach is oriented towards indoor scenes with well-defined room structures (e.g. office buildings). It is obviously not appropriate for outside environments, but occlusion management on outdoor scenes is not a critical problem. Our WIM revealing strategy is slightly sensitive to the offset used for comparisons against the LDI representation of the current cell. As a result, an object being manipulated might partially disappear when getting close to one of the frontmost walls of the cell. However, this can be avoided by simply rotating the hand-held WIM so that the wall becomes backmost geometry. The cell detection method is also limited by the size of the voxel grids that can be realistically managed. A solution for large-scale models is to split the model into smaller parts and build separate voxelizations for each part.

Figure 8. Rendering a WIM with several neighboring cells facilitates manipulation tasks among cells. The WIM revealing strategy has been modified to keep visible the objects inside the cell containing the user's hand (drawn as a red ball).

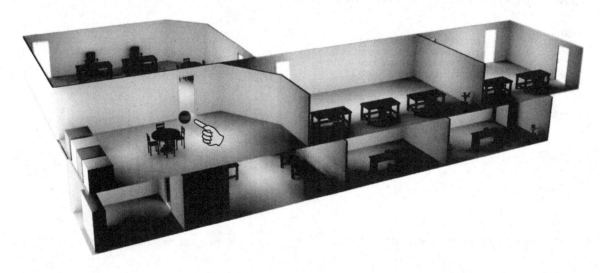

CONCLUSION AND FUTURE WORK

In this paper an enhanced version of the WIM metaphor has been presented. Our approach supports arbitrarily-complex, densely-occluded scenes by selecting the region to be included in the miniature copy using a semantic subdivision of the scene into logical structures such as rooms. The rationale of our approach is that matching the miniature copies with logical entities of the environment would help the user to accomplish spatial tasks. We have shown empirically that our approach facilitates accurate selection and manipulation of 3D objects through their WIM proxies, providing a clear, low-complexity view automatically adapted to the user's location. Our current system allows users to switch automatic WIM delimitation on and off; when turned off, the WIM shows a miniature replica of the whole scene, which can be more suitable for way-finding tasks at large scale levels. Unlike other WIM extensions using continuous scrolling, our approach preserves the extents of the miniature copy while the user remains in the same room. The room center instead of the current viewpoint is used as pivot point for hand-held manipulation and visualization of the miniature. We have found this behavior to be less distracting to the users.

There are several directions that can be pursued to extend the current work. It may be interesting to explore alternative visibility-aware decompositions of the scene suitable for outdoor environments, enabling fast identification and removal of occluding geometry, as well as cell decompositions requiring no preprocessing at all. Although we have focused on its implementation for the WIM, it may be interesting to explore the application of our revealing strategy to manipulate directly the objects shown in the immersive view.

ACKNOWLEDGMENT

This work has been partially funded by the Spanish Ministry of Science and Technology under grant TIN2007-67982-C02.

REFERENCES

Airey, J. (1990). *Increasing update rates in the building walkthrough system with automatic model-space subdivision and potentially visible set calculations.* Unpublished PhD thesis, Department of Computer Science, University of North Carolina at Chapel Hill.

Andújar, C., Ayala, D., & Brunet, P. (2002). Topology simplification through discrete models. *ACM Transactions on Graphics, 20*(6), 88–105.

Andújar, C., Vázquez, P., & Fairén, M. (2004). Way-finder: Guided tours through complex walkthrough models. *Computer Graphics Forum, 23*(3), 499–508. doi:10.1111/j.1467-8659.2004.00781.x

Burns, M., & Finkelstein, A. (2008). Adaptive cutaways for comprehensible rendering of polygonal scenes. *ACM Transactions on Graphics, 27*(5), 1–7. doi:10.1145/1409060.1409107

Chittaro, L., Gatla, V. K., & Venkataraman, S. (2005). The interactive 3d breakaway map: A navigation and examination aid for mult-ifloor 3d worlds. In *Proceedings of CW '05: 2005 International Conference on Cyberworlds* (pp. 59-66). Washington, DC: IEEE Computer Society.

Coffin, C., & Hollerer, T. (2006). *Interactive perspective cut-away views for general 3d scenes.* In *Proceedings of 3DUI '06: IEEE Symposium on 3D User Interfaces* (pp. 25-28).

Cohen-Or, D., Chrysanthou, Y., Silva, C., & Durand, F. (2003). A survey of visibility for walkthrough applications. *IEEE Transactions on Visualization and Computer Graphics, 9*(3), 412–431. doi:10.1109/TVCG.2003.1207447

Diepstraten, J., Weiskopf, D., & Ertl, T. (2003). Interactive cutaway illustrations. In *Proceedings of Eurographics, 2003*, 523–532.

Dong, Z., Chen, W., Bao, H., Zhang, H., & Peng, Q. (2004). Real-time voxelization for complex polygonal models. In *Proceedings of PG '04: 12th Pacific Conference on Computer Graphics and Applications* (pp. 43-50).

Eisemann, E., & Décoret, X. (2006). Fast Scene Voxelization and Applications. In *Proceedings of the 2006 ACM Symposium on Interactive 3D Graphics and Games* (pp. 70-78).

Elmqvist, N., Assarsson, U., & Tsigas, P. (2007). Employing dynamic transparency for 3d occlusion management: Design issues and evaluation. In *Proceedings of INTERACT, 2007*, 532–545.

Elmqvist, N., & Tsigas, P. (2008). A taxonomy of 3d occlusion management for visualization. *IEEE Transactions on Visualization and Computer Graphics, 14*(5), 1095–1109. doi:10.1109/TVCG.2008.59

Everitt, C. (2001). *Introduction to interactive order-independent transparency*. NVIDIA Corporation.

Feiner, S., & Seligmann, D. (1992). Cutaways and ghosting: satisfying visibility constraints in dynamic 3D illustrations. *The Visual Computer, 8*(5), 292–302. doi:10.1007/BF01897116

Hable, J., & Rossignac, J. (2005). Blister: Gpu-based rendering of boolean combinations of free-form triangulated shapes. *ACM Transactions on Graphics, 24*(3), 1024–1031. doi:10.1145/1073204.1073306

Haumont, D., Debeir, O., & Sillion, F. (2003). Volumetric cell-and-portal generation. In *Proceedings of the Computer Graphics Forum* (pp. 3-22)

Hong, L., Muraki, S., Kaufman, A., Bartz, D., & He, T. (1997). Virtual voyage: interactive navigation in the human colon. In *SIGGRAPH '97: Proceedings of the 24th annual conference on Computer graphics and interactive techniques* (pp. 27-34).

Jones, M., & Satherley, R. (2001). Using distance fields for object representation and rendering. In *Proceedings of Eurographics, 2001*, 37–44.

Kirsch, F., & Döllner, J. (2005). Opencsg: a library for image-based csg rendering. In *Proceedings USENIX 05* (p. 49).

LaViola, J. J., Jr., Feliz, D. A., Keefe, D. F., & Zeleznik, R. C. (2001). Hands-free multi-scale navigation in virtual environments. In *Proceedings of the Symposium on Interactive 3D Graphics '01* (pp. 9-15).

Shade, J., Gortler, S., He, L. W., & Szeliski, R. (1998). Layered depth images. In *Proceedings of SIGGRAPH, 98*, 231–242.

Stoakley, R., Conway, M. J., & Pausch, Y. (1995). Virtual reality on a wim: interactive worlds in miniature. In *Proceedings of SIGCHI'95: SIG on Human factors in computing systems* (pp. 265-272).

Teller, S. J., & Séquin, C. H. (1991). Visibility preprocessing for interactive walkthroughs. *SIGGRAPH Computer Graphics, 25*(4), 61–70. doi:10.1145/127719.122725

Wingrave, C. A., Haciahmetoglu, Y., & Bowman, D. A. (2006). *Overcoming world in miniature limitations by a scaled and scrolling wim. In 3D* (pp. 11–16). User Interfaces.

This work was previously published in International Journal of Creative Interfaces and Computer Graphics, Volume 1, Issue 2, edited by Ben Falchuk, pp. 1-14, copyright 2010 by IGI Publishing (an imprint of IGI Global).

Chapter 7

TagClusters:
Enhancing Semantic Understanding of Collaborative Tags

Ya-Xi Chen
Media Informatics, University of Munich, Germany

Rodrigo Santamaría
University of Salamanca, Spain

Andreas Butz
Media Informatics, University of Munich, Germany

Roberto Therón
University of Salamanca, Spain

ABSTRACT

Many online communities use TagClouds, an aesthetic and easy to understand visualization, to represent popular tags collaboratively generated by their users. However, due to the free nature of tagging, such collaborative tags have linguistic problems and limitations, such as high semantic density. Moreover, the alphabetical order of TagClouds poorly supports a hierarchical exploration among tags. This paper presents an exploration to support semantic understanding of collaborative tags beyond TagClouds. Based on the results of the authors' survey of practical usages of collaborative tags, they developed a visualization named TagClusters, in which tags are clustered into different groups, with font size representing tag popularity and the spatial distance indicating the semantic similarity between tags. The subgroups in each group and the overlap between groups are highlighted, illustrating the underlying hierarchical structure and semantic relations between groups. The authors conducted a comparative evaluation with TagClouds and TagClusters based on the same tag set. The results confirmed the advantage of TagClusters in facilitating browsing, comparing and comprehending semantic relations between tags.

DOI: 10.4018/978-1-4666-0285-4.ch007

INTRODUCTION

The advent of the next-generation Web has tremendously influenced our ways of dealing with online digital items. In today's online communities, people are allowed to sharing their content and access others' in turn. They are also encouraged to make contributions by tagging these digital items. The most representative websites are YouTube (http://www.youtube.com) for video sharing, Flickr (http://www.flickr.com/) for photo sharing, and the online music community Last.fm (http://www.last.fm). The general goal of making online search and browsing easier is the main motivation for tagging. Besides facilitating personal organizing, browsing and searching online items, such collaborative tags also help to discover new items, acquire knowledge and derive insights users may be not aware of before.

Currently, there are two main usages of collaborative tags. Users can use tags to conduct a keyword-based search to seek information on the web. Comparing tags generated by single users, large quantities of collaborative tags convey public interests and opinions in a general level. Therefore, TagClouds, a visualization for the most popular tags, has become a fashion in many websites. Although TagClouds is widely used, it still has some intrinsic limitations. Many researchers have already noticed this and dedicate to improve its effectiveness by proposing more aesthetical representations or providing a better semantic understanding. In this paper, we take Last.fm as our experiment platform and explore how to use an improved visualization to support the semantic understanding of collaborative tags. We are specifically interested in the hierarchical structures and relationships among tags, which might lead to more successful tag recommendation and visualization-based music retrieval.

In the remaining parts of this paper, TagClouds and their related work will first be discussed. Based on a survey among Last.fm users, some

possibilities to improve semantic understanding beyond TagClouds will be explored. Finally, a prototype named TagClusters and its evaluation will be presented. The discussions on the evaluation results and future work will conclude this paper.

TAGCLOUDS

TagClouds is a visualization of popular tags (see Figure 1). In this visualization, tags are normally ordered alphabetically, with font size representing their popularity. Additional information, such as recency can be illustrated with color lightness. Comparing with tags generated by single users, these popular tags in TagClouds have a higher degree of generality and accuracy. Such visualization facilitates quickly foraging an overall impression of the most popular items, and thus conveys the general interests among a large audience (Viégas & Wattenberg, 2008), (Hearst 2008), (Hearst & Rosner, 2008). TagClouds can be also used for keyword-based search by selecting one or multiple tags as input.

LIMITATIONS OF TAGCLOUDS

In most online communities, users are allowed to generate tags freely, without any restriction or quality control. This low usage barrier has attracted hundreds of millions users. However, due to the free nature of tagging, some problems are inevitable with these collaborative tags (Li, Bao, Yu, Fei & Su, 2007; Hassan & Herrero, 2006).

Linguistic Problems

Nielsen (2007) and Begelman, Keller and Smadja (2006) discovered educational and cultural background influence people's understanding of tags, which is one of the reasons for tag inconsistency among different users. With no input restrictions,

Figure 1. TagClouds in Last.fm

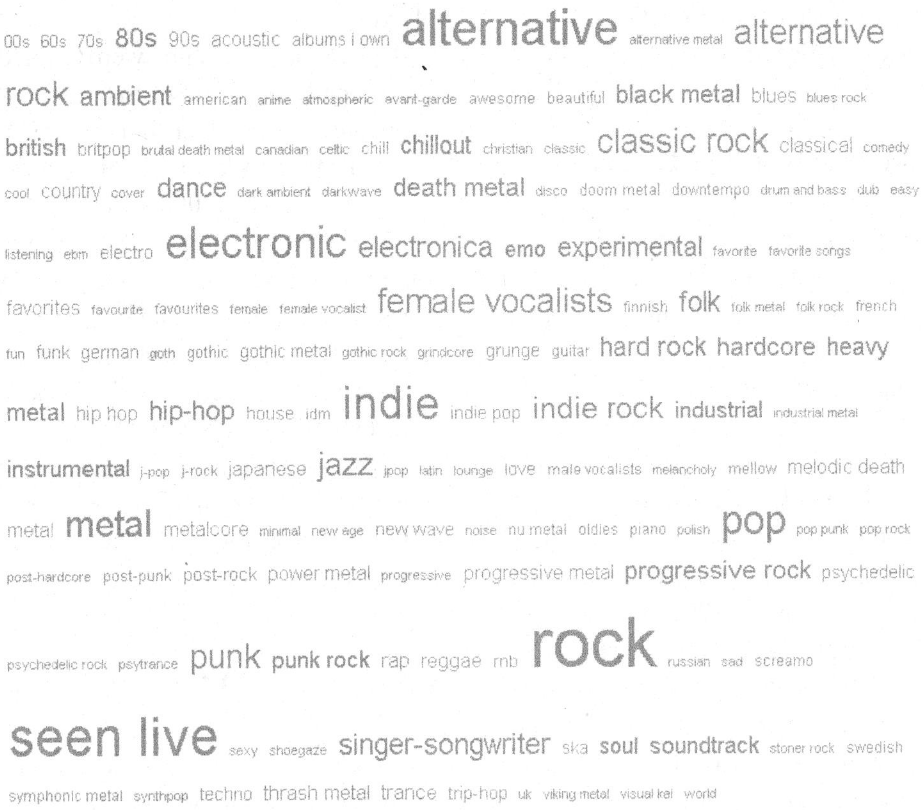

00s 60s 70s 80s 90s acoustic albums i own alternative alternative metal alternative rock ambient american anime atmospheric avant-garde awesome beautiful black metal blues blues rock british britpop brutal death metal canadian celtic chill chillout christian classic classic rock classical comedy cool country cover dance dark ambient darkwave death metal disco doom metal downtempo drum and bass dub easy listening ebm electro electronic electronica emo experimental favorite favorite songs favorites favourite favourites female female vocalist female vocalists finnish folk folk metal folk rock french fun funk german goth gothic gothic metal gothic rock grindcore grunge guitar hard rock hardcore heavy metal hip hop hip-hop house idm indie indie pop indie rock industrial industrial metal instrumental j-pop j-rock japanese jazz jpop latin lounge love male vocalists melancholy mellow melodic death metal metal metalcore minimal new age new wave noise nu metal oldies piano polish pop pop punk pop rock post-hardcore post-punk post-rock power metal progressive progressive metal progressive rock psychedelic psychedelic rock psytrance punk punk rock rap reggae rnb rock russian sad screamo seen live sexy shoegaze singer-songwriter ska soul soundtrack stoner rock swedish symphonic metal synthpop techno thrash metal trance trip-hop uk viking metal visual kei world

two general problems are hardly to avoid from the users' perspective (Wu, Zhang, & Yu, 2006): Synonymy, which is also termed as "inter-indexer inconsistency" by Nielsen (2007), appears when different terms are used to describe the same item. A term with several different meanings brings ambiguity (Mathes, 2008), which may reduce the precision of the retrieval results.

Visual Bias

In TagClouds the font size of tags is determined by their usage frequency, and popular tags with larger font size naturally draw more visual attention. It is easy to catch the most prominent topics, but on the other hand it also leads to a problem of visual bias: Tags with larger font size tend to dominate the visual attention of the whole visualization and other less important items with smaller size tend to be visually ignored (Hassan & Herrero, 2006), (Begelman, Keller, & Smadja, 2006) and (Hearst & Rosner, 2008). Moreover, small font size also makes the comparison of tags difficult (Hearst and Rosner, 2008).

Poor Semantic Understandability

Alphabetical order is one of the main features of TagClouds, which is an efficient assistance to ease the finding of tags. On the other hand it poorly supports a semantic exploration. Hearst and Rosner (2008) discovered in their user study that a significant proportion of participants did not even notice this alphabetical arrangement. Users also had difficulties to derive the underlying semantic relations among tags, and some of them misinterpreted the spatial distance between tags as their semantic relatedness. Therefore TagClouds is concluded as not appropriate to supporting understanding of structure and relations, which is also supported by Hassan and Herrero (2006).

IMPROVEMENTS OF TAGCLOUDS

Recently many researchers have started to improve TagClouds by enhancing their aesthetic appearance or supporting their semantic understanding.

Aesthetic Enhancements

Since several factors influence the effectiveness of TagClouds, such as font size and weight, some systems have already allowed the user to adjust these parameters, for example in PubCloud (Kuo, Hentrich, Good & Wilkinson, 2007).

Some algorithms have been introduced to improve the quality of TagClouds by packing the text in the visualization tighter. Kaser and Lemire (2007) used Electronic Design Automation (EDA) to improve the arrangement of TagClouds by avoiding large unused white space. Seifert, Kump and Kienreich (2008) presented a series of algorithms to display tags in arbitrary convex polygons with a self-adapting font size. A circular layout was developed in (Bielenberg & Zacher, 2005), in which both font size and distance to the center represent tag importance. It was claimed in (Lohmann, Ziegler & Tetzlaff, 2009) that sequential layout with alphabetical sorting is suitable for finding a specific tag, while a thematically clustered layout can facilitate finding tags which belong to a certain topic.

Supporting Semantic Understanding

In (Shaw, 2008) tags were visualized as a graph, in which length of edge represents similarity. TagOrbitals (Kerr, 2008) displays relevant tags in an atom metaphor, in which each primary tag was placed in the center, and other related tags were placed in surrounding bands. The main problem with this visualization is the varying orientation of texts.

Clustering algorithms were applied to gather semantically similar tags. In (Hassan & Herrero, 2006) the k-means algorithm was applied to group semantically similar tags. Similar work can be found in (Provost, 2008). Li, Bao, Yu, Fei and Su (2007) supported browsing large scale social annotations based on an analysis of semantic and hierarchical relations. The user's profile and the temporal dimension can be integrated for personalized or time-related browsing (Nielsen, 2007).

Most of the methods discussed above are static visualizations and lack interaction. The semantic representation should be further explored, which will help the user to form a better understanding of hierarchical structure and relations.

PRACTICAL TAG USAGE IN LAST.FM

As discussed above, TagClouds have distinct linguistic problems and poorly support the understanding of structure and relationships among tags. In this paper, we have chosen the tags in Last.fm as the experimental platform. It allows users to tag music-relevant information, such as tracks, albums and artists. These tags can then be used to produce a TagClouds (see Figure 1). The user can search with these collaboratively generated tags, and Last.fm will return a page with the retrieval results, in which relevant tags and artists will be displayed. For example, in the retrieval result for the tag "*rock*", one can see the related tags such as *alternative*, *indie* and *punk*.

In order to obtain a better understanding of the practical usage of User-Generate Content in Last. fm, we conducted a survey with Last.fm users. Based on these, we derived a number of design guidelines, which inspired our development of the semantic-based tag visualization. We reported this survey briefly in the following, and more details can be found in (Chen, Boring, & Butz, in press).

User Interview

In order to gain more insights on the effective use of tags contributed by the users, we need to explore the features and benefits of music-related tags, as well as the users' search and tagging behavior. In order to explore these, we conducted interviews with 13 Last.fm users, who were recruited in the Last.fm online forums. Three of them were female and 10 male, and their age varied from 18 to 26 with an average age of 23 years. Among these participants, there were 7 undergraduate students, 2 graduate students, 2 researchers and 2 employees in business. All the participants had a common knowledge about computers and the Internet. They had a relatively long listening history: all of them registered more than 2 years ago, 2 users even more than 3 years and one user more than 4 years ago.

During the interview, the participants were equipped with a PC, a keyboard and a mouse. They were given a list of all the questions to be discussed. While they were formulating their answers, the Think-Aloud protocol was applied, which helped them to express their answers in a more natural and flexible way. Participants could also freely browse their personal profiles and other services of Last.fm. The key aspects explored were the tagging and searching behavior and relevant user-generated tags. Example questions for searching behavior were: "How often do you search for music in Last.fm?", "How often do you use tags for searching?" and "What do you think about the TagClouds of Last.fm?". Example questions for the tagging behavior were: "How often do you tag music in Last.fm?", "Which kind of tags do you use for tagging?" and "Do you think tagging music is difficult?"

12 out of 13 participants used the search functionality frequently. Only one user looked for music by browsing the charts of popular artists. Besides standard keywords of artist, album and song, the participants did not search with tags very often and the average score for their usage

frequency was 2.2 (1 for never, 5 for daily). Genre was the most frequently used tag for keyword-based search. All participants felt that the too general tags might make them getting lost among too many less relevant results and thus find nothing specific.

When asked to comment the TagClouds shown in Figure 1, one prominent comment was the redundancy. The participants did not tag very often themselves, and the average tagging frequency was 1.1 (1 for never). Similarly to tags used for search, most of their actual input tags were also related to genre. Some other participants also use personalized tags for quick relocating, such as "listen again" and "Sunday morning". The majority of participants thought that tagging music is hard and one participant even postponed it as the last task because he thought it was a hard and serious job and he needed more time to think about it.

Online Survey

In order to validate the results of our interviews, we conducted an online survey with a larger population. The survey lasted for two months and 228 Last.fm users joined in it, 93 of which were female and 133 male (two gender identifiers were left blank). Their age varied from 16 to 36 with an average age of 22 years. The participants were mainly students and employees from North America and Europe. Participants reported themselves to be experienced Last.fm users with an average score of 3.8 (5 for very experienced). Their registration histories varied from 0.13 to 5.72 years with an average duration of 1.8 years.

The questions mainly covered the general experience with search and tagging. Their answers showed that they seek information quite often in Last.fm, with an average frequency of 4.0 (1 for never, 5 for daily). A significantly larger proportion of this time (with an average percentage of 64%) was spent in browsing-like filtering rather than specific search activities. Concerning keyword-based search, participants mostly search music-related information (4.0/5), such as names of artists, albums, songs, and less about social information of groups, users and events. Consistently with the interview result, tags were used much less for search (2.0/5).

The participants thought Last.fm TagClouds (as shown in Figure 1) offeres an efficient overview for the most popular items (3.6/5), but they also noticed the apparent linguistic problems. They commented that a too general selection of tags is counterproductive for tag-based search.

Participants did not tag very often (1.8/5) and they mainly tagged music in their own libraries. In the questionnaire, they were required to tag one specific artist and the top tags were genre-related, such as *pop*, *funk* and *soul*. The top motivations for tagging were easing browsing and searching, facilitating personal organization and searching, and conveying their musical knowledge.

Implications

Based on the results of the interview and the online survey, we derived some implications about the users' searching and tagging behavior. People's information seeking behavior is more alike to browsing than to specific keyword-based search. People rarely tag music and they tag it with different motivations. In Last.fm, most of the popular tags are genre-relevant. The personal understanding of genre is subjective and people might come up with different tags for the same music. Searching with tags is not common in Last.fm because these user-generated tags are normally too general to help users finding specific targets.

We believe that if the tags can be efficiently organized in a more understandable way, they will be more helpful for tag recommendation and tag-based music retrieval. We therefore explore the semantic aggregation of tags to support efficient hierarchical browsing and understanding the relations between tags.

Semantic Aggregation

Through an analysis of tag text, the problem of synonym can be efficiently alleviated by grouping semantically similar tags, such as *favorite* and *favorites*, *rock and roll* and *rock n roll*. This semantic aggregation can also help to remove the ambiguity. For example, a significantly number of users think "*electronic*" and "*IDM*" belong to the same genre. By grouping these similar concepts in one group, their relation can be clearly indicated and the user has a good chance to be "educated".

Hierarchy Exploration and Relation Visualization

The implicit hierarchical structure hidden inside the user-generated tag can also be extracted with the text analysis. By uncovering the underlying semantic relations, it is possible to derive a semantic understanding of tags, especially the important genre-relevant ones. With a clearly demonstrated hierarchical structure, the user can also search more efficiently with less ambiguity. By highlighting the overlapping areas between groups, the user can tell the relation between tags at a higher semantic level.

Possible Applications

With a hierarchical structure of tags, it is possible to offer efficient tag suggestions. Such assistance can efficiently help users to input more appropriate tags while avoiding possible spelling errors or redundancy. Both existing work and our survey have confirmed the importance of genre in conveying the general information of music (Cunningham, Bainbridge & Falconer, 2006). Due to the fact that there is no standard definition of genre, we expect such a tag suggestion facility would be especially useful to recommend genre-related tags. For example, if the user types in "*electronic*", the system can suggest "*IDM*" as a similar tag. If

Figure 2. The visualization of TagClusters (with the same tag set in Figure 1)

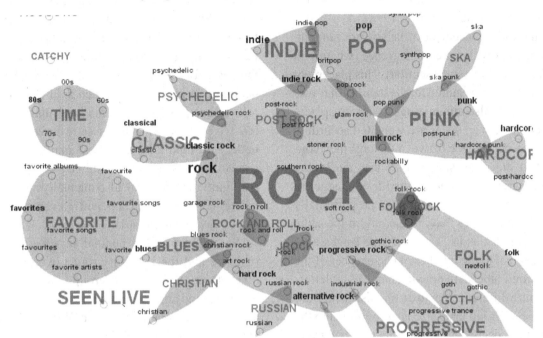

the hierarchical structure is achieved, it will help the user to conduct a more controlled tag-based search, which will yield retrieval results with higher relevance.

TAGCLUSTERS: SUPPORTING THE SEMANTIC UNDERSTANDING OF TAGS

We investigated the problems with user-generated tags in Last.fm and explored possibilities to improve the semantic understanding of these tags. Based on the aforementioned design considerations, we built a prototype named TagClusters to support the semantic understanding of tags (as shown in Figure 2).

TagClusters is implemented based on Overlapper (Santamaría & Therón, 2008), a graph-based visualization tool that highlights the connections and overlaps among entities (nodes) in data. TagClusters is an interactive interface in which tags are drawn as labels with different sizes (size

representing tag popularity, as in TagClouds), and tag groups are drawn as transparent colored areas (see Figure 2). TagClusters use the underlying visualization of Overlapper, based on a force-directed layout (Fruchterman & Reinhold, 1991) that does not use a typical node-link approach, but a Venn-diagram approach, in order to represent groups and group relationships. On a force-directed layout, two forces are typically computed within an iteration loop: a spring force is applied to connected nodes, keeping them close, while a repulsion force is applied among nodes, separating non-connected nodes. In our case, each node in the visualization corresponds to a tag, and two tags clustered in the same group are connected by an edge. In this schema, each group is a complete sub-graph joining every node in it, and it is represented by a transparent hull that wraps all of its nodes. This is achieved by using the outermost nodes of the groups as anchoring points for a spline curve which is drawn in a solid color to improve group traceability. Edges are only used to compute attraction forces among nodes in the same groups, but they are not drawn to avoid edge cluttering (Gansner & North, 1998).

The initial placement of tags is not random, but coherent with tag co-occurrence (which will be discussed in the next section). This placement reduces the time required for the stability of forces in the layout, also minimizing possible misplacements. Moreover, edges are weighted according to the co-occurrence between the tags they connect, so the more similar they are, the higher the attraction force represented by the edge. In this way, nodes will be separated proportionally to their similarities even if they are in the same group. Finally, as in TagClouds, the label size is proportional to the number of occurrences of the tag. Group labels are drawn using capital letters and with a different color to distinguish them from tag labels. Group label size is proportional to the sum of the occurrences of all the tags the group contains. This is done on a logarithmic scale to avoid very large tags. Therefore, TagClusters can be seen as TagClouds in which position is relevant and based on tag co-occurrence and tag groups. The visualization is further supported by group wrappers. These characteristics exploit human perception for traceability and group detection, improving the visual analysis (Ware, 2004).

In addition, the final user interface offers several interactions, such as panning and zooming without losing context (provided by an overview in the top-right corner), hiding or showing tags, groups and labels, searching tags by text, modifying the underlying forces, modifying node and group locations, changing color settings, and exporting the current visualization to an image. The system also provides multiple options for tag selection, which facilitate tag-based music retrieval. For example, the user can choose multiple tags or groups using both keyboard and mouse. She or he can also draw a shape manually and all the tags included in this shape will be selected. As pointed out in (Hearst & Rosner, 2008), it is difficult to compare or discover tags in small print,

so our interface also allows customized label font sizes. Although infrequently, the force-directed technique may misplace nodes, positioning them inside groups they do not belong to (this may be the case, for example, for elongated hulls connecting two other groups, such as the *goth* and *folk* groups in Figure 2). This particular issue is resolved by allowing the user to hover over a node. This highlights all nodes connected to the respective node, thereby resolving any possible ambiguity. The user can also manually adjust the positions of groups and tags, and relevant changes can be saved automatically.

Since most of the popular tags are related to genre and the relevant groups overlap each other, these genre-related groups are placed in the center and other semantically less related tags and groups are scattered around. Within a group, tags are further grouped into sub-groups. Since groups are represented as transparent colored areas, overlapping groups (groups that share one or more common tags) have intersecting, more opaque areas, thus highlighting the overlapping tags. With such assistance, the user can obtain a better understanding of structure and relation between tags. For example, in Figure 2, we can see that *rock* is the most popular genre group which is also related to several others, such as *pop*, *indie* and *punk*. Also we find several genres at the bottom right of the figure relating to both *metal* and *rock* groups, such as *progressive* and *goth* (see Figures 2 and 3).

UNDERLYING SEMANTIC ANALYSIS

The arrangement of tags in TagClusters is achieved based on a semantic analysis: The hierarchical structure is achieved based on a text analysis, which also helped to exclude redundancy. Then a calculation of the semantic similarity between each pair of tags helps to determine the initial position for each tag.

Figure 3. Examples of text analysis result

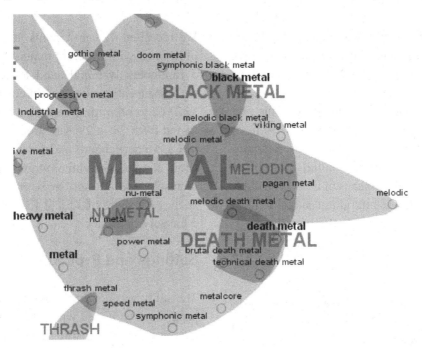

Text Analysis

With an observation of the Last.fm TagClouds (see Figure 1), we notice that synonymy is the most serious linguistic problem among these user-generated tags. Specifically, it is mainly caused by the issue of singular and plural, for example, "*favorite*" and "*favorites*", or by different spellings, such as "*favorite*" and "*favourite*". Besides, the usage of different separators produces another kind of redundancy, for example, "*rock and roll*" and "*rock n roll*".

We also discovered that many Last.fm tags, especially the genre-related tags, share a characteristic property: The tag at the lower semantic level almost always contains the tag at the higher level and the length of tag is roughly proportional to its semantic level, for example, "*metal*", "*death metal*" and "*brutal death metal*". This feature helps us to derive the hierarchical structure. In our system, after removal of different separators, such as "_" and "&", the Porter algorithm (Porter, 2006) is applied to detect the stem for each tag.

Tags with the same stem will be clustered into one group. Within one group, tags sharing other stems will be further clustered into sub-groups. For example, all the tags containing "*metal*" will be grouped in the *Metal* group and tags such as "*death metal*" and "*brutal death metal*" will be further placed into a sub-group (as shown in Figure 3). All tags related to gender will be clustered in a *Vocal* group, and a similar thing is done for the time-related tags, such as "*80s*" and "*00s*" (see left part of Figure 2). After the text analysis, most of the tags can be correctly grouped into a hierarchical structure. We notice that this basic technique has some limitations and should be further enhanced to distinguish the literally similar but musically different tags such as *classic* and *classic rock*

Calculation of Semantic Similarity

After achieving the hierarchical structure of tags, we calculate the semantic similarity between each pair of tags based on their co-occurrence. It is a metric widely used in the field of Information

Retrieval to determine the semantic relations between a pair of information items (Nielsen, 2007), (Begelman, Keller & Smadja, 2006). In our case, this semantic similarity (*Sim*) between tag A and B equals to the ratio between the number of resources in which these two tags co-occur and the number of resources in which any of the two tags appears (Nielsen, 2007), (Hassan & Herrero, 2006), as equation 1 shows. With the semantic similarity between tags, the initial location of each tag is assigned by means of a 2D projection based on a non-metric multidimensional scaling of co-occurrences (Sammon, 1969).

$$Sim(A, B) = |A \cap B| / |A \cup B| \qquad (1)$$

Through the approach of semantic analysis discussed above, all tags can be semantically organized into relevant groups and sub-groups, with the distance representing their semantic similarity. With interconnections with each other, the genre-relevant groups become prominent in the visualization. Other categories such as time- or emotion-related groups are scattered around, due to their less semantic relationship with the genre category.

USER STUDY

In order to evaluate our visualization tool, we conducted a comparative evaluation of TagClouds and TagClusters. We were specifically interested in the performance of our tool in supporting the perception of semantic relationships among tags.

User Study Design

TagClouds and TagClusters were evaluated using a repeated measures within participants factorial design. The independent variable was sysType (TagClouds and TagClusters). The order of sysType was counterbalanced between participants to minimize learning effects.

Participants

We recruited 12 participants at the University of Munich with different majors, 7 German and 5 foreigners, 4 female and 8 male. These 12 participants allowed a perfect counterbalance of sysType to minimize learning effects. Their age varied from 24 to 29 with an average age of 27 years. All participants had a common knowledge about computers and the Internet. They reported themselves to be familiar with TagClouds with an average score of 3.58 (1 for unfamiliar at all, 5 for very familiar).

Settings and Procedure

The study was conducted in our lab and participants were equipped with a PC, a keyboard and a mouse. On average the user study lasted about 35 minutes per participant. It was recorded on video and the Think-Aloud protocol was applied.

The user study consisted of a pre-questionnaire, an interview and a post-questionnaire. The participants were first asked to fill out a pre-questionnaire with demographic information and their general experience with tags. After a brief introduction of TagClouds and TagClusters, the participants were asked to execute 6 tasks, which mainly covered the aspects of searching, browsing, comparison and relation understanding. Each task consisted of two sub-tasks and the following are 6 example tasks:

Task 1: Single tag locating: Find a tag named "German".

Task 2: Tag ranking: List the top 5 popular tags.

Task 3: Tag comparison and filtering: List the top 5 tags related to genre.

Task 4: Structure deriving: Give a hierarchical structure for the *Metal* group.

Task 5: Tag relation detection: Is there an overlap between *pop* and *punk*?

Task 6: Similarity judgment: Is *indie* more similar to *punk* or *progressive*?

After completing each task, participants scored how easy the task was, and how helpful the system was in supporting the task. After completing all the tasks, participants filled out a post-questionnaire concerning the overall impression of both systems.

Hypotheses

Based on the main features of both visualizations (for example, tags are ordered alphabetically in TagClouds and semantically grouped in TagClusters), the following hypotheses were stated:

H1: TagClouds will outperform TagClusters in Task 1 regarding completion time, answer precision, task easiness and system usefulness.

H2: TagClouds will outperform TagClusters in Task 2 regarding completion time, answer precision, task easiness and system usefulness.

H3: TagClusters will outperform TagClouds in Task 3 regarding completion time, answer precision, task easiness and system usefulness.

H4: TagClusters will outperform TagClouds in Task 4-6 regarding completion time, answer precision, task easiness and system usefulness.

Results

The results are reported based on the 24 sessions performed by the participants. We analyzed the questionnaires, answers and the screen activities and discovered the following results. The comparison of the completion time, the answer precision, the task easiness and the system usefulness for both systems are shown in Figure 4.

For task 1, although the tags in TagClouds can be located by their alphabetical order, locating the first character still needed some time. A dependent t-test showed that TagClouds cost significantly more time with task 1 than TagClusters ($t(11)=3.131$, $p<0.05$). Furthermore, 25% of the participants did not realize that TagClouds are ordered alphabetically, thus they spent more time on tag locating. Participants claimed that the search functionality in TagClusters helped to locate the item quickly. Both systems received the same answer precision but TagClouds was rated lower in the aspects of task easiness and system usefulness. Thus hypothesis (H1) was rejected.

For task 2, TagClouds performed better concerning the time efficiency and answer precision, and participants spent significantly less time with TagClouds ($t(11)=3.92$, $p<0.05$). The scores for the task easiness and system helpfulness were also significantly higher with TagClouds ($t(11)=3.354$, $p<0.01$; $t(11)=3.139$, $p<0.05$). Since no significant difference of answer precision was revealed, Hypothesis (H2) cannot be proved.

For task 3, although TagClusters performed better in the aspects of answer precision, task easiness and system usefulness, it cost more time than with TagClouds. Thus Hypothesis (H3) was rejected.

TagClouds contain all the tags in a small graph and it is easier to scan and locate tags without panning or zooming. To present all the tags in groups and describe the similarity between tags as spatial distance, TagClusers need more space and thus create a larger graph in which the participants had to keep panning and zooming to get a complete overall impression. To form the correct impression, the participant also needed to mentally compare and memorize the relevant information which might slow down the response time and lead to answers with lower precision. Results for task 2 and 3 imply that we should make better usage of the space in TagClusters in order to create a smaller and more efficient visualization.

The results for task 4-6 were rather consistent: TagClusters received higher scores in all aspects. A dependent t-test showed that TagClusters worked significantly better with task 4 concerning both time efficiency ($t(11)=2.752$, $p<0.05$) and answer precision ($t(11)=4.077$, $p<0.01$). Since the tags are

Figure 4. Comparison of system performance. Top left: completion time. Top Right: answer precision. Bottom left: task easiness. Bottom right: system usefulness.

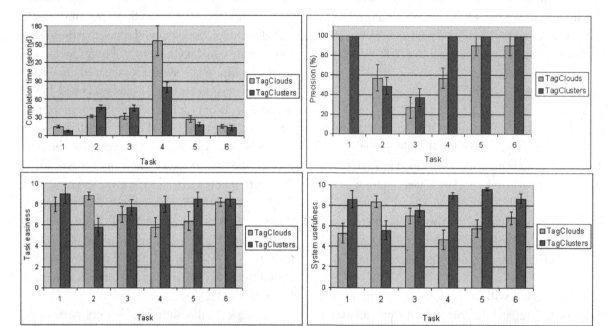

hierarchically organized and semantically similar groups are placed near to each other, it is easy to find the structure. With TagClouds, the semantically similar tags might be placed scattered all over the graph, and the participants had to scan all the tags to form a mental structure, which cost much more time and led to lower precision. To derive the complex structure for genre-related tags in task 4, the participants spent much more time with TagClouds but received lower precision in their answers. Since the semantically similar tags are hierarchically grouped and the overlapping part is visually highlighted, it is easier to determine the relation between tags. Thus Tag-Clusters worked better with task 5 and 6 which require understanding of semantic relation among tags. TagClusters also performed significantly higher in task 4-6 regarding the system usefulness (t(11)=4.872, p<0.01; t(11)=4.451, p<0.05; t(11)=2.526, p<0.05). Although TagClusters received higher scores in all aspects, it was not

proved to be significantly better in all aspects, thus hypothesis (H4) cannot be verified.

After completing all tasks, the participants filled out a post-questionnaire concerning the overall impression of both systems in the aspects of enjoyment, understandability, helpfulness and aesthetics (see Figure 5). TagClusters was scored overall scientifically higher (t(11)=4.358, p<0.01), and specifically significantly higher in the aspects of enjoyment (t(11)=2.905, p<0.05), understandability (t(11)=3.446, p<0.01) and helpfulness (t(11)=8.060, p<0.01).

DISCUSSION

Visualization Issue

The alphabetical arrangement in TagClouds is useful to ease the locating of specific tag. However, users who are unfamiliar with this visualization tend to ignore this characteristic. The font size

Figure 5. Overall impression of both systems

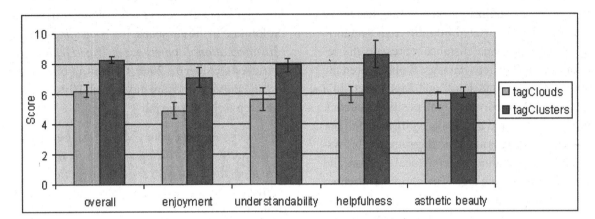

of tags is determined by their usage frequency, and more popular tags are more noticeable in the visualization. However, tags with smaller size are likely to visually fade out. The position of tags is also an influential factor to draw the user's visual attention. Some users claimed that the top half part seemed to be more visually prominent than other parts and the bottom half part was often ignored. Moreover, to make a better usage of the limited space in TagClouds, some long tags are truncated and placed into successive lines, which also led a misunderstanding. For example, *alternative rock* in the first line of Figure 1 was separated into 2 lines, and some participants thought they were two individual tags, which conflicts the alphabetization principle.

Instead of ordering tags alphabetically, Tag-Clusters groups tags based on their semantic relatedness, which helps to discover less popular tags. For example, there are many rock-related tags, which are hard to distinguish in Figure 1. But they are easier to be noticed in TagClusters, as they are group in the most prominent *rock* group.

Semantic Understanding

Without any assistance about semantic relations between tags, some participants misinterpreted a close position or similar font size in TagClouds as semantic similarity. To propose a semantic understanding of certain tags, sometimes the user has to scan linearly and might have difficulties in locating multiple tags which scattered all over the graph. Some participants even used the mouse to point at one tag or stared at the current focus tag on the screen while writing down the answers. Another problem is that, the users with less musical knowledge, especially with genres, may have problems to judge the relation between uncommon genre-related tags. This was especially the problem with our foreign participants. With the assistance in TagClusters, all of them could conduct the same tasks easier. The participants also came up with some aesthetical suggestions for TagClusters, such as stronger highlighting, color coding for different tag categories and the desire for a more compact graph.

CONCLUSION AND FUTURE WORK

TagClouds is a popular visualization for collaboratively generated tags. However, it has some distinct problems and poorly supports semantic understanding among tags. In this paper we investigate ways to support semantic understanding of collaboratively generated tags. We conducted a survey on practical tag usage in Last.fm, an online music community. Based on the results, we propose a visualization named TagClusters, in which tags are clustered into different semantic groups and the visual distance represents the semantic similarity between tags. We compared the performance of TagClouds and TagClusters in a user study. We received overall positive feedback on TagClusters and the results confirmed that our tool has advantages in supporting semantic browsing and understanding of hierarchical structure and relationships among tags. The semantic-oriented organization of tags can exclude redundancy effectively and may also facilitate tag recommendation and tag-based music retrieval, which will be explored in our future work. Besides, similarly to ThemeRiver (Westerman & Cribbin, 2000), the temporal dimension can be integrated to offer a time-based visualization which may indicate the hidden trends among general musical interests over time.

ACKNOWLEDGMENT

This research was funded by the Chinese Scholarship Council (CSC), the German state of Bavaria and the Spanish Ministerio de Educación y Ciencia (project CSD 2007-00067). We would like to thank the participants of our user study.

REFERENCES

Bateman, S., Gutwin, C., & Nacenta, M. (2008). Seeing things in the clouds: the effect of visual features on tag cloud selections. In *Proceedings of the 9th ACM conference on Hypertext and Hypermedia* (pp. 193-202). New York: ACM Press.

Begelman, G., Keller, P., & Smadja, F. (2006). Automated tag clustering: improving search and exploration in the tag space. In *Proceedings of the 15th international conference on World Wide Web*. Retrieved October 02, 2009, from http://citeseerx. ist.psu.edu/viewdoc/download?doi=10.1.1.120.5 736&rep=rep1&type=pdf

Bielenberg, K., & Zacher, M. (2005). *Groups in social software: Utilizing tagging to integrate individual contexts for social navigation*. Unpublished master's dissertation, University of Bremen, Germany.

Chen, Y.-X., Boring, S., & Butz, A. (in press). How Last.fm Illustrates the Musical World: User Behavior and Relevant User-Generated Content. In *Proceedings of the International Workshop on Visual Interfaces to the Social and Semantic Web*.

Cunningham, S. J., Bainbridge, D., & Falconer, A. (2006). 'More of an Art than a Science': Supporting the Creation of Playlists and Mixes. In *Proceedings of the 7th International Conference on Music Music Retrieval*. Retrieved October 02, 2009, from http://waikato.researchgateway.ac.nz/ bitstream/10289/77/1/content.pdf

Fruchterman, T. M. J., & Reinhold, E. M. (1991). Graph Drawing by Force-directed Placement. *Software, Practice & Experience, 21*(11), 1129–1164. doi:10.1002/spe.4380211102

Gansner, E. R., & North, S. C. (1998). Improved forced-directed layout. In *Proceedings of the 6th Symposium on Graph Drawing* (pp. 364-374). New York: Springer.

Golder, S. A., & Huberman, B. A. (2006). Usage Patterns of Collaborative Tagging Systems. *Journal of Information Science, 32*(2), 198–208. doi:10.1177/0165551506062337

Halpin, H., Robu, V., & Shepherd, H. (2007). The complex dynamics of collaborative tagging. In *Proceedings of the 16th International Conference on World Wide Web* (pp. 211-220). New York: ACM Press.

Halvey, M. J., & Keane, M. T. (2007). An assessment of tag presentation techniques. In *Proceedings of the 16th International Conference on World Wide Web* (pp. 1313-1314). New York: ACM Press.

Hassan, M. Y., & Herrero, S. V. (2006). Improving tag-clouds as visual Music Retrieval interfaces. In *Proceedings of the International Conference on Multidisciplinary Information Sciences & Technologies.*

Havre, S., Hetzler, B., & Nowell, L. (2000). ThemeRiver: Visualizing Theme Changes over Time. In *Proceedings of IEEE Symposium on Information Visualization* (pp. 115-123). Washington, DC: IEEE Computer Society.

Hearst, M. A. (2008). *What's up with Tag Clouds?* Retrieved October 02, 2009, from http://www.perceptualedge.com/articles/guests/whats_up_with_tag_clouds.pdf

Hearst, M. A., & Rosner, D. (2008). Tag Clouds: Data Analysis Tool or Social Signaller? In *Proceedings of the 41th International Conference on System Sciences* (pp. 1-10). Washington, DC: IEEE Computer Society.

Kaser, O., & Lemire, D. (2007). Tag-cloud drawing: algorithms for cloud visualization. In *Proceedings of the International Conference on World Wide Web.* New York: ACM Press.

Kerr, B. (2008). *TagOrbitals: tag index visualization.* Retrieved October 2, 2009, from http://domino.research.ibm.com/library/cyberdig.nsf/1e4115aea78b6e7c85256b360066f0d4/8e1905dc8b000673852571d800558654?OpenDocument

Kuo, B. Y. L., Hentrich, T., Good, B. M., & Wilkinson, M. D. (2007). Tag clouds for summarizing web search results. In *Proceedings of the 16th International Conference on World Wide Web* (pp. 1203-1204). New York: ACM Press.

Li, R., Bao, S., Yu, Y., Fei, B., & Su, Z. (2007). Towards effective browsing of large scale social annotations. In *Proceedings of the 16th International Conference on World Wide Web* (pp. 943-952). New York: ACM Press.

Lohmann, S., Ziegler, J., & Tetzlaff, L. (2009). Comparison of Tag Cloud Layouts: Task-Related Performance and Visual Exploration. In *Proceedings of the 12th International Conference on Human-Computer Interaction* (pp. 392-404). New York: Springer.

Mathes, A. (2008). *Folksonomies - cooperative classification and communication through shared metadata.* Retrieved October 2, 2009, from http://www.adammathes.com/academic/computer-mediated-communication/folksonomies.html

Nielsen, M. (2007). *Functionality in a second generation tag cloud.* Unpublished master's thesis, Gjøvik University College, Norway.

Porter, M. F. (2006). An algorithm for suffix stripping. *Program: electronic library and information systems, 14*(3), 211-218.

Provost, J. (2008). *Improved document summarization and tag clouds via singular value decomposition.* Unpublished master's thesis, Queen's University, Canada.

Rivadeneira, A. W., Gruen, D. M., Muller, M. J., & Millen, D. R. (2007). Getting our head in the clouds: toward evaluation studies of tagclouds. In *Proceedings of the SIGCHI Conference on Human Factors in Computing Systems* (pp. 995-998). New York: ACM.

Sammon, J. W. (1969). A non-linear mapping for data structure analysis. *IEEE Transactions on Computers*, *18*(5), 401–409. doi:10.1109/T-C.1969.222678

Santamaría, R., & Therón, R. (2008). Overlapping Clustered Graphs: Co-authorship Networks visualization. In *Proceedings of the 9th international Symposium on Smart Graphics* (pp.190-199). New York: Springer.

Seifert, C., Kump, B., & Kienreich, W. (2008). On the beauty and usability of tag clouds. In *Proceedings of the 12th International Conference on Information Visualization* (pp.17-25). Washington, DC: IEEE Computer Society.

Shaw, B. (2008). *Utilizing folksonomy: Similarity metadata from the del.icio.us system*. Retrieved October 2, 2009, from http://www.metablake.com/webfolk/web-project.pdf

Viégas, F. B., & Wattenberg, M. (2008). Tag Clouds and the Case for Vernacular Visualization. *Interaction*, *15*(4), 49–52. doi:10.1145/1374489.1374501

Ware, C. (2004). *Information Visualization: Perception for Design* (2nd ed.).

Wu, X., Zhang, L., & Yu, Y. Exploring social annotations for the semantic web. In *Proceedings of the International Conference on World Wide Web* (pp. 417-426). New York: ACM.

This work was previously published in International Journal of Creative Interfaces and Computer Graphics, Volume 1, Issue 2, edited by Ben Falchuk, pp. 15-28, copyright 2010 by IGI Publishing (an imprint of IGI Global).

Chapter 8
Magnet Mail:
A Visualization System for Emails

Paulo Castro
CITI-DI, FCT, Universidade Nova de Lisboa, Portugal

Adriano Lopes
CITI-DI, FCT, Universidade Nova de Lisboa, Portugal

ABSTRACT

Magnet Mail (MM) is a visualization system for emails based on a zoomable interface and on manipulation of objects. Users are able to search, analyze and understand relations among email messages as long as they provide searching keywords to do so, as well as interact with graphical objects in the display in a pro-active manner. The underlying concept is a magnet metaphor that relates user interaction, searching keywords and relations among emails. In this paper, the authors present a prototype that interacts with a mass-market email system and most of its graphical implementation relies on the Piccolo toolkit.

INTRODUCTION

Email is now part of our lives as a communication tool, whether if used in the working place or in the context of personal relationships. It is an efficient, fast and inexpensive mechanism to communicate. The downside of such remarkable success is that it leads to a large amount of data in the email boxes, some of which might be useless from a user's point of view. Hence, management problems arise when users need to search and to understand the similarity of topics and patterns among email messages.

Despite the lack of focus on visualization issues related to email applications, recent examples have shown some effort on adding user-friendly features, namely those related to sorting, filtering and searching messages. Even though, there is a long way to go until we provide users the so much needed help to manage messages conveniently.

Most of the current applications are failing on usability because they denote the use of hierarchical folders and also they do return results in a textual or list-based format. Some of them do not

DOI: 10.4018/978-1-4666-0285-4.ch008

even provide proper hints about email similarities or patterns, which can be dramatic when a particular inbox has got a huge collection of messages as it happens in these days. Rather than having some sort of add-ons, users would like to see real changes in the way email usability is delivered. They want to easily navigate across large email collections and to infer patterns. As a matter of a fact, proper usability can only be achieved if object manipulation is also considered.

A visualization system dealing with a large collection of documents, as it is the case of an email inbox, incorporates various techniques. The most important are the following ones: Firstly, automated methods for indexing documents and for decomposing them through statistics. There will be statistical data representing the documents as much accurately as possible. Secondly, techniques to map results into a sort of interactive display so users can visualize and interact with, redefining queries and so on. Moreover, an interesting feature is to give users a proficient overview of documents so they can have a quick understanding prior to any reading.

In this paper we propose Magnet Mail (MM), a document visualization system related to the email paradigm with emphasis on direct manipulation of graphical objects. The remaining of the paper is organized as follows: First, we highlight some related work, which is followed by a detailed description of MM. Then we present preliminary tests and results and finally we draw some conclusions and point out possible paths for further development.

RELATED WORK

A large majority of email client solutions seeking better user interaction rely not only on header information but message content. We envisage three major approaches as far as information visualization is concerned:

- Time-based visualization.
- Thread-based visualization.
- Social-based visualization.

First and foremost, these approaches can work together and can all be part of a particular email client application. For example, time-based visualization can easily be found alongside thread-based visualization so it is a matter of how much each one contributes to the final package.

Time-based visualization highlights the importance of timestamp in emails. Emails can be displayed chronologically so one can figure out how content have changed over time.

The Themail application shows this approach. It relies on the content of messages to display interactions over time. Its interface shows a series of columns of keywords arranged along a timeline. Keywords are shown in different colors and sizes depending on their frequency and distinct conversations over time (Viégas, Scott, & Donath, 2006). Mailview is another tool that display emails chronologically. It includes focus+context views, dynamic filters and coordinated views (Frau, Roberts, & Boukhelifa, 2005). Also, FaMailiar is a tool to visualize email data over time, focusing on discovering communication rhythms and patterns. Some features include daily email averages, daily quality of emails, frequency of email exchanges, comparative frequency of email exchanges (Mandic & Kerne, 2004).

Thread-based visualization focus on presenting relations among emails according to threads of replies. These systems highlight the progress of a particular set of email replies, seen by the user as a chain of related emails. Unlike the concept of threads in databases, email threads are not always complete. Displaying trees with the threads usually does its visualization.

The Thread Arcs tool is one example of thread-based visualization, where each message is a node and they are linked to each other according to the conversational thread they represent (Kerr, 2003). Another representative example is the EzMail tool (Samiei, Dill, & Kirkpatrick, 2004). It is a multi-view interface for email messages running in conjunction with an email client application, where messages are seen as components of threads and it also provides historical information.

Social-based visualization is supported by the fact that email messages are inherently examples of social behavior. In the end, there will be patterns in such social networks that can be quantified using graph theory and then be visualized accordingly.

The Enronic application is an interesting visualization and clustering tool representing this social-based approach. It unifies information visualization techniques with various algorithms for processing an e-mail corpus, including message categorization, social network inference and community analysis (Heer, 2005). This system uses the Prefuse toolkit (Heer, Card, & Landay, 2005).

Despite all these contributions, we think there is space for improvement. In particular when it comes to user interaction. For example, the tools using thread-based visualization may have difficulties to explaining its underlying concept, as most of email users are not familiarized with the idea of threads. We are in favor of a common day metaphor, easily understandable, as the underlying concept to display and to manage email messages. Moreover, tools not only should provide users meaningful information about the data under analysis but to allow direct user manipulation of graphical objects representing the data. In the end, users should be pro-active when dealing with their email archives but on the basis of helpful information.

Having set this research scenario, we were inspired by Dust and Magnet (Yi, 2005) (which is also based on the WebVIBE system (Mouse & Lewis, 1997)) to develop a new concept but totally focus on the email domain. The outcome is the Magnet Mail system we propose now.

The Dust and Magnet application uses the zoomable user interface toolkit called Piccolo (Bederson, Grosjean & Meyer, 2004) and applies a magnet metaphor to display multivariate information. The data is represented as particles of iron dust and data variables are represented as magnets. It also provides interactive techniques to display and to manipulate data in the display area.

It is worth mentioning an application in the email domain that uses Piccolo, proposed by Diep and Jacob. This application shows emails as rectangular nodes and users are allowed to drag them or pan the entire viewing area (Diep, 2004). Yet, users have no special hints about relations among emails.

MAGNET MAIL

As already mentioned, MM is a document visualization system targeting email archives. With this new approach we aim to reduce the user effort for searching and browsing email messages.

MM provides a comprehensible metaphor to interact with data. It also enables a global overview of an email collection instead of showing just a few blocks of results as many systems do. This implies the use of interactive and graphical capabilities, in particular direct manipulation of objects, although the typical textual list-based format is still preserved. The relations among emails are based on the concept of email importance in relation to user-defined searching keywords. For that purpose, MM needs to process email messages in order to generate term-frequency information about keywords.

Nonetheless, MM still provides the basic email functionalities found in common email systems, e.g. to preview an email message and to reply.

System Architecture

Figures 1 and 2 capture the underlying architecture of MM. The major software modules are: XML database, Data-Collector Management, Search & Results Management, Configuration Management and Display Management.

Figure 1. MM system architecture

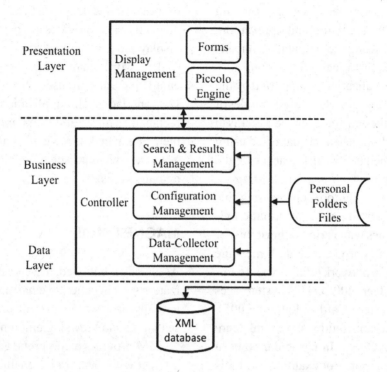

Figure 2. Detailed MM system architecture

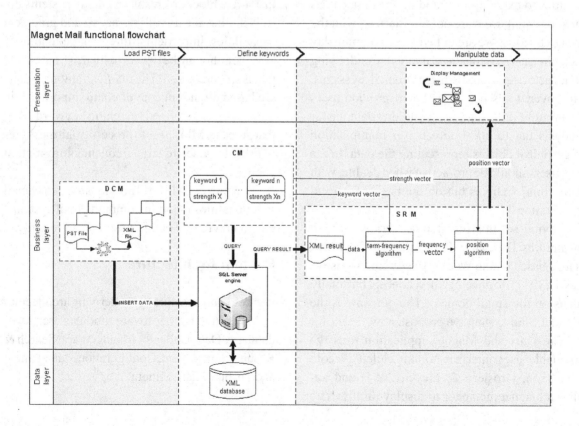

The XML database stores the users' email information originated from their personal folders. MM interacts with a mass-market email system, the Microsoft Outlook, a decision related to the fact that we pursue a broader usage. Hence, the target file archives are Microsoft Personal Storage files (PST). Quite understandably, most of the MM implementation relies on the Microsoft .NET framework.

The main task of the Data-Collector Management is to feed the SQL server engine with XML data representing the content of the PST files. As for the Configuration Management, it is responsible for establishing the framework for further queries to the database, based on user-defined keywords information.

The Search & Results Management deals with setting appropriate queries to the database and to process the results returned by the search engine. This processing includes computations required by the Display Management, the module where user activity takes place. Its implementation is also supported by the Piccolo toolkit so data is displayed and manipulated as graphical objects.

Figure 3 shows a screenshot capturing a high-level view of MM. The interface is divided into four main areas: on top, the (a) *Graphical interaction area*, where users visualize and manipulate graphical information and at the same time can interact with the system via zooming, panning and selecting features; on bottom-left, the (b) *Settings and results area*, for example to define a list of searching keywords and associated properties; fol-

Figure 3. An overall view of the MM, with four distinct areas: mails and keywords in the graphical interaction area; area of setting and results, including a tabular view of results; a detailed view of a particular email; and an overall view from where the display in the interaction area can be panned or zoomed.

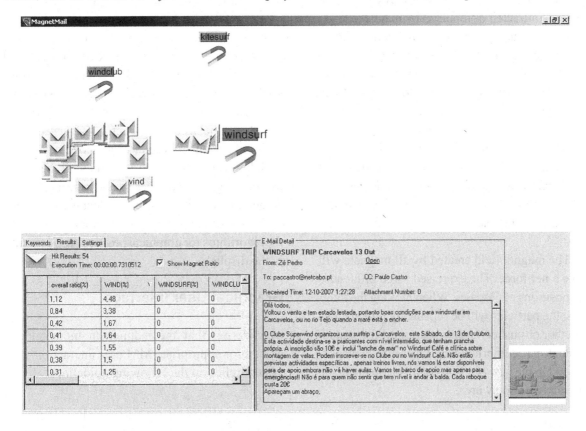

lowed by the (c) *Detail area*, containing detailed information about selected items of interest; and finally on bottom-right, the (d) *Overall view area* to give spatial context to data visualization. For the sake of screen space optimization, the *Settings and results area* is divided into three tabs: one tab for searching keywords, another one for MM settings and the last one for list-based viewing of information.

Emails and Keywords

The user interaction relies mostly on the relationship among emails and user-defined keywords. MM describes this relationship as a sort of magnetism and electromagnetism phenomena, that is, it borrows the idea that materials exert attractive and repulsive forces over other materials. On that basis, we have established the following:

a. Keywords play the role of magnets and email messages the role of particles, which are attracted or repulsed by magnets.
b. Each magnet creates a magnetic field to exercise a force over the particles.
c. The force exert by a magnet varies from strong to weak according to a user-defined parameter, which value can also be negative (attraction vs. repulsion).
d. Any magnet influences the position of every particle that lies on its magnetic field, but there is no influence on other magnets.
e. A particle has no influence at all on magnets or on other particles.

The magnet field created by all magnets will have a net force. The exercised force influences the positions of particles. When moving the magnets, the particles will be repeatedly pulled close together or pushed further apart until the system comes to an equilibrium state. Once that is reached, we obtain the new positions of all elements in the interactive display area.

The behavior of such system can be modeled through a graph, where the forces exerted by magnets are the edges and the particles are the nodes. Moreover, Force-Based algorithms can govern the equilibrium and/or position of the various elements so applying forces over edges and nodes can simulate graph dynamics.

In conclusion, the position of graph nodes can be computed if we rely both on mechanical and magnetic laws and considering edges as springs and nodes as electrically charged particles. Assuming that each node is located in a particular position, with velocity and mass, we then can compute the net force as the sum of total force on every node. This computation is done according to both Coulomb repulsion and Hooke attraction forces. Once the force is computed, we then obtain the velocity and the position of each node and the total kinetic energy using associated functions. This process is repeated until the total kinetic energy is less than a predefined value yielding to the equilibrium state of the graph.

Prior to the graphical simulation of the relationship among emails and keywords, it is required to query such information from the XML database. To do so, pairs of keyword and its importance value set by the user are stored in a keyword-vector, and then a statistical algorithm of term frequency calculates the frequency-vector. Basically, this algorithm obtains a vector of matched results of each keyword string within each email message by counting the search terms and returns the average of them within the email documents. Then both keyword and frequency vectors are used in the algorithms for graphical positioning of emails in the display.

Graphical User Interface

Considering that the magnetism metaphor is crucial for appropriate MM user interaction, the system relies on the following guidelines:

- To provide efficient interactivity so users can set and/or redefine queries through object manipulation and interaction.
- Use of meaningful icons and color, as well as adequate features provided by the underlying graphical framework, that is, the Piccolo toolkit. Recall that the Piccolo engine provides an intuitive user interaction, with visual effects such as zooming, navigation, animation and iconic data representations.
- Use of techniques to overcome screen limitation, such as zooming and panning techniques.
- To display both an overview and details of the email collection.
- To provide a multi-view display format, that is, to complement graphical information with common list-based format.

Figure 3 gives a glimpse of the MM graphical user interface. In the following we will discuss four major user interface characteristics: Magnetism metaphor, viewing, highlighting and data processing.

- *Magnetism metaphor*. Users are able to drag keywords in the visualization area. Each keyword will attract or repulse emails according to its attribute value. The higher the matched attribute is, the fastest the email is attracted to the corresponding keyword. The magnitude of attraction between both is computed via an appropriate algorithm. On the other hand, users can reformulate keyword strings and their attribute values in order to get more detailed and filtered results. That is why users can also set these values as negative, meaning repulsive forces.
- *Viewing*. The viewing facilities include (a) a multi-view approach mixing the typical list-based viewing information with the graphical-style display; (b) zooming-out to

get a better overview of the display zone and zooming-in to get a closer and detailed view; (c) panning; (d) overall view of email items on display and consequently providing context; (e) detailed view of emails contents.

In the case of graphical visualization, the displayed results depend almost on direct object manipulation of keywords. For list-based or tabular visualization, retrieved results are displayed as usual, that is, as a list-based view. Here, the results can be ordered according to the search frequency of emails in relation to each keyword.

The idea of providing both types of visualization does not necessarily imply that one overshadows the other. On the contrary, the goal is to be complementary. The graphical approach provides a user-friendly mechanism to analyze the information but the tabular approach provides more detailed information and can be easily ordered.

- *Highlighting*. The main visual attribute is the relative location in the display area among emails and keywords. Nonetheless, size and color are used to further distinguish the importance of the emails in relation to keywords. The underlying idea is to provide users extra help to track and to trace emails in the display area.

Hence, every keyword is associated to a color scale. The scale is mainly used to set the color of email objects. At any point in time, the color of each email object is defined on the basis of the relationship email-keyword and the color scale of the keyword under visual focus. For a particular keyword, the stronger the color the more related the email is to that keyword. As far as magnet color is concerned, it is used the "maximum" color of its scale. By default, the setting of color scale is an automatic process, but the user is entitled to change it if he/she wants to.

On the other hand, the color scale to be used may change if the user requires in the tabular view the sorting of frequencies in respect to a particular keyword. The new color scale is the one of the selected keyword, that is, the keyword currently under focus. But when there is no one selected, the color scale is considered to be neutral so color feature is somehow useless.

As far as size of graphical objects is concerned, we note that the size of each keyword object is proportional to its importance. Indeed, the bigger the object, the stronger the keyword, and consequently more easily it will attract or repulse email objects. Again, negative importance means the keyword will repel related emails. In respect to email object size, it only gets bigger when the user hovers the mouse over it so it is a short-lived visual effect.

- *Data processing*. MM provides a ranking system, based on the term frequency, for the most common searching keywords in emails. Thus, it is possible to compare the similarity of themes or topics among emails.

Finally, it is also important to point out that users can benefit from useful features available in Microsoft Outlook by linking a selected email with the Microsoft Outlook email message.

User Interaction Scenario

Let us now illustrate a typical use of MM. Recalling Figure 3, emails and keywords are placed in the interaction area, and users can interact with: (a) keywords, (b) a tabular view of results, (c) an area for a detailed view of a particular email, and (d) an overall viewing area from where they can pan or zoom the display where keywords and emails are drawn.

After defining or updating keywords, the keywords are placed in the interaction area, alongside the set of emails that match the query result (see

Figure 4). These keywords will attract or repel the returning results, based on the importance they have.

Initially, the email collection that is somehow related to the keywords that have been set is placed at one location, just as a pile of documents. Immediately after, it is the direct user manipulation of the keywords/magnets that changes the location of each email/particle. Users can grab and drag keywords as they want so they play an active role in the process of searching and understanding their own emails. For instance, with a new positioning of the email collection, a user can easily figure out that the closer an email is to a keyword, the greater the probability is that this particular keyword is the most related to the email (among all returning results) even if it suffers attraction and/or repulsion from other keywords.

Notice however that, if there are just few user actions and a couple of emails have exactly the same frequency related to a particular magnet, then those emails may stay at same location. To minimize such problem, when the user rolls the cursor over an email envelop, it will have bigger shape and it is shown snipped information. Hence, the email envelope is highlighted (see Figure 5).

As a final synopsis, Figure 6 shows four screenshots of MM depicting some steps of interaction with MM.

TESTS AND RESULTS

Evaluating a visualization system is a difficult task. We have not extensively evaluated MM yet but we have carried out some preliminary tests with users. At this point in time we are particularly keen on knowing how usable the prototype can be and to figure out its potentiality so we can improve it.

The case study consisted of experimentation, where a group of 30 users aged from 21 to 30 years old have followed a case scenario task list. Additionally, users could have watched a MM video demonstration if they choose to do so. Once

Figure 4. The user sets each keyword, as well as associated importance and color scale

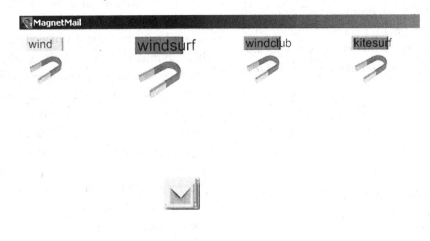

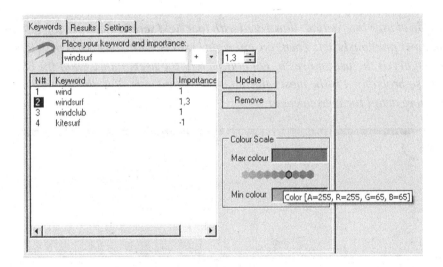

they performed their tasks, they were invited to fill in a simple questionnaire and to rate questions from 1 (min) to 5 (max).

This exercise allowed us to grasp major MM features, potentialities and pitfalls. Just to give a glimpse, we present the average marks we have obtained to the following questions:

- *How easy you found to use this interface?* 3.91
- *How satisfied you were with the search results set?* 3.73
- *How ambiguous you thought the search results set was?* 3.36
- *How do you rate the time spent to perform a search?* 3.27
- *How do you rate the potentialities of Magnet Mail?* 3.27
- *How do you rate the Magnet Mail originality?* 4.09

In general, users have classified MM as a useful and easy-to-use tool, and highlighted its originality. For example, some users have mentioned that

Figure 5. Example of a keyword (windsurf) as a magnet attracting or repulsing related email documents. When the user rolls the cursor over an email, its size increases and snippet information is shown. It is a mechanism to highlight that particular email.

direct manipulation and the possibility of setting positive and negative importance to various keywords broadens the scope of analysis, particularly if comparing with commercial email systems such as Microsoft Outlook and Apple Mail.

The users also felt that the time to return query results needs to be reduced. This is more problematic as the email collection gets bigger. Actually, from tests we carried out with query result sets of 55, 110, 165 and 220 email messages, the time costs to return results were respectively 1.77, 3.11, 4.98 and 6.07 seconds. These values were gathered using a PC Intel Pentium Centrino M 1.5 GHz, with 512 Mb RAM. This can be im-

Figure 6. Example of user interaction, illustrated with four MM screenshots. On top left, the user drags the keyword/magnet previously set. Then, on top right, emails with some kind of relationship are attracted to the magnet as the user moves it. On bottom left, the user realizes that the closer e-mail has a better ranking so probably it is the most relevant e-mail of interest. Finally, on bottom right, the user can analyze in more detail the chosen email.

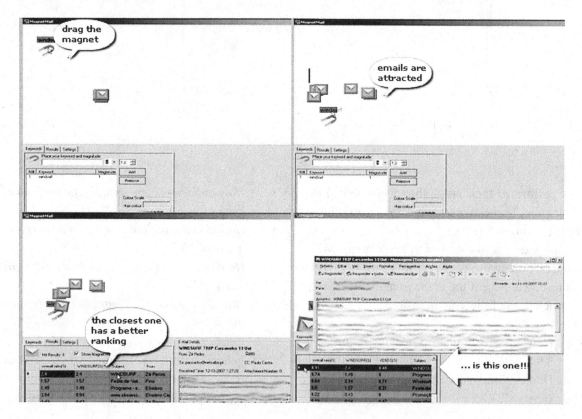

proved, at least if considering the use of parallel programming with GPUs.

On the other hand, users have pointed out that color mapping is not as effective as probably one would expect. They rather prefer the location attribute of graphical objects so coloring email objects is not helpful.

Also, they pointed out that tabular view should include more complex grouping, filtering and sorting features as one can experience with current spreadsheets. Actually, the use of brushing techniques on both views would help when the display area gets cluttered with many email objects.

CONCLUSION

We have presented a prototype to visualize email archives with emphasis on user-friendly graphical interaction based on direct manipulation of objects. It uses a common magnet metaphor, which translates relations among searching keywords and related email messages. Not only users can overview and understand an email collection with no reading effort but also to obtain details of email messages they query about. This is not the usual scenario found in many commercial tools such as Microsoft Outlook and Apple Mail. These tools use mainly textual and list-based representations of email collections.

Hence, the focus on MM is to allow users to get new insight data and to play an active role in the information retrieval process. For example, users can rate the importance of searching keywords they specify so ultimately they are able to better managing and understanding their own email archives.

Based on preliminary user tests we have carried out, we found that users are responsive to accept MM as an easy-to-use and original tool to analyze email collections. Nevertheless, as it stands now, there are a few problems to be solved.

The scalability is a major one: if a huge volume of search results is placed in the interaction area, many icons would overlap, so it makes difficult to interact with. In that respect, it is worth to study the idea of grouping emails and using brushing/linking data visualization techniques. On the other hand, more work needs to be done with positioning algorithms in order to lower time cost, including the help of parallel programming with GPUs.

The use of color to extend email codification is another aspect requiring further analysis. Users were not very sympathetic to its use so prior to an extensive evaluation task in the future, MM should be improved on that matter, maybe to restrain its use if that would be the outcome. Actually, the location attribute to codify emails has proven to be sufficiently effective.

Finally, we are considering the extension of MM to the web-search paradigm.

REFERENCES

Bederson, B. B., Grosjean, J., & Meyer, J. (2004). Toolkit Design for Interactive Structured Graphics. *IEEE Transactions on Software Engineering*, *30*(8), 535–546. doi:10.1109/TSE.2004.44

Diep, E., & Jacob, R. J. K. (2004). Visualizing E-mail with a Semantically Zoomable Interface. In *Proceedings of the IEEE Symposium on Information Visualization* (pp. 215-216). Washington, DC: IEEE Computer Society.

Frau, S., Roberts, J. C., & Boukhelifa, N. (2005). Dynamic coordinated email visualization. In V.Skala (Ed.), *Proceedings of the 13th International Conference on Computer Graphics, Visualization and Computer Vision,* Plzen, Czech Republic (pp. 187-193).

Heer, J. (2005). *Exploring Enron: Visual Data Mining of Email*. Retrieved January 2009, from http://jheer.org/enron

Heer, J., Card, S. K., & Landay, J. A. (2005). Prefuse: A Toolkit for Interactive Information Visualization. In *Proceedings of the SIGCHI Conference on Human Factors in Computing Systems* (pp. 421-430). New York: ACM.

Mandic, M., & Kerne, A. (2004). faMailiar & Intimacy-Based Email Visualization. In *Proceedings of the IEEE Symposium on Information Visualization* (pp. 14-14). Washington, DC: IEEE Computer Society.

Mouse, E., & Lewis, M. (1997). Why Information Retrieval Visualizations Sometimes Fail. In *Proceedings of the IEEE International Conference on Systems, Man, and Cybernetics* (Vol. 2, pp. 1680-1685). Washington, DC: IEEE Computer Society. Kerr, B. (2003). Thread arcs: An email thread visualization. In *Proceedings of the IEEE Symposium on Information Visualization* (pp. 27-38). Washington, DC: IEEE Computer Society.

Rojansky, V. (1979). *Electromagnetism Fields and Waves*. Mineola, NY: Dover Publications.

Samiei, M., Dill, J., & Kirkpatrick, A. (2004). EzMail: using information visualization techniques to help manage email. In *Proceedings of the 8th International Conference on Information Visualisation* (pp. 477-482). Washington, DC: IEEE Computer Society.

Viégas, F. B., Scott, G., & Donath, J. (2006). Visualizing email content: portraying relationships from conversational histories. In *Proceedings of the SIGCHI conference on Human Factors in Computing Systems* (pp. 979-988). New York: ACM.

Yi, J. S., Melton, R., Stasko, J., & Jacko, J. (2005). Dust & Magnet: multivariate information visualization using a magnet metaphor. *Information Visualization, 4*(4), 239–256.

This work was previously published in International Journal of Creative Interfaces and Computer Graphics, Volume 1, Issue 2, edited by Ben Falchuk, pp. 29-39, copyright 2010 by IGI Publishing (an imprint of IGI Global).

Chapter 9
An Assistant Interface to Design and Produce a Pop-Up Card

Sosuke Okamura
University of Tokyo, Japan

Takeo Igarashi
University of Tokyo, Japan

ABSTRACT

This article describes an assistant interface to design and produce pop-up cards. A pop-up card is a piece of folded paper from which a three-dimensional structure pops up when opened. The authors propose an interface to assist the user in the design and production of a pop-up card. During the design process, the system examines whether the parts protrude from the card or whether the parts collide with one another when the card is closed. The user can concentrate on the design activity because the error occurrence and the error resolution are continuously fed to the user in real time. The authors demonstrate the features of their system by creating two pop-up card examples and perform an informal preliminary user study, showing that automatic protrusion and collision detection are effective in the design process.

INTRODUCTION

A pop-up card is a piece of folded paper from which three-dimensional (3D) paper structures pop up when it is opened. The card can be folded flat again afterward. Pop-up cards, also called Origamic Architectures, find their origin in Japan (Chatani, 1985). People enjoy this interesting paper craft through the realization of pop-up books

DOI: 10.4018/978-1-4666-0285-4.ch009

(e.g. Baum, 2000; Sabuda & Carroll, 2003; Sabuda & Reinhart, 2005) and greeting cards. Figure 1 shows an example of pop-up books.

Constructing a pop-up card is relatively easier than designing one; anyone can simply cut out and fold the pieces and glue them together if a template, which is printed parts, is available. However, it is unfortunately much more difficult for nonprofessionals to design a pop-up card and make its templates from scratch. There are two reasons to this difficulty. The first difficulty is

Figure 1. "Alice's Adventures in Wonderland", a typical pop-up book (Sabuda & Carroll, 2003)

correctly understanding and designing the pop-up mechanisms. The book (Carter & Diaz, 1999) helps to understand mechanisms, but does not tell how to combine them to design a desired look. The second difficulty is determining the positions of pop-up parts so that they do not collide with each other. Professionals usually solve these problems through repetitive trial and error by drawing on their experience during design: cutting component parts out of paper, pasting them on the card, and checking whether they collide. If an error is found, they re-think the design and start over from the beginning. This process requires a lot of time, energy, and paper. Design and simulation in a computer help both nonprofessionals and professionals to design a pop-up card, eliminate the boring repetition, and save time.

Glassner (1998, 2002) proposed methods for designing a pop-up card on a computer. He introduced several simple pop-up mechanisms and

described how to use these mechanisms, how to simulate the position of vertices as an intersecting point of three spheres, how to check whether the structure sticks out beyond the cover or if a collision occurs during opening, and how to generate templates. His work is quite useful in designing simple pop-up cards.

In this article, we build on Glassner's pioneering work and introduce several innovative aspects. We add two new mechanisms based on the V-fold: the box and the cube. We present a detailed description of the interface for design, which Glassner did not describe in any detail. In addition, our system provides real-time error detection feedback during editing operations by examining whether parts protrude from the card when closed or whether they collide with one another during opening and closing. Finally, we report on an informal preliminary user study of our system involving four inexperienced users.

RELATED WORK

Glassner (1998, 2002) described a stable analytical solution for important vertices in the three main pop-up mechanisms (single-slit, asymmetric single-slit, and V-fold mechanisms) when a pop-up card opens and closes in interactive pop-up card design. In addition, he introduced two simple gimmicks (pull and whirligig gimmicks), but not the underlying calculations. He also implemented his methods in a small program and designed his original pop-up cards. However, he did not describe its interactive behavior in detail, nor did he report any user experience.

Mitani and Suzuki (2003) proposed a method for creating a 180° flat fold Origamic Architecture with lattice-type cross sections. Their system creates pop-up pieces from a 3D model. It used a mechanism similar to the angle fold open box mechanism described in next section. However, a 3D model is not always available. Furthermore, the pieces are set only on the center fold line, cannot be combined with other pieces and cannot represent movement.

Hendrix (2004, 2007) proposed a pop-up workshop system that enables the user to design pop-up cards by making two-dimensional (2D) cuts. The 3D result can be opened and closed on the Viewer window in her system. Hendrix and Eisenberg (2006) also showed that children could design pop-up cards using their system. However, the user edits 3D pop-up cards in a 2D interface. It is not intuitive and demands a highly skilled user to imagine the 2D images from the resulting 3D shape.

Lee, Tor, and Soo (1996) described calculations and geometric constraints for modeling and simulating multiple V-fold pieces. However, their system is limited to V-fold mechanisms and it is difficult to design a pop-up card only using V-fold mechanisms. In addition, it is not designed as an interactive system.

Aforementioned researches have aimed at the design of 180° pop-up cards. On the other hand, several interactive interfaces have been proposed for 90° pop-up cards. Mitani, Suzuki, and Uno (2003) proposed a method to design Origamic Architecture models with a computer using a voxel model representation. Using this method, the system can store 90° pop-up card models and display them using computer graphics. Their achievement is also commercialized (Tama Software Ltd., 2005). User operations are the interactive addition and deletion of voxels. They reported their system was used for graphics science education (Mitani and Suzuki, 2004). Mitani and Suzuki (2004) also proposed a method for designing Origamic Architecture models with a computer using a model based on a set of planar polygons. That system computes and imposes constraints to guarantee that the model can be constructed with a single sheet of paper. Thus, it enables the user to make more complex 90° pop-up cards interactively from the beginning through to the pattern printing stage. However, those system and interface are not available for 180° pop-up cards. Almost all of the 90° pop-up cards are made from only cutting and folding with a single sheet of paper and their constraints are strong and simple. For this reason, it is easy to treat 90° pop-up cards in a computer and above system works well given the constraint. On the other hand, 180° pop-up cards are made from cutting, folding and gluing with multiple pieces and it is difficult to design as a voxel model or planer polygon model.

ASSISTED POP-UP CARD DESIGN

Figure 2 shows a screenshot of our prototype system. Our system allows the user to design pop-up cards using a mouse and a keyboard. The system consists of a single window in which the user designs and simulates pop-up cards. Figure 3 shows the system functions; simulate, set, edit, delete, and put textures on. The user decides positions of parts, adjusts their properties (e.g., length, angle, position and pattern), and generates templates.

Figure 2. Prototype system

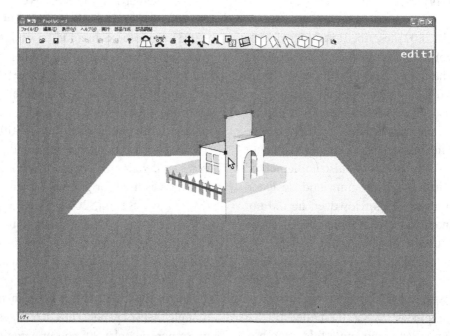

During the interactive editing, the system always examines whether parts protrude from the card or whether they collide with one another.

Five mechanisms are implemented in our system. They are the V-fold, the even-tent and the uneven-tent mechanisms which were introduced by Glassner (1998). Others are the angle fold open box and the angle fold cube mechanisms (Carter & Diaz, 1999) which are newly introduced in this article. They are based on the V-fold mechanism and add the V-fold to the tent backward. The former forms a box, which is an empty rectangular parallelepiped without a top and a bottom as

shown in Figure 4 (a). The latter is an angle fold open box with a lid as shown in Figure 4 (b). The lid is folded toward the inside of the box when a card is closed.

Constrained Editing

An unfolded card which has a center fold line is only displayed when the user executes our system. The user designs a pop-up card with the help of four functionalities: setting, editing, deleting, and mapping.

Figure 3. Prototype system functions

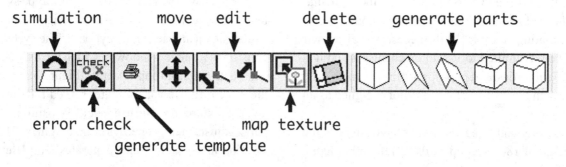

Figure 4. (a) Angle fold open box mechanism. (b) Angle fold cube mechanism

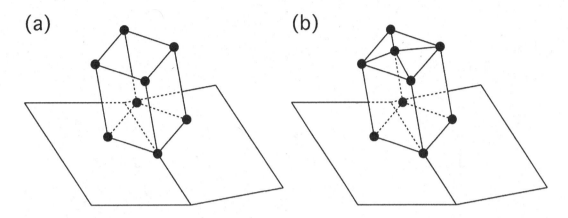

Set / Delete Parts: The user first selects a desired mechanism among V-fold, even-tent, uneven-tent, box, and cube, and moves the mouse cursor to a fold line. If the system permits to set a new part, a black point appears on a fold line. The system automatically generates a new part at that black point position if the user clicks the mouse button. Its parameter is set with the default length and angles that can be adjusted later (see Figure 5). The generated part makes several new fold lines where a new part can be set. The user can also delete an unnecessary or failed part by clicking the part. If other parts exist on the part when the part is deleted, they are also deleted because the pop-up card structure is broken.

Edit Shapes: The user can edit the shape of the parts by dragging their vertices as shown in Figure 6. When the user edits a part, the vertices of the selected part are highlighted and the user drags one of the vertices. There are two types of editing; editing a length and editing an angle. When editing a length, the user can change its value individually as shown in Figure 6 (d) and (e) or with maintaining the parallelogram shape by pressing the Shift key while dragging as shown in Figure 6 (c). When editing an angle, the user can change the angle between two planes or the inclination of the parts as shown in Figure 6 (f)-(i).

Map Textures: The user can put a texture on a part. Before mapping textures, the user has to

Figure 5. User interface for setting parts. (a) When the user clicks on a fold line, (b) the system generates a new part there

(a)   (b)

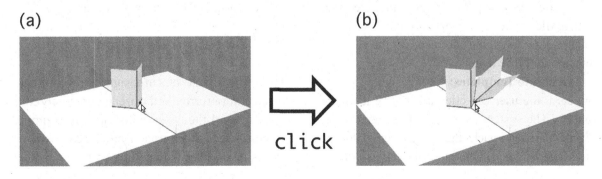

Figure 6. User interface to edit shapes. The user can (a)-(e) change lengths; (f), (g) change open angles; (h), (i) change gradient angles; and (j), (k) apply textures

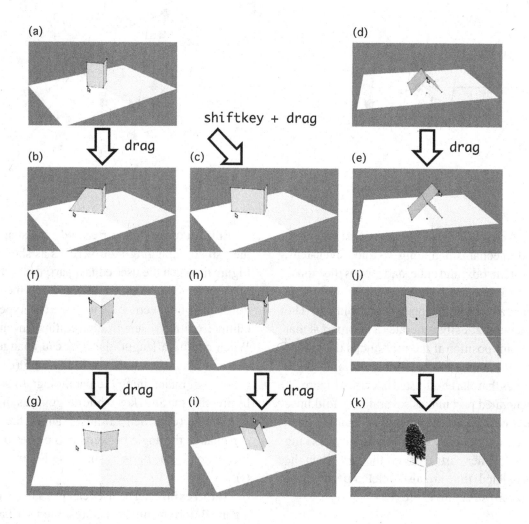

prepare them as square image file in advance (e.g. 256 pixel * 256 pixel). To put a texture on a part, the user clicks on a panel of a part and selects an image file as shown in Figure 6 (j) and (k). After mapping textures, the user can edit the part and change for other textures.

Generate Templates: After designing a pop-up card, the user can click a generate template button. The system automatically generates unfolded parts and packs them as 2D templates. In addition, it adds parts to glue tabs and guidelines to tell the user where to fold and glue them on. If the user finishes in this section, all the user has to do is print and construct the design.

Real Time Error Detection

The most difficult point in designing a pop-up card is detecting an error. As the user interactively edits a pop-up card, the system automatically examines whether the parts protrude from the card when it closes or whether they collide with one another during closing and opening. If the system detects such a protrusion or collision error, a message is displayed on the lower right of the window and the parts that caused the error are highlighted in yellow as shown in Figure 7 (c) and (d). This error detection process runs in real time. If the user resolves the error, the message and the highlights disappear immediately.

IMPLEMENTATION

We implemented our prototype system based on Glassner's work (1998, 2002) using Microsoft Visual C++ with the MFC platform. We also used OpenGL to render the scene and OpenCV to read images. Figure 3 shows the functions that were implemented in our system. A pop-up card is represented as a tree data structure. Pop-up card data consists of part data and fold line data. Each node of the tree corresponds to a part which contains fold lines relative to this part. Each node

Figure 7. User interface when the system detects errors. (a), (b) The user moves a part. (c), (d) The system displays a warning message and highlights the part if the system detects an error. (e) The part protrudes from the card if the card is closed. (f) The part collides with one another if the card is closed.

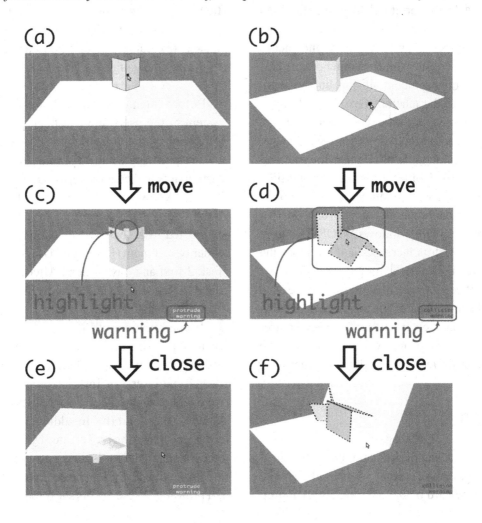

contains its relative position on the parent part and various parameters; lengths, angles and textures. The system first computes the card position, left half position of which is always fixed, based on its open angle and updates its vertices and center fold line information. The system next updates the 3D coordinates of the parts on the center fold line of the card. If this calculation is finished, information of the fold lines made by parts on the center fold line are updated. Next, the system calculates the coordinates of parts on their fold line. The system repeats this procedure recursively to determine the 3D coordinates of all parts.

We use a collision detection method proposed by Glassner (2002), in which the system simulates the card's opening by discretely changing the angle from 0° to 180° with a predefined interval because the cost of orbit calculation is too high to be executed in real time. For each angle, the system calculates all parts' positions and checks whether these collide with each other or not. This method may miss a minor collision, but this is not an issue due to the inherent flexibility of paper. Table 1 shows average time required to check the protrusion errors and collision errors. We changed the number of parts and the angle interval and averaged the result of ten trials in each condition. This experiment was conducted using a typical notebook personal computer with 2.10MHz CPU, 2G byte memory, and windows XP OS. The more the number of parts increases and the more the angle of step narrows, the more calculation time increases. Pieces of work in pop-up books we have consist of about 10 parts; we therefore decided to check collision at every 10° by default. The user can change this angle interval freely because the environment and feeling are different for each user.

RESULTS

Figure 8 shows examples of pop-up cards designed using our system. The first was based on "The Wonderful Wizard of OZ" (Baum, 2000) pop-up

book shown in Figure 8 (a). We designed the piece shown in Figure 8 (b) on our system in approximately 2 hr. Determining the heights and position was easy due to the error detection mechanism. Figures 8 (d)-(f) show the templates generated by our system, which required approximately 2 hr for assembly in the final form shown in Figure 8 (c). Figure 6 (g) shows another example. This required approximately 2 hr for the design and 2.5 hr for assembly into the final form shown in Figure 6 (h).

We also conducted an informal preliminary user study. The user test was conducted using a typical notebook personal computer with a mouse and a keyboard. We assigned the user two tasks to assess the features of our system.

Task 1: to create a pop-up card of a building you imagine without using our system

Task 2: to create a pop-up card of a building you imagine using our system

Before attempting Task 2, we detailed our system to the users and had them practice with it for approximately 5 minutes. Four users (User 1 ~ 4) participated in this study. None of the participants had created pop-up cards before and had little knowledge of them. Two of them (User 1 and User 2) first completed Task 1. Then they completed Task 2 before explanation and practice. Other two of them (User 3 and User 4) completed Task 2 first and Task 1 next. After they had finished both tasks, we conducted a brief interview to collect their feedback.

The left column of Figure 9 shows the cards created in Task 1 and the right column of Figure 9 shows ones in Task 2. The cards produced by User 1 and User 3 in Task 1 look good, but they were failed designs because of collision shown in Figures 10 (a) and (b). In addition, a protrusion error occurred in the card created by User 3. On the other hand, all the cards produced by participants in Task 2 with our system closed correctly and did not protrude. These results show that it is difficult

Table 1. Average time required to check errors (msec)

The number of parts	The angle interval				
	1°	5°	10°	15°	20°
5 parts	177.9	35.1	18.0	12.6	9.2
10 parts	662.3	129.2	65.5	46.6	33.6
15 parts	1389.9	282.7	143.3	100.7	74.7

Figure 8. Pop-up cards designed using our system

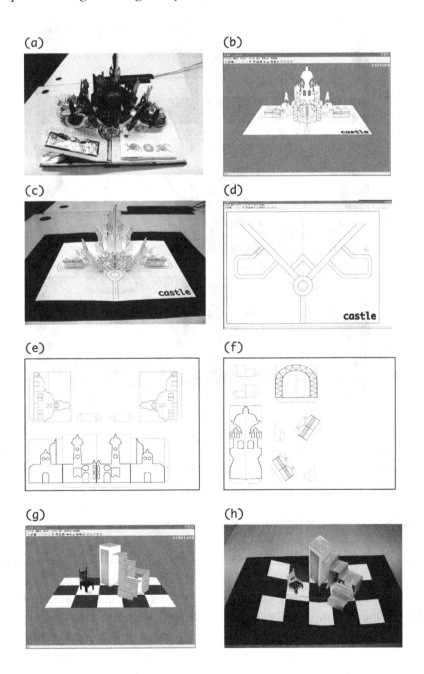

Figure 9. The result of the user study

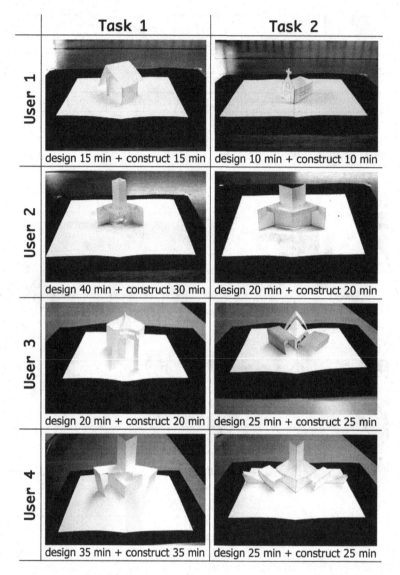

for nonprofessionals to design and construct valid pop-up cards by checking whether errors occur or not by themselves and our system is useful to make it easier.

Timing measurements show that three of four participants spent more time in Task 1 than in Task 2. This is because they need to think of how mechanisms work, how to manufacture the parts and then check that parts have no errors. On the other hand, in Task 2, the system frees the users from these time-consuming tasks by automati-

cally computing collision and protrusions and showing the results graphically. This enables the users to design pop-up cards easily and quickly.

The preliminary user study and the feedback from the users show the following advantages of our system. First, our system makes the design of a pop up card easier than using paper, scissors, and glue. Second, the pop-up cards designed using our system close correctly without protrusion or collision error. This system also saves time in the design process. In fact, the three of four us-

Figure 10. Error examples

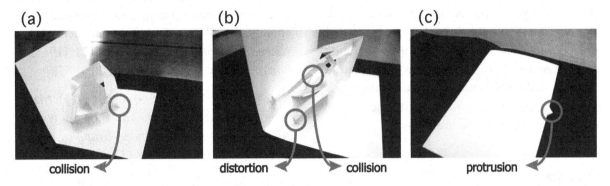

ers spent less time in the design stage because it was easy to adjust the height or the position of the pop-up parts that it would not protrude from the card, whereas the other user spent a long time adjusting the height in Task 1. In addition, User 1 and User 3 succeeded using our system even though they failed to make an acceptable pop-up structure manually.

Even so, there are two limitations to our system. First, there is a lack of a full editing system. Even though symmetrical design is frequently used in pop-up cards, symmetric editing is not directly supported. Because snapping is also not supported in our current implementation, it is difficult to align parent-child parts. Second, the direction that the user desires to move and the one that the user must move may be different because of displacement in 2D on the screen for editing.

CONCLUSION

Here we proposed an interface to help people to design and create pop-up cards. Our system examines whether the parts protrude from the card or whether they collide with one another during interactive editing, and it displays the result continuously to the user. This helps the user to concentrate on the design activity. We showed sample pop-up cards created using our system and reported the results of a preliminary user study. The preliminary user study shows that the protrusion and collision detection functions are very effective.

We plan to add new functions to the system in the future. We would like to improve our editing system. Mirror editing system in which the system changes values to maintain symmetry reduces user's work by half. A constraint editing system in which a pair of edges is always same length or parallel if the user marks two edges helps the user to design a better look. We could also create a function for the user to change lengths and angles by entering numerical values. Another feature would consist in allowing the user to paint textures directly or edit them, instead of preparing them in advance with a paint software. Finally, although we have implemented five mechanisms in this system, there are many possibilities and the user may conceive a new part while designing. Thus we would like to make part data a template the system can import or export.

We would not claim that our method (direct manipulation interface with continuous feedback) is the best interface for designing physical objects in general. There are many other methods for designing physical objects such as quick sketching or tangible interfaces. Each method has its own strength and weakness. Our experience is that sketching and tangible approaches are less constraining, so they are good for very early exploration. In contrast, our method is suitable for later stages of the design process or for the design of objects with complicated constraints. Pop-up card is an example of highly-constrained objects where one cannot design arbitrary shape and our approach works well. However, it is true that our method is a little bit too constraining for very initial exploration and we would like to work on this problem in the future.

REFERENCES

Baum, L. F. (2000). *The Wonderful Wizard of OZ*. New York: Elibron Classics.

Carter, D. A., & Diaz, J. (1999). *The Elements of Pop-up: A Pop-up Book for Aspiring Paper Engineers*. New York: Little Simon.

Chatani, M. (1985). *Origamic Archtecture Toranomaki*. Tokyo: Shokokusha.

Glassner, A. (1998). *Interactive Pop-up Card Design*. Miscrosoft Tech. Rep.

Glassner, A. (2002). Interactive Pop-up Card Design, 1. *IEEE Computer Graphics and Applications*, *22*(1), 79–86. doi:10.1109/38.974521

Glassner, A. (2002). Interactive Pop-up Card Design, 2. *IEEE Computer Graphics and Applications*, *22*(2), 74–85. doi:10.1109/38.988749

Hendrix, S. L. (2004). *Popup Workshop: Supporting and Observing Children's Pop-up Design*. Unpublished PhD dissertation, Department of Computer Science, University of Colorado.

Hendrix, S. L. (2007). *Popup Workshop*. Retrieved from http://l3d.cs.colorado.edu/~ctg/projects/popups/index.html

Hendrix, S. L., & Eisenberg, M. A. (2006). Computer-assisted pop-up design for children: computationally enriched paper engineering. *Advanced Technology for Learning*, *3*(2), 119–127. doi:10.2316/Journal.208.2006.2.208-0878

Lee, Y. T., Tor, S. B., & Soo, E. L. (1996). Mathematical modelling and simulation of pop-up books. *Journal of Computer Graphics*, *20*(1), 21–31. doi:10.1016/0097-8493(95)00089-5

Mitani, J., & Suzuki, H. (2003). Computer aided design for 180-degree flat fold origamic architecture with lattice-type cross sections. *Journal of Graphics Science of Japan*, *37*(3), 3–8.

Mitani, J., & Suzuki, H. (2004). Computer aided design for origamic architecture models with polygonal representation. In *Proceedings of the Computer Graphics International Conference* (pp. 93-99).

Mitani, J., & Suzuki, H. (2004). Making use of a CG based pop-up card design system for graphics science education. *Journal of Graphics Science of Japan*, *38*(3), 3–8.

Mitani, J., Suzuki, H., & Uno, H. (2003). Computer aided design for origamic architecture models with voxel data structure. *Transactions of Information Processing Society of Japan*, *44*(5), 1372–1379.

Sabuda, R., & Carroll, L. (2003). *Alice's Adventures in Wonderland*. New York: Little Simon.

Sabuda, R., & Reinhart, M. (2005). *Encyclopedia Prehistorica: Dinosaurs*. Somerville, MA: Candlewick Press.

Tama Software Ltd. (2005). *Pop-up card designer pro*. Retrieved from http://www.tamasoft.co.jp/craft/popupcard-pro/index.html

This work was previously published in International Journal of Creative Interfaces and Computer Graphics, Volume 1, Issue 2, edited by Ben Falchuk, pp. 40-50, copyright 2010 by IGI Publishing (an imprint of IGI Global).

Chapter 10
Organ Augmented Reality:
Audio–Graphical Augmentation of a Classical Instrument

Christian Jacquemin
LIMSI-CNRS, University of Paris Sud 11, France

Rami Ajaj
LIMSI-CNRS, France

Sylvain Le Beux
LIMSI-CNRS, France

Christophe d'Alessandro
LIMSI-CNRS, France

Markus Noisternig
IRCAM, France

Brian F.G. Katz
LIMSI-CNRS, France

Bertrand Planes
Artist, France

ABSTRACT

This paper discusses the Organ Augmented Reality (ORA) project, which considers an audio and visual augmentation of an historical church organ to enhance the understanding and perception of the instrument through intuitive and familiar mappings and outputs. ORA has been presented to public audiences at two immersive concerts. The visual part of the installation was based on a spectral analysis of the music. The visuals were projections of LED-bar VU-meters on the organ pipes. The audio part was an immersive periphonic sound field, created from the live capture of the organ sounds, so that the listeners had the impression of being inside the augmented instrument. The graphical architecture of the installation is based on acoustic analysis, mapping from sound levels to synchronous graphics through visual calibration, real-time multi-layer graphical composition and animation. The ORA project is a new approach to musical instrument augmentation that combines enhanced instrument legibility and enhanced artistic content.

DOI: 10.4018/978-1-4666-0285-4.ch010

INTRODUCTION

Augmented musical instruments are traditional instruments that are modified by adding controls and additional outputs such as animated graphics (Bouillot et al., 2009; Thompson et al., 2007). The problem with usual approaches to instrument augmentation is that it generally makes the instrument more complex to play and more complex to understand by the spectators. The enhanced functionality of the instrument often distorts the perceived link between the performer's actions and the resulting sounds and images. Augmentation is likely to confuse the audience because it lacks transparency and legibility.

In addition to augmenting traditional instruments with new controllers, like the hyper-kalimba (Rocha et al., 2009) which extends the kalimba (an instrument from the percussion family), Augmented Reality is also used to create new musical instruments. Some of these instruments mimic real music devices like the Digital Baton (Marrin et al., 1997), replicating the traditional conducting baton, or the AR scratching[1] imitating a DJ's vinyl scratch. Other musical instruments that use Augmented Reality are totally innovative and are not based on existing devices. The Augmented Groove (Poupyrev et al., 2001) is an example of such a device where novice users manipulate a physical object in space to play electronic musical compositions. The main difference between creating novel instruments and extending existing instruments is the level of familiarity with the instrument. Instrument extension seems more suitable for experimented performers rather than novice ones due to the experience level with the instrument and possibly a wider range of control.

Musical instrument augmentation is interesting because it extends a traditional instrument, while preserving and enriching its performance and composition practices. The Organ and Augmented Reality (ORA) project focuses on a rarely stressed use of augmentation, the enhanced comprehension and legibility of a music instrument without increasing its complexity and opacity. Our research on output augmentation follows the same purposes as (Jordà, 2003), making the complexity of music more accessible to a larger public. Jorda's work focused on the playing experience; similarly, we intend to improve and facilitate the listening experience. These principles have been used by Jordà et al. (2007) for the design of the ReacTable, an augmented input controller for electronic musical instruments. The ReacTable is a legible, graspable, and tangible control interface, which facilitates the use of an electronic instrument so as to be accessible to novices. Its use by professionals in live performances confirms that transparency is not boring and is compatible with long term use of the instrument.

This paper presents the issues and technical details of the ORA project and performance, the augmentation of an historical church organ for a better understanding and perception of the instrument through intuitive visual and audio outputs. It is based on the following achievements:

- The visuals are directly projected onto the organ pipes (not on peripheral screens),
- The visual augmentation is temporally and spatially aligned: the visual rendering is cross-modally synchronized with the acoustic signal and the graphical projection is accurately aligned with the organ geometry,
- The augmentation preserves the traditional organ play. Traditional compositions as well as new artworks can be played on the augmented instrument,
- The augmentation offers a better understanding of the instrument's principles by showing a visualization of hidden data such as the spectral content of the sound and its position inside the instrument.

The aim of the ORA project was to make an audio and visual Augmented Reality on the grand organ of the Sainte Elisabeth church in Paris. The

ORA project was supported by the City of Paris "Science sur Seine" program for bringing science closer to citizens. The pedagogical purpose was to present the basic principles of sound and acoustics, and illustrate them through audio and graphics live performances. The two concerts were complemented by a series of scientific posters explaining background knowledge and specialized techniques used in the ORA project. The project involved researchers in interactive 3D graphics and computer music, a digital visual artist, an organ player and composer, and engineers.[2] ORA has been presented to public audiences through two visually and acoustically augmented concerts at Church Sainte Elisabeth. The visual part of the installation was based on a spectral analysis of the music. The visuals were projections of LED-bar VU-meters on the organ pipes. The audio part was an immersive periphonic sound field, created from the live capture of the organ sound, so that the listeners had the impression to be placed inside the augmented instrument. This article presents in detail the visual augmentation; the audio part of this project is described in (d'Alessandro et al., 2009).

VISUAL AUGMENTATION OF INSTRUMENTS

Musical instrument augmentation can target the interface (the performer's gesture capture), the output (the music, the sound, or non-audio rendering), or the intermediate layer that associates the incoming stimuli with the output signals (the mapping layer). Since the ORA project approach tries to avoid modifying the instrument's playing techniques, it focuses on the augmentation of the mapping and output layers in order to enhance composition, performance, and experience.

About augmented music composition, Sonofusion (Thompson et al., 2007) is both a program-

Figure 1. ORA Concerts, Eglise Sainte Elisabeth de Hongrie, Paris, May 15th & 17th, 2008

ming environment and a physically-augmented violin used for composing and performing multimedia artworks. Sonofusion compositions are "written" through lines of code, and the corresponding performances are controlled in real-time through additional knobs, sliders, and joysticks on the violin. While addressing the question of multi- and cross-modal composition and performance in a relevant way, Sonofusion control system is complex and opaque. The many control devices offer multiple mapping combinations. Because of this diversity, the correlation between the performer's gestures and the multimedia outputs seems arbitrary to the audience at times. Musikalscope (Fels et al., 1998) is a cross-modal digital instrument that was designed with a similar purpose, and has been criticized by some users for its lack of transparency between the user's input and the visual output.

For teaching music to beginners, augmented reality can be used to project information onto the instrument about the playing of the instrument. For electric and bass guitar, Cakmakci et al. (2003) and Motokawa and Saito (2006) augment the instrument by displaying the expected location of the fingers onto the guitar fingerboard. The visual information is synchronized with audio synthesis and is available through direct projection on the instrument or via visual composition using a head-mounted display.

About augmenting a performance, the Synesthetic Music Experience Communicator (Lewis Charles Hill, 2006) (SMEC) is used to compose synesthetic cross-modal performances based on visual illusions experienced by synesthetes. When compared with Sonofusion, graphic rendering in SMEC is better motivated because it relies on reports of synesthetic illusions. SMEC however raises the question whether we can display and share perceptions which are deeply personal and intimate in nature.

Visually augmented performances have also addressed human voice augmentation. The Messa di Vocce installation (Levin & Lieberman, 2004)

was designed for real-time analysis of human voice and for producing visual representations of human voice based on audio processing algorithms. The graphical augmentation of the voice was autonomous enough to create the illusion of being an alter ego of the performer. Since it is governed by an "intelligent" program, Messa di Vocce graphical augmentation does not seem as arbitrary as other works on instrument augmentation (human voice is considered here as an instrument). When attending augmented instrument performance with insufficiently motivated augmentation, the spectators are immersed by a complex story which they would not normally expect when attending a musical event.

VIRTUAL AND AUGMENTED REALITY FOR THE ARTS AT LIMSI-CNRS

In 2003, LIMSI-CNRS launched a research program entitled *Virtuality, Interactivity, Design, and Art* (*VIDA*) to develop joint projects with artists, designers, and architects in Virtual and Augmented Reality, and, more generally, in arts/science projects on Human/Computer Interaction. Through artistic collaborations, new research themes have emerged which have fertilized research at LIMSI-CNRS and broadened the scope of our works. The developments enabled by these academic works have also provided artists with new software tools and new environments for their creative works. Without these developments, they would not have been able to realize such innovative artworks. A necessary engineering workforce has been involved in these collaborations so that scientific prototypes could be turned into usable applications for the artists whether on stage or in art installations.

The ORA project is part of a sub-theme in VIDA dealing with Augmented Reality in the arts. This theme was initiated through collaboration with the theater company Didascalie.Net (director Georges

Gagneré) concerning video-scenography for the performing arts. The question of "presence" in an artwork, smart projection on non-flat surfaces, and the interaction of performers with live image synthesis were among the issues addressed in this collaboration. Through live "experiments" with the stage director and actors, unexpected experimental configurations emerged which triggered innovative works. For instance, the combination of video-projection and conventional lighting raised new topics of research considering video-projection and performer's or spectator's shadows. Interaction of performers with live computer graphics has also led us to develop a dynamic multilayer model for video-scenography that parallels the layers of stage decoration (Jacquemin & Gagneré, 2007).

Augmented Virtualiy (closer to the digital world than Augmented Reality) has also be used in collaborations between the visual artist Bertrand Planes and LIMSI-CNRS for two digital art installations (Mar:3D and Gate:2.5) in which shadows of spectators were projected into the virtual scene (Jacquemin et al., 2007). Through these installations, we have addressed the issue of spectator presence in a Virtual Environment through the use of shadows, which also proved to be a good medium for non-tactile gestural exploration of a virtual world.

The ORA project was developed in 2008 to address issues of accurate spatial and temporal registration of video-projection in a real-time performance. It was the first time that LIMSI-CNRS was involved in a project with strong expectations for aligning real time graphics in space with a complex architecture and aligning them in time with a live sound production. This project has been followed since by works on Mobile Augmented Reality[3], in which the viewers' location in the scene changes with time. The artistic target of this work was an installation on the River Seine, for which spectators embarked on a boat cruise, viewing the river banks augmented with a re-projection of modified infrared video-capture of the riverside. As a first approach to mobile augmented reality, we have not dealt with the identification of mobile elements but only with the issues of dynamic calibration and live special effects. Future work will deal with more elaborate analysis of the mobile scene related to tracking and identification in the physical world allowing for semantic registration of virtual elements on the real-world.

ORA ARTISTIC DESIGN

Visual Design

The design of the ORA project visual artwork transforms the instrument in such a way that it appears as both classical and contemporary. The 20th century style of the visual augmentation contrasts with the baroque architecture of the instrument. The Sainte Elisabeth church organ is located high on the rear wall of the building. In this church, as it often occurs, the believers face the altar and listen to the music and cannot look at the instrument. Even if one looks at the organ, the organist cannot be seen, resulting in a very static visual experience. For the two ORA project concerts the seating was reversed, with the audience facing the organ at the gallery.

The church acoustics is an integral part of the organ sound as perceived by the listeners. Through the use of close multichannel microphone capture, rapid signal processing, and a multichannel reproduction system, the audience was virtually placed inside a modified "organ" acoustics, thereby providing a unique sound and music experience. To highlight the digital augmentation of the organ sound, VU-meters were displayed on the pipes of the organ facade through videoprojection, making a common reference to audio amplifiers. These VU-meters were dynamically following the music spectral composition and built a subtle visual landscape that was reported as "hypnotic" by some members of the audience. The traditionally static and monumental instrument was visually transformed into a fluid, mobile, and transparent contemporary art installation.

Sound Effects & Spatial Audio Rendering

The organ is one of the oldest musical instruments in Western musical tradition. It offers a large pitch range with high dynamics, and it can produce a large variety of timbres. An organ is even able to imitate orchestral voices. Because of the complexity of the pipe machinery, advances in organ design have been closely related to the evolution of associated technologies. During the second half of the 20th century electronics were applied to organs for two purposes:

- To control the key and stop electro-pneumatic mechanisms of the pipes,
- To set the registration (the combinations of pipe ranks).

However, very little has been achieved for modifying the actual sound of the organ. In the ORA project, the pipe organ sound is captured and processed in real-time through a sequence of digital audio effects. The transformed sound is then rendered via an array of loudspeakers surrounding the audience. Therefore, the sound perceived by the audience is a combination of the natural sound of organ pipes, the processed sound, and the room acoustics related to each of these acoustic sources. Spatial audio processing and rendering places the inner sounds of the organ in the outer space, radically changing their interaction with the natural room acoustic, and adding a new musical dimension.

Augmented Organ

Miranda and Wanderley (2006) refer to augmented instruments[4] as "the original instrument maintaining all its default features in the sense that it continues to make the same sounds it would normally make, but with the addition of extra features that may tremendously increase its functionality". With a similar intention in mind, the ORA project was designed to enrich the natural sound of organ pipes through real-time audio processing and multi-channel sound effects, to meet the requirements of experimental music and contemporary art.

ARCHITECTURE AND IMPLEMENTATION

The Instrument

The Sainte Elisabeth Church organ used for the ORA project is a large 19th century instrument (a protected historical monument), with three manual keyboards (54 keys), a pedal board (30 keys), and 41 stops with mechanical action. This organ has approximately 2500 pipes. Only 141 of the organ pipes are located on the facade and visible to the public. The front side of the organ case has a dimension of approximately 10x10m. The organ pipes are organized in four main divisions: the "Positif", a small case on the floor of the organ loft (associated with the first manual keyboard), the "Grand Orgue" and "Pédale" divisions at the main level (associated with the second manual keyboard and the pedal board), and the "Récit" division, a case of about the same size as the "Positif", crowning the instrument (associated with the third manual keyboard). The "Récit" is enclosed into a swell-box.

A set of 5 microphones was placed in the four instrument divisions (see Figure 2 left). These divisions are relatively sound isolated, and the near-field sound captured in one division was significantly louder than the sounds received from other ones. Hence, the captured sounds can be considered as being acoustically "isolated" from each other at least in the mid- and high-frequency ranges.

General Architecture

The organ pipes, despite their gray color and their slight specular reflection, were an appropriate surface for video-projection. The visual ornamentation of the instrument was made with three video-projectors: two for the upper part of the instrument and one for the lower part (see Figure 2).

The organ sound captured by the microphones was given as input to a digital signal processing unit for sound analysis and special effects. The processed sounds were then diffused back into the church over a loudspeaker array encircling the audience. The sound processing modules for graphical effects consisted of spectral analysis and sampling modules that computed the levels of the virtual VU-meters. These values were sent

over the Ethernet network to the 3D engine. The graphical rendering relied on Graphic Processing Unit programming: vertex and fragment shaders that used these values as parameters to animate the textures projected on the organ pipes to render the virtual LED-bars. The right part of Figure 2 shows the full hardware installation of the ORA project with the location of the video-projectors and loudspeakers, and the main data connections.

Graphic Rendering

Graphic rendering relies on Virtual Choreographer (VirChor)[5], a 3D graphic engine offering communication facilities with audio applications. The implementation of graphic rendering in VirChor involved the development of a calibration procedure and dedicated shaders for blending, masking, and animation. The architecture is divided into three layers: initial calibration, real-time compositing, and animation.

Calibration. The VU-meters are rendered graphically as quads that are covered by two samples of the same texture (white and colored LED-bars), depending on the desired rendering

Figure 2. Architecture of the installation: sound capture and video-projection

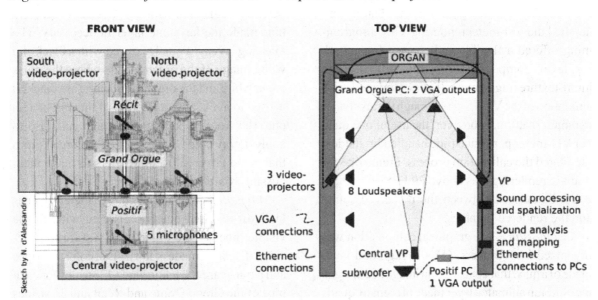

style. These quads must be registered spatially with the organ pipes. Due to the complexity of the instrument and its immobility, registration of the quads with the pipes was performed manually. Before the concert began, a digital photograph of the projection of a white image was taken with a camera placed on each video projector, near the projection lens. This photo was then used as a background image in Inkscape[6] to calibrate the projection of the virtual LED-bars on the organ pipes. The vector image in Inkscape contained as many quads as visible organ pipes in the background image. Each quad was manually aligned with the corresponding pipe of the background image in the vector image editor. Luckily, the amount of effort for this calibration work was only significant for the first edition of the vector image. Successive registrations (for each re-installation) amounted to a slight translation of the quads aligned in the previous edition, since attempts were made to relocate each video-projector in a similar position for each concert. The resulting Inkscape SVG vector image was then converted into an XML 3D scene graph through a Perl script and then loaded into VirChor.

During a concert, the VU-meter levels were received from the audio analysis component (section *Analysis and Mapping*) and transmitted to the Graphic Processing Unit (GPU) that in turn handled the VU-meter rendering. GPU programming offered a flexible and concise framework for layer compositing and masking through multi-texture fragment shaders, and for interactive animation of the VU-meters through vertex shader parameterization. Moreover, the use of one quad per VU-meter per visual pipe handled by shaders facilitated the calibration process. Frame rate for graphic rendering was above 70 FPS and no lag could be noticed between the perceived sound and the rendered graphics.

Compositing. The graphical composition was organized into 4 layers: (1) a background layer made of a quad that contained an image of the organ pipes, (2) an animated layer made of as many quads

as organ pipes, each quad was used to render one of the VU-meters, (3) a masking layer made of a single black and white mask, and used to avoid animated quads to be rendered outside the organ pipes, and (4) a keystone layer used to distort the output image and register it accurately on the organ pipes (see left part of Figure 3). The VU-meter animated layer is made of a set of multi-textured quads, and the background and mask layers are single quads that are parallel to the projection plane and that fill the entire display. Real-time compositing, keystone homography, and control of background color were made through vertex and fragment shaders applied on the geometrical primitives building these layers. The keystone layer (4) is a quad textured by the image generated by layers (1) to (3) that is oriented in such a way that it can correct the registration of the virtual VU-meters on the organ pipes. A modification of the keystone quad orientation is equivalent to applying an homography to the final image. This transformation enables slight adjustments in order to align the digital graphics with the organ and to compensate for calibration inaccuracies. It could also be computed automatically from real-time captures of calibration patterns (Raskar & Beardsley, 2001). Elaborate testing has shown that the background, VU-meter, and mask quads were perfectly registered with the physical organ, and thus made the keystone layer unnecessary. The masking layer is a quad textured with a black and white image of the organ facade where the pipes are in white and the organ wood parts are black. It is used to avoid any projection of the VU-meters onto the wooden parts of the organ, and also to apply a gray color on the part of the organ pipes that is not covered by VU-meters to make them possibly visible to the audience.

Animation. The animated VU-meter layer is made of textured quads registered with all the visible pipes of the organ. The texture for VU-meter display is made of horizontal colored stripes and a transparent background (42 stripes for each pipe of the Grand Orgue and Récit and 32 stripes

Figure 3. Multi-layer composition and VU-meter animation through sampling

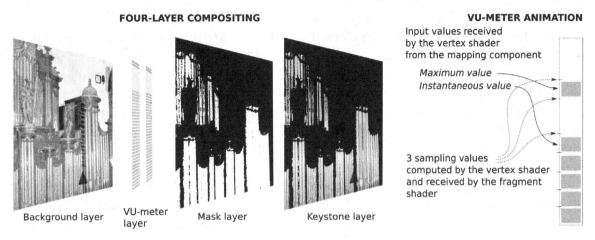

FOUR-LAYER COMPOSITING

Background layer   VU-meter layer   Mask layer   Keystone layer

VU-METER ANIMATION

Input values received by the vertex shader from the mapping component

Maximum value

Instantaneous value

3 sampling values computed by the vertex shader and received by the fragment shader

for each pipe of the Positif). The purpose of the animation of these VU-meter quads is to mimic real LED-bar VU-meters that are controlled by the energy of their associated organ sound spectral band (see next section).

Each VU-meter receives activation values from the sound analysis and mapping components: the instantaneous value and the maximum value for the past 500ms (typical peak-hold function). These values are received through UDP messages and represent the sound levels of the spectral bands associated with each pipe. These intensities are sampled in the vertex shader to show or hide whole texture stripes and to avoid displaying only fractions of them. The level sampling performed in the vertex shader and applied to each quad is based on a list of predefined *sampling values* loaded in the shader. Since the height of a VU-meter texture is clamped to [0, 1], each sampling value is the height between two stripes that represent two VU-meter bars (see right part of Figure 3). For example, a texture for 42 LED-bars has 43 sampling values. The sampling values are then transmitted from the vertex shader to the fragment shader that only displays the stripes below the received values and the top stripe associated with the maximal sampled value. The resulting perception by the audience is that each VU-meter is displaying a

number of LED-bar stripes that corresponds to the associated spectral band intensity.

Before describing how these instantaneous control values were generated by sound analysis, we first present the detailed content of the musical program and its motivation.

Musical Program

The ORA project was based on two organ concerts, with a bit of *strangeness* added by a virtual graphic animation of the organ facade and live electronic modifications of the organ sound. The musical program was a combination of a "classical" program and somewhat unusual digitally augmented pieces. The pieces of the great classical organ repertoire (Bach, Couperin Franck, Messiaen) were alternated with a piece in 12 parts especially written by Christophe d'Alessandro for this project. This piece exploited the various musical possibilities offered by the sound capture, its digital transformation, and the diffusion system.

A large majority of special effects cannot be applied to pieces of the classical repertoire without damaging their subtle musical content. Contrary to the aesthetics of classical music played on electronic instruments, we adopted the point of view of historically informed performances, privileging historical registrations. Along this line, the music played in the concert was chosen to fit the aesthetics of the specific organ considered. Only subtle spatial audio and reverberation effects were used in conjunction with classical music.

It must be pointed out that the application of electronic effects to classical music is somewhat paradoxical: the effects in this case are considered successful as long as they do not sound "electronic", or other words, as long as they are not noticed by the audience.

The main argument of the musical piece composed for the ORA project in 12 parts was to play with inner and outer spaces, capturing inside and playing outside the instrument. This argument is also a metaphor for the music itself, based on a short text by Dorothée Quoniam: *Les 12 degrés du silence* (the 12 degrees of silence). Quoniam, a 19th-century Carmelite, explained to a young sister the teachings of her inner voice. The cycle is about speech, silence, inner and outer voices. It was played in alternation with classical repertoire music. This piece makes use of several unusual sound possibilities offered by the system.

1. *Sound relocation in the church.* The sound captured in a given division is played at another place in the church.
2. *Dynamic sound location.* Sound motion is suited to music made of an accompanied solo voice (called "Récit" in the French organ literature), like a singer moving in the church. A more massive effect is the slow extension and retraction through variation of the spatial extent (width) of the sound of a division in the acoustic space, like a tide rising and falling.
3. *Virtual room augmentation.* Artificial reverberation enlarges the acoustic space. This can transform the acoustics of the relatively small church where the concert took place into that of a grand cathedral. At the same time, sounds presented to the audience through loudspeakers have less interaction with the natural room acoustics before arriving at the

audience, resulting in a perceived reduction in reverberation.

4. *"Additive" effects that enrich the original sound.* Additive effects work well when applied to flute pipes, adding artificial harmonics to sound. For instance, the inharmonicity provided by the harmonizer effect and reverberations can transform the pipe sounds into percussion-like sounds.
5. *"Subtractive" effects that spectrally reshape the original sound.* Subtractive effects work well when applied to spectrally rich sounds. For instance the spectrum shaping effect provided by the Kapkus-Strong algorithm can give a vocal quality to reed pipes.

Analysis and Mapping

This section describes the real-time audio analysis and mapping for VU-meter visualization. Most of the approximately 2500 organ pipes are covered by the organ case, while only the 141 of the facade pipes are seen by the audience. As such, a direct mapping of the frequency played to visual pipes is not relevant, due to the large number of hidden pipes. In the context of ORA, the main purpose of the correspondence between audio data and graphical visualization was:

1. To metaphorically display the energy levels of the lowest spectral bands on the largest pipes (resp. display the highest bands on the smallest pipes)[7],
2. To maintain the spatial distribution of the played pipes by separating the projected spectral bands in zones, corresponding to the microphone capture regions and thereby retaining the notion of played pipe location,
3. To visualize the energy of each spectral band in the shape of a classical audio VU-meter. The display was based on the instantaneous value of the energy and its last maximal value with a slower refreshing rate.

In order to estimate the mapping of sound level values to VU-meter heights, pre-recordings were analyzed (Figure 4). This analysis allowed for a rough estimate of the overall range of the various organ divisions and to separate these spectral ranges into different frequency bands according to the evolution of the harmonic amplitudes over frequency. The analysis resulted in a maximum spectral range of 16 kHz for the Positif and Récit divisions of the organ, and 12 kHz and 10 kHz for the central and lateral parts of the Grand Orgue.

Each spectral band was further divided into sub-bands corresponding to the number of visually augmented pipes, i.e. 33 for Positif and Récit, 20 and 35 for the lateral and central Grand Orgue. The sub-bands were not equally distributed over frequency range (warping) in order to gain a better energy balance between low and high frequencies. The spectral energy contained in the lowest

frequency range was much greater than in the highest one. Thus, the frequency bands widths for lower frequencies were narrower, so as to have approximately the same spectral dynamics over all frequency bands. The frequency band divisions are summarized in Table 1. The energy of the lowest sub-band (the largest pipe) was used as reference signal for re-calibration.

The real-time spectral analysis consists of three stages: estimation of the power spectral density for each sub-band, mapping, and broadcasting over IP. The concert mapping process is presented schematically in Figure 5.

Power spectral density (PSD). The PSD was estimated via periodograms as proposed by Welch (1967). The buffered and windowed input signal was Fourier transformed (Fast Fourier Transform, FFT) and averaged over consecutive frames. Assuming ergodicity, the time average provides a

Figure 4. Spectral sound analysis

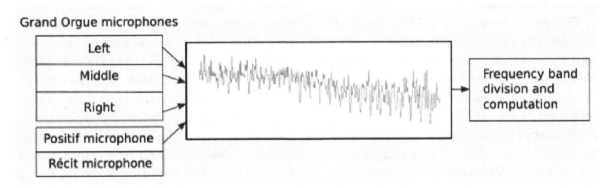

Table 1. Frequency bandwidths

Récit and Positif Bandwidth (33 bands)	Central Bandwidth (35 bands)	Lateral Bandwidth (20 bands)
0 - 600 Hz 5 x 120 Hz	0 - 1200 Hz 10 x 120 Hz	0 - 600 Hz 5 x 120 Hz
600 - 1600 Hz 5 x 200 Hz	1200 – 3200 Hz 10 x 200 Hz	600 - 2200 Hz 5 x 320 Hz
1600 - 5000 Hz 10 x 340 Hz	3200 - 6400 Hz 8 x 400 Hz	2200 - 5000 Hz 5 x 360Hz
5000 - 8000 Hz 5 x 600 Hz	6400 - 11000 Hz 5 x 900 Hz	5000 – 10000 Hz 5 x 1000 Hz
8000 - 12000 Hz 5 x 800 Hz	11000 – 12000 Hz 2 x 500 Hz	
12000 - 16000 Hz 3 x 1000 Hz		

Figure 5. Mapping between sound analysis and graphics

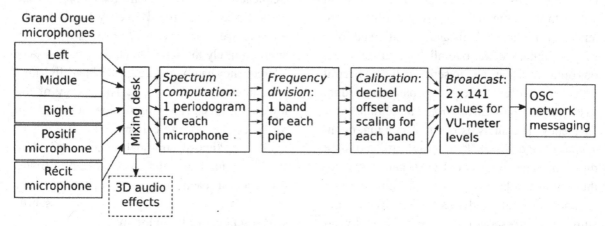

good estimation of the PSD. Through long term averaging, the estimated sub-band levels are not sensitive to brief peaks and represent the root mean square (RMS) value. The decay of the recursive averaging was adjusted such that the VU-meter values changed smoothly for visual representation. The actual averaging was such that every incoming frame was added to the last three buffered frames.

Frequency band division. The computed periodograms were transmitted to the frequency band division module as five 512-point spectra. This module, that represents the second part of sound signal processing, divided the Welch periodograms into 141 frequency bands. Since the number of visible pipes in each division of the organ was inferior to 512 (resp. 33, 20, 35, 20, and 33) an additional spectral averaging was necessary in order to map the entire frequency range to the pipes of the organ. According to the spectral tilt, lower frequency bands (below ~1.5 kHz) had more energy, thus only three frequency bands from the Welch periodograms were added for the largest pipes, whereas up to 30-40 bands were added for the highest frequency range (above ~8 kHz), as detailed in Table 1. For the central Grand Orgue, the last two bandwidths were smaller than the preceding ones. This choice was made in order to better match the number of visible pipes in this region. An alternate choice

could have been a doubled 1 kHz bandwidth only, essentially repeating the same values for the two last pipes. Nevertheless, due to the curved shape of the organ, the smallest pipes were often partly hidden by larger ones, and this issue was not too critical in the current installation.

Calibration. The third and most difficult part was the calibration of the VU-meter activations through a scaling of the frequency band dynamics to values ranging from 0 to 1. The null value corresponds to an empty VU-meter (no sound energy in this frequency band), and 1 to a full VU-meter (maximum overall amplitude for this frequency band). The sound output was calibrated by applying pre-calculated decibel shifts computed from spectral analysis of the preliminary recordings, so that 0 would correspond to the ambient sound with the air blower turned on. According to this analysis, each frequency band had approximately a 30 dB amplitude dynamics, therefore each VU-meter activation was divided by 30 so the VU-meter graphical rendering on the organ pipe would use the whole range of height positions during the entire course of the concert.

This technique for sound spectral analysis and calibration encountered the following difficulties:

1. The positions of the microphones varied slightly between each rehearsal and performance. Since the microphones could be

close to different pipes depending on their positions in the organ divisions, it resulted in slight changes in the amplitude levels of the sound spectral analysis.

2. The acoustics of the church produced a slight feedback effect between microphones and loudspeakers, and the offsets of the VU-meter calibration had to be readjusted for each concert.

3. Since the dynamics of the pipes depended on the loudness of each concert piece, and since the concert pieces varied from very loud to quiet ones, these variations resulted either in saturation or in a lack of reaction of the VU-meters.

4. The electric bellows system for air pressure generated a low-frequency parasite noise that was captured by the microphones and had to be taken into consideration for the minimal calibration level.

5. Even though the microphones were placed inside the organ divisions, the sound of the instrument could interfere with the church sounds such as audience applause and loud-speakers. Some of the spectators noticed the influence of their hand clapping on the virtual VU-meter levels, eventually using this unintended mapping to transform the instrument into an applause meter.

Because of these difficulties, approximately half an hour before the beginning of each concert was devoted to manual correction of the pipe calibration. The lowest activation level of the pipes was tuned with the bellows system switched on to cope with this background noise. In order to deal with the variations of dynamics between the concert pieces, the dynamics of each organ division was controlled by a slider on the audio monitoring interface. Last, the applause effects were avoided by manually shifting down all the division sliders after each piece.

Broadcast. The third and last module task was to concatenate all the frequency band values into a single message that could be sent through UDP over the Ethernet network. All the values were scaled to an numerical range [0, 1]. The real-time intensity values were doubled and a memory of the last maximal value was kept so that the audience would get the impression of a real VU-meter with an instantaneous value and a peak-hold maximum value. If no instantaneous value would overpass the peak-hold value for a half second, the current intensity value would replace the last peak-hold value. Thus two lists of 141 values were sent to the 3D graphical engine through UDP messages over the internal Ethernet network: 141 instantaneous frequency bands amplitudes and 141 associated last maximal values.

Audio Rendering

Algorithms were designed such that separate divisions of the organ were processed separately as they have different tonal properties (timbre, dynamics, and pitch range) and often contrast each other. Microphone signals were digitally converted via multi-channel audio cards with low-latency drivers; the real-time audio processing was implemented in Pure Data (Puckette, 1996). Selected algorithms included ring modulation, harmonizers, phasers, string resonators, and granular synthesis. Audio rendering was reproduced over an 8-channel full-bandwidth speaker configuration along the perimeter of the audience area and an additional high-powered subwoofer on the altar of the church, at the end opposite from the organ.

Historically, the rich variety of organ sounds is based on the combination of pipe ranks or registers. Various audio effects can be added as "electronic registers" to pipe organs, but their musical practicability strongly depends on the acoustics of the different pipes. Flue pipes, for example, have a frequency spectrum which is sparse and limited to a few harmonics for some stop ranks, e.g. the *Bourdon*; and as such are well suited to additive synthesis algorithms creating more harmonically rich sounds. On the contrary, reed pipes offer a very dense frequency spectrum with high dynamics that might "overload" additive audio effects, which could yield distortions and noise-like sounds. However, subtractive synthesis algorithms are well suited to reed pipes as they allow one to spectrally reshape the harmonically rich organ sounds.

Ring modulators and harmonizers fall into the category of additive effects and have been well studied in signal processing literature (Zölzer, 2002; Verfaille, 2006). Ring modulation, or double sideband (DSB) modulation, can be realized by multiplying two signals together producing components equal to two times the number of frequency components in one signal multiplied by the number of frequency components in the other. Harmonizing relates to adding several pitch-shifted versions of a sound to itself and various shifting ratios are used in order to produce different degrees of inharmonicity. In practice, microphones capture the global sound of each organ division, providing a polyphonic input signal to the harmonizers. The many inharmonic partials are added to the original signal spectrum to produce a very dense and inharmonic sound. The Karplus-Strong string resonator is a physical model-based algorithm simulating plucked string sounds, and is closely related to digital waveguide sound synthesis (Karjalainen et al., 1998) which provides a computationally efficient and simple approach to subtractive synthesis (Karplus & Strong, 1983). The algorithm consists of variable delay lines and low-pass filters arranged in a closed loop which allow dynamic control of resonance effects. When applied to the rich spectrum of reed pipes, this algorithm results in human voice like sounds with rapidly changing formants.

A large variety of multi-channel spatial audio systems have been developed recently such as quadrophony, vector base amplitude panning (VBAP), wave field synthesis (WFS), and Ambisonics. The sound spatialization environment used for the ORA project relied on third-order Ambisonics for 2D sound projection on the hori-

zontal plane only. Ambisonics was invented by Gerzon (1973). While the church room acoustic generates reverberation that is part of the organ sound, the presence of early reflections and late reverberation deteriorates sound localization accuracy. Different weighting functions described in (Noisternig et al., 2003) were applied prior to the Ambisonic decoding in order to widen or narrow the directional response patterns. The ORA sound design was made tolerant to reduced localization accuracy by employing non-spatially focused sounds, variable room reverberation algorithms, and spatial granular synthesis.

The classical repertoire organ pieces were spatialized and the reverberation time of the church acoustics was digitally increased. For these pieces, it made the organ sound independent from the organ location and it rendered the room sound much larger than the actual Sainte Elisabeth church. For the contemporary piece with audio digital effects, the captured sounds were distorted in real-time through signal processing algorithms.

CONCLUSION AND PERSPECTIVES

The audio and graphical calibrations of the installation involved manual adjustments that could be avoided through automatic calibration equipments and algorithms. By equipping the organ facade with fiducials (graphical patterns that can be captured by video camera and recognized by visual pattern-matching algorithms), the VU-meter quads could be automatically registered with the organ pipes. Such a realignment would make the installation more robust to slight displacements of the video-projectors between concerts and/or rehearsals. On the audio calibration side, background noise detection could be improved by automatically capturing the decibel amplitudes of the background noise frequency bands and by using these values to calibrate the minimal intensity values of the VU-meters. Similarly, automatic detection of spectral band maximal values could be used for amplitude calibration so that each VU-meter could use the full range of graphical heights during the concert.

The ORA project has shown that the audience is receptive to such a new mode of instrument augmentation that does not burden artistic expression with additional and unnecessary complexity, but instead subtly reveals hidden data, making the performance both more appealing and better understandable. The work presented in this article opens new perspectives in musical instrument augmentation. First, graphical ornamentation could be applied to smaller non-static musical instruments such as string instruments by tracking their spatial location. Second, digital graphics for information visualization could reveal other hidden physical data such as air pressure, keystrokes, or valve closings and openings. This could be made possible by equipping the instrument with other additional sensors in addition to the microphones. Information visualization could also deal with a fine capture of ambient sounds such as audience noise, acoustic reflections, or even external sound sources such as street noise, and use them as additional artistic elements.

In summary, this project has demonstrated that live electronics applied to the pipe organ can extend the musical capacities and repertoire of the instrument, while maintaining its historical character. As such, it is then possible to mix classical and contemporary music harmoniously. The ORA augmented instrument thus offers performers and composers new means of expression.

REFERENCES

Bouillot, N., Wozniewski, M., Settel, Z., & Cooperstock, J. R. (2007). A mobile wireless augmented guitar. In *Proceedings of the 7th International Conference on New Interfaces for Musical Expression NIME '07*, Genova, Italy.

Cakmakci, O., Bérard, F., & Coutaz, J. (2003). An augmented reality based learning assistant for electric bass guitar. In *Proceedings of the 10th International Conference on Human-Computer Interaction (HCI International 2003)*, Crete, Greece.

d'Alessando, C., Noisternig, M., Le Beux, S., Katz, B., Picinali, L., Jacquemin, C., et al. (2009). The ORA project: Audio-visual live electronics and the pipe organ. In *Proceedings of International Computer Music Conference ICMC 2009*, Montreal, Canada.

Fels, S., Nishimoto, K., & Mase, K. (1998). Musikalscope: A graphical musical instrument. *IEEE MultiMedia, 5*(3), 26–35. doi:10.1109/93.713302

Gerzon, M. A. (1973). Periphony: With-height sound reproduction. *Journal of the Audio Engineering Society. Audio Engineering Society, 21*(1), 2–10.

Jacquemin, C., & Gagneré, G. (2007). Revisiting the Layer/Mask Paradigm for Augmented Scenery. *International Journal of Performance Arts and Digital Media, 2*(3), 237–258. doi:10.1386/padm.2.3.237_1

Jacquemin, C., Planes, B., & Ajaj, R. (2007). Shadow casting for soft and engaging immersion in augmented virtuality artworks. In *Proceedings of 9th ACM Confernece on Multimedia 2007*, Augsburg, Germany.

Jordà, S. (2003). Interactive music systems for everyone: Exploring visual feedback as a way for creating more intuitive, efficient and learnable instruments. In *Proceedings of the Stockholm Music Acoustics Conference (SMAC 03)*, Stockholm, Sweden.

Jordà, S., Geiger, G., Alonso, M., & Kaltenbrunner, M. (2007). The ReacTable: exploring the synergy between live music performance and tabletop tangible interfaces. In *Proceedings of the 1st International Conference on Tangible and Embedded Interaction TEI '07* (pp. 139-146). New York: ACM.

Karjalainen, M., Valimi, V., & Tolonen, T. (1998). Plucked String Models: From the Karplus-Strong Algorithm to Digital Waveguides and Beyond. *Computer Music Journal, 22*(3), 17–32. doi:10.2307/3681155

Karplus, K., & Strong, A. (1983). Digital Synthesis of Plucked String and Drum Timbres. *Computer Music Journal, 7*(2), 43–55. doi:10.2307/3680062

Levin, G., & Lieberman, Z. (2004). In-situ speech visualization in real-time interactive installation and performance. In *Proceedings of the 3rd international symposium on Non-photorealistic animation and rendering NPAR '04* (pp. 7-14). New York: ACM.

Lewis Charles Hill, I. (2006). *Synesthetic Music Experience Communicator.* Unpublished doctoral dissertation, Iowa State University, Ames, IA.

Marrin, T., & Paradiso, J. (1997). The Digital Baton: a Versatile Performance Instrument. In *Proceedings of the International Computer Music Conference ICMC 1997.*

Miranda, E. R., & Wanderley, M. (2006). *New Digital Musical Instruments: Control and Interaction Beyond the Keyboard (Computer Music and Digital Audio Series).* Madison, WI: A-R Editions, Inc.

Motokawa, Y., & Saito, H. (2006). Support system for guitar playing using augmented reality display. In *Proceedings of the 2006 Fifth IEEE and ACM International Symposium on Mixed and Augmented Reality (Ismar '06)* (pp. 243-244). Washington, DC: IEEE Computer Society.

Noisternig, M., Sontacchi, A., Musil, T., & Höldrich, R. (2003). A 3D ambisonic based binaural sound reproduction system. In *Proceedings Audio Engineering Society AES 24th International Conference,* Banff, Canada.

Poupyrev, I., Berry, R., Billinghurst, M., Kato, H., Nakao, K., Baldwin, L., et al. (2001). Augmented Reality Interface for Electronic Music Performance. In *Proceedings of HCI 2001* (pp. 805-808).

Puckette, M. S. (1996). Pure data: Another integrated computer music environment. In *Proceedings of the International Computer Music Conference ICMC 1996,* Hong Kong, China (pp. 37-41).

Raskar, R., & Beardsley, P. (2001). A self-correcting projector. In *Proceedings of the 2001 IEEE Computer Society Conference on Computer Vision and Pattern Recognition CVPR 2001,* Kauai, HI (pp. 504-508). Washington, DC: IEEE Computer Society.

Rocha, F., & Malloch, J. (2009). The Hyper-Kalimba: Developping an Augmented Instrument from a Performer's Perspective. In *Proceedings of the 6th Sound and Music Computing Conference SMC 2009,* Porto, Portugal (pp. 25-29).

Thompson, J., & Overholt, D. (2007). Sonofusion: Development of a multimedia composition for the overtone violin. In *Proceedings of the International Computer Music Conference ICMC 2007 International Computer Music Conference,* Copenhagen, Denmark (Vol. 2).

Verfaille, V. (2006). Adaptive Digital Audio Effects (A-DAFx): A new class of sound transformations. *IEEE Transactions on Audio, Speech and Language Proc., 14*(5), 1817–1831. doi:10.1109/TSA.2005.858531

Welch, P. (1967). The use of Fast Fourier Transform for the estimation of power spectra: A method based on time averaging over short, modified periodograms. *IEEE Transactions on Audio and Electroacoustics, AU-15,* 70–73. doi:10.1109/TAU.1967.1161901

Zölzer, U. (2002). *DAFx – Digital Audio Effects.* New York: John Wiley and Sons.

ENDNOTES

1. http://toddvanderlin.com/2009/04/ar-scratching/http://www.synthtopia.com/content/2009/04/28/augmented-reality-dj-scratching/

2. The ORA project participants were: Organ performer: Christophe d'Alessandro; Live electronics performer: Markus Noisternig; Video installation: Bertrand Planes; Audio design: Christophe d'Alessandro, Markus Noisternig, Sylvain Le Beux, Lorenzo Piccinali, Brian Katz, Nicolas Sturmel, Nathalie Delprat; Video design: Rami Ajaj and Christian Jacquemin. The Musical Works were compositions of F. Couperin, J.S Bach, C. Franck, O. Messiaen, C. d'Alessandro. Videos of the event can be found at http://www.youtube.com/watch?gl=FR&hl=fr&v=JlYVUtJsQRk or in higher resolution at the project site http://vida.limsi.fr/doku.php?id=wiki:orgue_augmentee_fr

3. http://vida.limsi.fr/doku.php?id=wiki:realite_augmentee_mobile_fr

4. In scientific articles, augmented instruments are often called hybrid instruments, hyper-instruments, or extended instruments.

5. http://virchor.sf.net

6. Inkscape is a vector graphic editor: http://www.inkscape.org

7. Since only few pipes are visible, the exact note of a pipe was not necessarily falling into the frequency band displayed on its surface.

This work was previously published in International Journal of Creative Interfaces and Computer Graphics, Volume 1, Issue 2, edited by Ben Falchuk, pp. 51-66, copyright 2010 by IGI Publishing (an imprint of IGI Global).

Section 2
Volume 2

Chapter 11
Line Drawings that Appear Unsharp

Hans Dehlinger
University of Kassel, Germany

ABSTRACT

A straight line, pen-drawn and executed on a pen-plotter, is by default sharp and crisp. This is the nature of a straight line between two points. Likewise, drawings generated from such lines are by definition sharp. This paper considers generative line drawings, executed on a pen-plotter which appears to be wholly or in part unsharp when viewed. Described here are some strategies based on systematic experiments with geometric transformations to produce such drawings. The topic is approached from an artist's point of view with a focus on the generative and algorithmic issues involved, and the results are demonstrated by examples.

INTRODUCTION

Walking on a windy evening in winter at twilight, all trees without leaves, the landscape almost entirely gray, and the scene dominated by lines. Lines are everywhere. But the images are soft, often with unsharp contours. Although in reality, all these images are crisp and sharp, we see them blurred and soft, their shadows even more so. Viewing such scenes creates a specific mood in the viewer and therefore it is not surprising that artists have recognized the particular and interesting characteristics of such situations, and have tried to devise techniques to generate those effects.

Although a line is by definition *sharp*, and it seems to be illogical to imagine it otherwise, we attempt the generation of line-oriented images that *appear unsharp* to the viewer. This is an artistic challenge, and we will approach it experimentally. Being interested in computer generated algorithmic work, we restrict our experiments to pen-drawn, line-oriented drawings, coded as

DOI: 10.4018/978-1-4666-0285-4.ch011

Figure 1. Two unsharp photographic images of part of a tree in winter, photographed under insufficient light and strong wind

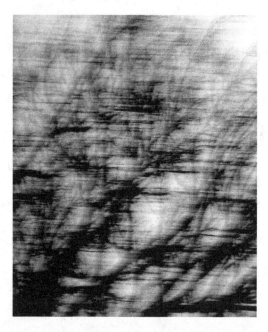 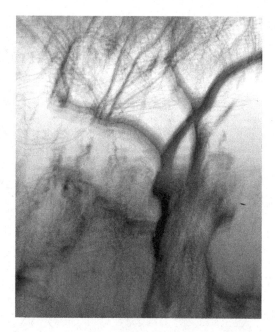

vectors and executed on pen-plotters. Such an unsharp line-drawing seems to be a contradiction in itself because it is composed of lines, which are always drawn as sharp and precise entities. In the light of such logic it is a particular challenge we try to achieve, and we follow this line of investigation out of artistic interest. In nature, due to conditions, unsharp images may be experienced in abundance. The two images in Figure 1, part of a tree photographed in insufficient light on a windy winter evening, and a willow tree, photographed under similar conditions may serve as examples. There is motion blur, transparency and gray-scaling, all contributing to the unsharp expression of the images. Unsharp images and images out of focus are known in contexts such as digital imagery, photography, painting, advertising, and science for example. When we talk about "unsharp vector-line-images", we always talk about images that *appear* unsharp. On close inspection their constituting entities, the lines are definitely sharp, as long as we view them under normal circumstances. The effect of "unsharpness"

is caused by insufficiencies of our perceptual systems to separate them properly, because of distance, interlacing, interferences and other factors. For the main topic of interest here – unsharp, line-oriented pen-drawn vector images, executed on pen-plotters – no algorithms formulated by computational experts are available, to the best of our knowledge. This is one of the reasons to choose an experimental approach, which seems justified as a beginning.

REMARKS ON THE PROBLEM

The systematic investigation of the problem in form of a sequence of experiments, carried out in 2009, can be seen as a follow-up on a few earlier attempts by the author: One of them exhibited at "intersections", the SIGGRAPH 2006 Art Show in Boston (http://www.siggraph.org/artdesign/gallery/S06/index.html), and others reported in Lieser (2009). The experiments were set up to systematically explore unsharp line drawings restricted to the rather narrow species of line-oriented, generative, pen-drawn, pen-plotter drawings. It is important to explicitly point to this restriction. Vector oriented data formats were widely in use in the first-generation of drawing-output-devices for which we have to count the pen-plotters we use to carry out the drawings. To generate drawings in vector-formats, instruction-commands are used to drive and control the movements of the pen on the plotter. Typically, to draw a line on such a plotter, instructions like *pen-up, pen-down,* and *move between x,y coordinate pairs* are executed. This generating code is strictly vector oriented and it is distinctly different from the pixel-oriented codes almost exclusively in use for image manipulation today. From an artist's point of view, the properties of a pen drawn line may just be what are wanted. And the resulting drawing may indeed be dramatically different from a pixel-based line-drawing. It may be of high aesthetic interest to be able to resort to a pen drawn vector line. Some artists from the Algorists Group (Beyls, 1988) actually insist to have it this way. The question posed here is: Can we generate drawings which *appear* to be unsharp or blurred, despite the sharp and crisp lines they are necessarily composed of? The question is justified, because blurred images are a particularly interesting class of images, and to generate or remove blur is a well researched field of study. Likewise, *unsharpness* as such is not a new phenomenon in art at all. We first will turn our attention to some of its appearances within this context.

UNSHARP IMAGES IN THE CONTEXT OF ART

In his 2004 treatise on the history of unsharpness, Ullrich refers to the painting *Las Hilanderas* by Diego Velásquez, dating from 1650, in which a spinning wheel in motion is depicted. Velázquez paints the inner part of the wheel unsharp in a sort of *motion blur* to indicate the movement.

Ullrich also notes that painters over centuries would definitely have had the technical ability and means to paint effects of unsharpness as we know them from photography, but they did not paint that way. Paintings were supposed to deliver sharp imagery throughout especially in the foreground. In situations where perspective depth and wide views were involved, for example in landscapes, we find unsharpness in form of the *sfumato*, perfected by Leonardo and his followers. Sfumato is a technique, by which contours are softened or blurred and appear like seen through a haze. It is applied to fuzzy-up objects and backgrounds. An example of an artist, who also made use of the concept of *unsharpness, is* William Turner (Joseph Mallord William Turner 1775 – 1851). In the younger history of art, unsharp images are found more frequently. Especially with the emergence of photography, unsharpness really became an artistic theme. In the beginning the shortcomings of equipment and processes led to unsharp images inevitably. But in due course and with those obstacles technically removed, unsharp or out-of-focus images were produced intentionally. And surprisingly early after photographic images appear on the scene, *unsharp images* intentionally made that way were presented. Examples are the soft photographic portraits of Julia Margaret Cameron (Gernsheim, 1975). Around 1890 unsharp-effects were quite popular, and it was considered naive to believe only a sharp photograph was a good photograph. An unsharp image in this sense is the result of a deliberate constructive effort by the artist. It is *designed* as unsharp to attract the attention of a viewer. By being *out of focus,* an irritation is caused, which the eye cannot resolve on the fly, and a second look is suggested. Unsharp images in photography can be achieved in numerous ways by manipulating the equipment, the film-material or the print. To deliver an unsharp image deliberately has also led to controversial debates in the scene on the legitimacy of such an approach as a valid picture-generation-process. Today, it seems, the pro unsharpness-faction among the photographers has decided this issue in its favor. Two recent photographers, using unsharpness as an artistic device, are Avedon (2009) and Sugimoto (1998), but there are many others too. A particular striking image is the 1962 portrait of dance teacher Killer Joe Piro (http://www.spaceagepop.com/piro.htm) by Richard Avedon. In contemporary painting, Gerhard Richter has used the concept of unsharpness widely in his photographic paintings, an example being his painting *Motor Boat* (Richter, 1965). But blur or fogginess in a wider sense is also found in Literature. We cite from *A Midsummer Night's Dream* by Shakespeare: "Or in the night, imagining some fear, how easy is a bush supposed a bear!" Induced by imagination and language, it appears a bush is turning into a bear.

UNSHARP LINE DRAWINGS

There are no *unsharp* line drawings, for obvious reasons. But can we generate them to *appear* unsharp? Finding out how is the motivation of the attempts presented here. Looking at Figure 1 again, we may hypothetically infer that slightly displaced copies of one and the same drawing, layered on top of each other may result in a new drawing that appears to be unsharp. This is our departure point for the experiments. It is fairly easy to make a copy of a program-generated drawing and subject this copy to various geometric transformations. Plain geometrical transformations like move, rotate, scale and shear are present in all image-processing systems. One of their main characteristics is their universal applicability, and we can readily use them in an experimental set-up. It does not matter in which data format an image is coded a scale or any other geometrical transformation is always applicable. In the photographs of Figure 1 each one of the "layers" has a different transparency, a feature difficult if not impossible to achieve with a pen-drawn line on a pen-plotter, especially when we make use of only one pen for

all the lines in a drawing. Transparency, as well as the fading gray-shades in Figure 1, are due to different exposure times on the film. They may also, and significantly so, be contributing to the blur, but we have to ignore them here. They cannot be achieved with a line.

Related Work

The transformation of images is a basic and important issue in image manipulation, and consequently, it is treated in an overwhelmingly large body of scholarly work from beginners (JH Labs, n. d.). to very sophisticated. We also have to recognize that there are plenty of methods and plenty of algorithms around the topic of blur in pixel based imagery. This also is an indicator that blurred images are interesting and that the problems around them have attracted many researchers. Besides the set of geometric transformations mentioned, we also know a large array of other transformations, and we usually find them packed into the *filters* of image manipulation application packages. Contrary to the first set, they are limited to operating on specific image-data-formats. To blur a pixel image, usually a frame, the *convolution kernel* is moved across the image, and each pixel within the kernel frame is changed according to an algorithm (example http://www.jhlabs.com/ip/blurring.html). To apply a blur algorithm to an image will require a pixel image. It makes no sense otherwise. Despite the large body of information available on pixel oriented imagery, it is of little relevance in the context of vector line images. We have to resort to other constructions to achieve the effects we want. There is another, quite different type of effect, which also renders line drawings to appear to be unsharp when viewed. It is known as Moiré effect (http://www.mathematik.com/Moire/), a visual irritation that occurs when viewing superimposed geometric line patterns where the lines differ slightly in angle, size, or spacing. The visual irritation is very similar to the effects we are trying to generate. But, instead of the strict geometrical patterns usually associated with Moiré effects, the drawings we are after use chaotic arrangements and controlled random processes (Dehlinger, 2004, 2007).

EXPERIMENTAL APPROACH

We first approach the problem with an experimental set-up. As a basic general assumption we use layers of one and the same drawing as suggested by the images in Figure 1. As for any scientifically valid experiment, we expect that the experiment is comprehensible, delivers measurable results, is repeatable and objective. Of course, this holds for art-experiments as well. Any experimentalist independent of location and time should obtain the same results. In each of the experiments, always *three layers* on top of each other have been used: the original drawing, and two distinctly transformed copies of the original drawing. The immediate question is of course: Why *three layers*? This decision was made for reasons of consistency and comparability in the experimental set-up, and as a measure of standardization. As for the transformations regarded suitable, the set of basic geometrical transformations (scale, move, rotate, and shear) have already been mentioned, and only they are used. We can apply them to entire drawings, parts of drawings or even a few singled out lines of drawings.

For the experiments we place one and the same drawing n x m times onto a virtual canvas. We can imagine this canvas as an n x m matrix, were each cell is occupied by one and the same drawing. And, conveniently, we will use matrix notation for the enumeration of drawings in cell-positions. If n = 1, and m = 1, we have one single drawing on our canvas. If n = 5, and m = 5, we have 25 identical drawings on our canvas. In each of the experiments the entire canvas is systematically subjected to transformations. It is important to remember that geometric transformations are applied relative to a point of origin. For a scaling

operation or a rotation, the point of reference for the transformation is by default assumed to be in the center of the canvas, but it can also be changed systematically to achieve other results.

We start with a first experiment on a single drawing, a 1 x 1 matrix. As in Figure 1, we use an image from nature: a tree-branch. But instead of using a photograph of the branch –a pixel image– we convert it to a line drawing fit for plotting on the pen-plotter. From left to right of Figure 2, we see the *converted drawing*, the *newly generated drawing,* and a close-up of a rectangular section as indicated. The new drawing is composed of three layers, the original and two slightly scale-reduced copies with scaling factors of 0.8 and 0.6 respectively. The point of reference for the transformations has been shifted to the bottom right corner of the drawing.

Viewing the center drawing of Figure 2 from a regular reading distance, it *appears* to be unsharp. Getting closer, or enlarging, as to the right, the effect disappears. Depending on the distance of viewing and some properties of layering, our visual system gets a *blur-like* impression from the vector-line-drawing on display.

In Figure 3, we place 25 identical drawings on a canvas of five by five meters. The entire canvas is systematically subjected to transformations and layering. On Figure 4, we see some of the results.

It is clearly visible that the experiments yield effects on the drawings which render them to *appear* unsharp. To systemize, we give the following sequence of operations which was carried out for each experiment.

1. Set up matrix M_1 with n x m identical drawings on a virtual canvas
2. Copy the entire matrix as C and keep it stored
3. Apply a geometrical transformation to C
4. Draw C, obtained in step 3, as an additional layer on top of M_1 and get as result M_2
5. *Apply a second geometrical transformation to C*

Figure 2. Vector-line drawing of a tree-branch. From left to right: A line-conversion from a digital photograph; three layers of the drawing - the conversion, and two slightly scale-reduced copies with scaling factors of 0.8 and 0.6; and a close-up. The bottom right corner is the point of reference for both scaling-transformations.

Figure 3. Identical images on a 5 x 5 matrix and a canvas size of 5 by 5 meters

Figure 4. Examples (4.1-4.8) of drawings from the matrix of Figure 3

6. Draw it on top of M_2 and get as a result M_3

7. Inspect M_3 for unsharp images and record their positions within the matrix

In successively numbered runs, the parameters for the transformations are changed systematically. The results are then inspected and unsharp drawings are identified. The decision on what to finally consider as *unsharp* has to be made as an *offhand, overall aesthetic judgment*, based on a seriatim inspection of the experimental results. The only relevant question in this context is: Have unsharp images been generated and in which position of the matrix are they located? An example of an experimental record is given in Table 2. In this particular experiment, only *scaling* was used as a transformation. A total of eight runs were carried out. In each run the same matrix of twenty-five drawings was transformed.

The generation of unsharp drawings on a penplotter is the sole interest of this experimental effort. As can be seen from Table 2, runs 1 to 4 did deliver unsharp images. Not so runs 5 to 8; they were unsuccessful attempts. Table 2 also shows that for the test drawing of this experiment, only very small differences in the two applied scaling operations were generating the desired results.

The center of scaling for the above experiment is located in the center of the matrix, and the displacements due to scaling will change for an image depending on its position in the matrix. The effects of the displacements will get stronger the farther away a drawing is located from the center. Examples of unsharp line drawing from the experiment recorded in Table 2 are displayed in Figure 5. If the displacements relative to a viewing distance are below the threshold of visual discrimination, the image may appear to be sharp despite being transformed. As an example, we point to a transformed drawing in Figure 6 of the matrix from Figure 1, which is taken from Pos. 3.3, the center of the matrix, and is not considered unsharp. A larger drawing using the settings from another experiment is shown in Figure 7.

ADDRESSING PARTITIONS

Besides subjecting an entire drawing to the transformations we may also choose to subject portions of a drawing to transformations. With his strategy a broader mix of transformations can be applied; either to a single drawing or to a matrix. The fol-

Table 1. Legend to Figures number 4.1 to 4.8 in Figure 3

Drawing ID E_BL M 5x5	run	1st transformation, scaling by a factor of	2nd transformation, scaling by a factor of	No. of unsharp images generated	Matrix positions for unsharp images
	1	100,3	99,8	12	*1.1; 1.2; 1.5; 2.1; 2.5; 3.1; 3.5; 4.1; 4.5; 5.1; 5.2; 5.3;*
	2	100,4	99,7	22	*all except 2.3; 3.3; 4.3*
	3	100,5	99,6	24	*all except 3.3*
	4	100.6	99,5	5	*2.3; 3.3; 4.1; 4.2; 4.3*
	5	101	99	1	*3.3*
	6	102	98	1	*3.3*
	7	103	97	1	*3.3*
	8	104	96	1	*3.3*

Figure 5. Examples of unsharp line drawing from the experiment recorded in Table 1. Left image: run_2_position_1.1; middle: run_4_position_2.3; right: run_4_position_4.1

Figure 6. Drawing with scaling factors of 1.003 / 0.997 from position 3.3 of a 5 x 5 matrix which is not considered to be unsharp

Table 2. Record of an experiment with 8 runs. Scaling is applied as transformation. The scaling factors are changed systematically from run to run. The resulting drawings have three layers: Original drawing, drawing resulting from 1st transformation, and drawing resulting from 2nd transformation

Num-ber	Matrix	Position in matrix	Transformations applied in order of execution
4.1	5 x 5	Pos. 3.3	Rotation by 1 degree, Rotation by 2 degrees
4.2	5 x 5	Pos. 4.3	Rotation 20°, Horizontal sheer 2, Horizontal sheer 4,Rotation by -20°
4.3	5 x 5	Pos. 5.4	Horizontal and vertical move by 1 cm, Rotation by -3.9°
4.4	5 x 5	Pos. 3.4	Rotation by 0.2°, Rotation by 0.6°
4.5	4 x 8	Pos. 5.2	Rotation by 1°, Rotation by 2°
4.6	5 x 5	Pos. 3.2	Rotation by 0.7°, Horizontal shear 3
4.7	5 x 5	Pos. 4.5	Scale 1.005, Scale 1.006
4.8	5 x 5	Pos. 3.2	Scale 1.005, Scale 0.996

Figure 7. Unsharp Drawing (2009), plotter-drawing, pencil on paper, 80 cm x 80 cm

lowing experiment is set up along this line. Three copies of the original were placed into the positions 1.4, 1.8, and 8.7 respectively of an 8 x 8 matrix on a virtual canvas of 500 x 500 cm. From each of the three drawings, a local partition, roughly indicated by the inscribed rectangle (top of Figure 8), was removed for separate treatment. The removed parts were different in size and boundary for each of the drawings. The matrix was subjected to a rotation of +0.3 degrees and to a second rotation of -0.3 degrees. The cut-outs were placed on a separate canvas in the same positions and subjected to a scaling transformation with a factor 0.99 and then to one of factor 1.003 respectively. Again, all the resulting drawings here are composed of the standard three layers: the original and two trans-formations. The bottom row of Figure 8 shows the reassembled drawings after the transformations have been applied to the separated parts.

ADDRESSING SINGLE LINES

Not only arbitrary regions of a drawing, but also in-dividual lines or groups of lines located anywhere in a drawing can be the target for transformations. With a strategy to address single line-elements in a drawing, we operate on a detail level, and a number of further and quite different possibilities for manipulations become available. For example, a rotate-transformation applied to a single line can mean: place the center for the rotation into the center of the line, into the starting point or the end point of the line, or place it into any other point. But also, and aside from the geometrical transformations used so far, an entire different class of manipulations becomes accessible which we may call *programmed transformations,* because they rely on the design of special programs and transform lines by physically changing them, as

Figure 8. Drawings with different transformations applied to parts of a drawing. In the top row the original drawing. In the bottom row the drawings resulting from positions 1.4, 1.8, and 8.7 of the 8 x 8 matrix

for example when adding short fractions of all sorts on or very close to a line. Such purposefully designed elements will make the line appear fuzzy in character to enhance the illusion of unsharpness. For an illustration of this strategy we turn to Figure 9 which shows photographic images taken from a pencil-plotter-drawing. We recall that all of the lines in the drawings are coded as vectors. Essentially, such a code is a list of character strings stored as an ASCII text file and it contains x,y coordinate-pairs, pen-up and pen-down commands. For further processing, the code strings can be easily manipulated by a suitable program. We can even use the search and replacement functions of a standard word processing system for such manipulations. The drawing displayed to the left of Figure 9 has been subjected to such a *programmed transformation*. The program was written to accept as an input file the x,y coordinates obtained from the code of the original drawing. The program successively changes a *line-object* of the original drawing, according to specified parameter settings, and produces as output a *fuzzy line-object*

for plotting. This new line-object is vector-based as well, but it is more "complicated" as a shape. Each one of the addressed lines is manipulated on the code level with the purpose to render it fuzzy, obscuring its sharp line-nature. The effect on the resulting drawing viewed from a proper distance relative to the size of the plotted image (which is 80 x 80 cm) *appears* to be unsharp.

A MEASURE OF UNSHARPNESS

One has to remember that there is no formal measure for *unsharpness*. Human vision is actually a complex matter, influenced by a number of factors like, but not limited to, the field of vision, concerned with the scope of what we see; the sensitivity to contrast which addresses the ability to distinguish objects at the same distance; and the perception of depth, which is the ability to judge the relative distance of objects. In ophthalmology, a normal visual acuity (http://webvision.med. utah.edu/book/part-viii-gabac-receptors/visual-

Figure 9. Fuzzy_1, pen-plotter drawing, pencil, 80 x 80 cm, 2009 (left), and a detail (right)

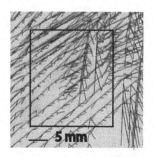

5 mm

acuity/) is usually defined according to Snellen (1862) and tested with a Snellen Chart (http://www.mdsupport.org/snellen.html). Two point-objects, or the gap *g* between two lines can be separated by the eye with what is known as the *minimum separabile* and is given by:

$$g = 2 * d * \tan(\partial/2) \qquad (1)$$

With *d* being the distance of viewing and ∂ the view-angle, which is approximately 1 minute of arc. At a distance of *3000 mm*, and with $\partial = 57$, we get:

$$g = 2 * 3000 * tan(1/114) = 0,918 \text{ mm}$$

In the *unsharp* drawings we want to generate, we are interested to control and predict the displacement of lines in a drawing due to transformations. For example, consider as a transformation a uniform scaling by a factor *s* relative to the center *C* of a drawing. A point *P* at distance *r* from the center will be displaced as *P′* at distance *r′* from *C:*

$r′ = r * s$ $s > 1$ will enlarge (move P′ away from C)

$s < 1$ will reduce (move P′ closer to C)

$|g| = |r′ - r|$

$$g = r * s - r \qquad (2)$$

Together with *(1)*

$$s = 1 + (2 * d * \tan(\partial/2)) / r \qquad (3)$$

The lowest threshold for scaling to deliver visually separable images depends on the limits of normal acuity, the distance *d* of viewing a drawing, and the size of the drawing as represented by *r*. Given a drawing size, represented by *r* and a scaling factor *s*, we can calculate the maximum distance d of viewing for which we barely will be able to separate two close lines. The density of the lines and the chaotic nature of their arrangements in the drawings involved may most likely demand a much smaller *d*. At any rate, with the above formulas, we can get an approximate range for predicting the effects we want to generate. For example, a drawing such as the one displayed in Figure 7 with a size of *800 x 800* mm, assuming *r = 400 mm*, viewed from a distance *d = 3000 mm* should according to *(3)* apply a scaling factor of at least *s = 1.002* to appear to be unsharp. This is in line with our experimental findings. In a matrix the images affected most by *s* are located in the corners of the canvas. Since we are operating on the lowest possible acuity-threshold, lines will barely be separable and tend to merge to deliver a gray shape instead. To generate the desired effects especially small transformation factors will have to be used. In addition and besides the effects generated by the transformations proper we will most likely encounter some Moiré effects as a wanted byproduct. The superimposition of line-patterns is one of the conditions for Moiré effects to occur. Since we use one and the same drawing for layering, a sort of "line pattern" may be present.

CONCLUSION

Generating fine-art line drawings on a pen-plotter that appear to be unsharp, despite being composed of crisp lines was experimentally tested using geometric transformations and layering. The experiments were cast into a rigid framework. For reasons of experimental consistency, and to proper compare and evaluate the effects generated by the transformations, the original drawing and two slightly different transformations of the original drawing where mapped onto each other. The results were drawn out on a pen-plotter with pencil. Transformations were applied globally, effecting an entire drawing, and locally, addressing a region of a drawing. For these two cases, only the geometric transformations scale, rotate, move, and shear have been applied. In addition, *programmed transformations* were designed to manipulate individual lines at the level of their codes. Unsharpness is caused by two factors: the limits of human vision to properly separate two closely located lines from a given distance, and, linked to this factor, the visual irritations caused by what is known as *Moiré effect*. The experiments showed that especially small displacements create the wanted effects, given a minimum viewing distance. As to our knowledge, the algorithmic generation of vector line based fine-art drawings that appear unsharp, has not been addressed by the literature.

REFERENCES

Art Cyclopedia. (n. d.). *Julia Margaret Cameron (British photographer, 1815-1879)*. Retrieved from http://www.artcyclopedia.com/artists/cameron_julia_margaret.html

Beyls, P. (1988). *The Algorists, historical notes by Roman Verostko*. Retrieved from http://www.verostko.com/algorist.html

Brostow, G. J., & Essa, I. (2001). Image-based motion blur for stop motion animation. In *Proceedings of the ACM 28th Annual Conference on Computer Graphics and Interactive Techniques* (pp. 107-116).

Cameron, M. (2008). *Introduction to the history of photography*. Retrieved from http://photographyhistory.blogspot.com/2008/01/julia-margaret-cameron.html

Dehlinger, H. (2004). *Zeichnungen*. Kassel, Germany: Kassel University Press.

Dehlinger, H. (2007). On fine art and generative line drawings. *Journal of Mathematics and the Arts, 1*(2), 97–111.

Gernsheim, H. (1975). *Julia Margaret Cameron: Her life and photographic work*. New York, NY: Millerton.

Hewlett-Packard Company. (1983). *Interfacing and programming manual, HP7475A graphics plotter*. San Diego, CA: Hewlett-Packard Company.

Labs, J. H. (n. d.). *Java imaging processing.* Retrieved from http://www.jhlabs.com/ip/blur-ring.html

Lieser, W. (2009). *Digital art.* Königswinter, Germany: H. Fullmann.

Olga's Gallery. (n. d.). *Joseph Mallor William Turner (1775-1851).* Retrieved from http://www. abcgallery.com/T/turner/turner.html

Snellen, H. (1862). *Probebuchstaben zur Betimmung der Sehschärfe.* Utrecht, The Netherlands: P. W. van de Weijer.

Sugimoto, H. (1998). *Architecture.* Retrieved from http://www.sugimotohiroshi.com/architecture.html

Ullrich, W. (2002). *Die Geschichte der Unschärfe.* Berlin, Germany: Wagenbach.

Wikipedia. (n. d.). *Julia Margaret Cameron.* Retrieved from http://de.wikipedia.org/wiki/Julia_Margaret_Cameron

This work was previously published in International Journal of Creative Interfaces and Computer Graphics, Volume 2, Issue 1, edited by Ben Falchuk, pp. 1-13, copyright 2010 by IGI Publishing (an imprint of IGI Global).

Chapter 12
Materials of the Data Map

Brian Evans
The University of Alabama, USA

ABSTRACT

Data mapping is the essence of being human. This report follows the process of data mapping; the transmission of a structured utterance from one domain to another. It starts with signals in the world and moves through experience and engagement with the world through those signals. The paper develops descriptions of the materials and mechanisms of data mapping. The descriptions are aids and conveniences in the effort to understand the systemic workings of the process of communication. From a systems perspective one might find points of leverage in their own involvement with the processes of communication and data mapping. Recognizing these leverage points can help in activities of art making, information design and in simply living.

INTRODUCTION

This paper is an artist statement of sorts, an informal excursion exploring the process of communication—tracing the passage of a message or signal from transmission to reception. Receiving messages is one half of living. Responding to messages is the other half. This paper concerns itself with the materials and mechanisms of the former. It offers and advances simple and useable definitions to help artists and designers as they develop and create their own messages. From an analytical perspective these ideas can become quite difficult to understand, but I believe that there is perhaps a less rigorous yet practical way to think about how we engage the world. The hope is to provide a "clear portrayal of the complexity" that is the process of data mapping, from our visualizations and sonifications of information to the more fundamental ways that we experience life (Tufte, 1983).

DOI: 10.4018/978-1-4666-0285-4.ch012

DATA MAPPING

Being human is data mapping and information processing—processes both basic and complex. Data mapping does two things to a signal.

1. A data map *abstracts* the signal. This abstraction accommodates mediation, fitting the format of the medium that will carry the signal.
2. Abstraction *reduces* the content of the signal and reduces the amount of data carried in the signal, facilitating its transference and possibly its eventual comprehension when received further along the signal path.

Each medium is itself mediated, again abstracting and reducing a signal. Sound for example starts as a vibrating object. Vibrations are transduced into changing pressure moving through the medium of air. That energy is transduced again into the tension of the eardrum, carried as mechanical energy by the ossicles of the inner ear, which is mediated through the cochlear fluid into the complexities of the auditory nerve and the brain. Often signals are abstracted into many maps in parallel, which we then receive synchronously—hearing and seeing for example. A signal that is simultaneously seen and heard (perhaps also felt and smelt) is a common example and a daily experience for all of us. By the time we receive signals from the world we are far removed from the source of the transmissions. All we receive are shadows, abstractions, maps of data being sent across the distances between us and the real we are immersed in. The signal loss over these distances is immense, yet miraculously communication still occurs.

To begin this excursion some informal definitions will help. What follows are some lists, some charts, some conveniences that are themselves maps of how we wade in the ebb and flow of the ocean of information surrounding us. Processing this information is the essence of being alive.

THE INFORMATION FOOD CHAIN

The terms data, information and knowledge are often used erroneously as synonyms. Their use in this paper has them situated in a dependent relationship similar to organisms on a food chain (Figure 1). The discussion begins at the base of the chain where no signal exists. Here there is unfocused energy and the promise of a signal—noise.

Noise

Noise is the primitive, the base upon which everything depends. Without noise there is nothing. Noise is the fundamental utterance of difference. *It manifests as randomness.* For example, in audio synthesis noise is simply created by mapping a sequence of random numbers into amplitude, as seen in Figure 2 (Dodge & Jerse, 1985). We essentially hear all frequencies at once. If this sequence changes at rates within the audio spectrum the sound is a rumble or hiss, perhaps the "shhh" of the ocean or the rustling of leaves. Some believe this will be the sound of the universe at the end, at maximum entropy. The visual equivalent is usually described as white light, the seeing of all frequencies of the visible spectrum at once. Perhaps a more accurate equivalent might be the snow we see on a TV screen that has no signal, which would average out to gray light (Figure 3).

Noise is essentially a non-signal (but not nothing) that is always different so paradoxically always the same. The most important thing to understand about noise is that, if measured, at any given moment its value is random. Difference is constant. There is no relationship between any two values from one instant to the next. From the ground of noise as defined here we move up the chain to data.

Data

Data then is what noise is not. Data is the opposite of constant difference. It brings in sameness

Figure 1. The information food chain. New knowledge can change the context for data, thus changing the information, thus creating new knowledge (an ongoing feedback loop).

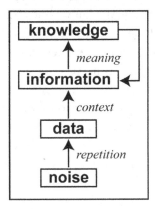

Figure 2. A graph of a white noise audio signal in the time domain—amplitude on the y-axis (randomly changing) and time on the x-axis

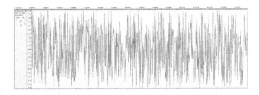

Figure 3. White noise from randomly colored pixels that will visually average to gray. The insert shows a magnification of a small square of pixels from the image.

or *repetition*. Data is a signal with structure. Without repetition there is no structure. There are an infinite number of ways that aspects of a signal can repeat. Many are subtle. But if there is no repetition then each instant of an utterance is random and thus noise.

In a binary world we see the difference between tossing a true coin (heads or tails, zero or one) or tossing a weighted coin. With the true coin each toss is random and there is no structure. If one side is weighted or favored then we will have some repetition and a pattern will emerge—noise has becomes data. Another paradox here is that repetition establishes a difference that stands out from the noise (the random ground of constant difference). Consider the SETI project listening to the vast universe of difference that is cosmic noise, searching for a signal, a structured utterance—seeking to "find constant or slowly pulsed [repeating] carrier signals, something like a flute tone against the noise of a waterfall" (http://www.seti.org).

Usually it is data that is mediated along a signal path. Data manifests in various ways. In a digital space it is simply on and off coded as the binary 0 and 1 (Petzold, 2000). Action potentials in the neuronal networks of our brain are data too, manifested as the electro-chemical spikes that move through those networks. It is data, abstracted (and encoded) the moves most efficiently along a signal path.

Information

Information is where a signal becomes useful for us. Data, a structured utterance, becomes information when it situates within a *context*. Consider for example the binary information stored on the hard drive of a computer. If we have a tool that will allow us to look at the data we can see the structure there. We will see a pattern in the zeros and ones. While we may see structure in the data there is no useful content until we put the data into a context. Before a context is established, data from a digital audio file or an image will look pretty much the same. If we open the data in iTunes it becomes audio information and we can hear it. If we open the data in Photoshop it becomes a visual image.

It is here at the stage of information, when we process data within a context that we begin to understand something such that we might choose to respond. Data must sit within a context and become information before we can do anything useful with it. Abstract data can be mapped into many contexts. This is a point of leverage and the basis of visualization and sonification in information design and in digital art.

"In a digital space we have data abstracted to number. Number can then map into a variety of outputs. The number 255 can represent a saturated red, heard as middle C, or both simultaneously! Thus any image can be heard, any sound can be seen. Here we find the true power of mathematical abstraction, and a way to integrate the visual arts and music. Using digital technology to map (or re-map) mathematical descriptions or numerical models, we can bridge music and visual art. We can see Beethoven's Ode to Joy. We can hear Monet's Water Lilies. Once visual art and music are reduced to number they are the same. A digital synaesthesia occurs. With our ability to map numbers as we please mathematics becomes a metaphoric language from which we can create poetry" (Evans, 2005).

Knowledge

Knowledge results from learning, when information is stored in our brain and made available for use in either short or long term memory. *We metabolize information into knowledge from the catalyst of meaning.* When information has value for us we store it. We remember it. There are evolutionary mechanisms at the base of this process, unfolding from instincts for survival and the genetic mechanisms of fear and pleasure (Zull, 2002). During our development as individuals, and as a species, the processes of valuation and meaning have become quite complex. These processes are the core of much of what we call culture.

A key thing here is the difference between teaching and learning. Teachers pass on information while trying to make it meaningful for the student. It is the student that learns—the student alone converts information into knowledge. Knowledge is personal. It cannot be shared. That new knowledge can now be used in the construction of future knowledge. This is an important thing to consider as *all knowledge is built on prior knowledge.*

HOW WE READ THE WORLD (THE EXPERIENTIAL CHAIN)

Again there are some terms here that are frequently used erroneously as synonyms—sensation, perception and cognition. These processes are different, individual links along the experiential chain (Figure 4). They engage data, information and knowledge at different stages of a signal transmission. Here too are some conveniences for thinking about the mechanisms of information processing in life and specifically the process of data mapping.

Reality—What is There

First and foremost is reality—what is really out there. It is crucial to understand that we cannot wholly know what is out there. (This is not just a philosophical stance it is a fact.) Energy from our world enters our bodies through our senses. We are removed from that energy in both space and time. We are always and forever experiencing the past not the present, and the 'there' not the 'here'. We experience signals once removed from the source, abstracted and mediated through the physical soup in which we exist. These mediated

Figure 4. The experiential chain. Note the similarity to the structure of the information food chain. Our concepts can change our perceptions, which can change our concepts (another ongoing feedback loop). The distances cover what 'is' (the ontological), to what we believe is (the epistemological, the foundation of knowledge building), to the connections (interpretations, the hermeneutic) that are the materials of knowledge and the basis of our actions.

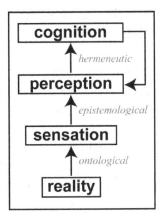

signals are further abstracted and reduced by the mechanisms of our bodies. (Here we see again the idea that a medium is itself mediated.)

Sensation—What We See

Our senses are our first stage of data mapping. Reality transmits signals via various substances or media. These transmissions are abstractions of the source. (Just as *any* signal we transmit is an abstraction/reduction of who we are.) Information from a reality source is reduced/abstracted to data that accommodates the medium of transmission. If that mediated data falls within the limits of our senses then we can receive the data and map it into a form that we can use. For example, when objects move in our atmosphere the pressure of air molecules around those objects changes in response to that movement. The changing air pressure is *not* the motion of the object. The changing air pressure is an analog, a model, a mapping of the

motion of the object. The object and its motion are already displaced in space and time from the map of changing air pressure. All we have is the trace, the index of the motion moving through the air.

If that motion is close to us, is of sufficient amplitude, and occurs at a rate of vibration between 20 and 20,000 cycles per second our eardrums will respond to the vibration manifested as the acoustic energy of changing air pressure. From the eardrum the energy is converted into electrochemical energy through various mechanisms and is eventually transmitted over the auditory nerve to the brain. The thalamus in the brain is a key step on the signal path, functioning as a relay from the senses to the cerebral cortex (Carter, 2009). In the cortex the data is contextualized.

Perception—What We Think We See

From the thalamus sensory signals are distributed throughout the brain (primarily the cortex) for further processing. Visual sensory information, for example, is divided across many layers of the cortical brain for processing. Our older brain (on the evolutionary scale) processes "where" information such as motion, depth and position, while our higher, newer brain processes "what" information such as object recognition, color and faces (Livingstone, 2002). At the perceptual level information is processed unconsciously and automatically. We also create schema or preconceptions (perceptions) about the world. These schema filter our responses to the signals coming in. Sometimes these schema are not accurate, but they still impact how we perceive the world.

Consider that perspective drawing was developed in the 15th century. How was it that it took so long for Western civilization to realize that visual distance does not equal actual distance? (Kemp, 1990). What we actually see is a wall getting shorter from base to roof as it gets further away, but we know (or assume) it is the same height in physical space so we think we see them as parallel Based on that perception we draw the walls as parallel lines. The essence of learning to draw is "learning to see"—understanding and traversing the divide between sensation and perception. "This tendency to form schematic representations [what we think we see] appears to interfere with our ability to draw, and by inference, to see what in fact may be there to be seen. Only when one takes deliberate steps to bypass or otherwise disconnect this tendency…does the true nature of the subject emerge" (Hoffman, 1989).

Cognition—What We Think About What We Think We See

Cognitive science and neuroscience are developing a growing understanding of how we think.

"The mind is inherently embodied.

Thought is mostly unconscious.

Abstract concepts are largely metaphorical.

These are the three major findings of cognitive science. More than two millennia of a priori philosophical speculation about these aspects are over. Because of these discoveries, philosophy can never be the same again" (Lakoff & Johnson, 1999).

We construct our cognitive reality out of the sensations we record, matched against the networks of connections (knowledge) we have stored in our memories. Our knowledge impacts how the new sensory information is perceived, and as the pattern matching continues, abstraction of patterns continues and the mapping goes deeper into our neuronal networks. We can begin to reason based on these metaphoric matches—we conceptualize.

We desire, fueled by the instinct to survive, and so we make predictions and we act based on those predictions. "Pain and pleasure are the levers the organism requires for instinctual and acquired strategies to operate efficiently. In all probability they were also the levers that controlled the de-

velopment of social decision-making strategies" (Domasio, 1994). Pattern matching, reasoning and predicting define our interpretations of the present in relation to the past (what we know) and the future (what we predict). Those conceptual metaphors, those pattern matches are data maps. They are the devices of our desire and the drivers of our actions.

BRIDGING THE DISTANCES (NAVIGATING INTENTION)

Now we are at the core of the data map, as we move from one process to another the signal must be reduced, abstracted and mapped. For example electro-magnetic energy in the real world hits the retina of our eye where a small subset of the spectrum is sensed, transduced (mapped from one form of energy into another) and sent over the optic nerve to the brain (again mostly to the thalamus where signals are divided and dispatched for further processing). The familiar signal path starts in reality, is mediated into energy mapped into sensation, which is mediated into energy mapped into perception. Human experience is a constant navigation across these mediations—distances traversed on the vehicle of the data map. Also along the entire signal path there is noise in each stage of the transmission—noise from the physical imperfections of our senses and from the chemical, biological and psychological imperfections of our bodies and our brains. Curiously, in many ways, it is this noise that defines us as individuals and makes life interesting.

The Ontological Distance (Reality→Sensation)

This is the divide between what is and what we can actually experience—from reality to sensation. We are at the mercies of our bodies (of which the brain is a part). We are not able to receive reality complete and in toto. We can only receive the abstracted subset of signals to which our senses respond. The reduction of data here is dramatic—from the infinite information around us to the small finite subset that is processed by our limited, highly restricted senses! And, constrained by the laws of physics, we can only experience our embodied responses to what exists outside our bodies and across the nerve pathways within our bodies. Those signals take time to travel to us and through us; hence we can only receive what occurred in the past.

The Epistemological Distance (Sensation→Perception)

This is the divide between what we sense and what we will eventually process as information and metabolize as knowledge—from sensation to perception. The gap between what we see and what we think we see is large. This distance involves genetic and cultural factors. Habituation for example is hardwired, allowing us to dismiss signals that are constant and understood to not be a threat to our survival. Imagine a mechanical clock in your living room. In a matter of minutes you no longer hear the tick-tock of its gears and pendulum. You eardrum is still responding, still sensing the signal, but your perceptions have filtered it out such that you no longer hear it.

The Hermeneutic Distance (Perception→Cognition)

Here is where we bridge perception and cognition. We begin in earnest to connect the new information to what we already know. We *interpret* our new perceptions within the network of neural connections and the glial landscape of cells that comprise the material basis of who we are (Edelman, 2007; Fields, 2009). We make connections, matching the patterns in a perceived signal to patterns stored as synaptic connections in our short and long-term memories (Kandel, 2006).

The conceptual domain (the firing neuronal connections in our brain) is a substrate of meaning allowing the new signal ("the strange") to be understood in the context of the known ("the familiar"). New synapses form in the brain connecting the new to the old. Knowledge is constructed. The steps of data mapping from sensation to the new cognitive connections formed in our neural networks are the means of that construction. Each step is a metaphor—an analogy accomplished with an abstraction that allows an association, a pattern match from one conceptual domain to another.

THE METAPHORIC LOOP

Maps are metaphors and metaphors are the basis of the construction of knowledge (Lakoff & Johnson, 1980). As all knowledge builds on prior knowledge, metaphor is the glue that connects and binds the known to the new. The mechanism of the metaphor is a process of association, a constant loop of compare and contrast of the old and the new, the familiar and the strange. When metaphor is a mapping across conceptual domains it is possible to reason about one domain from knowledge of the other.

For example I can reason about an emotional space based on my embodied understanding of physical space. I understand 'in' as the experience of being physically contained, such as 'in' a room. I have physically, with my body, experienced 'in'. I also physically experienced and know that I can exit and get outside the room that I am 'in'. My friend says he is "in a bad mood." This is a metaphor that maps an emotional space into a known experience of physical space. I can reason from the mapping of emotional space to physical space that he might be able to exit the emotional space he is 'in', and so hopefully the bad mood is temporary. The map provides a mechanism for reasoning from my embodied knowledge to an understanding my friends current emotional state, to predicting his future state (Johnson, 2007).

The Loop

A Metaphor is a pattern match found between conceptually unlike things. It manifests as a loop of desire that is the essence of being cognitively alive. It parallels our more basic desires for food, and sleep (Evans, 2009). Our survival instincts have us scanning our environment in search of difference. If something changes it might be a threat to survival (fear) or enhance survival (pleasure). We compare and contrast signals coming in to signals stored, looking for a pattern match. If there is no match then the incoming signal is new and strange. We need to know and so search more deeply for a match. Some dimension of the new must match something in memory or we cannot know the new. The search for knowledge is ongoing—a constant process of neural computation—a continual search for "*a best match* between the [sensory] inputs and current brain state" (Feldman, 2006). Desire to know the new is strong. Our survival might depend on it. Life is the constant processing of our surroundings in support of this desire.

"The relation between what we see and what we know is never settled" (Berger 1972). This is a relation of the strange and the familiar—the loop of creativity (manifested as innovation) and learning (Figure 5).

Figure 5. The metaphoric loop of learning (new knowledge from new information) and creating (new knowledge from known information)(Gordon, 1961)

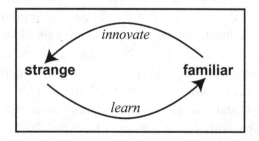

Learning

The tension inherent in desire is a motivation for learning. A fundamental mechanism for learning is analogic thinking through metaphor. "In regards to cognition analogy is everything" (Hofstadter, 2001). All knowledge builds on prior knowledge though the pattern match of conceptual metaphor. New information enters the system and is understood in relation to the already known. The strange is connected, compared and contrasted with the familiar (Gordon, 1961).

Creativity

Creativity is also a process in the metaphoric loop, but here new connections are found within the already known. What is required is seeing the known in new ways—making the strange familiar. In developing "the creative habit… Metaphor is the lifeblood of all art, if it is not art itself" (Tharp, 2003).

THE STRUCTURES OF CONNECTION

Recent research in network structure provides insights into the mechanisms of connection and communication, and also can help us to understand them as a system. Recognizing points of leverage in the system brings an ability to enhance and foster the key components of the system—learning and creativity. Of specific interest are the traces of signals through our neuronal networks that are the materials of cognition. Conceptual metaphors are the key connectors at the cognitive level. How is it that metaphor is such a powerful tool in our engagement with the world? An understanding of network structures can help answer the question. The following network structures provide simple models that can serve as maps of information flows (Newman, Barabási, & Watts, 2006).

Clustered Networks (High Structure/Low Communication)

Figure 6 is an illustration of a clustered graph or network. The figure shows a network of one hundred agents or nodes, with each node connected to its four closest neighbors. A cluster shows a high structure of repetition as each node has many nodes in common with each linked neighbor. The clustered nodes could represent a close circle of friends or perhaps a group of wired neurons. What the graph shows is that while clusters are tightly structured, information does not flow through the network very effectively. To move a signal from the source node (#0) to the target node farthest away from the source (#50), will take at minimum twenty-five steps.

Random Networks (Low Structure/ High Communication)

Figure 7 is an illustration of a random network, with properties that are exactly opposite those of a clustered network. Here each node is *randomly* linked to four other nodes. Linked neighbors will rarely have other nodes in common. Signals will move through this network with little coherence, but will traverse the network quickly as it is highly connected.

Small-World Networks (High Structure / High Communication)

A small-world network is one that is clustered and so highly structured, with just a small amount of randomness (Watts & Strogatz, 1998). Figure 8 is an illustration of a small-

Figure 6. Graph of a100 node clustered network, showing the 25 steps needed to traverse the network from the source to the target. Clustered networks are highly structured but poorly connected

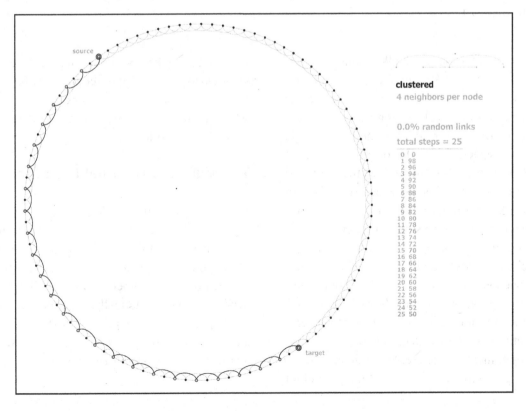

Figure 7. Graph of a 100 node random network, showing the 3 steps needed to traverse the network from the source to the target. Random networks are not very structured but highly connected.

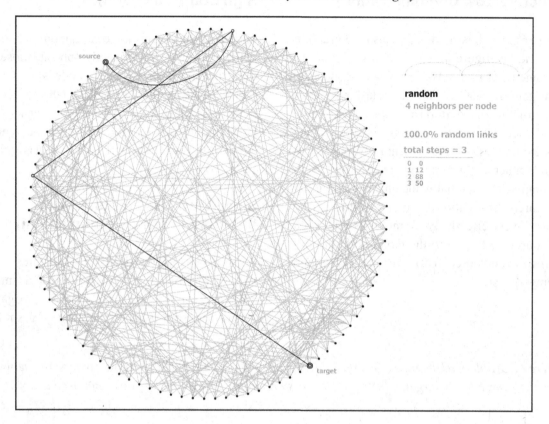

world network, based on the Watts and Strogatz model, with just 5% randomness in the links. Note that the network is nearly as effective as the random network in regards to moving a signal quickly through the network while nearly as structured as the original clustered graph. Evidence is growing that the neuronal networks of our brains are structured this way (Bassett & Bullmore, 2006). While most linking is clustered there are a small number of seemingly random connections as well.

Hebb's law states that "cells that fire together wire together" (LeDoux, 2002). Our brain's network is built on associations. Some associations have the appearance of randomness. However a connection is a pattern match. Pattern match means repetition, means structure. Some times what is repeating might be subtle, seemingly random

when out of context. When two neurons are firing simultaneously a synaptic connection begins to form—two nodes of a network are linked and some essence of structure is recorded for later recall. The brain learns.

The Multi-Dimensional Utterance

A conceptual point on a picture plane requires at least six values to define it—the x,y coordinates of the diagonal of the plane and the x,y location of the point on the plane. If we are describing a visible point the number of defining dimensions needed grows dramatically. At a minimum we must specify color, shape, size, texture, location and so forth. *Any utterance is an expression in many, many quantifiable dimensions.*

Figure 8. Graph of a 100 node small-world network with 5% random links. This graph needs only 5 steps to traverse the network from the source to the target. This is an illustration of the unique nature of small-world networks, highly structured and highly connected

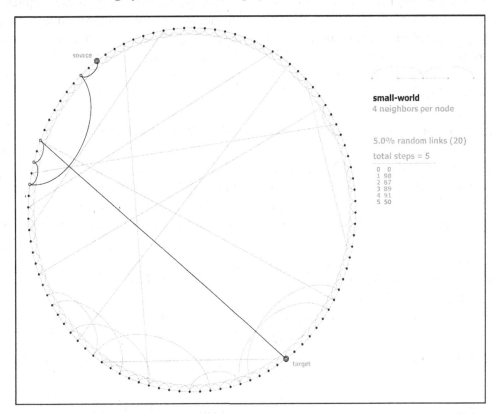

As sensory information continues along the signal path any and all of the dimensions are potentially abstracted and they then traverse that path in parallel, eventually spreading through the dense networks in the brain. Any single dimension or combination of dimensions might fire another network of connections based on pattern matches. Maybe the color of the point is the color of a rose. Maybe it is egg-shaped, the size of a pinhead, a golf ball. Maybe it's rough like sandpaper, situated next to a similar point, but two inches to the right. Any one of the associations will set off their own unique set of neuronal connections.

Pattern matches are repetition hence they are structure. Patterns, dimensions, attributes, qualities, they are all mapped, as they are all processed along the experiential chain. They make other connections and other matches, which make more connections and more matches in the deeply recursive poetry that is the constant flow of human individual consciousness.

Metaphor as Connection and the Mechanism of Creativity

The human brain is made up of billions of neurons and trillions of synaptic connections (Edelman, 1992). We see in the structure of the small-world network the power of the metaphor as an efficient way to move signals through those trillions of connections in new configurations, showing us new ways to think about what we know. The "leap of intuition" the "aha moment" can be seen to be random links in our mostly clustered and highly structured brains.

A primary means through which we can reason and through which we can imagine. A new idea is a neuronal circuit that we may not have noticed before (a forgotten memory, a weak link) or in our plastic brains a newly grown synaptic connection.

A pattern match fires through new or newly discovered circuits of neurons such that we attend to old knowledge in new ways or use new data to make new knowledge. As circuits fire the connections get stronger, firing more easily the next time. Eventually the wiring joins the cluster as part of the structured brain, no longer strange. New pattern matches or other forgotten memories continue to occur. These new associations, seemingly random links (to the clustered brain) empower us again to tap our creative potentials. The effectiveness of the small-world structure continues as long as we embrace the new and learn. Association, manifested within this small-world substrate, is recognized as an effective model of how we think and especially the neural process of "cognitive insight"—creativity (Schiller, 2005).

CONCLUSION

This brief excursion along the communication path shows the significance of abstraction and connection. These are the basis of the data map. Maps are metaphors and they provide a repetition of generalized aspects of an utterance across conceptual space. This repetition protects us from the phenomenological chaos around us. We are accosted by infinite amounts of data and information—way more that we can possibly process. Along the experiential chain what is useable for us in understanding the moment is a reduction and abstraction sent forward along the signal paths. We must make sense of things to function as living beings. Our sanity and survival depend on it.

A data map, manifested as a rich metaphor can enhance that process. We map the abstraction back into a sensory experience, making new metaphors and new maps. We make images. We make sounds.

It is a constant process of feedback. Sometimes the feedback is loud and clear and necessary to make quick decisions or to excite quick action. Sometimes we see a more subtle mapping. We recognize the poetry of our existence as we find the resonances and understand the responsibilities we share with everyone and everything around us.

ACKNOWLEDGMENT

This work is done with the project support of the US National Science Foundation (award IIS 1002758) and the Leadership Board of the College of Arts and Sciences, The University of Alabama.

REFERENCES

Bassett, D. M., & Bullmore, E. (2006). Small-world brain networks. *The Neuroscientist, 12*(6).

Berger, T. (1972). *Ways of seeing* (p. 7). London, UK: Penguin Books.

Carter, R. (2009). *The human brain book*. New York, NY: Darling Kindersley.

Damasio, A. (1994). *Descartes error, emotion, reason and the human brain*. New York, NY: Penguin Press.

Dodge, C., & Jerse, T. A. (1985). *Computer music* (pp. 86–88). New York, NY: Schirmer Books.

Edelman, G. M. (1992). *Bright air, brilliant fire: On the matter of the mind* (pp. 16–30). New York, NY: Basic Books.

Edelman, G. M. (2007). *Second nature: Brain science and human knowledge* (p. 262). New Haven, CT: Yale University Press.

Evans, B. (2005, June). Numbers to neurons: Digital synaesthesia. In *Proceedings of the Art+Math=X Conference*, Boulder, CO.

Evans, B. (2009). Loop theory. *Wig: Journal of Experimental Scholarship, 1*(1).

Feldman, J. A. (2006). *From molecule to metaphor: A neural theory of language* (p. 5). Cambridge, MA: MIT Press.

Fields, R. D. (2009). *The other brain: From dementia to schizophrenia, how new discoveries about the brain are revolutionizing medicine and science*. New York, NY: Simon & Schuster.

Gordon, W. J. J. (1961). *Synectics* (pp. 33–37). New York, NY: Harper & Row.

Hoffman, H. S. (1989). *Vision and the art of drawing*. Upper Saddle River, NJ: Prentice Hall.

Hofstadter, D. (2001). Epilogue: Analogy as the core of cognition. In Gentner, D., Holyoak, K. J., & Kokinov, B. N. (Eds.), *The analogical mind: Perspectives from cognitive science* (pp. 499–538). Cambridge, MA: MIT Press.

Johnson, M. (2007). *The meaning of the body: Aesthetics of human understanding*. Chicago, IL: University of Chicago Press.

Kandel, E. R. (2006). *In search of memory: The emergence of a new science of mind*. New York, NY: W. W. Norton & Company.

Kemp, H. S. (1990). *The science of art*. New Haven, CT: Yale University Press.

Lakoff, G., & Johnson, M. (1980). *Metaphors we live by*. Chicago, IL: University of Chicago Press.

Lakoff, G., & Johnson, M. (1999). *Philosophy in the flesh: The embodied mind and its challenge to western thought*. New York, NY: Basic Books.

LeDoux, J. (2002). *The synaptic self: How our brains become who we are*. New York, NY: Penguin Books.

Livingstone, M. (2002). *Vision and art: The biology of seeing*. New York, NY: Harry N. Abrams.

Newman, M., Barabási, A.-L., & Watts, D. J. (Eds.). (2006). *The structure and dynamics of networks*. Princeton, NJ: Princeton University Press.

Petzold, C. (2000). *Code: The hidden language of computer hardware and software*. Redmond, WA: Microsoft Press.

Schilling, M. A. (2005). A 'small-world' network model of cognitive insight. *Creativity Research Journal, 17*(2-3), 131–154.

Tharp, T. (2003). *The creative habit: Learn it and use it for life* (p. 64). New York, NY: Simon & Schuster: The SETI Institute. (n. d.). *FAQ*. Retrieved from http://www.seti.org/Page.aspx?pid=558

Tufte, E. (1983). *The visual display of quantitative information*. Cheshire, CT: Graphic Press.

Watts, D. J., & Strogatz, S. H. (1998). Collective dynamics of 'small-world' networks. *Nature, 393*, 440–442.

Zull, J. (2002). *The art of changing the brain* (pp. 47–69). Sterling, VA: Stylus Publishing.

This work was previously published in International Journal of Creative Interfaces and Computer Graphics, Volume 2, Issue 1, edited by Ben Falchuk, pp. 14-26, copyright 2010 by IGI Publishing (an imprint of IGI Global).

Chapter 13
Digital Images:
Interaction and Production

Linda Matthews
University of Technology, Sydney, Australia

Gavin Perin
University of Technology, Sydney, Australia

ABSTRACT

The valence of any visual paradigm and its accompanying technologies is subject to the contingencies of political regimes and cultural shifts. The instigation, implementation and even reconfiguring of any associated technological system effects a translation and adjustment to the structure and use of these supporting mechanisms that both re-defines the relationship between object and viewer and ultimately influences its translation into material form. The permeation of digital systems throughout contemporary urban space is typified by Internet Protocol webcam systems, instigated by civic authorities for surveillance and the imagistic promotion of iconic city form. This paper examines how this system's reception and subsequent translation of transmitted data signals into digital information not only presents new material to mediate people's engagement with public space, but moreover, how it presents new opportunities for the designer to materialize its three-dimensional form within the spatial ambiguity of virtual and real-time environments.

INTRODUCTION

The visuality regimes that work to compose the contemporary paradigm are both numerous and, above all, highly competitive. According to Jay (1988) this is a desirable and, more importantly,

DOI: 10.4018/978-1-4666-0285-4.ch013

a productive condition which presents opportunities to shape the ways in which landscape and its habitable space are mediated to the viewer via constantly evolving technologies.

In light of this, the ubiquitous implementation of the webcam network within contemporary urban environments is a technology that mediates the city image to the public domain to support diverse but simultaneously occurring subcultures. This system is traditionally a surveillance mechanism instigated by civic authorities as a response to the spatial complexity of the modern city and its inability to be observed from a single vantage point. However, the distinction here is, unlike the panoptic scheme devised by Bentham (1995), the technological transportability of the image facilitated by the Internet Protocol network allows captured 'content' to re-enter public space rather than remain the property of a privileged minority.

Furthermore, the implementation of these high volume data networks has overridden the former limitations of closed circuit surveillance systems and extended the reach of their remote capacities into the area of urban tourism. Recent observations reveal that authorities strategically site network cameras as imagistic purveyors of significant city sights. In this new dual role, these pervasive digital systems are able to provide a new privileged, albeit highly orchestrated, vantage point from which the 'remote' tourist is able to view the city landscape.

However, the most important and enriching aspect of this type of visual regime is contingent upon the very diversification of its systemic architecture: upon the reflexive capacity of webcam technology which offers viewers an opportunity to adapt and mediate their visual experience of the urban environment, and also upon aspects of its operation which can be exploited by the designer to materialize three-dimensional form.

This paper, therefore, will discuss how the webcam's conversion of the actual into the virtual provides an engagement with urban space that is both qualitative and experiential. The disruption of the regulatory control of the webcam images opens a space for productive engagement with the making of city images that both exceeds the intention to privilege sanctioned forms and to render stable representations of the urban landscape.

Also it will discuss how the technologies of the virtual can provoke a springboard from which to intervene within this landscape, and more impor-tantly, it will show how the geometry instigated by the camera governs this intervention. With specific focus on the productive exploitation of specific aspects of translational camera hardware: the re-arrangement of the colour filter array pat-terns located within colour sensor mechanism and the adaptation of aberrant diffraction effects, the paper will reveal how their potential incorpora-tion into design composition can have a material effect upon urban form. The outcomes of tests outlined in this paper thus initiate just some of a potentially diverse range of new opportunities for the composition of a dynamic and diverse urban space.

IMAGING SPACE

Politics and Image-Making

The right to select projective images of the city is underscored by the same type of highly determined and politically sanctioned power structures that have always governed this type of representation. Both Louis Marin in his book, *Utopics: Spatial play*, (1984) and and W.J.T Mitchell in his essay, *Imperial Landscapes*, (2002) establish how control of the production and dissemination of representa-tions of landscape, both 'natural' and urban, can be deliberately exploited to achieve control of that space. For Marin, this notion is predicated not only upon the prohibitive expense of manufacturing the city portrait or map, but to an even greater extent upon the fact that the framing of the city view is always dependent upon the acquiescence of those who control the viewpoint. Possession is not the same as access, and in this type of scenario, one might indeed occupy the space but is in no way empowered to curate or alter the view. However, the most important issue here is that in both cases the exercise of political control gained through the 'right' to image inhabitable space is linked to the control and propagation of these socially sanctioned images

However, in contemporary environments, the advent of digital image fabrication technology has meant that both the capacity and the entitlement for imaging space have been extended beyond the civic power brokers to the individual. The recent implementation of network cameras for the promotion of tourism instigates a performative role for this system as a propagandising tool not only to the real but also to the virtual tourist. This new role also imbues such sites with a visibility that potentially overrides the traditional physical considerations involved in the making of city form by creating new prime 'marketable' sites. Sites such as Earthcam (http://www.earthcam.com/), a global network of live webcams, comprise an exhaustive search engine of internet cameras offering an equally extensive range of urban, natural or domestic views to engage the remote viewer.

At this point it is important to define the types of camera technologies that comprise the webcam network which has evolved as a response to the increasingly diverse requirements of urban imaging. In this paper the term 'webcam' is used generically to describe IP-based cameras that connect directly to IP networks. Contrary to the types of devices designed for online socializing, these cameras record at high frame rates, have good resolution and have multiple, user-end manipulable functions. Also, because these systems are IP-based, it is possible to monitor, store, and archive video, audio and associated application data over the Internet or across private data networks. In fact, it is possible for anyone with the proper security clearance and a standard browser to control and configure the cameras on the network (although in some cases, even this security wall is vulnerable and can be perforated by hackers). The video is transportable anywhere within the extent of the IP network unlike closed-circuit television (CCTV) systems that require proprietary equipment and dedicated coaxial cabling (Dunn, 2006).

Therefore, what was originally a simple mechanism devoted to surveillance and operating within multiple, individual closed circuit systems, has, with the advent of the IP network, been extended into an open circuit and globally available platform. This not only extends the reach of image data to a worldwide audience, but more importantly, it begins to blur the boundaries between what has hitherto been regarded as an imaging tool specific to the maintenance of civic control and ownership and its newfound entrepreneurial capacity serving a range of unprecedented functions. An illustration of this extended function concerns its performative capacity which is exploited by groups like New York's Surveillance Camera Players (http://www.notbored.org/the-scp.html), who employ webcam camera views at high visibility traffic locations to stage performances, effectively subverting the surveillant intent of these systems. The camera view, literally transformed into a performance venue, allows individuals to become producers rather than consumers of content, thereby creating a very different mode of engagement with public space. A further example of this development of overlapping and sometimes conflicting functions is the tourist webcam view of the Sydney Opera House operated by the Sydney Harbour Foreshore Authority (http://www.therocks.com), whose alternative surveillant role was revealed when it was closed to public viewing during the 2007 APEC Conference.

This performative aspect of technology as a projected 'prosthesis' of human expression is discussed by Marc Hansen in, *New Philosophy for New Media*, where he describes this new type of engagement with the computer 'as an embodied prosthesis, a catalyst for bodily self-transformation' (Hansen, 2004, p.120). In this scenario, the body becomes 'virtualised' as a result of its engagement with the virtual world. This sets up a cycle wherein the Internet user navigates a new topology through a third party system: the Internet to engage with public space and in this sense the viewing of the space becomes performative, i.e. it is the doing of something rather than projecting form from outside.

Disrupting the View

To contextualize digital image-making and to provide a background against which the performance and content of contemporary two-dimensional representations of urban space might be assessed, it is worth drawing upon two particular interpretations of pictorial tradition.

In his essay *Prospect, Perspective and the Evolution of the Landscape Idea*, Dennis Cosgrove argues that the implementation of linear perspective and the ensuing two-dimensional representation of three-dimensional space reveals a manipulation of the viewer/object relational field which ensures that landscape, or more specifically property, is in 'its correct relationship with other things' (Cosgrove, 1985, p. 55), or in other words, in line with the concerns of a specific minority group. Cosgrove goes on to discuss how the normalization of the view creates stasis or 'a static pattern or picture whose internal relations and constituent forms are understood, but which lacks process or change' (Cosgrove, 1985, p. 57).

In a similar way, W.J.T Mitchell's essay, *Imperial Landscapes* traces how different political regimes control the means of production and dissemination of landscape representations to deliberately maintain control of territory. However, Mitchell's discussion of Augustus Earle's 1827 painting 'Distant View of the Bay of Islands, New Zealand' (http://www.nla.gov.au/exhibitions/earle/nz.html), reveals that images disruptive to the authorized view of landscape have long existed beside their more traditional counterparts. According to Mitchell, Earle's subversive use of the Maori totem disrupts the picturesque tradition, observing that it stands outside convention: 'It does not… provide a dark refuge for the viewer to hide behind, nor does it provide a convenient stand-in for the beholder's gaze within the composition. On the contrary, it is a hazard, an emblem of an alien vision that stares back into the space of the beholder' (Mitchell, 2002, p. 25). For Mitchell, the issue is about contesting the conventions of

the representation, adding that this is 'another convention for organizing and perceiving the landscape, one that contends with and reshapes the convention that Earle carries as picturesque traveller' (Mitchell, 2002, p. 25). The main thrust of his argument here is that this Maori carved figure not only subverts European picturesque conventions, but it also demonstrates that this tradition is not necessarily exclusively western. While the figure departs in its orientation from western tradition, it nevertheless reveals that "stopping still just to look at the land is so important to the Maoris that they erect a statue to keep surveillance over a place" (Mitchell, 2002, p. 26). The consequence of this revelation is therefore that all representation of landscape is universally skewed or 'contaminated' by the projected semantics of its inherent social and cultural values (Matthews & Perin, 2010).

The Digital Picturesque

It is fair to say that while the webcam system, as the modern technology of image-making and transmission, is equally as susceptible to the exertion of spatial control by authoritarian bodies as was the traditional picturesque, it is also susceptible to the same kind of extension and diversification of its content as illustrated by Mitchell.

To explore this concept further, an urban webcam site available globally was selected as the basis for a range of speculative design scenarios which would not only test the capacity of this system to diversify and extend its primary function as a tourist/security webcam but which would also establish a *modus operandi* for doing this.

In the first instance, the webcam view of Sydney Harbour Foreshore (Figure 1) was used to explore specific conditions relating to the authorization of the image. The distinguishing condition that led to selection of the Circular Quay site was in part the regulatory by-law that attempted to regularize and control form and image to avoid any contestation of the iconic status of the Sydney Opera House. The visual scope of

Figure 1. Webcam view of Sydney Harbour with grid and subdivisions applied

the webcam view of the Sydney Opera House and the wider Circular Quay precinct is subject to the regulatory framework of the City of Sydney Council's Development Control Plan and vicinity controls which ensure that this view is conserved by legislation.

An initial test, therefore, explored the actual physical structure of image fabrication by this system and looked at new ways in which the webcam image might serve as a platform for generating form. In accordance with this idea, the initial step taken was to spatialize the image of the Circular Quay Foreshore site by placing a linear grid over the 'conflated' webcam view. The consequence of this tactic was that because the virtual image is composed of a series of equally sized information pixels, then any design element applied at a uniform scale to this virtual image would manifest at different scales in its real-time physical counterpart. In addition, the site image was subdivided mathematically from its mid-point to determine locations for intervention while remaining faithful to the notion that inherent, subjective hierarchies needed to be avoided or at least minimised within the experimental process.

To provide further detail beyond an abstract spatial delineation the gridded space was rescaled by superimposing an optical illusion pattern, the Münsterberg pattern (Figure 2), over the original image. This pattern, selected for its optical instability, was anamorphically projected across this three-dimensional space which meant that each unit of the façade of any formal intervention would vary in scale in direct relation to its location within the camera field of view. The consequence of this was that any user-end action of manipulating the field of the camera would also be accompanied by a shifting in and out of focus of that façade. This action creates a strong blurring effect which could be further enhanced by the action of the pattern in material form.[1]

Furthermore, the optical instability of this pattern challenges not only the promotional agency of the webcam system, but it also addresses the issue of pictorial and, consequently, cultural stasis raised by Cosgrove. It is precisely because the content of the webcam image is constantly changing that the problem of being locked into a single orchestrated visual narrative is avoided and the possibility of exploring opportunities raised by its dynamic qualities is opened up.

Figure 2. Top: Webcam view of Sydney Harbour showing projection of Münsterberg pattern and Below left to right: Development of Münsterberg pattern (far left) into 3D form

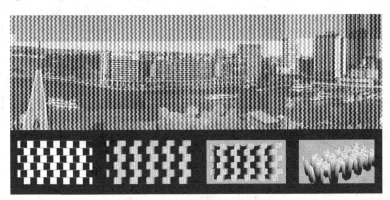

The disjunctive and disruptive effects of all of these tactics deployed on the Sydney webcam image are the modern counterpart of Earle's totem within the picturesque tradition: they disrupt the experience of viewing on site, both as a physical real-time and a 'virtual' visual experience. The difference here, however, is that their potency is attributable to the inability of the imagistic content to stabilize or form rather than to any figurative disruption of meaning and signification.

Also, paradoxically, while the webcam view relies upon the same visual transmission of the representation of power structures as does the picturesque image, unlike the latter, it is not derived from two-dimensional modes of representation. Significantly, unlike the traditional notion of the picturesque wherein the image 'pre-forms' the real, the Sydney webcam view test literally 'un-forms' the virtual image and, by extension, the power structures which govern its real-time counterpart.

MATERIALIZING THE ANAMORPHIC VIEW

The Geometry of the Camera View

In order to assess the capacity of an imaging mechanism to depart from its prescribed role, it is essential first to explore the operational frame of its viewer/object relational field. Within the constraints of Cartesian geometry, the generative platform of the webcam mechanism operates from an anamorphic perspective. This has profound and extensive consequences for the type of imagistic product of this process.

James Elkins' discourse on this subject sheds some light on what the exploration of this issue within a modern digital context might offer. Elkins uses the term 'fossilization of perspective' (Elkins, 1994) to refer to the modern failure to exploit fully the implications of anamorphic perspective within contemporary visuality paradigms. Elkins uses Lacan's chiasmatic perspective diagram (Figure 3) to illustrate precisely this failure to extend the observer/object viewing field beyond a single prescribed viewing condition.

The Lacanian diagram conceptually reverses the relation between observer and object: the visual field of the observer is expanded and that of the object contracted. This has a clear parallel in the type of viewing relationship that occurs in an Internet context wherein the viewer's visual field is determined by that of the wide webcam camera lens and the object is the focal point with the intermediate image becoming literally the Lacanian screen. However, this diagram too falls short of describing accurately the viewing ambit of the webcam platform. Lacan's failure to incorporate anamorphic perspective into his chias-

Figure 3. Top left: Lacan's chiasmatic diagram showing inversion of viewer/object relational field; Top right: Revised two-dimensional Lacanian diagram showing base of triangle or "V" the viewer as a circular viewing field and the vertex "O" as the object or "point of light"; Bottom: Three-dimensional representation of revised Lacanian diagram showing expanded viewing field "V" and its correlation with the webcam view

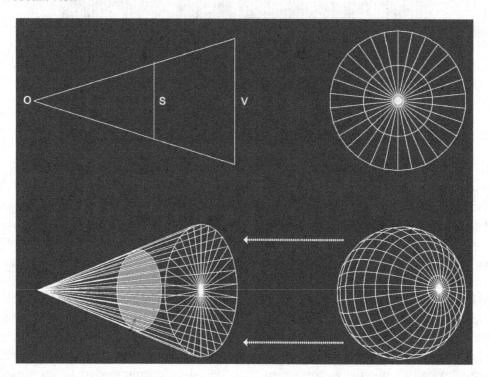

matic diagram accounts for only one, not the countless viewpoints from which an object is viewed by this modern technology. Nevertheless, a simple transformation of the geometry of this diagram into a three-dimensional sphere is able to account for this new condition. In the revised diagram, the viewing field is extended to represent the innumerable, unauthorized views of an object which might stand outside the intended visual narrative and contribute to the imagistic representation of a cityscape.*ve.*

Anamorphic Form

The formal implications of utilizing this image-making technology as a generative platform in fact lie within this revised Lacanian diagram. If once again we use the Sydney webcam view as a site

within which to intervene, then any formal intervention therein will be driven by the geometrical constraints of the camera view as demonstrated by this diagram.

To refer back to the initial formal manoeuvres and the application of the Münsterberg pattern to generate spatial intervention, the formal translation of this pattern across any site selected within the camera view would inevitably be dictated by the site's orientation to the camera. Put simply, because the integrity of the pattern can only be achieved when it is flat to the camera lens, then any consequent built form would have to be twisted at a perpendicular angle to the camera to achieve a legible reading of its façade (Figure 4).

A projective design scenario can best illustrate the effect of this principle using two separate but neighbouring sites within the Sydney webcam

Figure 4. Left: Twisting of material surface according to site location and Right: Orientation map of camera angles

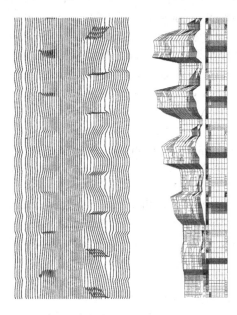 

view. Initially, the Münsterberg pattern was used to produce a displacement field created in the 3D modelling program, Rhinoceros. The different response to camera angles is clearly reflected in the façade of each intervention: the angle determines the degree of morphing required achieving a legible reading of the applied Münsterberg pattern and in each of these cases the extent of twisting has specific implications for the distribution of internal program. For example, in the projective form situated at a more acute angle to the camera lens, the twisting action, taking place along the entire vertical axis of the building, establishes a direct relationship between the extent of distortion and the utility of the space: in this scenario a more intimate space would be produced by greater distortion or twisting, while conversely, less twisting would result in a more open or public space (Figure 5).

In contrast to this, the second projective intervention revealed something quite different. Because the façade of this intervention is situated at an almost perpendicular angle to the camera, it is able to disguise large discrepancies between the

Figure 5. Street (left) and webcam views (right) of intervention located at an acute angle to the camera lens

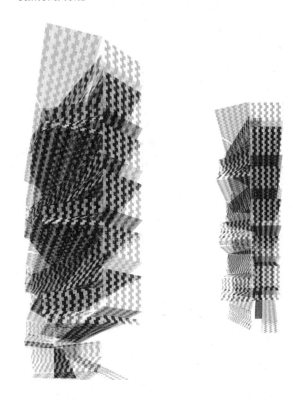

view presented to the camera and the view presented to the street. In this case, the application of the pattern might require a disruption of its scale to facilitate the design brief such as a duplication of the pattern to achieve an appropriate façade response. In this situation, the pattern would appear flat to the camera view, while in contrast it exposes its extensive programmatic projections only to the street view (Figure 6).

According to Hansen, the effect of these types of visual discrepancies which are hitherto part of an uncharted topology generated by the computer, is both disconcerting and disorienting to both the virtual and the real-time viewer. Certainly the form here is reframed around affect rather than symbolic signification, but its uncanny optical illusion distortion produces, both virtually and physically, a type of bodily sensation that Hansen describes as 'proprioception' wherein 'our visual faculties are rendered useless and we experience a shift to an alternate mode of

perception' (Hansen, 2004, p. 203). Also *Also*, importantly, in the same type of dual environment signalled by the representation of the anamorphic skull in Hans Holbein's painting 'The Ambassadors', the existence of multiple viewpoints also means that these worlds are visually interdependent: that they can only ever be understood and resolved in conjunction with each other.

Reference to this type of discomfort or disorientation is also made in Lyle Massey's essay Configuring Spatial Ambiguity: Picturing the Distance Point from Alberti to Anamorphosis (2003). Massey argues that the disjunctive effect of anamorphosis is to engage rather than distance the viewer, 'Forcing the viewer both to succumb to and resist absorption into the picture plane, the anamorphic distortion makes the viewer aware of phenomenal as well as representational space' (Massey, 2003, p. 172). Massey uses the diagrams of a seventeenth century French scientist to argue that this bodily sensation is the result of the

Figure 6. Street (left) and webcam views (right) of intervention located perpendicular to the camera lens

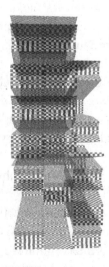

conflation of the viewer and the picture plane, or the conflict between represented and embodied space. To quote him, it is an, 'oblique slide into the perspective grid or the space of representation itself' (Massey, 200, p. 171). Consequently, in terms of the output of the digital webcam network, governed as it is by the camera geometry, the virtual view completes the viewer's understanding of the real-time experience and vice versa. *er.*

EXPLOITING TECHNOLOGY

Manipulating Visibility: Sensors

The distribution of elements within the Münsterberg pattern also has an interesting coincident dynamic with the fundamental building block of the image itself: the pixel. It is the arrangement of these smallest addressable elements in varying intensities of red, green and blue elements that are the atomic basis of digital colour composition and whose various combinations comprise the additive colour system or RGB.

Translational hardware mechanisms such as colour sensors which operate within input devices (the camera), rely upon specific arrangements of the colour elements red, blue and green to achieve image results that are pre-determined by proprietary companies. Generally speaking, the sensor arrangement is geared to optimise both brightness (luminosity) and intensity (chroma), particularly in conditions where the received image is distributed to a global audience to enhance opportunities for tourism and the like.

The CCD sensor is a device containing grids of individual pixels arranged horizontally and vertically with a colour filter mosaic or array located above the grid to capture colour information and convert it to a full-colour image. There are many optional arrangements for these arrays but the traditional arrangement is the Bayer filter array with a pattern of 50% green, 25% red and 25% blue. This particular arrangement is used for a number of reasons: because it targets the capacity of the human eye to resolve green above other colours, but, more insidiously, because it produces a stable, predictable outcome and it is compatible with the numerous software applications made available for image translation.

However, recent tests reveal that there are multiple alternative array assembly options that have the potential to produce diverse and highly strategic chromatic outcomes within the viewing environment of the digital webcam network and which ultimately offer the viewer or the designer more autonomy.

The operational procedure of the sensor creates an immediate relationship between the composition pattern of received virtual image and its colour filter array counterpart. The camera lens directs the light from a single image point onto each pixel which in turn generates a corresponding charge. This means that because the charges created by the pixel array mirror the pattern of the transmitted image, then any deliberate manipulation of the pattern within the physical view will also affect its virtual counterpart.

One way of demonstrating this would be to incorporate a physical representation of variations of the Bayer pattern array (Figure 7) in a building façade viewed by an IP webcam network. Because within an additive colour system, the superimposition of all three RGB colours produces white or maximum luminance, then in a projective design scenario, the addition of two complementary colours to a third at an intended or strategic location would produce white or invisibility i.e. no chrominance, just luminance, when it is captured by the image sensor. Similarly, the addition of complementary colours to a third colour at random would also deliver variable chromatic results.

Figure 7. Bayer array pattern (left) with variations combining to produce white and new colour options

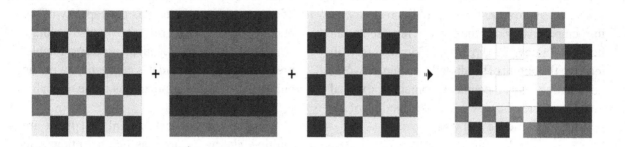

Sensor Tests

Tests were conducted using a Sony SX43E Handycam Digital Video Recorder whose operational technology replicates that of the Sony SNC-RZ50N network camera. Compensations were made for specific differences between the two when calculating results. The comparative features critical to these tests were the zoom factor; the f-stop range which determines the amount of light that can pass through the lens; and the sensor size which determines both the number and size of the pixels. In these tests, the network camera's reduced depth of field or ability to resolve images was offset by its larger sensor size and lower f-range which increases its ability to absorb light. In other words, discrepancies within the capacities of the two cameras result in a similar output: the main parity issue is that the network camera is designed for low light conditions and therefore is susceptible to fewer light aberrations because of security issues; however its ability to resolve images and colours is much the same as that of the Handycam.

The tests utilized the Bayer array pattern itself and two other variations of it translated into a scaled translucent material form. These patterns measured 150mm x 150mm to correspond to a typical building façade element of one and a half metres in height. Similarly, the light source/aperture plane distance was conducted at a projective scale of 1:10, for example, a three metre

light source/aperture plane distance in the test corresponds to a thirty metre distance in the urban environment. The other additional operational criterion was the lighting sources which were three American DJ FS-1000 Followspots with ZB-HX600, 120V 300W Halogen Lamps operating in reduced light conditions to simulate urban night-time conditions.

The objective of the test was to explore the combined light transmission effects of three individual array patterns in response to both camera location and angle (Figure 8). Each of the patterns is a complementary derivative of the Bayer array pattern and, in fact, if all were directly superimposed their combined effect would produce reduced chroma, and with intense amounts of luminosity, white or zero visibility. In addition to this, the test would also look for strategic distances or critical angles at which this might occur, thereby providing a template of opportunities or moments by means of which decisions for strategic design intervention and exploitation could be implemented.

The patterns were each placed at a thirty degree angle to the camera and their collective light emission patterns were recorded on a white board at a standard three metre distance over a range of zoom factors. The camera was then placed at exactly the same three metre distance from the light sources previously occupied by the board which also coincided with the point at which their combined emission had produced white (Figure 9).

Figure 8. Diagram showing the material implementation of the performance of three Bayer variations combining to produce white as they are viewed within an RGB environment

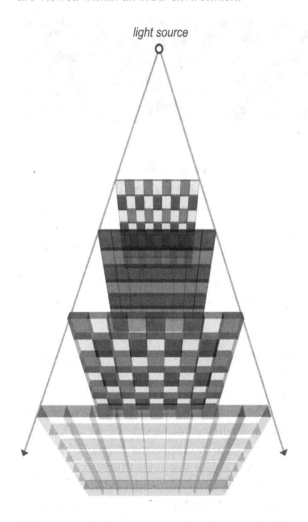

The results showed that when the patterns were projected individually on the board the pattern was clearly defined with strong chromatic intensity. However, when the projection of the patterns was combined, both the pattern definition and the strength of the chroma were severely diminished and began to approach white. The same effect was repeated when the camera replaced the board at exactly the same three metre distance from the light source. However, what became apparent in the latter test was that not only was the effect of producing white stronger, but it was visible only at specific moments of the 'zoom' factor or f-stop [aperture] intervals, and in addition to this it was not visible to the naked eye. In other words, this opened up several opportunities: to tabulate specific moments where the operation of the camera's mechanism translates an image reduced in both form and visibility; and to exploit the differences in a building's visibility between duplicate, simultaneously occurring environments (Figure 10).

It is not difficult to see the potential for the Münsterberg pattern to be adapted into this context. Its anamorphic formal projection into selected locations within the three-dimensional Sydney webcam site using a range of different assembly pattern variations could be used projectively as a device for determining different programmatic configurations. At one extent of the zoom range,

Figure 9. Bottom far left: RGB colour emission onto board without pattern; Top left to right: Bayer array variations combining to produce white. Bottom centre: Three individual pattern colour emissions onto board; Bottom far right: Combined pattern emission onto board showing diminished intensity of colour.

Figure 10. Far left: Camera view of light emitting patterns when placed in exactly the same location as the board. Second left to right: Camera view of light emitting patterns showing varying degrees of pattern visibility at different f-stop or zoom factors. The camera remained at a standard distance from the light source during this test.

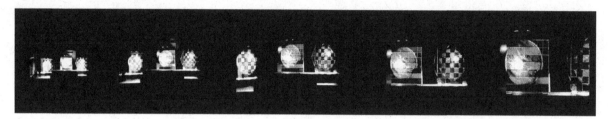

the pattern would produce an individual façade element while at the other extent of its range, the same diminished pattern might determine floor and wall division. However, more significantly, it is the deliberate assembly of the façade pattern according to programmatic activity and consequently particular levels of luminance that allows it to perform within a temporal context with varying degrees of selective visibility. In this specific way, the strategic location of programmatic activity can drive the visibility of the interior spaces translated into the materiality of the façade.

Manipulating Visibility: Diffraction

Further tests revealed that the camera lens mechanism offers other opportunities for design intervention. These show that aspects of the camera's image-making process traditionally regarded as aberrations are able to be productively exploited by again capitalizing upon the discrepancies that occur between the virtual and actual views of a site. Fraunhofer diffraction patterns produced by the incidence of the luminance of an image on the camera lens over a range of different lens apertures are a common kind of visual idiosyncrasy that occurs within the camera's recording of a selected viewing field. The same principle that operated in the previous tests was again used to demonstrate how the incorporation of design elements into a façade intervention allows the designer to manipulate its visibility and prominence

across simultaneous environments. In this case, the façade itself acted as a giant diffraction grating intervening as an aperture between a light source [emitted by the program within the building] and the camera. Also, importantly, this phenomenon occurred only in the camera-mediated view, the effect was not visible to the naked eye (http://www.flickr.com/photos/not-bernard/5389607903/in/photostream/).

Diffraction Tests

Five patterns were used in the tests; all were based upon optical illusion patterns or were derived from Fraunhofer diffraction patterns extracted from the open-source software program Fresnel Diffraction Explorer (Dauger Research, 2005).

While the tests were conducted using the same equipment and conditions of the sensor test (Figure 11), the Sony Handycam has a similar low-end f-range capacity and a greater high-end f-range capacity: almost twice that of the network camera. Because the high-end range is where diffraction effects are most likely to occur, this means that the Handycam is more susceptible to effects of diffraction when its lens aperture exceeds f3.8 at the high end. Therefore only diffraction effects that occur between the range of f1.8 and 3.8 were used to support any observations made.

The tests revealed a recurrence of abnormal or idiosyncratic behaviour in the camera's translation of the image in the following ways:

Figure 11. Patterns used as diffraction gratings: From left to right: Centre to far right: diffraction patterns extracted using Fresnel Diffraction Explorer

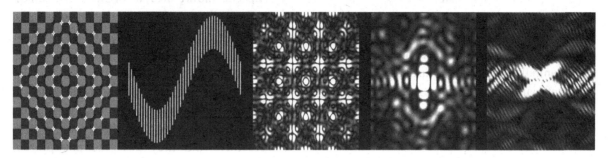

The strongest diffraction effect occurred on the inward zoom between f 1.8 and f 3.4 and occurred in all instances over a range of different diffraction gratings. In some instances the effect extended beyond the immediate grating zone to include the area around the grating. However, the aspect of the effect that was most unexpected was that the diffraction effect in all cases was absent on the outward zoom trajectory. Therefore it can be said that not only does the grating pattern determine the type of diffraction effect, but moreover, that this pattern, because of the camera's aberrant performance, displays varying degrees of visibility at different points within the webcam's trajectory (Figure 12).

The inclusion of these types of patterns into the types of formal interventions framed within

Figure 12. Test using an optical illusion pattern as a diffraction grating showing varying diffraction effects at different f-stop intervals. The test images were processed as montages of successive frames using ImageJ non-proprietary software (Source: http://rsbweb.nih.gov/ij/).

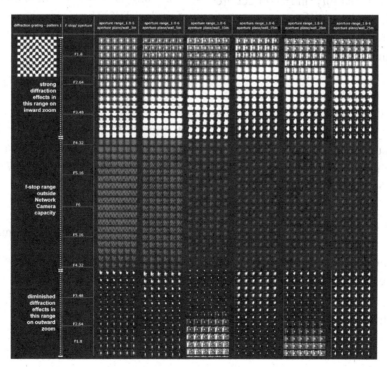

a webcam view has, of course, similar implications for manoeuvring visibility as does the introduction of sensor array patternings. In both cases, it is the idiosyncrasies of the image-making technology that allow the designer to strategically manipulate the relationship between a building's materiality and its performance and to exploit the discrepancies that might arise between the two worlds it inhabits.

CONCLUSION

The preliminary tests outlined in this paper, therefore, reveal how the technology that mediates the representation of contemporary urban environments is able to offer unprecedented opportunities for intervention within civic space to both the individual and the designer. Techniques outlined in this paper which manipulate the camera's internal mechanism, seen in the non-traditional assembly of colour array patterns and which capitalize upon the recurrence of abnormal or idiosyncratic behaviour, demonstrated in the use of diffraction patterns, mean that both a building's visibility and its effect are able to be deliberately controlled by the incorporation of these features into formal facades, or put simply, by managing the relationship between its materiality and its mediating technology.

The departure from traditional architectural form-making practices and the establishment of these new techniques directly challenges the ideologies behind these practices, and ultimately suggests a more contextual response to urban intervention. Also, more importantly, it dismantles the agency of the political structures which govern both actual and virtual form.

The utilization of the digital image to determine programmatic hierarchies and by extension, its mediating technology, not only liberates the designer from the spatial dictates of abstract geometries, but also, unlike picturesque representation, it escapes the constraints of a two-dimensional representation which pre-figures the real. Instead, the architecture of this new medium makes it possible to intervene simultaneously in both environments: the actual and the virtual, to 'deconstruct' the urban image, and moreover, to subvert its underlying power structures.

The types of initial manoeuvres discussed in this paper link the fabrication of urban form to the conceptual heart of this technology's architecture, and they navigate unexplored environments to chart a new digital topology. The fact that these tactics are also coupled with the creation of a type of unstable experiential affect in the viewer is an inevitable and yet productive consequence of a more liberating paradigm which does not operate according to reliance upon any stable figural narrative, but instead is delineated by the creation of a productive and performative space that is constantly evolving.

REFERENCES

Bentham, J. (1995). *The Panopticon writings*. London, UK: Verso.

Berry, J. (2003). *Bare code: Net art and the free software movement*. Retrieved from http://www.uoc.edu/artnodes/espai/eng/art/jberry0503/jberry0503.html

Cosgrove, D. (1985). Prospect, perspective and the evolution of the landscape idea. *Transactions of the Institute of British Geographers*, *10*(1), 45–62.

Damjanovski, V. (2005). *CCTV: Networking and digital technology. Amsterdam, The Netherlands: Elsevier*. Butterworth: Heinemann.

Dauger Research. (2005). *Fresnel diffraction*. Retrieved from http://daugerresearch.com/fresnel/index.shtml

Dunn, P. (2006). *How to: Set up an IP-based camera surveillance system*. Retrieved from http://www. crn.com/news/channel-programs/192203498/ how-to-set-up-an-ip-based-camera-surveillance-system.htm

Elkins, J. (1985). *The poetics of perspective*. Ithaca, NY: Cornell University Press.

Hansen, M. B. N. (2004). *New philosophy for new media*. Cambridge, MA: MIT Press.

Hérault, J. (2010). *Vision: Images, signals and neural networks*. Singapore: World Scientific.

Jay, M. (1999). Scopic regimes of modernity. In Foster, H. (Ed.), *Vision and visuality* (pp. 2–23). New York, NY: New Press.

Kruegle, H. (2007). *CCTV surveillance: Analog and digital video practices and technology*. Amsterdam, The Netherlands: Elsevier Butterworth Heinemann.

Macarthur, J. (2007). *The Picturesque: Architecture, disgust and other irregularities*. London, UK: Routledge.

Marin, L. (1984). *Utopics: Spatial play*. London, UK: Macmillan.

Massey, L. (2003). Configuring spatial ambiguity: Picturing the distance point from Alberti to anamorphosis. In Massey, L. (Ed.), *The treatise on perspective*. Washington, DC: National Gallery of Art.

Massumi, B. (2002). *Parables for the virtual, movement, affect, sensation*. Durham, NC: Duke University Press.

Matthews, L. (2010). Virtual sites: Performance and materialization. *Technoetic Arts: A Journal of Speculative Research, 8*(1), 55-65.

Matthews, L., & Perin, G. (2010, November). *The modern picturesque and techniques of adaptation*. Paper presented at the First International Conference on Transdisciplinary Imaging at the Intersections between Art, Science and Culture, Sydney, Australia.

McConnell, J. (2008). *Computer graphics: Theory into practice*. Sudbury, MA: Jones and Bartlett.

Mitchell, W. J. T. (2002). Imperial landscapes. In Mitchell, W. J. T. (Ed.), *Landscape and power* (pp. 5–34). Chicago, IL: University of Chicago Press.

Panofsky, E. (1997). *Perspective as symbolic form*. New York, NY: Zone Books.

Savard, J. (2009). *Colour filter array designs*. Retrieved from http://www.quadibloc.com/other/ cfaint.htm

ENDNOTE

[1] The designation of the white sections of the pattern as transparent panelling by the designer would also enhance the blurring effect because light would then bleed around the edges of the solid black panels. In this way the discrepancies between the two environments would be able to be controlled by material decisions: the actual physical experience of the pattern at a 1:1 scale would be very different from the experience of the webcam view.

This work was previously published in International Journal of Creative Interfaces and Computer Graphics, Volume 2, Issue 1, edited by Ben Falchuk, pp. 27-41, copyright 2010 by IGI Publishing (an imprint of IGI Global).

Chapter 14
Creative Interfaces:
Development of New Integrated and Visual Solutions

Ioana Armiano
EON Reality, Sweden

ABSTRACT

Recent developments in process interaction solutions are helping companies and educational institutions to reduce training costs, enhance visualization, and increase communication. Service personnel can make more informed decisions by allowing a broad range of employees to access data instantly. New 3D interactive technologies incorporated into training applications and learning environments together with the introduction of the one projector 3D solution is rapidly changing the landscape for education. Over the last 10 years, virtual reality applications have been applied in various industries; medical, aircraft computer modeling, training simulations for offshore drilling platforms, product configuration, and 3D visualization solutions for education and R&D. This paper examines emergent visualization technologies, their influence on market growth and on new perceptions of learning and teaching. It describes the interrelationship between technology development, technology providers, product launches, R&D, and the motivation to learn and teach new skills. The paper incorporates social, technological, and global markets growth drives, describing the pull and drag synergy between these forces.

INTRODUCTION

In his "Strategy for America Innovation, Grand Challenges" of the 21st century" President Obama identified the following grand challenge: "Develop an Educational software that is as compelling as the best video game and as effective as a personal tutor; online courses that improve the more students use them; and a rich, interactive digital library at the fingertips of every child." The society is in the aftermath of the industrial revolution, which creates new opportunities for learning, community development, and trade. One of the main social factors is

DOI: 10.4018/978-1-4666-0285-4.ch014

technology as an agent of change in interaction between people. This new society requires new approaches in a number of areas for people to identify themselves in their surroundings and to further develop interdisciplinary knowledge sharing. Today we live in an interaction society, which means a fundamental change, as great as when society went from newspapers and printed media to movable and auditory media. Though, the difference is far greater this time because the shift is much faster when decentralization of information means an exponential spreading effect. This article tells about some new integrative and visual solutions in creating interfaces, networking engines, visualization technologies, and 3D interactive virtual-world platforms exemplified by new technologies developed at EON Reality, Inc.

1. DEVELOPMENT OF NEW CREATIVE INTERFACES

Interactive 3D and innovative visualization technologies, including Virtual Reality, are a part of the infrastructure platform that supports 21st century training and development in the global competitiveness. Technology companies are collaborating with educational institutions and governments all over the world to develop new applications, and thus unfold new solutions for learning and training.

While the Internet has reduced communication barriers across geographical boundaries, effective communication remains a challenge when there is a lack of consistent, scalable and illustrative interfaces. The issues and gaps include:

- Integrated communication and end work flow
- Scalable and integrated configurations for planning and design
- Remote information exchange and access to diverse global networks without traveling
- Integration with large-scale displays (from laptop to "CAVE" solutions) to further reinforce understanding and create a pedagogical experience that is easy to understand and remember longer.

Collaborative 3D solutions/immersive 3D communication, virtual meetings and events technology aim to fill this gap by providing a platform where people can present their ideas, communicate complex concepts and collaborate using rich media objects such as web pages, presentation slides, video, live feeds and interactive 3D content (Figure 1).

Figure 1. Development of new creative interfaces

2. FOCUS AREAS

3D / VR interfaces are aimed to provide effective visual communication and knowledge transfer solutions for cooperation, prototyping new models, and cultivating open and collaborative approaches to learning and training. Focus areas for the new developments include, among other domains, cooperation with educational and research institutions, medical and pharmaceutical companies, digital design studios and architectural or urban planning, virtual product development, information and R&D information visualization, and energy or petrochemical companies.

Cooperation with Educational and Research Institutions

IDC Asia is a collaboration formed between three parties: Temasek Polytechnic, IM Innovations and EON Reality Inc. The project was initiated in 2005 when Temasek Polytechnic (TP) started working with IM Innovations Pte Ltd to promote the pervasive use of 3D visualization and digital media solutions and services. Their Engineering School has been using virtual reality in its project work and curriculum since early 2000. Focusing on developmental projects for the industry, training and education, the IDC Asia has established relationships with government and research grant agencies such as the Infocomm Development Authority (IDA), the Media Development Authority (MDA), the Ministry of Education and National Research Foundation.

Tan Hock Soon, manager of Interactive Digital Centre Asia in Temasek; we see education as a key market sector and we will direct our applications, research and developmental work towards this area".

- Spin off incubator start-up enterprise ca support and create opportunities to develop entrepreneurial communities around the multi-disciplinary interactive 3D technology.

- Development of rich media content can easily be adapted for use at trade shows, websites, etc.

New IT jobs can be generated for IT and media professionals, along with education and resource support, in the areas of the interactive 3D modeling, data base creation, Web & media implementation, business development, marketing, and interactive media services within education, energy, and medical sectors (Figure 2).

2.1. Education and Training

Virtually environments can help teachers use new methods more aligned with the way the mind learns (Jacobson, 2010). Recent research demonstrates that people learn best with methods where you do not just transmit information—and then see if they can sort it out, but where you find ways to scaffold and support learners for a while, then fade it out over time. Here is where technology can be very helpful. Learners can accomplish and engage in ways they might otherwise not been able to. Michael J. Jacobson, Professor and Chair of Education at The University of Sydney, is a forerunner in the research of learning in the world of 3D virtual reality. His latest research involves several projects on how virtual learning experiences may support innovative pedagogical approaches in the increasingly technology rich classrooms in Australia and around the world. Some of the learning activities are conducted in the virtual world and include "productive failure" - a pedagogical approach where learners are given challenging tasks or problems that they initially fail at, which, under certain circumstances, can lead to long term learning gains.

"Our current educational system has failed to engage many students and help them succeed. Even by middle school, many children give up the belief that learning within the educational system is motivating and possible for them" (Dede, 2007).

Figure 2. Collaboration with education and research institutions is aimed at production of self-sustaining experiential learning environments incorporating new technologies. It is also aimed at creating new programs or enhancing existing graphics, animation, and other multi-media related programs. Within the walls of innovation–industry, government, educators, artists and entrepreneur's generated ideas lay the capability to create innovative self-sustainable support resources. Here partners can innovate, customize, design, and create solutions to meet local needs

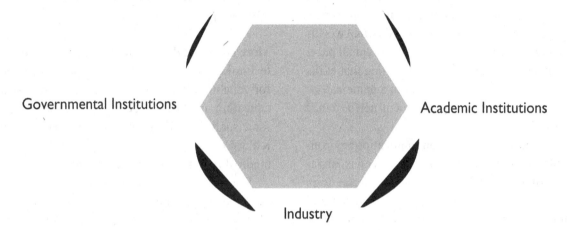

In Africa, where poor literacy skills and language barriers are huge challenges to learning and skills development, Virtual Reality comes into its own. Together with partners such as UNESCO, the WK Kellogg Foundation and World Links of Harare, - Naledi3d Factory - a VR based technology company in South Africa has successfully used VR to communicate concepts and practices in a wide range of disciplines. Their projects include rural hygiene in Uganda; Malaria; HIV/AIDS awareness for Ethiopian educators, sanitation in Mozambique and supporting emerging farmers in Zimbabwe on a range of agricultural issues (http://www.naledi3d.com).

Three-dimensional spatial visualization training has been found to improve educational outcomes, such as helping college students complete engineering degrees (Newcombe, 2010). Dr. Hilliard Jason (M.D., Ed.D.) clinical professor with the School of Medicine at the University of Colorado-Denver and the former editor of "Education for Health" offers an interesting explanation as to why 3D may be so appealing to our younger generations. "A lot of the way our brain is shaped

and functions can be understood in terms of the survival aspects of evolution. For our earlier ancestors the 3D moving imagery was vital to life – it made the difference whether they found lunch or became lunch" (http://future-talk.net).

2.1.2. Social and Computer Games

Because of the web based, social networking world that brings to youth MySpace, Facebook and Twitter, computer games and other mediated technologies, there is a phenomenon of teens across the globe using social networking sites and on line computer games to build community and connect with their peers. These teens bring to today's classroom a different skill set for engaging with their peers and also the expectation that their learning environment will provide that same level of engagement in learning – and, for the most part, it does not.

One of the ideas that computer games bring to the foreground is the role of play and having fun in a learning experience (Scacchi, Nideffer, & Adams, 2008). According to Professor Walt Scacchi, "computer games are really online information systems or online information environments. In a game environment, the learner gains an incentive to engage in the material and wants to figure out how to best solve the challenges that the game is placing before them, says. Besides providing the learner with a more engaging learning experience, computer games or computer based virtual worlds also allow learners to work at an individual pace. A game can be foundational, meaning that skills or results accomplished earlier in a game can be used as a platform for subsequent performance later on".

Development of new communication environments that incorporate 3D interactive visualization solutions and Virtual Reality technology into learning and training applications can add value to Academic institutions. Schools and local businesses become important hubs of designing skills, rapid prototyping, and problem solving that will increase local interdependencies and redefine relationships with the broader economy (Knowledgeworks, 2001).

- Enhanced learning opportunities appropriate to individual needs, aspirations and abilities.
- Resources can be made more readily available to provide enterprises access to the skills, knowledge and values needed in a knowledge-based economy
- Dangerous or sensitive tasks can be simulated in a virtual learning environment (VLE, SLB).

The Interactive Digital Center of the Kentucky Community and Technical College System (KCTCS) in collaboration with EON Reality launched its first visualization project for simulation based learning by developing a training application for coal miners. The simulation-based training application can be viewed on a laptop or can be projected using 3D stereographic technology so that the learning objects appear to float in space in 3D. Real-time, interactive, and photo-realistic visualizations are used to present the subject content and miners interact with the visualization at their own pace to accomplish training tasks (Figure 3).

2.2. Medical Visualization and VR Therapy

More and more doctors are using Virtual Reality technologies in surgical equipment, equipment for rehabilitation and therapy, for training and educating medical students and surgeons and for visualization of 3D medical data (Rydmark, Kling-Petersen, Pascher, & Philip, 2001). For the medical field this is a paradigm shift.

Eliot Winer, an Iowa State professor of mechanical engineering and James Oliver, director of the university's CyberInnovation Institute, have developed technology that converts 2D medical scans into detailed 3D images that can be used to plan a surgery or teach a lesson in anatomy. The software is based on virtual reality and uses real patient data from CT and MRI scans.

"Snow world" is an immersive virtual reality pain distraction system originated and developed by Hoffman & Patterson at the Univ. of Washington Seattle and Harborview Burn Center. The program helps ease pain of treatment by immersing patients in a wintry, computer-generated environment. During treatment, a patient wears a position-tracking helmet that displays a world of 3D graphics. Early results with two combat burn patients were published in the "Journal of Cyber Therapy and Rehabilitation". The results demonstrated that immersive VR reduced the reported amount of time patients with burn injury spent thinking about their pain and VR reduced pain unpleasantness (Figure 4).

2.2.1. VR Therapy

By applying techniques used in cognitive behavior therapy into an immersive virtual environment, researchers at the Babes-Bolyai University, in Romania has developed a program that promises great success for ADHD treatment. Professor Daniel David, a specialist on virtual reality therapy at the Department of Clinical Psychology and Psychotherapy, has together with a team of researchers developed a new concept for a "Virtual Classroom Intervention" system for ADHD (Anton, Opris, Dobreani, David, & Rizzo, 2009).

An example where virtual reality training has been successfully implemented is in the procedure used to reduce fear. Case studies have shown that ten to twelve training sessions in a virtual reality environment can eliminate or reduce one's fear or phobia. But, until now researchers didn't know the reason why virtual reality therapy works so well. Researcher Claude Frasson and his colleagues at the Department of Computer Science and Operations Research at the University of Montreal, have been analyzing the reaction of the brain in relation to specific stimuli through the use of EEG (Chaouachi, Heraz, Jraidi, & Frasson, 2009). Claude

Figure 3. In 2008, the U.S. Department of Labor recognized the value of this training application in promoting improved health and safety for mine workers by awarding KCTCS and the Kentucky Coal Academy its Grand Prize and Mixed Media Public Award in their annual Materials Training national competition sponsored by the Mine, Safety and Health Administration division

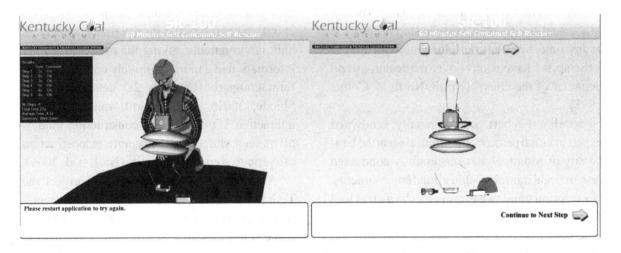

Figure 4. Virtual reality technologies are used to plan a surgery, perform radiation therapy and teach physiology and anatomy

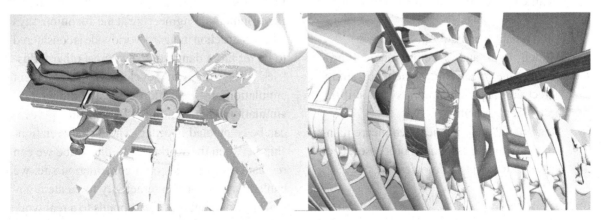

Frasson explains, "What is being analyzed is how certain stimuli that activates fear affects the brain and the reaction that comes out can be measured. In this stage we can see that the communication between the two functions in the brain is being developed and improved.

I am able to tell you that measurements have been made where it is shown that the fear and stimulus are reduced by being enrolled in VR-training," Claude Frasson says.

Fear of heights, posttraumatic stress and the fear of public speaking are symptoms that are being treated in a virtual, immersive "Cube" environment at the Babes-Bolyai University. Professor Daniel David explains; "The virtual ICube simulates in a very realistic way, the environment that could be stressful for the clients. Taking in account that in a virtual environment you can stop the process at any time, you can control the medium, and as a therapist I have control over the reactions and behavior of the client" (North, North, & Coble, 1998).

Jocelyn Faubert, internationally renowned expert in visual perception and professor at the University of Montreal, has successfully conducted research and training within virtual environments. "Perception training has proven to be a great tool for athletes that want to improve their game and reaction capacity and their ability to absorb and process infield information" (Greffou, Bertone, Hanssens, & Faubert, 2008).

Ways that visualization technologies can benefit patient care and the pharmaceutical sector:

- VR Therapy and Pain relive
- Model, train and develop medical procedures in virtual environment to rapidly detect and resolve temporary and shifting bottleneck capacities
- Operational and logistical healthcare planning – including associated processes, people and medical technologies

- Virtual consultations, interactive and visual diagnostic tools that provide self explanatory treatment procedures
- Leverage tele- presence to proactively engage patients and colleagues
- Collaboratively gather integrated patient information and efficiently attend to specific need

2.3. Digital Design Studios and Architectural or Urban Planning

Urban Planning brings together issues of planning, transportation, architectural design, development economics, urban design landscape architecture and engineering to create a vision for an area and then ensure it is delivered (White & Engelen, 2000). 3D can be used in visualizing urban and built environments, giving the option to deliver information in a more intuitively comprehensive form compared to static 2D data (Narushige Shiode, 2001). Architectural walk-through of interactive 3D digital city construction models offers an architecturally accurate reconstruction of a proposed construction site (Broll et al.,2004).

As a part of a Virtual Construction project, the Technion (Israel Institute of Technology) recently installed an immersive VR environment, the EON Icube (Figures 8 and 9). The immersive laboratory will serve as a simulator for constructors to train for potential dangers and learn how take precautions in their day to day work. Associate Professor Rafael Sacks at the Faculty of Civil and Environmental Engineering at the Technion, says "the construction industry worldwide is considered to be far more dangerous than most other industries". The aim is to develop a "discrete event simulation" for operation control and operation simulation where a number of steps in a process can be calculated in order to help study relationship between the workers. "In the ICube we can recreate the activities on a construction site, we can add avatars and interactivity to create a virtual environment that corresponds to a real work environment. By simulating dangerous situations we can study how construction workers perceive hazards in their every day work". Professor Rafael Sacks continues; "Workers can learn to identify and understand specific dangers that they generally are not aware of. This type of research relates to industrial psychology and has significant value when it comes to evaluating stressful situations and when there is an inclination to take unnecessary risks due to concerns for productivity".

Similar projects have been conducted in a Cave environment at the University of Reading in England. "We collaborate to bring architects and designers together with safety experts into the Cube environment", Professor Sacks says. "They walk through the 3D building and can discuss possible problems in order to improve the design so that the buildings can be built and function safer". Advantages and benefits include:

- 3D multi-user virtual communication environments where architects and interior designers can communicate their designs to their clients through active real time walk through.
- Planners can study the impact of urban development planned and the effects of proposed 3D development activities at any particular site.
- CAVE environments can be used for architects and customers to immerse themselves within their designs allowing walk or fly through the building, while selecting different design options.

2.4. Virtual Product Development

Virtual product development and interactive 3D digital models enable designers to communicate their designs through active real time demonstrations. Design, installation difficulties and servicing issues can be detected long before the first prototype is manufactured. The advantages become:

- Reduce of costly physical prototypes
- A cost effective way of visualizing a product that helps minimize design errors before actually rolling out for production
- Improved innovation through the interactive design process, engaging all stakeholders
- Increased product development using digital validation
- Large scale immersive display system (EON ICube environment, CAVE system) can be used in engineering evaluations allowing a better insight in the position of the different components

Virtual product development (Figure 5) and interactive 3D digital models enable designers to communicate their designs through active real time demonstrations. Design and installation difficulties and servicing issues can be detected before the first prototype is manufactured. An interactive 3D environment (from laptop to immersive CAVE environment) (Figure 6) can be used in engineering evaluations for a better insight in the position of the different components.

2.5. Information and R&D Visualization

Scientific visualization is an area where 3D environment particularly useful (George, Robertson, Jock, Mackinlay, & Stuart, 1991). When there are multiple correlated variables involved, displaying only raw data is not sufficient; it still requires the user to derive meaningful conclusions from large amount of data. Information visualization becomes a useful tool when it comes to understanding new knowledge from large amounts of simulation data. High Performance Computing and massive data sets are difficult to understand intuitively. This becomes especially important in the research and development domain, as multiple visual information and design visualization can support decision-making and allow users to comprehend

Figure 5. Virtual product development; Paccar engine

and compare content and visual data. Users can see conception of a 3D content and draw plans and graphs simultaneously.

2.6. Energy and Petrochemical Companies

Energy is fundamental to economic growth and sustainable expansion; therefore the development of sustainable energy system solutions is high on the political agenda. Visualization technologies, together with innovation and policy responses based on solid research, shared knowledge and strong initiatives can produce beneficial advantages for the Oil and Gas industries such as:

- Quicker roll out, and official launch of a new product
- Reduced instruction time
- Faster, more informed decision-making self-study
- Effective knowledge transfer of safety procedures

- Increased return on investment (ROI) of enterprise information and data between classroom and on the job
- Improved maintenance, repair operation and risk managing
- More effective and efficient research

An example of VR training implementation for the energy sector is the Aramco Oil Rig simulation developed by EON Reality. Aramco's personnel are provided realistic interaction in 3D with environments, equipments and hundreds of components covering all stages of training from: Rock Outcrop Simulation Vertical Seismic Profile Acquisition, Borehole visualizations, Wellhead and Gate Valve, lesson guides and 3D walkthroughs (Figure 7).

3. MACRO TRENDS

"So many students who come out of the current education system say 'Give me the instruction book

that shows me how to do that. We tell them, 'There is no book. You need to think on your own and then you have to write the book'' (George Lucas).

Virtual Reality is becoming a multi-billion-dollar field with uses in education, health care, training and maintenance, design, military, information processing and entertainment. Why is this happening right now? Several forces have accelerated the growth in elementary VR technology and expanded its application.

Knowledge-based economy and global information society are pushing us to examine the role of educational institutions, as we know them today. Our ability to meet the social, economic, health, and environmental challenges over the next several decades depends on our contribution, creation, and exchange of learning resources. Rapid knowledge transfer and a workforce that continuously acquires and adapts new skills underlie the "learning economy." Attention is now focused on the role of information and technology in modern economies and the transmission of knowledge through communication and computer networks. Here education is a key market sector that will move into application development, research and developmental work. The evidence for this includes:

- Recent trends in projection hardware, avatar development, and interactivity have made it possible for cost effective immersive virtual interactive solutions. Sales of 3D displays are projected to grow from 2 million units in 2003 to 8 million units in 2010 (http://www.digitimes.com/index.asp).
- 2009 Cisco Systems canceled its sales training and Apple is pulling out of future Macworld and instead of spending $1 million for sales training, the billion-dollar company will hold its training virtually
- A monumental shift in pricing and quality is taking place in the 3D projection space

– In 2009, Texas Instruments released a new 3D Single DLP chip target to the 3D education mass market with a 90% cost reduction

- 2009 Microsoft announces a new interactive 3D gesture & body interaction control, Natal, targeted at the volume market
- As more people embrace a technology-filled lifestyle including cell phones, smart phones and other wireless devices, traditional learning methodologies no longer satisfy the needs of today's learners. There is an ongoing validation of the teaching potential of SBL and the adoption of 3D products in colleges and universities worldwide. JTM Concepts recently conducted independent studies in the state of Illinois to compare the results of grade school classes taught with 3D curriculum versus standard lecture teaching methods. The research, supported by state funding, showed that students taught using one of JTM's Classroom 3D simulations had an average increase in test scores of up to 35 percent versus the 9.8 percent score increase from traditional teaching methods. In the first school, the control group test scores increased 9.7 percent. But the group that received its lesson in 3D saw a 35 percent increase. And in the second school with low-income students, the score improvements were 9.7 percent for the control group and 23 percent for students who received the 3D lesson (Texas Instruments, 2010).
- Environmental challenges and economic restrictions are driving the demand for reducing travel time and costs spent on meetings and events. UN demands virtual meetings to help reduce carbon footprints. The aim is to reduce travel costs by 50% to 80% and emissions by 15%.
- The Avatar 3D Movie; this type of movie is generating increasing consumer expectations and demand for 3D technologies,

Figure 6. An interactive 3D environment (from laptop to an immersive CAVE environment) can be used in engineering evaluations for a better insight in the position of the different components

immersions and interaction that in turn drive companies' demand for interactive 3D products, virtual meetings, training and communication environments.

3.1. Problems and Considerations

Globally, increased competition demands greater productivity and efficiency. As a result, innovation and adaptability have become critical sources of competitive advantages. In an ever-accelerating world economy, companies are learning faster about new trends, products, and production methods, yet teachers do not have the right tools to leapfrog to 21-century classroom. Needs and problems for consideration comprise several issues, mainly in the areas of training and education, as well as immersive 3D communication.

The training and education issues are:

- Need to motivate and engage learners in effective knowledge transfer
- Effectively minimize accidents and train people in "what if" scenarios
- Today's traditional online meetings are not able to address the need for VLE or SBL
- Increase in health care costs forces the industry to focus on streamlining capital investments for equipment and training

Immersive 3D communication issues are:

- System costs are high
- Lack of software solutions that are easy to use, scalable, integrated, collaborative, and work cross platform
- Lack of content and applications

Figure 7. The Virtual Reality Training System (VRTS) – Interactive interface developed for the oil and gas industry

Figure 8. The Icube the EON Icube is an interactive visualization solution and a collaborative environment similar to a CAVE system. The head and the Xbox 360 controllers, which use optical motion tracker systems, are navigation devices calculating the 3D perspective view in real-time.

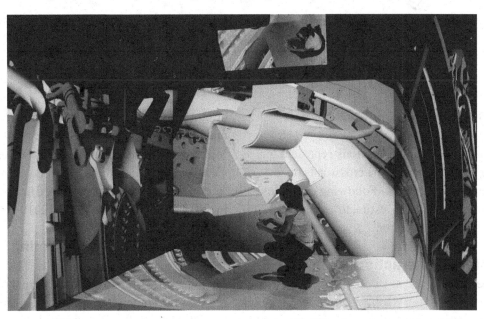

Figure 9. EON Icube configuration; The "Cube" environment can be configured in 4-wall and 6-wall versions or be integrated into several stereoscopic environments, shaped into a star shaped cluster, where participants can enter their own "cube reality" and simultaneously interact with others in that same world. The technology is an interactive multi-user concept with the purpose to engage visitors in a collaborative experience.

3.2. Technology Applications

Visualization technology solutions represent an emerging market that is at the crossroads of several different growth areas. Following examples endeavors to provide an estimate that may be useful as a market indicator.

3D Customer Interaction Management

The 3D Customer Interaction is a segment that reuses existing CAD assets developed for product design in the area of sales, marketing, training, maintenance and support. Still the 3D Customer Interaction market segment is in an emerging stage and the adoption rate will take some time. The total CAD market is estimated to reach $8.2B by 2012 (Jon Peddie Research, 2010).

Interactive 3D Virtual Meeting

The market for Interactive 3D Virtual Meetings is a subset to the traditional online meeting market. The online Web presentation sessions and various video meetings -- logged their first $1 billion quarter in 2007, according to Wainhouse Research. Wainhouse researchers project that in North America alone, revenue from audio, video, and Web collaboration services will reach $4.4 billion by 2011.

3.2.1. The EON Coliseum

EON Coliseum is a networking engine that optimizes multi-modal communication. It is a PC based online 3D interactive virtual-world platform that provides realistic communication capabilities between multiple users, incorporating 3D worlds, slideshows, videos, and, most important, the ability to interact with 3D objects virtually from anywhere in the world. With an ability to communicate with one too many from any "environment" you wish to "be in" and interaction through personalized 3D avatars with gestures, voice and chat, the platform is a tool aimed to accelerate learning anywhere and anytime while using interactive 3D objects in simulated environments.

EON Coliseum (Figure 10) has the following competitive advantages:

- Multi-user environment with avatars that focuses on business and education
- Remote 3D simulation/interaction with 3D objects
- Real-time voice communication - Voice-over-IP (devices that support Internet Protocol) network, which secures peer-to-peer/conference
- Streaming video
- Virtual presentation surface supporting major formats for text and imagery, any software via TCP/UDP (transmission control protocol and user diagram protocol), providing multi-format document viewing
- DataLink node extends connectivity to virtually any software (TCP/UDP), e.g. Matlab
- Hotspots/transparent layers/oblique profiles/animation
- Dynamic Download

Figure 10. The EON Coliseum A PC based platform that combines rich media with personalized interaction through avatars, voice and chat, while using interactive 3D objects in simulated environments

- Ability to record a presentation
- Scalable publishing formats.

Simulation Based Learning

Simulation-Based Learning ("SBL") where learning is conducted with a computer or a mobile device that benefit from the interactivity of an online environment. Simulation Based Learning (SBL), incorporates interactive 3D visualization into game-like remote info learning applications and learning environments. The SBL market ranges from multi-disciplinary university research education to technical education programs for plant maintenance, product support, and other visual applications, expanding in education for more advanced, simulation based 3D learning experiences. Further on the video game industry is fueling and setting the expectations for SBL interactive experiences through new technologies like Nintendo Wii, PlayStation 3, and Xbox 360.

Simulation Based Learning (SBL) provides content, applications and real-time interactive visualizations, utilizing multi-modality and multi-dimensional data from any file format, such as CAD data, GIS data, MRI data, etc. Users engage in a scalable, Internet connected network. Advantages comprise possibilities for repetition and assessment, safe and realistic hazardous situation training, and 24-hour accessibility.

Serious Games

There is now an emergent supply chain for corporate Serious Games with a number of corporations taking the first steps by commissioning Serious Games development. The same demand applies to Healthcare providers (e.g., training for surgery, for emergency medical response, and for managing surgical teams). The Serious Games market in 2007 was estimated to be around $400 million per year – just in the US (mostly Educational and Military).

Additionally, Serious Games are gaining solid traction in Europe and the video game industry is finding more and more business outside the entertainment sector – both indicators of a growing demand for interactive, experiences from the consumer to the learner to the corporate environment (Alhadeff, 2007).

Immersive 3D Solutions

By integrating 3D software and applications with various immersive and stereoscopic display systems (from portable Tablet PCs and glass free stereo display systems to curved-screen and immersive rooms consisting of multi-channel projection walls,) this market is today a subset of the AV and Projection market and estimated to grow to $15.8 billion market in 2015 from $140 million in 2008, with a compound annual growth rate (CAGR) 95% for the period, according to Displaybank. Displaybank said by 2015, 3D displays will account for 9.2% of the total display market (Digitimes.com).

3.2.2. The Icube

By using a set of synchronized PCs linked together in a local area network running on a UNIX platform, high-resolution 3D, rear projected digital imagery and stereoscopic glasses, users are immersed in what appears to be a very engaging VR experience. Objects can be manipulated through gesture-enabled gloves with force feedback, while 3D sound can be synchronized with the imagery for an extraordinary experience. The system uses electromagnetic 6DOF trackers to determine the user's position and work in unison with the glasses to produce a true stereoscopic perspective. No shadows are visible because each of the screens is rear projected. A 3-wall Icube system consists of three rear-projected screens and one front projected floor screen set-up in a fixed U-shape configuration where each screen is 96″ by 72″.

4. AUGMENTED REALITY, TELE-PRESENCE AND MOBILE IMMERSION

Other technologies are also allowing people to move away from purely physical communication to "augmented/mixed" reality communication and interaction. Tele-Presence is one of these technologies – it is the real-time display of 3D information and images that assists and enhances collaboration and interaction. Augmented reality/mobile immersive devices are visualization devices that provide added contextual information to functions like communication, product development and medical imaging. Connected with 3D glasses they provide real time guidance and explanation by for example superimposing a video image with a 3D model overlaying and augmenting the real world. Input that contains additional hidden information is accessible from sensors like RFID. Target use for Augmented reality//mobile immersion:

- Education and location based information
- Installation and Support - Assisting difficult tasks
- Medical Visualization
- Construction, Infrastructure

A report from market intelligence firm ABI Research forecasts the global RFID market to grow to $5.35 billion in 2010 (http://www.idtechex.com/products/en/articles/00000169.asp).

Augmented Reality & Head Mounted Display Technology Implementations for Education

AR has a variety of implementations in education including:

- As a study and self-learning tool (potential for mobile learning)
- Facilitating classroom projects and enhance classroom reflection
- Guiding classroom field trips
- As an exploratory game
- Situated learning

4.1. Survey

University of New Mexico (non-3D) (http://chronicle.com/article/Augmented-Reality-on-Smar/65991/ ; http://www.digitaltech-frontier.com)

Design: The University uses an augmented reality (integrated mobile computing & physical surroundings) educational game for second-year Spanish class students called ARIS (Augmented Reality and Interactive Storytelling). ARIS lets designer's link text, images, video, or audio to a physical location, making the real world into a map of virtual characters and objects that people can navigate with iPhones, iPads, or iPod Touches. The tool is open-source and was developed by Madison research group.

Augmented Reality Development Lab from Digital Tech Frontier

(http://augmentedrealitydevelopmentlab.com/products/)

Facilitate classroom learning includes:

- ARDL Core Software
- Student sets interaction paddles
- PDF templates
- 5 cameras
- Google Sketchup model exporter and viewer
- Augmented reality module builder
- Module pack one includes content for the following: Discover the Planets, Build The Human Heart, 3D Multiplication, Moon Phases, Moon Eclipse, Virtual Creature mask, Discover Chemical Molecules, Exploring Volcanoes & Terrain, Earth Surface

Visualization, Math-Fractions: 3D Sphere, Wearing Maori Artifacts, Build A Maori Village, Nasa, ARDL Art Selection. The ARDL Module Creation Tool [teacher edition] Teachers can develop a module, and if it's designed to ARDL standards, then ARDL will distribute the new module at a cost to other users. The profits will be split with the developer and Digital Tech Frontier, LLC.

Pricing: 5 user licenses for 2,999 USD

Conceptual Design of AR in Education (Guides a Classroom Field Trip)

(http://educationstormfront.wordpress.com/2010/09/20/viddler-com-barras-andrew-final-project-uploaded-by-gamestrategies/)

Concept: The concept uses AR smart phones, a game server, gps, and possible AR HMD. This is a futuristic concept that does not currently hold analysis value.

Conceptual Design of a Civil War AR (Guides a Classroom Field Trip)

(http://www.kickstarter.com/projects/jmummert/the-civil-war-augmented-reality-project)

Concept: The concept uses an AR device (preferably an iPad-like device) with GPS. GPS locations trigger the display of photographs, text, and digital overlay (location-based information). Learners trace the steps of Confederate and Union Calvary men.

GE Smart Grid Augmented Reality (Facilitate Classroom Learning)

(http://ge.ecomagination.com/smartgrid/#/augmented_reality)

Design: The Smart Grid site can also be used when teaching students about alternative energy sources like wind turbines and solar energy. They can actually see 3-D models of each and interact with them. This would be a great introduction and attention grabber for an energy unit in science classes.

Cyber-Anatomy (Individual Learning – Classroom Learning)

(http://www.cyber-anatomy.com/)

Design: Cyber-Anatomy produces 3 stereoscopic solutions: human anatomy, cyberscience 3D, and custom solutions. The Cyber-Anatomy Med™ product is claimed to be the world's most advanced virtual cadaver for interactive anatomy education. The modules are available in two formats. Cyber-Science 3D™ is a suite of interactive 3D software in the areas of biology, human anatomy, zoology, micro-biology, chemistry and others that allow the user to explore, control, and manipulate virtual 3D models.

LarnGear Technology

(http://www.larngeartech.com)

Design: The company advertises its products noting that users can either use a PC, handheld device, or HMD to view the AR environment.

Molecular structure – Accommodates both self-study and may be used as a classroom tool. Users may view molecules. They may zoom in an out of a molecule. They can add elements to a molecule. And, they can view information on the molecules and elements. The molecules are in a continuous state of rotation.

- Earth structure – Presented as a book AR self-study book. The company also has a book on Robots. Thailand's Institute for the Promotion of Teaching Science and Technology supported and/or developed this 3D augmented reality textbook on geology

- House Floor Plan – for showcasing the levels of a house.

LearnAR

(http://www.augmatic.co.uk/work.html)

Design: Learners can hold up markers to their body and their organs and bones will display in 3D. The system also contains game elements. The AR module asks the learner a question and they have to hold up one of several color marked marker cards as the answer. The system keeps track of the number of questions asked, their score, and will respond as to whether the selected answer (i.e., marker) is correct.

The value of these technologies to the education system are:

- **Learning styles:** The ability to provide visual and time lapse examples allows for rich examples of complex phenomena (engineering, earth sciences, medicine, environmental applications to name a few) while engaging many styles of learners.
- **Authentic Learning:** AR provides a form of situated learning. For example, AR can tremendously enhance vocational studies for those wishing to enter the trades: auto and aviation mechanics, electricians, carpenters, etc... The ability to annotate real elements and the ability to add to reality by superimposing virtual aids, will aid in instruction and learning for those disciplines where a specific spatial configuration of elements must be learned and remembered (auto mechanics, medicine, chemistry).

- **Realistic models:** For students in K-12, AR provides a means of "seeing" phenomena in 3D, thereby bringing the contextual three dimensional nature of the real world to the their learning. Textual and pictorial information in the typical 2 dimensional print-based resources loses much of the richness of the "real" world elements, and involves an element of interpretation that is difficult for some students (http://www // augreality.pbworks.com/w/page/9469033/ Classroom-Learning-with-AR).
- **Engagement/Interactivity:** Illustrations in books can come to life with AR technology and can captivate readers of all ages.

The challenges of the industry include:

- Lack of funding in educational institutions.
- Lack of training in digital literacy skills (Johnson, Smith, Levine, & Haywood, 2010).
- Little agreement in the educational industry to the path to reform and a slow path to reform (Johnson, Smith, Levine, & Haywood, 2010).
- Perception of games as only entertainment – People have grown up with the understanding that games and interactive experiences are the realm of fun, play time or vacation and education is the realm of receiving information in a serious, no-nonsense, static, non-interactive fashion with little feedback or immediate consequences for incorrect assumptions or answers
- Lack of experience learning via games/ simulations combined with playing "games" only for fun leads to a perception that games/simulations aren't a serious way to learn. Unfamiliarity with development process - This is due in a large part to the time the design team doesn't understand how to create a game/simulation or the nature of non-linear content and thus

causes delays, false starts and cost overrun. They don't have experience learning from games/simulations and their educational models are lecture-focused and centered on linear delivery of content.

- Not understanding the mechanisms in games/simulations that make them educational.

4.1.1. Online Virtual Worlds for Education

There are numerous virtual worlds that children and teens may participate in including but not limited to Second Life, Tootsville, Mokitown, Nicktropolis, Cybertown, JumpStart, and Whyville. Some of these virtual worlds, such as Whyville and Second Life are well-established. Users can interact with one another in these words and can often complete learning activities together.

JumpStart (jumpstart.comis marketed as 3D interactive, adventure, learning games that stimulate the mind through critical thinking skills, math and reading, allowing a child to "get a real jumpstart in life". The intended audience for the virtual world is children 3-12 years old. Children "start the adventure" into JumpStart by designing their very own "jumpee" (i.e., avatar). JumpStart markets the virtual world to both parents and teachers. JumpStart has been in existence for approximately 20 years and claims to be trusted by over 30 million parents. For a fee of fee of $7.99, parents can register their kids at JumpStart.com to become members of the fully interactive 3D virtual world.

4.1.2. Consoles

A wide-variety of edutainment-type games exist for the numerous game consoles. In the education sector, these games are known as "serious games".

The most popular consoles that maintain a selection of games for learning include:

- Nintendo DS
- Nintendo Wii
- Sony PSP
- PC

The Nintendo console is by far the most populated with children's educational games. Educational games on the Nintendo DS include but are not limited to: Art Academy, Brain Age,

Personal Trainer: Math Nintendo, Jumpstart: Escape From Adventure Island (JumpStart games associated with JumpStart.com), I.Q. Trainer, Learn Science.

Sony PSP Educational games include but are not limited to: Hot Brain, Spelling Challenges and More, Brain Quest: Grades 3 & 4, Brain Quest: Grades 5 & 6, Mind Quiz: Your Brain Coach, Brain Assist, Brain Age: Train Your Brain in Minutes a Day, Brain Age 2: More Training in Minutes a Day, Brain Challenge, Math Play, Margot's Word Brain, Big Brain Academy, Animal Genius.

Nintendo is expected to release a 3D version of their highly popular and successful Nintendo DS, referred to as the Nintendo 3DS in February – March of 2011. The 3D-enabled screen doesn't require the user to wear glasses. The device also has the ability to turn the 3D offering off completely. New to the 3DS and not present on the DSi is a motion sensor and gryoscope for physical, three-dimensional gaming. The 3DS will be able to run all current games on the market for the Nintendo DS, however it's not the case the other way around. The 3DS comes with cameras and allows for augmented reality. The console allows for creating Miis (personalized digital avatar). You can point the outer cameras at someone's face, snap a photograph of them, and the 3DS automatically creates a Mii for you based on their facial features.

Gaming on PCs has been available for a while due to nVidia's 3D vision, and with their 3DTV Play technology users can hookup an HDTV via HDMI to their GeForce enabled 3D pcs.

The PlayStation 3 system is already equipped with everything it needs to play stereoscopic 3D games. Due to a free firmware update released this past April, the PS3 system is the only console on the market that can support full stereoscopic 3D gaming. Sony also has a collection of 3D games for the PS3 system. Online discussion has indicated that it is possible to play Xbox Kinect with a 3D TV doing 2D to 3D conversion. However, it is generally understood that the Xbox does not currently support 3D TV. The Nintendo Wii does not currently support 3D. The Microsoft Kinect project was previously known as project Natal. Rumors exist that the original Natal project consisting of augmented reality, gesture control, and artificial intelligent tutors is still ongoing. Many believe that great potential exists for the application of Kinect to an AR environment.

For further analysis of projectors, laptops, and other products in the commercial space please see Appendices A and B.

SUMMARY

Consoles. Primarily the handheld consoles, currently represent the largest market for edutainment-based learning. There exist a wide and varied number of edutainment titles for at least 4 different gaming platforms: Nintendo DS, Nintendo Wii, Sony PSP, and the PC. It is most important to note herein that from December of 2010 to February of 2011 Nintendo is expected to release the Nintendo 3DS. The 3DS is a mobile 3D gaming/learning environment. Out of all the technologies reviewed it is the game console technology that has the greatest share of the edutainment market.

CAVE environments. Have primarily been used for research and not as commercial education-based learning environments. The author of this document was unable to find any CAVEs which were deployed solely for purposes of K-12 education. This is likely due to the fact that CAVEs are costly in concern to other classroom based technologies and that CAVEs can generally only accommodate one individual at a time, and therefore, scheduling complications arise. CAVEs may be implemented with both a 3D stereoscopic and 3D non-stereoscopic features.

Several **3D stereoscopic content providers** currently exist for the individual learning and instructor led environments. Most of the 3D content available is for math and science, although Amazing Interactives offers some history and geography content. Bloggers noted that at the InfoComm International 2010 conference that was supposed to promote 3D learning that there was a noticeable lack of content available. The only companies offering 3D content at the conference were Tactus Technologies, JTM Concepts, and Amazing Interactives Ltd. JTM Concepts bundles its Classroom3 solution with XpanD's 3D glasses and Sharp's PG-D2500x projector. Amazing Interactives has both classroom and individual tutor-based content. The company has the largest range of educational solutions on the market..

AR. Augmented reality appears to have the greatest potential and due to several initiatives is gaining increasingly widespread adoption. Out of all of the technologies, augmented reality has seen the greatest implementation in schools; however, it is typically implemented for high school age groups and not the age group currently under consideration. Proponents of augmented reality technology in education say augmented reality differs from virtual reality in that while virtual reality aims to replace a person's perception of the world with an artificial world, augmented reality enhances a person's perception of his or her surroundings. ARDL was created in part to respond to the challenge that lecture-based learning does not affect students in the same way that technology-infused learning experiences can't. AR HMD devices also present an alternative to CAVEs (http://www.3davatarschool.com).

SUMMARY

Technology progresses has cut the cost and improved the performance of virtual reality systems, making the technology available for education and training. While the overall 3D market is still in its early stages, the *Customer interaction management* and *Simulation Based Learning (SBL)* segments have found (CIM) considerable traction particularly in the sales and marketing operations of heavy manufacturers (aerospace, automotive, defense) and other industries (construction, engineering, commercial development) where complex products are not easily presented. According to leading interactive 3D technology providers the 3D immersion is here to stay; "3D is a mass market phenomena and is increasingly being adopted in a widening range of applications. The way 3D has impacted the world of cinema is clear, but there are other applications where 3D breaks new boundaries, improving the aspirations, viewing, learning, or commercial experience for those involved." NEC Display Solutions Europe.

Visualization has found a range of support in Academia and R&D is supporting th and the market follows. 3D cameras, 3D projectors and 3D TV.

The aspect of using interactive 3D worlds online is probably the largest application area,

where the internet is converted from a 2D world to a interactive 3D world, blending video, tele presence, 3D communication and rich media publishing. 3D and its deployment has become an imperative in a wide-variety of industries:

- Visualization of large data and R&D within a stereo 3D immersive (virtual reality) environment.
- Visualization of design concepts and layout prior to production. Photo-realistic 3d models and animations for marketing and advertising needs (Figure 11).
- Virtualization of design elements simultaneously to accelerate the design process. Demonstrate complex solutions and create an immersive technological infrastructure to increase the probability of securing grants.
- Simulation-based learning/training, 3D content and curriculum; Risk management solutions and support of faster, more informed decision-making.
- Interactive 3D visualization support of maintenance, repair, and overhaul (MRO) operation.
- 3D multi-user virtual and collaboration solutions (teleimmersion) Reduced travel time and costs.
- Construction designs with stereo 3D architectural renderings. Visualization of proposed changes to existing buildings and structures in 3D prior to construction. Publish architectural renderings to a wide array of virtual reality and immersive hardware platforms, and online.
- Classroom initiative rolls out 3D simulations. There is an ongoing validation of the teaching potential of SBL and the adoption of 3D products in colleges and universities worldwide. (Classroom3® 3D, 2010).
- Multi-million-dollar, state of the art edutainment facilities using 3D stereoscopic audio and immersive visual technology

Figure 11. Design concepts for commercial aircraft; build see, modify, experience and accept products in a Real Time virtual environment prior to manufacturing. These services include interactive product configurations, merging of technologies and processes together with realism of the models.

are breaking a new ground in the entertainment segment. Combining educational and entertainment values from other forms of attractions, such as museums and theme parks with the use of advanced multimedia and Virtual Reality technologies, the new "edutainment" attractions are growing in popularity.

The educational or edutainment market is growing faster than others. More and more products and venues are marketing themselves as edutainment to increase their perceived value. New Discovery and Experience centers launch over the world with the sponsorship from local industry, retailers and governmental institutions. In return they get brand recognition and increased levels of recruitment to technical colleges, universities and so into industry.

While in the manufacturing economy, work was associated with self-improvement and leisure with purposeless relaxation, today many people see leisure time as an opportunity to improve themselves and their children.

- Every year, more than 100 million people visit 400 IMAX theatres in over 40 countries to be edutained. Half of the screens are in informal learning institutions such as museums, zoos and planetariums, while half are part of commercial cinema complexes.
- Major universities like MIT, Stanford and Duke are using iTunesU podcasts and YouTube for their distribution of free online courses while the App Store is being marketed as a "24/7 learning store at your fingertips".
- The worldwide market for edutainment toys reached $2.35 billion in 2007. In-Stat expects this figure to reach $9 billion by 2012.

REFERENCES

Alhadeff, E. (2007). *$9 Bi: Microsoft's conservative estimate for the serious games market.* Retrieved from http://www.futurelab.net/blogs/marketing-strategy-innovation/2007/12/9_bi_microsofts_conservative_e.html

Alhadeff, E. (2007). *Serious games, serious money: A sizeable market.* Retrieved from http://elianealhadeff.blogspot.com/2007/03/serious-games-serious-money-sizeable.html

Annett, M. K., & Bischof, W. F. (2010). Investigating the application of virtual reality systems to psychology and cognitive neuroscience research. *Presence (Cambridge, Mass.), 19*(2), 131–141.

Anton, R., Opris, D., Dobreani, A., David, D., & Rizzo, A. S. (2009). Virtual reality in the rehabilitation of attention deficit/ hyperactivity disorder/ instrument construction principles. *Journal of Cognitive and Behavioral Psychotherapies, 9*(2), 235.

Balding, J. J. (2009). *Incorporating innovative and immersive technologies: Changing the art of design.* Union City, CA: AECbytes.

Blog, E. O. N. (2010). *New aspects of brain research reveals impact of VR training.* Retrieved from http://eonrealityblog.wordpress.com/2010/04/07/new-aspects-of-brain-research-reveals-impact-of-vr-training/

Broll, W., Lindt, I., Ohlenburg, J., Wittkämper, M., Yuan, C., & Novotny, T. (2004). ARTHUR: A collaborative augmented environment for architectural design and urban planning. *Journal of Virtual Reality and Broadcasting, 1*(1), 1–10.

Chaouachi, M., Heraz, A., Jraidi, I., & Frasson, C. (2009). Influence of dominant electrical brainwaves on learning performance. In *Proceedings of the World Conference on E-Learning in Corporate, Government, Healthcare and Higher Education,* Montreal, QC, Canada.

Cheng, R. (2006, August 31). No-contact technology. *Wall Street Journal.*

Da Costa, C. (2009). *EON's ICube is the apple of virtual reality.* Retrieved from http://www.gadgetreview.com/2009/04/eons-icube-is-the-apple-of-virtual-reality-video.html#ixzz0uFicOgl

Dalgarno, B., & Harper, B. (2004). User control and task authenticity for spatial learning in 3D environments. *Australian Journal of Educational Technology, 20*(1), 1–17.

Dalgarno, B., Hedberg, J., & Harper, B. (2002). The contribution of 3D environments to conceptual understanding. In *Proceedings of the Annual Conference of the Australasian Society for Computers in Learning in Tertiary Education,* Auckland, New Zealand.

Davies, A., & Dalgarno. B. (2009). Learning fire investigation the clean way: The virtual experience. *Australasian Journal of Educational Technology, 25*(1).

Dede, C. (2007). Reinventing the role of information and communications technologies in education. *Yearbook of the National Society for the Study of Education, 106*(2), 11–38.

Gann, D., & Dodgson, M. (2008). Innovate with vision. *Ingenia, 36,* 45–48.

Greffou, S., Bertone, A., Hanssens, J.-M., & Faubert, J. (2008). Development of visually driven postural reactivity: A fully immersive virtual reality study. *Journal of Vision (Charlottesville, Va.), 8*(11), 1–10.

Jacobson, M. J. (2010). *Learning in virtual reality environments.* Retrieved from http://eonrealityblog.wordpress.com/2010/02/28/learning-in-virtual-reality-environments/

Johnson, L., Smith, R., Levine, A., & Haywood, K. (2010). *The 2010 horizon report: K-12 edition.* Austin, TX: The New Media Consortium.

Jon Peddie Research. (2010). *CAD report.* Retrieved from http://www.jonpeddie.com/publications/cad_report/

Knowledgeworks. (2008). *2020 forecast: Creating the future of learning.* Retrieved from http://www.futureofed.org/pdf/forecast/2020_forecast.pdf

Leybovich, I. (2010). *RFID market projected to grow in 2010.* Retrieved fromhttp://news. thomasnet.com/IMT/archives/2010/03/radio-frequency-identification-rfid-market-projected-to-grow-in-2010-beyond.html

Newcombe, N. S. (2010). Picture this increasing: Math and science learning by improving spatial thinking. *American Educator*, 2010.

North, M. M., North, S. M., & Coble, J. R. (1998). Virtual reality therapy: An effective treatment for psychological disorders. In Riva, G. (Ed.), *Virtual reality in neuro-psycho-physiology*. Amsterdam, The Netherlands: IOS Press.

Prensky, M. (2002). *What kids learn that's POSITIVE from playing video games.* http://www. cyber-spy.com/ebooks/ebooks/What-Kids-Learn-Thats-POSITIVE-from-Playing-Video-Games-(ebook).pdf

Raynor, W. (2005). *Globalization and outsourcing in a flat, but unbalanced world.* Retrieved from http://www.newwork.com/Pages/Opinion/Raynor/Unbalanced.html

Real Vision Consultancy. (2009). *Re-creating natural environments using real-time 3D engines.* Retrieved from http://docs.google.com/viewer?a=v&q=cache:cDfULwxqUeUJ:www. realvision.ae/pdf/3D_engines_stereo3d.pdf+cr yengine+cave+virtual+environment+stereosco pic&hl=en&gl=us&pid=bl&srcid=ADGEESiY LDqcWuKux9D_OGengCtliHRFS_buk7hlDN-zN1kOJm12HXh-4gzHz8yslVj3PueT71Fu-5CIZ4tQ1jFUdrK6L5EIGf5miuA7Abosz09ni_ euekSysXA0wQ-CKH8sbDhYgoYGXQ&sig= AHIEtbQQTRQiDIdbTPk97ebbI4kT7JBhlg

Rydmark, M., Kling-Petersen, T., Pascher, R., & Philip, F. (2001). 3D visualization and stereographic techniques for medical research and education. *Studies in Health Technology and Informatics, 81*, 434–439.

Scacchi, W., Nideffer, R., & Adams, J. (2008). A collaborative science learning game environment for informal science education: DinoQuest online. *New Frontiers for Entertainment Computing, 279*, 71–82.

Scrogan, L. (2010). *Beyond the red carpet: 3D comes to school.* Retrieved from http://bvsd.org/ bvs3d/Documents/BEYOND THE RED CAR-PET - BVS3D.pdf

Shiode, N. (2000). 3D urban models: Recent developments in the digital modelling of urban environments in three-dimensions. *GeoJournal, 52*(3), 263–269.

Texas Instruments. (2010). *Classroom3® 3D case study.* Retrieved fromhttp://www.dlp. com/downloads/DLP_3D_Classroom3_Case_ Study.pdf

White, R., & Engelen, G. (2000). High-resolution integrated modeling of the spatial dynamics of urban and regional systems. *Computers, Environment and Urban Systems, 24*(5), 383–400.

Wong, G. (2009). *EON Coliseum: Pioneering multi-modal communication in virtual reality.* Retrieved from http://www.eonreality.com/ brochures/EON_Coliseum_Whitepaper.pdf

APPENDIX A

Terminology

Augmented Reality (AR) is an interactive 3D environment that blends with our physical reality; the capability to link the virtual world with the physical world through for example a "superman vision" where a video image is superimposed with a 3D model of the same environment and adding hidden information accessible from sensors like RFID.

Avatar is a computer user's representation of himself/herself or alter ego, whether in the form of a 3D (three dimensional) model used in computer games, a two-dimensional picture used on Internet forums and other communities. The term "avatar" can also refer to the personality connected with the screen name, or handle, of an Internet user.

CAVE (Cave Automatic Virtual Environment) is an immersive virtual reality environment where projectors are directed to three, four, five or six of the walls of a room-sized cube. The name is also a reference to the allegory of the Cave in Plato's Republic where a philosopher contemplates perception, reality and illusion. CAVE technical specifications:

- ○ Utilizes 4 screens, 3 rear and 1 front projection
- ○ Tracks the user with 12 tracking cameras
- ○ Can be used in either a 90°, 135°, or 180° configuration
- ○ The total viewing area enclosed by the four screens is nearly 8'x10'x10' or 800 cubic feet
- ○ Each screen is controlled by its own computer and these computers are all synced with one another

CAI Computer-assisted instruction

Customer Interaction Management is in this context defined as the use of interactive 3D technology to effectively capture, propose and validate customer needs thus improving the customer journey and end state.

EON Coliseum application framework, built on top of EON Reality's base generic 3D product platform. The technology combines videoconference, screen sharing, and 3D interaction.

Game engine is a software system designed for the creation and development of video games. These tools are an integrated development environment to enable simplified, rapid development of specific interactive models and environments.

GPS Global Positioning System

ICT Information and communication technologies

Interactive Digital Centers (IDC) are worldwide collaborative partnerships focusing on visualization and 3D Interactive Digital Media solutions and services for various industries.

Interactive 3D virtual meeting is a 3D Web conferencing tool that allows users to virtually meet online rather than in a physical conference room and learn, present, demonstrate, collaborate and train.

ITS Intelligent tutoring systems

Information Society The emerging term "information society" comes from the new focus on the role of information and technology in modern economies and the transmission of knowledge through communication and computer networks.

Immersive 3D solution is defined as an integrated system consisting of software, computers, displays, projectors or glasses that provide a state of consciousness where an immersant's awareness of physical self is diminished by being surrounded in an engrossing total environment.

Interactive 3D Virtual Meeting is a 3D Web conferencing tool that allows users to virtually meet on line to learn, present, demonstrate, collaborate and train. Features can include Shared Virtual Worlds, Communication with Voice-over-IP, Live video support, Virtual Presentation Surface, and Multi-format document viewing.

Knowledge-based Economy The term "knowledge-based economy" stems from the recognition of the place of knowledge as the driver of productivity and growth in modern economics. Rapid knowledge transfer and a workforce that continuously acquires and adapts new skills underlie the "learning economy".

LMS Learning management systems.

MMO Massively multi-user online environments.

MUVE Multi-user virtual environment.

Simulation Based Learning is an extension of e learning that provides an interactive learning experience combining the sophistication of simulator technology with the ease of use and scalability of video game industry.

Virtual Learning environment (VLE) is a computerized environment designed to support teaching and learning in an educational setting which involves distance learning. In a virtual learning environment, where virtual reality mimics the real world, learners can perform experiments otherwise dangerous or impossible to do in reality.)

Virtual Reality (VR) allows a user to interact with a computer-simulated environment, whether simulation of the real world or an imaginary world displayed either on a screen or through stereoscopic displays.

Virtual Reality exposure Therapy places the client in a computer-generated world where they "experience" the various stimuli related to their phobia. The client wears a head-mounted display with stereo earphones to receive both visual and auditory cues. In careful, controlled stages, the client is exposed to these virtual experiences that elicit increasingly higher levels of anxiety

Virtual world is a computer-based simulated environment where interaction takes place in real time with digital personas (Avatars). Some, but not all, virtual worlds allow for multiple users. There are elements of interactivity, collaboration, immersion and immediacy, which distinguish virtual worlds from regular webinars.

WHD Wireless handheld device.

APPENDIX B

3D Content for Projectors and Laptops

Safari Montage (CLAIM) (http://www.safarimontage.com/)

Products and Solutions

- Digital curriculum presenter – a classroom lesson presentation tool. Digital Curriculum Presenter provides a platform for teachers to present a complete digital curriculum, capable of supporting the playback of over 40 of the most popular media and document file formats. Integrated with Moodle® and other Learning Management Systems (LMS), Digital Curriculm Presenter provides a single intuitive and attractive interface that allows teachers to deliver a lesson without the burden of having to switch between multiple media players and technologies. The Digital Curriculum Developer™ feature provides the tools to build or import the scope and sequence of a course, add important visual assets to a lesson and create robust formative assessments.

- Digital content – from well-known content providers including PBS, ABC News, and Sesame Street. It is also claimed to be a 3D content creator, but this claim is only referenced in Web articles and the company's website makes no such claim nor does it identify any 3D products or services

Discover Education (CLAIM) (http://www.discoveryeducation.com/)

Products and Solutions

- It is also claimed to be a 3D content creator, but this claim is only referenced in Web articles and the company's website makes no such claim nor does it identify any 3D products or services

Google SketchUp (FREE 3D CONTENT) (sketchup.google.com)

Products and Solutions

- Allows students to easily create 3D models of everything from simple geometric forms to complex communities.

Reallusion 3DXchange allows user to import free SKP 3D models from Google's 3D Warehouse.

Tactus Technologies (INDIVIDUAL LESSON) (http://www.tactustech.com/)

Products and Solutions

- V-Frog 2 virtual dissection software – is for those beyond the age of 12 and allows students to virtually dissect a frog. Students can animate their specimen: see the heartbeat, see how muscles work, and watch digestion. Every layer of the specimen can be made transparent. Also features comparative anatomy to help students understand the differences and similarities between the systems of different species.

JTM Concepts (INSTRUCTOR LED) (http://www.jtmconcepts.com)

The company bundles its content with XpanD's 3D glasses and Sharp's PG-D2500X projector.

Products and Solutions

- Classroom3 – a library of interactive simulations for education. Library access is web-based and is updated regularly. Classroom provides content in four different subject areas including math, botany, astronomy, and biology (http://www.dlp.com/projector/case-studies/improved-test-scores-3d.aspx).

Amazing Interactives (http://www.amazing-int.com/)

Products and Solutions

- 2D & 3D Explorer (interactive) for supporting the delivery of the following subject areas maths, English, geography, ICT (computing technology), biology, physics, chemistry, history and art & design. This is an individual, interactive and explorable environment, which may also be instructor led.
- 2D and 3D Tutor for full narration and interactivity of the subject matter. This is an individual tutor-based environment.
- 2D and 3D Sen for highly interactive sensory experiences. Note: This is a research project and not a commercial product.

Competitive Stereoscopic Engines

Unity3D Gaming Engine (http://unity3d.com/) Not a content provider.

Products and Solutions

Unity 3 is a game development tool that has been designed to let you focus on creating amazing games. Unity has multi-platform development and is publishable to its Web player, PC and Mac, iOS, Android, Xbox 360, and PS3.

Note: Has 3D workarounds, but does not yet have native stereoscopic 3D support.

Cryengine automatic Virtual Environment (CryVE) (http://cryve.id.tue.nl/)

yengine automatic Virtual Environment (CryVE) http://cryve.id.tue.nl/

Products and Solutions

CryVE is based on the game engine CryEngine2. The improved visuals and performance of the CryEngine2 over the game engines used by similar systems like CAVEUT, confirm CryVE system as a solid alternative to bring state of the art technology and photorealistic graphics to low-cost CAVE systems. CryVE is a low-cost implementation that offers advantages to the scientific, gaming, and graphics enthusiasts communities (VE Engines).

This work was previously published in International Journal of Creative Interfaces and Computer Graphics, Volume 2, Issue 1, edited by Ben Falchuk, pp. 42-67, copyright 2010 by IGI Publishing (an imprint of IGI Global).

Chapter 15
Criteria for the Creation of Aesthetic Images for Human–Computer Interfaces:
A Survey for Computer Scientists

Gabriele Peters
FernUniversität in Hagen, Germany

ABSTRACT

Interaction in modern human-computer interfaces is most intuitively initiated in an image-based way. Often images are the key components of an interface. However, too frequently, interfaces are still designed by computer scientists with no explicit education in the aesthetic design of interfaces and images. This article develops a well-defined system of criteria for the aesthetic design of images, motivated by principles of visual information processing by the human brain and by considerations of the visual arts. This theoretic disquisition establishes a framework for the evaluation of images in terms of aesthetics and it serves as a guideline for interface designers by giving them a collection of criteria at hand; how to deal with images in terms of aesthetics for the purpose of developing better user interfaces. The proposed criteria are exemplified by an analysis of the images of the web interfaces of four well known museums.

1. INTRODUCTION

Images are often the key components of user interfaces. Examples of such interfaces from several applications of augmented reality (i.e., geovisualization, navigation, maintenance, mu-seum guides, etc.) are shown in Figures 1 and 2. Figure 1 shows an image of the environment which is augmented by data indicating a possible path for a boat.

One could be of the opinion that such a real-time navigation system has to show "just the image the camera captures". But the interface

DOI: 10.4018/978-1-4666-0285-4.ch015

Figure 1. Images as key components of user interfaces: navigation (Adapted from WisdomTools LLC, 2009)

designer has to decide for the specification of numerous variables that determine how the captured image is presented in the user interface. To name but a few, she has to choose color space, contrast, dynamic range, spatial arrangement of the image components (e.g., the position of the horizon), depth of field, and focal length. Figure 2 shows an example for maintenance instructions for an engine. The previous statements hold true for this example, as well. Even in a case where *some* parameters of an image are user-controlled - as is the case for the maintenance example, where the viewing direction is user-controlled – the interface designer still has to control other image

Figure 2. Images as key components of user interfaces: maintenance (Adapted from Ecole Polytechnique Federale de Lausanne, Automatic Control Laboratory, 2011)

parameters (such as the color space or the dynamic range in this example). There are still voices claiming that images in augmented reality applications are "literal depictions of the real-world scene". However, there is no such thing as a "literal depiction of the real-world". It simply does not exist, because *every* image (independent of whether it was generated by a human or by a technical device) can depict only a part and only a particular view or perspective of the real-world. Among the many parameters that determine the appearance of an image are those mentioned earlier (contrast, depth of field, etc.). For a concrete image these parameters have concrete, determined values. The *choice* of these values is in the responsibility either of the human who generates the image or (in the case of augmented reality applications) in the responsibility of the designer of the computer system which generates the image, and this choice should be a conscious and well-considered decision rather than being left to chance.

Topics such as the importance of aesthetic qualities of graphical elements of user interfaces (Tufte, 1990), the aesthetics of interaction (Norman, 2002), or the aesthetics of websites in particular (Lavie & Tractinsky, 2004) have frequently been addressed. There are also early publications on aesthetics in general, even in the context with mathematics (Birkhoff, 1933), (Bense, 1965). What is underrepresented in the literature is the role of *image* aesthetics in interfaces. This paper is an attempt to fill this gap. The roles of images in human-computer interaction are manifold. Stone et al. (2005) name four main benefits. Images motivate and attract the attention of the user and have the function to persuade her. They communicate information, which is often exploited in computer-based learning. Furthermore, they have the great power to overcome language barriers, and last but not least they support interaction. Images are especially powerful whenever it is difficult to describe the depicted information by

words or numbers. This is the paradigm for most human-computer interaction applications.

In Section 2 we propose aesthetic categories that, on the one hand, allow for the evaluation of the aesthetic qualities of an image (and thus of an important component of human-computer interfaces) and, on the other hand, enable an interface designer to adapt her tools to the needs of the user. Section 2 closes with an analysis of the images of the web interfaces of four well known museums to exemplify the described criteria by means of practical instances, where images are key components of human-computer interfaces. Furthermore, to justify the proposed categories we take a closer look at the user and her visual system in Section 3, where we describe basics about human visual processing and the possible connections to our aesthetic experience. We summarize results from cognitive neuroscience and psychology, that give an understanding of the basic principles of the human visual system. This system solves a perceptual problem by filtering out the salient features of an object from the details and varieties of its appearance. This is akin to visual artist's abilities to cull from the sensory manifolds those image features that enhance the clarity of the representation. Thus, cognitive neuroscience as well as artistic principles represent the foundations for the defined categories and criteria of visual aesthetics.

2. CRITERIA FOR THE CREATION AND ASSESSMENT OF IMAGES IN TERMS OF AESTHETICS

In this section we will consider which criteria of image composition are capable of evoking an aesthetic sensation. We divide these criteria into six categories, the motivation of which is described later in Section 3. Many books have been filled with principles of art work of images, i.e., the layout and arrangement of color and form in visual arts, whether it is drawing, painting, or photography.

In this section we refer to the classic benchmark by Feininger (1961) as it summarizes the most basic principles of aesthetic composition and is still a reference for photographers and artists. For each criterion described in this section we give an example, mostly in form of a photograph, but the described principles hold true for all kinds of images.

Reading only the captions of this section it can be regarded as a quick guide for the creation and assessment of images in terms of aesthetics. In the last subsection we analyze the images of websites of four museums with respect to the introduced criteria.

2.1. Category Color

Many examples of color-blind animals support the opinion that color is not the most important feature of the visual world. Even humans with an impairment of their color sense are able to cope excellently with the requirements of life. Nevertheless, color is a modularity of the visual system, which just in the context of beauty is an important means to evoke aesthetic experiences. Three criteria of color and its distribution in an image, which are known to appeal to our aesthetic sense, are examined in this subsection.

2.1.1. Usage of a Few Strong Colors

The maximum number of strong colors for an image still to be pleasant to the eyes usually is two to three. If more than a few strong colors occur in an image usually the effect of beauty is lost. (Maybe this corresponds to the isolated process in the human visual system triggered by only one special visual attribute which will be explained in subsection 3.2.) In principle, color in an image should correlate with its content (Feininger, 1961). If color is not the salient feature of an object depicted in the image, as it holds true, for example, for a butterfly, the visual system of the observer is overcharged and an aesthetic impression is missed. The left image of Figure 3 shows an example. The orange color of the turbans of the musicians is the dominant property of them in this image. Thus, as a consequence they are depicted in such a way that the orange color is also the dominant property of the whole image itself. All other colors of the image are subordinate or even non-colors (white). Also the right image of Figure 3 gets by with only a few strong colors, the yellow of the taxis and the red rear lights of the cars.

The deliberate choice of only one main color in an image, called monochromaticity, represents an extreme variation of this rule. Quite aesthetic results can be achieved if only a small range of colors adjacent in the color circle are chosen, e.g.,

Figure 3. Usage of a few strong colors and application of complementary contrast

only red, brown, and orange tones in a picture of autumn foliage. The images of Figure 4 shows an extreme example of this principle, where only a brown tone is used and this even in a quite unsaturated way.

Such a subtle monochrome coloration allows for the accentuation of important elements which come to the fore, as the bench and the person in these examples.

2.1.2. Application of Complementary Contrast

Pairs of colors that are in some way opposites of each other are called complementary colors. The traditional sets of complementary pairs in art are red and green, blue and orange, and yellow and purple. They face each other in the color circle, as for example advocated by van Goethe (1810) or Itten (1961) (Figure 5).

Two complementary colors reinforce themselves mutually in their luminance. By a moderate application of this effect the attention of the observer can be directed, which is especially important for human interaction with information systems. The most beautiful effect often is achieved if the complementary colors are the only strong colors. The hindu picture of Figure 3 with the dominant orange of the turbans and the zither and the contrasting blue tone of the blanket may hold as an example for this effect, as well. The complementary contrast becomes evident in two phenomena, the simultaneous and the successive contrast, where the nonexistent complementary color is anticipated either simultaneously in the environment of an existent color or immediately after the exposure of a color, respectively. Colloquially speaking, the human visual system requests the complementary completion and generates it on its own authority if it is not present. This can hold as another argument that supports the thesis of the foundation of aesthetics in cognitive neuroscience, as exposed in Section 3.

2.1.3. Exploitation of the Dynamic Range

The distribution of tonal values in an image is characterized by the dynamic range. Although it applies for colored as well as for black and white images the principle is best explained by means of gray value images. The dynamic range describes

Figure 4. Subtle monochrome coloration

Figure 5. Color circles from the 18th century (left) and by Josef Itten, 1961 (right)

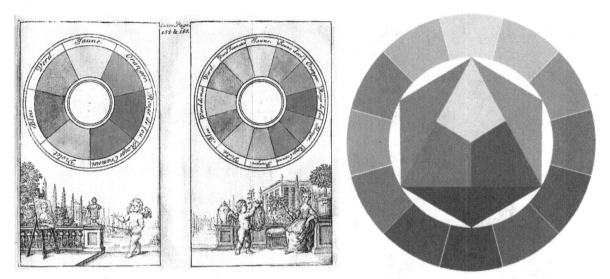

the ratio of luminance values from the brightest highlights to the deepest shadows in an image (i.e., white and black, respectively).

Our visual system can perceive much a greater dynamic range than that which can be rendered in an image via a monitor or a print.

When we consider the instantaneous dynamic range (where our pupil opening is unchanged) this ratio is indicated between 1:1000 and 1:10,000 (McHugh, 2010). But our visual system is extremely adaptive and the dynamic range actually changes depending on brightness and contrast of a scene. If we consider situations where our pupil opens and closes for varying light, we can see over a range of nearly 1:1,000,000. In contrast to this, the dynamic range of prints is about 1:250 and those of monitors can reach values of about 1:1000.

One can say that an image looks pleasing to the eye if the display medium (print or monitor) is able to render the dynamic range of the depicted scene in a similar way as it is perceived by the human visual system. The contrast ratio of an image should be controlled in such a way that the wide range of intensity levels from the brightest light to the deepest shadow is represented in an image. As a rule of thumb, an image is said to be aesthetic only if the full tonal range is present and,

in addition, the tonal values are distributed in a well-balanced manner. The images of Figure 6 can pass off as examples for that. As an indicator for an advantageous distribution of the tonal values the histogram of an image can serve (Figure 7).

In the first example the dynamic range of the image is smaller than the dynamic range of the scene. The histogram indicates that some shadow and highlight detail is lost. The second histogram is one of an image of low contrast. The dynamic range of the scene is smaller than the dynamic range of the image. In contrast to this, a histogram shape which covers the whole range of gray level values as depicted in the last example is a good precondition for an aesthetic image. It indicates that both shadow and highlight detail is captured. In general, the very bright and dark parts of an image should only take up small portions of an image, just as it holds true for the images of Figure 6. A technique that should be mentioned in this context is Ansel Adams' zone system (Adams, 1981). With this system he gave a recipe to bridge the gap between the limited dynamic range of prints or monitors in comparison to our visual system. The zone system allows for the prints or monitor displays to approximate the way the world looks to our eyes. It does this by providing a

Figure 6. Exploitation of the dynamic range

simple way to control the contrast of images. Although originally developed for film negatives, its principles can easily be adopted for digital imaging.

A temporary fashion worth mentioning is high dynamic range imaging (Reinhard et al., 2005; Brown, 2006). As a field primarily evolved in computer graphics, it provides a set of methods to generate an image of high dynamic range from multiple exposures of the same scene. The source images are overlapped and masked appropriately so that the resulting composite represents a wider gamut of colors and tones. However, images generated with this technique often evoke an artificial impression and the effect tends to become stale if exaggerated.

2.2. Category Form

More important than color perception, form perception is one of the most basic visual functions, to master the demands of the environment. It provides the source of information necessary for basic survival functions such as navigation, recognition of prey, predators, and mates, as well as for high level behaviors such as reading. But form and shape of objects do not only allocate essential information on the world surrounding us, they are also a source of aesthetic sensation.

Two aesthetic criteria of form, clarity and silhouettes, are known to be judged as being beautiful and are described in the following.

2.2.1. Forms Should Be Clear and Simple

Speaking about form in the context of elements constituting an image usually lines and surfaces are meant. Lines can actually be present by the contrast gradient or color changes or they can emerge through our perception. For example, elements of an image can be arranged in such a way that they are connected by imaginary lines. Those can be attributed by their orientation, as well. It is known since a long time, that an image, that appeals favorably to our visual system,

Figure 7. Histograms as indicators for image quality

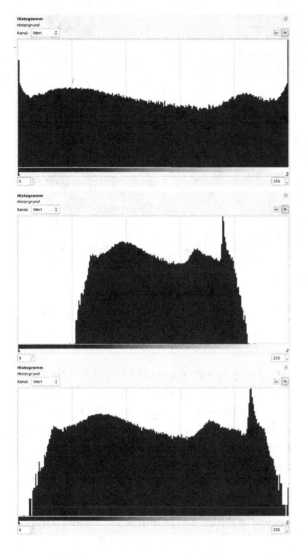

should comprise only a few predominant orientations in any case, either evolving from actual lines, by edges and boundaries of surfaces, or by imaginary lines. The main orientations in the left image of Figure 8, for example, are constituted only by straight lines (verticals, horizontals, and diagonals), those of the right image by straight and curved lines and concentric ovals.

The few and overall shapes of both images are consistent, simple, and clearly recognizable. This is what Feininger means when he speaks of clarity and simplicity of form (Feininger, 1961).

To put forward a few generalizations, one can say that horizontal lines tend to evoke emotions of stability, constancy, and reliability. Vertical lines can induce the impression of rigidity and strength, whereas diagonals, besides of their graphical appeal, are adequate if a feeling of tension has to be created. If curved lines obey a continuous function in a mathematical sense and if they take a uniform course within the image as a whole they seem to appear beautiful.

2.2.2. Silhouettes Evoke Aesthetic Impressions

Silhouettes are explicitly listed by Feininger as components of aesthetic images (outlines which are typical for an object, vigorous and unusual; clear silhouettes) (Feininger, 1961).

Also artists from other disciplines have realized the value of silhouettes for the visual effect. Giacometti with his sculptures of men and animals can hold as an example. The strong impact of his works is achieved mainly by their silhouettes, viewed from a distance (Sartre, 1948), rather than by their three-dimensionality. Giacometti was a master in reducing objects (mainly humans and animals) to their characteristic outlines. Figure 9 shows an example.

Another prominent example is the series of photographs of moving humans and animals by Muybridge (1887) (Figure 10). Here the outlines of the objects play a decisive role in the aesthetic classification of his works, as well.

But not only shapes of animals and humans are perceived as being beautiful, also the silhouettes of other objects can be aesthetic elements of an image, such as the bench or the couple under the umbrella in Figure 11.

As a rule of thumb, one can say that silhouettes appear beautiful, if they capture the main characteristics of an object. The outline of the object should either be clearly identifiable or graphi-

Figure 8. Clarity and simplicity of form

cally interesting. In addition, silhouettes are supposed to be sharp-edged and clearly distinct from the background rather than ambiguous and bleary. However, this last rule does not apply unrestrictedly. The shape of the human body can be regarded as an exception to this rule, as already indicated by the fact that the human brain handles body shapes separately. This is pointed out in more detail in Section 3. Apparently, even if human silhouettes are depicted in a blurry fashion (Figure 12), they can evoke a sense of beauty.

2.3. Category Spatial Organization

A major role for the aesthetics of an image as a whole is not only played by the shapes of the elements constituting an image, rather also their mutual spatial relations in the two-dimensional surface of the image are of importance for its aesthetic appearance. Analogously to the form criterion *clarity* in the last subsection, we will here comment on the aesthetic criterion *clarity of spatial organization*. Other criteria of spatial organization are the *golden mean*, *texture* and *pattern*, *rhythm*, *repetition*, and *variation*, described next.

2.3.1. Clarity of Spatial Organization of Image Elements

According to Feininger clarity and simplicity of spatial organization are the silver bullet for an aesthetic image (Feininger, 1961). Too many objects in a single image cause confusion and derangement. An image should not be overloaded by details, as well. Figure 13 shows an example which demonstrates the power of spatial organization.

The attention of the viewer is focused on the person in the center, although the visible parts of the boy occupy only a very small portion in the image. This effect is only in part due to the form contrast between curved and straight lines, but mainly due to the spatial arrangement of the image elements. In general, an image appears aesthetically, if no element be omitted or be added without destroying the visual balance. There are also some more restrictive rules concerning the distribution of light and dark parts of an image. The usual way to scan an image is supposed to be from the left upper part diagonally to the right lower part. Accordingly, the most important portion of an image is the left upper part, because

Figure 9. Animal Silhouettes (Replica of the sculpture "Cat" by Alberto Giacometti, original sculpture from 1954)

Figure 10. Animal silhouettes (Adapted from The Horse in Motion by Eadweard Muybridge, 1887)

here the image inspection starts. As exemplified by the pictures of Figure 8, an image should have its lighter parts in the upper left and its darker parts in the lower right, because humans are more inclined to examine lighter parts of an image rather than darker parts.

2.3.2. Application of the Golden Mean

A particular ratio of an asymmetric line division is defined by the so-called golden mean or golden section. Whereas symmetry appears rather static and boring, divisions in accordance with the golden mean are considered as being harmonic and interesting. A line should be divided in such

Figure 11. Silhouettes of other objects

a way that the ratio of the smaller part a to the larger part b is the same as the ratio of the larger part b to the whole $a+b$. Put in formulas it reads like this:

$$\varnothing = \frac{a}{b} = \frac{b}{a+b} \qquad (1)$$

As solutions for the ratio $\varnothing$ we obtain the two possibilities

$$\varnothing_1 = \frac{\sqrt{5}-1}{2} \approx 0.618 \text{ and}$$

$$\varnothing_2 = -\frac{\sqrt{5}+1}{2} \approx -1.618 \qquad (2)$$

As we deal only with positive lengths here, solution 2 drops out and the geometric definition of the golden mean is

$$\varnothing = -\frac{\sqrt{5}-1}{2} \approx 0.618 \qquad (3)$$

Figure 12. Human silhouettes- Dark Days - Venice, 2006 (Photographs taken from Peters, 2011)

Figure 13. Clarity of spatial organization of image elements

It has the continued fraction expansion

$$\varnothing = \frac{\sqrt{5}-1}{2} = \cfrac{1}{1+\cfrac{1}{1+\cfrac{1}{1+\dots}}} \qquad (4)$$

and the best rational approximations to $\varnothing$ are given by the convergents of this infinite continued fraction, arrived at by cutting it off at different levels in the expansion: 1/1, 1/2, 2/3, 3/5, 5/8,... Thus, the convergents of the golden mean are the ratios of successive Fibonacci numbers (Cartwright, 2002). Therefore, a division of a line,

surface, or volume in the ratio of about 3:5 appears harmonic, i.e., aesthetic. From antiquity until today $\varnothing$ has constantly been present in art. Even ancient Chinese paintings show the golden section in an accuracy of three decimal places. Examples from architecture are the Great Pyramid of Cheops and the Parthenon of Athens. The main explanation for the usage of this proportion in art is that it is found frequently in nature, e.g., in sea shells or in human proportions (for example in the ratio of finger limbs).

An image constructed according to the rule of the golden mean is shown in Figure 14. The woman is approximately placed in the golden mean. The majority of the images in this article obey this construction rule.

2.3.3. Wholistic Impression by Textures and Patterns

Texture denotes the structural characteristics of a surface. In a classical study (Tamura, 1978) texture was classified into 6 dimensions, namely coarseness, contrast, directionality, line-likeness, regularity, and roughness. *Patterns* are regular visible surface structures which underlie a more or less repetitive entity. These structures can be graphical ones, which means that they are arrangements of combinations of certain visual themes (e.g., stripes, zigzags, or checked patterns). Patterns are not to be confused with noise, which are visual signals without a recognizable pattern.

Nature is full of patterns. Sand dunes, tree branches, snowflakes, or crystals display most beautiful patterns, to name but a few. It is an open question as to why patterns evoke aesthetic feelings in humans, but our visual system seems to look for patterns in visual stimuli even if they are actually not present. For example, we are able to detect an organizing principle (i.e., something meaningful) even in arbitrary structures of low information content such as clouds. This phenomenon is known as *clustering illusion* (Gilovich,

Figure 14. Application of the Golden mean

1985). For Feininger (1961) "pattern, rhythm, and repetition of interesting, related forms" is one of the ten most important properties of an aesthetic image. Examples for images which appeal mainly because of their overall pattern and texture character are given in Figures 15 and 16.

The images in Figure 15 are made up of fairly regular patterns, those in Figure 16 display more random textures, but for all holds true that the entire image plane is filled with consistent structure and thus evokes a wholistic impression. Other examples of images mainly being effective because of patterns are given in Figure 18, and maybe even the images of Figure 8 works partly because of their pattern character.

2.3.4. Repetition of Image Elements

Many visual patterns are strongly related to repeated shapes or objects, sometimes referred to as elements of a series. These copies can occur in regular spatial distances or they can be arranged arbitrarily. All things significant for animals or humans show a minimum of *repetition*. However, only those (not only visual) patterns seem to be essentially relevant, the complexity of which ranges somewhere *between* perfect symmetry (e.g., the ticking of a clock) and noise without any structure (e.g., the rush of a stream). Patterns of largest relevance for animals are those of a medium amount of information. Regarding aesthetics conditions are similar. Perfect symmetry in images as well as chaos (or noise) is not ranked beautiful. Figure 17 demonstrates the beauty of repetition by copying single slices of an image and combining them without modification. Repeated structures are also present in the images of Figure 8 and contribute to their aesthetic appeal.

2.3.5. Application of Variations to Patterns

As pure repetition often is said to be monotonous and thus boring another principle of art consists in *variation*, which means an instance of change in present structures. This is usually applied to increase the visual interest. Figure 18 shows variations over a theme, namely stripe patterns in animal fur. Another example is given in Figure 15. Variation of a pattern is realized here in the right image by the details of the different letters.

2.3.6. Rhythm Induced by the Repetition of Elements

Visual rhythm is the last aesthetic primitive of spatial organization we will explain. It is an artistic principle closely connected to repetition and often

Figure 15. Wholistic impression by patterns

described by the flow of how the viewer's eye is drawn across an image, for example, whether the eye is forced to jump rapidly or glide smoothly from one image element to the next. The most common explanation as to why humans appreciate rhythm, either in music or in the visual arts, is that it recalls how we walk and the heartbeat we heard in the womb.

An art dictionary defines visual rhythm as "regularities of repetition of image elements to produce the look and feel of movement" (Delahunt, 2010). There are several types of visual rhythm. These include:

1. *Regular Rhythms: ab ab ab ...* is the most common type. Another example is *abbb abbb abbb ...* The picture in Figure 17 exploits the schema *aaa bbb ccc ...*

2. *Alternating Rhythms*: for example: *aba cdc aba efe aba ...*

3. *Progressive Rhythms*: Progression occurs when there is a gradual increase or decrease in the size, number, or some other quality of the elements repeated. A sample pattern would be: *ab aabb aaabbb aaaabbbb ...* The left image of Figure 8 displays a progressive rhythm.

Figure 16. Wholistic impression by textures

   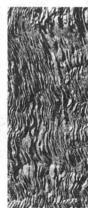

Figure 17. Repetition of image elements

In these examples the letters *a, b*, etc. stand for visual elements of any sort. In Figure 18 the effect of visual rhythm is even more evident: in the left image of the first row the viewer's gaze is led horizontally from the left to the right by the arrangement of the vertical stripes, whereas in the middle picture of the same row it is directed diagonally from the upper left to the lower right.

2.4. Category Motion

Motion refers to life and action. As this article is about images rather than movies, we will illuminate the means by which motion can be conveyed in an image. Calder, most famous for inventing the mobile, used black, white, and red as the only colors for his kinetic sculptures, because he was

Figure 18. Rhythm by repetition of patterns and application of variations. Selection of the collection "Streifzüge", 2000 (Photographs taken from Peters, 2011)

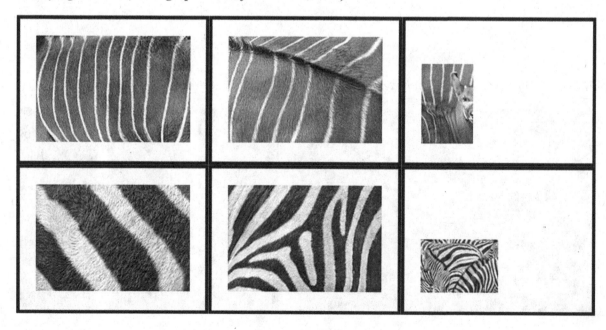

of the opinion that all other colors would confuse the clarity of motion (Calder, 1952). This opinion is interesting because of the coincidence with the functional specialization of the color and motion pathways in our visual system, mentioned at the end of subsection 3.1. According to Calder, motion is most effectively represented by placing highly contrastive surfaces side by side. Translated into images, this means that motion is best expressed in an image (even a color image), if it is based on contrast changes, rather than color. The graphical means by which this can be realized are manifold. For example, motion can be "freezed". This can be effective if an unusual phase of a moving object is catched, such as a horse jumping. But we will concentrate here on *blur* and the depiction of *distinct motion phases*, which are two of the most expressive motion symbols.

2.4.1. Expression of Motion by Blur of High Contrast

A strong indicator for movement is given by blur. Feininger defines it as "unsharpness in one direction", namely the direction of the moving object (Feininger, 1961). The stronger the blur, the stronger the impression of speed. In photography it can be achieved either by a static camera taking a moving object (so-called *motion blur*) or panning the camera with a moving object (so-called *panning blur*).

Blur as an indicator for motion is an aesthetic primitive if the blurred parts of the image contain lines or stripes of high contrast rather than being of homogeneous luminance. Figure 19 shows two examples of motion blur.

Note the high contrast changes in the blurred regions. The same holds true for the images of Figure 20. Here the blur was induced by a panning of the camera. In the upper image it was panned with the walking woman, thus she is depicted almost sharply. In the lower image the camera was panned with the right car. For both images it is essential for the evocation of an aesthetic impression that the blurred regions exhibit high contrasts.

2.4.2. Depiction of Distinct Motion Phases

The depiction of a number of distinct motion phases in a single image represents another technique to illustrate movement in images. Its high aesthetic appeal is probably partly due to the element of repetition. A series of sharp, slightly different, partly overlapping copies of an object, which is captured in different phases of movement, can symbolize the concept of motion in a graphically smart way. Marcel Duchamp practiced this

Figure 19. Motion blur of high contrast

Figure 20. Expression of motion by panning blur

principle in his famous painting pictured in Figure 21. As shown in Figure 22, in photography distinct motion phases are usually obtained by multiple exposures of a not necessarily moving object.

2.5. Category Depth

To depict the three-dimensional world in the two-dimensional image plane it has to be simulated by means of artistic devices. A number of basic techniques of picture language can be used to create the illusion of depth in an image. Examples of these techniques are: controlling the variation between sizes of depicted objects, overlapping them, and placing those that are on the depicted ground as lower when nearer and higher when deeper (Delahunt, 2010).

We concentrate her on the *visualization of linear perspective*, the *exploitation of the contrast between sharpness and unsharpness*, and *the light and shadow distribution*.

2.5.1. Visualization of Linear Perspective

Filippo Brunelleschi's experiments in perspective painting in the early 1400s mark the invention of linear perspective. It works by following geometric rules for rendering objects as they appear to the human eye. For instance, we see parallel lines as

Figure 21. Depiction of distinct motion phases. Marcel Duchamp's Nude Descending a Staircase No. 2, 1912 (Source: http://www.philamuseum. org used with permission)

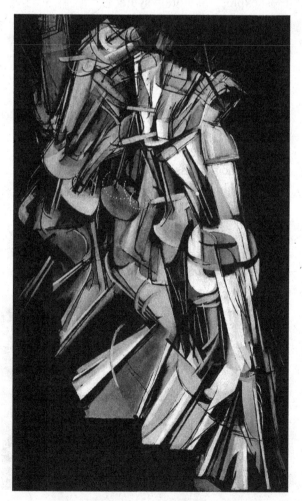

Figure 22. Depiction of distinct motion phases. Double exposure indicating slight movement

converging in the distance, although in reality they do not. The lines of buildings and other objects in a picture are slanted inward making them appear to extend back into space. If lengthened, these lines will meet at the vanishing point along an imaginary horizontal line representing the eye level (Delahunt, 2010). Figures 23 and 24, each with its vanishing point in the center, give examples for images composed in linear perspective.

2.5.2. Exploitation of the Contrast between Sharpness and Unsharpness

Blur can be interpreted as unsharpness in one direction. In this subsection we consider unsharpness more generally as absence of high frequency content. The visual impression of the contrast between sharp and unsharp parts of an image can affect quite aesthetic to the viewer. This can be exploited for the purpose of focusing attention to the important image elements. The most common application of this principle can be found in portrait photography, where a large aperture is used to obtain a small depth of field, which results in an unsharp background and thus emphasizes the portrayed person as seen in Figure 25.

2.5.3. Depth by the Distribution of Light and Shadow

A large field of research in machine vision, called *shape from shading* (Zhang, 1999), still considers the question how the shape of a three-dimensional object can be recovered from shading in a two-dimensional image. Different illumination conditions cause different shadings of the objects we perceive. Somehow our brain is able to suggest the form of an object from this shading. Put in terms of image areas, the human visual system is able to perceive depth from the distribution of light

Figure 23. Visualization of linear perspective

Figure 24. Visualization of linear perspective

and shadow in an image. A strong visual effect is achieved, for example, if objects are depicted as if illuminated under extreme conditions. We often find sharp contrasts then on the surface of the object, and our recognition is accompanied by a feeling of beauty.

The pictures of Figure 26 give examples of this principle.

2.6. Category Human Body

The human body represents the last aesthetic category we turn to in this section. As will be explained in subsection 3.1 the body and its parts such as hands and heads take up a special position in visual information processing, which reflects the importance of these visual stimuli for our survival. Analogously, also in our aesthetic

Figure 25. Contrast between sharpness and unsharpness

sensation it seems to be worth to be regarded as a separate category. *Principal axes* of an object are a particularly important concept in this context.

2.6.1. Visibility of the Principal Axes of a Body

Axes of symmetry or elongation around which the local parts of objects are grouped in order to constitute their global form are called *principal axes*. If an object is enlarged, shrunk, or rotated around its principal axis the relationship between the parts and the principal axis remains constant across all variations. Principal axes are considered as being aesthetically relevant (Latto, 1995). Supporting arguments for this opinion can be derived from the arts as well as from cognitive neuroscience. Stick figures have been used by artists ever since, even humans in cave paintings have been depicted by means of their principal axes. On the other hand, it has been shown in a study that little animal models made of pipe-cleaners are sufficient to represent the animals (Marr & Nishihara, 1978). They are easily recognizable although no information on the surface of the shape is present. The authors supposed that the success is due to the correspondence between the pipe-cleaners and the axes of the volumes they stand for.

To name yet another argument, theories of object recognition can be divided into two types: view-centered and object-centered (Peters, 2000). In order to accommodate novel views, they both must appeal to a minimal set of structural descriptions defining the global form of an object. Principle axes representations are thought of as likely candidates for structural descriptions appealed to by both theories (Tarr & Bülthoff, 1998). To come back to aesthetics, Giacometti again provides examples for the thesis that the human body intrinsically is capable of evoking a feeling of beauty. What distinguishes his human statues is the fact that they almost only consist of their principal axes. Giacometti reduces the human body to its basic shape, and thus we recognize the concept of a human at once (Figure 27). He creates the "idea" of man or woman with his works (Gross, 2002). Sartre put this as follows: "As soon as I see them [these figures], they spring into my visual field as an idea before my mind; the idea alone is at one stroke all that it is" (Sartre, 1948).

Other examples are given again by a motion study of Muybridge in Figure 28, this time boxing

Figure 26. Depth by the distribution of light and shadow

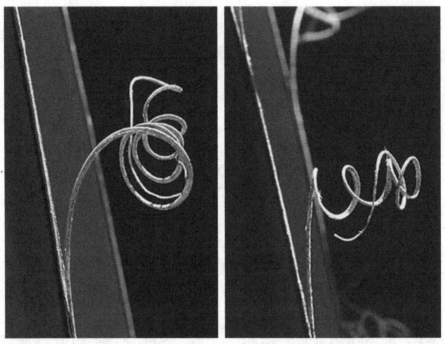

men, and the shapes of humans in Figure 29, which illustrate both, the aesthetic criterion of silhouettes dealt with in subsection 2.2, as well as the beauty of the human body defined by its principal axes.

Summarizing, it seems that the human body does not appear beautiful arbitrarily, but because its shape, especially in the extreme version of principal axes, corresponds to the simplifications and transformations our visual system performs to analyze and represent it. We will address this issue in more detail in Section 3.

2.7. Instances from Practice

To exemplify and concretize the described criteria we will describe some practical instances in this section, where images are key components of human-computer interfaces. For the clarification of the established rules we present examples which meet the rules as well as examples which do not. Generally, websites of museums are good examples as they usually avail themselves of images to attract visitors. The websites of the following four museums are considered: Josef Albers Museum Quadrat, Bottrop, Germany (Figure 30), Wallraf-Richartz-Museum, Cologne, Germany (Figure 31), Deutsches Museum, Berlin, Germany (Figure 32), and Tate, London, UK (Figure 33) (The main Tate home page will be changing within the next months). We analyze the main images of two screenshots for each museum. The left parts of the figures show the main webpages, the right parts show subordinate webpages of the same website, respectively. For this analysis we chose only such museums that are well known and thus promise to meet already a certain design standard. Although images are only one of many aspects that contribute to a website's success, the overall web design is not the concern of this article. We refer to the aesthetic appeal of the used *images*, only. Thus, from the results of this analysis one cannot deduce anything relating to the usability of the considered *website as a whole*.

Figure 27. Human body (Replica of the sculpture "Walking Man" by Alberto Giacometti, original sculpture from 1961)

2.7.1. Color

Josef Albers Museum: In the only image of the main website (Figure 30a) brown and gray tones are dominant; the only strong color is the green color of the lawn. Thus the rule to use only a small number of strong colors is fulfilled. Monochromaticity is given inherently in Figure 30b as the portrait is a black and white photograph.

Wallraf-Richartz-Museum: In Figure 31a also only one strong color appears, namely the blue color of the sky. The rest of this image has gray and almost black tonality, giving the image an almost graphical appearance. The images of Figure 31b display monochrome values; the color is even repeated between both images, establishing a relationship between them. Thus, here the single images also correspond in the context of the interface, yielding a consistent overall impression of the webpage.

Deutsches Museum: Many strong colors (red, turquoise, yellow, pink) are visible in the four center images of Figure 32a. The main image of Figure 32b is a collage in form of a panorama that slowly runs through from right to left. Many colors appear in this panorama and a design matching between the tones of the single components of the collage is not recognizable.

Tate: Both Figures, 33a and 33b, are variations of the main webpage of Tate, in the sense that the main image cycles through a total number of six images. For both of these screenshots we refer to this large main image, only. For the main image of Figure 33a holds, as for Figure 32a, that many strong colors are visible in this collage, even red letters are superimposed (Note that this is not the website of the Tate Online Shop but the main webpage of Tate). In contrast, the image of Figure 33b displays unobtrusive shades of gray in the black and white photograph.

As the exploitation of the dynamic range is a minimal requirement for an image, and as these museums are top ranking museums, this criterion is met for all images of the four discussed websites.

2.7.2. Form

Josef Albers Museum: The dominant form of the photograph of Figure 30a is the spherical sculpture, which is a very simple form. The visible elements of the portrait (Figure 30b) are given by the person, one straight,

Figure 28. Human body (Adapted from Two Nude Men Wrestling by Eadweard Muybridge, 1887).

Figure 29. Silhouettes of the human body. Selection of the Collection "Dark Days - New York", 2007 (Photographs taken from Peters, 2011)

Figure 30. Website of the Josef Albers Museum Quadrat Bottrop, Germany. a) Main webpage, b) Subordinate webpage. Screenshots from 2011-02-02 (© 2011, www.quadrat-bottrop.de, used with permission).

and one curved boundary of the sofa, which are very clear and simple forms, as well.

Wallraf-Richartz-Museum: Even more simple than the photograph of the sculpture (Figure 30a) appears the image of Figure 31a. With its strong contrast between light and shadow it takes almost an abstract effect. Also the photographs of Figure 31b, especially the upper one, display clearly visible forms with the nested rectangles of the alley through the exhibition halls.

Deutsches Museum: Whereas in the images of the Figures 30 and 31 simple and clearly visible forms – spheres (with curves) and cuboids (with verticals and diagonals) - catch the eye, almost no such simple forms can be detected in the images of the website shown in Figure 32. For each of the four center images of Figure 32a it is difficult to say at a glance what they depict. Only at a closer look one can recognize a section of a close-up view of a jukebox, the front view of a classic car, a boy in front of an airplane, and a comic-strip character. Also

the main image of Figure 32b, i.e., the collage of several exhibits, is not composed with simplicity in mind.

Tate: For the main image of Figure 33a the same holds true. Again in contrast to this image, the image of Figure 33b consist of rather simple forms, i.e., the ellipses that are made of the shapes of the sunflower seeds.

2.7.3. Spatial Organization

Josef Albers Museum: The photograph of the sculpture in the garden (Figure 30a) as well as the portrait of Josef Albers (Figure 30b) are composed in a clear and simple way. The sculpture is placed in the golden mean, and the spatial arrangement of the portrait ensures that possible superfluous and disturbing forms are excluded from the image.

Wallraf-Richartz-Museum: The image of Figure 31a is also composed according to the rule of the golden mean. It appears almost like a pattern with repetitions and variations, even more when viewed from a distance

Figure 31. Website of the Wallraf-Richartz-Museum, Cologne, Germany. a) Main webpage, b) Subordinate webpage. Screenshots from 2011-02-02. (© 2011, www.wallraf.museum, used with permission).

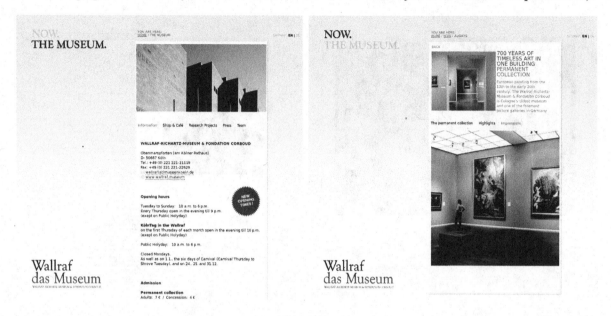

Figure 32. Website of Deutsches Museum, Berlin, Germany. a) Main webpage, b) Subordinate webpage. Screenshots from 2011-02-02. (© 2011, Deutsches Museum, www.deutsches-museum.de, used with permission).

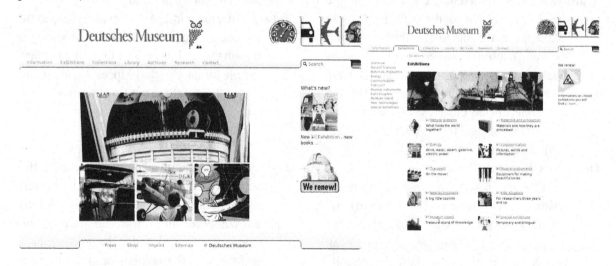

or with slightly slitted eyes. There is also rhythm in this image; the eye is drawn from the upper left to the lower right. Rhythm is also induced in the upper image of Figure 31b by the repetition of the nested frames of the passage way.

Deutsches Museum: In the images of Figure 32 none of the designing principles for the arrangement of image components, as proposed earlier in this section, can be recognized.

Figure 33. Website of Tate, London, UK. a) Main webpage, b) Variation of the main webpage. Screenshots from www.tate.org.uk, 2011-02-04. (© Copyright Tate, 2011, used with permission)

Tate: The same holds true for the main image of Figure 33a. But again, the photograph of Figure 33b, where the organizing principle consists in the completely homogeneous distribution of the texture in the image plane, appears well-organized.

2.7.4. Motion

Classical means of motion cannot be detected in any image of any of the four websites. Only the images of Figure 32 and 33a at least convey less stability than those of Figures 30 and 31 by showing more clutter or, e.g., by the skewed diagonals of the jukebox image. If motion was intended it could have been communicated more compelling, though.

2.7.5. Depth

Josef Albers Museum: The distribution of light and shadow on the sphere in Figure 30a

brings out its three-dimensional shape very well.

Wallraf-Richartz-Museum: The central perspective is able to convey an impression of depth in the image of Figure 31a and even more in the upper image of Figure 31b. Another stylistic device used to create the impression of depth in Figure 31a is the distribution of light and shadow.

Deutsches Museum: In the images of Figure 33, depth is hardly conveyed. Considering the main image of Figure 33b, one can say that for the different components of the collage different viewing angles of the objects have been chosen. The white rodent, for example, is viewed from above, whereas the ship is viewed from the side. This impedes a unified perspective of the panorama and thus prevents the emergence of the impression of depth. Also the distribution of light and shadow is disadvantageous. The light comes from different angles for different components. For example, the ship is lit from right behind, whereas the man is lit from the right front. Another factor that deranges the impression of depth is the inconsistent adoption of sharpness and unsharpness. As an example it can be mentioned that the fur of the rodent is depicted sharply, whereas the ship is displayed in a more unsharp manner.

Tate: Also the main image of Figure 33a does not convey the impression of depth. In Figure 33a this has obviously not been intended, because the collage is mostly an overlay of several two-dimensional things such as books or pictures. In Figure 33b the absence of depth is not a disadvantage because of the inherently two-dimensional character of the photograph.

2.7.6. Human Body

To complete the list of aesthetic categories, the lower image of Figure 31b demonstrates very well the power of the visibility of the principal axes of the human body. The woman can be recognized at once although she takes only a small part of the image. She is in the exact position of this image. Especially, she does not have one of the paintings in her background, but she stands with the homogenous surface of the walls in her back, thus the shape of her body is clearly visible.

2.7.7. Summary

A good indicator for a clear and simple structure of an image is the fact that it does not lose anything when viewed from a larger distance. Then clear forms and a simple structure remain visible as in the examples of the Josef Albers Museum and the Wallraf-Richartz-Museum. On the other hand, one has to take into account that these four museums probably intend to address a different public. Certainly the target audience of the Deutsches Museum is a more infantine one than for example that of the Josef Albers Museum. So, maybe it is just consequent not to obey the classic aesthetic

rules of image design. By the way, the overall layout (which is not the subject of this article) of the webpages of the Deutsches Museum is quite simple and well arranged. As mentioned earlier, to assess the usability of an interface as a whole, a deeper analysis of more parameters than just the aesthetics of images has to be carried out. The role of the interface as a whole has to be considered in such an analysis as well as the target audience of an interface. The webpages of the Deutsches Museum probably can hold as an example for the fact that an interface still can be usable quite well and still can be attractive for a special target group even if the images, if considered individually, are not designed according to the rules presented in this article. To make firm statements on the usability of the whole interface, further analysis of the role of the interface as a whole would be necessary which is not the scope of this article.

Summarizing, one can say that for the more aesthetic images (in the sense of aesthetics as defined in this article), i.e., those of the webpages of the Josef Albers Museum, the Wallraf-Richartz-Museum, and the second variation of the Tate's main webpage, not only a few of the earlier defined criterions for an aesthetic appeal of an image are met, but usually many of them. For example, the image of Figure 31a displays only one strong color, it consists of simple rectangular forms, the spatial organization of the image elements is clear and simple, the repetition and variations of the rectangular forms create a rhythm in the image, and the distribution of light and shadow conveys the impression of depth. The presence of one design principle seldom comes alone, and so does their absence in the less convincing examples.

3. FOUNDATIONS OF THE PROPOSED CRITERIA IN THE HUMAN VISUAL SYSTEM

In this section we start with an overview of the human visual system in subsection 3.1 and draw the conclusion in subsection 3.2 that the basic categories of visual aesthetics introduced in Section 2 can directly be derived from the modularity of our visual system.

3.1. Modularity of the Human Visual System

The human visual system is organized as a parallel, modular system. It processes different attributes of a visual scene, such as color and motion, in different, specialized subdivisions of the brain. These cortical areas are dedicated to the analysis of a single property of the visual scene, only. The left part of Figure 34 shows a human brain from the medial side with some of these areas.

From the retina in the eyes the visual information is carried along the major visual pathway, called *optic pathway*, to the *primary visual cortex* (V1) at the back of the brain. Signals carrying information on, e.g., *color*, *motion*, *form*, and *depth* are transported to V1 and are collected into specialized compartments in V1. Both, directly and via an intermediate area called V2, V1 sends this information further on to other specialized

areas. For example, a colored stimulus leads to an activation in V1 and in a complex of areas called V4. Analogously, a moving visual pattern activates V1 and an area called V5 located on the outside surface of the hemispheres (see right part of Figure 34). Form is processed in several parts spread out over the cortex. There are cells in V1 that respond to oriented lines, but also cells in other areas such as V2 and V3 respond selectively to orientation. Another interesting modularity that has its own representation in the brain is the body and parts of it, such as faces and hands. In the monkey temporal cortex cells have been identified which are responsive to different body posture and movement (Perrett et al., 1990). The human fusiform gyrus (in the left part of Figure 34 marked by the turquoise color), for example, is important for the perception of faces. The functional specialization of the human visual system and the independence of its modules are also reflected by the fact that the brain needs different amounts of time to perceive color, form, and motion. Color is perceived before form which is perceived before motion. The difference between color and motion perception is about 60-80

Figure 34. Cortical areas of the human visual system dedicated to different visual modularities (Adapted from Zeki, 1999)

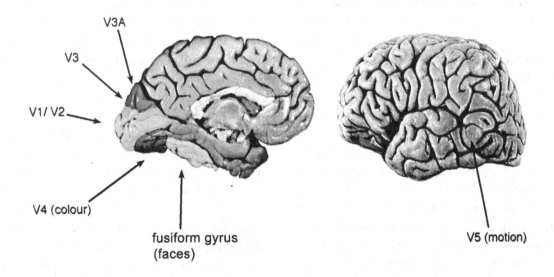

milliseconds (Moutoussis, 1997). In addition, motion perception is sensitive to luminance, but not to color cues, which has been shown in a behavioral study (Ramachandran et al., 1978).

3.2. Foundations of the Proposed Criteria in the Visual System

We speak of the aesthetics of color or the aesthetics of portrait painting, as if there are also different categories of aesthetics. These categories seem to correspond to the modules of visual perception (Latto, 1995; Zeki, 1999). The above mentioned modules of the human visual system (color, form, motion, body parts) and other not mentioned ones such as *depth* and *spatial organization* of objects are also attributes that have been important for the formal aspects of visual arts, and thus for aesthetics. Neuroscience studies revealed that the judgment of a painting as beautiful or ugly correlates with specific brain structures, principally the orbito-frontal cortex (Kawabata & Zeki, 2004). But Zeki suggests that there is not one visual aesthetic "sense" only but many, each tied to a different specialized processing system. Different attributes of the formal aspect of art excite different groups of cells in the brain, thus there is also a functional specialization in aesthetics (Zeki, 1999). It is interesting to study patients with brain lesions in different parts of the visual system. A patient of Oliver Sacks suffered from achromatopsia due to damage to area V4, which is dedicated to color processing (Sacks et al., 1987). This patient was an artist and before his attack he had a preference for the colorful paintings of the Impressionists. However, the deterioration of V4 changed the aesthetic quality of these works for him, as he could not perceive color anymore. Also his own paintings became grayish and dirty, but his form vision was not impaired, so he still could sketch objects and enjoy the aesthetic quality of forms. Latto posed the question as to why some features - the aesthetic criteria in our context - of the modularities are more effective, i.e., provoke a

stronger aesthetic impression, than others (Latto, 1995). He came to the conclusion that a property of a stimulus is intrinsically interesting if it resonates with mechanisms of the visual system. To be more concrete, the more effective features isolate or exaggerate one of the processes of the human visual system, e.g., by evoking maximal responses of those cells in the brain dedicated to that special attribute. This effect can occur at any level in the visual system, e.g., lines and edges are low-level, human shapes are high-level aesthetically effective features. They are aesthetically moving not because they reflect properties of the world but because they blend with our brains.

Summarizing, we suggest that the categories of visual aesthetics proposed in Section 2, i.e., *color*, *form*, *spatial organization*, *motion*, *depth*, and the *human body*, correspond to the different modularities of the human visual system.

4. CONCLUSION

We proposed a well-defined system of criteria for the aesthetic design of images for human-computer interfaces. In the context of human-computer interaction users are more willing to adopt a product if it evokes pleasurable feelings. In addition, the acceptance of an application has severe implications for its safety. Disregarded for a long time, the aesthetic appeal of interfaces recently becomes more important. In this article we addressed only one element of interfaces, namely images. The best content of an image does not reach the recipient, if the image is designed poorly and thus appears confusing or ugly.

We have proposed six categories of visual aesthetics. For each category we explored the conditions and properties that enhance the clarity or vividness of the visual presentation. These *aesthetic criteria* are, on the one hand, presented in the form of a quick guide for interface designers for the creation of images in interfaces and, on the other hand, they can be used for the assessment of the usability of given interfaces. In addition, the proposed criteria are justified in an interdisciplinary fashion by the way how sensory information is processed by our visual system, as well as by approved practices of artists.

Summarizing, the contributions of this article are the following. It gives a *concise* compilation of a set of aesthetic rules for images to be used in interfaces (in contrast to probably already existing, but circumlocutory descriptions in the literature of visual arts). These rules are justified not only artistically (by the fact that artists apply them since a long time), but for the first time in this context also *scientifically* (by drawing parallels to principles of visual information processing by the human brain). These rules are discussed in the context of interface design. By publishing them in a computer science context the benefit consists in the circulation of knowledge maybe well-known in the arts and design community but maybe little-known in the computer science community. Thus, there is reasonable hope that this article is able to promote development in an *interdisciplinary* manner.

REFERENCES

Adams, A. (1981). The negative. In Baker, R. (Ed.), *The new Ansel Adams photography series, book 2*. Waterbury, CT: New York Graphic Society.

Bense, F. (1965). *Aesthetica: Einführung in die neue Ästhetik*. Baden-Baden, Germany: Agis.

Birkhoff, G. D. (1933). *Aesthetic measure*. Cambridge, MA: Harvard University Press.

Brown, G. J. (2006). High dynamic range digital photography. *Royal Photographic Society Journal*, 428-431.

Calder, A. (1952). Temoignages pour l'art abstrait. In Alvard, J., & Gindertael, R. (Eds.), *Editions art d'aujourd'hui*. Paris, France: Editions d'Art Charles Moreau.

Cartwright, J., Gonzalez, D., Piro, O., & Stanzial, D. (2002). Aesthetics, dynamics, and musical scales: A golden connection. *Journal of New Music Research, 31*, 51–58. doi:10.1076/jnmr.31.1.51.8099

Delahunt, M. R. (2010). *Rhythm: ArtLex art dictionary*. Retrieved from http://www.artlex.com

Feininger, A. (1961). *Die hohe Schule der Fotografie*. Düsseldorf und Wien, Germany: ECON.

Gilovich, T., Vallone, R., & Tversky, A. (1985). The hot hand in basketball: On the misperception of random sequences. *Cognitive Psychology, 17*, 295–314. doi:10.1016/0010-0285(85)90010-6

Gross, F. (2002). Mathieu paints a picture. *Journal of the City University of New York's Graduate Center Ph.D. Program in Art History, 8*.

Itten, J. (1961). *Kunst der Farbe*. Ravensburg, Germany: Otto Maier Verlag.

Kawabata, H., & Zeki, S. (2004). Neural correlates of beauty. *Journal of Neurophysiology, 91*(4), 1699–1705. doi:10.1152/jn.00696.2003

Latto, R. (1995). The brain of the beholder. In *The artful eye* (pp. 66–94). Oxford, UK: Oxford University Press.

Lavie, T., & Tractinsky, N. (2004). Assessing dimensions of perceived visual aesthetics of web sites. *International Journal of Human-Computer Studies, 60*(3), 269–298. doi:10.1016/j.ijhcs.2003.09.002

Marr, D., & Nishihara, H. K. (1978). Representation and recognition of the spatial organization of three-dimensional shapes. *Proceedings of the Royal Society of London. Series B. Biological Sciences, 200*, 269–294. doi:10.1098/rspb.1978.0020

McHugh, S. T. (2010). *Cambridge in color*. Retrieved from http://www.cambridgeincolour.com

Moutoussis, K., & Zeki, S. (1997). A direct demonstration of perceptual asynchrony in vision. *Proceedings. Biological Sciences, 264,* 393–397. doi:10.1098/rspb.1997.0056

Muybridge, E. (1887). *Animal locomotion: An electro-photographic investigation of consecutive phases of animal movement.* Philadelphia, PA: J. B. Lippincott Company.

Norman, D. A. (2002). Emotion and design: Attractive things work better. *Interactions Magazine, 9*(4), 36–42.

Perrett, D. I., Rolls, E. T., & Caan, W. (1990). Three stages in the classification of body movements by visual neurons. In Barlow, H., Blakemore, C., & Weston, M. (Eds.), *Images and understanding* (pp. 94–107). Cambridge, UK: Cambridge University Press.

Peters, G. (2000). Theories of three-dimensional object perception- a survey. In *Recent research developments in pattern recognition* (*Vol. 1*, pp. 179–197). Kerala, India: Transworld Research Network.

Peters, G. (2011). *Eyeszeit Fotografie.* Retrieved from http://www.eyeszeit.net

Ramachandran, V. S., & Gregory, R. L. (1978). Does colour provide an input to human motion perception? *Nature, 275,* 55–56. doi:10.1038/275055a0

Reinhard, E., Ward, G., Pattanaik, S., & Debevec, P. (2005). *High dynamic range imaging: Acquisition, display, and image-based lighting.* San Francisco, CA: Morgan Kauffman.

Sacks, O., & Wasserman, R. (1987). The painter who became color blind. *The New York Review of Books, 34,* 25–33.

Sartre, J.-P. (1948). The search for the absolute. In Alberto, G. (Ed.), *Exhibition of sculptures, paintings, drawings.* New York, NY: Pierre Matisse Gallery.

Stone, D., Jarett, C., Woodfoffe, M., & Minocha, S. (2005). *User interface design and evaluation.* San Francisco, CA: Morgan Kauffman.

Tamura, H., Mori, S., & Yamawaki, T. (1978). Textural features corresponding to visual perception. *IEEE Transactions on Systems, Man, and Cybernetics, 8*(6), 460–472. doi:10.1109/TSMC.1978.4309999

Tarr, M. J., & Bülthoff, H. H. (1998). Image-based object recognition in man, monkey and machine. *Cognition, 67*(1), 1–20. doi:10.1016/S0010-0277(98)00026-2

Tufte, E. R. (1990). *Envisioning information.* Cheshire, CT: Graphics Press.

van Goethe, J. W. (1810). *Zur Farbenlehre.* Retrieved from http://www.mathpages.com/home/kmath608/kmath608.htm

Zeki, S. (1999). *Inner vision.* Oxford, UK: Oxford University Press.

Zhang, R., Tsai, P.-S., Cryer, J. E., & Shah, M. (1999). Shape from shading: A survey. *IEEE Transactions on PAMI, 21*(8).

This work was previously published in International Journal of Creative Interfaces and Computer Graphics, Volume 2, Issue 1, edited by Ben Falchuk, pp. 68-98, copyright 2010 by IGI Publishing (an imprint of IGI Global).

Chapter 16
On Not Being Able to Draw a Mousetrap

James Faure Walker
CCW Graduate School, University of the Arts, London, UK

ABSTRACT

A hundred years ago officers entering the Royal Navy took an exam where they had to draw a mouse-trap. At the time there was much discussion, and some despair, about competence, and about teaching. For amateurs, drawing manuals provided instructions on how to render a still life in 3D, or draw a running figure, tasks that would now be effortless given current software. Today much debate about drawing, its purpose, and about 'digital drawing', and de-skilling. Graphics programs are designed for 'realism'. But contemporary drawing looks in the opposite direction: into the processes of drawing; the expressive mark; and the structure and character of the line. Those who deal with the evolving gadgetry of digital drawing have had to contend both with unhelpful software, and with an art world that has yet to realise the scope of this new visual universe.

THE INAUTHENTIC DIGITAL DRAWING

In our normal way of thinking, a 'fine art' drawing involves direct observation, even if it is 'abstract' or made by collecting raindrops. It is something for the viewer to linger over: the sensitive touch of brush, pen or pencil on paper, the illusion of

DOI: 10.4018/978-1-4666-0285-4.ch016

light and shade, that timeless moment of the Rembrandt drawing of a child learning to walk. Such drawings are intimate, tied to a certain place and time, as if we are seeing something through the artist's own eyes. It is not the type of drawing that we would associate with anything digital. Frank Auerbach's drawings are regularly described as 'intensely seen'. I am not sure what that actually means – you can stare at something intensely, but can see something intensely? – but I cannot imagine anyone describing a digital drawing in those terms. The phrase crops up in a recent how-to-draw book, and it is no surprise that there is no mention in this quite thorough book of any kind of drawing involving a computer (Micklewright, 2005). In other words, if we are looking to make a drawing that is intimate, personal and expressive we are not talking about laptops and drawing tablets.

I am here embarking on an essay about 'digital' drawing because the context is 'visualisation'. That sounds like a more objective pursuit than drawing in a 'fine art' way. I am assuming that by writing about drawing here there is some common ground between the artist, the architect and the engineer. I acknowledge, too, that the approach of the artist in thinking about drawing has its own set of priorities, which have less to do with objective rigour than with throwing a few ideas up in the air to see what happens. Much of the 'digital drawing' discussed here has been made in that playful spirit. It has not been made to demonstrate a point, illustrate how a machine works, or to depict anything at all. I should stress that when I speak of the tensions between traditional and digital approaches, I am not really speaking of technical problems that can be resolved through an improved interface. It is more a matter of changing attitudes, changing atmospheres, and the way drawings are seen and used. It is not just about how they are made. It is the perception of 'technology'- or rather the misconception of what digital drawing involves - that gets us into trouble. Drawing software will not 'solve' that all by itself. In most contexts a digital drawing is still seen as 'impersonal', particularly among those attuned to traditional ways of thinking about drawing.

If I 'draw' an object digitally, a cup on my desk, I am not telling you what I feel about it, or what it feels like to stare at it. I just want to tell you what it is like, perhaps give you its dimensions, or show it in 3D so you can turn it about. I may photograph the cup and process it to give it an expressive 'hand-drawn' look, but if you see the

telltale texture of the paint program, you won't be fooled into sensing my sensitivity. Nor, if you see it as a linear diagram of a cup, as an 'illustration', will you believe there was necessarily an actual cup there in the first place. There is no witness. I could have made it up.

Artists who have adapted to digital tools can find themselves hampered by this stereotype, as if they are working within an untrustworthy medium: to draw 'digitally' means to draw without the expressive power, the music, the personality, the honesty of the pencil drawing. Even the etching, which is mechanically produced, is popularly considered to guarantee an authenticity – that dark inkiness of the line – that is beyond the digital print. I have come across this perception so many times that I consider it as a reflex, triggered by paper texture and pencil workings, blind to any other qualities the image may show. The reflex rejects high tech to protect the sacred flame of the drawing tradition[1]. Equally, some digital artists – if I can still use that phrase – do work in a colder, or more raucous tone, and that conforms to the prejudice that digital equals an alienated and unreal world.

What I am suggesting here, by looking at a few how-to-draw books of a hundred or so years ago that have long fallen out of use, is that a cold, impersonal, accurate 3D representation was consistently aimed for, and was well within the fine art repertoire. Generally, there was less tolerance of the subjective and playful. Drawing was an accomplishment, a skill requiring hard work and discipline. It was also conceived as quite a mechanical process. They would have been quite at ease with Illustrator. Figure 1 shows the Cylindrical and Conical Objects, Plate 6 from Glass (1920).

In brief then, the story of the draw program, of the opportunities that all of a sudden expanded the repertoire tenfold, is something of a non-story. Drawing as a whole has not been transformed. Instead, you may have to ask why it was that 'fine art' drawing has been so little affected.

Figure 1. Cylindrical and Conical Objects, Plate 6 (adapted from Glass, 1920, p. 16)

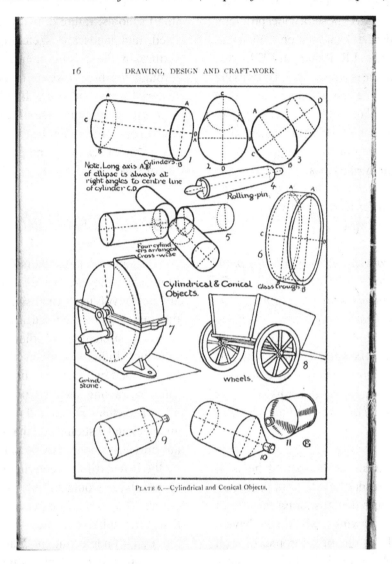

Here are the drawing tools, laid out on the screen as toolboxes, menus of effects and transformations, with layers, endless permutations available, and yet this amazing invention has not supplanted pencil and paper; it has not been taken up as much as it might have been. If anything, through being rejected in this unthinking manner, it has reinforced the 'traditionalist' position. Figure 2 shows Colour and Drawing: From a Garden Table, 32" x 22" giclee iris print.

OBSERVING THE MOUSETRAP

A hundred years ago the teaching of drawing - at the time a proper school subject with examinations, boards, and a legacy of rigorous methods of copying geometry - had reached something of a crisis. Disciplinarians, intent on accurate measurement, vied with libertarians, who felt children should be left to express their natural instincts. Competence in drawing was required in professions where nowadays the computer is indispensable – architecture, engineering, map-making, sign-writing, advertising. But there was one particular exam that exposed a wider problem: the Royal Navy entrance examination. "What was most striking," writes H.R. Rankin in 1924, "was the number of candidates who obtained in drawing *no marks at all. …* The test given was to draw a mousetrap, the actual object being placed before each candidate" (Rankin, 1928). He goes on to make a case, and this argument seems at odds with the assumptions many of us make today about the basis of 'observational' drawing. You might say this is an argument for learning how to draw by first learning 3D software.

All drawing is a convention: therefore the pupil must know the rules. (This) writer would never think of treating pupils who are beginning the subject as certain theorists have advised, viz., to let each draw what he sees. It is his opinion, and a well fixed one, that the beginner does not know what he sees, and therefore how can he draw it? To express three dimensions in terms of two is at first utterly beyond the power of the beginner (Rankin, 1928).

Like other manuals of the period he is at pains to show the reader how to hold the pencil (Figure 3). The pages demonstrating this are of course themselves drawings, which now have a period flavour. This is one of the ironies of such approaches to teaching drawing, which constantly allude to its universal nature, the enduring truths, the classical tradition, and so on. Even the most 'neutral' outline drawings can be dated to their decade. In that respect, Rankin is quite correct to in saying we do not necessarily 'see' what is in front of us, but notice only what we are capable of seeing, what we expect to see. Figure 4 shows 'I wish I could Draw (a system of art teaching by natural methods)' from Bradshaw (1941).

From where I am writing this, in London, there is little evidence of digital and non-digital drawing concepts coming together. The default teaching method is to draw what is set in front of you – the model or the still life. This is what is taught in art schools; figure drawing classes are advertised, and landscape sketching is an essential fixture in the leisure-painting industry. Look through the how-to-draw books on sale in art material stores and you will not find chapters on digital drawing. But these stores do sell specialist inkjet paper. Increasingly, the inkjet print is simply a way of scanning and printing off your watercolours.

DIGITAL DE-SKILLING

Art students are inducted into Adobe's Creative Suite, and if they are to work in design, the web, in any field involving 'visualising' information, then that may well be their starting-point in drawing. It may be stretching the point to say that they are drawing 'digitally' – much of that material will be provided by texts and photos. But when they think of drawing, they will probably think first of all of a sketch - pencil and paper, simple, direct and personal. I should add that were some graduate drawing students to sit that same test faced by the Boy Artificers entering the Royal Navy, I suspect there would still be failures. I would not enforce the teaching of perspective to the extent that H.R. Rankin advocates – he fulminates against the 'evil' of neglecting the grammar – but I have noticed that few students – digital or non-digital specialists - can draw a convincing table from memory in perspective.

Now, I am not complaining about any of this, just pointing out that somehow or other some of the supposedly 'empowering' ideas that accompanied the initial wave of digital art have run into the sand. Generally, we may be a 'de-skilled' society when it comes to handicrafts compared with a hundred years ago. Why, anyway, would you want to make an observational drawing on a laptop? Wouldn't a student learning the programs want to go the whole distance, and work in 3D motion graphics, or at least on the web? Where

Figure 2. James Faure Walker, 1998, Colour and Drawing: From a Garden Table, 32" x 22" giclee iris print

is the attraction in keeping to the 2D still image? So, yes, I recognize there are some apparent contradictions in applying such a liberating set of tools to the rigid format of a drawing. And then there are the anachronisms, the assumed sense of scale, a conception of 'nature' that accommodates what can be seen with the naked eye, within a few feet, or a few miles if it is a landscape, but has no credible way of picturing the micro scale of DNA or the macro scale of light-years. For that we do need visualisation. Our pictures of planets and the galaxies beyond are fabricated through computer graphics. They simply could not be drawn any other way more directly.

Perhaps the mismatch between new knowledge and old drawing methods does not matter. Even the drawing most engaged with contemporary art tends to be low tech, to be emphatically physical,

with more in common with cave painting than with high-end rendering. For the moment the paraphernalia of drawing, the rows of easels in the life room, remain in use. Drawing, it seems, represents permanence, the fixed centre of art. The great majority of amateurs, students, teachers, or professional artists, have little interest in drawing with the computer. They keep faith with the tried and tested, carrying on much the same as if the world had not changed in a hundred years. They use cell phones, email, Facebook, and probably don't write letters anymore. Yet for drawing they prefer paper, specialised cartridge paper.

There has long been a division between the graphic and the fine arts. By neglecting digital media, the fine arts here look decidedly conservative. The graphic arts are about printing, communication, animation, the web, and getting the message across as economically as possible. For those purposes the pencil has had its day. The flight controller needs a 'real time' display on the screen. There is no way that data could be processed and rushed out by a team of draughtsmen, dependent on plane spotters and equipped just with pencil and paper. But the shifting lines they track on the screen had to be designed by someone – they don't just 'happen' because they are digital. Maps, IKEA instructions, silicon chips, all need to be drawn, but no handiwork is evident and none of the data is observed with the naked eye.

MASTERPIECES OF DIGITAL DRAWING

What have 'fine' artists achieved through digital drawing? Or – as the question has been put more pointedly – where are the masterpieces? If you were in a hurry to find such a collection of 'digital drawing', without any ambiguity in the term, you could turn to the 'algorist' group of computer art pioneers: Harold Cohen, Roman Verostko, Frieder Nake, Manfred Mohr, Paul Brown, and others, recently exhibited at the Victoria and

Figure 3. Pencil Drawing (adapted from Rankin, 1928)

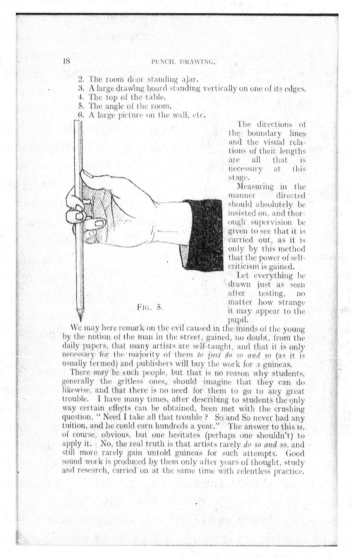

Albert Museum's 'Digital Pioneers' exhibition in London (http://www.vam.ac.uk/exhibitions/future_exhibs/Digital%20Pioneers/index.html). These are certainly drawings, abstract and linear for the most part, drawn by mechanical pens, by plotters. Derived from homemade programs, drawn by robotic movement, in no sense were they 'seen' before they emerged on paper (Though Harold Cohen's Aaron program does make its own judgments about shapes and colour.) Generally, the 'systematic' look of these pieces is indebted to the idealism of the Constructivists - particularly to Naum Gabo. It is an aesthetic that endeavoured to eliminate aesthetics, in the sense that rather than depending on an individual's tastes, the forms are articulated according to a pre-arranged scheme that had to balance out and run its course. What you encountered would be as anonymous and impersonal as a mathematical formula, driven by its own rationale. In theory – and as ever it is only a theory - this would bypass the taste of the individual artist, and produce an art form of universal appeal. 'Computer art' of this genre goes back to the 1960's, but its roots go back

Figure 4. I wish I could Draw (a system of art teaching by natural methods) (adapted from Bradshaw, 1941)

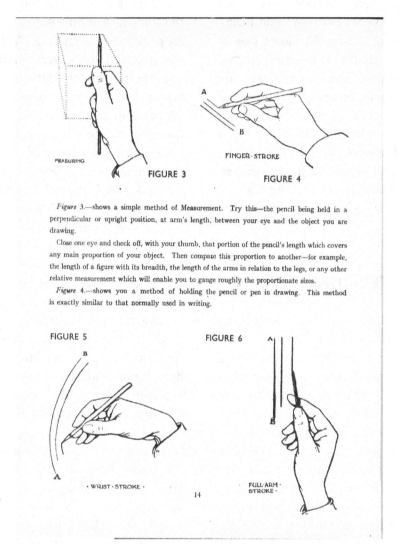

Figure 3.—shows a simple method of Measurement. Try this—the pencil being held in a perpendicular or upright position, at arm's length, between your eye and the object you are drawing.

Close one eye and check off, with your thumb, that portion of the pencil's length which covers any main proportion of your object. Then compare this proportion to another—for example, the length of a figure with its breadth, the length of the arms in relation to the legs, or any other relative measurement which will enable you to gauge roughly the proportionate sizes.

Figure 4.—shows you a method of holding the pencil or pen in drawing. This method is exactly similar to that normally used in writing.

much further, at least to Mondrian and the ultra classical traditions.

It represents only a fraction of what can be done with the power of computer graphics. By the mid-nineties the 'algorithmic' approach was falling out of favour with advocates of newer forms of digital art. Shows of interactive art were billed as 'the art of the future'. It is worth emphasising just how much was expected of 'virtual art'. Futurologists regularly spoke of 'virtual' art displacing object-based art: art would soon 'go digital' wholesale, disembodied from its physical shell, like the medieval soul breaking free from corrupted flesh. Come the millennium 'traditional' art forms would fade away.

Twenty years later, the millennium was of little consequence in comparison with 9/11, and we look back on those predictions as follies of their time, when words like 'hyper', 'cyber', 'wired' had a neon aura. That future has been whisked away. Now we talk of global warming, financial meltdown, and militant fundamentalism. Nor has the technology advanced as expected: we have iPhones and Facebook, not VR glasses. Traditional art has retained its physical shell. The 'mainstream' art world has been smart enough to adapt. Digital photography and websites are taken for granted as no more special than digital watches. It is only within the last ten years or so that we have come to see the digital world as normal. The very term 'digital' has come to be embarrassing – I recall being in a run-down optician's and seeing the slogan 'to the digital future' about some gadget, faded and covered in dust, and it looked comical. The label 'digital art' may have already suffered the same fate.

NO PLACE FOR DIGITAL DRAWING

As far as I can recall, no one spoke earnestly about drawing – either about its future or its past – at any of the conferences on digital art I attended during the past twenty years. Painting was often mentioned, standing as it did for an obsolete delivery format. Compared with the wonders of immersive virtual reality, a painting didn't talk back to you, move about, open its doors, or connect with a remote sensor in the desert. But some colleagues, who like me had spent some years introducing art students to Photoshop, admitted that they resorted to setting up basic drawing classes - just a simple still life - because it was the best way of introducing them to the principles of figure/ground, composition, tonality, and perspective.

I had been involved in attempting – with limited success – to introduce students to the joys of drawing digitally. On occasion I have given presentations at drawing conferences, cautiously worded – 'digital drawing: does it exist?' - and have had colleagues tell me that they would like to come along but this is a something they have no interest in. Ten years ago I helped start a Drawing M.A. and I have also taught on other M.A. courses. The spectre of technology as 'inhuman' and lacking in any aesthetic potential was ingrained in the students' minds. Equally, when teaching on a graphics, or digital course, the students had little use for 'arty' drawing, or its pretentious theorising. With some irony, it was precisely this stereotype of a still life with a few bottles on a table that advocates of a new type of drawing want to avoid. They speak of 'drawing in an expanded field', ways of drawing that embrace video and performance art; but rarely do they touch on computer graphics. Sometimes it is the 'graphic' component they want to avoid. Indeed, questions such as do you need to be 'able to draw' before you work digitally, or "are traditional approaches to drawing still valid given new digital tools?" take you round and round in circles (Ursyn, 2008). It depends on what being 'able to draw' means, what counts as 'traditional', and what counts as 'drawing' in the first place.

So the story of the connections and disconnections between 'traditional' and 'digital' drawing does not follow a straight line where new tech replaces old technology. Drawing with a computer may be considered 'advanced', and we still use the term 'new technology'. The 'digital pioneers' exhibition showed a phase that is now being documented as history, though artists are still making 'drawings' using plotters, an output device that has become technologically obsolete but still has potential. You might also say that the uncritical enthusiasm for virtual art, the idealism of taking physical art forward into a non-material world, that is also from a different age. All of this means that we need to think of the impact of digital tools in more subtle terms. They have not transformed art in the manner some envisaged, nor does it now make sense to speak of 'digital' art as an independent form of art. So if – like me – you feel at ease drawing both through the screen and on a sketchbook, where do you belong? Is it best to forget about the techniques you use and just concentrate on how the drawing/picture/painting works on the eye?

DRAWING BOOKS, THE MISSING CHAPTER

There are books titled the 'complete' book of drawing, yet drawing is not a subject that neatly settles inside fixed borders. A hundred years ago there was more interest in botanical studies, drawing from memory, and developing motifs for wallpaper, architectural decoration, and so on. Today the books are more centred on fine art, often conservative and aimed at the modest amateur; they keep their distance from what used to be called 'commercial' art, or graphics, which would now mean digital visuals of all kinds. On the other hand, within the agreed drawing territory there are long-running debates that surface at drawing conferences - such as whether drawing is an art form in its own right, or just a means to an end used by designers and architects as much as by artists. There are questions such as whether knowledge of anatomy is essential for life drawing, whether the same goes for drawing a tree, or, at the other extreme, whether drawing can be taught at all. Then there are discussions about whether road markings can count as drawings, whether going for a walk is a drawing, whether drawings can be made collaboratively. These discussions are more academic than practical, but keep online forums busy (Ursyn, 2008). From following these you get a sense of what practitioners are thinking about. There is much interest in the 'phenomenology' of drawing, in recounting what the drawer experiences in making a life drawing, and sometimes this interior monologue compensates for what – to my mind at least – is a dull drawing. Perhaps in the West we hang on to the familiar - the meditation of the life room - rather than engage with the weird and wonderful ways of drawing with software. Or, perhaps there is something misconceived about the software itself, along with the interface. It does not feel 'direct'. Whatever the reason, and in whatever form, digital drawing still remains beyond the pale.

Twenty years ago, if you were teaching art students how to draw with the computer, the first lesson would be about using the mouse. This would also be explained in diagrams in the manual. Students would regularly say 'I am not a computer person'. This was the equivalent of the student saying 'I can't draw'. Some people may be born with an aptitude – whether it is for computer graphics, drawing, or both. But what one generation considers an admirable skill another will take for granted. As already mentioned, a hundred years ago how-to-draw books devoted several pages to the art of holding the pencil correctly. It might be strange today to give a lesson on how to move the mouse; it would be stranger still to devote a lesson to holding the pencil. In twenty, fifty years time a future generation will look at the layout of Adobe's Creative Suite and perhaps smile at our terminology – those 'workflow pipelines'.

The how-to-draw books of the last century were often aimed at the amateur and tended to keep 'modern' art off the agenda. From the 1920's up to the 1960's you find little mention of abstraction. Authors dismiss all those now considered modern masters as bad examples to follow, and modern art as an experiment that led its followers away from the proper business of art, namely, depicting nature correctly and without distortion. There are parallels with the way anything digital is kept off limits in contemporary drawing books, with real drawing preoccupied with the outline of that yacht, oak tree or spaniel - or experimenting with flicked ink. Recent publications rarely mention drawing programs, but earlier on there were some examples. This is from 1984:

"I include one example of linear computer graphics... to illustrate that these drawings can offer us some ideas and inspiration. A computer can be regarded as just another instrument which it is possible to use to create a work of art. On the other hand, there are those who feel that work

resulting from a machine is denied expression and creative thought and that it is too clinical and cold in appearance" (Capon, 1984) (Figure 5).

The illustration is of a digital watch, at the time more high tech then than it would be today, when few teenagers have watches at all as they take the time from cell phones. What is fascinating about the examples these books cite is that they are often so much imbued with their own time and place. The typical objects of 1920 – coalscuttle, handcart, wagon wheel, water pump – are not the typical objects of today. The pointillist technique for drawing a car in 1984 is dated partly by the technique, but also by the style of car. One lesson I take from this is to be sceptical of any pronouncement about drawing – or digital art – that claims to be true for all times and all places. I suspect we are all more of our time than we may realise. Another lesson is that some of the dilemmas we face in bringing 'art' and 'technology' together have a long history of fierce argument and raised blood pressure.

Figure 5. Basic Drawing (adapted from Capon, 1984)

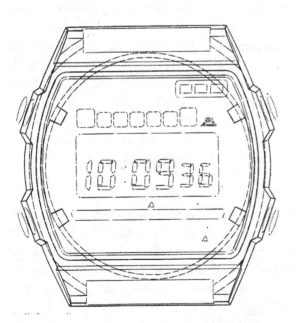

"Sometimes in a painting, buildings also are sketched in with the aid of ruler and protractor. But many artists are enraged at the mere mention of the ruler. In this matter you must not be influenced by the expression of other people's feelings, but do what you feel is right for you in your own work" (Jaxtheimer, 1962).

There was always controversy as to how drawing should be taught, particularly between those who advocated exact measuring and correcting your drawing in relation to the model, and those who preferred fluency and expression. The dry, uninteresting exercises of measuring, testing, with perspective vanishing points – whether a ruler was used or not - were insisted upon as the necessary groundwork. Today we can leave all that to a labour-saving program. H.R. Rankin cited the 'golden words': "Clear view, exact measurement, precise statement" (Rankin, 1928). The discipline was to be enforced. He was no friend of free improvisation: "the idle, aimless scribble that some children indulge in must be sternly repressed" (Rankin, 1928).

CHEATING

Some traditionalists regard a drawing program as cheating – at root the same abhorrence as that directed against using the ruler, though it does not take much study to work out how compasses were used for circles on Greek vases, stencils in medieval painting, and so on. The complaints about falling standards, modern shortcuts, probably go back beyond antiquity. Some manuals justified their attention to the detail of technique by pointing to the damage wrought by the cult of modern art. This remark is typical:

"No artist in any medium can satisfactorily express himself without an adequate knowledge of

the techniques called for in its use. This truth can rarely have been more neglected than it is today" *(Alston, 1954).*

The drawing books evolved from the 'secrets of the studio' handed down from the masters, to the much friendlier you-can-do-it-too tone of the nineteen twenties, where song sheets were promising 'instant' success from their piano 'lessons', and easy to follow dance step notations. Here the reader could acquire the essence of drawing from a sequence of exercises. These manuals echo the 'instant impressionism' you find in programs today, and the tips in computer graphics magazines: turn a photo into an oil painting; compose with an automated golden section. This only works if you have modest expectations, and a superficial notion of art history. The drawing manuals, like the paint programs, depended on volume sales to the hobbyist market. Because of that, they are a prime source for uncovering the fads of the time. In addition, they are full of drawings, and these are fascinating in their own right.

I have taken this brief excursion into the world of drawing manuals partly because of the parallels with the present: the exchanges between liberals and disciplinarians about the ruler, these have similarities with the dispute as to whether the 'computer artist' was cheating if he or she used an off the shelf program. But a further reason is because of the drawings themselves. They are a species unto themselves: a drawing showing how to hold the pencil has also to be a clear and accurate drawing itself. They aim to be as straightforward and unaffected by style, but in most cases they can be pinned down to their decade. They may declare that the nude is the most timeless and universal subject known to man, but the pose, the hairstyle, the degree of idealisation or characterisation, make it 1900, 1925 or 1950. A social history – including attitudes to authority, class, sexuality, fashion, education - could be worked out just from such a sequence of published life-drawings (Figure 6).

When the look of the drawings changed, many factors other than drawing technology had a part to play. The familiar subject matter of the 1880's – where the same page would have examples of sheep and sailing ships - is not the familiar subject matter of today (Chapman, 1873). The point here is that it would be a mistake to put too much of the credit – or blame – for what is occurring today on digital drawing alone, that is to say on one technology making another one redundant.

REALITY CHECK

The urban world most of us inhabit is so markedly different from that world that, if anything, we should really be surprised that so many of the techniques have persisted, and are still being taught. I am in two minds about this. Does it really matter that the landscape books with detailed explanation of how to convey aerial perspective using a 2B pencil have nothing to say about how the Hubble 'photos' are produced? Shouldn't we celebrate the fact that drawing pedants still insist on studying anatomy, while surgeons themselves depend on scanners, lasers, visualised data? The visualisation methods for interpreting data from remote galaxies, stock markets, traffic, and the alimentary canal – none of these call for the 'direct seeing' of the traditionally trained draughtsman. If we were having a serious operation, calculating a Mars mission, or held in a stack over JFK, we might be grateful for that.

There is no need for a digital work of art to be any more rigorous, any more 'rational', than any other form of art. It could have the apparent fluent abandon of calligraphy, the obsessive fixation of a Giacometti, the fickle spontaneity of Picasso. One of the obstacles in understanding the real scope -perhaps I should say the potential scope - of digital drawing is that the available models, such as algorithmic art, give the impression that every dot, every line, derives from some legacy of the underlying algorithm. When exhibiting

Figure 6. Drawing Without a Master, Plate XVII (adapted from Trew, 1936)

at SIGGRAPH, artists have had to itemise the techniques and ideas behind their work. It is as if these 'intentions' are expressed in the work, as if without knowing the program, and the artists' manifesto, the viewer will have nothing to go by. In recent years the artists are provided with a theme, as if it were a student project, a visualisation exercise, a chance to demonstrate a new facet of the ever-advancing technology. This is now an outdated conception of how artists operate, especially artists using digital tools. A successful visual work should be respected for holding its own. No explanations should be necessary. It should be up to the viewer, or critic, to make sense of it, to offer an interpretation, or if necessary to reject it.

My own interests here in drawing, and generally in the great variety of visualisation images, are those of the painter. I am fascinated by complex diagrams, maps, cut-away drawings, as images in their own right (http://www.visualcomplexity. com/vc/). I work with paint programs, as well as with conventional paints, so I have some understanding of how these diagrams, these linear meshes came about. If necessary, I can recreate the look of these patterns. They become source material, possible components in a visual mix. I can play around with them with no particular end in view, but I can also have in mind how much more complex a journey to work – by car, bus, subway - is in 2010 than in, say, 1870. At that time there would have been some connection between what you could observe and what an artist might produce on a canvas. Today that would seem only possible using some deliberately archaic style. Besides, it would be an irrelevant project, given the ever-present CCTV, cell-phone cameras, and stream of adverts and travel information competing for your attention.

I wonder whether this is still possible, but recall that at the Prince's Drawing School - an institution set up to preserve 'traditional' observational drawing - I have seen drawings of railway stations in smoky charcoal, evoking the era of steam. Travelling by subway, a sketchbook would be out of place, and a snapshot or video might not capture the sense of the milling crowd. For example, if you observe for half an hour the flow of commuters through a ticket barrier – in London we have electronic Oyster cards – you lose the sense of people as individuals. You see how a transport system has been designed to deal with statistics, with average dimensions, to cope with the flow of so many thousands per hour. I am not suggesting a flow chart of a subway system is any better than a series of portraits of commuters; nor am I suggesting that there is a pressing need to make a work 'visualising' the daily commute. My point is that this is a common experience now beyond the reach of the older methods of drawing. Perhaps this is where the repeats, patterns, and complexities that can be manipulated in a drawing program come into their own, not necessarily to illustrate the toiling commuters, but to provide a visual analogy.

DIAGRAMS AND OVERHEAD VIEWS

If you were making notes observing an ant's nest, you would not be preoccupied with close-up portraits, or action shots, but with a 'visualisation' of their routes and activities. An all-seeing god looking down on us might come to the same conclusion, and just study the tracks we make, the roles we play. On occasion an artist may hit upon a human subject that is best seen in this way, from above. If we set ourselves the task of depicting a soccer game we might have these same thoughts. The players are defined by roles – forward, midfield, defence, goalkeeper – and each role has its particular choreography. A forward stands, alert and ready to pounce. A goalkeeper scans the field, always waiting. Most of us watch the action on TV, and we look down from above. Though we may be aware of the star players, and their idiosyncrasies, we are caught up in the fortunes of the team, the balance of play shifting this way and that. We may have seen the same patterns of play countless times before, but it is the unpredictable twists and turns that keep us glued to the screen. It is like high-speed chess.

In fact I did receive such a commission out of the blue in 2009. I was one of five English artists commissioned via FIFA to make a print celebrating the South African World Cup (http://www.2010fineart.com/international-fine-art.php). There were some interesting conditions, such as that individual celebrity footballers could not be represented because of copyright issues, nor could team colours. As the commission came in the summer, with no football on TV, I had to resort to watching a match between the USA and Brazil on the web. I made some quick sketches in pencil and from this I devised six characteristic positions, or actions, and the position of the

arms was as significant as the legs. Luckily, I had photographed a fifties soviet textile design of football players in an exhibition in Boston some years before, and this helped me develop a design that expressed something of the rhythm of a game, without portraying specific players or nationalities. I could claim that this was as much a visualisation as a drawing (Figure 7).

There is no need to depict such a subject and present it as a 'still image', but there is also no reason not to attempt such an enterprise. There are in fact numerous projects where artists and scientists collaborate, and gradually we may find a more visually sophisticated way of depicting, or making visible what we could never see with our naked eyes. One consequence is that some of the most spectacular images available – those Hubble pictures – don't resonate as much as they might amidst the drawing community. Judging from the debates on the Drawings Research Network, and the topics that come up at drawing conferences, the themes are introspective, and philosophical, especially the phenomenology invoked in drawing the posed figure. Little comes up about how we might make use of the knowledge we now have about the cosmos, or about the micro worlds revealed through the electron microscope. One artist who has worked for a decade on visualising the secrets of seeds and pollen is Rob Kesseler (http://www.robkesseler.co.uk/). The colour he uses is not 'seen' because that is not what the microscope senses. The Hubble images, incidentally, are received as grey scale via colour filters and the colour is reconstructed. Microscopic images have been a source for abstract painters for almost a hundred years now – Paul Klee is the obvious example, and he remarked that art was about making something visible, not just transcribing the visible.

As I stressed at the beginning of this essay, though there is common ground across several disciplines that make use of drawing in the sense of visualisation, the artist may use the grammar of drawing – the lines, the geometry, the tonal-

Figure 7. James Faure Walker, 2010 Fine Art, South African World Cup commission archival inkjet print 33" x 24"

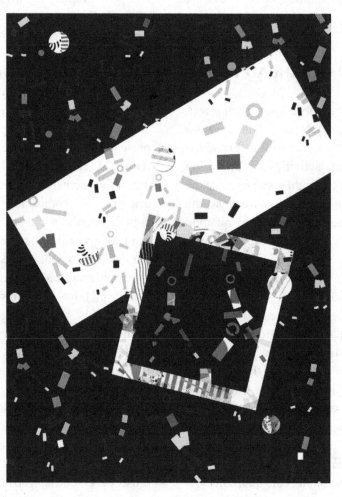

ity – in a far more playful manner. In my own case I tend to improvise without any end in view, though I may begin from a biological illustration, such as the malarial mosquito's life-cycle, an old botanical illustration, or something I have read about in an astronomical publication. This was the case in a large digital print, 'Dark Filament' (Figure 8), where I had to think of a title at short notice for an upcoming exhibition in 2006. It was in fact exhibited in the Digital Pioneers exhibition at the Victoria and Albert Museum in 2009. But these connections are not meant to be taken literally, and for the most part I prefer paintings to be seen as primarily paintings, and whether they are

produced using 'hand painting' – as in 'November 13' (Figure 9) – or through paint programs is beside the point.

CONCLUSION

In sum then, there are three lessons to be learned from the uneasy exchanges between digital and non-digital drawing. First, technology is never going to come to the rescue and solve the difficulty of drawing a mousetrap. If we give up on the task of drawing it directly from observation, and rely on photos, or on 3D prefab models, then we are

Figure 8. James Faure Walker, Dark Filament, 2006, archival Epson print 44" x 53" (exhibited in the Digital Pioneers exhibition, collection Victoria and Albert Museum, London, 2009)

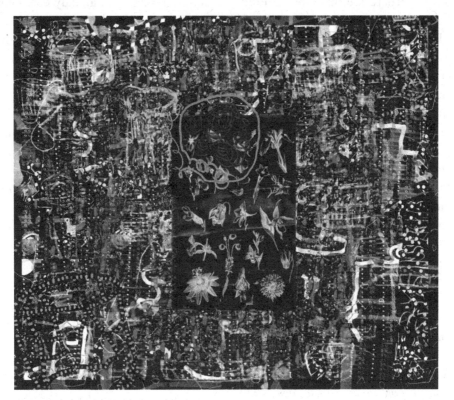

Figure 9. James Faure Walker, November 13, 2009, 42" x 56" oil on canvas

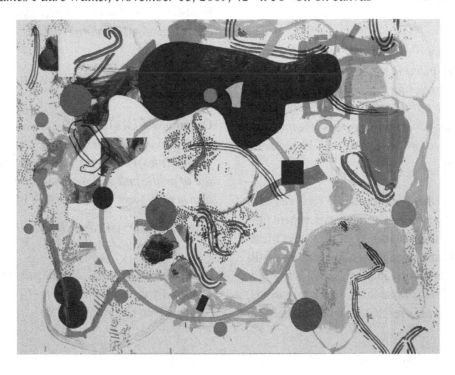

admitting that in this respect we already have become de-skilled. There are numerous useful gadgets, and ways tedious tasks can be automated and improved ways of presenting complex data, but this should not mean we become entirely dependent on them. It doesn't take much to learn the rules of perspective.

Second, the foundations of drawing, its basic principles are not always as permanent and fixed as they seem at the time. When we look back at previous certainties we find quite peculiar assumptions, assumptions that we would not make now - particularly about the purpose of art to represent 'nature', and about what counts as a 'doctrine'. For example, Matisse's drawing may today be the gold standard, but there was a different view in 1925:

He abandoned in 1900 and the following years, the aspect of nature; he dealt in mere arabesques of tint, formless, artificial. He exaggerated, with full knowledge of what he was doing, what Van Gogh had done in part and unconsciously. We have now entered fully upon the period of 'doctrines' that Impressionism had inaugurated forty years before....

In countries such as England and Germany it is not fully realized that the French people are much too matter of fact to have taken seriously the greater part of this unmeasured folly. These various '-isms' have been staged as an attraction for foreigners as are the cabarets of Montmartre (Blake, 1925).

And this is the third point. The received idea that modern art was a misguided experiment persisted in drawing manuals right up to the fifties and sixties. That conventional idea of drawing, still found in contemporary manuals, pushes any talk of digital drawing, of visualisation, to the margins. In fifty years time, a researcher will look back on

those publications, and the ways drawing programs simply imitated an already dated conception of drawing, and wonder how we could have all been so blind. And finally, a word of advice for any impatient draughtsman tempted by the example of Auerbach, or any modern expressionist:

Softness and clearness should first be aimed at, without, of course, any lack of decision. The thickness of the line is perhaps immaterial. Digging the pencil in ought to be rigidly prohibited, just as much as indiscriminate thumping on a piano (Rankin, 1928).

REFERENCES

Alston, R. W. (1954). *Painter's idiom*. London, UK: Staples.

Blake, V. (1925). *The way to sketch (notes on the essentials of landscape sketching; particular reference being made to the use of water-colour)* (pp. 113–116). Oxford, UK: Clarendon Press.

Bradshaw, P. V. (1941). *I wish I could draw (a system of art teaching by natural methods)*. London, UK: The Studio.

Capon, R. (1984). *Basic drawing* (p. 47). London, UK: Batsford.

Chapman, J. G. (1873). *The American drawing-book: A manual for the amateur, and basis of study for the professional artist: Especially adapted to the use of public and private schools, as well as home instruction.* New York, NY: A.S. Barnes & Co.

Dexter, E. (2005). *Vitamin D: New Perspectives in Drawing*. London: Phaidon Press.

Faure Walker, J. (2006). *Painting the Digital River: How an Artist Learned to Love the Computer*. Upper Saddle River, NJ: Prentice Hall.

Garner, S. (Ed.). (2008). *Writing on Drawing: Essays on Drawing Practice and Research*. Bristol: Intellect.

Glass, F. J. (1920). *Drawing design and craft-work, for teachers, students, etc*. London, UK: Batsford.

Jaxtheimer, B. W. (1962). *How to paint and draw* (p. 34). London, UK: Thames & Hudson.

Lieser, W. (2010). *The World of Digital Art*. Potsdam, Germany: Ullmann.

Micklewright, K. (2005). *Drawing: Mastering the language of visual expression*. London, UK: Laurence King.

Morgan Spalter, A. (1998). *The Computer in the Visual Arts*. Boston, MA: Addison-Wesley Professional.

Rankin, H. R. (1924). *Pencil drawing* (p. 1). London, UK: Sir Isaac Pitman.

Trew, G. C. (1936). *Drawing without a master*. London, UK: A. & C. Black.

Ursyn, A. (2008). Digital drawing, graphic storytelling and visual journalism. In Garner, S. (Ed.), *Writing on drawing: Essays on drawing practice and research* (pp. 169–177). Bristol, UK: Intellect.

Wands, B. (2007). *Art of the Digital Age*. London: Thames and Hudson.

ENDNOTE

[1] An example of the prevalent antipathy towards the 'digital mark' in drawing came up on the Drawing Research Network, June 14 2010. This statement received more than a dozen responses within a day, all of them agreeing that a digital mark was to some degree inauthentic:

"The immediacy of the drawn, painted or sculpted mark is an act or great power. As an expression of an artist's intent, it makes real what is until that point a mere concept, an idea, without being. Yet once that mark is placed, the artwork is tangible and holds a meaning to both artist and viewer.

These marks are refined and collected into the final work and this has a value, both artistically and financially. This is the creation of art.

Yet place those marks with a mouse, graphics tablet or touch screen and their value is degraded. What was a primal, expressive act, becomes a fad, a gimmick, a lesser action. Where is the sacred in the digital mark? What is its value?"

James Horn, Senior Research Artist, Freestyle Games Ltd.

https://www.jiscmail.ac.uk/cgi--bin/webadmin?A1=ind1006&L=DRAWING-RESEARCH

This work was previously published in International Journal of Creative Interfaces and Computer Graphics, Volume 2, Issue 1, edited by Ben Falchuk, pp. 105-121, copyright 2010 by IGI Publishing (an imprint of IGI Global).

Chapter 17
User Experiences and Differences in Viewing Architectural Images with Various Interfaces

David Fonseca
La Salle Universitat Ramon Llull, Spain

Oscar García
La Salle Universitat Ramon Llull, Spain

Marc Pifarré
La Salle Universitat Ramon Llull, Spain

Eva Villegas
La Salle Universitat Ramon Llull, Spain

ABSTRACT

This paper proposes an empirical approach to the visualization phase of architectural images, employing established concepts, methodologies, and measurement techniques found in media psychology and user-centered studies. The paper proposes a human-centered approach for conceptualizing visualization technologies and evaluating the quality concept of images to simulate a satisfactory architectural experience. The authors use psychophysiological measures to capture the affective component of image quality experience facilitated by different displays, including immersive and nonimmersive displays. These types of visualizations are important for empirically evaluating the experiential aspects of an architectural space and other types of images.

DOI: 10.4018/978-1-4666-0285-4.ch017

INTRODUCTION

The visualization of architectonic projects has evolved over the past 20 years due to 2D and 3D CAD-CAM technologies. Traditional photography and *maquettes* (French for scale model of buildings) are still employed as aesthetic resources for examining spaces and shapes. However, the use of infographic techniques allows the generation of images and animations, enabling professionals or architects to examine details and change textures or illuminations in a more rapid, interactive, and comfortable manner.

Today's professionals are increasingly employing the latest technologies to work and communicate on projects. However, taking into account a number of experiences gathered from the university environment, it has been found that users do not apply these technologies optimally. They do not control the size or resolution of the images, and in the majority of the cases, they do not consider the final user or the type of screen where these images will appear. This absence of resource optimization is disturbing, mainly due to the employment of digital images, which are considered essential in understanding the space and presentation of architectonic ideas. In this specific sector where visualization is crucial, we have found that there is a remarkable deficiency of usability studies that, which focus on the manner in which information should be presented. The impact that information has on a user is based on the effectiveness of the mode of communication employed and on the user's own preferences.

The research community is exploring the different possibilities that mobile or immersive devices offer users, producing studies ranging from optimizing the presentation of information, thereby creating an augmented reality, to those more focused on user interaction. Undoubtedly, one of the most investigated themes on the use of these new technologies is that of information visualization (IV). IV is a well-established discipline that proposes graphical approaches to help users better understand and make sense of large collections of information. The small screens of handheld or immersive devices provide a clear imperative to design visual information carefully and with the goal of presenting it most effectively. The limited screen size makes it difficult to display large information, and the device capability and the network bandwidth are other important factors to take into account at the moment of the image creation. The main problems associated with vision in immersive and mobile devices are related to the distance of image visualization (away from the optimal range of screen visualization according to recommendations that fix the distance between 8–10 cm per inch of a screen's diagonal distance, http://www.hdtv-expertos.com/2008/05/distancia-ngulo-y-altura.html). A higher resolution is necessary to maintain the quality perception in a head-mounted display, but this slows down the load on a mobile device, a device that does not require this high resolution.

This paper includes a multidisciplinary approach that intends to examine a user's emotional response according to the technical features of an image and its display where it is visualized, in order to make headway in generating images with accurate parameters that will optimize the manner in which the user visualizes an architecture project.

The main goal of the study is to quantify and evaluate the differences in emotional behavior and the perceived quality of architectural images, based on the user experience and the type of device. The results will allow us to propose new compression rates or resolutions to adapt any image to different devices without reducing its communication without reducing its integrity.

We will apply techniques already employed in usability studies and examine a user's interaction with computing systems (HCI– HCC) to measure the user's emotional response (psychological and neuropsychological) according to technical aspects such as the digital image and the type of display (information technology). This relationship between visualization and emotional response has been extensively studied during the previous years (as indicated in the Literature Review section). The purpose of these studies was to demonstrate the manner in which an image is capable of evoking emotional states in and reactions from a user based on the user's perception. We will employ clear techniques of different areas as a starting point for an in-depth study of architectural images in a professional environment.

LITERATURE REVIEW

Image Classification

In the past 20 years and due to the popularization of digital images, we can find innumerable approaches to classifying digital images according to their contents, typology, and format, among other characteristics (Enser & Armitage, 1997; Hollink, A.Th, Wielinga, & Worring, 2004). Based on these studies and other studies with users such as interviews and different user experiences (Kennedy, 2005), we can define different concepts such as the information stored in an image, including shapes, objects, people, and locations. New types of classifications have been developed through the Internet, where several image banks exist and users share millions of pictures by themes using applications such as Flickr (http://www.flickr.com/), Getty Images (http://www.gettyimages.es), and Fotosearch (http://www.fotosearch.es). This development initiated relentless research aimed at identifying new methods and applications for resolving the issue of inclusion of descriptive parameters in images, termed metadata (Lieberman & Liu, 2002). A majority of the referred references and other studies conducted during the last decade (Eakins, 2002) have based their efforts on extracting descriptors automatically, which better defines an image from an objective point of view; that is, it better describes the elements that compose the image (Enser, 2000; Lim & Jin, 2005). Very few studies have correlated ideas or

concepts of a user's specific topics to an image or have personalized the result according to the needs of a user (Hollink, Wielinga, & Worring, 2004).

In all of the cases that were referenced, image information was stored either as a series of labels associated with the image according to a specific metadata model (for example, the IPTC Header, which is used to include all authorship data of images used by the Associated Press; Exif, a format in which digital cameras store all data related to an image; MPEG-7, which is used in content description of audiovisuals; multimedia or XMP developed by Adobe, which supports a great number of extensions) or as an additional characteristic of the image in a database that could even restrain it. This is common in large image repositories and other resources typical of Web 2.0 and 3.0 such as Flickr, which stores an image externally but stores the address and metadata associated with the image in a database (http://highscalability.com/flickr-architecture).

Emotional Visualization and User Experience

It is extremely difficult to identify emotional and subjective elements for describing images. This type of information could affect the user's image perception due to cultural factors such as gender, age, and education (Tractinsky, 1997). In fact, emotions have a considerable influence over other psychological processes including perception, memory, apprenticeship, and thought (Dolcos, 2002).

Emotion is an affective state that humans experience; it is a subjective reaction to the environment that accompanies organic changes of innate origin and is influenced by a person's experience (Lang, Greenwald, Bradley, & Hamm, 1993). Each user has different emotions depending on previous experiences, apprenticeship, character, and specific situations in which they are evoked. There exist six basic emotions: fear, surprise, aversion, wrath, happiness, and sadness (Ekman,

1992), an evolution of initial view of Ekman who enunciated those emotions can be studied using a simplified method based on three levels and discussed in Ekman (1999):

- By employing a "pleasant-unpleasant" scale.
- By employing an "active-passive" scale.
- By studying cultural and social differences, as emotional reactions are learned in a specific environment.

Based on these three basic levels we can find a multitude of studies primarily in psychological and neuropsychological frameworks to measure emotions (Clough, Müller, & Sanderson, 2004; Hong, Ahn, Nah, & Choi, 2005; Boehner, DePaula, Dourish, & Sengers, 2007). Many of these studies have used a series of images with different semantic features in a perception exercise to measure the emotional impact that images have on the user.

The most important system based on digital images to measure emotions replicated in many scientific studies is the International Affective Picture System (IAPS) (Lang, Bradley, & Cuthbert, 2005), which measures the emotional response of a user to viewing images in different environments. The IAPS is an established method for identifying emotional dysfunction, or different behaviors in several types of users and conditions (Houtveen, Rietveld, Schoutrop, Spiering, & Brosschot, 2001; Mikels, Fredrickson, Larkin, Lindberg, Maglio, & Reuter-Lorenz, 2005; Verschuere, Crombez, & Koster, 2007). The IAPS measures the emotional response of a user based on the simplification of Ekman's scales, which assign different levels of valence and arousal, together with a third level of a less important concept, such as dominance.

Color and Quality Perception

When we focus on images, the most significant aspect that influences an emotional state is color (Jacobson & Bender, 1996). The perception of

color, as with any other sense is subordinated to subjective analysis criteria and depends on personal preferences, the relationship of the color with other colors, shapes in the line of sight, contrast, lighting, the perceiver's health and frame of mind, and other factors. It must be noted that a few experts cite the Hypothesis of Linguistic Relativism: which states that languages can affect chromatic perception in certain aspects, as different languages divide the spectrum received by a user in different ways. Psychology and experimentation with colors and photographic images confirm that colors influence a user's emotional responses (Chen, 2006; Coursaris, Swierenga, & Watrall, 2008; Xin, 2004). The evaluation of the differences between images in color or in black and white and its impact on the user is an area completely contemporary with relevant applications (Winn & Everett, 1979; Cano, Quetzal, & Polich, 2008; Stahre, Billger, & Anter, 2009). Color design for illustrative visualization is a dynamic and actual framework with which to create new research (Wang et al., 2008) and new approaches such a as in our work, as not only color but also personal profiles of the user within a gender based and cultural environment will affect the communicative ability of the image (Fernández, Carrera, Sánchez, & Paéz, 1997; Porras & Pereyra, 2001).

Currently, the study of the quality perception of images has generated considerable interest due to business requirements. However, it is extremely difficult to define and measure the concept of quality in an image (Fairchild, 2002; Vansteenkiste, Van der Weken, Philips, & Kerre, 2006). Initially, quality depends on physiological aspects of each user (Coursaris, Swierenga, & Watrall, 2008); however, it becomes increasingly complicated when subjective aspects, such as the user's society or culture are taken into account (Tractinsky, 1997). Peter Engeldrum (2004) described a systematic method known as the Image Quality Circle (IQC), which organizes the primary elements that define image quality. These elements comprise technological variables, physical parameters of an image, and, finally, human determinants of the perception process, which determine the quality of an image. The correlation among these variables enables the creation of a "psychometric scale" based on user evaluations and different cultural variables. To work with users for defining a few quality perception scales (Fairchild, 2002), it is necessary to define different stages in the following manner:

- Psychophysical study to quantify perception scales. In other words, empirically examine human visual response models, in which different concepts such as color, special and temporal sight, and different iterations that lead to the conclusion, are interrelated.
- The modeling of visualization to include all stimuli.
- Iteration for verification.

The study and understanding of the relationship among different elements, by which the quality of a perceived image can be determined, enables us to define all the features that an image possesses that enable the user's visualization to be satisfactory and adaptable to every requirement, an assertion on which this study is based.

Moreover that, this study is related to the way a user analyzes architectural imagery on the basis of merge the color model and compression options. We need to take into consideration that black and white images are still widely used within several applications such as infographical creations and compositing panels where there's a significant percentage (80%) of this type of content.

The Effects of Screen Size Visualization Distance

Currently, there is a large variety of screens with different profiles (size, resolution, and range of colors) and that require different viewing approaches. Many studies have concentrated on

resolving specific issues related to visualization due to requests from users (Bellman, Schweda, & Varan, 2009). The visualization of advertisements on different types of screens is an example that has been extensively studied in the communication framework (Heppner, Benkofske, & Moritz, 2004; Knoche, McCarthy, & Sasse, 2005; Knoche & Sasse, 2008). As indicated, studies conducted for evaluating differences in the effectiveness of generic visual messages due to differences in the screen size and the image quality are currently a matter of great interest for modeling communication and improving empathy between users and messages.

Compared to smaller screens, larger screens magnify images of objects, and thus appear closer, which implies that attractive or aversive stimuli from the depicted images appear closer, thus increasing the urgency and intensity of responses to those stimuli (Bellman, Schweda, & Varan, 2009). Larger images increase the automatic allocation of resources to attention because the peripheral vision is influenced, increased visual processing is required, and larger images generate larger mental visions (Reeves, Lang, Kim, & Tatar, 1999). If we employ immersive technology, the size and details of the image and peripheral vision of a user increases, thereby increasing the communicative capacity of the environment and message, as the user is mentally absorbed by the environment (Henden et al., 2008).

However, what is a large or small screen? To set the screen size, it is necessary to observe the distance of observation and the resolution of the screen. The perception of an image or a screen varies between users, and we can find several recommendations that provide advice regarding the optimum distances to see a screen (http://www.casadomo.com). Previous studies (Fonseca, García, Duran, Pifarré, & Villegas, 2008) have described an index of optimum visualization (IOV) as the result of dividing the diagonal distance of the image in the screen among the distance visualization (both in cm). After cheking the recommendations of different devices an average factor of 0.31 emerges as the optimum rate of visualization regardless of screen size. For extreme values of IOV a natural trend is to perceive a reduction in quality because we cannot see the details from far away or because pixels and errors of the compression are very apparent from a small distance. Emotional responses are stronger when negative or positive stimuli appear closer, as with those evoked by images on large screens. Previous studies (Codispoti & De Cesarei, 2007) determined the effects of screen size on valence, which were comparable to its effect on arousal; namely, positive and negative images on larger screens evoked stronger positive and negative responses, respectively. Other studies (Mühlberger, Neumann, Wieser, & Pauli, 2008) measured responses to negative stimuli and found that larger images reflecting larger objects generated a stronger startled response to smaller images reflecting smaller objects. Other studies associated large format displays with more positive reactions regardless of the stimulus (Reeves & Nass, 1996).

Working Hypotheses

To achieve the main objectives of our study, we have defined a set of working hypotheses. These hypotheses are based on an analysis of previous interdisciplinary frameworks and are described as follows.

- **H1:** Previous experience visualizing a particular type of image is an emotional factor that must be considered.
- **H2:** Gender and age are factors that influence both generic and specific emotional responses.
- **H3:** Viewing high-quality images in high resolution yield more positive emotional reactions in the presence of images with a small format or low resolution.

- **H4:** Low-quality images with compression errors or pixelation on a large screen or that are viewed near the screen will evoke a strong negative response compared to those on a small screen or that are viewed far from the screen

The following section describes the experiment and corresponding steps that we have implemented to test our hypotheses for determining the manner in which the type of screen and image and the typology of the user influences the visualization of architectural images. According to our knowledge, this is the first study that compares the effects of three screen devices (computer screen, projector screen and head-mounted display) and focuses on the visualization of images related to architectural frameworks. Previous research studies focusing on the television framework (Bellman, Schweda, & Varan, 2009) assessed the behavior of users viewing advertisements on different types of screens; however, they did not evaluate the quality of the displayed image, which is the main differentiating factor of our study.

In our study, we analyzed whether or not visualization in black and white or in color and the quality of an image influence the emotional responses of a user by enlarging the scope of and improving upon previous studies (Winn & Everett, 1979; Levkowitz, Holub, Meyer, & Robertson, 1991; Canoa, Classa, & Polich, 2009). Additionally, we examined the importance of color as a discursive and communicative element for representing a project with regard to real, virtual, and photorealistic images in the architectural framework by complementing other previous studies (Genov, Schnall, & Laird, 1999; Cleempoel & Van, 2008). To fulfill our objectives, we also analyzed the differences in the visualization and evaluation of images in a specific immersive environment between classical visualization (projector or computer screens) and visualization with a specific HMD model (5DT HMD 800-40, http://www.5dt.com/products/phmd.html) (Figure 1).

Figure 1. Users realizing architectonic test on Computer Screen and HMD (© 2009-2010, David Fonseca. Used with permission).

The undergraduate students (second year, degree on Architecture) learn to create infographical images where they compose both Din-A3 and Din-A2 panels (60% of the content is B/W) and virtual tours. All the content will be projected onto a PC screen. There is also the possibility to deliver this content to some other interesting devices such as Virtual Reality HMDs (Head Mounted Displays) or Augmented Reality platforms (already present in mobile devices and smartphones). In order to increase the end-user satisfaction besides the adaptation of the content, several usability studies are mandatory. It is interesting to mention that these are not usually applied within the architectural teaching framework.

To arrive to this point, we previously divided our research into two phases:

Phase 1: Replication and evaluation of the IAPS model and the online test system of the project. We chose test 1 of the IAPS model, replicated the test specifications provided in the technical report to subsequently implement it into our online system, compare whether or not our results are consistent with those of previous studies (Ramirez et al., 1999), and validated our system at subsequent stages.

Phase 2: Implementation of a model that combines original images of the IAPS model and images modified in terms of color and compression, i.e., JPG changes into JPG2000 with compression rates between 80% and 95% (Fonseca, Fernández, & García, 2008). The criterion for selecting modified images is based on image evaluations in phase 1 with respect to both positive and negative emotional values. In addition, we have started examining the manner in which visualization distance influences perception, in terms of both quality and emotional components of an image vis-à-vis compression rates.

Brief Summary of Previous Phases

The initial two phases were conducted from 2007 to 2009. The complete methodology and results can be found in the aforementioned references. The main objective of these two phases was to work with the IAPS system, replicating the test system and comparing the results of American and Spanish studies to validate our methodology (Fonseca, García, Pifarré, Villegas, & Duran, 2008).

In phase one, we worked with a total of 143 users, of which 67 were women and 76 were men (all Spanish nationalities, between the ages of 18–81 years, and from different educational and professional backgrounds). The main conclusions of the initial phase are as follows:

- The results obtained are analogous to those of normalized Spanish study, which validates our test system. Furthermore, a difference in the emotional evaluation of images that are not commonly associated with culture (for instance, poisonous animals, firearms, mutilations; in other words, the capability of negative images to evoke strong emotional responses) was confirmed.
- A difference was observed in user evaluations based on their age group. The users in the first subgroup (18–30 years), assigned higher scores to images reflecting strong emotional content (either positive or negative) than users in the second subgroup (30 years and above).
- Similar results have been obtained depending on the gender of the user. For example, women valued images that reflected strong emotions more highly than men.

Overall, factors such as cultural differences, gender, and age group influence the visualization and emotional evaluation of a photographic image. This difference must be taken into account in subsequent stages for further study, as the reaction reflects different types of users. These early results seem to validate hypotheses H1 and H2, pending confirmation from the results that will be received from new iterations employing additional images.

In phase 2, we made the first step to study the perceived quality. This study has been conducted with a total of 77 users (belonging to different countries, between the ages of 18–35 years, and all University students). The following is the summary of results and conclusions of this phase as

extended in (Fonseca, García, Duran, Pifarré, & Villegas, 2008):

- Users can easily perceive both black-and-white and color images, although they assign a greater value to the color-compressed rather than black-and-white images. Another interesting result associated with responses from women is that they assign higher values to quality as compared to men. This finding initiates a future line of research for examining whether or not a physiological differentiation in vision by gender exists and the requirement for product differentiation based on the gender of the end-user, as we shall see later.
- Emotional data (valence and arousal) revealed no significant differences between color or black-and-white images. However, changes were observed when images were highly compressed; for example, positive images in black-and-white with a lower quality resulted in a minor valence as compared to color images in previous studies.
- A decrease in the quality of an image can weaken its emotional impact due to the loss in the level of detail that the eye perceives. This situation is equivalent to increasing or decreasing the distance between a user and screen. Too much distance between a user and screen leads to a loss of perceived detail and too little distance leads to the user perceiving unintended compression errors and details.

Overall, these conclusions validate hypotheses H1, H2, and H4.

METHODOLOGY AND IMPLEMENTATION

Based on the literature, we can summarize the stages of our research in the following steps:

- Generate a new image classification system based on user responses, storing information in an on line dynamic database. We have employed a system similar to Flicker, where the image is stored externally and the database remains linked to users' evaluations of visualized images.
- The IAPS is a reference for employing images to measure a user's emotional responses. The NIMH (http://www.csea. phhp.ufl.edu), located at the center of the University of Florida and where the IAPS was created, provides the IAPS set of images to any research group that seeks to study any matter related to the measurement of emotions and some levels associated with the digital image and user behavior. This service has yielded numerous studies focused on psychology, neuropsychology, communications, and technology. Based on this standardization, we used these images to recreate new test environments and compared the data with that of the original study (Lang, Bradley, & Cuthbert, 2005) and of the Spanish iteration (Moltó et al., 1999). Having found the methodology of the test is stable and generates homogeneous data compared with the previous studies, we have created the new test with a certain number of IAPS images as control images and the main group of images related to an architectural framework.
- The assessment of a user's emotional response using images is a current and relevant line of research. Among these studies, the evaluation of color and its parameters to show related images of architectural framework is an emergent research area (Recayte & Bund, 2005) where our work can contribute new data.
- Given the importance of the image inside the screen and its relationship with the perceived quality and emotional level,

we studied the differences between users based on the devices, focusing on architectural images a new area with interesting opportunities to make new contributions (Eilouti, 2009).

In this present phase, we have carried out an implementation of a model that combines images from phase 2 as control images and original pictures related to architecture: infographic, phototypesetting, and real digital images of projects. Architectural images, both original as well as modified in terms of compression and color (similar to the modifications made to images in phase 2) are presented.

Designing an Open Source System to Classify and Store Data Online

We have created a new web application that permits image indexing based on users' personal evaluations, and both expert and nonexpert users can easily use this application. Using this web application, we can extract any user-related information from any device with the help of an Internet connection. We have developed this web application based on the open source technology employing the following services:

- HTTP Server - Apache HTTP Server.
- Program system - PHP Hypertext Processor.
- Database - MySQL Server.

Figure 2 provides a detailed explanation of the logic structure of the web application, which has been explained in detail in previous publications (Fonseca, 2008), and also indicates an example of the front office of the application.

Users' information and evaluations of each image are stored inside a database and related to each image in a tabular manner, which permits us to extract and consult results in a simple and swift manner.

Figure 2. Internal Open Source Technology applied to Web page of the test implemented and screenshot of the architectonic test number (© 2009-2010, David Fonseca. Used with permission)

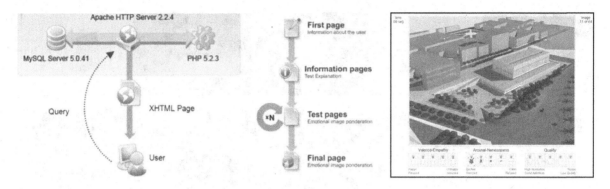

PHASE 3: IMAGE QUALITY IN ARCHITECTURE IMAGES, NORMAL ENVIRONMENT VS. IMMERSIVE DISPLAYS, AND USER EXPERIENCE RESULTS

Procedure

We have employed two models of images in the test design: the first is a representative selection from the IAPS, which was used as a set of control images and placed at the beginning (7 images) and at the end (7 images) of the test. The use of these images and their placement within the test can be explained as it follows. Firstly we intend to maintain an opened research line related to the visualization of the IAPS pictures. Secondly we are truly interested in the analysis and gathering of information related to non-specific images where the topic is not restricted (for instance related to the architectural field). Therefore we can compare the results according to the different user's profiles, as a parallel research track.

The second group of images related to the architectural project were split into the following diverse sub-groups: infographic images generated by a computer (18 images), explanatory photographic images of a concrete project (Bridge AZUD, Ebro River in Zaragoza, Spain, Isidro Navarro, 2008; 19 images), composition panels

(used in the course "Informatics Tools, Level 2," Architectural Degree, La Salle, Ramon Llull University; 7 images), and HDR photographic images (6 images).

Our two models combined original images of the IAPS, color images with a resolution of 1024x768, and architectural color images, which had resolutions between 800x600 and 4900x3500. There were also images that were modified in black and white and underwent different levels of compression; for example, JPG images were transformed to JPG2000 format at compression rates of between 80% and 95%. We used the JPEG 2000 format because it is an international standard ISO-15444 developed in open source code due to the benefit (Bernier, 2006) in its increased compression capability, which is especially useful in high-resolution images (Rosenbaum & Schumann, 2005). Another interesting aspect of the JPG2000 format is the ROI (region-of-interest) coding scheme and spatial/SNR scalability, which provide a useful functionality of progressive encoding and display for fast database access as well as for delivering various resolutions to devices with different capabilities in terms of display, resolution or connection bandwidth (Chen et al., 2003). In Figures 3, 4, and 5, we can see some examples of the different types of images used in this test.

Regarding the types of images, the test method involved the following steps:

Figure 3. Infographic images of test 3. The type of images samples 4 basic situations: indoor, outdoor, day and night scenes (© 2008, Isidro Navarro. Used with permission)

Figure 4. Real photographic images of test 3 (© 2008, Isidro Navarro. Used with permission.)

Figure 5. Composition Panels of test 3 with different type of designs to evaluate what type of composition works better in the different displays and users (© 2008, Isidro Navarro. Used with permission.)

1. The test facilitator explained the basic objective of individually evaluating each image based on various aspects as well as the various phases of the test and collected general information about the test environment including local time, date, place, and screening conditions (type, size, resolution, and room illumination).

2. The user provided some personal information, such as gender, age, country, and educational qualifications.

3. The user evaluated the viewing conditions (such as distance from the screen and projector viewing angle) for the paper test in phase 1. For the subsequent phases, in which we employed an on line test (http://www.salle.url.edu/mid), the user was required to only evaluate the displayed distance and screen size because the resolution and other statistical data such as date, local time, and display time of each image were automatically captured by the system. The facilitator displayed the two previous images. Without providing a definite time limit, the facilitator explained the manner in which the user must evaluate the images.

4. In phase 3, where the web system was employed, the user was given 20 seconds to evaluate three parameters (valence, arousal and quality). Once the user completed the three evaluations, the system automatically jumped to the subsequent image. If the user was unable to complete the evaluation, the concepts were left unmarked within the system.

This test was conducted in two environments. The first test was conducted using a computer screen with 12 women (average age: 27.7; standard deviation: 7.2) and 22 men (average age: 28.86; standard deviation: 7.01). The second test was conducted using an immersive head screen employing 6 women (average age: 25.83; standard deviation: 6.36) and 8 men (average age: 27.25; standard deviation: 6.45). We worked with three types of users: architecture teachers and professionals, architecture students, and other professionals employed in fields unrelated to the above-mentioned fields (administrative professionals, engineers, lawyers, doctors, and other professionals). We have taken into consideration the resolution of the screen, visualization distance, and image size—information that we will subsequently use for examining the importance of the above-mentioned parameters in the visualization process. The value of the estimated error for phase 3 was 1.6%, considering the total sample size of 2980 valid punctuations, bearing in mind the response time of the user.

Based on the design of the test performed, we had samples of unrelated groups, which mean that the observations were made on different sampling units and with different averages. To evaluate the results from a statistical point of view the first step was to define the significance level (α) with which we would work. This level was used both for the comparison of averages and for assessing the confidence level of the selected samples. This is usually done with values greater than or equal to 90% ($\alpha = 0.1$), but doing so would require a large number of samples to reduce the margin of error. Because we are using a qualitative sample, this can lower the levels of significance assessed to those at a value of $\alpha = 0.4$, which signifies a reasonable margin of error. Our study assessed the level of significance with $\alpha = 0.2$ (Grenacre, 2007). Lower values (below 0.2) indicate that the differences observed within the sample comparatives show a differential behavior depending on different users and/or environments. This information is relevant and it should be considered for the design of any image.

PHASE 3: OVERALL RESULTS

Focusing on the two main devices tested of this phase and simplifying the data viewing only the average by gender of the three levels measured, the standard deviation and the variance between them, Table 1 was derived.

There are several methods to compare the differences between two averages. We can study the differences between the variances using ANOVA, or we can directly analyze the difference of the averages by the "Student's t distribution". The latter method varies the formula of calculation based on the variance of the samples, which in our case is different as can be seen in Table 1. The Student's distribution is also better suited for small samples, which is why this method was selected. Performing an overall analysis of the values obtained by architectural images for a significance level of 80% ($\alpha = 0.2$) and comparing the results based on the users' experiences with those im-

ages (experts or non-experts), we obtained the results in Table 2 separated by gender.

As can be seen from the results in Table 2, which were compared statistically, emotional behavior among users by gender and user experience is differentiated at a level of significance greater than 80% ($p = \alpha = 0.2$ or less) on the computer screens; this must not be extrapolated to the case of HMDs, where the differences are relevant in specific cases. This information reflects some important findings, namely, the device and environment where an image is displayed affects the user's emotional response. Because the quality of the display increases, allowing higher image quality, previous user experience on the subject of the picture is noteworthy, especially in the case of male users.

Table 1. Global comparison of the levels measured in terms of gender and user experience

	Computer Screen								Head Mounted Display							
	Female				Male				Female				Male			
	N:5 (No Arq)		N:7 (Arq)		N:11 (No Arq)		N:11 (Arq)		N:2 (No Arq)		N:4 (Arq)		N:2 (No Arq)		N:6 (Arq)	
	Av.	SD	Av.	SD	Av.	SD	Av.	SD	Av.	SD	Av.	SD	Av.	SD	Av.	SD
Valence	5.53	1.56	5,87	1.76	4,92	1.67	5,57	1.68	5,88	2.04	5,35	1,76	4,40	1.08	5,48	1.43
Arousal	4.32	1.53	3.77	1.49	3,78	1,60	3,05	1.71	3,66	1,60	3,40	1.22	3,12	1.11	2,37	0.97
Quality	6.22	1.86	5.90	1.83	5.70	1.90	6,24	1.74	6,48	1.54	5,59	1.83	4,56	1.41	6.26	1.59
Variance V	2.50		3.14		3.11		2.90		4.17		3.24		1.20		2.20	
Variance A	2.44		2.46		2.80		3.02		2.58		1.70		1.27		1.21	
Variance Q	3.50		3.44		3.60		3.14		2.39		3.41		2.15		2.67	

Table 2. Statistical analysis of the average differences between expert and non expert users

	Computer Screen			Head Mounted Display		
FEMALE	*Valence*	*Arousal*	*Quality*	*Valence*	*Arousal*	*Quality*
Student's t	1,34	-0,8	-0,4	-0,6	-0,2	-1,2
P(T<=t)	0,10	0,20	0,32	0,32	0,41	0,15
Critic Value	0,87	0,89	0,88	1,38	0,94	0,98
MALE	*Valence*	*Arousal*	*Quality*	*Valence*	*Arousal*	*Quality*
Student's t	1,47	-1,40	0,97	0,92	-0,94	1,27
P(T<=t)	0,07	0,08	0,17	0,26	0,19	0,21
Critic Value	0,86	0,85	0,86	1,37	0,90	1,37

PHASE 3: INFOGRAPHIC IMAGES

Concentrating on architectural images, we analyzed the behavior of users according to the typology of images, their technical characteristics (resolution and color model), and the display. The average perceived quality of computer-generated images (infographic images) is discussed in Figure 6 and the following paragraphs.

The perceived quality of the image decreases according to its level of compression. Further, significant observations indicate the reduction in perceived quality in the case of uncompressed black-and-white images (computer screen average (CS Av): 5.67; SD: 0.24; HMD average (HMD Av): 4.99; SD: 0.26) as compared to the same images in color (CS Av: 6.28; SD: 0.34; HMD Av: 6.18; SD: 0.48). The mentioned decrease is more accentuated in HMD (23.97%) as compared to CS visualization (10.67%) and is statistically significant at a level of $\alpha = 0.01$.

As shown in Figure 6, there are no statistically significant differences in the results comparing visualization on a computer screen and on a HMD

Figure 6. Infografic Images, Quality perceived in function of color and compression (1: Color without compression, 2: Color with 80% compression, 3: Color with 95% compression, 4: B&W without compression), user sex (F:female – M:male) and type of display (Comp. Screen and HMD). (© 2009-2010, David Fonseca. Used with permission.)

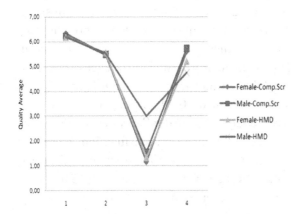

($\alpha = 0.48$ in women and $\alpha = 0.46$ in men). We also found no significant differences by gender when using the same device ($\alpha = 0.47$ on the computer screen and 0.41 on the HMD). We will analyze whether the decrease in the quality of black-and-white and compressed images affects the emotional framework:

Focusing on the valence graph (Figure 7) and comparing the results between the computer screen and the HMD, there are no statistically significant differences by gender ($\alpha = 0.39$ for women, and $\alpha = 0.37$ for men).

If we compare the results between males and females on the same device, there are also no statically significant differences ($\alpha = 0.26$ on the computer screen and $\alpha = 0.28$ on the HMD). Focused on the arousal, there are no statistical differences by gender between different devices ($\alpha = 0.33$ in women and $\alpha = 0.30$ in men), but we found an interesting result when comparing responses for the same display but between genders: $\alpha = 0.26$ on the computer screen and $\alpha = 0.002$ on the HMD.

Graphical results show some visual differences that are not statically significant for the case of arousal between males and females when using the HMD. This result with infographic images confirms that negative stimuli generate a higher negative response (H4 confirmation), especially among women, meaning that there is some difference between males and females in function of the device (H2 confirmation).

PHASE 3: PHOTOGRAPHIC IMAGES

The subsequent step verifies whether the results and conclusions arrived at regarding infographic images are comparable with photographic images of a real project.

For this study, we increased the number of black-and-white images with compression modifications. The average results of perceived quality according to the gender of the user, the visualiza-

Figure 7. Infografic Images, Valence and Arousal values according to color, compression, gender of user (F:female – M:male) and type of display (Comp. Screen and HMD) (© 2009-2010, David Fonseca. Used with permission.)

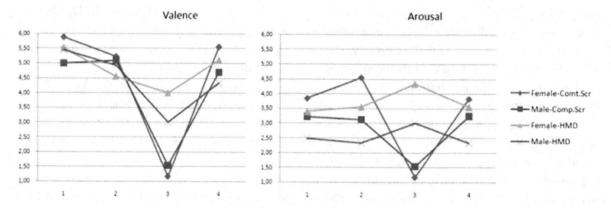

tion display and the level of compression are as follows in Figure 8 and subsequent paragraphs.

The first interesting result indicated in the graph is the evaluation with a superior quality (approximately 7.5%) of color images that were compressed to 80% in the JPG2000 format (X-Axis point n°2, Av: 6.67; SD: 0.35), as compared

Figure 8. Quality of photographic architectural image according to compression and model color (X-axis: 1:Color without compression, 2: 80% rate JPG2000 compression, 3: 95% rate JPG2000 compr., 4:Black and white without compression, 5:80% rate JPG2000 B&W compr., 6: 95% rate JPG2000 B&W compr.), gender (F:female – M:male) and the display (Computer Screen and HMD) (© 2009-2010, David Fonseca. Used with permission.)

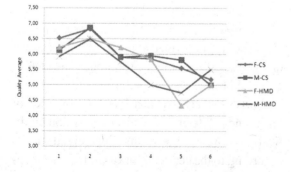

to the original uncompressed images (X-Axis point n° 1, Av: 6.21; SD: 0.40), displayed on both a computer screen and a HMD. The similarity of the values allows us to affirm that it will be indistinct between formats, leaving the perceived quality unaffected. Furthermore, we can verify a similar behavior in the evaluation of quality when the images are in color, irrespective of the level of compression (Av: 6.27; SD: 0.36).

There is a significant difference at a level greater than 90% ($\alpha = 0.10$) in the overall assessment of image quality between color and grey-scale images. The significance levels for the computer screen and HMD are $\alpha = 0.045$ and $\alpha = 0.018$, respectively, values that indicate a loss of perceived quality in black-and-white images higher for the HMD than for the computer screen regardless of their level of compression. Studying the results by gender for both devices analyzed, there was no statistical difference in perceived quality (gender differences associated with the CS and HMD had significance levels of $\alpha = 0.47$ and $\alpha = 0.39$, respectively). However, if we analyze the differences between users of the same gender in screen function, there is a significance difference in the case of male users, where the significance level is $\alpha = 0.15$ ($\alpha = 0.24$ for the female users).

The results reflecting the relationship between the perceived quality and the emotional framework provide us with the information seen in Figure 9.

As experienced in previous studies, the behavior of valence is comparable to that of the perception of quality, especially in the case of computer screen visualization, with a sensitive reduction (8%) for black-and-white images (Av: 4.71; SD: 1.16), compared to original colored images (Av: 5.08; SD: 0.26). This reduction is significantly different at a level greater than 90% ($\alpha = 0.10$) to the overall assessment of image valence between color and grey-scale images. The significance levels for the computer screen and HMD are $\alpha = 0.062$ and $\alpha = 0.038$, respectively, values that indicate a greater overall valence for color images in both devices. The respective significance levels of the arousal are $\alpha = 0.17$ for computer and $\alpha = 0.32$ for HMD, indicating a greater reaction in the comparison of image color under devices with high-resolution displays.

Studying the emotional data separately by gender and device, the valences associated with computer screens and HMDs were valued more highly by the females than by the males, with significance levels of $\alpha = 0.047$ and $\alpha = 0.036$, respectively. Arousal was also more highly indicated by females, with significance levels of $\alpha = 0.0004$ and $\alpha = 0.0001$ on computers and HMDs, respectively.

Analyzing the data for the same gender and the different displays, the valences of females and males were not significantly different between computer screens and HMDs (where the level of significance between values are $\alpha = 0.38 > 0.2$ our limit, and 0.47), but arousal was higher for both females and males on computer screens compared with HMDs (with significance levels of $\alpha = 0.00006$ and $\alpha = 0.001$, respectively).

This study validates hypotheses H2, H3 and H4, and we can conclude that black-and-white images are not "usable" for the visualization of an architectural project (infographic or realistic). Color is necessary to understand the lighting model and texture of surfaces. The perception of surface shapes of objects is simpler in color models, representing the major reason for eliminating the usage of black-and-white images.

PHASE 3: COMPOSITION PANELS

To evaluate computer-generated images, characteristics such as their composition, text, and use of real images were used to assess the importance of highlighting the basic model of the project in front of a background and other complementary elements of the panel.

Based on the findings of the previous study, which appears to demonstrate the importance of

Figure 9. Valence and Arousal of Architectural and photographic image, according to compression level, color, user profile and type of display (© 2009-2010, David Fonseca. Used with permission.)

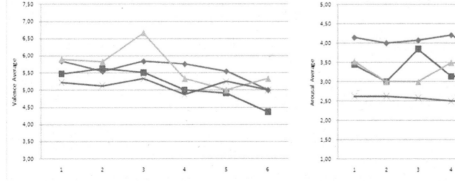

viewing large images, especially architectural images, the hypothesis is made that for those images with less information, quality, empathy and emotion ratings made by the user will be higher than they will be for those that incorporate text or other "sub images" complementing the panel.

Analysis of the data yields interesting results, starting from the initial point that all the compositions have similar resolutions, and the panels presented in positions 5 and 6 (images 49 and 50 of the test) are those with a larger component of the text. These panels can be visible and understandable in the printed version of the same, but it is difficult to read in the digital environment:

- All graphs starting from the middle point (average valence: 5.16; SD: 1.68; and average quality: 5.32, SD: 2.21). This information, compared with the results obtained from the following images, can be understood as indicating that in front of a particular type of image, users intermediately evaluate the expected stimulus to the next stimulus presented.
- Analyzing the responses of the valence: the data collected from female users are in line with the working hypothesis for this study, especially in the environment of the

HMD (green graph), where the values obtained for the panels with more text are significantly lower than the rest.

- The responses of the valence for male users are more homogeneous, with similar behaviors found between the two environments studied (computer screen: 5.14 – standard deviation: 1.93 to HMDs: 5.36 – standard deviation: 1.59, difference of less than 5%). Additionally, note that for these users there was no decrease in the emotional level for images with much text, but in terms of perceived quality, regardless of the environment, behavior that in the case of females only met in the HMD device.
- The highest-rated valence image was the last image presented (No. 7 of Figure 10, with an average of 5.70 and SD: 1.63, which is more than 10% better than the average rating of 5.18). This image does not have large text or an excessive overlap of photographic elements, and here, the graphics are freer of additional information. Likewise, and reaffirming our previous studies it is the highest rating of perceived quality (6.25 – SD: 2.08, approximately 15% above the average quality of all the compositions at 5.50).

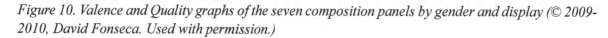

Figure 10. Valence and Quality graphs of the seven composition panels by gender and display (© 2009-2010, David Fonseca. Used with permission.)

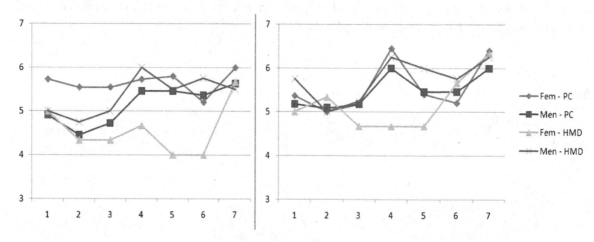

Analyzing the results statistically between devices (computer screen vs. HMD), there is a significant difference in all levels and users, based on our initial level of significance of $\alpha = 0.2$, as we can see in Tables 3 and 4.

From those results, we can conclude that the infographic composition of panels does not require text, inaccurate perspectives, or excessive details to produce a positive visual experience. The average rating for all images in this group are below those of the global average test, indicating that such images are not suitable for viewing in digital environments that yield reductions in perceived size compared to the traditional view in printed panels. The local hypothesis is confirmed, and we also observed a greater difference in users' behaviors between the two environments for the rest of the architectural images.

CONCLUSION

Based on the results obtained and the working hypothesis discussions, we will begin extracting the first group of recommendations, which will undoubtedly have to be corroborated by further studies.

After analyzing the methodological design of this phase, we find a clear discrepancy within the users if taking into account the gender. This is especially important when testing with the HMD device. This difference generates more statistically significant differences easily. Therefore we will confirm it upon the following phases while applying an accurate design based on the selection of a more balanced amount of samples.

In architectural project visualization, and as happens with an image in general, we can distinguish the behaviors of users according to their gender and their experience. As we can see in Tables 1 and 2, there is a differentiated visual behavior between the users, especially in the case of computer screens:

- High-definition screens generate a greater differentiation between the qualities perceived, especially to male users. The expert users give a higher rating in valence and quality, with a minor increase in arousal, than non-expert users. It seems that female users do not perceive the quality differences on computer screens and that their emotional evaluation is more similar.

Table 3. Statistical analysis of the differences between computer screen and HMD based on gender

	Computer Screen vs. HMD		
FEMALE	*Valence*	*Arousal*	*Quality*
P(T<=t)	0.001	0.166	0.136
MALE	*Valence*	*Arousal*	*Quality*
P(T<=t)	0.193	0.024	0.132

Table 4. Statistical analysis of the differences female and male based on the type of screen

	Female vs. Male		
Computer Screen	*Valence*	*Arousal*	*Quality*
P(T<=t)	0.013	0.047	0.370
HMD	*Valence*	*Arousal*	*Quality*
P(T<=t)	0.009	0.003	0.044

- In immersive environments, the female users more clearly perceive the quality differences, but this information does not affect their emotional response. Only the expert and non-expert male users show a significant difference in arousal.

As Arnheim (1954/1974) asserted, *"...perception is influenced by two vital forces, the psychological and the physical that make dynamic viewing experience."* The results of this study confirmed this statement, as each user's reaction to an image varies and is influenced by his or her experience and relationship with the environment.

Recommendation 1

It is necessary to increase the quality of architectural images when they are viewed by experts as producing the same emotional reaction compared to non-experts. To achieve this effect, the images should be displayed in color, and we can compress them into the JPG2000 format at a compression ratio of no more than 80%.

Another interesting result is the gender-differentiated behavior that was found. A recent study (Correa, 2007) identified a variable in visualization based on the gender and age of the user, namely, the presence of estrogen receptors in the retina. In these studies, the same shades of colors appeared lighter to younger users (without gender distinction) compared to older users, possibly because of the darkening of the corneas and lenses of people over the age of 35 years. Older users tend to perceive images to be darker than they actually are. This can be explained by hormonal changes in women because of their estrogen levels and justifies the requirement for making a clear distinction between the age and gender of users prior to adapting new information.

A direct relationship exists between the perceived quality and emotional evaluation of an image by a user. While a user does not perceive a quality loss, the user values the image with a high valence (irrespective of the semantic category that circumscribes the image). However, the perception of compression errors reduces the user's "affinity" with the image and increases the activation of the user (especially for women). This behavior is more prominent in immersive environments as compared to classical visualization situations. In summary, valence and arousal are statistically higher when using computer screens compared to HMDs, especially for female users.

Recommendation 2

It is necessary to increase the quality or the resolution of architectural images when they are viewed on devices at low resolutions or close to the screen to produce the same emotional reaction compared to screens with high resolution. To achieve this effect, images should be displayed in color, and we can compress them into the JPG2000 format at a compression ratio of no more than 80%.

The visualization of black-and-white images in architectural projects generates lower values than colored images of equal resolution and compression level, thereby generating a decreased emotional response. This can be attributed to poorer visualization of the object textures in black-and-white images, a very important consideration in design and architectural projects. The importance of "chroma" and contrast has also been studied as differential factors in perception (McManus, Jones, & Cottrell, 1981; Zemach, Chang, & Teller, 2007) and is an area with an interesting potential for future study because color may play an important role in affective picture processing, as the manipulation of hue, saturation, brightness, contrast and compression of an image can influence emotional responses (Canoa, Classa, & Polich, 2009).

The compression of infographic images must be more restrictive than for photographic images, as the evaluation of both the quality and the valence of infographic images is lower than that of photographic images at equal levels of compression (from JPG to JPG2000 to 80%). This observation not only supports values but also, according to the typology of the image, increases them. The fact that the image generated by a computer "lacks realistic imperfections" that correspond to the real image is responsible for this situation, making it more sensitive to the errors produced by pixelation or compression.

The latest affirmation reaffirms the relationship between perceived quality and emotional valence as well as a differential behavior between female and male users in front of devices with low-quality resolutions or negative stimuli.

Recommendation 3

If the final user is a male, and the viewing environment has a low resolution or is seen up close (based on IOV; see the literature review), it is necessary to increase the quality of the image by about 20% to yield similar results compared with those of female users.

To conclude, and on the basis of this experience, we can affirm that it is necessary to examine the real usability and consequences of employing immersive screens, as 64% of the users who undertook the HMD test felt "cyber sickness" after the test was completed. This indicates how difficult it is to create an appropriate project in an immersive environment. The application of the "traditional" techniques of usability (such as personal questionnaires and task test) and the latest advances in analyzing users' experiences such as Bipolar Interview Laddering (Pifarré, Sorribas, Villegas, Fonseca, & García, 2009), will be immensely useful in developing further studies, that do not have unpleasant side effects.

REFERENCES

Arnheim, R. (1954/1974). *Art and visual perception: A psychology of the creative eye.* Berkeley, CA: University of California Press.

Bellman, S., Schweda, A., & Varan, D. (2009). Viewing angle matters-screen type does not. *The Journal of Communication*, 609–634. doi:10.1111/j.1460-2466.2009.01441.x

Bernier, R. (2006). An introduction to JPEG 2000. *Library Hi Tech News*, 23(7), 26–27. doi:10.1108/07419050610704349

Boehner, K., DePaula, R., Dourish, P., & Sengers, P. (2007). How emotion is made and measured. *International Journal of Human-Computer Studies*, 65(4), 275–291. doi:10.1016/j.ijhcs.2006.11.016

Canoa, M., Classa, Q., & Polich, J. (2009). Affective valence, stimulus attributes, and P300: Color vs. black/white and normal vs. scrambled images. *International Journal of Psychophysiology*, 71(1), 17–24. doi:10.1016/j.ijpsycho.2008.07.016

Chen, L., Xie, X., Fan, X., Ma, W.-Y., Zhang, H.-J., & Zhou, H. (2003). A visual attention model for adapting images on small devices. *Multimedia Systems*, 9(4), 353–364. doi:10.1007/s00530-003-0105-4

Chen, L. O. (2006). *World of colour emotion.* Retrieved May 22, 2008, from http://colour-emotion.co.uk/whats.html

Cleempoel, K., & Van, Q. A. (2008). The influence of lighting in the build environment: a study to analyse human behaviour and perception as measured by mood and observation. In *Proceedings of the Conference on Measuring Behavior*, Maastricht, The Netherlands (pp. 385-388).

Clough, P., Müller, H., & Sanderson, M. (2004). *The CLEF 2004 cross-language image retrieval (Vol. image and video retrieval).* Berlin, Germany: Springer-Verlag.

Codispoti, M., & De Cesarei, A. (2007). Arousal and attention: Picture size and emotional reactions. *Psychophysiology*, 680–686. doi:10.1111/j.1469-8986.2007.00545.x

Correa, V., Estupiñán, L., Garcia, Z., Jimenez, O., Fernanda Prada, L., & Rojas, A. (2007). Percepción visual del rango de color: Diferencias entre género y edad. *Revista Med de la Facultad de Medicina*, *15*(1), 7–14.

Coursaris, C., Swierenga, S., & Watrall, E. (2008). An empirical investigation of color temperature and gender effects on web aesthetic. *Journal of Usability Studies*, *3*(3), 103–117.

Dolcos, F. C. (2002). Event-related potentials of emotional memory: encoding pleasant, unpleasant, and neutral pictures. *Cognitive, Affective & Behavioral Neuroscience*, *2*(3), 252–263. doi:10.3758/CABN.2.3.252

Eakins, J. P. (2002). Towards intelligent image retrieval. *Pattern Recognition*, (35): 3–14. doi:10.1016/S0031-3203(01)00038-3

Eilouti, B. (2009). A digital incorporation of ergonomics into architectural design. *International Journal of Architecture Design*, 235-253.

Ekman, P. (1992). A set of basic emotions. *Psychological Review*, 550–553. doi:10.1037/0033-295X.99.3.550

Ekman, P. (1999). Basic emotions. In Dalgleish, T., & Power, M. (Eds.), *Handbook of cognition and emotion*. Chichester, UK: John Wiley & Sons.

Engeldrum, P. (2004). A theory of image quality: The image quality circle. *Journal of Imaging Science and Technology*, *48*(5), 446–456.

Enser, P. (2000). Visual image retrieval: seeking the alliance of concept-based and content-based paradigms. *Journal of Information Science*, *26*(4), 199–210. doi:10.1177/016555150002600401

Enser, P., & Armitage, L. (1997). Analysis of user need in image archives. *Journal of Information*, *23*(4), 287–299. doi:10.1177/0165551974231830

Fairchild, M. D. (2002). Image quality measurement and modeling for digital photography. *Japan Hardcopy, 2002*, 318–319.

Fernández, I., Carrera, P., Sánchez, F., & Paéz, D. (1997). Prototipos emocionales desde una perspectiva cultural. *Revista electrónica de Motivación y Emoción, 4*(8-9), 1-14.

Fonseca, D., Fernández, A., & García, O. (2008). Comportamiento plausible de agentes virtuales: Inclusión de parámetros de usabilidad emocional a partir de imágenes fotográficas. Extensión. *Revista Iberoamericana de Sistemas, Cibernética e Informática, 3*(2).

Fonseca, D., García, O., Duran, J., Pifarré, M., & Villegas, E. (2008). An image-centred "search and indexation system" based in user's data and perceived emotion. In *Proceedings of the 3rd ACM International Workshop on Human-centered Computing*, Vancouver, BC, Canada (pp. 27-34).

Fonseca, D., García, O., Pifarré, M., Villegas, E., & Duran, J. (2008). Propuesta gráfica de "clasificación y búsqueda emocional de imágenes por Internet" adaptadad para usuarios discapacitados o no expertos. *Iberoamerican Journal of Systemics. Cybernetics and Informatics, 5*(2), 1–9.

Genov, A., Schnall, S., & Laird, J. (1999). *In search of the intrinsic emotional meaning of color - Implications for design.* Retrieved June 18, 2008, from http://www.emotion-research.net

Grenacre, M. (2007). *Estadistica*, 1. Barcelona, Spain: Apuntes UOC.

Henden, C., Champion, E., Muhlberger, R., & Jacobson, J. (2008). A surround display warp-mesh utility to enhance player engagement. In *Proceedings of the 7th International Conference on Entertainment Computing* (pp. 46-56).

Heppner, C., Benkofske, M., & Moritz, R. (2004). Mobile video: A study of quality perception. In *Proceedings of the Human Factors and Ergonomics Society 48th Annual Meeting*, New Orleans, LA (pp. 1865-1869).

Hollink, L. A., Wielinga, B., & Worring, M. (2004). Classification of user image descriptions. *International Journal of Human-Computer Studies*, *61*(5), 601–626. doi:10.1016/j.ijhcs.2004.03.002

Hong, S., Ahn, C., Nah, Y., & Choi, L. (2005). Searching color images by emotional concepts. In S. Shimojo, S. Ichii, T.-W. Ling, & K.-H. Song (Eds.), *Proceedings of the 3rd International Conference on Web and Communication Technologies and Internet-Related Social Issues* (LNCS 3597, p. 921).

Houtveen, J., Rietveld, S., Schoutrop, M., Spiering, M., & Brosschot, J. (2001). A repressive coping style and affective, facial and physiological responses to looking at emotional pictures. *International Journal of Psychophysiology*, *42*, 265–277. doi:10.1016/S0167-8760(01)00150-7

Jacobson, N., & Bender, W. (1996). Color as a determined communication. *IBM Systems Journal*, 526–538. doi:10.1147/sj.353.0526

Kennedy, M. R. (2005). *Informing content and concept-based image indexing and retrieval through a study of image description.* Chapel Hill, NC: School of Information and Library Science, University of North Carolina.

Knoche, H., McCarthy, J., & Sasse, M. (2005). Can small be beautiful? Assessing image resolution requirements for mobile TV. In *Proceedings of the 13th Annual ACM International Conference on Multimedia* (pp. 829-838).

Knoche, H., & Sasse, M. (2008). Getting the big picture on small screens: Quality of experience in mobile TV. *Interactive Digital Television: Technologies and Applications*, 242-260.

Lang, P., Bradley, M., & Cuthbert, B. (2005). *International Affective Picture System (IAPS): Affective ratings of pictures and instruction manual.* Gainesville, FL: University of Florida.

Lang, P., Greenwald, M., Bradley, M., & Hamm, A. (1993). Looking at pictures: affective, facial, visceral, and behavioral reactions. *Psychophysiology*, 261–273. doi:10.1111/j.1469-8986.1993.tb03352.x

Levkowitz, H., Holub, R., Meyer, G., & Robertson, P. (1991). Color vs. black-and-white in visualization. In *Proceedings of the 2nd Conference on Visualization*, San Diego, CA (pp. 336-339).

Lieberman, H., & Liu, H. (2002). Adaptative linking between text and photos using common sense reasoning. In P. De Bra, P. Brusilovsky, & R. Conejo (Eds.), *Second International Conference on Adaptive Hypermedia and Adaptive Web-Based Systems* (LNCS 2347, pp. 2-11).

Lim, J.-H., & Jin, J. (2005). A structured learning framework for content-based image indexing and visual query. *Multimedia Systems*, *10*(4). doi:10.1007/s00530-004-0158-z

Maya, E. C., Quetzal, A. C., & Polich, J. (2009). Affective valence, stimulus attributes, and P300: Color vs. black/white and normal vs. scrambled images. *International Journal of Psychophysiology*, *71*(1), 17–24. doi:10.1016/j.ijpsycho.2008.07.016

McManus, I., Jones, A., & Cottrell, J. (1981). The aesthetics of colour. *Perception*, *10*(6), 651–666. doi:10.1068/p100651

Mikels, J. A., Fredrickson, B. L., Larkin, G. R., Lindberg, C. M., Maglio, S. J., & Reuter-Lorenz, P. A. (2005). Emotional category data on images from the IAPS. *Behavior Research Methods*, *37*(4), 626–630. doi:10.3758/BF03192732

Moltó, J., Montañés, S., Poy, R., Segarra, P., Pastor, M., & Tormo, M. (1999). Un nuevo método para el estudio experimental de las emociones: El international affective picture system (IAPS). *Revista de Psicología General y Aplicada*, *55*(1), 55–87.

Mühlberger, A., Neumann, R., Wieser, M., & Pauli, P. (2008). The impact of changes in spatial distance on emotional responses. *Emotion (Washington, D.C.)*, 192–198. doi:10.1037/1528-3542.8.2.192

Pifarré, M., Sorribas, X., Villegas, E., Fonseca, D., & García, O. (2009). BLA (Bipolar Laddering) applied to YouTube. Performing postmodern psychology paradigms in user experience field. *Journal of Behavioral, Cognitive, Educational and Psychological Sciences, 1*(2), 76–82.

Porras, M., & Pereyra, M. (2001). El valor psicológico del color y su uso en la comunicación. *HUELLAS-Búsquedas en Artes y Diseño*, (1), 141-145.

Ramirez, O. (1999). Un nuevo método para el estudio experimental de las emociones: El international affective picture system (IAPS). *Revista de Psicología General y Aplicada, 55*(1), 55–87.

Recayte, P., & Bund, E. (2005). La imagen digital en la mediación Arquitecto-Usuario. In *Proceedings of the 9th Iberoamerican Congress on Digital Graphics*, Lima, Peru (pp. 1-5).

Reeves, B., Lang, A., Kim, E., & Tatar, D. (1999). The effects of screen size and message content or attention and arousal. *Media Psychology*, 49–67. doi:10.1207/s1532785xmep0101_4

Reeves, B., & Nass, C. (1996). *The media equation: How people treat computers, television, and new media like real people and places*. Cambridge, UK: Cambridge University Press.

Roscoe, S. (1991). The eyes prefer real images. In Ellis, S. (Ed.), *Pictoral communication in virtual and real environments* (pp. 577–585). London, UK: Taylor and Francis.

Rosenbaum, R., & Schumann, H. (2005). JPEG2000-based image communication for modern browsing techniques. In *Proceedings of the SPIE Image and Video Communications and Processing Conference* (pp. 1019-1030).

Stahre, B., Billger, M., & Anter, K. F. (2009). To colour the virtual world: Difficulties in visualizing spatial colour appearance in virtual environments. *International Journal of Architectural Computing, 7*(2), 289–308. doi:10.1260/147807709788921949

Tractinsky, N. (1997). Aesthetics and apparent usability: Empirically assessing cultural and methodological issues. In *Proceedings of the SIGCHI Conference on Human Factors in Computing* (pp. 115-122).

Vansteenkiste, E., Van der Weken, D., Philips, W., & Kerre, E. (2006). Perceived image quality measurement of state-of-the-art noise reduction schemes. In J. Blanc-Talon, W. Philips, D. Popescu, & P. Scheunders (Eds.), *Proceedings of the 8th International Conference on Advanced Concepts for Intelligent Vision Systems* (LNCS 4179, pp. 114-126).

Verschuere, R., Crombez, G., & Koster, E. (2007). *Cross cultural validation of the IAPS*. Ghent, Belgium: Ghent University.

Wang, L., Giesen, J., McDonnell, K. T., Zolliker, P., & Mueller, K. (2008). Color design for illustrative visualization. *IEEE Transactions on Visualization and Computer Graphics, 14*(6), 1739–1754. doi:10.1109/TVCG.2008.118

Winn, W., & Everett, R. (1979). Affective rating of color and black-and-white pictures. *Educational Technology Research and Development, 27*(2), 148–156.

Xin, J. H. (2004). Cross-regional comparison of colour emotions part I. Quantitative analysis. *Color Research and Application, 29*(6), 451–457. doi:10.1002/col.20062

Zemach, I., Chang, S., & Teller, D. (2007). Infant color vision: prediction of infants' spontaneous color preferences. *Vision Research*, 1368–1381. doi:10.1016/j.visres.2006.09.024

This work was previously published in International Journal of Creative Interfaces and Computer Graphics, Volume 2, Issue 2, edited by Ben Falchuk, pp. 1-22, copyright 2010 by IGI Publishing (an imprint of IGI Global).

Chapter 18
Rain Simulation in Dynamic Scenes

Anna Puig-Centelles
Universitat Jaume I, Spain

Nicolau Sunyer
Universitat de Girona, Spain

Oscar Ripolles
Universidad Politécnica de Valencia, Spain

Miguel Chover
Universitat Jaume I, Spain

Mateu Sbert
Universitat de Girona, Spain

ABSTRACT

Rain is a complex phenomenon and its simulation is usually very costly. In this article, the authors propose a fully-GPU rain simulation based on the utilization of particle systems. The flexibility of CUDA allows the authors to include, aside from the rainfall simulation, a system for the detection and handling of the collisions of particles against the scenario. This detection system allows for the simulation of splashes at the same time. This system obtains a very high performance because of the hardware programming capabilities of CUDA.

INTRODUCTION

The use of an efficient and realistic rain simulation system increases the realism of outdoor scenes. The problem of depicting atmospheric precipitations has been approached in many occasions, not only for rain visualization (Tatarchuk, 2006; Wang et al., 2008), but also for its interaction with other surfaces (Kaneda, Ikeda, & Yamashita, 1999; Stuppacher & Supan, 2007) or even for the accumulation of water on the ground (Fearing, 2000).

Most of the systems proposed for real-time rain simulation are based on the use of particle systems (Kusamoto, Tadamura, & Tabuchi, 2001; Wang et al., 2006; Tariq, 2007). These systems have been successfully employed in previous solutions to

DOI: 10.4018/978-1-4666-0285-4.ch018

simulate several types of diffuse phenomena, such as smoke or fire (Reeves, 1983). Nevertheless, the use of particle systems to represent rain has significant limitations due to the cost involved in handling the great quantity of particles that is necessary to offer scenarios of intense rain with realistic appearance. As a consequence, virtual environments which integrate particle systems have serious performance problems, as rain simulation consumes a very important part of the computer resources.

A possible solution to overcome this limitation is the exploitation of graphics hardware, since its constant evolution continuously offers new possibilities. Following this idea, there are many techniques which use GPU programs (*shaders*) in order to alleviate the CPU load and to speed up rain visualization (Tatarchuk, 2006; Tariq, 2007). Moreover, some of the latest proposals also include the use of the *Geometry Shader* (Iwasaki, Dobashi, Yoshimoto, & Nishita, 2008; Puig-Centelles, Ripolles, & Chover, 2009).

In this work we propose a rain simulation system, which is managed and updated only on graphics hardware. The solution suggested is based on the utilization of particle systems to simulate rain. It includes the management of rain under variable wind conditions and also the detection and handling of collision of raindrops against the scenario to generate splashes. Figure 1 shows an image of the proposed simulation system in an intense rain environment.

Developing this system by means of the traditional graphics pipeline would be very complex. Our proposal offers a very flexible framework which obtains a very high performance through the use of CUDA. CUDA (Compute Unified Device Architecture) is a technology created by NVIDIA with the objective of making the most of the great processing capacity of current graphics cards to solve problems with a high computational load (Nvidia, 2007). In the specific case of the rain simulation that we propose, the use of CUDA considerably frees the CPU from an enor-

mous number of operations. In this sense, the framework that we propose in this paper offers three main advantages with respect to previous GPU methods:

1. It does not introduce the overhead of using a graphics library for a task independent of graphics, as is the case of the calculations made for the particle simulation. Moreover, our framework provides methods for the direct visualization of the results, given the memory interoperability between OpenGL and CUDA within the graphics card.

2. In contrast to previous solutions, it is not necessary to perform two passes of the graphics hardware to make the calculations that update the positions of particles. All the calculations can be made in one single pass, leaving the second pass only for visualizing the geometry obtained.

3. It is possible to add more natural effects related to the precipitation, such as the dynamic generation of geometry to simulate splashes. As we will see in the following sections, the simulation of splashes requires a third rendering pass to prepare the calculations of the collisions in a dynamic environment.

This article is organized using the following structure. The next section summarizes the previous work in rain simulation, concentrating on those models that use graphics hardware to accelerate and to improve rain visualization; we also address those systems that detect and handle collisions of raindrops. Then, we present an overview of the main features of the framework which we have developed, comparing its characteristics with the solutions previously developed. The following section describes in detail our rain model, including the subsystem in charge of the calculation of collisions. Later, the results are presented, regarding both performance and visual quality. Finally, we summarize the contributions of our proposal and outline future lines of work.

Figure 1. Intense rain environment

PREVIOUS WORK

During the last few years several approaches have been developed in the field of computer graphics to render rainfall. Some of those methods have been devised in order to add rain to a single image of a scene or to a captured video with moving objects and sources (Stanik & Werman, 2003; Garg & Nayar, 2004). Nevertheless, real-time rain has been traditionally rendered in two ways, either as a camera-centered geometry with *scrolling textures* or as *particle systems*.

- **Scrolling textures:** The solutions used by this family of techniques displace a texture of rain which covers the whole scene, simulating the falling movement (Wang & Wade, 2004). These methods are not capable of creating a really convincing impression of precipitation due to the lack of depth sensation that they offer. To

overcome this limitation, some authors (Tatarchuk, 2006) have developed more complex solutions which include different layers of scrolling textures to simulate rain at different distances, although the problem has not been completely solved. Another problem in this kind of methods is the fact that the camera movements are limited; if the observer looks towards the sky, the realistic sensation of the falling rain is completely lost.

- **Particle systems:** The techniques using particle systems efficiently depict rainy scenes (Kusamoto, Tadamura, & Tabuchi, 2001; Rousseau, Jolivet, & Ghazanfarpour, 2006; Wang et al., 2006; Tariq, 2007; Wang et al., 2008). However, this group of methods is that they are not suitable for scenarios where the user moves fast, such as computer games. This is due to the fact that adjusting all the particles to the new camera conditions is very costly. To alleviate this problem, several proposals use the computational capacities of graphics cards to simulate rainy environments. The more recent ones (Tariq, 2007; Puig-Centelles, Ripolles, & Chover, 2009) propose solutions that maximize the use of the GPU to process and to simulate rain by working uniquely on the graphics card.

Table 1 summarizes the features of the rain simulation techniques which exploit graphics hardware. The description of each solution presented includes different aspects of rain precipitation:

- **Technique:** indicates if the technique employed to represent rain uses particle systems or scrolling textures.
- **Collisions:** states whether the authors consider that the particles collide between them or with some other surface.
- **Rendering:** indicates what kind of use the models make of current GPU possibilities.

- **Wind:** indicates whether the system considers the alteration in the falling movement of the drops due to the wind.
- **Others:** this field includes various characteristics that can be considered in the different models, such as snow, depth of field, ripples or puddles.

Collision Detection

The splashing of a raindrop is a complex phenomenon where the distribution of droplets of a splash depends on many different features of the elements involved. In this sense, Garg et al. (2007) measured the water drops on different surfaces to offer a physically realistic simulation. This high degree of physical simulation is usually beyond real-time applications. In this sense, the solution proposed by Feng et al. (2006) presents a method for detecting collisions and it includes a subsystem to simulate the splashes of drops after collision. Later, the method introduced in Tariq (2007) suggests the simulation of the splashes by applying

Table 1. Characterization of rain solutions

Authors	Technique	Collisions	Rendering	Wind	Others
(Wang & Wade, 2004)	Scrolling Textures	No	Vertex	No	Snow
(Feng, Tang, Dong, & Chou, 2006)	Particle System	Yes	Vertex, Pixel	Yes	Splashes, Depth of Field
(Wang et al., 2006)	Particle System	No	Vertex, Pixel	Yes	Splashes
(Tatarchuk, 2006)	Scrolling Textures / Particle System	Yes	Vertex, Pixel	Yes	Splashes Puddles, Dripping
(Rousseau, Jolivet, & Ghazanfarpour, 2006)	Particle System	No	Vertex, Pixel	No	Snow
(Tariq, 2007)	Particle System	No	Vertex, Pixel, Geometry, Texture Arrays	Yes	Splashes
(Wang et al., 2008)	Particle System	No	Not indicated	Yes	Rainbow, Scattering
(Rousseau, Jolivet, & Ghazanfarpour, 2008)	Particle System	Yes	Vertex, Pixel	Yes	Snow
(Puig-Centelles, Ripolles, & Chover, 2009)	Particle System	No	Vertex, Pixel, Geometry	No	Level of Detail
Our Proposal	Particle System	Yes	Vertex, Pixel, Geometry, CUDA	Yes	Splashes

a displacement texture over the scenario. This method is not very precise, although the results obtained are visually satisfactory. More recently, Rousseau et al. (2008) described a method for collision detection based on capturing the normal and the height of each point in the scenario with a camera above the scene. Thus, by using this texture in rendering time they are capable of detecting collisions and to calculating the rebound direction of the splashes by means of the surface normals.

GENERAL FEATURES

The use of graphics hardware allows us to accelerate rain visualization considerably. In this sense, other authors have contributed with methods where particles are displaced in the graphics card itself, saving the positions calculated by using techniques as *render-to-vertex* (Rousseau, Jolivet, & Ghazanfarpour, 2006) or the more recent *Stream Output* (Tariq, 2007) introduced in the Shader Model 4.0.

Usually, rain simulation models on graphics hardware needed two passes of the graphics pipeline to obtain the geometry. Figure 2 shows a diagram that summarizes these two traditional passes:

- The first pass moves the particles following the falling movement of the drop with a certain velocity, which can be defined as constant for all the particles or vary for each element of the particle system. Furthermore, in this pass the system repositions those particles that have come out of the scenario to continue with the simulation without losing the sensation of a continuously falling rain.

- In the second pass, the system creates the four points forming the quad used to simulate the drops. The calculation of these new positions takes into account the current position of the camera to orient the *quads* towards the user as an impostor would do. At this point, some models choose to texturize the *quad* and others assign a final color to it.

To improve this two-pass technique, we decided to use CUDA to optimize the use of the graphics card. It will still be necessary to make two passes. The first one will be made with CUDA and the second one with OpenGL, since CUDA is not a graphics library that allows the visualization of the updated geometry. Moreover, as we commented in

Figure 2. Rendering passes that are necessary to obtain the geometry in previous solutions

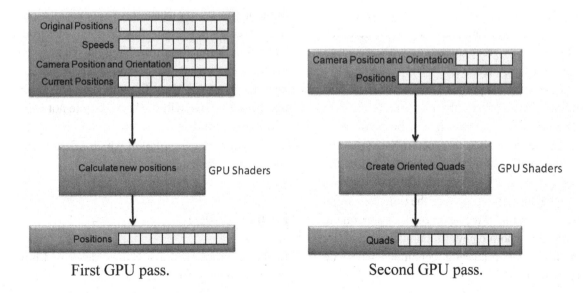

First GPU pass. Second GPU pass.

the introduction, the simulation of splashes requires a third rendering pass to prepare the calculations of the collisions in a dynamic environment

CUDA Usage

The concept of GPGPU (General Purpose Computing on Graphics Processing Units) was presented as a low-cost alternative to parallel processing systems (Dokken, Hagen, & Hjelmervik, 2005). Hence, instead of employing a large number of computers, several authors resorted to graphics processors to make mathematical calculations.

The problems presented by graphics applications do not generally require a very high processing capacity, contrary to the problems that have been traditionally solved through GPGPU techniques. The use of CUDA in a graphics application is very interesting because of the way in which information can be accessed and shared among the different processes running in parallel. In CUDA, a thread has its own processor, variables (registers), processor states, etc. A block of threads is represented as a virtual multiprocessor. The blocks can be run in any order in a concurrent or sequential way. The memory is shared among the threads; in a similar way, there is shared memory among the blocks of a kernel. This means that it is possible to work on the same data in different threads and in different blocks, besides being able to do it in an asynchronous way with the CPU. This supposes a great advantage with respect to the previous architecture.

In our work we propose the use of CUDA to optimize the update of the particles in the rain simulation system. Thus, it will be possible to write at the same time the vector that stores the updated positions and the vector that stores the generated *quads*. The use of this framework allows us, on the one hand, to reduce the time consumed in the calculation of the new positions and, on the other, to incorporate new functionalities that, by using traditional rendering techniques, would be very complex to obtain.

The main advantage offered by our solution is that all the calculations are made in only one CUDA kernel. The way CUDA works with memory positions allows us to save information in several buffers at the same time, to employ read/write buffers and to decide in which buffer position the generated information should be saved. A more detailed description of our proposed solution will be presented in the following section.

Raindrops Perception

Another feature that traditionally defined a rain simulation framework is the use of a visually-satisfying simulation of the raindrops. The retinal persistence of the human eye (or the motion blur of the shutter of a camera) makes the raindrops to be perceived as streaks. This is due to the fact that when observing rain, a drop keeps falling for a time lapse that is not perceived neither by the retina nor the shutter. Thus, in order to represent this effect in a realistic way, rain particles are shaped as vertical streaks, whose pixels receive contributions of the successive positions of the drop. It is possible to find methods that have tried to capture in a texture the appearance of these streaks (Rousseau, Jolivet, & Ghazanfarpour, 2006). The complexity resulting from incorporating these textures into the real-time rain simulation increases the cost of the system without offering a considerably better visual aspect in contrast to the systems that do not use textures. Therefore, in our system we have chosen to assign the *quads* a color with a certain level of transparency to give them their final appearance. In the results section we will see how, despite not using textures to simulate drops, our system is capable of offering a rain simulation which offers a high sensation of realism to the final user.

RAIN MODEL

In the previous section we have described how rain was managed in previous solutions and how we propose to improve these solutions. In this section we will thoroughly describe how we have implemented the aforementioned contributions.

One of the aims of our suggested system is to offer better capabilities. In this sense, we consider that the calculation of collisions is a very important requirement in a complete solution to the problem of rain simulation. The calculation of collisions offers advantages in two senses. On the one hand, it allows us to optimize the update of the positions of the particles as it avoids moving those drops that have already collided, as happens with mountains or buildings, and that are not visible anymore. On the other hand, the main contribution refers to realism, since the generation of splashes is a fundamental part in rain simulation.

In our framework we propose a simple system, although it would be possible to use more complex methods with no technical difficulty. Similarly to Rousseau et al. (2008), the method we have applied consists in making a capture of the heightmap of the scene we are visualizing. This capture is made for every image we create, so that the system is capable of adapting the calculation of the collisions to the state of the scene in each moment, considering the movements of the characters and other objects in the environment. This heightmap is stored as a texture inside the graphics card memory. Figure 3 shows the process of obtaining the heightmap from a camera positioned at such height and distance that allows us to observe the whole scene.

The solution proposed will detect if a raindrop collides with the environment by accessing this texture. Thus, when detecting a collision we decide to create a quad in that position and texturize it with an image that simulates water dispersion after the collision. Currently, the splashes last a single frame, although a more complex animation could be used. In this way, it would be possible to create several particles that simulate the drops created from the collided drop, which could follow a new trajectory. Nevertheless, in the system we

Figure 3. Diagram of the capture of the heightmap

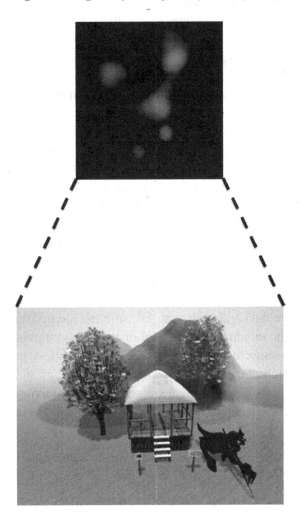

present we have chosen to apply a simpler method, as it is capable of offering a realistic sensation with a lower cost

In addition to the simulation of splashes, we have also included the effect of the wind on the falling raindrops. The wind simulation implies altering the falling vector of the raindrops, so that they do not fall completely vertical. Moreover, it is also necessary to perform a small modification of the algorithm in charge of generating the oriented quads. This way, it will be necessary to consider the falling direction of the particles so that the quad is also oriented following this direction. Figure 4 presents a snapshot of our rain simulation system where wind has been added. It can be seen how the shape of the quads has been adapted to the new falling direction of the raindrops.

Data Structures and Algorithms

Figure 5 summarizes the data distribution in the graphics card memory that we propose for our approach. This figure includes, shaded in red, the structures that are necessary to make the calculation of collisions and the simulation of splashes. In this figure we can see how it will be necessary to store in memory the original position of the drops and their speed, which are calculated stochastically. Moreover, we need a buffer to store the current position of the particles, which will be read and written at the same time to update the raindrops location. From a slightly different perspective, we will also need two buffers to store the generated *quads* for the raindrops and the collisions, which are generated considering the orientation and position of the camera. These

buffers are shared with OpenGL to visualize the obtained geometry. It is important to comment that if the particle suffers a collision it is necessary to reposition it above the field of vision of the user in order to continue with the rain simulation.

Algorithm 1 offers the whole rain simulation process in a detailed way through its description by using pseudocode. The *kernel* proposed includes the calculation of collisions, so that every time we displace a particle, we compare its resulting position with the height stored in the previously commented texture. If a collision is detected, the system repositions the particle in the upper area of the scene considering the current camera position, so that the rain system follows the movements of the user. Moreover, we will add a new particle to our particle subsystem in charge of collisions. One of the aims of the system is to keep the volume of raindrops constant, so that the rain sensation is maintained. This is the reason why we do not change the falling particles into splashing ones. In situations where a large amount of splashes are produced, our proposal is capable

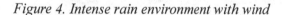

Figure 4. Intense rain environment with wind

Figure 5. Diagram of memory usage

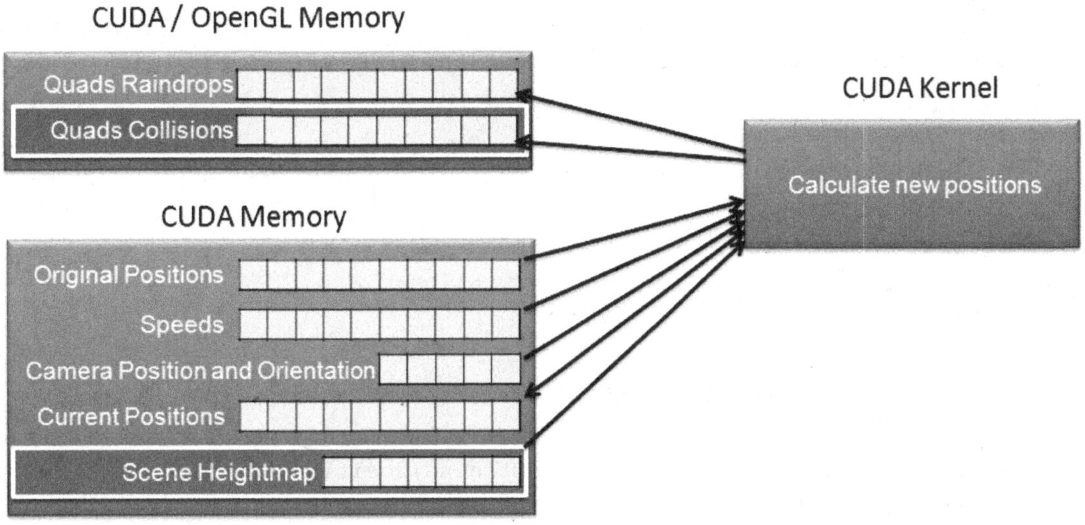

CUDA / OpenGL Memory

Quads Raindrops
Quads Collisions

CUDA Memory

Original Positions
Speeds
Camera Position and Orientation
Current Positions
Scene Heightmap

CUDA Kernel

Calculate new positions

of maintaining the rain intensity without limiting the amount of splashes to visualize.

The subsystem of collisions needs some specific considerations. The amount of collisions that are generated at each frame is variable and, therefore, we need some techniques to manage this variable amount of geometry. One of the features of CUDA that allows the efficient calculation of collisions are atomic operations, specifically the instruction *atomicInc()* (CUDA, 2007). This instruction reads the contents of a register in memory, it adds one integer and it writes the result in the same memory direction. Atomic operations guarantee that there are no interferences between execution threads, so that a specific memory position is not accessed by other thread until the operation is finished. In our case, we can maintain a single collision counter which is also used to store the position where the collision happens in a correct and subsequent way inside the collision vector. Thus, as output of the *kernel* we will obtain a vector of *quads* located in the positions where collisions have happened and oriented again towards the observer. This vector will have a fixed size in memory, but its content will have a variable size, depending on the characteristics of the scene.

Finally, it is important to comment that our framework follows the movements of the user. If the user modifies its position, the whole rain container is modified to locate the raindrops according to the new camera position. In this sense, the system works as a sliding cloud that permanently tracks the viewer. This is the reason why the camera position and orientation are necessary in the first rendering pass. The shape of the rain container can affect the performance of the system. Using the frustum to locate the raindrops can pose a problem when performing fast changes in the viewing direction. This is the reason why we use a rain container which is shaped as an elliptical semicylinder, which can be understood as an extended frustum. This rain container was introduced in Puig-Centelles, Ripolles, and Chover (2009), where a more detailed explanation and comparison of different rain containers can be found.

RESULTS

In this section we will analyze the solution proposed from several perspectives, since, apart from

Algorithm 1. Pseudo-code of the position update process

```
// Scene capture
heightMap=renderTexture();

// Process of raindrops update
FOR particle IN Particles
  // Scroll the particle
  particlePositions[particle] -=particleSpeeds[particle];
  IF {collision(particlePositions[particle],heightMap)}
    numCollisions++;
    quadsCollisions[numCollisions] =
calculateQuadparticlePositions[particle],cameraPosition);

    particlePositions[particle]= particleOriginalPositions[particle];
    translate(particlePositions[particle],cameraPosition);
    rotate(particlePositions[particle],cameraOrientation);
  ENDIF
  quadsParticles[particle]=
                calculateQuad(particlePositions[particle],cameraPosition);
ENDFOR
```

the performance, we are interested in analyzing the visual quality of the obtained simulation. The scene used in the various tests is the one presented in Figure 1. All the tests have been conducted on Windows XP Professional in a computer with an Intel QuadCore Q6600 at 2.4GHz processor, 4 GB RAM and a GeForce GTX280 graphics card with 1 GB RAM.

Visual Quality

One of the main objectives of the proposed work is to offer a rain simulation method which is realistic to the human eye. In this sense, Figure 1 presented an intense rain environment where we simulated 2 million particles in real time. To this simulation we have to add the calculation of collisions for each raindrop and the splash generation. Despite the great amount of particles to manage, the simulation process is performed in real time.

Figure 6 shows several screen captures of our rain simulation method. Each of them represents a different number of particles, which will give way to a different perception of rain intensity.

A video of our simulation can be found in http://graficos.uji.es/videos/videoIJCICG.avi, where the reader can appreciate the visual quality of the technique we present. As it happens in Figure 6, in the video we also render the scenario with different rain intensities.

Collisions and Splashes

As we have already mentioned, the inclusion of splashes adds realism to the final scene. The images introduced until now allowed us to observe how the splashes are distributed in the scene. In this section we want to especially remark that the selected method for the calculation of collisions allows us to easily detect the surfaces on which drops collide.

Figure 6. Rain environments with different intensities

a) Rain appearance with 512,000 particles.

b) Rain appearance with 1 million particles.

c) Rain appearance with 2 million particles.

d) Rain appearance with 4 million particles.

Figure 7 shows two images detailing the scene. In this case, splashes have been coloured in red so that it is easier to distinguish them from the environment. The first one shows a perspective of the scene, where we can see how splashes are never generated inside the hut or under the trees, since the drops collide on the roof or on the foliage. In addition, Figure 7b allows us to see how the system adapts to the geometry of the scene, since it can be observed how the splashes take place following the shape of the palm tree.

Finally, it is important to note that our method captures the heightmap in every frame rendered, so that the calculation of collisions adapts to the movements of characters and objects in the scenario.

Performance

The utilization of CUDA for the simulation of the raindrops offers significant advantages regarding performance. Figure 8 presents a study of the performance (in frames per second) of our system when simulating various amounts of rain. In this case, the intensities chosen are the ones presented in Figure 6. Furthermore, we also include separately the cost of the collisions calculation, in order to be able to analyze how much the simulation of splashes affects the performance of our proposal.

From the results shown in Figure 8 we can conclude that the simulation system proposed is capable of simulating a high quantity of drops in real time. Regarding the calculation and the visualization of the splashes, it increases the processing time by 15% on average. It is important to remark that, the more particles the rain system handles, the more percentage of time is necessary

Figure 7. Rain simulation examples with collision detection

a) Scene perspective.

b) Detail of the collisions detected on a palm tree.

Figure 8. Performance comparison for rain environments with different intensities

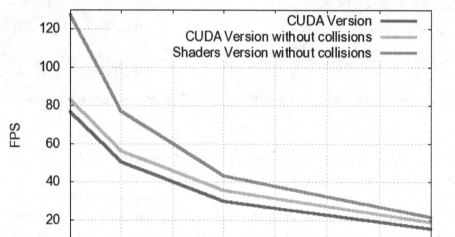

to dedicate to collisions. For this reason, for the simulation which works with 500,000 particles the system slows down by 8%, whereas if we want to visualize 4 million particles we will have to consider that the performance is affected in a 21%.

In this test we also want to compare our proposal with the methods based on the use of the traditional graphics pipeline (Tariq, 2007). Thus, we have also included the results of a *shaders*-based implementation of our rain framework without collisions. We can say that the performance obtained with *shaders* increases by 30% on average. In this case, the difference between both methods decreases as we visualize more particles, so if we want to simulate 4 million particles the performance difference will be only a 14%.

Otherwise, it is important to comment that the use that the rain system makes of the CPU in

Figure 9. Percentage of CPU use during 30 seconds of animation

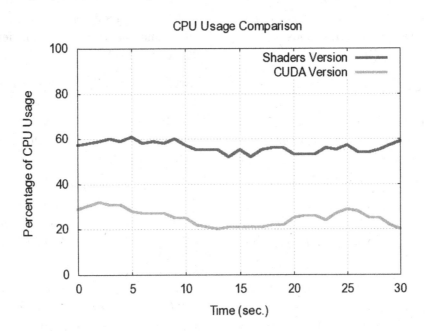

one case and in the other is very different. Figure 9 shows the percentage of use of the CPU for 30 seconds of the simulation. We can see that the rain simulation based on *shaders* consumes 57% of the CPU time, whereas with CUDA this occupation is reduced to 26%. The function calls by CUDA are asynchronous, allowing the simulation to be more fluent.

CONCLUSION

In this paper we have presented a set of techniques to efficiently visualize scenarios with rain of different intensities and different falling directions with a realistic appearance. The improvement of the simulation has been possible thanks to the use of new techniques for GPU programming, as their flexibility allows us to offer advanced techniques such as the collisions detection. Thus, the quality obtained in the different tests is due to the possibility of including a high quantity of particles and splashes. Moreover, CUDA enables the graphics application to reduce by half the use

of CPU time if compared with the *shaders* version, which allows the application to dedicate that time to make other calculations.

The solution we have described offers great advantages and encourages us to continue improving the simulation. In this sense, we plan to use the collision detection for further effects, like the accumulation of rain on the ground and the alteration of the properties of the surfaces depending on the amount of water received. This latter line of work is especially interesting as it can considerably contribute to the development of a physically and visually realistic rain simulation. Finally, we consider interesting to study the alteration of the precipitation and the splashes in situations of wind, so that the system solves correctly situations where drops do not fall in a totally vertical way.

ACKNOWLEDGMENT

This work has been funded by the Spanish Ministry of Science and Technology (TIN2010-21089-C03-01, TIN2010-21089-C03-03 and

TSI-020400-2009-0133), by the European Union (ITEA2 IP08009), by the Generalitat de Catalunya (2009-SGR-643) and by FEDER funds.

REFERENCES

Dokken, T., Hagen, T., & Hjelmervik, J. (2005). The GPU as a high performance computational resource. In *Proceedings of the 21st Spring Conference on Computer Graphics* (pp. 21-26).

Fearing, P. (2000). Computer modelling of fallen snow. In *Proceedings of the 27th Annual Conference on Computer Graphics and Interactive Techniques* (pp. 37-46).

Feng, Z., Tang, M., Dong, J., & Chou, S. (2006). Real-time rain simulation. In W. Shen, K.-M. Chao, Z. Lin, J.-P. A. Barthès, & A. James (Eds.), *Proceedings of the 9th International Conference on Computer Supported Cooperative Work in Design II* (LNCS 3865, pp. 626-635).

Garg, K., Krishnan, G., & Nayar, S. (2007). Material based splashing of water drops. In *Proceedings of the Eurographics Symposium on Rendering*.

Garg, K., & Nayar, S. K. (2004). Detection and removal of rain from videos. In *Proceedings of the IEEE Conference on Computer Vision and Pattern Recognition, 1*, 528–535.

Iwasaki, K., Dobashi, Y., Yoshimoto, F., & Nishita, T. (2008). GPU-based rendering of point-sampled water surfaces. *The Visual Computer, 24*(2), 77–84. doi:10.1007/s00371-007-0186-8

Kaneda, K., Ikeda, S., & Yamashita, H. (1999). Animation of water droplets moving down a surface. *Journal of Visualization and Computer Animation, 10*(1), 15–26. doi:10.1002/(SICI)1099-1778(199901/03)10:1<15::AID-VIS192>3.0.CO;2-P

Kusamoto, K., Tadamura, K., & Tabuchi, Y. (2001). A method for rendering realistic rainfall animation with motion of view. *IPSJ SIG, 2001*(106), 21-26.

Nvidia. (2007). *CUDA: Compute unified device architecture - programming guide.* Retrieved April 2, 2010, from http://developer.download.nvidia.com/compute/cuda/1 0/NVIDIACUDAProgrammingGuide1.0.pdf

Puig-Centelles, A., Ripolles, O., & Chover, M. (2009). Creation and control of rain in virtual environments. *The Visual Computer, 25*(11), 1037–1052. doi:10.1007/s00371-009-0366-9

Reeves, W. T. (1983). Particle systems: a technique for modeling a class of fuzzy objects. *ACM Transactions on Graphics, 2*(2), 91–108. doi:10.1145/357318.357320

Rousseau, P., Jolivet, V., & Ghazanfarpour, D. (2006). Realistic real-time rain rendering. *Computers & Graphics, 30*(4), 507–518. doi:10.1016/j.cag.2006.03.013

Rousseau, P., Jolivet, V., & Ghazanfarpour, D. (2008). GPU rainfall. *Journal of Graphics, GPU, and Game Tools, 13*(4), 17–33. doi:10.1080/2151237X.2008.10129270

Stanik, S., & Werman, M. (2003). Simulation of rain in videos. *International Journal of Computer Vision Texture*, 95-100.

Stuppacher, I., & Supan, P. (2007). Rendering of water drops in real-time. In *Proceedings of the Central European Seminar on Computer Graphics for Students*.

Tariq, S. (2007). *Rain nvidia whitepaper.* Retrieved April 2, 2010, from http://developer.download.nvidia.com/whitepapers/2007/SDK10/RainSDKWhitePaper.pdf

Tatarchuk, N. (2006). Artist-directable real-time rain rendering in city environments. In *Proceedings of the ACM SIGGRAPH Courses* (pp. 23-64).

Wang, C., Wang, Z., Zhang, X., Huang, L., Yang, Z., & Peng, Q. (2008). Real-time modeling and rendering of raining scenes. *The Visual Computer*, *24*, 605–616. doi:10.1007/s00371-008-0241-0

Wang, L., Lin, Z., Fang, T., Yang, X., Yu, X., & Kang, S. (2006). Real-time rendering of realistic rain. In *Proceedings of the ACM SIGGRAPH Sketches* (p. 156).

Wang, N., & Wade, B. (2004). Rendering falling rain and snow. In *Proceedings of the ACM SIGGRAPH Sketches* (p. 14).

This work was previously published in International Journal of Creative Interfaces and Computer Graphics, Volume 2, Issue 2, edited by Ben Falchuk, pp. 23-36, copyright 2010 by IGI Publishing (an imprint of IGI Global).

Chapter 19
A Simple Physically– Based 3D Liquids Surface Tracking Algorithm

Gonçalo N. P. Amador
Universidade da Beira Interior, Portugal

Abel J. P. Gomes
Instituto de Telecomunicações, Portugal

ABSTRACT

Navier-Stokes-based methods have been used in computer graphics to simulate liquids, especially water. These physically based methods are computationally intensive, and require rendering the water surface at each step of the simulation process. The rendering of water surfaces requires knowing which 3D grid cells are crossed by the water's surface, that is, tracking the surface across the cells is necessary. Solutions to water surface tracking and rendering problems exist in literature, but they are either too computationally intensive to be appropriate for real-time scenarios, as is the case of deformable implicit surfaces and ray-tracing, or too application-specific, as is the case of height-fields to simulate and render water mantles (e.g., lakes and oceans). This paper proposes a novel solution to water surface tracking that does not compromise the overall simulation performance. This approach differs from previous solutions in that it directly classifies and annotates the density of each 3D grid cell as either water, air, or water-air (i.e., water surface), opening the opportunity for easily reconstructing the water surface at an interactive frame rate.

INTRODUCTION

Visual plausibility is the ultimate goal in liquid simulations, and has been one of the biggest challenges in computer graphics since the mid of 1960's (Iglesias, 2004; Tan & Yang, 2009). In

DOI: 10.4018/978-1-4666-0285-4.ch019

fact, the realistic simulation of water is necessary in the production of movies, animation systems, video games, and virtual environments. Currently, there are three major approaches for the simulation of liquids, those that resort to the physical principles that govern fluids motion (i.e., Navier-Stokes equations), those that are simplifications or approximations of the Navier-Stokes equations (i.e., Euler equations, Swallow Water equations, and the Lattice Boltzmann Method), and those that solely represent the geometry of the water mantles with no physical simulation whatsoever (i.e., procedural methods).

The focus of this paper is on the Navier-Stokes-based simulation of liquids. Depending on how the evolution of the liquid is observed in time and space, a Navier-Stokes-based simulation can be classified as either Eulerian or Lagrangian. In computer graphics, the Navier-Stokes-based simulation of a liquid consists in an alternate sequence of two steps: physically-based simulation and surface rendering. To achieve this, the Navier-Stokes-based simulation and rendering of a liquid requires the tracking and reconstruction of its surface somewhere in the overall simulation pipeline. Solutions addressing these tracking and reconstruction problems already exist (Enright & Fedkiw, 2002; Enright et al., 2002; Fleck, 2007; Müller, 2009). However, these techniques have the disadvantage of being computationally intensive, that is, they negatively affect the overall frame rate of simulation, making them inappropriate for real-time simulations.

Within the family of Lagrangian methods (i.e., particle approach) we find two major methods, that had their origins in computational fluid dynamics, to model the shape of liquids, namely: the Smoothed Particle Hydrodynamics (SPH) (Müller et al., 2003; He et al., 2010; Maruzewski et al., 2010), and the Moving Particle Semi-Implicit (MPS) method (Premoze, 2003; Yamamoto, 2009). These models use two different approaches to approximate the solution of partial differential equations, as those used to solve the Navier-Stokes equations. In both methods, a smooth kernel is assigned to each particle (i.e., liquid element). After each physical simulation time step, within which tracking is also done, those kernels are used to identify and reconstruct the elements that are isolated liquid particles or regions of multiple liquid particles. Lagrangian methods allow for complex

water effects such as splashes, spray, or puddles. However, large water mantles require prohibitive amounts of particles, in terms of computation and memory resources.

When the simulation is limited to water mantles (e.g., ocean surface near shore, rivers, and pounds), it is enough to use procedural methods (Belyaev, 2003) or simplified Eulerian methods (e.g., Shallow Water Equations (SWE) (Miklós, 2004; de la Asunción et al., 2010), Euler equations (Fedwik, 2002; Elsen et al., 2008), or 2D Navier-Stokes (Stam 2002, 2003a, 2003b; Elcott et al., 2007) together with height-fields (Miklós, 2004; Baboud & Décoret, 2006). Note that height-fields only allow the representation of water mantles for one liquid, that is, no multiphase liquid simulation can be performed with them. Regardless of all these issues, the physical simulation is the most costly computation part of any liquid simulation in terms of time performance, in part because of the calculations carried out by linear solvers to solve the Navier-Stokes equations (Amador & Gomes, 2010a, 2010b). Therefore, simplified Eulerian methods constitute an attempt to reduce the time spent with the physical simulation, thus providing more time for the surface tracking, reconstruction and/or direct rendering.

For more complex types of simulations, one uses some Eulerian method or LBM together with level sets (Foster & Fedwik, 2001; Sussman, 2003; Thürey & Rüde, 2004; Lossasso et al., 2006; Keenan et al., 2007; Bridson & Müller, 2007). Another alternative is to use a hybrid approach (Lossasso et al., 2004; Cline et al., 2005; Kim et al., 2007) that combines an Eulerian method or LBM coupled with Lagrangian simulation. Implicit surface-based methods (e.g., level sets, SPH, and MPS) add more computations after the physical simulation step. These additional computations arise from the fact that, after updating the velocity field, several entities need to be updated before rendering the water surface. First, the candidates to liquid surface markers must be updated. Secondly, we need to check whether or not such candidates are surface markers using numerical interpolation. Third, it is required to reconstruct the implicit surface that describes the updated water surface. Thus, implicit surface-based methods are time-consuming. Besides, they have the additional disadvantage of generating bulged water surfaces (i.e., blobby surfaces).

Real-time liquid simulations as those needed in games and virtual environments, and depending on the liquid behaviour intended to simulate, make usage of either SPH, or height-fields combined with procedural methods or with simplified Navier-Stokes equations. But, when several real-time special effects are necessary simultaneously, we need to use hybrid techniques (Losasso et al., 2004; Cline et al., 2005; Baboud & Müller, 2007; Müller et al., 2008; Nätterlund, 2008; Gjermudsen, 2009).

The main contribution of this article is a simple surface tracking algorithm for Eulerian methods with negligible penalties on the frame rate. With this purpose in mind, we modified the semi-Lagrangian density advection (Stam, 1999) to allow 3D coupled water-air physically-based simulations surface tracking. Interestingly, the presented solution applies not only to implicit or backward integration algorithms, but also to explicit or forward integration algorithms. Moreover, if the physical simulation step were implemented in parallel and run in real-time, then our algorithm would also run in real-time even for finer grids than 32^3 because the rendering step has a negligible impact on the overall performance of the algorithm. As far as the authors are aware, this novel approach tracks altogether at most two liquids, air, and liquids-air surface cells, without using any implicit surface-based approach.

The presented algorithm resembles to another due to (Foster & Fedkiw, 2001). Nevertheless, our approach deals with more data than mere water and air cells, since our solution was designed to further store data required to perform the rendering of one or two liquid surfaces. Besides, while our approach follows a Eulerian simulation method,

the approach due to (Foster & Fedkiw, 2001) is essentially a hybrid approach because it combines a Eulerian method to simulate the velocity field of the liquid, and a Lagrangian method, together with level sets, to rendering and tracking of liquid surface. Also, when compared to level set-based techniques, our method requires a less amount of computations. However, this is achieved at the cost of more memory read/write accesses.

This article is organized as follows. In the next section, the physically-based Eulerian fluid simulations are briefly explained, focusing more on the stable fluids approach. The implementation of the surface tracking algorithm is then presented and the performance of water simulations using our algorithm is analyzed. The final section draws relevant conclusions and points out new directions for future work.

FLUID SIMULATOR

As previously mentioned, our surface tracking algorithm was implemented modifying the stable fluids algorithm (Stam, 1999), which follows an Eulerian approach. More specifically, we changed the stable fluids implementation due to Ash (Ash, 2005), which is a 3D implementation of the original 2D Stam's stable fluids without obstacles (Stam, 2003b). The second version of 2D stable fluids, due to Stam, could have been extended to support obstacles, but such was not performed in his work or in Ash's work. Our implementation differs from Ash's implementation in the sense that our fluid simulation includes the tracking algorithm, as well as obstacles.

As an Eulerian method, our algorithm makes usage of a grid of 3D cells, some of which are filled in with water, totally or partially. Algorithmically speaking, this grid is mapped to a 1D array, as illustrated in Figure 1.

The difference between stable fluids and other Eulerian methods lies in the fact that stable fluids method solves fluid simulation equations

Figure 1. 3D grid (left) represented by a 1Dar-ray (right)

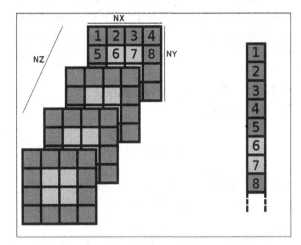

using implicit integration rather than explicit integration. In this way, the simulation can be carried out with large steps in time, without causing numerical instability.

Our tracking algorithm was implemented by modifying the density advection step. Therefore, before proceeding any further, let us briefly describe Eulerian simulations underlying the stable fluids, in particular the specific step of advection.

The motion of fluids (e.g., water or air) can be described by the following set of partial differential equations, known as the Navier-Stokes equations (Eqs. 1, 2 and 3):

$$\frac{\partial \vec{u}}{\partial t} = -\left(\vec{u} \cdot \nabla\right)\vec{u} + v\nabla^2\vec{u} + \vec{f} \qquad (1)$$

$$\frac{\partial \acute{A}}{\partial t} = -\left(\vec{u} \cdot \nabla\right)\acute{A} + k\nabla^2\acute{A} + S \qquad (2)$$

$$\nabla \vec{u} = \vec{0} \qquad (3)$$

where $\vec{u}$ stands for the velocity field, v denotes the value of the kinematic viscosity of the fluid, $\vec{f}$ represents the external accelerations added to the velocity field (e.g., gravity), $\acute{A}$ is the density of

the field, k is a scalar that describes the rate at which density diffuses, S is the external source added to the density field, $\nabla = \left(\frac{\partial}{\partial x}, \frac{\partial}{\partial y}, \frac{\partial}{\partial z}\right)$ is the gradient operator, and $\nabla^2 = \nabla \cdot \nabla = \left(\frac{\partial^2}{\partial x^2}, \frac{\partial^2}{\partial y^2}, \frac{\partial^2}{\partial z^2}\right)$ is the Laplacian operator.

Eqs. 1 and 2 describe the evolution of velocity and density of the fluid over time. Eq. 3 states that the velocity field, where the fluid flows, must be mass/energy conservative. In general, an Eulerian solver updates the velocity field where the fluid moves, and then it updates the quantities (density) of the fluid or fluids. Finally, the fluid is visualized using direct rendering or reconstruction techniques.

In the simulation of liquids for computer graphics, often only the surface of the liquid or liquids is required to be visualized. Our algorithm differs from other Eulerian algorithms in the way it updates the fluid density, and by not using any kind of simplification of the Navier-Stokes equations. Unlike the level set approach, our algorithm does not compute the evolution of an implicit function that represents the surface of a fluid over time.

The stable fluids method estimates the next value of velocity in a given cell by interpolating its previous and current values. Other Eulerian solutions extrapolate the next position based on its current position. But, as mentioned above, the stable fluids method has the advantage of permitting large time steps during the simulation. However, although this method allows time steps that are longer than those used in explicit methods, numerical errors may pop up in the advection if the method uses too large time steps, what may lead to an unstable simulation, not to say unpredictable simulation.

In order to solve Equations 1 and 3, first we have to solve each of the terms in the velocity field equation (Equation 1) and in the mass/energy conservation equation (Equation 3). To solve each of the terms, we proceed with the following three steps: addition of external accelerations $\left(\vec{f}\right)$, diffusion $\left(\dfrac{\partial \vec{u}}{\partial t} = v\nabla^2\vec{u}\right)$, and move $\left(-\left(\vec{u}\cdot\nabla\right)\vec{u} \text{ and } \nabla\vec{u} = \vec{0}\right)$. Afterwards, each of the terms of the density equation (Equation 2) is solved. These terms are solved in three steps, namely: addition of external sources $\left(S\right)$, diffusion $\left(\dfrac{\partial \acute{A}}{\partial t} = k\nabla^2\acute{A}\right)$, and advection $\left(-\left(\vec{u}\cdot\nabla\right)\acute{A}\right)$. Notice that, if the kinematic viscosity $\left(v\right)$ in Equation 1 is discarded, the fluid is classified as inviscid, and the resulting equations are referred to as the Euler equations.

To include our surface tracking algorithm in the simulation step we only had to modify the step of density advection (term $\left(-\left(\vec{u}\cdot\nabla\right)\acute{A}\right)$ in Equation 2). All the remaining physical simulation steps, regardless of using stable fluids or not, aside the generalization from 2D to 3D, required no other changes. Therefore, the reader is referred to (Stam, 2003b; Ash, 2005; Cline et al., 2005) for further explanations on the discretization of Equations 1 to 3.

Let us now pay attention on the modified advection step, for the specific case of stable fluids. When a fluid flows out, solid objects, densities, the fluid itself, and other quantities (i.e., other fluids) are advected or transported, as a result of the fluid velocity when it's moving. To better understand the advection, let us consider that each cell of the 3D grid represents a fluid particle, and that each particle travels along a velocity field. The advection of a stable fluid is performed using an implicit formulation, overcoming this way the instability that results from using explicit methods with large steps in time. Stam's method, also referred as semi-Lagrangian advection, is illustrated in Figure 2. For each cell, and assuming that a particle is moving in an uniform velocity field (green arrows), Stam's method starts by moving

the particle (gray arrow) to its former position (black circle), and then estimates the next value of velocity of particle in the current cell using linear interpolation of its previous and current velocities.

SURFACE TRACKING AND RENDERING

Often, in computer graphics, we only need to render the surface of a liquid, not its interior. Anyway, the realistic light effects either in the surface or inside the liquids are dealt using computational techniques that are not addressed in this paper (for further details on light effects on water, see Darles et al., 2011).

Two steps are necessary to render the surface of one or more liquids in 3D using Eulerian simulations: surface tracking and surface rendering. First, the grid cells crossed by the liquid surface must be identified or tracked. A liquid surface cell is a cell that has at least one neighbouring cell filled with air, other liquid, or an obstacle. Second, the rendering/reconstruction of the water surface is carried out from those liquid surface cells. For the

Figure 2. Illustrating the semi-Lagrangian advection

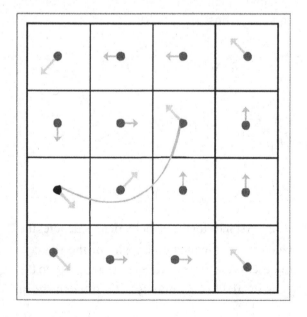

time being, our algorithm only addresses the first step fully, while the second step is done in a non-realistic manner using splat rendering.

Surface Tracking

The liquid surface tracking step makes part of the density advection algorithm of our modified stable fluids:

1. For each simulation time step
2. For each grid cell
3. Trace a virtual particle back in time from its current position (B) to its former position (A)
4. Estimate the new density value in position B using linear interpolation of its former value in position A and its current value in position B
5. Mark all cell's with density greater than 0.2 as liquid
6. End For
7. Reset the number of surface cells (S_Cells) and liquid cells (L_Cells) to 0
8. For each grid cell
9. If the cell is a liquid cell increment by one the value of L_Cells
10. If any of the cell's 26 neighbours is not liquid mark the cell as liquid surface and increment by one the value of S_Cells
11. End if
12. End if
13. End For
14. Enforce boundary conditions
15. End For

More specifically, the liquid surface tracking comprises the steps 7 to 13 of the previous algorithm (density advection). In order to track the liquid surface, we changed the density advection step of the fluid simulation to determine whether a cell is a liquid surface cell, a liquid cell, or a bounding cell (i.e., moving or static obstacles). It is clear that the remaining cells are air cells. This information about the types of cells is stored in the first 6 bits of a 32 bits hexadecimal flag, as illustrated in Figure 3.

Note that our algorithm at most admits two liquids that may or may not mix themselves. So, the first 6 bits of the hexadecimal flag indicate if the corresponding cell is 1-type liquid cell (i.e., a cell filled in with the first liquid), 2-type liquid cell (i.e., a cell filled in with the second liquid), 1-type surface cell, 2-type surface cell, a moving bound cell, or a static bound cell. The remaining 26 flag bits, which are not currently being used by our algorithm, comprise a way to classify each out of the 26 neighbouring cells as a surface cell or anything else. This means that data about these neighbouring 26 cells could be used to render the liquid surface more realistically.

Figure 3. 32-bit hexadecimal flag of a grid cell

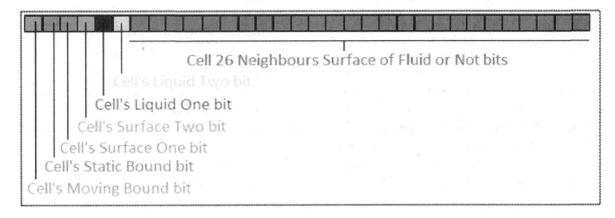

In our implementation, the simulation data is stored in a data structure (GRID), where we find data concerning the total number of grid cells (GRID_cells), the total number of surface cells (S_cells), also called partially liquid cells, the total number of partially and totally liquid cells (L_cells), the cell size in the direction of each coordinate axis (sizeX,sizeY,sizeZ), the previous and current velocity and density values associated to each cell (cvx,cvy,cvz,pvx,pvy,pvz,d,pd), and the 32-bit flag for each cell (FLAG).

Let us come back to Figure 3, where the 32-bit hexadecimal flag associated to a generic cell is shown. In order to change a property bit to '1', we have to combine a specific bit mask with the flag through the bit-to-bit OR operation. There are six masks to set the six most significant bits of the flag to '1'. For example, to set the 1-type liquid bit (the 5-th bit from the left) to '1', we apply such an OR operation to the 32-bit flag and the mask '0x08000000'. Similarly, to set a specific property bit to '0', we use the bit-to-bit AND operation. For example, to set the 2-type surface bit (the 4-th bit from the left) to '0', we combine the 32-bit flag and the mask '0xEFFFFFFF' as operands of the bit-to-bit AND operation. Note that all the cells marked as static boundaries are read from a disk file before starting the simulation. Consequently, only the flags of remaining cells are updated at each time step of the physical simulation.

After updating the velocity field during the density advection step, it comes the time of tracking partially liquid cells concerning the surface of the liquid. The tracking algorithm proposed here can be divided in two parts. In the first part, for each advected cell, if the cell is neither a moving boundary cell nor a static boundary cell, and if the cell density value is higher than 0.2, the cell is marked as a 1-type liquid cell. In order to consider two liquids in the simulation, there must be two distinct density ranges for which a liquid is either of 1-type, 2-type, or none (i.e., air).

Having completed the advection for all cells (steps 1-6), and before enforcing the boundary conditions (step 14), the surface tracking of the liquid starts off. For that purpose, the number of partially liquid cells (S_cells) and the number of totally liquid cells (L_cells) are first reset to zero. Therefore, the surface tracking (steps 7-13) of the liquid aims at identifying which cells are partially and totally filled in with liquid. To achieve this, for each cell that is marked as liquid, one has to increment the L_cells variable by one. Afterwards, if at least one out of its 26 neighbouring cells is an air cell, the cell is marked as a surface cell, and the L_cells counter is incremented by one.

Surface Rendering

To render the liquid surface, exclusively cells marked as surface cells (or partially liquid cells) are drawn as discs, a technique that is commonly referred as splat rendering. The OpenGL-based algorithm used in the splat rendering of the liquid surface is as follows:

1. Create buffer object (glGenBuffers)
2. While graphics application requires rendering do
3. For each grid cell
4. If the cell is liquid surface, store the (x,y,z) position of the cell in a vertex temporary array
5. End for
6. Select color of the liquid
7. Bind the buffer object (glBindBuffer)
8. Upload data from the client to the buffer (glBufferData)
9. Point to the buffer data to draw (glVertexPointer)
10. Draw data in the buffer (glEnableClientState, glDrawArrays, and glDisableClientState)
11. End while
12. Delete buffer object (glDeleteBuffers()).

EXPERIMENTAL RESULTS

The presented algorithm was tested on a Intel(R) Core(TM) i7 CPU 920@2.67GHz, with 8.0Gbytes of DDR3 RAM, an NVIDIA GTX 295 graphics card, running the Windows 7 Enterprise 64 bits operating system with SP1. Despite the high-performance computing capabilities of the graphics card, our surface tracking algorithm was implemented as a non-parallel, single-core CPU code.

In order to test our algorithm, we designed a graphics simulation scenario, in which we see a pipe pouring water into a box (Figure 4). That is, this scenario concerns the simulation of only one liquid (i.e., water). Figure 4 shows all cells that are partially or fully filled in with water (i.e., a 1-type liquid), regardless of being surface cells

or not, which appear rendered as white disks. In Figure 5, only the cells crossed by the water surface are drawn. Every cell, having a density value higher than 0.2, is marked as a 1-type liquid cell, regardless of whether it is partially or fully filled in with water. Since this scenario only involves one liquid, the density value of 0.2 in the range (0,1) was chosen as the minimum value for a liquid be considered as a liquid in a given cell; otherwise, the cell does not contain any liquid, it is either filled with air or it is an obstacle cell. It is clear that, in simulations involving multiple liquids, we have to consider different physical densities for different liquids.

To better assess the impact of the water surface tracking algorithm on the overall fluid simulation pipeline, we carried out experiments using two different sub-scenarios: one scenario without

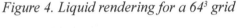

Figure 4. Liquid rendering for a 64³ grid

surface tracking (WOST) and another scenario with surface tracking (WST), as illustrated in Figures 4 and 5. In each simulation scenario, we carried out three tests, a test for a distinct grid that divides the 3D scene into cells. These tests were accomplished using grids with 32^3, 64^3, and 128^3 cells.

The experimental results are presented in Table 1, where #PFPS denotes the number of frames per second resulting from only running the physical simulation step, #FPS stands for the number of frames per second obtained from running the overall simulation pipeline, which includes physical simulation and rendering of water, #TLC counts the biggest number of liquid cells obtained in some simulation step, and #TLSC represents the corresponding number of liquid surface cells.

Based on the results shown in Table 1, three conclusions can be drawn. First, and taking into consideration the grids used in the simulation, the surface tracking algorithm does not penalize the total frame rate of the simulation because the difference #FPS-#PFPS is negligible. Second, the total number of liquid cells (#TLC) and the total number of liquid surface cells (#TLSC) to be rendered is a negligible portion of the total number of cells, respectively less than 13% and less than 2% of the total number of cells. Third, the sequential CPU-based code of our algorithm runs in real-time for small grids, that is, a grid of 32^3 cells.

Altogether, the first and third conclusions allow us to envision a possible algorithm for rendering water in real-time, at least in high-performance computing devices such as, for example, GPUs (Graphics Processing Units). By shortening the performance time of the physical simulation for finer grids, we could even think

Figure 5. Surface liquid rendering for a 64^3 grid

Table 1. Comparison between all water cells rendering and surface rendering scenarios

	Grid Size	#PFPS	#FPS	#TLC	#TLSC
WOST	32^3	30	30	2946	-
WST		30	30	2946	393
WOST	64^3	5	5	30193	-
WST		5	5	30193	1502
WOST	128^3	<1	0	260344	-
WST		<1	0	260344	16206

of running an entirely sequential algorithm in real-time on CPU.

The first two conclusions also favour the possibility that, if our algorithm were extended to also update the remaining 26 bits of the 32-bit flag of each cell, a realistic liquid surface rendering could be performed. Besides, the second conclusion opens up the possibility for a better memory management scheme of cells, thus reducing the memory required by the physical simulation. In fact, the algorithm may be modified in order to dynamically use as much memory as required to store the cell data in real-time.

CONCLUSION AND FUTURE WORK

In this paper, we have proposed a novel liquid surface tracking algorithm. As shown above, our algorithm does not penalize the overall performance of the fluid simulation. The proposed technique was implemented using a semi-Lagrangian, Eulerian fluid solver. Nevertheless, it can be also implemented using explicit solvers. It diverges from other surface tracking approaches (e.g., level sets), in the sense that it does not compute the evolution of an implicit function that describes the liquid surface shape. Instead, the proposed technique directly carries out the tracking of the liquid surface during the modified density advection step.

There are several directions for future work. First, we can use the data in the remaining 26 bits of the 32-bit flag of each cell in order to change the velocity diffusion step, density diffusion step, and velocity projection step, as needed to simulate multiphase fluids interaction. Second, this data can also be used to produce realistic liquid surface rendering, and add light effects (e.g., refraction and reflection). Third, we intend to re-implement and optimize the sequential CPU-based simulator in CUDA, MPI, OpenMP, and OpenCL. Finally, we intend to perform a comparative study among these parallel implementations for real-time purposes.

ACKNOWLEDGMENT

This work has been partially supported by the Fundação para a Ciência e a Tecnologia (FCT) and the Instituto de Telecomunicações (IT), in the context of the MOGGY Project (A Browser-Based Massive Multiplayer Online Game Engine Architecture), PTDC/EIA/70830/2006.

REFERENCES

Amador, G., & Gomes, A. (2010a, March). A CUDA-based implementation of stable fluids in 3D with internal and moving boundaries. In *Proceedings of the International Conference on Computational Science and its Applications* (pp. 118-128). Washington, DC: IEEE Computer Society.

Amador, G., & Gomes, A. (2010b, April). CUDA-based linear solvers for stable fluids. In *Proceedings of the International Conference on Information Sciences and Applications* (pp. 1-8). Washington, DC: IEEE Computer Society.

Ash, M. (2005). *Simulation and bisualization of a 3D gluid.* Unpublished master's thesis, Université d'Orléans, Orléans, France.

Asunción, M., de la Mantas, J., & Castro, M. (2010, September). Programming CUDA-based GPUs to simulate two-layer shallow water flows. In P. D'Ambra, M. Guarracino, & D. Talia (Eds.), *Proceedings of the 16th International EURO-PAR Conference on Parallel Processing* (LNCS 6272, pp. 353-364).

Baboud, L., & Décoret, X. (2006). Realistic water volumes in real-time. In *Proceedings of the EUROGRAPHICS Workshop on Natural Phenomena*.

Belyaev, V. (2003). Real-time simulation of water surface. In *Proceedings of the International Conference on Computer Graphics & Vision* (pp. 131-138).

Bridson, R., & Müller, M. F. (2007, August). Fluid simulation. In *Proceedings of the ACM SIGGGRAPH Course Notes* (pp. 1-81). New York, NY: ACM Press.

Cline, D., Cardon, D., & Egbert, P. K. (2005). *Fluid flow for the rest of us: Tutorial of the marker and cell method in computer graphics.* Unpublished manuscript.

Darles, E., Crespin, B., Ghazanfarpour, D., & Gonzato, J. (2011). A survey of ocean simulation and rendering techniques in computer graphics. *Computer Graphics Forum, 30,* 43–60. doi:10.1111/j.1467-8659.2010.01828.x

Elcott, S., Tong, Y., Kanso, E., Schröder, P., & Desbrun, M. (2007). Stable, circulation-preserving, simplicial fluids. *ACM Transactions on Graphics, 26.*

Elsen, E., LeGresley, P., & Darve, E. (2008). Large calculation of the flow over a hypersonic vehicle using a GPU. *Journal of Computational Physics, 227*(24), 10148–10161. doi:10.1016/j.jcp.2008.08.023

Enright, D., & Fedkiw, R. (2002, July). Robust treatment of interfaces for fluid flows and computer graphics. In *Proceedings of the 9th International Conference on Hyperbolic Problems Theory, Numerics, Applications* (pp. 153-164).

Enright, D., Marschner, S., & Fedkiw, R. (2002). Animation and rendering of complex water surfaces. *ACM Transactions on Graphics, 21,* 736–744. doi:10.1145/566570.566645

Fedkiw, R. (2002). Coupling an Eulerian fluid calculation to a Lagrangian solid calculation with the ghost fluid method. *Journal of Computational Physics, 175*(1), 200–224. doi:10.1006/jcph.2001.6935

Fleck, B. (2007). *Real-time rendering of water in computer graphics.* Unpublished manuscript.

Foster, N., & Fedkiw, R. (2001, August). Practical animation of liquids. In *Proceedings of the 28th Annual Conference on Computer Graphics and Interactive Techniques* (pp. 23-30). New York, NY: ACM Press.

Gjermundsen, A. (2009). *LBM vs. SOR solvers on GPUs for real-time snow simulations.* Unpublished master's thesis, Norwegian University of Science and Technology, Trondheim, Soer-Troendelag, Norway.

He, J., Chen, X., Wang, Z., Cao, C., Yan, H., & Peng, Q. (2010). Real-time adaptive fluid simulation with complex boundaries. *The Visual Computer, 26,* 243–252. doi:10.1007/s00371-010-0426-1

Iglesias, A. (2004). Computer graphics for water modeling and rendering: a survey. *Future Generation Computer Systems, 20,* 1355–1374. doi:10.1016/j.future.2004.05.026

Keenan, C., Ignacio, L., & Sarah, T. (2007). Real-time simulation and rendering of 3D fluids. In *GPU gems 3* (pp. 633–675). Reading, MA: Addison-Wesley.

Kim, B., Liu, Y., Llamas, I., Jiao, X., & Rossignac, J. (2007). Simulation of bubbles in foam with the volume control method. *ACM Transactions on Graphics, 26.*

Losasso, F., Gibou, F., & Fedkiw, R. (2004). Simulating water and smoke with an octree data structure. *ACM Transactions on Graphics, 23,* 457–462. doi:10.1145/1015706.1015745

Losasso, F., Shinar, T., Selle, A., & Fedkiw, R. (2006). Multiple interacting liquids. *ACM Transactions on Graphics, 25,* 812–819. doi:10.1145/1141911.1141960

Maruzewski, P., Le Touzé, D., Oger, G., & Avellan, F. (2010). SPH high-performance computing simulations of rigid solids impacting the free surface of water. *Journal of Hydraulic Research, 48,* 126–134. doi:10.1080/00221686.2010.9641253

Miklós, B. (2004). *Real time fluid simulation using height fields.* Unpublished manuscript.

Müller, M. (2009, August). Fast and robust tracking of fluid surfaces. In *Proceedings of the ACM SIGGGRAPH/EUROGRAPHICS Symposium on Computer Animation* (pp. 237-245). New York, NY: ACM Press.

Müller, M., Charypar, D., & Gross, M. (2003, July). Particle-based fluid simulation for interactive applications. In *Proceedings of the ACM SIGGGRAPH/EUROGRAPHICS Symposium on Computer Animation* (pp. 154-159). Aire-la-Ville, Switzerland: Eurographics Association Press.

Müller, M. F., Stam, J., James, D., & Thürey, N. (2008, August). Real time physics. In *Proceedings of the ACM SIGGGRAPH Course Notes* (pp. 1-90). New York, NY: ACM Press.

Nätterlund, M. (2008). *Water surface rendering.* Unpublished master's thesis, Umeå University, Umeå, Sweden.

Peachey, D. R. (1986). Modeling waves and surf. *ACM SIGGRAPH Computer Graphics, 20,* 65–74. doi:10.1145/15886.15893

Premoze, S., Tasdizen, T., Bigler, J., Lefohn, A. E., & Whitaker, R. T. (2003). Particle-based simulation of fluids. *Computer Graphics Forum, 22,* 401–410. doi:10.1111/1467-8659.00687

Stam, J. (1999, August). Stable fluids. In *Proceedings of the 26th Annual Conference on Computer Graphics and Interactive Techniques* (pp. 121-128). New York, NY: ACM Press

Stam, J. (2002). A simple fluid solver based on the FFT. *Journal Graphics Tools, 6,* 43–52.

Stam, J. (2003a, July). Flows on surfaces of arbitrary topology. In *Proceedings of the ACM SIGGGRAPH Papers* (pp. 724-731). New York, NY: ACM Press.

Stam, J. (2003b, March). Real-time fluid dynamics for games. In *Proceedings of the Game Developer Conference.*

Sussman, M. (2003). A second order coupled level set and volume-of-fluid method for computing growth and collapse of vapor bubbles. *Journal of Computational Physics, 187*(1), 110–136. doi:10.1016/S0021-9991(03)00087-1

Tan, J., & Yang, X. (2009). Physically-based fluid animation: A survey. *Science in China Series F: Information Sciences, 52*(5), 723–740. doi:10.1007/s11432-009-0091-z

Thürey, N., & Rüde, U. (2004, November). Free Surface Lattice-Boltzmann fluid simulations with and without level sets. In D. Amsterdam, The Netherlands: IOS Press.]. *Proceedings of the International Workshop on Vision, Modeling, and Visualization, 2,* 199–207.

Yamamoto, K. (2009, December). Real time two-way coupling of fluids to deformable bodies using particle method on GPU. In *Proceedings of the ACM SIGGRAPH Asia Posters.* New York, NY: ACM Press.

This work was previously published in International Journal of Creative Interfaces and Computer Graphics, Volume 2, Issue 2, edited by Ben Falchuk, pp. 37-48, copyright 2010 by IGI Publishing (an imprint of IGI Global).

Chapter 20
Accurate Infrared Tracking System for Immersive Virtual Environments

Filipe Gaspar
ADETTI-IUL / ISCTE-Lisbon University Institute, Portugal

Rafael Bastos
Vision-Box & ADETTI-IUL / ISCTE-Lisbon University Institute, Portugal

Miguel Sales
DiasMicrosoft Language Development Center & ISCTE-Lisbon University Institute, Portugal

ABSTRACT

In large-scale immersive virtual reality (VR) environments, such as a CAVE, one of the most common problems is tracking the position of the user's head while he or she is immersed in this environment to reflect perspective changes in the synthetic stereoscopic images. In this paper, the authors describe the theoretical foundations and engineering approach adopted in the development of an infrared-optical tracking system designed for large scale immersive Virtual Environments (VE) or Augmented Reality (AR) settings. The system is capable of tracking independent retro-reflective markers arranged in a 3D structure in real time, recovering all possible 6DOF. These artefacts can be adjusted to the user's stereo glasses to track his or her head while immersed or used as a 3D input device for rich human-computer interaction (HCI). The hardware configuration consists of 4 shutter-synchronized cameras attached with band-pass infrared filters and illuminated by infrared array-emitters. Pilot lab results have shown a latency of 40 ms when simultaneously tracking the pose of two artefacts with 4 infrared markers, achieving a frame-rate of 24.80 fps and showing a mean accuracy of 0.93mm/0.51° and a mean precision of 0.19mm/0.04°, respectively, in overall translation/rotation, fulfilling the requirements initially defined.

DOI: 10.4018/978-1-4666-0285-4.ch020

INTRODUCTION

During the last decade, Virtual and Augmented Reality technologies have became widely used in several scientific and industrial fields. Large immersive virtual environments like the CAVE (Cave Automatic Virtual Environment) (Cruz-Neira, 1992), can deliver to the users unique immersive virtual experiences with rich HCI modalities that other environments cannot achieve. In this context, through a collaboration of a large group of Portuguese and Brazilian entities namely, institutional (Portuguese Ministry of Science, Grândola City Hall), academic (ISCTE-IUL, IST, FCUL, PUC Rio), and industrial (SAPEC, Fundação Frederic Velge, Petrobrás, Microsoft), the first large scale immersive virtual environment installed in Portugal, "CaveHollowspace of Lousal" or "CaveH" in short (Dias, 2007), started its operation in the end of 2007. The CaveH of Lousal (situated in the south of Portugal, near Grândola) is part of an initiative of the National Agency for the Scientific and Technological Culture, in the framework of the Live Science Centres network. CaveH aims at bringing to the educational, scientific and industrial sectors in Portugal, the benefits of advanced technologies such as, immersive virtual reality, digital mock-up and real-size interactive simulation. Its physical configuration is a 4-sided cave assembling six projection planes (2 for the floor, 2 for the front, and 1 for each side) in a U

topology with 5.6 m wide, 2.7 m height and 3.4 m in each side (Figure 1), giving a field of view of more than 180°, with a resolution of 8.2 mega pixel in stereoscopy for an audience of up to 12 persons (where one is being tracked). It is worth mentioning that each front and floor projection planes of the installation have 2 x 2 associated projectors (in a passive stereo set-up), with a blending zone that creates the impression of a single projection plane each.

The range of critical industries where simulation and real-size digital mock-up observation are imperative, extends the CaveH applicability to several fields such as, entertainment, aerospace, natural resources exploration (oil, mining), industrial product design (automotive, architecture, aeronautics), therapy (phobia, stress), etc. In most of these applications, the interaction with the user is crucial to fulfill the application purpose.

A CAVE is an immersive virtual environment, which largely benefits from the ability of human brain to process the depth perception. However this awareness can be lost and the full immersion can be compromised, if the several 3D view frustums of the set-up (truncated pyramids usually associated to visualization volume of a virtual camera in rigorous perspective), and corresponding viewports, are not correctly adjusted to the main user's head position, while he/she is in inside the physical space of the immersive space (Figure 2) during interactive sessions.

Figure 1. CaveHollowspace of Lousal physical set-up

Figure 2. Dynamically adjustment of view frustums and viewpoints required to correctly display images on several projection planes, when the user moves from a) to b)

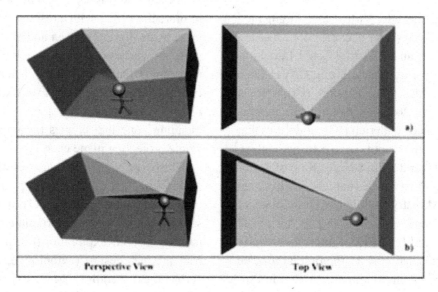

For this reason, it is essential to integrate in an infrastructure like the CaveH, an accurate tracking system that follows an artefact attached to user's head position, enabling the underlying distributed 3D graphics system to adjust the image on the CaveH displays in real-time (6 in total for the case in study, Figure 1), to reflect perspective variations (Figure 2). In this paper we describe in detail a prototype of an infrared-optical tracking system capable of tracking in real-time a set of artefacts that the user can adjust to stereo glasses, thus tracking his/her pose or use as 3D input device, while interacting in virtual environments. The rigid body artefacts are made of spherical infrared markers, allowing the system to detect 6DOF motion in a three-dimensional space in respect to a reference coordinate system, i.e., translation across X, Y and Z axis and rotation over X, Y and Z axis. This system can be used in virtual reality settings such as the CaveH or in augmented environments, being an alternative in this last case to video-based tracking (Dias, 2006).

The paper starts by summarizing the related state-of-the-art work in infrared and vision-based tracking systems (*Related Work*) and then pres-

ents a *System Overview* of the chosen hardware configuration as well as the developed software architecture. Subsequently, we describe the proposed infrared *Camera Calibration* technique and present the in-house developed algorithms that solve three common problems found in infrared tracking systems: *Feature Segmentation and Identification, 3D Reconstruction via Triangulation* and *Model Fitting*. Then, in *Results and Discussion* section, we present and discuss our results and, in last section we extract conclusions and plan for future research directions.

RELATED WORK

Several commercial tracking systems can be found in the market. Vicon (2011) or ART (2011) propose systems with configurations that usually allows 4 to 16 cameras, with update rates from 60Hz to 120Hz. However, due the high cost of these commercial solutions, we turned to the scientific community and have analysed the literature regarding the availability of accurate and precise algorithms to track independent rigid body markers and artefacts. We found out that the multi or single camera systems, using infrared or vision-based tracking technologies share the same problem formulation: the need of computing the position and orientation of a rigid body target or artefact relatively to a reference co-ordinate system. To solve this problem a sufficient number of geometric correspondences between a real feature in the world reference space and its 2D projection in the camera's image space, is required. Several approaches to the tracking problem can be found in the literature. In PTrack (Santos, 2006), a marker-based infrared single-camera system is presented. Similar to ARToolKit (Kato, 1999), this contribution takes advantage of a non-symmetric square geometric arrangement label in object space (an infrared marker) and its correspondence in projected image space. PTrack uses an iterative approach to twist the square label projection in order to derive a correct orientation, and then performs iterative scaling to the label, to correct the position of the square infrared marker. Another single-camera tracking contribution is ARTIC (Dias, 2004), where the marker design is based on colour evaluation. Each marker has a different colour which can be segmented using vision-based-techniques and a 3D artefact structure has been designed with five of such markers. The algorithm used to estimate the artefact pose, is PosIT (DeMenthon, 1992). Analogous to Lowe (1991), PosIT is an iterative algorithm but does not require an initial pose. The algorithm needs four non-coplanar points as features in image space and the knowledge of the corresponding object model points. The object pose is approximated through scaled orthographic projection. Another well-known example of a multi-camera infrared tracking system is the ioTracker (nowadays is a commercial system, even though it started as a research project) (Pintaric, 2007). This system uses rigid body spherical infrared markers (targets) that take advantage of the following constraint: every pair-wise Euclidean distance between features associated to markers, is different and the artefacts construction is done to maximize the minimum difference between these features'

pair-wise distances. By having several cameras, the feature information in several image spaces is correlated via Epipolar Geometry (the geometry of stereoscopic projection) and the 3D reconstructed feature in object space is performed via Singular Value Decomposition (Golub, 1993). The pose estimation is a 3D-3D least square pose estimation problem (Arun, 1987) and requires the object model points and at least 3 reconstructed points to estimate a 6DOF pose. In Santos (2010), an extension of PTrack system for multiple cameras is presented. Several independent units of PTrack are combined to track several square infrared marker labels via multiple cameras. Camera calibration is achieved via traditional techniques. The breakthrough of this work is in the sensor fusion module, which receives tracking information from PTrack units and groups it by label identification. The final 3D position of each marker is obtaining by averaging the marker positions in each camera, projected in the world coordinate system. Each label orientation is computed as the normal vector of the label, from the cross-product of two perpendicular edges of the label. Our work has been largely influenced by the ioTracker, especially in two specific algorithms: Multiple-View Correlation and Model Fitting, where we follow the complexity reduction approach proposed by Pintaric and Kaufmann (*Model Fitting* Section) with two important modifications and advances, to avoid superfluous computational time (for further details see Section *Candidate Evaluation via Artefact Correlation*).

SYSTEM OVERVIEW

In order to develop a tracking system our first step was to create a comparative assessment between different tracking technologies that can be used in immersive virtual environments such as the CaveH, based on a clear definition of system requirements which are:

1. Real time update rate (at least 25 Hz, which is the maximum supported by affordable infrared cameras);
2. Without major motion constraints: this means that the tracking technology shall be less obtrusive as possible, allowing the user to interact with the CaveH environment through several artefacts and enabling the best freedom of movement;
3. Robust to interference of the environment, that is, the technology chosen should not have interferences with system materials and hardware (e.g., acoustic interference, electromagnetic interference);
4. Without error accumulation in the estimated poses, that is, the accuracy of the estimated artefact pose should be below 1 mm and 0.5°, respectively, for the overall translation (average over the 3DOF in translation) and overall rotation (average over the 3DOF in rotation);
5. No significant drift of the estimated pose, that is, the precision of the estimated

artefact 3D pose (position and orientation) should be below 0.1mm and 0.1°, respectively, for the overall translation (average over the 3DOF in translation) and overall rotation (average over the 3DOF in rotation).

In the following sub-sections we present an evaluation of several tracking technologies regarding their performance and reliability (*Tracking Technologies Assessment*), followed by the hardware components of our system (*Hardware Setup*) and the software architecture and workflow. In Figure 3 is depicted a high level diagram representing the key concepts and the CaveH technologies used to enable an immersive virtual environment.

Tracking Technologies Assessment

In Table 1, we present a summarized comparison between the main advantages and drawbacks of different available tracking technologies. By

Figure 3. Key concepts and CaveH technologies to enable immersion in a virtual reality environment

Immersion in virtual reality User's feeling of being part of the represented world	
Key concepts	**CaveH technologies to enable key concepts**
Simulation include consistent sensory stimulation of life-size scenes	**Visual stimulation:** Stereoscopic high resolution imaging projection **Auditory stimulation:** 3D auralization **Visual viewports and viewpoints correction:** IR tracking system

Interaction
real-time, easy, natural and rich interaction, irrespectively of the photorealism of the VE
	Multimodal interfaces:
	    Speech control
	    IR tracking system artefacts
	    Wiimote & Nunchuck from Nintendo Wii

Applications in immersive virtual environments Entertainment, aerospace, natural resources exploration (oil, mining), industrial product design (ergonomics, automotive, architecture), therapy (phobia, stress), mission critical industry (aerospace), cultural heritage	

analysing this table, we can conclude that only optical technology can cover all our specified requirements. However, this option highlights three problems to be addressed: (1) line of sight occlusion; (2) ambient light interference; and (3) infrared radiation in the environment, which we will tackle through the hardware configuration chosen. Considering the nature of our problem (tracking artefacts poses in a room-sized environment), an outside-in tracking approach is the best fit solution. Outside-in tracking employs an external active sensor (usually a video camera) that senses artificial passive sources or markers over the body of a person or on an artefact, and retrieves its pose in relation to a reference coordinate system.

Hardware Setup

Once the technology to be used has been defined, the hardware setup was chosen based on a strategy to minimize costs, without compromising the system reliability and performance and the specified requirements.

Cameras

To minimize the line of sight occlusion problem, at least two cameras are required. We have opted to use a setup of four cameras, AVT Pike F-032 B, with IEEE 1394b interface (AVT, 2011), with a maximum resolution of 640x480 at a capture rate of 209 fps. We have also assessed several lens models for the selected camera model in order to choose the optimal overture angle at best precision, since precision and operational volume are inversely proportional. The multiple cameras create a volume of diamond shape where artefacts can be seen (of diamond shape). In Figure 4 we see a simulation, with:

a) 3.5 mm Lens, field of view of 81.20° and resolution at the centre of 3.50 mm;
b) 4.5mm Lens, field of view of 67.40° and resolution at the centre of 2.70 mm.

The retained solution was the left one. Despite the reduced resolution comparing to the right solution, we have selected the configuration that allows a larger tracking volume.

IR Filters and IR LEDs

Most CCD-based cameras are sensitive to the infrared spectrum. Usually these sensors come with an attached infrared filter, which can be replaced by an infrared band-pass filter – we have selected

Table 1. Tracking technologies requirements comparison

Technologies	Accuracy and Precision	Real Time Update Rate	Robust to Interference	Motion Constraints	Additional Problems
Acoustic	Low, Low (centimetres, degrees)	No (speed of sound variation)	No (acoustic interference)	Yes (line of sight occlusion)	None
Electromagnetic	High, High (sub-millimetre, sub-degree)	Yes (>100Hz)	No (interference with metal objects)	No	Small working volume
Inertial	High, Low (error accumulation)	Yes (>100Hz)	No (graviton interference)	No	Limited by cabling
Mechanical	High, High (sub-millimetre, sub-degree)	Yes (100Hz)	Yes	Yes (mechanical arm paradigm)	Small working volume
Optical	High, High (sub-millimetre, sub-degree)	Yes (>=25Hz)	No (ambient light and infrared radiation)	Yes (line of sight occlusion)	None

Figure 4. Simulation of CaveH "diamond shape volume", created by multiple cameras, where artefacts can be seen. a) 3.5mm Lens: larger tracking volume but lower resolution at the centre – the retained solution; b) 4.5mm Lens: lower tracking volume but higher resolution at the centre

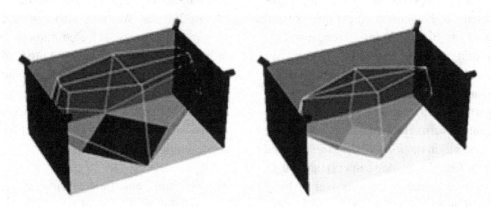

a Schneider Kreuznach IR filter (Schneider, 2011) (cut-on wavelength 725 ±10 nm). This gives us the ability of obtaining finer measurements in the infrared spectrum. To enhance infrared detection by light reflection, we have chosen to mount an infrared light ring emitter in each camera (Figure 5). Since the CaveH in operation is completely absent of environmental light (the CaveH room is in total darkness and usually with a room temperature of 21° C), we have a controlled lighting setting. With this set-up the only relevant source of infrared light is emitted by the LED arrays, which is subsequently detected by the applied infrared band-pass filters.

Shutter Controller

In order to synchronize the cameras frame grabbers, we need to use a shutter controller. We have opted by a National Instruments USB shutter controller NI-USB6501 (NI, 2011), a digital and programmable device that triggers camera's capture on varying or static periods of time.

Artefacts

Artefacts are made of a set of infrared markers arranged in space with known pair-wise Euclidean distances in a pre-defined structure. Each artefact

is a unique object with a detectable pose within a tracking volume. We have opted by passive retro-reflective markers instead of active markers because the last ones require an electric source, which would become more expensive, heavy and intrusive. Our lab-made markers are built from plastic spheres with 20 mm of radius and covered with retro-reflective self-adhesive paper. We have chosen spheres since it is a geometric form that allows an approximation to an isotropic reflection system.

Figure 5. Hardware components of the Infrared Camera system. a) AVT Pike Camera; b) Infrared LED emitter; c) Shutter controller; d) Artefact for IR tracking

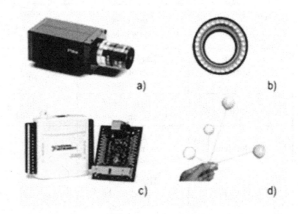

Software Architecture and Process Workflow

Our software architecture comprises a real-time and threaded oriented pipeline. The diagram in Figure 6 illustrates the full real-time infrared tracking pipeline process since multiple frames (one per camera), synchronously reach the application to generate the final output: the pose of each target in a known reference coordinate system.

However, two other important steps are done previously during an off-line stage:

- *Camera calibration* – For each camera, we determine its intrinsic parameters (focal length, the principal point, pixel scale factors in the image domain and the non-linear radial and tangential distortion parameters), and extrinsic parameters (position and orientation in relation to a reference coordinate system);
- *Artefact calibration* – For each artefact structure, we compute the Euclidean distances between each pair of markers. This procedure allows us to use artefacts with different and non-pre-defined topologies (under some constraints, see *Candidate Evaluation via Artefact Correlation* Section) and overcomes the precision error

in their construction. A "reference pose" is also computed for comparison with poses retrieved by application.

Each on-line pipeline cycle in Figure 6 starts when multiple frames are grabbed by the application (Multiple Video Input). For each frame an image segmentation algorithm identifies the 2D image coordinates of every blob feature, i.e., the 3D real infrared marker projected in the image, and recovers its centre and radius (Feature Segmentation). Through epipolar geometry (Hartley, 2003), the recovered 2D features are correlated from the different views establishing feature correspondences (Multiple View Correlation). Via Singular Value Decomposition (SVD) Triangulation (Golub, 1993), we are then able to reconstruct 3D markers through n multiple projected views of each marker, where the n range is [2; number of cameras] (3D Metric Reconstruction). The resulting 3D point collection is examined in order to determine which points belong to each artefact (Model Fitting), following Pintaric's approach. Finally, for each discovered artefact, its position and orientation in relation to a reference coordinate system or, in relation to "reference pose", are estimated (Pose Estimation).

Figure 6. Infrared tracking process

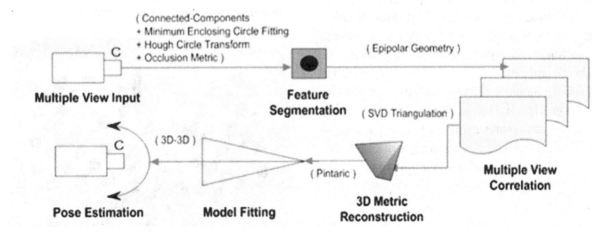

Camera Calibration

Camera calibration is a critical step in many computer vision applications. Considerable effort has been made on the development of effective and accurate procedures to address this problem since the reliability of computer vision systems, such as optical tracking, are highly dependent on the camera calibration phase. Several approaches can be found in the literature (Wang, 2004; Zhao, 2007), to evaluate the internal camera geometric and optical characteristics (intrinsic parameters) and to find the three-dimensional position and orientation of the camera reference frame in relation to a reference coordinate system (extrinsic parameters). We have decided to solve the two problems separately, essentially because intrinsic parameters have to be determined only once (ideally) and combined solutions to solve intrinsic and extrinsic parameters tend to be more imprecise. Our camera calibration offline approach was entirely based on the technique developed by Zhang (1999) available in the OpenCV (2011) library.

Intrinsic Calibration

Using a classical pinhole camera model (Heikkila, 1997) it is possible to find a set of parameters which define a 3D transformation matrix that maps pixel coordinates of an image point into the corresponding coordinates in the camera reference frame. The method used, allows finding the focal length, the principal point, the pixel scale factors and the non-linear radial and tangential distortion using a chessboard pattern (Figure 7). The chessboard has known geometric and topological properties– its squares width and height, the number of horizontal and vertical squares – which allows extracting the object corners and determining intrinsic parameters through projective transformation.

Extrinsic Calibration

In multi-camera systems, to perform reliable 3D point's reconstruction from a scene, all cameras' extrinsic parameters have to be calibrated under the same world coordinate system. The used method requires at least four 3D-2D correspondences between the world reference frame and each camera image plane, in order to compute the camera extrinsic parameters through a well-documented computer vision algorithm: Direct Linear Transform (Abdel-Aziz, 1971). The DLT performs a homography that transforms a 3D object plane into 2D image coordinates. In order to establish 3D-2D correspondences we have used a co-planar square arrangement of five markers as presented in Figure 8, with known positions in world space. In image space, by means of our *Feature Segmentation and Identification* algorithm, we can identify the markers centre and radius via a projective transformation. By observing Figure 8, we see that our markers' distribution takes advantage of two important constraints: the "orientation point" is the one with smaller Euclidean distance to the average of all points; the remaining points are identified by their proximity to the image corners; the point of index 1 has the smaller Euclidean distance

Figure 7. Camera Intrinsic Calibration. a) 6x8 chessboard calibration pattern. b) Calibration output: chessboard corners extraction

Figure 8. Extrinsic calibration marker

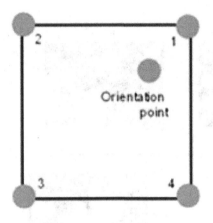

to the "orientation point". With the presented constraints we easily order the points from the "orientation point" to the fifth point following an anti-clockwise order. The result achieved with extrinsic calibration is within a re-projection error of 0.92 pixels/mm.

FEATURE SEGMENTATION AND IDENTIFICATION

In this work, as well as within the scope of infrared tracking systems, we define "feature" as a region of interest (ROI) of an image, whose centre corresponds to the infrared marker (blob centre) projection in the camera 2D image space. Our feature segmentation and identification algorithm comprises several techniques to approximate blobs to circles recovering the feature's radius and centre.

Feature Segmentation through Non-Destructive Threshold

After acquisition, the first image processing operation is a non-destructive image thresholding. Since our work environment is lighting controlled and most of information is filtered by infrared filters, we have used a threshold operation to eliminate noise and discard possible false artefacts in the image. The output of the IR camera is a grey-scale image where the retro-reflective markers have extremely high value of luminance (>65% of the maximum value). It is straightforward to segment our features establishing a static threshold value (discovered experimentally), where the pixels with luminance value below the threshold are forced to zero (Figure 9). We have decided to use a non-destructive operation because in an algorithm used later in our pipeline, the Hough Circle Transform (Kimme, 1975), the gradient information will be extremely useful to accelerate circles searching.

Feature Identification

A classic approach to identify the retro-reflective markers in image space is the adoption of Hough Circle Transform (HCT) (Kimme, 1975; Duda, 1972). HTC is a well-known technique to find geometric primitives in an image (in our case, circles). The principle of this technique is to transform the image space into a tri-dimensional accumulator, where each entry of the accumulator is a potential circle parameterized by its centre (x, y coordinates) and radius. The local-maxima entries on the accumulator will be the retrieved circles. Our features can assume a wide range of radii in the image (especially if the image space has partially-occluded features), which turns the Hough accumulation highly demanding, in terms of memory, to be applied in a real-time application with the robustness and the precision needed. Therefore, instead of applying HCT to the whole image (640 x 480 of resolution), our feature identification algorithm consists in a combination of one technique to identify ROIs containing features (Connected-Components Algorithm) and one decision metric (Occlusion Metric), to select the best algorithm to be applied to the image to recover the features centres and radius from two possible algorithms (Minimum Enclosing Circle Fitting or Hough Circle Transform), depending on whether occluded features exist or not. For

Figure 9. Feature segmentation workflow. Solid bounding boxes represent features extracted through MECF, while dashed bounding boxes depicts features extracted via HCT.

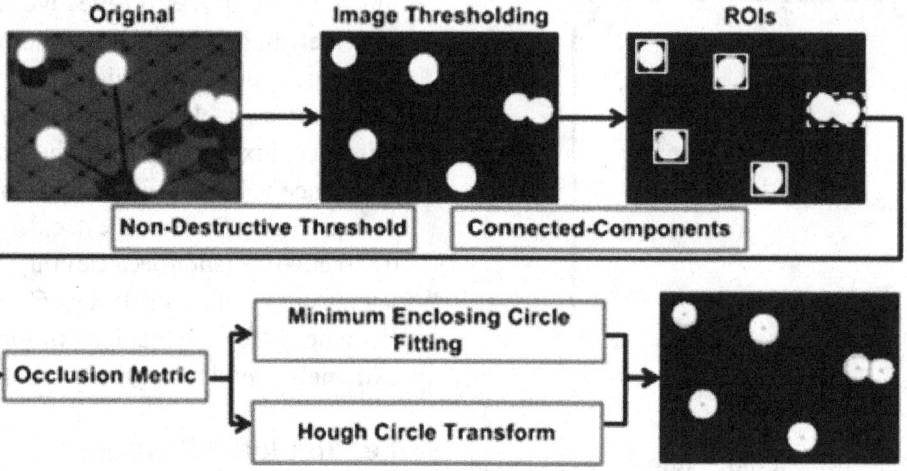

the HCT algorithm we use a bi-dimensional accumulator approach (Kimme, 1975). The feature segmentation workflow can be seen in Figure 9.

Connected-Components Algorithm

Instead of analysing the whole image, the purpose of this "in-house" developed algorithm is to isolate image regions of interest (ROIs) for further examination. The statement is: by analysing pixel by pixel, a blob can be seen as a set of adjacent pixels with luminance values greater than zero. The Connected-Components (CC) technique used is a recursive algorithm that analyses each pixel of an image, from left to right and from top to bottom, using a pixel map with the same size of the image to mark the visited pixels. The recursion works as follows. For the selected pixel, the algorithm marks its coordinates in the pixel map to guarantee that that pixel is not visited again. Then, if the pixel luminance value is larger than zero, its coordinates in the image are collect in an array structure that keeps record of the current ROI. Finally, for each adjacent coordinates of the current pixel, the algorithm repeats the entire process. The recursion rolls back when all adjacent pixels are visited. The result is a vector

of bounding boxes where each one includes a set of pixels (a minimum of 9 pixels) belonging to one ROI, i.e., a Connect-Component, which contains at least one feature (can possibly include more too, when features are occluded). In Figure 9 each bounding box represents the limits of the connected-components.

Minimum Enclosing Circle Fitting

One of the alternative techniques to the HCT used to retrieve the feature's radius and circle is the Minimum Enclosing Circle Fitting (MECF) algorithm (Fitzgibbon, 1995). Since the Connected-Components output is a set of 2D points belonging to the same ROI in image, the problem can be stated by defining three distinct entities. A set of n 2D data points, P:

$$P = \left\{ p_i \right\}_{i=1}^{n} \qquad (1)$$

Where p_i is an image point defined by its x and y pixel coordinates, (x_i, y_i), and n is the number of points in the set P. Also, a family of curves, $F_c(a, p)$, parameterized by the vector a and passing through the point p are mathematically defined in the following form:

$$Fc(a, p) = a_1(x^2 + y^2) + a_2x + a_3y + a_4 \qquad (2)$$

Finally we have the distance metric, $d(C(a), p_i)$, which defines the distance from a point p_i and the curve $C(a)$. The aim of this algorithm is to find the value a_{min} for which the following error function is globally minimized:

$$\varepsilon^2 = \sum_{i=1}^{n} d(C(a), p_i) \qquad (3)$$

The four points p_i that define the width and height limits of set P are recorded, i.e., the points with minimum and maximum width and height. Then, the algorithm searches for curves passing through these points, and orders them according to the number of intersections between points and curves. For each curve defined by a vector a, the error function presented in Equation (3) is computed. The a_{min}, i.e., the curve that minimizes the error function is selected and the respective radius and the centre are retrieved. The algorithm is more efficient than HCT and accurate but not applicable to occluded features, which would result in circles containing two features (Figure 10 b) (3)).

Occlusion Metric

Having two different techniques able to find feature's radius and centre, we have decided to add to our feature identification workflow an occlusion metric in order to determine whether or not a ROI of the image has occlusions, and select the appropriate technique (MECF or HCT) to apply in real-time.

During the development of our feature identification technique, we have observed several proprieties regarding the outputs of both CC and MECF algorithms which allows us to distinguish between "normal and "occluded" features. Examples, quite evident in Figure 10, and are: occluded features usually show a lower percentage of white pixels inside the bounding box; in occlusion cases, MECF area is normally larger than the bounding box area; occluded features normally have a higher difference between bounding box width and height sizes; etc. Considering these observations, we have performed a series of test cases, analysing both the image bounding box defined by the CC algorithm and the MECF output, aiming to label features in two distinct categories: "occluded" or "normal". The performed tests comprised 200 different samples, with 50% of the samples being the output from "normal" features cases and the remaining samples, the output from "occluded" features cases. As a result of the performed tests, we have proposed an empirical occlusion metric, comprising five rules in an OR logic operation, to label features as "occluded" when:

Figure 10. Occluded and normal features comparison. a) Single feature example. b) Overlapped features example. The three algorithmic phases in feature identification algorithm can be observed: (1) original feature; (2) ROI in the image delimited by a bounding box; (3) MECF with retrieved centre and radius.

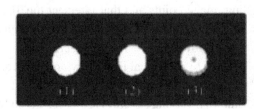 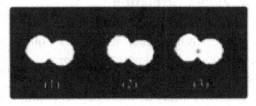

1. Its bounding box retrieved by CC algorithm has less than 65% of white pixels;
2. The bounding box has a width and height difference greater than 1.5 pixels;
3. The MECF and ROI radius difference is greater than 0.9 pixels;
4. MEFC and bounding box area difference is greater than 60 pixels;
5. MEFC circle exceeds the ROI limits in more than 2.5 pixels.

Although we need to run MECF always to verify the last three rules, this strategy of using HCT depending on the Occlusion Metric results, allows us saving 10.06 ms (see *Results and Discussion* Section) per frame with a robustness of 97%, since MECF is faster and accurate but only HCT is applicable to overlapped features.

3D RECONSTRUCTION VIA TRIANGULATION

Once identified the feature's position in different views, the subsequent problem is to use these information to reconstruct the markers position in 3D-scene space. In this section we cover the geometry of several perspective views. First, we clarify how to establish correspondences across imaged features in different views by using epipolar geometry (Hartley, 2003): we call it Multiple View Correlation. Therefore, having groups of correspondent features, we present our 3D metric reconstruction to recover the marker position in 3D space via Singular Value Decomposition (SVD) (Golub, 1993), the 3D Metric Reconstruction (Dias, 2007).

Multiple View Correlation

A useful and widely used mathematical technique to solve feature's correlation from two or more views is epipolar geometry (Hartley, 2003). The epipolar geometry theory defines that a 3D point,

X, imaged on the first camera view of a stereo pair, as x_1 restricts the position of the correspondent point x_2 in the second camera view to a line (epipolar line), if we know the extrinsic parameters of the stereoscopic camera system. This allows us to discard features as possible correspondences whose distance to the epipolar line are above a certain threshold. Our multiple-view correlation is based in this constraint and works as follows. We define a set of stereo pairs between the reference camera the camera with most features in the current frame) and the remaining ones. For every stereo pair and for each feature in the first view (reference camera image), we compute the distance between the features centres in the second view and the epipolar line that corresponds to the feature in the first view. All features with a distance above our threshold are discarded. The corresponding feature is the one with the smallest distance to the epipolar line. The result is a set of feature correspondences between the reference camera and the remaining ones which can be merged giving a Multiple-View Correlation.

3D Metric Reconstruction

By setting a well-known camera topology during the camera calibration step and by establishing optimal feature's correlation through multiple view correlation, we are able to perform the 3D metric reconstruction of the artefact. This process can be obtained in two different methods: by triangulation or via SVD. When we have correspondences between only two views, we can use triangulation instead of SVD to obtain the 3D point location, i.e., the 3D point can be computed directly through epipolar geometry as the intersection of rays fired from the camera positions that hit the corresponding image points and that intersect the 3D point. This analytic method is clearly faster than using SVD. However, the line intersection problem can lead us to numerical instability and subsequently to numerical indeterminacies which affect system stability. Having several views for a given feature correspondence, several possible solutions for the reconstruction derive from epipolar geometry and we are left with a set of linear equations that can be solved to compute a metric reconstruction for each artefact feature via SVD (presented also in Dias, 2007). The SVD usually denotes that a matrix A, can be decomposed as $A = V \Lambda U$. Using each camera's intrinsic and extrinsic parameters, we stack into matrix A the existing information for each i view (2D point location $-x, y$). Solving the A matrix by SVD and retaining the last row of the V matrix, the reconstruction point coordinates (x, y, z) are the singular values in Λ. The matrices sizes vary with the number of views used to re-construction the 3D points coordinates: $A_{[2i \times 4]}$; $V_{[2i \times 2i]}$; $\Lambda_{[2i \times 4]}$; $U_{[4x4]}$. After testing both solutions in the two viewing scenarios, we have decided to preserve the system reliability using the SVD technique, despite the computational cost.

MODEL FITTING

The purpose of model fitting is to determine which set of reconstructed 3D points belongs to each artefact (Figure 11), labelling its spatial model and estimating the relative pose of the artefact. Fitting a model to a cloud of points is typically a NP-hard problem. However, Pintaric and Kaufmann have proposed an approach to reduce the complexity of this problem (Pintaric, 2007) combining Candidate Evaluation via Artefact Correlation and Maximum Clique Search. Our model fitting technique is largely influenced by Pintaric and Kaufmann. In the following sections the technique is presented, focusing in our proposed improvements.

Candidate Evaluation via Artefact Correlation

The candidate evaluation goal is to decide which points are "good candidates" to belong to the specific artefacts. The metric used to compare pairs of 3D points is the Euclidean distance between them, where we can take advantage of three important constraints: artefacts are rigid-body objects with constant Euclidean distances between pair-wise markers; since we control the artefacts construction, its design can be done to maximize the minimum difference between Euclidean distances across all targets; knowing the minimum Euclidean distance detectable by our system we maintain the previous constraint above this value. This Euclidean distance constraint does not allow arbitrarily designed artefacts but, according to

Figure 11. Rigid body artefacts. a) 6 DOF artefact used as 3D input device. b) 3 DOF artefact attached to user's stereo glasses

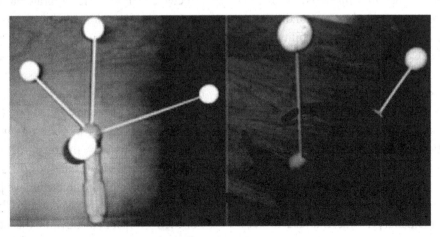

Pintaric (2007), the computational complexity reduction that arises is worthwhile.

The candidate evaluation technique is divided into two phases (Figure 12). For each artefact, an offline calibration process (*0. Calibration*) is needed in order to construct a Correlation Score Look-up Table (CSLT) with all artefact Euclidean distances between all pair-wise markers, given the N distances $[d_0, ..., d_N]$. Let's follow the example of artefact depicted in Figure 12 where $N = 6$. At runtime (*Online*), for each system pipeline cycle, an Euclidean Distance Matrix (EDM) of size M x M is constructed, containing distances between all pairs of the M points reconstructed ($M = 8$ in the given example). For each calibrated artefact, a Correlation Score Matrix (CSM) of size N x N is computed (*1.Correlation*). Each entry of CSM corresponds to a correlation between the EDM corresponding entry and the artefact's Euclidean distances stacked in the CSLT. In other words, each entry of CSM represents the probability of a pair of makers to belong to the artefact concerned. The result is a set of connection edges between markers with high probability distances (*b. High probability edges*). Then, from the CSM, a vector containing the accumulated correlation scores (ACS) is computed through row or column-wise summation (*2. Accumulation*). Since each CSM row or column represents a 3D reconstructed point, each entry of the ACS vector represents the probability of the respective point to belong to the artefact. Finally the ACS vector passes through a threshold (*3. Threshold*), to determine which points are candidates to belong to the artefact (c. High probability lines), resulting in the ACST vector of size K (accumulated correlation scores with a threshold), which is the number of correctly labelled points for the concerned artefact. Our approach differs from Pintaric's original formulation in two main aspects. First, despite each Correlation Score Matrix entry represents the probability of a pair of makers to belong to a certain artefact, there is no information about which artefact' markers are responsible for this high probability. The CSM implementation was changed to keep

record of the artefact markers indexes with high correlation score, the number of these markers, as well their probability. This information avoids the introduction of an additional processing step to establish point's correspondences between the output of Candidate Evaluation and the calibrated artefact (mandatory for pose estimation), which is not possible in Pintaric's formulation. Additionally, this simple change allows the introduction of our second improvement; the definition of a threshold for accepting/discarding candidate points, not only by high correlation probability but also taking into account the number of indexes connected to the concerned point. Any point with less than two high correlation entries in the CSM (which means, linked to less than 2 edges) is discarded in the algorithm pass, i.e. any point that can't belong to a set of at least three points, since we need a minimum of three points to retrieve 6DOF pose estimation. Obviously, specially designed 3DOF (in translation) artefacts with less than three markers, do not follow this rule. The final output of Candidate Evaluation is a list of points, each one with a reference to a set of connected points to which it is linked (Figure 12). However, our implemented technique might still leave points with just one link, as depicted in Figure 12 - *c. High probability lines*. Additionally, despite the fact that our Candidate Evaluation algorithm greatly reduces the complexity of the problem of labelling artefact points, it is still not sufficient to establish the optimal match between the reconstructed points and the calibrated artefacts. In the evaluation of candidate points for this match, our used metric is based in Euclidean distances between pairs of points, and since there are always precision errors/accuracy, it is necessary to set an error margin to accept the matches. With the increase in the number of reconstructed points so does the likelihood of having more points with the same matches. In this way, the result of the Candidate Evaluation might have false positives that can only be eliminated with the algorithm we present in the next section (the MCS – Maximum Clique Search). For each artefact in evaluation, this new algorithm

Figure 12. Candidate Evaluation workflow

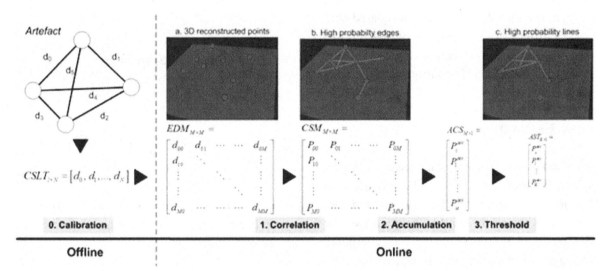

determines the largest set of vertices, where any pair is connected by an edge, which shows the highest probability of matching that artefact.

Maximum Clique Search

The output of the previous step can be actually seen as a graph, where each candidate marker is a vertex and has a connection with a set of other markers, creating with each one an edge. Given a graph, which can be denoted by $G = (V, E)$, where V is a set of vertices and E is a set of edges, a clique is a set of vertices where any pair of two is connected by an edge. In the Maximum Clique Search problem (MCS), the goal is to find the largest amount of cliques, i.e., find the largest sub-graph of G, denoted by $C = (V_c, E_c)$, where any pair of vertices V_c are connected by an edge E_c. To address this problem we have developed an algorithm based on (Konc, 2007). The markers with high probability to belong to a certain artefact are the input of maximum clique search algorithm. The vertex-clique returned is the set of points more probable to be the corresponding artefact.

Analysis Algorithm Input and Output

Developing metrics to deal with the model fitting algorithm input and output is desirable, in order to decrease the required computational time. A simple input metric can be followed. For an artefact with N markers and M vertices in the input, only one of the subsequent scenarios can happen:

- *Unique maximum-clique:* $N \leq M \geq 2$ and each Mth vertex have exactly $M - 1$ edges. In this case there is no need to run the MSC algorithm;
- *No maximum-clique:* $M < 3$, we need at least 3 points to estimate the 6DOF pose;
- *Find maximum-clique:* we need to run the MCS to determine the maximum vertex-clique.

Also important is the output metric. We account for three possible outcomes:

- *Single solution:* The graph has exactly one vertex-clique of size $N \geq 3$. No further processing is needed;
- *Multiple solutions:* The graph has multiple vertex-cliques of size $N \geq 3$. We compute

the pose estimation for each solution and choose the one with minimal squared sum of differences from the last retrieved pose;

- *No solutions:* Any vertex-cliques of size $N \geq 3$ in the graph. The last pose retrieved is shown.

Pose Estimation

After achieving a solution with a set of adjacent points, the pose estimation is the procedure to determine the transformation (translation and rotation) between the runtime solution and the "reference pose" (of the model points) computed during the Artefact Calibration step. We have developed the 3D-3D least square pose estimation presented by Haralick (1989). The pose estimation problem is to compute a rotation matrix R, and a translation vector T, for solution points which transform them into the model points. Three non-collinear correspondences are required to estimate a 6DOF pose. Assuming our model points which define the "reference pose" denoted by $\{x_1, x_2, ..., x_N\}$ and the corresponding solution points denoted by $\{y_1, y_2, ..., y_N\}$, where N define the number of correspondences, the pose is estimated using a least square error minimization approach based on points re-projection error and solved by Single Value Decomposition, SVD. Here we provide an overview of the technique, which is described in detail in Arun (1987). The least square problem can be expressed to minimize:

$$\sum_{n=1}^{N} w_n \| y_n - R x_n + T \|^2 \qquad (4)$$

Where w_i represent the weight given to the ith point based on its re-projection error. To simplify the problem we can compute the mean values of each set of points (centroid) and translate them to the reference coordinate system origin, eliminating the translation T:

$$\sum_{n=1}^{N} w_n \| y_n - R x_n \|^2 \qquad (5)$$

Expanding equation (5) we have:

$$\sum_{n=1}^{N} w_n \left(\| y_n \|^2 - 2(y_n, Rx_n) + \| Rx_n \|^2 \right) =$$
$$\sum_{n=1}^{N} w_n \| y_n \|^2 - 2trace \left(R^T \sum_{n=1}^{N} w_n y_n x_n^T \right) + \sum_{n=1}^{N} w_n \| Rx_n \|^2 \qquad (6)$$

In order to minimize the general equation, we want to maximize the second term. Defining K as a correlation matrix:

$$K = \sum_{n=1}^{N} w_n y_n x_n^T \qquad (7)$$

The problem can be now stated as:

$$trace(R^T K) \to maximum \qquad (8)$$

The solution to the correlation matrix can be found by SVD, where the correlation matrix can be decomposed into the form:

$$K = W \Lambda V \qquad (9)$$

Here Λ represents the singular values. The rank of K is equal to the number of linearly independent columns or rows of K. Since $RR^T = 1$, the equation (5) is maximized if:

$$R = V \begin{pmatrix} 1 & & \\ & 1 & \\ & & \det(VU^T) \end{pmatrix} U^T \qquad (10)$$

This gives a unique solution to the rotation matrix. The translation vector, T, is given by:

$$T = \bar{y} - R\bar{x} \qquad (11)$$

Where $\bar{x}$ and $\bar{y}$ represent the centroids of each set of points computed previously. To improve this method, the weight w_i, of each reconstructed point y_i, is indirectly proportional to its re-projection error rp_i:

$$w_i = \left(rp_i \ / \ Rp \right)^{-1} \qquad (12)$$

Where Rp defines the sum of re-projection errors across all points y_i. The major phases of the tracking algorithm can be observed in Figure 13 where the poses of two independent artefacts are evaluated.

RESULTS AND DISCUSSION

In order to assess the system accuracy and precision we have assembled a preliminary setup in our Computer Graphics lab at ISCTE-IUL, of size 4m x 2m x 2m.

Frame Rate and Latency

To determine the system performance we have executed our application during 10 minutes moving two artefacts inside the tracking volume. The mean frame rate measured was 24.80 fps which gives a mean latency of 40.32 ms.

Feature Segmentation Analysis

In *Feature Segmentation and Identification* Section we have presented a combination of three different techniques and one metric to solve feature segmentation problem – Connect-Components (CC), Minimum Enclosing Circle Fitting (MECF), Hough Circle Transform (HCT) and Occlusion Metric (OM). Now

Figure 13. Software main stages. a) Feature Segmentation output in each view (each one represented by a colour); b) Epipolar lines from all views projected in each view; c) 3D Reconstruction of markers; d) Artefacts' pose retrieval after Model Fitting

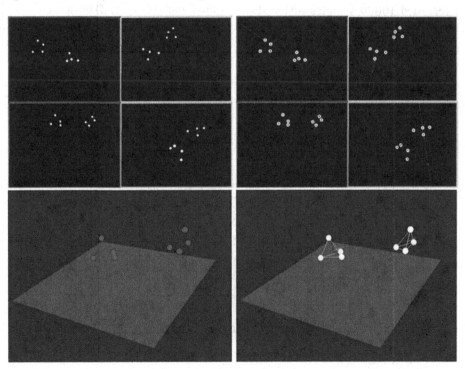

we base our choices through algorithms comparison, summarized in Table 2. All results presented on this sub-section result from an analysis of 10000 frames.

By analysing the table above it is easy to conclude that our final retained technique is faster than the two others. The comparison between the implemented approach and the similar version only with CC and HCT is relevant to prove that Occlusion Metric is important when choosing the algorithm to identify a feature in a certain ROI. The difference between the two last approaches presented in Table 2 in terms of computational time needed, is largely due the fact that MECF and OM only requires an average of 0.02 ms to process a ROI, while HCT takes about 0.82 ms to analyse a ROI. As mentioned, HCT is sensible to occlusions.

Precision in Artefact Pose Retrieval

To measure the system's precision, where we want to sense the deviation of the estimated pose of the artefact relatively to the average estimation, we have placed a static single marker on the working volume and recorded 10000 samples of its 3D reconstruct position. We have then measured its deviation in relation to the average reconstructed position across all samples. The histogram in Figure 14 shows this deviation. The mean devia-

Table 2. Different feature segmentation techniques and its computational time required to process one image

Technique	Mean Time [ms]
HCT applied to the whole image	37.59
Our technique with CC+HCT only	21.13
Our final technique using HCT or MECF depending in the OM	11.07

tion computed was 0.35 mm and the maximum deviation in the experiment was 0.82 mm.

Following the same reasoning, we have placed a four-marker artefact (Figure 11) in the working volume. Next, we have calibrated the pose and estimated the same pose 10000 times, using our technique, for a unique pose in the real space. The histogram on Figure 15 shows the deviation of the estimated translation (in this case, the Euclidian distance between the calibrated geometric centre of the artefact and the estimated centre). The mean and maximum translation deviations were 0.19 mm and 0.55 mm. In Figure 16 we present the overall rotation error (average rotation error over the three axes X, Y, Z) between the calibrated and estimated poses. The mean and maximum overall rotation errors were, respectively, 0.04° and 0.12°.

Figure 14. Single marker deviation to mean value

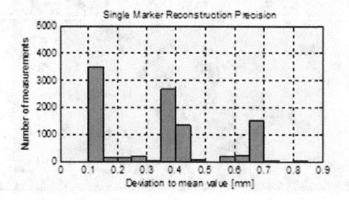

Accuracy in Artefact Pose Retrieval

With the accuracy tests we want to evaluate the mean error in translation and rotation of the estimated pose and for that, we have designed several experiments. The first of such experiments provided us with the computation of the re-projection error of a single marker in all images. We have moved the object during 10000 frames across the working volume. The re-projection error histogram is shown in Figure 17. The mean and maximum re-projection error measured were, respectively, 3.49 mm and 6.86 mm.

Another experiment to determine the system's accuracy consisted in assembling a two-marker artefact with a known Euclidean distance (15 cm). Subsequently, we have recorded the estimated distance between the markers while moving the artefact across the working volume during 10000 frames. The histogram in Figure 18 shows the quadric error of the 3D Reconstruction (deviation of the estimated distance from 15 cm). The mean and maximum quadratic reconstruction errors in this trial were, respectively, 2.44 mm and 49.75 mm.

In another experiment aiming at determining the tracking algorithms errors (feature segmentation error, re-projection error and reconstruction error), we have performed the following steps. By having a calibrated (virtual) artefact, we have

Figure 15. Deviation between the calibrated and estimated translation

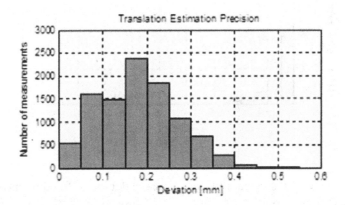

Figure 16. Deviation between the calibrated and estimated rotation

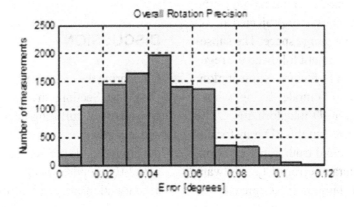

Figure 17. Histogram of the re-projection error

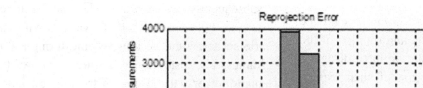

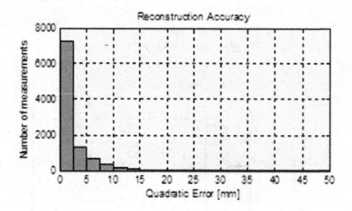

Figure 18. Reconstruction accuracy

applied to it a series of 3D transformations (a concatenation of translations and rotations, during a period of time) as a ground truth, keeping record of the original points. First we have computed a ground truth 3D transformation and have applied it to the calibrated points, keeping record of the original points. Next we have re-projected all 3D features in each camera image space. The subsequent steps of this experiment followed the regular system workflow: (1) feature segmentation; (2) 3D reconstruction; (3) model fitting, whose output is a pose, i.e., a 3D transformation. The absolute difference between this 3D transformation and the known ground truth transformation, defines the pose accuracy error of the software component of our technique. Experiments over

each degree of freedom have been performed. In Figures 19 and 20, we show the observed errors in translation along the *Y* axis and, in rotation over the *Y* axis.

The mean accuracy errors can be seen in Table 3.

DISCUSSION

Comparing the requirements established in *System Overview* Section, the achieved results can be considered as fulfilling them from the qualitative and quantitative perspectives, with some minor deviations to the pre-set values. We have achieved a real-time update rate, without noticeable error accumulation and drift in the estimation of two

Table 3. Absolute pose estimation accuracy over the 6DOF

Mean Error	Over X	Over Y	Over Z	Overall
Translation [mm]	1.09	0.85	0.85	0.93
Rotation [deg]	0.55	0.39	0.60	0.51

artefacts poses. During all experiments, no major constraints or interferences were noticed. However, concerning the experiments described in this section, our major issues are related with some accuracy errors found in pose estimation that largely exceeds the expected values (Figures 19 and 20). To identify the origin of the high errors obtained in the performed trials, the whole application pipeline was traced. We have concluded that in 93.43% of severe error cases – errors higher than 5.0mm / 2.0°, which only represent 0.80% of all tested cases – the origin of the problem starts when an occluded feature in the image space, is not identified by the Hough Circle Transform. This causes a missing feature and an error in computing the feature centre in the same bounding box. The missing feature when is projected in the other cameras images is correctly reconstructed, but the feature that suffers from the centre calculation error, leads to a 3D point reconstruction error originated from the view where the occlusion happens. When the set of 3D reconstructed points reaches the model fitting algorithm, they generates some "awkward"

Euclidean distances that cause a change in the "normal" correspondences between reconstructed points and calibrated artefact and therefore the pose computation presents a high error, in that case. In fact the high errors observed in reconstruction quadratic-error (Figure 18) can be justified by the use of two markers in this experiment, which increases the probability of having occlusions. In synthesis, two problems can be extracted. First, the Hough Circle Transform does not always provide the needed robustness and accuracy to identify overlapped features. The second related issue, which affects the Model Fitting correspondence, relates to our manual and error-prone artefact construction and design, which does not maximize the minimum Euclidean distance between artefact markers. Both problems will be addressed in the following chapter.

By comparing the general specifications of our system with ioTracker – one of the most relevant works found in the state-of-the-art – our system is outperformed in terms of performance, number of artefacts simultaneous tracked and precision (in 3D reconstruction and pose estimation). In the

Figure 19. Translation accuracy in Y axis

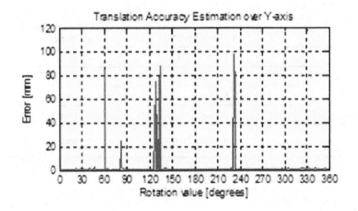

Figure 20. Rotation accuracy over Y axis

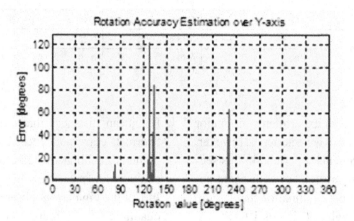

other hand, we achieve better accuracy, both in 3D reconstruction and pose estimation – see Table 4 for details.

CONCLUSIONS AND FUTURE WORK

In this paper a complete hardware and software architecture of an infrared tracking system was presented and some advances in the current state-of-the-art have been identified. The presented tracking system is appropriate for large scale immersive virtual reality environments or augmented reality settings. A full engineering approach was addressed, from clear user requirements to system specifications, development and testing plans, software and hardware design and engineering, followed by an

analysis of system performance, precision and accuracy. Although we have achieved sufficient performance, precision and accuracy according to the requirements previously set and well comparable with ioTracker in terms of accuracy, we still have several ideas to improve the system in the future and solve the identified problems in the previous chapter. One of such issues is of recovering the features centres in the presence of feature occlusions in the image space, by using the Hough Circle Transform, which shows only moderate robustness and accuracy. Common approaches found in the literature (Kimme, 1975; Duda, 1972) address this problem by calculating the pixels gradient direction which should have the opposite direction of the circle centre. However, due to the presence of noise, arising from the image acquisition and

Table 4. Infrared Tracking systems specifications comparison

	Our System	ioTracker
Performance	Up to 25 Hz	Up to 60 Hz
No. simultaneous artefacts	2	10
3D Reconstruction Precision	0.35 mm	0.04 mm
3D Reconstruction Accuracy	3.49 mm	5.30 mm
Pose Retrieval Precision (translation / rotation)	0.19mm / 0.04°	0.05mm/ 0.02° [a]
Pose Retrieval Accuracy (translation / rotation)	0.93mm / 0.51°	± 5.0 mm [a]

[a] This Experiment was not explained by the authors.

from markers prone-error manufacturing, these approaches tend to compromise the robustness. On the other hand, techniques that fit 2D data points in geometric shapes (e.g. a circle), have shown better accuracy and speed. One of the future research directions to address this problem is the topic of data fitting applicable to feature occlusion cases. Recent scientific contributions have shown the effectiveness of maximum likelihood estimation to fit a cloud of 2D points with occlusions, in several circles (Frosio, 2008). Another alternative way to develop the feature detection is through hardware segmentation. The CCD cameras allow us to regulate the light that enters through the camera lens or to change the exposure time. These two changes usually create a detectable gradient between two features that were previously occluded, avoiding the utilization of the costly Hough Circle Transform. However, the artefacts' support infrastructure should be made of a material that should not reflect light, and should ideally be transparent and rigid to support the markers, or otherwise would create even more unpredictable occlusions. We would need to find or create such material, with the aid of a Materials Engineering Department of a well ranked University. A parallel approach is the introduction of predicting filters, such as the Kalman Filter (Welch, 2004), to perform comparisons between estimated and predicted poses and develop heuristics to choose the best fit, in order to minimize the pose error. Additionally, by analysing the pose changes between frames, cut-off translations and rotations could be defined, since there is certainly a change limit for both transformations, in a time interval of 40 ms (25 Hz) which corresponds to the time between two frames. Another envisaged improvement is a better artefact design based on topology assessment. Our lab-made artefacts do not have the sub-millimetre precision required to enhance the model fitting complexity reduction, which force us to have an off-line artefact calibration phase. We hope to achieve a precise artefact construction which will allow us to suppress the artefact cali-

bration phase and introduce artefacts in the system only by its geometric and topological description. Approaches to design artefacts that maximize the minimal Euclidean distance across all markers (Pintaric, 2008) are foreseen and for that, collaboration with the Architecture department of ISCTE-IUL is envisaged. By reducing the size of markers, which reduce the probability of occlusion, we could improve the features detection. Alternatively, we could combine information from several cameras. This is especially beneficial when, in a certain view a feature is occluded and, in another view, the same feature is detected only through the pixel-connected algorithm. This information could be correlated in the Multiple View Correlation phase and used to solve the feature segmentation problem in a robust way. We also plan to investigate the applicability of GPU computing and advanced parallel programming in our system, namely in algorithms with no interwork dependences (e.g., Feature Segmentation, Candidate Evaluation) which could benefit from the number of pipelines available in modern GPUs. There are several examples in literature of faster implementations in GPU than CPU (Yang, 2002; Moreland, 2003). Moreover, each module develop in our system can be applied in several fields. The feature identification algorithm can be integrated in any problem that needs to identify circular primitives (e.g., medical imaging). Any problem regarding 3D reconstruct of world point from several views can use our approach of Multiple View Correlation. Examples of such problems can be found in object tracking for augmented reality, 3D object and scene reconstruction for SLAM (Simultaneous Localization and Mapping) in robotics, general 3D scene reconstruction and mapping or image stitching.

ACKNOWLEDGMENT

We would like to thank Rui Varela and Pedro Martins, of ISCTE-IUL for designing and developing the system's electronics and to thank Luciano Pereira Soares of PUC Rio de Janeiro and Petrobrás for the lens model simulation.

REFERENCES

Abdel-Aziz, Y. I., & Karara, H. M. (1971). Direct linear transformation into object space coordinates in close-range photogrammetry. In *Proceedings of the Symposium on Close-Range Photogrammetry* (pp. 1-18).

ART. (2011). *Advanced Realtime Tracking GmbH.* Retrieved July 5, 2011, from http://www. ar-tracking.de

Arun, K. S., Huang, T. S., & Blostein, S. D. (1987). Least-squares fitting of two 3-D point sets. *IEEE Transactions on Pattern Analysis and Machine Intelligence*, 698–700. doi:10.1109/TPAMI.1987.4767965

AVT. (2011). *Allied vision technologies.* Retrieved July 5, 2011, from http://www.alliedvisiontec.com

Cruz-Neira, C., Sandin, D., DeFanti, T., Kenyon, R., & Hart, J. (1992). The CAVE: Audio visual experience automatic virtual environment. *Communications of the ACM, 35,* 72–65. doi:10.1145/129888.129892

DeMenthon, D., & Davis, L. S. (1992). Model-based object pose in 25 lines of code. In *Proceedings of the European Conference on Computer Vision* (pp. 335-343).

Dias, J. M. S. et al. (2007). CAVE-HOLLOW-SPACE do Lousal – Príncipios teóricos e desenvolvimento. *Encontro Português de Computação Gráfica, 15.*

Dias, J. M. S., & Bastos, R. (2006). An optimized marker tracking system. In *Proceedings of the 12th Eurographics Symposium on Virtual Environments* (pp. 1-4).

Dias, J. M. S., Jamal, N., Silva, P., & Bastos, R. (2004). ARTIC: Augmented reality tangible interface by colour evaluation. In *Proceedings of the Conference on Advances in Computer Graphics.*

Duda, R. O., & Hart, P. E. (1972). Use of the Hough transformation to detect lines and curves in pictures. *Communications of the ACM, 15,* 11–15. doi:10.1145/361237.361242

Fitzgibbon, A. W., & Fisher, R. B. (1995). A buyer's guide to conic fitting. In *Proceedings of the 5th British Machine Vision Conference* (Vol. 5, pp. 513-522).

Frosio, I., & Borghese, N. A. (2008). Real-time accurate circle fitting with occlusions. *International Journal of Pattern Recognition, 41*(3), 1041–1055. doi:10.1016/j.patcog.2007.08.011

Golub, G. H., & Van Loan, C. F. (1993). *Matrix computations.* Baltimore, MD: Johns Hopkins University Press.

Haralick, R. M., Joo, H., Lee, C. N., Zhuang, X., Vaidya, V. G., & Kim, M. B. (1989). Pose estimation from corresponding point data. *IEEE Transactions on Systems, Man, and Cybernetics, 19,* 1426–1446. doi:10.1109/21.44063

Hartley, R., & Zisserman, A. (2003). *Multiple view geometry in computer vision.* Cambridge, UK: Cambridge University Press.

Heikkila, J., & Silven, O. (1997). A four-step camera calibration procedure with implicit image correction. In *Proceedings of the Conference on Computer Vision and Pattern Recognition* (pp. 1106-1112).

Kato, H., & Billinghurst, M. (1999). Marker tracking and HMD calibration for a video-based augmented reality conferencing system. In *Proceedings of the 2nd IEEE and ACM International Workshop on Augmented Reality.*

Kimme, C., Ballard, D. H., & Sklansky, J. (1975). Finding circles by an array of accumulators. *Communications of the ACM, 18,* 120–122. doi:10.1145/360666.360677

Konc, J., & Janežiči, D. (2007). An improved branch and bound algorithm for the maximum clique problem. *MATCH Communications in Mathematical and in Computer Chemistry, 58,* 569–590.

Lowe, D. G. (1991). Fitting parameterized three-dimensional models to images. *IEEE Transactions on Pattern Analysis and Machine Intelligence, 13,* 441–450. doi:10.1109/34.134043

Moreland, K., & Angel, E. (2003). The FFT on a GPU. In *Proceedings of the SIGGRAPH/Eurographics Workshop on Graphics Hardware* (pp. 112-119).

NI. (2011). *National instruments.* Retrieved July 5, 2011, from http://www.ni.com/

Open, C. V. (2011). *Open computer vision library.* Retrieved July 5, 2011, from http://sourceforge.net/projects/opencvlibrary/

Pintaric, T., & Kaufmann, H. (2007). Affordable infrared-optical pose-tracking for virtual and augmented reality. In *Proceedings of the Trends and Issues in Tracking for Virtual Environments Workshop.*

Pintaric, T., & Kaufmann, H. (2008). A rigid-body target design methodology for optical pose tracking systems. In *Proceedings of the 15th ACM Symposium on Virtual Reality Software and Technology* (pp. 73-76).

Santos, P., Buanes, A., & Jorge, J. (2006). PTrack: Introducing a novel iterative geometric pose estimation for a marker-based single camera tracking system. In *Proceedings of the IEEE Virtual Reality Conference* (pp. 143-150).

Santos, P., Stork, A., Buaes, A., Pereira, C., & Jorge, J. (2010). A real-time low-cost marker-based multiple camera tracking solution for virtual reality applications. *Journal of Real-Time Image Processing, 5*(2), 121–128. doi:10.1007/s11554-009-0138-9

Schneider. (2011). *Schneider Kreuznach.* Retrieved July 5, 2011, from http://www.schneider-kreuznach.com

Vicon. (2011). *Motion capture systems from Vicon.* Retrieved July 5, 2011, from http://www.vicon.com

Wang, F. (2004). A simple and analytical procedure for calibrating extrinsic camera parameters. *IEEE Transactions on Robotics and Automation, 20,* 121–124. doi:10.1109/TRA.2003.820919

Welch, G., & Bishop, G. (2004). *An introduction to the Kalman Filter* (Tech. Rep. No. 95-041). Chapel Hill, NC: University of North Carolina.

Yang, R., & Welch, G. (2002). Fast image segmentation and smoothing using commodity graphics hardware. *Journal of Graphics Tools, 7*(4), 91–100.

Zhang, Z. (1999). Flexible camera calibration by viewing a plane from unknown orientations. In *Proceedings of the International Conference on Computer Vision, 1,* 666–673. doi:10.1109/ICCV.1999.791289

Zhao, J., Yan, D., Men, G., & Zhang, Y. (2007). A method of calibrating intrinsic and extrinsic camera parameters separately for multi-camera systems. In *Proceedings of the Sixth International Conference on Machine Learning and Cybernetics* (Vol. 3, pp. 1548-1553).

This work was previously published in International Journal of Creative Interfaces and Computer Graphics, Volume 2, Issue 2, edited by Ben Falchuk, pp. 49-73, copyright 2010 by IGI Publishing (an imprint of IGI Global).

Compilation of References

Abdel-Aziz, Y. I., & Karara, H. M. (1971). Direct linear transformation into object space coordinates in close-range photogrammetry. In *Proceedings of the Symposium on Close-Range Photogrammetry* (pp. 1-18).

Adams, L., Montanaro, M., & Sha, X. W. (2009). *Frankenstein's Ghosts*. Montreal, Quebec, Canada: Blue Riders and Topological Media Lab.

Adams, A. (1981). The negative. In Baker, R. (Ed.), *The new Ansel Adams photography series, book 2*. Waterbury, CT: New York Graphic Society.

Agarawala, A. (2006). *Enriching the Desktop Metaphor with Physics, Piles and the Pen* (Master's Thesis, University of Toronto). Retrieved May 10, 2009, from http://www.dgp.toronto.edu/~anand/big/Thesis-BumpTop.pdf

Agarawala, A., & Balakrishnan, R. (2006, April 22-27). Keepin' it real: Pushing the desktop metaphor with physics, piles and the pen. In R. Grinter, T. Rodden, P. Aoki, E. Cutrell, R. Jeffries, & G. Olson (Eds.), *Proceedings of the SIGCHI Conference on Human Factors in Computing Systems (CHI '06),* Montréal, Québec, Canada (pp. 1283-1292). New York: ACM Publishing. Retrieved from http://doi.acm.org/10.1145/1124772.1124965

Airey, J. (1990). *Increasing update rates in the building walkthrough system with automatic model-space subdivision and potentially visible set calculations.* Unpublished PhD thesis, Department of Computer Science, University of North Carolina at Chapel Hill.

Alhadeff, E. (2007). *$9 Bi: Microsoft's conservative estimate for the serious games market.* Retrieved from http://www.futurelab.net/blogs/marketing-strategy-innovation/2007/12/9_bi_microsofts_conservative_e.html

Alhadeff, E. (2007). *Serious games, serious money: A sizeable market.* Retrieved from http://elianealhadeff.blogspot.com/2007/03/serious-games-serious-money-sizeable.html

Alston, R. W. (1954). *Painter's idiom*. London, UK: Staples.

Amador, G., & Gomes, A. (2010a, March). A CUDA-based implementation of stable fluids in 3D with internal and moving boundaries. In *Proceedings of the International Conference on Computational Science and its Applications* (pp. 118-128). Washington, DC: IEEE Computer Society.

Amador, G., & Gomes, A. (2010b, April). CUDA-based linear solvers for stable fluids. In *Proceedings of the International Conference on Information Sciences and Applications* (pp. 1-8). Washington, DC: IEEE Computer Society.

Andújar, C., Ayala, D., & Brunet, P. (2002). Topology simplification through discrete models. *ACM Transactions on Graphics, 20*(6), 88–105.

Andújar, C., Vázquez, P., & Fairén, M. (2004). Wayfinder: Guided tours through complex walkthrough models. *Computer Graphics Forum, 23*(3), 499–508. doi:10.1111/j.1467-8659.2004.00781.x

Annett, M. K., & Bischof, W. F. (2010). Investigating the application of virtual reality systems to psychology and cognitive neuroscience research. *Presence (Cambridge, Mass.), 19*(2), 131–141.

Anton, R., Opris, D., Dobreani, A., David, D., & Rizzo, A. S. (2009). Virtual reality in the rehabilitation of attention deficit/ hyperactivity disorder/ instrument construction principles. *Journal of Cognitive and Behavioral Psychotherapies, 9*(2), 235.

Arnheim, R. (1954/1974). *Art and visual perception: A psychology of the creative eye*. Berkeley, CA: University of California Press.

Art Cyclopedia. (n. d.). *Julia Margaret Cameron (British photographer, 1815-1879)*. Retrieved from http://www.artcyclopedia.com/artists/cameron_julia_margaret.html

ART. (2011). *Advanced Realtime Tracking GmbH*. Retrieved July 5, 2011, from http://www.ar-tracking.de

Arun, K. S., Huang, T. S., & Blostein, S. D. (1987). Least-squares fitting of two 3-D point sets. *IEEE Transactions on Pattern Analysis and Machine Intelligence*, 698–700. doi:10.1109/TPAMI.1987.4767965

Ash, M. (2005). *Simulation and bisualization of a 3D gluid*. Unpublished master's thesis, Université d'Orléans, Orléans, France.

Asunción, M., de la Mantas, J., & Castro, M. (2010, September). Programming CUDA-based GPUs to simulate two-layer shallow water flows. In P. D'Ambra, M. Guarracino, & D. Talia (Eds.), *Proceedings of the 16th International EURO-PAR Conference on Parallel Processing* (LNCS 6272, pp. 353-364).

AVT. (2011). *Allied vision technologies*. Retrieved July 5, 2011, from http://www.alliedvisiontec.com

Azuma, R. (1997). A Survey of Augmented Reality. *Presence (Cambridge, Mass.)*, *6*(4), 355–385.

Baboud, L., & Décoret, X. (2006). Realistic water volumes in real-time. In *Proceedings of the EUROGRAPHICS Workshop on Natural Phenomena*.

Balding, J. J. (2009). *Incorporating innovative and immersive technologies: Changing the art of design*. Union City, CA: AECbytes.

Banissi, E. (2008). *Preface, 12th International Conference Information Visualisation*. Retrieved April 22, 2009, from http://www2.computer.org/portal/web/csdl/abs/proceedings/iv/2008/3268/00/3268toc.htm

Barad, K. M. (2007). *Meeting the universe halfway: Quantum physics and the entanglement of matter and meaning*. Durham, NC: Duke University Press.

Bassett, D. M., & Bullmore, E. (2006). Small-world brain networks. *The Neuroscientist*, *12*(6).

Bateman, S., Gutwin, C., & Nacenta, M. (2008). Seeing things in the clouds: the effect of visual features on tag cloud selections. In *Proceedings of the 9th ACM conference on Hypertext and Hypermedia* (pp. 193-202). New York: ACM Press.

Baum, L. F. (2000). *The Wonderful Wizard of OZ*. New York: Elibron Classics.

Bederson, B., & Shneiderman, B. (2003). *The Craft of Information Visualization: Readings and Reflections*. San Francisco: Morgan Kaufmann Publishers.

Bederson, B. B., Grosjean, J., & Meyer, J. (2004). Toolkit Design for Interactive Structured Graphics. *IEEE Transactions on Software Engineering*, *30*(8), 535–546. doi:10.1109/TSE.2004.44

Begelman, G., Keller, P., & Smadja, F. (2006). Automated tag clustering: improving search and exploration in the tag space. In *Proceedings of the 15th international conference on World Wide Web*. Retrieved October 02, 2009, from http://citeseerx.ist.psu.edu/viewdoc/download?doi=10.1.1.120.5736&rep=rep1&type=pdf

Bellman, S., Schweda, A., & Varan, D. (2009). Viewing angle matters-screen type does not. *The Journal of Communication*, 609–634. doi:10.1111/j.1460-2466.2009.01441.x

Belyaev, V. (2003). Real-time simulation of water surface. In *Proceedings of the International Conference on Computer Graphics & Vision* (pp. 131-138).

Benko, H., Ishak, E. W., & Feiner, S. (2004, November 2-4). Collaborative Mixed Reality Visualization of an Archaeological Excavation. In *Proceedings of the 3rd IEEE/ACM International Symposium on Mixed and Augmented Reality* (pp. 132-140). Washington, DC: IEEE Computer Society. Retrieved from http://dx.doi.org/10.1109/ISMAR.2004.23

Bense, F. (1965). *Aesthetica: Einführung in die neue Ästhetik*. Baden-Baden, Germany: Agis.

Bentham, J. (1995). *The Panopticon writings*. London, UK: Verso.

Berger, T. (1972). *Ways of seeing* (p. 7). London, UK: Penguin Books.

Bernier, R. (2006). An introduction to JPEG 2000. *Library Hi Tech News, 23*(7), 26–27. doi:10.1108/07419050610704349

Berry, J. (2003). *Bare code: Net art and the free software movement.* Retrieved from http://www.uoc.edu/artnodes/espai/eng/art/jberry0503/jberry0503.html

Beyls, P. (1988). *The Algorists, historical notes by Roman Verostko.* Retrieved from http://www.verostko.com/algorist.html

Bielenberg, K., & Zacher, M. (2005). *Groups in social software: Utilizing tagging to integrate individual contexts for social navigation.* Unpublished master's dissertation, University of Bremen, Germany.

Birkhoff, G. D. (1933). *Aesthetic measure.* Cambridge, MA: Harvard University Press.

Bishop, C. (2006). *Participation (Documents of Contemporary Art).* Cambridge, MA: MIT Press.

Blais, J., & Ippolito, J. (2006). *At the Edge of Art.* London: Thames & Hudson.

Blake, V. (1925). *The way to sketch (notes on the essentials of landscape sketching; particular reference being made to the use of water-colour)* (pp. 113–116). Oxford, UK: Clarendon Press.

Blog, E. O. N. (2010). *New aspects of brain research reveals impact of VR training.* Retrieved from http://eonrealityblog.wordpress.com/2010/04/07/new-aspects-of-brain-research-reveals-impact-of-vr-training/

Boehner, K., DePaula, R., Dourish, P., & Sengers, P. (2007). How emotion is made and measured. *International Journal of Human-Computer Studies, 65*(4), 275–291. doi:10.1016/j.ijhcs.2006.11.016

Bolter, J. D., & Grusin, R. (2000). *Remediation: Understanding New Media.* Cambridge, MA: MIT Press.

Bonanni, L., Alonso, J., Chao, N., Vargas, G., & Ishii, H. (2008, April 5-10). Handsaw: Tangible exploration of volumetric data by direct cut-plane projection. In *Proceedings of the Twenty-Sixth Annual SIGCHI Conference on Human Factors in Computing Systems (CHI '08),* Florence, Italy (pp. 251-254). New York: ACM Publishing. Retrieved from http://doi.acm.org/10.1145/1357054.1357098

Bonanni, L., Xiao, X., Hockenberry, M., Subramani, P., Ishii, H., Seracini, M., et al. (2009, April 4-9). Wetpaint: Scraping through multi-layered images. In *Proceedings of the 27th international Conference on Human Factors in Computing Systems (CHI '09),* Boston (pp. 571-574). Retrieved from http://doi.acm.org/10.1145/1518701.1518789

Bouillot, N., Wozniewski, M., Settel, Z., & Cooperstock, J. R. (2007). A mobile wireless augmented guitar. In *Proceedings of the 7th International Conference on New Interfaces for Musical Expression NIME '07,* Genova, Italy.

Bradshaw, P. V. (1941). *I wish I could draw (a system of art teaching by natural methods).* London, UK: The Studio.

Bridson, R., & Müller, M. F. (2007, August). Fluid simulation. In *Proceedings of the ACM SIGGGRAPH Course Notes* (pp. 1-81). New York, NY: ACM Press.

Broll, W., Lindt, I., Ohlenburg, J., Wittkämper, M., Yuan, C., & Novotny, T. (2004). ARTHUR: A collaborative augmented environment for architectural design and urban planning. *Journal of Virtual Reality and Broadcasting, 1*(1), 1–10.

Brostow, G. J., & Essa, I. (2001). Image-based motion blur for stop motion animation. In *Proceedings of the ACM 28th Annual Conference on Computer Graphics and Interactive Techniques* (pp. 107-116).

Brown, G. J. (2006). High dynamic range digital photography. *Royal Photographic Society Journal,* 428-431.

Brown, S. F. (2008). Hands-On Computing: How Multi-Touch Screens Could Change the Way We Interact with Computers and Each Other. *Scientific American, July.*

Bullivant, L. (2006). *Responsive Environments: Architecture, Art and Design.* London: Victoria and Albert Museum.

Burkhard, R. (2006). Is it Now Time to Establish Visualization Science as a Scientific Discipline? In *Proceedings of the 10th International Conference on Information Visualisation* (pp. 189-194). Washington, DC: IEEE Computer Society

Burns, M., & Finkelstein, A. (2008). Adaptive cutaways for comprehensible rendering of polygonal scenes. *ACM Transactions on Graphics, 27*(5), 1–7. doi:10.1145/1409060.1409107

Cakmakci, O., Bérard, F., & Coutaz, J. (2003). An augmented reality based learning assistant for electric bass guitar. In *Proceedings of the 10th International Conference on Human-Computer Interaction (HCI International 2003)*, Crete, Greece.

Calder, A. (1952). Temoignages pour l'art abstrait. In Alvard, J., & Gindertael, R. (Eds.), *Editions art d'aujourd'hui*. Paris, France: Editions d'Art Charles Moreau.

Cameron, M. (2008). *Introduction to the history of photography*. Retrieved from http://photographyhistory.blogspot.com/2008/01/julia-margaret-cameron.html

Canoa, M., Classa, Q., & Polich, J. (2009). Affective valence, stimulus attributes, and P300: Color vs. black/white and normal vs. scrambled images. *International Journal of Psychophysiology*, *71*(1), 17–24. doi:10.1016/j.ijpsycho.2008.07.016

Capon, R. (1984). *Basic drawing* (p. 47). London, UK: Batsford.

Card, S., Mackinlay, J., & Sheniderman, B. (1999). *Readings in Information Visualization: Using vision to think*. San Francisco: Morgan Kaufmann.

Carter, D. A., & Diaz, J. (1999). *The Elements of Pop-up: A Pop-up Book for Aspiring Paper Engineers*. New York: Little Simon.

Carter, R. (2009). *The human brain book*. New York, NY: Darling Kindersley.

Cartwright, J., Gonzalez, D., Piro, O., & Stanzial, D. (2002). Aesthetics, dynamics, and musical scales: A golden connection. *Journal of New Music Research*, *31*, 51–58. doi:10.1076/jnmr.31.1.51.8099

Cassinelli, A., & Ishikawa, M. (2005, July 31-August 4). Khronos projector. In D. Cox (Ed.), *ACM SIGGRAPH 2005 Emerging Technologies*, Los Angeles (pp. 10). New York: ACM Publishing. Retrieved from http://doi.acm.org/10.1145/1187297.1187308

Cawthon, N., & Vande Moere, A. (2007). The Effect of Aesthetic on the Usability of Data Visualization. In *Proceedings of the 11th International Conference on Information Visualisation* (pp. 637-643). Washington, DC: IEEE Computer Society.

Chalmers, M. (1996, October 27-November 1). A Linear Iteration Time Layout Algorithm for Visualising High-Dimensional Data. In *Proceedings of IEEE Visualization*, San Francisco (pp. 127-132).

Chalmers, M., & Chitson, P. (1992, June 23). Bead: Explorations in Information Visualisation. In *Proceedings of SIGIR '92*, Copenhagen, Denmark (pp. 330-337). ACM Publishing.

Chaouachi, M., Heraz, A., Jraidi, I., & Frasson, C. (2009). Influence of dominant electrical brainwaves on learning performance. In *Proceedings of the World Conference on E-Learning in Corporate, Government, Healthcare and Higher Education*, Montreal, QC, Canada.

Chapman, J. G. (1873). *The American drawing-book: A manual for the amateur, and basis of study for the professional artist: Especially adapted to the use of public and private schools, as well as home instruction*. New York, NY: A.S. Barnes & Co.

Chatani, M. (1985). *Origamic Archtecture Toranomaki*. Tokyo: Shokokusha.

Chen, L. O. (2006). *World of colour emotion*. Retrieved May 22, 2008, from http://colour-emotion.co.uk/whats.html

Chen, Y.-X., Boring, S., & Butz, A. (in press). How Last.fm Illustrates the Musical World: User Behavior and Relevant User-Generated Content. In *Proceedings of the International Workshop on Visual Interfaces to the Social and Semantic Web*.

Cheng, R. (2006, August 31). No-contact technology. *Wall Street Journal*.

Chen, L., Xie, X., Fan, X., Ma, W.-Y., Zhang, H.-J., & Zhou, H. (2003). A visual attention model for adapting images on small devices. *Multimedia Systems*, *9*(4), 353–364. doi:10.1007/s00530-003-0105-4

Chittaro, L., Gatla, V. K., & Venkataraman, S. (2005). The interactive 3d breakaway map: A navigation and examination aid for mult-ifloor 3d worlds. In *Proceedings of CW '05: 2005 International Conference on Cyberworlds* (pp. 59-66). Washington, DC: IEEE Computer Society.

Chorin, A. J., & Marsden, J. E. (1998). *A Mathematical Introduction to Fluid Mechanics* (3rd ed.). Berlin: Springer.

Cleempoel, K., & Van, Q. A. (2008). The influence of lighting in the build environment: a study to analyse human behaviour and perception as measured by mood and observation. In *Proceedings of the Conference on Measuring Behavior*, Maastricht, The Netherlands (pp. 385-388).

Cline, D., Cardon, D., & Egbert, P. K. (2005). *Fluid flow for the rest of us: Tutorial of the marker and cell method in computer graphics.* Unpublished manuscript.

Clough, P., Müller, H., & Sanderson, M. (2004). *The CLEF 2004 cross-language image retrieval (Vol. image and video retrieval)*. Berlin, Germany: Springer-Verlag.

Codispoti, M., & De Cesarei, A. (2007). Arousal and attention: Picture size and emotional reactions. *Psychophysiology*, 680–686. doi:10.1111/j.1469-8986.2007.00545.x

Coffin, C., & Hollerer, T. (2006). *Interactive perspective cut-away views for general 3d scenes.* In *Proceedings of 3DUI '06: IEEE Symposium on 3D User Interfaces* (pp. 25-28).

Cohen, J., Olano, M., & Manocha, D. (1998). Appearance-preserving simplification. In *SIGGRAPH '98: Proceedings of the 25th Annual Conference on Computer Graphics and Interactive Techniques* (pp. 115-122). New York: ACM Publishing.

Cohen-Or, D., Chrysanthou, Y., Silva, C., & Durand, F. (2003). A survey of visibility for walkthrough applications. *IEEE Transactions on Visualization and Computer Graphics*, *9*(3), 412–431. doi:10.1109/TVCG.2003.1207447

Cohn, J. P. (2008). Citizen Science: Can Volunteers Do Real Research? *Bioscience*, *58*(3). doi:10.1641/B580303

Correa, V., Estupiñán, L., Garcia, Z., Jimenez, O., Fernanda Prada, L., & Rojas, A. (2007). Percepción visual del rango de color: Diferencias entre género y edad. *Revista Med de la Facultad de Medicina*, *15*(1), 7–14.

Cosgrove, D. (1985). Prospect, perspective and the evolution of the landscape idea. *Transactions of the Institute of British Geographers*, *10*(1), 45–62.

Coursaris, C., Swierenga, S., & Watrall, E. (2008). An empirical investigation of color temperature and gender effects on web aesthetic. *Journal of Usability Studies*, *3*(3), 103–117.

Crane, K., Llamas, I., & Tariq, S. (2007). Realtime Simulation and Rendering of 3D Fluids. In *GPU Gems 3* (1st ed., pp. 633-675). Reading, MA: Addison-Wesley.

Cruz-Neira, C., Sandin, D., DeFanti, T., Kenyon, R., & Hart, J. (1992). The CAVE: Audio visual experience automatic virtual environment. *Communications of the ACM*, *35*, 72–65. doi:10.1145/129888.129892

Cunningham, S. J., Bainbridge, D., & Falconer, A. (2006). 'More of an Art than a Science': Supporting the Creation of Playlists and Mixes. In *Proceedings of the 7th International Conference on Music Music Retrieval*. Retrieved October 02, 2009, from http://waikato.researchgateway.ac.nz/bitstream/10289/77/1/content.pdf

Cycling '. 74. (2009). *jit.repos*. Retrieved June 14, 2009, from http://www.cycling74.com/docs/max5/refpages/jit-ref/jit.repos.html

d'Alessando, C., Noisternig, M., Le Beux, S., Katz, B., Picinali, L., Jacquemin, C., et al. (2009). The ORA project: Audio-visual live electronics and the pipe organ. In *Proceedings of International Computer Music Conference ICMC 2009*, Montreal, Canada.

Da Costa, C. (2009). *EON's ICube is the apple of virtual reality.* Retrieved from http://www.gadgetreview.com/2009/04/eons-icube-is-the-apple-of-virtual-reality-video.html#ixzz0uFicOgl

Dalgarno, B., Hedberg, J., & Harper, B. (2002). The contribution of 3D environments to conceptual understanding. In *Proceedings of the Annual Conference of the Australasian Society for Computers in Learning in Tertiary Education*, Auckland, New Zealand.

Dalgarno, B., & Harper, B. (2004). User control and task authenticity for spatial learning in 3D environments. *Australian Journal of Educational Technology*, *20*(1), 1–17.

Damasio, A. (1994). *Descartes error, emotion, reason and the human brain.* New York, NY: Penguin Press.

Damjanovski, V. (2005). *CCTV: Networking and digital technology.* Amsterdam, The Netherlands: Elsevier. Butterworth: Heinemann.

Darles, E., Crespin, B., Ghazanfarpour, D., & Gonzato, J. (2011). A survey of ocean simulation and rendering techniques in computer graphics. *Computer Graphics Forum*, *30*, 43–60. doi:10.1111/j.1467-8659.2010.01828.x

Dauger Research. (2005). *Fresnel diffraction.* Retrieved from http://daugerresearch.com/fresnel/index.shtml

Davies, A., & Dalgarno. B. (2009). Learning fire investigation the clean way: The virtual experience. *Australasian Journal of Educational Technology, 25*(1).

Dede, C. (2007). Reinventing the role of information and communications technologies in education. *Yearbook of the National Society for the Study of Education, 106*(2), 11–38.

Dehlinger, H. (2004). *Zeichnungen.* Kassel, Germany: Kassel University Press.

Dehlinger, H. (2007). On fine art and generative line drawings. *Journal of Mathematics and the Arts, 1*(2), 97–111.

Delahunt, M. R. (2010). *Rhythm: ArtLex art dictionary.* Retrieved from http://www.artlex.com

DeMenthon, D., & Davis, L. S. (1992). Model-based object pose in 25 lines of code. In *Proceedings of the European Conference on Computer Vision* (pp. 335-343).

Desain, P., & Honing, H. (1992). Music, Mind, and Machine: Studies in Computer Music, Music Cognition, and Artificial Intelligence (Kennistechnologie). *Thesis Pub.* ISBN-10: 9051701497.

Desain, P., & Honing, H. (1996). Physical motion as a metaphor for timing in music: The final ritard. In *Proceedings of the 1996 International Computer Music Conference,* San Francisco (pp. 458-460). ICMA.

Dexter, E. (2005). *Vitamin D: New Perspectives in Drawing.* London: Phaidon Press.

Dias, J. M. S. et al. (2007). CAVE-HOLLOWSPACE do Lousal – Princípios teóricos e desenvolvimento. *Encontro Português de Computação Gráfica, 15.*

Dias, J. M. S., & Bastos, R. (2006). An optimized marker tracking system. In *Proceedings of the 12th Eurographics Symposium on Virtual Environments* (pp. 1-4).

Dias, J. M. S., Jamal, N., Silva, P., & Bastos, R. (2004). ARTIC: Augmented reality tangible interface by colour evaluation. In *Proceedings of the Conference on Advances in Computer Graphics.*

Diep, E., & Jacob, R. J. K. (2004). Visualizing E-mail with a Semantically Zoomable Interface. In *Proceedings of the IEEE Symposium on Information Visualization* (pp. 215-216). Washington, DC: IEEE Computer Society.

Diepstraten, J., Weiskopf, D., & Ertl, T. (2003). Interactive cutaway illustrations. In *Proceedings of Eurographics, 2003,* 523–532.

Dodge, C., & Jerse, T. A. (1985). *Computer music* (pp. 86–88). New York, NY: Schirmer Books.

Dokken, T., Hagen, T., & Hjelmervik, J. (2005). The GPU as a high performance computational resource. In *Proceedings of the 21st Spring Conference on Computer Graphics* (pp. 21-26).

Dolcos, F. C. (2002). Event-related potentials of emotional memory: encoding pleasant, unpleasant, and neutral pictures. *Cognitive, Affective & Behavioral Neuroscience, 2*(3), 252–263. doi:10.3758/CABN.2.3.252

Dong, Z., Chen, W., Bao, H., Zhang, H., & Peng, Q. (2004). Real-time voxelization for complex polygonal models. In *Proceedings of PG '04: 12th Pacific Conference on Computer Graphics and Applications* (pp. 43-50).

Dorin, A., & Korb, K. (2007). Building Artificial Ecosystems from Artificial Chemistry. In *Proceedings of the 9th European Conference on Artificial Life* (pp. 103-112). Berlin, Germany: Springer-Verlag.

Dourish, P. (2001). Where the Action Is. Cambridge, MA: MIT Press.

Dragicevic, P. (2004, October 24-27). Combining crossing-based and paper-based interaction paradigms for dragging and dropping between overlapping windows. In *Proceedings of the 17th Annual ACM Symposium on User interface Software and Technology,* Santa Fe, NM (pp. 193-196). Retrieved from http://doi.acm.org/10.1145/1029632.1029667

Duda, R. O., & Hart, P. E. (1972). Use of the Hough transformation to detect lines and curves in pictures. *Communications of the ACM, 15,* 11–15. doi:10.1145/361237.361242

Dunn, P. (2006). *How to: Set up an IP-based camera surveillance system.* Retrieved from http://www.crn.com/news/channel-programs/192203498/how-to-set-up-an-ip-based-camera-surveillance-system.htm

Dunn, R. (2002, July 21-26). The virtual dig. In *Proceedings of the ACM SIGGRAPH 2002 Conference Abstracts and Applications,* San Antonio, TX (pp. 122-123). Retrieved from http://doi.acm.org/10.1145/1242073.1242139

Eakins, J. P. (2002). Towards intelligent image retrieval. *Pattern Recognition,* (35): 3–14. doi:10.1016/S0031-3203(01)00038-3

Edelman, G. M. (1992). *Bright air, brilliant fire: On the matter of the mind* (pp. 16–30). New York, NY: Basic Books.

Edelman, G. M. (2007). *Second nature: Brain science and human knowledge* (p. 262). New Haven, CT: Yale University Press.

Eilouti, B. (2009). A digital incorporation of ergonomics into architectural design. *International Journal of Architecture Design,* 235-253.

Eisemann, E., & Décoret, X. (2006). Fast Scene Voxelization and Applications. In *Proceedings of the 2006 ACM Symposium on Interactive 3D Graphics and Games* (pp. 70-78).

Eisenberg, M., Eisenberg, A., Blauvelt, G., Hendrix, S., Buechley, L., & Elumeze, N. (2005). Mathematical Crafts for Children: Beyond Scissors and Glue. In *Proceedings of the Art + Math = X, Special Year in Art & Mathematics International Conference* (pp. 61-64).

Ekman, P. (1992). A set of basic emotions. *Psychological Review,* 550–553. doi:10.1037/0033-295X.99.3.550

Ekman, P. (1999). Basic emotions. In Dalgleish, T., & Power, M. (Eds.), *Handbook of cognition and emotion.* Chichester, UK: John Wiley & Sons.

Elcott, S., Tong, Y., Kanso, E., Schröder, P., & Desbrun, M. (2007). Stable, circulation-preserving, simplicial fluids. *ACM Transactions on Graphics,* 26.

Elkins, J. (1985). *The poetics of perspective.* Ithaca, NY: Cornell University Press.

Elmqvist, N., Assarsson, U., & Tsigas, P. (2007). Employing dynamic transparency for 3d occlusion management: Design issues and evaluation. In *Proceedings of INTER-ACT,* 2007, 532–545.

Elmqvist, N., & Tsigas, P. (2008). A taxonomy of 3d occlusion management for visualization. *IEEE Transactions on Visualization and Computer Graphics,* 14(5), 1095–1109. doi:10.1109/TVCG.2008.59

Elsen, E., LeGresley, P., & Darve, E. (2008). Large calculation of the flow over a hypersonic vehicle using a GPU. *Journal of Computational Physics,* 227(24), 10148–10161. doi:10.1016/j.jcp.2008.08.023

Engeldrum, P. (2004). A theory of image quality: The image quality circle. *Journal of Imaging Science and Technology,* 48(5), 446–456.

Enright, D., & Fedkiw, R. (2002, July). Robust treatment of interfaces for fluid flows and computer graphics. In *Proceedings of the 9th International Conference on Hyperbolic Problems Theory, Numerics, Applications* (pp. 153-164).

Enright, D., Marschner, S., & Fedkiw, R. (2002). Animation and rendering of complex water surfaces. *ACM Transactions on Graphics,* 21, 736–744. doi:10.1145/566570.566645

Enser, P. (2000). Visual image retrieval: seeking the alliance of concept-based and content-based paradigms. *Journal of Information Science,* 26(4), 199–210. doi:10.1177/016555150002600401

Enser, P., & Armitage, L. (1997). Analysis of user need in image archives. *Journal of Information,* 23(4), 287–299. doi:10.1177/0165551974231830

Erbacher, R. F. (2007). Exemplifying the Inter-Disciplinary Nature of Visualization Research. In *Proceedings of the 12th International Conference on Information Visualisation* (pp. 623-630). Washington, DC: IEEE Computer Society.

European Network of Excellence in Evolutionary Computing. (2008). *EvoWeb.* Retrieved January 04, 2009, from http://evonet.lri.fr

Evans, B. (2005, June). Numbers to neurons: Digital synaesthesia. In *Proceedings of the Art+Math=X Conference,* Boulder, CO.

Evans, B. (2007a). Artist Statement. *Electronic Art and Animation Catalog, A Computer Graphics Annual Conference Series,* 264-265.

Evans, B. (2007b). *Visual Music*. Retrieved May 11, 2009, from http://www.lightspace.com

Evans, B. (2009). Loop theory. *Wig: Journal of Experimental Scholarship, 1*(1).

Everitt, C. (2001). *Introduction to interactive order-independent transparency*. NVIDIA Corporation.

Fairchild, M. D. (2002). Image quality measurement and modeling for digital photography. *Japan Hardcopy, 2002*, 318–319.

Faure Walker, J. (2006). *Painting the Digital River: How an Artist Learned to Love the Computer*. Upper Saddle River, NJ: Prentice Hall.

Fearing, P. (2000). Computer modelling of fallen snow. In *Proceedings of the 27th Annual Conference on Computer Graphics and Interactive Techniques* (pp. 37-46).

Fedkiw, R., Stam, J., & Jensen, H. W. (2001, August). Visual simulation of smoke. In *Proceedings of SIGGRAPH Computer Graphics Annual Conference* (pp. 15-22). New York: ACM Publishing.

Fedkiw, R. (2002). Coupling an Eulerian fluid calculation to a Lagrangian solid calculation with the ghost fluid method. *Journal of Computational Physics, 175*(1), 200–224. doi:10.1006/jcph.2001.6935

Feiner, S., & Seligmann, D. (1992). Cutaways and ghosting: satisfying visibility constraints in dynamic 3D illustrations. *The Visual Computer, 8*(5), 292–302. doi:10.1007/BF01897116

Feininger, A. (1961). *Die hohe Schule der Fotografie*. Düsseldorf und Wien, Germany: ECON.

Feldman, J. A. (2006). *From molecule to metaphor: A neural theory of language* (p. 5). Cambridge, MA: MIT Press.

Fels, S., Nishimoto, K., & Mase, K. (1998). Musikalscope: A graphical musical instrument. *IEEE MultiMedia, 5*(3), 26–35. doi:10.1109/93.713302

Feng, Z., Tang, M., Dong, J., & Chou, S. (2006). Real-time rain simulation. In W. Shen, K.-M. Chao, Z. Lin, J.-P. A. Barthès, & A. James (Eds.), *Proceedings of the 9th International Conference on Computer Supported Cooperative Work in Design II* (LNCS 3865, pp. 626-635).

Fernández, I., Carrera, P., Sánchez, F., & Paéz, D. (1997). Prototipos emocionales desde una perspectiva cultural. *Revista electrónica de Motivación y Emoción, 4*(8-9), 1-14.

Fields, R. D. (2009). *The other brain: From dementia to schizophrenia, how new discoveries about the brain are revolutionizing medicine and science*. New York, NY: Simon & Schuster.

Fishwick, P. (Ed.). (2006). *Aesthetic Computing*. Cambridge, MA: MIT Press.

Fitzgibbon, A. W., & Fisher, R. B. (1995). A buyer's guide to conic fitting. In *Proceedings of the 5th British Machine Vision Conference* (Vol. 5, pp. 513-522).

Fleck, B. (2007). *Real-time rendering of water in computer graphics*. Unpublished manuscript.

Fonseca, D., Fernández, A., & García, O. (2008). Comportamiento plausible de agentes virtuales: Inclusión de parámetros de usabilidad emocional a partir de imágenes fotográficas. Extensión. *Revista Iberoamericana de Sistemas, Cibernética e Informática, 3*(2).

Fonseca, D., García, O., Duran, J., Pifarré, M., & Villegas, E. (2008). An image-centred "search and indexation system" based in user's data and perceived emotion. In *Proceedings of the 3rd ACM International Workshop on Human-centered Computing*, Vancouver, BC, Canada (pp. 27-34).

Fonseca, D., García, O., Pifarré, M., Villegas, E., & Duran, J. (2008). Propuesta gráfica de "clasificación y búsqueda emocional de imágenes por Internet" adaptadad para usuarios discapacitados o no expertos. *Iberoamerican Journal of Systemics Cybernetics and Informatics, 5*(2), 1–9.

Foster, N., & Fedkiw, R. (2001, August). Practical animation of liquids. In *Proceedings of the 28th Annual Conference on Computer Graphics and Interactive Techniques* (pp. 23-30). New York, NY: ACM Press.

Frau, S., Roberts, J. C., & Boukhelifa, N. (2005). Dynamic coordinated email visualization. In V. Skala (Ed.), *Proceedings of the 13th International Conference on Computer Graphics, Visualization and Computer Vision*, Plzen, Czech Republic (pp. 187-193).

Frosio, I., & Borghese, N. A. (2008). Real-time accurate circle fitting with occlusions. *International Journal of Pattern Recognition, 41*(3), 1041–1055. doi:10.1016/j.patcog.2007.08.011

Fruchterman, T. M. J., & Reinhold, E. M. (1991). Graph Drawing by Force-directed Placement. *Software, Practice & Experience, 21*(11), 1129–1164. doi:10.1002/spe.4380211102

Fry, B. (2008). *Visualizing Data: Exploring and Explaining Data with the Processing Environment*. Sebastopol, CA: O'Reilly.

Gann, D., & Dodgson, M. (2008). Innovate with vision. *Ingenia, 36*, 45–48.

Gansner, E. R., & North, S. C. (1998). Improved forced-directed layout. In *Proceedings of the 6th Symposium on Graph Drawing* (pp. 364-374). New York: Springer.

Garg, K., Krishnan, G., & Nayar, S. (2007). Material based splashing of water drops. In *Proceedings of the Eurographics Symposium on Rendering*.

Garg, K., & Nayar, S. K. (2004). Detection and removal of rain from videos. In *Proceedings of the IEEE Conference on Computer Vision and Pattern Recognition, 1*, 528–535.

Garner, S. (Ed.). (2008). *Writing on Drawing: Essays on Drawing Practice and Research*. Bristol: Intellect.

Gaviria, A. R. (2008). When Is Information Visualization Art? Determining the Critical Criteria. *Leonardo, 41*(5), 479–482. doi:10.1162/leon.2008.41.5.479

Geiss, R. (n.d.). *Milkdrop*. Retrieved November 5, 2009, from http://www.nullsoft.com/free/milkdrop

Gendlin, E. T. (1997). *Experiencing and the Creation of Meaning: A Philosophical and Psychological Approach to the Subjective*. Evanston, IL: Northwestern University Press.

Genov, A., Schnall, S., & Laird, J. (1999). *In search of the intrinsic emotional meaning of color - Implications for design*. Retrieved June 18, 2008, from http://www.emotion-research.net

Gernsheim, H. (1975). *Julia Margaret Cameron: Her life and photographic work*. New York, NY: Millerton.

Gerzon, M. A. (1973). Periphony: With-height sound reproduction. *Journal of the Audio Engineering Society. Audio Engineering Society, 21*(1), 2–10.

Gilovich, T., Vallone, R., & Tversky, A. (1985). The hot hand in basketball: On the misperception of random sequences. *Cognitive Psychology, 17*, 295–314. doi:10.1016/0010-0285(85)90010-6

Gjermundsen, A. (2009). *LBM vs. SOR solvers on GPUs for real-time snow simulations*. Unpublished master's thesis, Norwegian University of Science and Technology, Trondheim, Soer-Troendelag, Norway.

Glass, F. J. (1920). *Drawing design and craft-work, for teachers, students, etc*. London, UK: Batsford.

Glassner, A. (1998). *Interactive Pop-up Card Design*. Miscrosoft Tech. Rep.

Glassner, A. (2002). Interactive Pop-up Card Design, 1. *IEEE Computer Graphics and Applications, 22*(1), 79–86. doi:10.1109/38.974521

Glassner, A. (2002). Interactive Pop-up Card Design, 2. *IEEE Computer Graphics and Applications, 22*(2), 74–85. doi:10.1109/38.988749

Golder, S. A., & Huberman, B. A. (2006). Usage Patterns of Collaborative Tagging Systems. *Journal of Information Science, 32*(2), 198–208. doi:10.1177/0165551506062337

Golub, G. H., & Van Loan, C. F. (1993). *Matrix computations*. Baltimore, MD: Johns Hopkins University Press.

Gordon, W. J. J. (1961). *Synectics* (pp. 33–37). New York, NY: Harper & Row.

Gosling, J., Joy, B., Steele, G., & Bracha, G. (2005). *Java(TM) Language Specification* (3rd ed.). Reading, MA: Addison-Wesley.

Grau, O. (2004). *Virtual Art: From Illusion to Immersion*. Cambridge, MA: MIT Press.

Grau, O. (Ed.). (2007). *Media Art Histories*. Cambridge, MA: MIT Press.

Greffou, S., Bertone, A., Hanssens, J.-M., & Faubert, J. (2008). Development of visually driven postural reactivity: A fully immersive virtual reality study. *Journal of Vision (Charlottesville, Va.), 8*(11), 1–10.

Grenacre, M. (2007). [Barcelona, Spain: Apuntes UOC.]. *Estadistica, 1*.

Gross, F. (2002). Mathieu paints a picture. *Journal of the City University of New York's Graduate Center Ph.D. Program in Art History, 8*.

Hable, J., & Rossignac, J. (2005). Blister: Gpu-based rendering of boolean combinations of free-form triangulated shapes. *ACM Transactions on Graphics, 24*(3), 1024–1031. doi:10.1145/1073204.1073306

Halpin, H., Robu, V., & Shepherd, H. (2007). The complex dynamics of collaborative tagging. In *Proceedings of the 16th International Conference on World Wide Web* (pp. 211-220). New York: ACM Press.

Halvey, M. J., & Keane, M. T. (2007). An assessment of tag presentation techniques. In *Proceedings of the 16th International Conference on World Wide Web* (pp. 1313-1314). New York: ACM Press.

Han, J. Y. (2005, October 23-26). Low-cost multi-touch sensing through frustrated total internal reflection. In *Proceedings of the 18th Annual ACM Symposium on User interface Software and Technology,* Seattle, WA (pp. 115-118). New York: ACM Publishing. Retrieved from http://doi.acm.org/10.1145/1095034.1095054

Hansen, M. B. N. (2004). *New philosophy for new media*. Cambridge, MA: MIT Press.

Haralick, R. M., Joo, H., Lee, C. N., Zhuang, X., Vaidya, V. G., & Kim, M. B. (1989). Pose estimation from corresponding point data. *IEEE Transactions on Systems, Man, and Cybernetics, 19*, 1426–1446. doi:10.1109/21.44063

Harris, M. J. (2004). Fast Fluid Dynamics Simulation on the GPU. In *GPU Gems - Programming Techniques, Tips, and Tricks for Realtime Graphics*. Reading, MA: Addison-Wesley.

Harrison, B. L., Ishii, H., Vicente, K. J., & Buxton, W. A. (1995, May 7-11). Transparent layered user interfaces: An evaluation of a display design to enhance focused and divided attention. In I. R. Katz, R. Mack, L. Marks, M. B. Rosson, & J. Nielsen (Eds.), *Proceedings of the SIGCHI Conference on Human Factors in Computing Systems,* Denver, CO (pp. 317-324). New York: ACM Publishing. Retrieved from http://doi.acm.org/10.1145/223904.223945

Hartley, R., & Zisserman, A. (2003). *Multiple view geometry in computer vision*. Cambridge, UK: Cambridge University Press.

Hartman, N. W., & Bertoline, G. R. (2005). Spatial Abilities and Virtual Technologies: Examining the Computer Graphics Learning Environment. In *Proceedings of the 9th International Conference on Information Visualisation* (pp. 992-999). Washington, DC: IEEE Computer Society.

Hassan, M. Y., & Herrero, S. V. (2006). Improving tag-clouds as visual Music Retrieval interfaces. In *Proceedings of the International Conference on Multidisciplinary Information Sciences & Technologies*.

Hathaway, D. (1985). A Manifesto for Cyborgs: Science, Technology and Socialist-Feminism in the 1980s. *Socialist Review, 80*, 65–108.

Haumont, D., Debeir, O., & Sillion, F. (2003). Volumetric cell-and-portal generation. In *Proceedings of the Computer Graphics Forum* (pp. 3-22)

Havre, S., Hetzler, B., & Nowell, L. (2000). ThemeRiver: Visualizing Theme Changes over Time. In *Proceedings of IEEE Symposium on Information Visualization* (pp. 115-123). Washington, DC: IEEE Computer Society.

Hearst, M. A. (2008). *What's up with Tag Clouds?* Retrieved October 02, 2009, from http://www.perceptualedge.com/articles/guests/whats_up_with_tag_clouds.pdf

Hearst, M. A., & Rosner, D. (2008). Tag Clouds: Data Analysis Tool or Social Signaller? In *Proceedings of the 41th International Conference on System Sciences* (pp. 1-10). Washington, DC: IEEE Computer Society.

Heer, J. (2005). *Exploring Enron: Visual Data Mining of Email*. Retrieved January 2009, from http://jheer.org/enron

Heer, J., Card, S. K., & Landay, J. A. (2005). Prefuse: A Toolkit for Interactive Information Visualization. In *Proceedings of the SIGCHI Conference on Human Factors in Computing Systems* (pp. 421-430). New York: ACM.

Heikkila, J., & Silven, O. (1997). A four-step camera calibration procedure with implicit image correction. In *Proceedings of the Conference on Computer Vision and Pattern Recognition* (pp. 1106-1112).

He, J., Chen, X., Wang, Z., Cao, C., Yan, H., & Peng, Q. (2010). Real-time adaptive fluid simulation with complex boundaries. *The Visual Computer, 26*, 243–252. doi:10.1007/s00371-010-0426-1

Henden, C., Champion, E., Muhlberger, R., & Jacobson, J. (2008). A surround display warp-mesh utility to enhance player engagement. In *Proceedings of the 7th International Conference on Entertainment Computing* (pp. 46-56).

Hendrix, S. L. (2004). *Popup Workshop: Supporting and Observing Children's Pop-up Design.* Unpublished PhD dissertation, Department of Computer Science, University of Colorado.

Hendrix, S. L. (2007). *Popup Workshop.* Retrieved from http://l3d.cs.colorado.edu/~ctg/projects/popups/index.html

Hendrix, S. L., & Eisenberg, M. A. (2006). Computer-assisted pop-up design for children: computationally enriched paper engineering. *Advanced Technology for Learning, 3*(2), 119–127. doi:10.2316/Journal.208.2006.2.208-0878

Heppner, C., Benkofske, M., & Moritz, R. (2004). Mobile video: A study of quality perception. In *Proceedings of the Human Factors and Ergonomics Society 48th Annual Meeting*, New Orleans, LA (pp. 1865-1869).

Hérault, J. (2010). *Vision: Images, signals and neural networks.* Singapore: World Scientific.

Hewlett-Packard Company. (1983). *Interfacing and programming manual, HP7475A graphics plotter.* San Diego, CA: Hewlett-Packard Company.

Hinckley, K., Pausch, R., Goble, J. C., & Kassell, N. F. (1994, April 24-28). Passive real-world interface props for neurosurgical visualization. In C. Plaisant (Ed.), *Conference Companion on Human Factors in Computing Systems,* Boston, (pp. 232).New York: ACM Publishing. Retrieved from http://doi.acm.org/10.1145/259963.260443

Hoffman, H. S. (1989). *Vision and the art of drawing.* Upper Saddle River, NJ: Prentice Hall.

Hofstadter, D. (2001). Epilogue: Analogy as the core of cognition. In Gentner, D., Holyoak, K. J., & Kokinov, B. N. (Eds.), *The analogical mind: Perspectives from cognitive science* (pp. 499–538). Cambridge, MA: MIT Press.

Hollink, L. A., Wielinga, B., & Worring, M. (2004). Classification of user image descriptions. *International Journal of Human-Computer Studies, 61*(5), 601–626. doi:10.1016/j.ijhcs.2004.03.002

Hong, L., Muraki, S., Kaufman, A., Bartz, D., & He, T. (1997). Virtual voyage: interactive navigation in the human colon. In *SIGGRAPH '97: Proceedings of the 24th annual conference on Computer graphics and interactive techniques* (pp. 27-34).

Hong, S., Ahn, C., Nah, Y., & Choi, L. (2005). Searching color images by emotional concepts. In S. Shimojo, S. Ichii, T.-W. Ling, & K.-H. Song (Eds.), *Proceedings of the 3rd International Conference on Web and Communication Technologies and Internet-Related Social Issues* (LNCS 3597, p. 921).

Houtveen, J., Rietveld, S., Schoutrop, M., Spiering, M., & Brosschot, J. (2001). A repressive coping style and affective, facial and physiological responses to looking at emotional pictures. *International Journal of Psychophysiology, 42*, 265–277. doi:10.1016/S0167-8760(01)00150-7

Husserl, E. (1982). *Ideas pertaining to a pure phenomenology and to a phenomenological philosophy. Vols. 1-2. Collected works of Edmund Husserl.* The Hague, The Netherlands: M. Nijhoff.

Iglesias, A. (2004). Computer graphics for water modeling and rendering: a survey. *Future Generation Computer Systems, 20*, 1355–1374. doi:10.1016/j.future.2004.05.026

Ippolito, J. (2002). Ten Myths of Internet Art, Tenth New York Digital Salon. *Leonardo, 35*(5), 485–498. doi:10.1162/002409402320774312

Irving, G., Guendelman, E., Losasso, F., & Fedkiw, R. (2006). Efficient simulation of large bodies of water by coupling two and three dimensional techniques. *ACM Transactions on Graphics, 25*(3), 805–811. doi:10.1145/1141911.1141959

Ishak, E. W., & Feiner, S. K. (2004, October 24-27). Interacting with hidden content using content-aware free-space transparency. In *Proceedings of the 17th Annual ACM Symposium on User interface Software and Technology,* Santa Fe, NM (pp. 189-192). New York: ACM Publishing. Retrieved from http://doi.acm.org/10.1145/1029632.1029666

Ishii, H., & Ullmer, B. (1997, March 22-27). Tangible bits: Towards seamless interfaces between people, bits and atoms. In S. Pemberton (Ed.), *Proceedings of the SIGCHI Conference on Human Factors in Computing Systems*, Atlanta, GA (pp. 234-241). New York: ACM Publishing. Retrieved from http://doi.acm.org/10.1145/258549.258715

Ittelson, W. H. (2007). The Perception of Nonmaterial Objects and Events. *Leonardo, 40*(3), 279–283. doi:10.1162/leon.2007.40.3.279

Itten, J. (1961). *Kunst der Farbe*. Ravensburg, Germany: Otto Maier Verlag.

Iwasaki, K., Dobashi, Y., Yoshimoto, F., & Nishita, T. (2008). GPU-based rendering of point-sampled water surfaces. *The Visual Computer, 24*(2), 77–84. doi:10.1007/s00371-007-0186-8

Jacobson, M. J. (2010). *Learning in virtual reality environments*. Retrieved from http://eonrealityblog.wordpress.com/2010/02/28/learning-in-virtual-reality-environments/

Jacobson, N., & Bender, W. (1996). Color as a determined communication. *IBM Systems Journal*, 526–538. doi:10.1147/sj.353.0526

Jacquemin, C. (2008). Allegra: A new instrument for bringing interactive graphics to life. In *Proceedings of the 16th ACM International Conference on Multimedia* (pp. 961-964). New York: ACM Publishing.

Jacquemin, C., Planes, B., & Ajaj, R. (2007). Shadow casting for soft and engaging immersion in augmented virtuality artworks. In *Proceedings of 9th ACM Confernece on Multimedia 2007*, Augsburg, Germany. Jordà, S. (2003). Interactive music systems for everyone: Exploring visual feedback as a way for creating more intuitive, efficient and learnable instruments. In *Proceedings of the Stockholm Music Acoustics Conference (SMAC 03)*, Stockholm, Sweden.

Jacquemin, C., & Gagneré, G. (2007). Revisiting the Layer/Mask Paradigm for Augmented Scenery. *International Journal of Performance Arts and Digital Media, 2*(3), 237–258. doi:10.1386/padm.2.3.237_1

Jaxtheimer, B. W. (1962). *How to paint and draw* (p. 34). London, UK: Thames & Hudson.

Jay, M. (1999). Scopic regimes of modernity. In Foster, H. (Ed.), *Vision and visuality* (pp. 2–23). New York, NY: New Press.

Johnson, L., Smith, R., Levine, A., & Haywood, K. (2010). *The 2010 horizon report: K-12 edition*. Austin, TX: The New Media Consortium.

Johnson, M. (2007). *The meaning of the body: Aesthetics of human understanding*. Chicago, IL: University of Chicago Press.

Jon Peddie Research. (2010). *CAD report*. Retrieved from http://www.jonpeddie.com/publications/cad_report/

Jones, M., & Satherley, R. (2001). Using distance fields for object representation and rendering. In *Proceedings of Eurographics, 2001*, 37–44.

Jordà, S., Geiger, G., Alonso, M., & Kaltenbrunner, M. (2007). The ReacTable: exploring the synergy between live music performance and tabletop tangible interfaces. In *Proceedings of the 1st International Conference on Tangible and Embedded Interaction TEI '07* (pp. 139-146). New York: ACM.

Kac, E. (2006). *Signs of Life: Bio Art and Beyond*. Cambridge, MA: MIT Press.

Kandel, E. R. (2006). *In search of memory: The emergence of a new science of mind*. New York, NY: W. W. Norton & Company.

Kaneda, K., Ikeda, S., & Yamashita, H. (1999). Animation of water droplets moving down a surface. *Journal of Visualization and Computer Animation, 10*(1), 15–26. doi:10.1002/(SICI)1099-1778(199901/03)10:1<15::AID-VIS192>3.0.CO;2-P

Karjalainen, M., Valimi, V., & Tolonen, T. (1998). Plucked String Models: From the Karplus-Strong Algorithm to Digital Waveguides and Beyond. *Computer Music Journal, 22*(3), 17–32. doi:10.2307/3681155

Karplus, K., & Strong, A. (1983). Digital Synthesis of Plucked String and Drum Timbres. *Computer Music Journal, 7*(2), 43–55. doi:10.2307/3680062

Kaser, O., & Lemire, D. (2007). Tag-cloud drawing: algorithms for cloud visualization. In *Proceedings of the International Conference on World Wide Web*. New York: ACM Press.

Kato, H., & Billinghurst, M. (1999). Marker tracking and HMD calibration for a video-based augmented reality conferencing system. In *Proceedings of the 2nd IEEE and ACM International Workshop on Augmented Reality*.

Kawabata, H., & Zeki, S. (2004). Neural correlates of beauty. *Journal of Neurophysiology, 91*(4), 1699–1705. doi:10.1152/jn.00696.2003

Keenan, C., Ignacio, L., & Sarah, T. (2007). Real-time simulation and rendering of 3D fluids. In *GPU gems 3* (pp. 633–675). Reading, MA: Addison-Wesley.

Kemp, H. S. (1990). *The science of art*. New Haven, CT: Yale University Press.

Kennedy, M. R. (2005). *Informing content and concept-based image indexing and retrieval through a study of image description*. Chapel Hill, NC: School of Information and Library Science, University of North Carolina.

Kerr, B. (2008). *TagOrbitals: tag index visualization*. Retrieved October 2, 2009, from http://domino.research. ibm.com/library/cyberdig.nsf/1e4115aea78b6e7c85256 b360066f0d4/8e1905dc8b000673852571d800558654? OpenDocument

Kim, T. (2008). Hardware-aware analysis and optimization of stable fluids. In *I3D '08: Proceedings of the 2008 Symposium on Interactive 3D Graphics and Games* (pp. 99-106). New York: ACM Publishing.

Kim, B., Liu, Y., Llamas, I., Jiao, X., & Rossignac, J. (2007). Simulation of bubbles in foam with the volume control method. *ACM Transactions on Graphics, 26*.

Kimme, C., Ballard, D. H., & Sklansky, J. (1975). Finding circles by an array of accumulators. *Communications of the ACM, 18*, 120–122. doi:10.1145/360666.360677

Kirsch, F., & Döllner, J. (2005). Opencsg: a library for image-based csg rendering. In *Proceedings USENIX 05* (p. 49).

Knoche, H., & Sasse, M. (2008). Getting the big picture on small screens: Quality of experience in mobile TV. *Interactive Digital Television: Technologies and Applications*, 242-260.

Knoche, H., McCarthy, J., & Sasse, M. (2005). Can small be beautiful? Assessing image resolution requirements for mobile TV. In *Proceedings of the 13th Annual ACM International Conference on Multimedia* (pp. 829-838).

Knowledgeworks. (2008). *2020 forecast: Creating the future of learning*. Retrieved from http://www.futureofed. org/pdf/forecast/2020_forecast.pdf

Konc, J., & Janežiči, D. (2007). An improved branch and bound algorithm for the maximum clique problem. *MATCH Communications in Mathematical and in Computer Chemistry, 58*, 569–590.

Kosara, R. (2007). Visualization Criticism – the Missing Link between Information Visualization and Art. In *Proceedings of the 11ᵗʰ International Conference on Information Visualisation* (pp. 631-636). Washington, DC: IEEE Computer Society.

Kosara, R., Bendix, F., & Hauser, H. (2006). Parallel Sets: Interactive exploration and visual analysis of categorical data. *Transactions on Visualization and Computer Graphics, 12*(4), 558–568. doi:10.1109/TVCG.2006.76

Kruegle, H. (2007). *CCTV surveillance: Analog and digital video practices and technology*. Amsterdam, The Netherlands: Elsevier Butterworth Heinemann.

Kuo, B. Y. L., Hentrich, T., Good, B. M., & Wilkinson, M. D. (2007). Tag clouds for summarizing web search results. In *Proceedings of the 16th International Conference on World Wide Web* (pp. 1203-1204). New York: ACM Press.

Kusamoto, K., Tadamura, K., & Tabuchi, Y. (2001). A method for rendering realistic rain-fall animation with motion of view. *IPSJ SIG, 2001*(106), 21-26.

Labs, J. H. (n. d.). *Java imaging processing*. Retrieved from http://www.jhlabs.com/ip/blurring.html

Lagus, K., Honkela, T., Kaski, S., & Kohonen, T. (1996, August 2-4). Self-Organizing Maps of Document Collections: A New Approach to Interactive Exploration. In *Proceedings of KDD '96: Second International Conference on Knowledge Discovery and Data Mining*, Portland, OR (pp. 238-243).

Lakoff, G., & Núñez, R. E. (2001). *Where Mathematics Comes from: How the Embodied Mind Brings Mathematics Into Being*. New York: Basic Books.

Lakoff, G. (1990). The Invariance Hypothesis: Is Abstract Reason Based on Image-Schemas? *Cognitive Linguistics, 1*(1), 39–74. doi:10.1515/cogl.1990.1.1.39

Lakoff, G., & Johnson, M. (1980). *Metaphors we live by*. Chicago, IL: University of Chicago Press.

Lakoff, G., & Johnson, M. (1999). *Philosophy in the flesh: The embodied mind and its challenge to western thought*. New York, NY: Basic Books.

Lang, P., Bradley, M., & Cuthbert, B. (2005). *International Affective Picture System (IAPS): Affective ratings of pictures and instruction manual*. Gainesville, FL: University of Florida.

Lang, P., Greenwald, M., Bradley, M., & Hamm, A. (1993). Looking at pictures: affective, facial, visceral, and behavioral reactions. *Psychophysiology*, 261–273. doi:10.1111/j.1469-8986.1993.tb03352.x

Latto, R. (1995). The brain of the beholder. In *The artful eye* (pp. 66–94). Oxford, UK: Oxford University Press.

Lau, A., & Vande Moere, A. (2007). Towards a Model of Information Aesthetics in Information Visualization. In *Proceedings of the 11th International Conference on Information Visualisation* (pp. 87-92). Washington, DC: IEEE Computer Society.

Lavie, T., & Tractinsky, N. (2004). Assessing dimensions of perceived visual aesthetics of web sites. *International Journal of Human-Computer Studies, 60*(3), 269–298. doi:10.1016/j.ijhcs.2003.09.002

LaViola, J. J., Jr., Feliz, D. A., Keefe, D. F., & Zeleznik, R. C. (2001). Hands-free multi-scale navigation in virtual environments. In *Proceedings of the Symposium on Interactive 3D Graphics '01* (pp. 9-15).

LeDoux, J. (2002). *The synaptic self: How our brains become who we are*. New York, NY: Penguin Books.

Lee, Y. T., Tor, S. B., & Soo, E. L. (1996). Mathematical modelling and simulation of pop-up books. *Journal of Computer Graphics, 20*(1), 21–31. doi:10.1016/0097-8493(95)00089-5

Lengler, R. (2006). Identifying the Competencies of 'Visual Literacy' - a Prerequisite for Knowledge Visualization. In *Proceedings of the 10th International Conference on Information Visualisation* (pp. 232-236). Washington, DC: IEEE Computer Society.

Lengler, R., & Eppler, M. (2006). *Towards A Periodic Table of Visualization Methods for Management*. Retrieved April 22, 2009, from http://www.visual-literacy. org/periodic_table/periodic_table.pdf

Levin, G., & Lieberman, Z. (2004). In-situ speech visualization in real-time interactive installation and performance. In *Proceedings of the 3rd international symposium on Non-photorealistic animation and rendering NPAR '04* (pp. 7-14). New York: ACM.

Levkowitz, H., Holub, R., Meyer, G., & Robertson, P. (1991). Color vs. black-and-white in visualization. In *Proceedings of the 2nd Conference on Visualization*, San Diego, CA (pp. 336-339).

Levoy, M., Pulli, K., Curless, B., Rusinkiewcz, S., Koller, D., Pereira, L., et al. (2000). The digital Michelangelo project: 3D scanning of large statues. In *Proceedings of the 27th Annual Conference on Computer Graphics and interactive Techniques* (pp. 131-144). Retrieved from http://doi.acm.org/10.1145/344779.344849

Lewis Charles Hill, I. (2006). *Synesthetic Music Experience Communicator*. Unpublished doctoral dissertation, Iowa State University, Ames, IA.

Leybovich, I. (2010). *RFID market projected to grow in 2010*. Retrieved from http://news.thomasnet.com/IMT/archives/2010/03/radio-frequency-identification-rfid-market-projected-to-grow-in-2010-beyond.html

Li, R., Bao, S., Yu, Y., Fei, B., & Su, Z. (2007). Towards effective browsing of large scale social annotations. In *Proceedings of the 16th International Conference on World Wide Web* (pp. 943-952). New York: ACM Press.

Lieberman, H., & Liu, H. (2002). Adaptative linking between text and photos using common sense reasoning. In P. De Bra, P. Brusilovsky, & R. Conejo (Eds.), *Second International Conference on Adaptive Hypermedia and Adaptive Web-Based Systems* (LNCS 2347, pp. 2-11).

Lieser, W. (2009). *Digital art*. Königswinter, Germany: H. Fullmann.

Lieser, W. (2010). *The World of Digital Art*. Potsdam, Germany: Ullmann.

Lim, J.-H., & Jin, J. (2005). A structured learning framework for content-based image indexing and visual query. *Multimedia Systems*, *10*(4). doi:10.1007/s00530-004-0158-z

Livingstone, M. (2002). *Vision and art: The biology of seeing*. New York, NY: Harry N. Abrams.

Lohmann, S., Ziegler, J., & Tetzlaff, L. (2009). Comparison of Tag Cloud Layouts: Task-Related Performance and Visual Exploration. In *Proceedings of the 12th International Conference on Human-Computer Interaction* (pp. 392-404). New York: Springer.

Loke, L., Larssen, A. T., Robertson, T., & Edwards, J. (2007). Understanding movement for interaction design: frameworks and approaches. *Personal and Ubiquitous Computing*, *11*(8), 691–701. doi:10.1007/s00779-006-0132-1

Losasso, F., Gibou, F., & Fedkiw, R. (2004). Simulating water and smoke with an octree data structure. *ACM Transactions on Graphics*, *23*, 457–462. doi:10.1145/1015706.1015745

Losasso, F., Shinar, T., Selle, A., & Fedkiw, R. (2006). Multiple interacting liquids. *ACM Transactions on Graphics*, *25*, 812–819. doi:10.1145/1141911.1141960

Lovejoy, M. (2004). *Digital Currents: Art in the Electronic Age* (3rd ed.). London: Routledge.

Lowe, D. G. (1991). Fitting parameterized three-dimensional models to images. *IEEE Transactions on Pattern Analysis and Machine Intelligence*, *13*, 441–450. doi:10.1109/34.134043

Lynn, G. (1999). *Animate Form*. New York: Princeton Architectural Press.

Macarthur, J. (2007). *The Picturesque: Architecture, disgust and other irregularities*. London, UK: Routledge.

Maeda, J. (2004). *Creative Code: Aesthetics + Computation*. London: Thames & Hudson.

Mandic, M., & Kerne, A. (2004). faMailiar & Intimacy-Based Email Visualization. In *Proceedings of the IEEE Symposium on Information Visualization* (pp. 14-14). Washington, DC: IEEE Computer Society.

Manovich, L. (2008). *Software Takes Command*. Retrieved April 26, 2009, from http://lab.softwarestudies.com/2008/11/softbook.html

Marin, L. (1984). *Utopics: Spatial play*. London, UK: Macmillan.

Marr, D., & Nishihara, H. K. (1978). Representation and recognition of the spatial organization of three-dimensional shapes. *Proceedings of the Royal Society of London. Series B. Biological Sciences*, *200*, 269–294. doi:10.1098/rspb.1978.0020

Marrin, T., & Paradiso, J. (1997). The Digital Baton: a Versatile Performance Instrument. In *Proceedings of the International Computer Music Conference ICMC 1997*.

Maruzewski, P., Le Touzé, D., Oger, G., & Avellan, F. (2010). SPH high-performance computing simulations of rigid solids impacting the free surface of water. *Journal of Hydraulic Research*, *48*, 126–134. doi:10.1080/00221686.2010.9641253

Massey, L. (2003). Configuring spatial ambiguity: Picturing the distance point from Alberti to anamorphosis. In Massey, L. (Ed.), *The treatise on perspective*. Washington, DC: National Gallery of Art.

Massumi, B. (2002). *Parables for the virtual, movement, affect, sensation*. Durham, NC: Duke University Press.

Mateo, J., & Sauter, F. (Eds.). (2007). *Natural Metaphor: Architectural Papers III*. Zurich, Switzerland: ACTAR & ETH Zurich.

Mathes, A. (2008). *Folksonomies - cooperative classification and communication through shared metadata*. Retrieved October 2, 2009, from http://www.adammathes.com/academic/computer-mediated-communication/folksonomies.html

Matthews, L. (2010). Virtual sites: Performance and materialization. *Technoetic Arts: A Journal of Speculative Research*, *8*(1), 55-65.

Matthews, L., & Perin, G. (2010, November). *The modern picturesque and techniques of adaptation.* Paper presented at the First International Conference on Transdisciplinary Imaging at the Intersections between Art, Science and Culture, Sydney, Australia.

Maturana, H. R., & Varela, F. J. (1980). Autopoiesis and Cognition: The Realization of the Living. In *Boston Studies in the Philosophy of Science* (Vol. 42). Dordrecht, The Netherlands: D. Reidel Publishing Company.

Maya, E. C., Quetzal, A. C., & Polich, J. (2009). Affective valence, stimulus attributes, and P300: Color vs. black/white and normal vs. scrambled images. *International Journal of Psychophysiology, 71*(1), 17–24. doi:10.1016/j.ijpsycho.2008.07.016

McConnell, J. (2008). *Computer graphics: Theory into practice.* Sudbury, MA: Jones and Bartlett.

McHugh, S. T. (2010). *Cambridge in color.* Retrieved from http://www.cambridgeincolour.com

McManus, I., Jones, A., & Cottrell, J. (1981). The aesthetics of colour. *Perception, 10*(6), 651–666. doi:10.1068/p100651

Merleau-Ponty, M. (1945). *Phenomenology of perception.* London: Routledge.

Micklewright, K. (2005). *Drawing: Mastering the language of visual expression.* London, UK: Laurence King.

Mikels, J. A., Fredrickson, B. L., Larkin, G. R., Lindberg, C. M., Maglio, S. J., & Reuter-Lorenz, P. A. (2005). Emotional category data on images from the IAPS. *Behavior Research Methods, 37*(4), 626–630. doi:10.3758/BF03192732

Miklós, B. (2004). *Real time fluid simulation using height fields.* Unpublished manuscript.

Miranda, E. R., & Wanderley, M. (2006). *New Digital Musical Instruments: Control and Interaction Beyond the Keyboard (Computer Music and Digital Audio Series).* Madison, WI: A-R Editions, Inc.

Mitani, J., & Suzuki, H. (2004). Computer aided design for origamic architecture models with polygonal representation. In *Proceedings of the Computer Graphics International Conference* (pp. 93-99).

Mitani, J., & Suzuki, H. (2003). Computer aided design for 180-degree flat fold origamic architecture with lattice-type cross sections. *Journal of Graphics Science of Japan, 37*(3), 3–8.

Mitani, J., & Suzuki, H. (2004). Making use of a CG based pop-up card design system for graphics science education. *Journal of Graphics Science of Japan, 38*(3), 3–8.

Mitani, J., Suzuki, H., & Uno, H. (2003). Computer aided design for origamic architecture models with voxel data structure. *Transactions of Information Processing Society of Japan, 44*(5), 1372–1379.

Mitchell, W. J. T. (2002). Imperial landscapes. In Mitchell, W. J. T. (Ed.), *Landscape and power* (pp. 5–34). Chicago, IL: University of Chicago Press.

Moggridge, B. (2007). *Designing Interactions.* Cambridge, MA: MIT Press.

Möller, C., & Seracini, M. (1996, August 4-9). The third dimension of "Ritratto di gentiluomo". In B. Blau, C. Dodsworth, L. Branagan, J. Ippolito, K. Musgrave, & W. Waggenspack (Eds.), *ACM SIGGRAPH 96 Visual Proceedings: the Art and interdisciplinary Programs of SIGGRAPH '96,* New Orleans, LA (pp. 11). Retrieved from http://doi.acm.org/10.1145/253607.253614

Moltó, J., Montañés, S., Poy, R., Segarra, P., Pastor, M., & Tormo, M. (1999). Un nuevo método para el estudio experimental de las emociones: El international affective picture system (IAPS). *Revista de Psicología General y Aplicada, 55*(1), 55–87.

Moreland, K., & Angel, E. (2003). The FFT on a GPU. In *Proceedings of the SIGGRAPH/Eurographics Workshop on Graphics Hardware* (pp. 112-119).

Morgan Spalter, A. (1998). *The Computer in the Visual Arts.* Boston, MA: Addison-Wesley Professional.

Morris, C., Ebert, D., & Rhengans, P. (1999, October 13-15). *An Experimental Analysis of the Pre-Attentiveness of Features in Chernoff Faces.* Paper presented at Applied Imagery Pattern Recognition '99, Washington, DC.

Morse, E. (1998). *Document Visualization.* Retrieved June 13, 2000, from http://www.lis.pitt.edu/~elm2/DocumentVisualization.htm

Mostafavi, M., & Leatherbarrow, D. (1993). *On Weathering: The Life of Buildings in Time*. Cambridge, MA: MIT Press.

Motokawa, Y., & Saito, H. (2006). Support system for guitar playing using augmented reality display. In *Proceedings of the 2006 Fifth IEEE and ACM International Symposium on Mixed and Augmented Reality (Ismar '06)* (pp. 243-244). Washington, DC: IEEE Computer Society.

Mouse, E., & Lewis, M. (1997). Why Information Retrieval Visualizations Sometimes Fail. In *Proceedings of the IEEE International Conference on Systems, Man, and Cybernetics* (Vol. 2, pp. 1680-1685). Washington, DC: IEEE Computer Society. Kerr, B. (2003). Thread arcs: An email thread visualization. In *Proceedings of the IEEE Symposium on Information Visualization* (pp. 27-38). Washington, DC: IEEE Computer Society.

Moutoussis, K., & Zeki, S. (1997). A direct demonstration of perceptual asynchrony in vision. *Proceedings. Biological Sciences*, *264*, 393–397. doi:10.1098/rspb.1997.0056

Mühlberger, A., Neumann, R., Wieser, M., & Pauli, P. (2008). The impact of changes in spatial distance on emotional responses. *Emotion (Washington, D.C.)*, 192–198. doi:10.1037/1528-3542.8.2.192

Müller, M. (2009, August). Fast and robust tracking of fluid surfaces. In *Proceedings of the ACM SIGGGRAPH/ EUROGRAPHICS Symposium on Computer Animation* (pp. 237-245). New York, NY: ACM Press.

Müller, M. F., Stam, J., James, D., & Thürey, N. (2008, August). Real time physics. In *Proceedings of the ACM SIGGGRAPH Course Notes* (pp. 1-90). New York, NY: ACM Press.

Müller, M., Charypar, D., & Gross, M. (2003, July). Particle-based fluid simulation for interactive applications. In *Proceedings of the ACM SIGGGRAPH/EUROGRAPHICS Symposium on Computer Animation* (pp. 154-159). Aire-la-Ville, Switzerland: Eurographics Association Press.

Muybridge, E. (1887). *Animal locomotion: An electrophotographic investigation of consecutive phases of animal movement*. Philadelphia, PA: J. B. Lippincott Company.

Nätterlund, M. (2008). *Water surface rendering*. Unpublished master's thesis, Umeå University, Umeå, Sweden.

Neal Brill, J. L. (2009). *Linking the Study of Visual Arts and Improved Reading Comprehension*. Unpublished master's thesis, University of Northern Colorado.

Newcombe, N. S. (2010). Picture this increasing: Math and science learning by improving spatial thinking. *American Educator*, 2010.

Newman, M., Barabási, A.-L., & Watts, D. J. (Eds.). (2006). *The structure and dynamics of networks*. Princeton, NJ: Princeton University Press.

Neyret, F., & Praizelin, N. (2001). Phenomenological simulation of brooks. In *Proceedings of the Eurographic Workshop on Computer Animation and Simulation* (pp. 53-64). New York: Springer-Verlag.

NI. (2011). *National instruments*. Retrieved July 5, 2011, from http://www.ni.com/

Nielsen, M. (2007). *Functionality in a second generation tag cloud*. Unpublished master's thesis, Gjøvik University College, Norway.

Noisternig, M., Sontacchi, A., Musil, T., & Höldrich, R. (2003). A 3D ambisonic based binaural sound reproduction system. In *Proceedings Audio Engineering Society AES 24th International Conference*, Banff, Canada.

Norman, D. A. (2002). Emotion and design: Attractive things work better. *Interactions Magazine*, *9*(4), 36–42.

North, M. M., North, S. M., & Coble, J. R. (1998). Virtual reality therapy: An effective treatment for psychological disorders. In Riva, G. (Ed.), *Virtual reality in neuro-psycho-physiology*. Amsterdam, The Netherlands: IOS Press.

Nvidia. (2007). *CUDA: Compute unified device architecture - programming guide*. Retrieved April 2, 2010, from http://developer.download.nvidia.com/compute/cuda/1 0/ NVIDIACUDAProgrammingGuide1.0.pdf

Olga's Gallery. (n. d.). *Joseph Mallor William Turner (1775-1851)*. Retrieved from http://www.abcgallery. com/T/turner/turner.html

Oliver, E. (2009). A survey of platforms for mobile networks research. *ACM SIGMOBILE Mobile Computing and Communications Review*, *12*(4), 7. doi:10.1145/1508285.1508292

Open, C. V. (2011). *Open computer vision library.* Retrieved July 5, 2011, from http://sourceforge.net/projects/opencvlibrary/

Panofsky, E. (1997). *Perspective as symbolic form.* New York, NY: Zone Books.

Paton, R. C., Nwana, H. S., Shave, M. J. R., Bench-Capon, T. J. M., & Hughes, S. (1991). Transfer of Natural Metaphors to Parallel Problem Solving Applications. In *Parallel Problem Solving from Nature* (LNCS 496, pp. 363-372).

Peachey, D. R. (1986). Modeling waves and surf. *ACM SIGGRAPH Computer Graphics*, *20*, 65–74. doi:10.1145/15886.15893

Perrett, D. I., Rolls, E. T., & Caan, W. (1990). Three stages in the classification of body movements by visual neurons. In Barlow, H., Blakemore, C., & Weston, M. (Eds.), *Images and understanding* (pp. 94–107). Cambridge, UK: Cambridge University Press.

Peters, G. (2007). Aesthetic Primitives of Images for Visualization. In *Proceedings of the 11ᵗʰ International Conference on Information Visualisation* (pp. 316-325). Washington, DC: IEEE Computer Society.

Peters, G. (2011). *Eyeszeit Fotografie.* Retrieved from http://www.eyeszeit.net

Peters, G. (2000). Theories of three-dimensional object perception- a survey. In *Recent research developments in pattern recognition* (*Vol. 1*, pp. 179–197). Kerala, India: Transworld Research Network.

Petitot, J. (2004). *Morphogenesis of meaning.* Bern, Switzerland: P. Lang.

Petzold, C. (2000). *Code: The hidden language of computer hardware and software.* Redmond, WA: Microsoft Press.

Pifarré, M., Sorribas, X., Villegas, E., Fonseca, D., & García, O. (2009). BLA (Bipolar Laddering) applied to YouTube. Performing postmodern psychology paradigms in user experience field. *Journal of Behavioral, Cognitive. Educational and Psychological Sciences*, *1*(2), 76–82.

Pintaric, T., & Kaufmann, H. (2007). Affordable infrared-optical pose-tracking for virtual and augmented reality. In *Proceedings of the Trends and Issues in Tracking for Virtual Environments Workshop.*

Pintaric, T., & Kaufmann, H. (2008). A rigid-body target design methodology for optical pose tracking systems. In *Proceedings of the 15th ACM Symposium on Virtual Reality Software and Technology* (pp. 73-76).

Popper, F. (2005). *From Technological to Virtual Art* (2ⁿᵈ ed.). London: Thames & Hudson.

Porras, M., & Pereyra, M. (2001). El valor psicológico del color y su uso en la comunicación. *HUELLAS-Búsquedas en Artes y Diseño*, (1), 141-145.

Porter, M. F. (2006). An algorithm for suffix stripping. *Program: electronic library and information systems, 14*(3), 211-218.

Porter, M. F. (1980). An algorithm for suffix stripping. *Program, 14*(3), 130–137.

Poupyrev, I., Berry, R., Billinghurst, M., Kato, H., Nakao, K., Baldwin, L., et al. (2001). Augmented Reality Interface for Electronic Music Performance. In *Proceedings of HCI 2001* (pp. 805-808).

POV-Ray Documentation. (2000). *Version 3.1g "Blob" POV-Ray Scene Language Help.*

Premoze, S., Tasdizen, T., Bigler, J., Lefohn, A. E., & Whitaker, R. T. (2003). Particle-based simulation of fluids. *Computer Graphics Forum*, *22*, 401–410. doi:10.1111/1467-8659.00687

Prensky, M. (2002). *What kids learn that's POSITIVE from playing video games.* http://www.cyber-spy.com/ebooks/ebooks/What-Kids-Learn-Thats-POSITIVE-from-Playing-Video-Games-(ebook).pdf

Provost, J. (2008). *Improved document summarization and tag clouds via singular value decomposition.* Unpublished master's thesis, Queen's University, Canada.

Puckette, M. S. (1996). Pure data: Another integrated computer music environment. In *Proceedings of the International Computer Music Conference ICMC 1996,* Hong Kong, China (pp. 37-41).

Puig-Centelles, A., Ripolles, O., & Chover, M. (2009). Creation and control of rain in virtual environments. *The Visual Computer, 25*(11), 1037–1052. doi:10.1007/s00371-009-0366-9

Ramachandran, V. S., & Gregory, R. L. (1978). Does colour provide an input to human motion perception? *Nature, 275,* 55–56. doi:10.1038/275055a0

Ramirez, O. (1999). Un nuevo método para el estudio experimental de las emociones: El international affective picture system (IAPS). *Revista de Psicología General y Aplicada, 55*(1), 55–87.

Rankin, H. R. (1924). *Pencil drawing* (p. 1). London, UK: Sir Isaac Pitman.

Raskar, R., & Beardsley, P. (2001). A self-correcting projector. In *Proceedings of the 2001 IEEE Computer Society Conference on Computer Vision and Pattern Recognition CVPR 2001,* Kauai, HI (pp. 504-508). Washington, DC: IEEE Computer Society.

Raynor, W. (2005). *Globalization and outsourcing in a flat, but unbalanced world.* Retrieved from http://www.newwork.com/Pages/Opinion/Raynor/Unbalanced.html

Real Vision Consultancy. (2009). *Re-creating natural environments using real-time 3D engines.* Retrieved from http://docs.google.com/viewer?a=v&q=cache:cDfULwxqUeUJ:www.realvision.ae/pdf/3D_engines_stereo3d.pdf+cryengine+cave+virtual+environment+stereoscopic&hl=en&gl=us&pid=bl&srcid=ADGEESiYLDqcWuKux9D_OGengCtli-HRFS_buk7hlDNzN1kOJm12HXh-4gzHz8yslVj3PueT71Fu5CIZ4tQ1jFUdrK6L5EIGf5miuA7Abosz-09ni_euekSysXA0wQ-CKH8sbDhYgoYGXQ&sig=AHIEtbQQTRQiDIdbTPk97ebbI4kT7JBhlg

Reas, C., & Fry, B. (2007). *Processing: A Programming Handbook for Visual Designers and Artists.* Cambridge, MA: MIT Press.

Recayte, P., & Bund, E. (2005). La imagen digital en la mediación Arquitecto-Usuario. In *Proceedings of the 9th Iberoamerican Congress on Digital Graphics,* Lima, Peru (pp. 1-5).

Reeves, B., Lang, A., Kim, E., & Tatar, D. (1999). The effects of screen size and message content or attention and arousal. *Media Psychology,* 49–67. doi:10.1207/s1532785xmep0101_4

Reeves, B., & Nass, C. (1996). *The media equation: How people treat computers, television, and new media like real people and places.* Cambridge, UK: Cambridge University Press.

Reeves, W. T. (1983). Particle systems: a technique for modeling a class of fuzzy objects. *ACM Transactions on Graphics, 2*(2), 91–108. doi:10.1145/357318.357320

Reinhard, E., Ward, G., Pattanaik, S., & Debevec, P. (2005). *High dynamic range imaging: Acquisition, display, and image-based lighting.* San Francisco, CA: Morgan Kauffman.

Rieser, M., & Zapp, A. (Eds.). (2008). *The New Screen Media: Cinema/art/narrative.* London: British Film Institute.

Rivadeneira, A. W., Gruen, D. M., Muller, M. J., & Millen, D. R. (2007). Getting our head in the clouds: toward evaluation studies of tagclouds. In *Proceedings of the SIGCHI Conference on Human Factors in Computing Systems* (pp. 995-998). New York: ACM.

Rocca, A. (2007). *Natural Architecture.* Princeton, NJ: Princeton Architectural Press.

Rocha, F., & Malloch, J. (2009). The Hyper-Kalimba: Developping an Augmented Instrument from a Performer's Perspective. In *Proceedings of the 6th Sound and Music Computing Conference SMC 2009,* Porto, Portugal (pp. 25-29).

Rohrer, M. R., Ebert, D. S., & Sibert, J. L. (1998, October 19-20). The Shape of Shakespeare: Visualizing Text using Implicit Surfaces. In *Proceedings Information Visualization 1998,* Durham, NC (pp. 121-129).

Rojansky, V. (1979). *Electromagnetism Fields and Waves.* Mineola, NY: Dover Publications.

Roscoe, S. (1991). The eyes prefer real images. In Ellis, S. (Ed.), *Pictoral communication in virtual and real environments* (pp. 577–585). London, UK: Taylor and Francis.

Rosenbaum, R., & Schumann, H. (2005). JPEG2000-based image communication for modern browsing techniques. In *Proceedings of the SPIE Image and Video Communications and Processing Conference* (pp. 1019-1030).

Rousseau, P., Jolivet, V., & Ghazanfarpour, D. (2006). Realistic real-time rain rendering. *Computers & Graphics*, *30*(4), 507–518. doi:10.1016/j.cag.2006.03.013

Rousseau, P., Jolivet, V., & Ghazanfarpour, D. (2008). GPU rainfall. *Journal of Graphics, GPU, and Game Tools*, *13*(4), 17–33. doi:10.1080/2151237X.2008.10129270

Rydmark, M., Kling-Petersen, T., Pascher, R., & Philip, F. (2001). 3D visualization and stereographic techniques for medical research and education. *Studies in Health Technology and Informatics*, *81*, 434–439.

Sabuda, R., & Carroll, L. (2003). *Alice's Adventures in Wonderland*. New York: Little Simon.

Sabuda, R., & Reinhart, M. (2005). *Encyclopedia Prehistorica: Dinosaurs*. Somerville, MA: Candlewick Press.

Sacks, O., & Wasserman, R. (1987). The painter who became color blind. *The New York Review of Books*, *34*, 25–33.

Salton, G. (1995). Automatic Analysis, Theme Generation, and Summarization of Machine-Readable Text. *Science*, *264*(3), 1421–1426.

Samiei, M., Dill, J., & Kirkpatrick, A. (2004). EzMail: using information visualization techniques to help manage email. In *Proceedings of the 8th International Conference on Information Visualisation* (pp. 477-482). Washington, DC: IEEE Computer Society.

Sammon, J. W. (1969). A non-linear mapping for data structure analysis. *IEEE Transactions on Computers*, *18*(5), 401–409. doi:10.1109/T-C.1969.222678

Santamaría, R., & Therón, R. (2008). Overlapping Clustered Graphs: Co-authorship Networks visualization. In *Proceedings of the 9th international Symposium on Smart Graphics* (pp.190-199). New York: Springer.

Santos, P., Buanes, A., & Jorge, J. (2006). PTrack: Introducing a novel iterative geometric pose estimation for a marker-based single camera tracking system. In *Proceedings of the IEEE Virtual Reality Conference* (pp. 143-150).

Santos, P., Stork, A., Buaes, A., Pereira, C., & Jorge, J. (2010). A real-time low-cost marker-based multiple camera tracking solution for virtual reality applications. *Journal of Real-Time Image Processing*, *5*(2), 121–128. doi:10.1007/s11554-009-0138-9

Sartre, J.-P. (1948). The search for the absolute. In Alberto, G. (Ed.), *Exhibition of sculptures, paintings, drawings*. New York, NY: Pierre Matisse Gallery.

Savard, J. (2009). *Colour filter array designs.* Retrieved from http://www.quadibloc.com/other/cfaint.htm

Scacchi, W., Nideffer, R., & Adams, J. (2008). A collaborative science learning game environment for informal science education: DinoQuest online. *New Frontiers for Entertainment Computing*, *279*, 71–82.

Schilling, M. A. (2005). A 'small-world' network model of cognitive insight. *Creativity Research Journal*, *17*(2-3), 131–154.

Schmalstieg, D., & Wagner, D. (2007). Experiences with Handheld Augmented Reality. In *Proceedings of the Symposium on Mixed and Augmented Reality* (pp. 12).

Schneider. (2011). *Schneider Kreuznach.* Retrieved July 5, 2011, from http://www.schneiderkreuznach.com

Schnoor, J. L. (2007). Citizen Science. *Environmental Science & Technology*, *41*(17), 5923–5923. doi:10.1021/es072599+

Scrogan, L. (2010). *Beyond the red carpet: 3D comes to school.* Retrieved from http://bvsd.org/bvs3d/Documents/BEYOND THE RED CARPET - BVS3D.pdf

Seifert, C., Kump, B., & Kienreich, W. (2008). On the beauty and usability of tag clouds. In *Proceedings of the 12th International Conference on Information Visualization* (pp.17-25). Washington, DC: IEEE Computer Society.

Sekuler, R., & Blake, R. (2002). *Perception* (4th ed.). Boston: McGraw Hill.

Sha, X. W. (2001). *Topological Media Lab* (Tech. Rep.). Atlanta, GA: Georgia Institute of Technology.

Sha, X. W., Sutton, T., Rousseau, J. S., Smoak, H. C., Fortin, M., & Sutherland, M. (2009). *Ozone: A continuous state-based approach to media choreography* (Tech. Rep.). Montreal, Quebec, Canada: Concordia University, Topological Media Lab.

Shade, J., Gortler, S., He, L. W., & Szeliski, R. (1998). Layered depth images. In *Proceedings of SIGGRAPH, 98*, 231–242.

Shaw, B. (2008). *Utilizing folksonomy: Similarity metadata from the del.icio.us system*. Retrieved October 2, 2009, from http://www.metablake.com/webfolk/web-project.pdf

Sha, X. W. (2002). Resistance is fertile: Gesture and agency in the field of responsive media. *Configurations, 10*(3), 439–472. doi:10.1353/con.2004.0006

Shiode, N. (2000). 3D urban models: Recent developments in the digital modelling of urban environments in three-dimensions. *GeoJournal, 52*(3), 263–269.

Singhal, A., & Salton, G. (1995, May 22-25). Automatic Text Browsing Using Vector Space Model. In *Proceedings of the Dual-Use Technologies and Applications Conference,* Utica, NY (pp. 318-324).

Skog, T., Ljungblad, S., & Holmquist, L. E. (2003). Between aesthetics and utility: Designing ambient information visualizations. In *Proceedings of the IEEE Symposium on Information Visualization (InfoVis)* (pp. 30-37).

Snellen, H. (1862). *Probebuchstaben zur Betimmung der Sehschärfe*. Utrecht, The Netherlands: P. W. van de Weijer.

Soddu, C. (2009) *Argenia, Generative Art and Science*. Retrieved April 23, 2009, from http://www.celestino-soddu.com/

Solé, R. (2008). On Networks and Monsters: The possible and the actual in complex systems. *Leonardo, 41*(5), 456–460.

Stahre, B., Billger, M., & Anter, K. F. (2009). To colour the virtual world: Difficulties in visualizing spatial colour appearance in virtual environments. *International Journal of Architectural Computing, 7*(2), 289–308. doi:10.1260/147807709788921949

Stam, J. (1999). Stable fluids. In *SIGGRAPH '99: Proceedings of the 26th Annual Conference on Computer Graphics and Interactive Techniques* (pp. 121-128). New York: ACM Publishing.

Stam, J. (2003a, July). Flows on surfaces of arbitrary topology. In *Proceedings of the ACM SIGGGRAPH Papers* (pp. 724-731). New York, NY: ACM Press.

Stam, J. (2003b, March). Real-time fluid dynamics for games. In *Proceedings of the Game Developer Conference*.

Stam, J. (2002). A simple fluid solver based on the FFT. *Journal Graphics Tools, 6*, 43–52.

Stanik, S., & Werman, M. (2003). Simulation of rain in videos. *International Journal of Computer Vision Texture*, 95-100.

Starner, T., Mann, S., Rhodes, B., Levine, J., Healey, J., & Kirsch, D. (1997). Augmented Reality Through Wearable Computing. *Presence (Cambridge, Mass.), 6*(4), 386–398.

Stoakley, R., Conway, M. J., & Pausch, Y. (1995). Virtual reality on a wim: interactive worlds in miniature. In *Proceedings of SIGCHI '95: SIG on Human factors in computing systems* (pp. 265-272).

Stone, D., Jarett, C., Woodfoffe, M., & Minocha, S. (2005). *User interface design and evaluation*. San Francisco, CA: Morgan Kauffman.

Stuppacher, I., & Supan, P. (2007). Rendering of water drops in real-time. In *Proceedings of the Central European Seminar on Computer Graphics for Students*.

Sugimoto, H. (1998). *Architecture*. Retrieved from http://www.sugimotohiroshi.com/architecture.html

Sussman, M. (2003). A second order coupled level set and volume-of-fluid method for computing growth and collapse of vapor bubbles. *Journal of Computational Physics, 187*(1), 110–136. doi:10.1016/S0021-9991(03)00087-1

Tama Software Ltd. (2005). *Pop-up card designer pro*. Retrieved from http://www.tamasoft.co.jp/craft/popupcard-pro/index.html

Tamura, H., Mori, S., & Yamawaki, T. (1978). Textural features corresponding to visual perception. *IEEE Transactions on Systems, Man, and Cybernetics, 8*(6), 460–472. doi:10.1109/TSMC.1978.4309999

Tan, J., & Yang, X. (2009). Physically-based fluid animation: A survey. *Science in China Series F: Information Sciences, 52*(5), 723–740. doi:10.1007/s11432-009-0091-z

Tariq, S. (2007). *Rain nvidia whitepaper.* Retrieved April 2, 2010, from http://developer.download.nvidia.com/whitepapers/2007/SDK10/RainSDKWhitePaper.pdf

Tarr, M. J., & Bülthoff, H. H. (1998). Image-based object recognition in man, monkey and machine. *Cognition, 67*(1), 1–20. doi:10.1016/S0010-0277(98)00026-2

Tatarchuk, N. (2006). Artist-directable real-time rain rendering in city environments. In *Proceedings of the ACM SIGGRAPH Courses* (pp. 23-64).

Teller, S. J., & Séquin, C. H. (1991). Visibility preprocessing for interactive walkthroughs. *SIGGRAPH Computer Graphics, 25*(4), 61–70. doi:10.1145/127719.122725

Texas Instruments. (2010). *Classroom3® 3D case study.* Retrieved from http://www.dlp.com/downloads/DLP_3D_Classroom3_Case_Study.pdf

Tharp, T. (2003). *The creative habit: Learn it and use it for life* (p. 64). New York, NY: Simon & Schuster: The SETI Institute. (n. d.). *FAQ.* Retrieved from http://www.seti.org/Page.aspx?pid=558

Thom, R. (1983). *Mathematical models of morphogenesis.* Chichester, UK: Ellis Horwood.

Thom, R. (1989). *Structural stability and morphogenesis: An outline of a general theory of models.* Reading, MA: Addison-Wesley.

Thompson, J., & Overholt, D. (2007). Sonofusion: Development of a multimedia composition for the overtone violin. In *Proceedings of the International Computer Music Conference ICMC 2007 International Computer Music Conference,* Copenhagen, Denmark (Vol. 2).

Thürey, N., & Rüde, U. (2004, November). Free Surface Lattice-Boltzmann fluid simulations with and without level sets. In []. Amsterdam, The Netherlands: IOS Press.]. *Proceedings of the International Workshop on Vision, Modeling, and Visualization, 2,* 199–207.

Tractinsky, N. (1997). Aesthetics and apparent usability: Empirically assessing cultural and methodological issues. In *Proceedings of the SIGCHI Conference on Human Factors in Computing* (pp. 115-122).

Trew, G. C. (1936). *Drawing without a master.* London, UK: A. & C. Black.

Tufte, E. R. (1997). *Visual explanations. Images and quantities, evidence and narrative.* Cheshire, CT: Graphics Press.

Tufte, E. (1983). *The visual display of quantitative information.* Cheshire, CT: Graphic Press.

Tufte, E. R. (1990). *Envisioning information.* Cheshire, CT: Graphics Press.

Turner, D. (2007). Hack: The Nintendo Wii. *MIT Technology Review, July.*

Ullrich, W. (2002). *Die Geschichte der Unschärfe.* Berlin, Germany: Wagenbach.

Ursyn, A. (1994). *Student Perception of Computer Art Graphics Integration of Art & Science.* Washington, DC: American Educational Research Association. (ERIC Document Reproduction Service No. ED 374 773)

Ursyn, A., & Scott, T. (2006). *Overlap between thinking in terms of art and computer science.* Paper presented at the Consortium for Computing Sciences in Colleges (CCSC), Durango, CO.

Ursyn, A., & Scott, T. (2007) Web with Art and Computer Science. In *Proceedings of the ACM SIGGRAPH Education Committee.* ISBN 978–1–59593–648–6.

Ursyn, A., & Sung, R. (2007). Learning Science with Art. In *Proceedings of ACM SIGGRAPH Education Committee Proceedings.* ISBN 978–1–59593–648–6.

Ursyn, A. (1997). Computer Art Graphics Integration of Art and Science. *Learning and Instruction, 7*(1), 65–87. doi:10.1016/S0959-4752(96)00011-4

Ursyn, A. (2008). Digital drawing, graphic storytelling and visual journalism. In Garner, S. (Ed.), *Writing on drawing: Essays on drawing practice and research* (pp. 169–177). Bristol, UK: Intellect.

Ursyn, A., Mills, L., Hobgood, B., & Scott, T. (1997). Combining Art Skills with Programming in Teaching Computer Art Graphics. *Computer Graphics, 25,* 3.

van Goethe, J. W. (1810). *Zur Farbenlehre.* Retrieved from http://www.mathpages.com/home/kmath608/kmath608.htm

Vande Moere, A. (2005). Form follows Data: The Symbiosis between Design and Information Visualization. In *Proceedings of the International Conference on Computer-Aided Architectural Design (CAADfutures '05),* Vienna, Austria (pp. 31-40). Retrieved January 3, 2009, from http://Web.arch.usyd.edu.au/~andrew/publications/caadfutures05.pdf

Vande Moere, A. (2008). Beyond the Tyranny of the Pixel: Exploring the Physicality of Information Visualization. In *Proceedings of the 12th International Conference on Information Visualisation* (pp. 469-474). Washington, DC: IEEE Computer Society.

Vansteenkiste, E., Van der Weken, D., Philips, W., & Kerre, E. (2006). Perceived image quality measurement of state-of-the-art noise reduction schemes. In J. Blanc-Talon, W. Philips, D. Popescu, & P. Scheunders (Eds.), *Proceedings of the 8th International Conference on Advanced Concepts for Intelligent Vision Systems* (LNCS 4179, pp. 114-126).

Verfaille, V. (2006). Adaptive Digital Audio Effects (A-DAFx): A new class of sound transformations. *IEEE Transactions on Audio, Speech and Language Proc., 14*(5), 1817–1831. doi:10.1109/TSA.2005.858531

Verschuere, R., Crombez, G., & Koster, E. (2007). *Cross cultural validation of the IAPS.* Ghent, Belgium: Ghent University.

Vesna, V. (2007). *Database Aesthetics: Art in the Age of Information Overflow (Electronic Mediations).* Twin Cities, MN: University of Minnesota Press.

Vicon. (2011). *Motion capture systems from Vicon.* Retrieved July 5, 2011, from http://www.vicon.com

Viégas, F. B., Scott, G., & Donath, J. (2006). Visualizing email content: portraying relationships from conversational histories. In *Proceedings of the SIGCHI conference on Human Factors in Computing Systems* (pp. 979-988). New York: ACM.

Viégas, F. B., & Wattenberg, M. (2008). Tag Clouds and the Case for Vernacular Visualization. *Interaction, 15*(4), 49–52. doi:10.1145/1374489.1374501

Wands, B. (2007). *Art of the Digital Age.* London: Thames and Hudson.

Wang, L., Lin, Z., Fang, T., Yang, X., Yu, X., & Kang, S. (2006). Real-time rendering of realistic rain. In *Proceedings of the ACM SIGGRAPH Sketches* (p. 156).

Wang, N., & Wade, B. (2004). Rendering falling rain and snow. In *Proceedings of the ACM SIGGRAPH Sketches* (p. 14).

Wang, C., Wang, Z., Zhang, X., Huang, L., Yang, Z., & Peng, Q. (2008). Real-time modeling and rendering of raining scenes. *The Visual Computer, 24,* 605–616. doi:10.1007/s00371-008-0241-0

Wang, F. (2004). A simple and analytical procedure for calibrating extrinsic camera parameters. *IEEE Transactions on Robotics and Automation, 20,* 121–124. doi:10.1109/TRA.2003.820919

Wang, L., Giesen, J., McDonnell, K. T., Zolliker, P., & Mueller, K. (2008). Color design for illustrative visualization. *IEEE Transactions on Visualization and Computer Graphics, 14*(6), 1739–1754. doi:10.1109/TVCG.2008.118

Wardrip-Fruin, N. (2003). *The New Media Reader.* Cambridge, MA: MIT Press.

Ware, C. (2004). *Information Visualization: Perception for Design* (2nd ed.).

Wattenberg, M. (2007). *Many Eyes.* Retrieved May 11, 2009, from http://www.bewitched.com/manyeyes.html

Watts, D. J., & Strogatz, S. H. (1998). Collective dynamics of 'small-world' networks. *Nature, 393,* 440–442.

Welch, G., & Bishop, G. (2004). *An introduction to the Kalman Filter* (Tech. Rep. No. 95-041). Chapel Hill, NC: University of North Carolina.

Welch, P. (1967). The use of Fast Fourier Transform for the estimation of power spectra: A method based on time averaging over short, modified periodograms. *IEEE Transactions on Audio and Electroacoustics, AU-15,* 70–73. doi:10.1109/TAU.1967.1161901

White, R., & Engelen, G. (2000). High-resolution integrated modeling of the spatial dynamics of urban and regional systems. *Computers, Environment and Urban Systems, 24*(5), 383–400.

Wikipedia. (n. d.). *Julia Margaret Cameron.* Retrieved from http://de.wikipedia.org/wiki/Julia_Margaret_Cameron

Wikipedia. (n.d.). Retrieved June 20, 2009, from http://wikipedia.com/

Wingrave, C. A., Haciahmetoglu, Y., & Bowman, D. A. (2006). *Overcoming world in miniature limitations by a scaled and scrolling wim. In 3D* (pp. 11–16). User Interfaces.

Winn, W., & Everett, R. (1979). Affective rating of color and black-and-white pictures. *Educational Technology Research and Development, 27*(2), 148–156.

Wise, J. A., et al. (1995, October 20-21). Visualizing the Non-Visual: Spatial Analysis and Interaction with Information from Text Documents. In *Proceedings of IEEE Information Visualization '95,* Atlanta, GA (pp. 51-58).

Wong, G. (2009). *EON Coliseum: Pioneering multi-modal communication in virtual reality.* Retrieved from http://www.eonreality.com/brochures/EON_Coliseum_Whitepaper.pdf

Woolford, K. A., & Guedes, C. (2007). Particulate matters: Generating particle flows from human movement. In *Multimedia '07: Proceedings of the 15th International Conference on Multimedia* (pp. 691-696). New York: ACM Publishing.

Wu, X., Zhang, L., & Yu, Y. Exploring social annotations for the semantic web. In *Proceedings of the International Conference on World Wide Web* (pp. 417-426). New York: ACM.

Xin, J. H. (2004). Cross-regional comparison of colour emotions part I. Quantitative analysis. *Color Research and Application, 29*(6), 451–457. doi:10.1002/col.20062

Yamamoto, K. (2009, December). Real time two-way coupling of fluids to deformable bodies using particle method on GPU. In *Proceedings of the ACM SIGGGRAPH Asia Posters.* New York, NY: ACM Press.

Yang, R., & Welch, G. (2002). Fast image segmentation and smoothing using commodity graphics hardware. *Journal of Graphics Tools, 7*(4), 91–100.

Yi, J. S., Melton, R., Stasko, J., & Jacko, J. (2005). Dust & Magnet: multivariate information visualization using a magnet metaphor. *Information Visualization, 4*(4), 239–256.

Zbikowski, L. M. (1998). Metaphor and Music Theory: Reflections from Cognitive Science. Music Theory Online. *Online Journal of the Society for Music Theory, 4*(1).

Zbikowski, L. M. (2005). *Conceptualizing Music: Cognitive Structure, Theory, and Analysis.* Oxford, UK: Oxford University Press.

Zeki, S. (1999). *Inner vision.* Oxford, UK: Oxford University Press.

Zemach, I., Chang, S., & Teller, D. (2007). Infant color vision: prediction of infants' spontaneous color preferences. *Vision Research,* 1368–1381. doi:10.1016/j.visres.2006.09.024

Zhai, S., Buxton, W., & Milgram, P. (1996). The partial-occlusion effect: Utilizing semitransparency in 3D human-computer interaction. *ACM Transactions on Computer-Human Interaction, 3*(3), 254-284. Retrieved from http://doi.acm.org/10.1145/234526.234532

Zhang, R., Tsai, P.-S., Cryer, J. E., & Shah, M. (1999). Shape from shading: A survey. *IEEE Transactions on PAMI, 21*(8).

Zhang, Z. (1999). Flexible camera calibration by viewing a plane from unknown orientations. In *Proceedings of the International Conference on Computer Vision, 1,* 666–673. doi:10.1109/ICCV.1999.791289

Zhao, J., Yan, D., Men, G., & Zhang, Y. (2007). A method of calibrating intrinsic and extrinsic camera parameters separately for multi-camera systems. In *Proceedings of the Sixth International Conference on Machine Learning and Cybernetics* (Vol. 3, pp. 1548-1553).

Zölzer, U. (2002). *DAFx – Digital Audio Effects.* New York: John Wiley and Sons.

Zull, J. (2002). *The art of changing the brain* (pp. 47–69). Sterling, VA: Stylus Publishing.

About the Contributors

Ben Falchuk has a long and diverse background in computer systems and middleware, human computer interaction, multimedia systems, and graphical and creative applications. He has over ten US patents pending and fifty publications, including peer-reviewed conferences, journals, and books, including an anticipated one titled "The Fabric of Mobile Services". He sits on the committees of prestigious international conferences and journals. Dr. Falchuk holds a Bachelor's of Applied Mathematics and Computer Science degree from the University of Waterloo, a Master's of Science degree from Carleton University, and a PhD in Electrical and Computer Engineering from the University of Ottawa. He also holds certificates in computer animation and HCI from Sheridan College and Rutgers, respectively. Thanks to his Sheridan experiences, his studies in the Fine Arts Studio, and many years of evaluating and devising novel creative systems, he brings a unique perspective. Dr. Falchuk is currently Senior Research Scientist in the Advanced Technology Solutions Lab of Telcordia Technologies (New Jersey). In this role, he develops new technologies, software, systems, and services. He architects and implements innovative software and develops intellectual property revolving around communications, multimedia, and creative applications.

Adérito Fernandes Marcos graduated in Computer Science Engineering from the Nova University of Lisbon; got a Ph.D. *suma cum laude in* Computer Graphics and Information Systems from the Technical University of Darmstadt, Germany; and Habilitation, an academic degree for Full Professorship (Agregação) in Technology and Information Systems from the University of Minho. Between November 1997 and October 2005 he has been a Departments Head, then Executive Director of the Computer Graphics Centre (CCG), an Interface Institute of the University of Minho. On behalf of CCG he received the European IST Prize 2000: Grand Prize Winner for the TeleInViVo project and also the LAVAL Virtual 2002 – "Science et education" and "GRAND PRIX DU JURY 2002", by the Laval Academy, Mayenne França, for the European project ARCHEOGUIDE. Since September 2009, he assumed the position of Associate Professor with Habilitation at the Portuguese Open University, Department of Sciences and Technology, Lisbon, Portugal. He is the head of this department since November 2010. In this university he is the principal mentor and founder of the Doctoral Program in Digital Media-Art and has been appointed for its Director. Previously, he was an Assistant Professor at University of Minho, where he was responsible for the design of a variety of curricula in the fields of Multimedia, Information Systems and Computer Graphics, Technology and Digital Art for undergraduate and post-graduate courses. At this university, he was co-founder of the Masters Course in Computer Graphics and Virtual Environments (with three editions) and founder and first director of the Masters Course in Technology and Digital Art, actually in its third edition. He integrated the Executive Board of Eurographics from January 2002 until

August 2005 and again since October 2008. Since October 2008, he became President of the Executive Board of the Eurographics Portuguese Chapter and reelected for a second term in 2010. He is chairman of Artech-International, an initiative in the field of digital/computer arts, that is responsible for the Artech - International Conference on Digital Arts. Since 2000, he is working as a regular consultant of Agency for Innovation, the European Association INTAS, European Commission and ZGDV (German Institute for Computer Graphics, Darmstadt, Germany). He is a member of Artech-International, Eurographics, ACM, IEEE and SIGRAPH. He is author and co-author of more than six dozen articles in refereed magazines, conference proceedings and book chapters.

* * *

Gonçalo Amador is currently a project researcher at the Instituto de Telecomunicações, at the Universidade da Beira Interior. His research interests, to name just a few, are Game Applied A.I., natural phenomena simulation, HCI tangible user devices/interfaces (e.g., touch devices, 2D/3D cameras, game console controllers such as the Wiimote), and distributed/parallel computing using technologies, such as, CUDA, OpenMP, OpenCL, MPI, and the GridGain middleware. Aside from Game Applied A.I., he possesses publications related to all the mentioned research areas. He currently is a researcher in the last year of the MOGGY (A Browser-Based Massive Multiplayer Online Game Engine Architecture) project. MSc Gonçalo holds a MSc (2009) in Engenharia Informática, and two BSc one in Engenharia Informática (2007) and another in Tecnologias e Sistemas de Informação (2011), all from Universidade da Beira Interior in Portugal.

Marko Balabanovic is the Head of Innovation at lastminute.com, and has worked in innovation at startups, corporate R&D labs and universities. His interests include interaction design, personalisation and recommendation systems, and the process of innovation. He holds a PhD from Stanford University and an MA from Cambridge University.

Russell Beale leads the Advanced Interaction Group in the School of Computer Science at the University of Birmingham. His interests range broadly across the border between interactive systems and society, with a particular focus on using artificial intelligence to create more usable interactive systems. As well as being a full-time academic, Russell has founded four companies and run two of them, provides consultancy services on projects he's interested in, and used to race yachts competitively until a toddler and twins needed his attention – but once they have learned to sail, he'll return to that as well.

Leonardo Bonanni is a PhD candidate at the MIT Media Lab's Tangible Media Group. His research is concerned with the social roles of artifacts; he is currently developing tools for transparency and for cultural sustainability. He teaches a product design curriculum at the Media Lab on the future of craft and the role of designers in shaping cultures of production. Prior to this he worked in the Media Lab's future home and kitchen projects. Leonardo has a background in sculpture and architecture and has a design practice that deals with interaction, products and architecture.

Bianca Cheng Costanzo is an undergraduate student at MIT working on tangible interfaces for art restoration at the MIT Media Lab's Tangible Media Group.

Mathias Dahlström holds an M.sc in Computer Science from Blekinge Institute of Technology and a M.A Diploma in Interaction Design from Interaction Design Institute Ivrea. His research interest lies in understanding our social interactions, specifically the importance of embodied interactions, in the context of designing mobile user experiences.

Filipe Gonçalves Gaspar is Reseacher in Virtual Media Lab, ADETTI-IUL, Portugal, since 2008. Received a BSc (2007) and an MSc (2009) in Telecommunications and Computer Science Engineering, field of Computer Graphics and Multimedia, both from ISCTE-IUL. In the last two years he has been lecturing in PIAGET Institute, Portugal, as Assistant Professor in courses such as: Computer Graphics, Human-Computer Interaction, and Multimedia. His main research interests are image processing, computer vision, augmented and virtual reality. He is starting his PhD thesis in Augmented Reality field: 3D Object Reconstruction and Tracking through Sensor Fusion.

Abel Gomes took a BSc degree (5 years) in electrical engineering and an MSc in computer graphics at University of Coimbra, Portugal. He also obtained a PhD degree in geometric modeling at Brunel University, England. His current research interests include geometric modeling, implicit curves and surfaces, molecular modeling, 3D biomedical visualization, multiresolution models, simulation and modeling of natural phenomena, computer graphics, and MMOGs (massively multiplayer online games). He has also served as a member of several international committees and editorial review boards related to computer graphics and computational science. His list of publications includes a book published by Springer-Verlag in 2009. He is a licensed Professional Engineer and he is member of the ACM and IEEE. He is also now the Head of Department of Computing at the University of Beira Interior, Covilhã, Portugal.

Robert Hendley is a researcher and lecturer in Computer Science at The University of Birmingham and previously at The University of Leeds. He is deputy director of CERCIA (The Centre of Excellence in Research in Computational Intelligence and Applications). He has led research projects funded by UK research councils, EU R&D programmes and industry. His work has included investigations into the underlying technologies and practice of the interaction between computer systems and people (especially the use of Artificial Intelligence techniques to support intelligent and adaptive interaction) user interface design, adaptive interfaces and information browsing, visualisation and discovery.

Matthew Hockenberry is a visiting scientist for the Center for Future Civic Media and holds an appointment in the Tangible Media Group as well. He is a researcher particularly interested in the social, technical and philosophical implications of the web.

Hiroshi Ishii is the Muriel R. Cooper Professor of Media Arts and Sciences, at the MIT Media Lab. He currently directs the Tangible Media Group, and he co-directs the Things That Think (TTT) consortium. Hiroshi's research focuses upon the design of seamless interfaces between humans, digital information, and the physical environment. His team seeks to change the "painted bits" of GUIs to "tangible bits" by giving physical form to digital information. Ishii and his team have presented their vision of "Tangible Bits" at a variety of academic, design, and artistic venues, emphasizing that the development of tangible interfaces requires the rigor of both scientific and artistic review.

Richard Lewis Jones is a senior innovation developer at lastminute.com labs in London. He has previously worked for Xerox and the Financial Times.

Maurizio Seracini is the director of the Center for Interdisciplinary Science for Art, Architecture, and Archaeology (CISA3) at the University of California San Diego's California Institute for Telecommunications and Information Technology (Calit2). He is a pioneer in the use of multispectral imaging and other diagnostic tools as well as analytical technologies as applied to works of art and structures. He has studied more than 2,500 works of art and historic buildings, ranging from Leonardo Da Vinci's "Last Supper" and Botticelli's "Allegory of Spring", to Da Vinci's "Adoration of the Magi".

Andrew Shum is an undergraduate student at MIT working on tangible interfaces for art restoration at the MIT Media Lab's Tangible Media Group.

Antony Speranza is an undergraduate student at MIT working on tangible interfaces for art restoration at the MIT Media Lab's Tangible Media Group.

Romain Teil is an undergraduate student at MIT working on tangible interfaces for art restoration at the MIT Media Lab's Tangible Media Group.

Anna Ursyn, Ph.D, is a Professor and Computer Graphics Area Head at the School of Art and Design, University of Northern Colorado. She combines programming with software and printmaking media, to unify computer generated and painted images, and mixed-media sculptures. Ursyn had over 30 single juried and invitational art shows and participated in over 100 fine art exhibitions. Her articles and artwork have been published in books and journals. Research and pedagogy interests include integrated instruction in art, science, and computer art graphics. She serves as a Liaison, Organizing and Program Committee member of IEEE Conferences on Information Visualization – iV: London, UK, and Computer Graphics, Imaging and Visualization Conferences – CGIV, and as Chair of the Symposium and Digital Art Gallery – D-ART iV. Website: Ursyn.com.

Sha Xin Wei, Ph.D., is Canada Research Chair in media arts and sciences, and Associate Professor of Fine Arts and Computer Science at Concordia University in Montréal, Canada. He directs the Topological Media Lab, a studio-laboratory for the study of gesture and materiality from computational and phenomenological perspectives. With degrees in Mathematics from Harvard and Stanford, Dr. Sha also worked more than 12 years in the areas of visualization, scientific and social simulation, humanities computing and distributed multimedia in collaborations with researchers from Apple, Xerox PARC, IBM Research, Interval Research, Sony, and Intel Labs. Prior to Concordia, Dr. Sha was faculty at the Georgia Tech, and a Visiting Scholar at Stanford, Harvard and MIT. Sha's creative works include the TGarden responsive environments, Hubbub speech-sensitive urban surfaces, Membrane calligraphic video, Softwear gestural sound instruments, the WYSIWYG sounding tapestry, and collaborations with a contemporary music ensemble and a choreographer in the Frankenstein's Ghosts performance work. Dr. Sha's technical areas of research include the realtime, continuous mapping of features extracted from expressive movement, using for example two-dimensional soft controllers made from woven or non-woven materials, into parameters modulating the continuous synthesis of video, sound, and physical or software control systems. In parallel Sha has published critical and philosophical essays in *Configurations, Modern Drama*, and *AI and Society,* drawing from and motivating these experiments. He serves as an editor of the *AI and Society, FibreCulture*, and the Rodopi Press book series: *Experimental Practices in Art, Science, and Philosophy*. He is writing a book on poiesis and enchantment in topological media.

Barry Wilkins has a BSc. in Computer Science and Software Engineering from The University of Birmingham. After several years of work in industry he returned and completed his PhD in Computer Science with work on pattern supported methodologies for visualisation design.

Xiao Xiao is a Master's student in the MIT Media Lab's Tangible Media Group, where she is inventing user interfaces to remote social interactions and musical performance. In her spare time, Xiao Xiao plays the piano, draws in her Moleskine, and spins poi on fire.

Index